"It is hard to overstate the impact that William Lane Craig has had for the cause of Christ. He is simply the finest Christian apologist of the last half century, and his academic work justifies ranking him among the top 1 percent of practicing philosophers in the Western world. Besides that, he is a winsome ambassador for Christ, an exceptional debater, and a man with the heart of an evangelist. I know him well and can say that he lives a life of integrity and lives out what he believes. I do not know of a single thinker who has done more to raise the bar of Christian scholarship in our generation than Craig. He is one of a kind, and I thank God for his life and work."

—J. P. Moreland, Distinguished Professor of Philosophy,
Talbot School of Theology

"In admirably clear prose, Professor Craig presents important philosophical and historical issues relevant to Christian beliefs. With extraordinary erudition, he sketches the arguments of major thinkers of both past centuries and recent times, and he presents his own reasons for concluding that traditional Christian doctrines about God and Jesus are credible. His replies to those skeptical of the existence of God, of historical knowledge, of the occurrence of miracles, and in particular of the resurrection of Jesus, take debates over those difficult topics an important stage further. Here is an admirable defense of basic Christian faith."

—C. Behan McCullagh, Philosophy Program, La Trobe University

"*Reasonable Faith* is a much-needed book for our times. It overflows with cogent and compelling argument presented in accessible and irenic language. University and seminary students will find this book especially helpful in exposing the fallacies and lack of evidence in the many and various challenges that have been leveled against historic Christian claims. Craig offers solid, convincing argument for and evidence of the trustworthiness of the New Testament Gospels and the ancient, credible witness of the resurrection of Jesus from the dead. I highly recommend this book."

—Craig A. Evans, Payzant Distinguished Professor of New Testament,
Acadia Divinity College; author, *Fabricating Jesus:
How Modern Scholars Distort the Gospels*

"Although my philosophical predilections often differ from Dr. Craig's (as they do from those of everyone else I know), I have found that he is very knowledgeable about science and current cosmological ideas. He provides interesting insights into their implications for our shared Christian beliefs."

—Don Nelson Page, Professor of Physics, University of Alberta

Crossway books by William Lane Craig:

*Two Tasks of the Christian Scholar: Redeeming the Soul,
    Redeeming the Mind* (co-editor)
Hard Questions, Real Answers
Time and Eternity: Exploring God's Relationship to Time

Reasonable Faith

Christian Truth
and Apologetics

Third Edition

WILLIAM LANE CRAIG

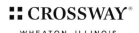
CROSSWAY®

WHEATON, ILLINOIS

Reasonable Faith: Christian Truth and Apologetics

Copyright © 1984, 1994, 2008 by William Lane Craig

Published by Crossway
        1300 Crescent Street
        Wheaton, Illinois 60187

Third edition 2008

Edited by John S. Feinberg and Leonard Goss

First printing, revised edition, 1994

First printing 2008

Printed in the United States of America

Cover design: Amy Bristow

Scripture quotations marked ESV are from the ESV® Bible (The Holy Bible, English Standard Version®), copyright © 2001 by Crossway, a publishing ministry of Good News Publishers. Used by permission. All rights reserved.

Scripture references marked RSV are from *The Revised Standard Version*. Copyright © 1946, 1952, 1971, 1973 by the Division of Christian Education of the National Council of the Churches of Christ in the U.S.A.

Scripture quotations marked AT are the author's translation.

Trade paperback ISBN: 978-1-4335-0115-9
PDF ISBN: 978-1-4335-0452-5
MobiPocket ISBN: 978-1-4335-0453-2
ePub ISBN: 978-1-4335-2118-8

Library of Congress Cataloging-in-Publication Data

Craig, William Lane.
   Reasonable faith : Christian truth and apologetics /
William Lane Craig.—3rd ed.
     p. cm.
   Includes index.
   ISBN 978-1-4335-0115-9 (tpb)
   1. Apologetics. I. Title.
BT1103.C74   2008
239—dc22   2007051433

Crossway is a publishing ministry of Good News Publishers.

For Jan, my love

"Many women have done excellently,
but you surpass them all." (Prov. 31:29)

Contents

Table of Figures

Preface to the Third Edition

I'm grateful to Crossway Books for offering me the opportunity to revise *Reasonable Faith* for this third edition. *Reasonable Faith* has become, I suppose, my signature book, and we're grateful for the way the Lord has used it in the lives of many. In the providence of God, the invitation to produce this revised edition comes at roughly the same time as the launch of our new web-based ministry Reasonable Faith at www.reasonablefaith.org, where a wide variety of supplementary material may be found. The launch of Reasonable Faith makes especially apropos the appearance of a fresh edition of this book.

Changes in the third edition consist largely of expansions and updates of the content rather than, I'm happy to say, of retractions. In revising the book I could not help but be struck by the fact that although the names have changed, the objections and their answers remain largely the same. The crucial chapter on the existence of God has been expanded into two. Keeping the book at approximately the same length was made possible by the deletion of the chapter on the historical reliability of the New Testament, a chapter which a former editor had insisted, despite my protestations, be inserted into the second edition. The inclusion of this chapter (itself a solid piece of work written at my invitation by Craig Blomberg) perpetuated the misimpression, all too common among evangelicals, that a historical case for Jesus' radical self-understanding and resurrection depends upon showing that the Gospels are generally reliable historical documents. The overriding lesson of two centuries of biblical criticism is that such an assumption is false. Even documents which are generally unreliable may contain valuable historical nuggets, and it will be the historian's task to mine these documents in order to discover them. The Christian apologist seeking to establish, for example, the historicity of Jesus' empty tomb need not and should not be saddled with the task of first showing that the Gospels are, in general, historically reliable documents. You may be wondering how it can be shown that the Gospel accounts of the discovery of Jesus' empty tomb can be shown to be, in their core, historically reliable without first showing that the Gospels are, in general, historically trustworthy. Read chapter 8 to find out.

Reasonable Faith is intended primarily to serve as a textbook for seminary level courses on Christian apologetics. Indeed, the book began as a set of lectures for my own class on apologetics. It has been further shaped by years of experience lecturing and debating on the relevant issues on university campuses throughout North America and Europe. The course it offers represents my personal approach to providing a positive apologetic for the Christian faith. I cover neither the history of apologetics nor options in evangelical apologetic systems; supplementary reading must be assigned to students to cover these two areas. For the history of apologetics, I recommend Avery Dulles, *History of Apologetics* (Philadelphia: Westminster, 1971), a scholarly masterpiece and an invaluable reference work. As for evangelical systems, Kenneth Boa and Robert Bowman Jr. survey the approaches of the most prominent evangelical apologists of our day in their *Faith Has Its Reasons* (Colorado Springs: NavPress, 2001). In order to round out your knowledge of the field of apologetics, you should avail yourself of this adjunct reading.

I've structured *Reasonable Faith* around the *loci communes* of systematic theology. The *loci communes* were the so-called "common places" or chief themes or topics of post-Reformation Protestant theology. It was Luther's colleague Melanchthon who first employed these "common places" as the framework for writing his systematic theology. Some of the most frequently discussed *loci* included *de Scriptura sacra* (doctrine of Scripture), *de creatione* (doctrine of creation), *de peccato* (doctrine of sin), *de Christo* (Christology), *de gratia* (soteriology), *de ecclesia* (ecclesiology), and *de novissimus* (eschatology).

In almost all of these *loci* apologetical issues confront the Christian theologian. I've heard it said that contemporary theology has become so irrational and fideistic that apologetics no longer finds a place in the course offerings of mainline theological schools. But that is not exactly correct. Having done my doctoral work in theology in Germany, I can say that while it is true that no courses in apologetics *per se* are offered in German departments of theology, nevertheless German theological instruction is itself very apologetically oriented. In classes on, say, Christology or soteriology, one will discuss as a matter of course various issues and challenges raised by non-Christian philosophy, science, history, and so forth, to Christian doctrine. (Unfortunately, the result of this interaction is inevitably capitulation on the part of theology and its retreat into non-empirical doctrinal sanctuaries, where it achieves security only at the expense of becoming irrelevant and untestable.) It bothered me that in evangelical seminaries our theology courses devote so little time to such issues. How much time is spent, for example, in an evangelical course on the doctrine of God on arguments for God's existence? Then it occurred to me: maybe the theology professors are expecting *you* to handle those issues in the apologetics class, since at my institution apologetics *is* offered as a separate course. The more I thought about this, the more sense it made. Therefore, in order to integrate apologetics into the theological curriculum I've structured this book around various apologetic issues which arise in the *loci communes theologiae*.

In our limited space, I've chosen to discuss several important issues in the *loci de fide* (faith), *de homine* (man), *de Deo* (God), *de creatione* (creation), and *de Christo* (Christ). I've taken the liberty to rearrange these *loci* from their normal order in a systematic theology into an order following the logic of apologetics. That is to say, our goal is to build a case for Christianity, and that determines the order in which we'll consider the issues. I'm painfully aware of other issues that are also interesting and important but that I have omitted. Still, we shall be considering the most crucial issues involved in building a positive case for the Christian faith.

Under *de fide,* I shall consider the relation between faith and reason; under *de homine,* the absurdity of life without God; under *de Deo,* the existence of God; under *de creatione,* the problem of historical knowledge and the problem of miracles; and finally, under *de Christo,* the personal claims of Christ and the historicity of the resurrection of Jesus. Our consideration of each question will fall into four sections. First, we shall take a look at the historical background of the issue in question to see how past thinkers have dealt with it. Second, I shall present and defend my personal views on the topic at hand, seeking to develop a Christian apologetic on the point. Third, I shall share some thoughts and personal experiences on applying this material in evangelism. Fourth, I provide bibliographical information on the literature cited or recommended for your future reading.

It is my earnest hope that God will use this material to help equip a new generation of intelligent, articulate Christians who are filled with the Spirit and burdened to see the Great Commission fulfilled.

William Lane Craig
Talbot School of Theology

Introduction

What is apologetics? Apologetics (from the Greek *apologia*: a defense) is that branch of Christian theology which seeks to provide a rational justification for the truth claims of the Christian faith. Apologetics is thus primarily a theoretical discipline, though it has a practical application. In addition to serving, like the rest of theology in general, as an expression of loving God with all our minds, apologetics specifically serves to show to unbelievers the truth of the Christian faith, to confirm that faith to believers, and to reveal and explore the connections between Christian doctrine and other truths. As a theoretical discipline, then, apologetics is not training in the art of answering questions, or debating, or evangelism, though all of these draw upon the science of apologetics and apply it practically. This implies that a course in apologetics is not for the purpose of teaching you, "If he says so-and-so, then you say such-and-such back." Apologetics, to repeat, is a theoretical discipline that tries to answer the question, What rational warrant can be given for the Christian faith? Therefore, most of our time must be spent in trying to answer this question.

Now this is bound to be disappointing to some. They're just not interested in the rational justification of Christianity. They want to know, "If someone says, 'Look at all the hypocrites in the church!' what do I say?" There's nothing wrong with that question; but the fact remains that such practical matters are logically secondary to the theoretical issues and cannot in our limited space occupy the center of our attention. The use of apologetics in practice ought rather to be an integral part of courses and books on evangelism.

What Good Is Apologetics?

Some people depreciate the importance of apologetics as a theoretical discipline. "Nobody comes to Christ through arguments," they'll tell you. "People aren't interested in what's true, but in what works for them. They don't want intellectual answers; they want to see Christianity lived out." I believe that the attitude expressed in these statements is both shortsighted and mistaken. Let me explain three vital roles which the discipline of apologetics plays today.

1) *Shaping culture.* Christians need to see beyond their immediate evangelistic contact to grasp a wider picture of Western thought and culture. In general Western culture is deeply post-Christian. It is the product of the Enlightenment, which introduced into European culture the leaven of secularism that has by now permeated the whole of Western society. The hallmark of the Enlightenment was "free thought," that is, the pursuit of knowledge by means of unfettered human reason alone. While it's by no means inevitable that such a pursuit must lead to non-Christian conclusions and while most of the original Enlightenment thinkers were themselves theists, it has been the overwhelming impact of the Enlightenment mentality that Western intellectuals do not consider theological knowledge to be possible. Theology is not a source of genuine knowledge and therefore is not a science (in German, a *Wissenschaft*). Reason and religion are thus at odds with each other. The deliverances of the physical sciences alone are taken as authoritative guides to our understanding of the world, and the confident assumption is that the picture of the world which emerges from the genuine sciences is a thoroughly naturalistic picture. The person who follows the pursuit of reason unflinchingly toward its end will be atheistic or, at best, agnostic.

Why are these considerations of culture important? They're important simply because the gospel is never heard in isolation. It is always heard against the background of the cultural milieu in which one lives. A person raised in a cultural milieu in which Christianity is still seen as an intellectually viable option will display an openness to the gospel which a person who is secularized will not. For the secular person you may as well tell him to believe in fairies or leprechauns as in Jesus Christ! Or, to give a more realistic illustration, it is like our being approached on the street by a devotee of the Hare Krishna movement who invites us to believe in Krishna. Such an invitation strikes us as bizarre, freakish, even amusing. But to a person on the streets of Delhi, such an invitation would, I assume, appear quite reasonable and be serious cause for reflection. I fear that evangelicals appear almost as weird to persons on the streets of Bonn, Stockholm, or Paris as do the devotees of Krishna.

What awaits us in North America, should our slide into secularism continue unchecked, is already evident in Europe. Although the majority of Europeans retain a nominal affiliation with Christianity, only about 10 percent are practicing believers, and less than half of those are evangelical in theology. The most significant trend in European religious affiliation is the growth of those classed as "non-religious" from effectively 0 percent of the population in 1900 to over 22 percent today. As a result evangelism is immeasurably more difficult in Europe than in the United States. Having lived for thirteen years in Europe, where I spoke evangelistically on university campuses across the continent, I can personally testify to how hard the ground is. It's difficult for the gospel even to get a hearing.

The United States is following at some distance down this same road, with Canada somewhere in between. If the situation is not to degenerate further, it is imperative that we shape the intellectual climate of our nation in such a way that Christianity remains a live option for thinking men and women.

It is for that reason that Christians who depreciate the value of apologetics because "no one comes to Christ through arguments" are so shortsighted. For the value of apologetics extends far beyond one's immediate evangelistic contact. It is the broader task of Christian apologetics to help create and sustain a cultural milieu in which the gospel can be heard as an intellectually viable option for thinking men and women.

In his article "Christianity and Culture," on the eve of the Fundamentalist Controversy, the great Princeton theologian J. Gresham Machen solemnly warned,

> False ideas are the greatest obstacles to the reception of the Gospel. We may preach with all the fervor of a reformer and yet succeed only in winning a straggler here and there, if we permit the whole collective thought of the nation to be controlled by ideas which prevent Christianity from being regarded as anything more than a harmless delusion.[1]

Unfortunately, Machen's warning went unheeded, and biblical Christianity retreated into the intellectual closet of Fundamentalism. Anti-intellectualism and second-rate scholarship became the norm.

Already in his day, Machen observed that "many would have the seminaries combat error by attacking it as it is taught by its popular exponents" instead of confusing students "with a lot of German names unknown outside the walls of the university." But to the contrary, Machen insisted, it is crucial that Christians be alert to the power of an idea before it reaches its popular expression. The scholarly method of proceeding, he said,

> is based simply upon a profound belief in the pervasiveness of ideas. What is to-day a matter of academic speculation begins to-morrow to move armies and pull down empires. In that second stage, it has gone too far to be combated; the time to stop it was when it was still a matter of impassionate debate. So as Christians we should try to mold the thought of the world in such a way as to make the acceptance of Christianity something more than a logical absurdity.[2]

In Europe we have seen the bitter fruit of secularization, which now threatens North America as well.

---

1. J. Gresham Machen, "Christianity and Culture," *Princeton Theological Review* 11 (1913): 7.
2. Ibid.

Fortunately, in the United States in recent decades a revitalized evangelicalism has emerged from the Fundamentalist closet and has begun to take up Machen's challenge in earnest. We are living at a time when Christian philosophy is experiencing a veritable renaissance, reinvigorating natural theology, at a time when science is more open to the existence of a transcendent Creator and Designer of the cosmos than at any time in recent memory, and at a time when biblical criticism has embarked upon a renewed quest of the historical Jesus which treats the Gospels seriously as valuable historical sources for the life of Jesus and has confirmed the main lines of the portrait of Jesus painted in the Gospels. We are well poised intellectually to help reshape our culture in such a way as to regain lost ground, so that the gospel can be heard as an intellectually viable option for thinking people. Huge doors of opportunity now stand open before us.

Now I can imagine some of you thinking, "But don't we live in a postmodern culture in which these appeals to traditional apologetic arguments are no longer effective? Since postmodernists reject the traditional canons of logic, rationality, and truth, rational arguments for the truth of Christianity no longer work! Rather in today's culture we should simply share our narrative and invite people to participate in it."

In my opinion this sort of thinking could not be more mistaken. The idea that we live in a postmodern culture is a myth. In fact, a postmodern culture is an impossibility; it would be utterly unlivable. Nobody is a postmodernist when it comes to reading the labels on a medicine bottle versus a box of rat poison. If you've got a headache, you'd better believe that texts have objective meaning! People are not relativistic when it comes to matters of science, engineering, and technology; rather, they're relativistic and pluralistic in matters of religion and ethics. But that's not postmodernism; that's modernism! That's just old-line Positivism and Verificationism, which held that anything you can't prove with your five senses is just a matter of individual taste and emotive expression. We live in a cultural milieu which remains deeply modernist. People who think that we live in a postmodern culture have thus seriously misread our cultural situation.

Indeed, I think that getting people to believe that we live in a postmodern culture is one of the craftiest deceptions that Satan has yet devised. "Modernism is passé," he tells us. "You needn't worry about it any longer. So forget about it! It's dead and buried." Meanwhile, modernism, pretending to be dead, comes around again in the fancy new dress of postmodernism, masquerading as a new challenger. "Your old arguments and apologetics are no longer effective against this new arrival," we're told. "Lay them aside; they're of no use. Just share your narrative!" Indeed, some, weary of the long battles with modernism, actually welcome the new visitor with relief. And so Satan deceives us into voluntarily laying aside our best weapons of logic and evidence, thereby ensuring unawares modernism's triumph over us. If we adopt this suicidal course of action, the consequences for the church in the next generation will be catastrophic. Christianity will be reduced to but another voice in a cacophony of competing voices, each sharing its own narrative and none commending itself as the objective truth about reality, while scientific naturalism shapes our culture's view of how the world really is.

Now, of course, it goes without saying that in doing apologetics we should be relational, humble, and invitational; but that's hardly an original insight of post-modernism. From the beginning Christian apologists have known that we should present the reasons for our hope "with gentleness and respect" (1 Pet. 3:15–16 ESV). One needn't abandon the canons of logic, rationality, and truth in order to exemplify these biblical virtues.

Apologetics is therefore vital in fostering a cultural milieu in which the gospel can be heard as a viable option for thinking people. In most cases, it will not be arguments or evidence that bring a seeker to faith in Christ—that is the half-truth seen by detractors of apologetics—but nonetheless it will be apologetics which, by making the gospel a credible option for seeking people, gives them, as it were, the intellectual permission to believe. It is thus vitally important that we preserve a cultural milieu in which the gospel is heard as a living option for thinking people, and apologetics will be front and center in helping to bring about that result.

2) Strengthening believers. Not only is apologetics vital to shaping our culture, but it also plays a vital role in the lives of individual persons. One such role will be strengthening believers. Contemporary Christian worship tends to focus on fostering emotional intimacy with God. While this is a good thing, emotions will carry a person only so far, and then he's going to need something more substantive. Apologetics can help to provide some of that substance.

As I speak in churches around the country, I frequently meet parents who approach me after the service and say something like, "If only you'd been here two or three years ago! Our son [or our daughter] had questions about the faith which no one in the church could answer, and now he's lost his faith and is far from the Lord."

It just breaks my heart to meet parents like this. Unfortunately, their experience is not unusual. In high school and college Christian teenagers are intellectually assaulted with every manner of non-Christian worldview coupled with an over-whelming relativism. If parents are not intellectually engaged with their faith and do not have sound arguments for Christian theism and good answers to their children's questions, then we are in real danger of losing our youth. It's no longer enough to teach our children Bible stories; they need doctrine and apologetics. Frankly, I find it hard to understand how people today can risk parenthood without having studied apologetics.

Unfortunately, our churches have largely dropped the ball in this area. It's insufficient for youth groups and Sunday school classes to focus on entertainment and simpering devotional thoughts. We've got to train our kids for war. We dare not send them out to public high school and university armed with rubber swords and plastic armor. The time for playing games is past.

We need to have pastors who are schooled in apologetics and engaged intellectually with our culture so as to shepherd their flock amidst the wolves. For example, pastors need to know something about contemporary science. John La Shell, himself the pastor of a Baptist church, warns that "pastors can no longer afford to ignore the results and the speculations of modern physics. These ideas are percolating down into the common consciousness through magazines, popularized treatises, and even novels. If we do not familiarize ourselves with them we may find ourselves in an intellectual backwater, unable to deal with the well-read man across the street."[3] The same goes for philosophy and for biblical criticism: what good does it do to preach on, say, Christian values when there is a large percentage of people, even Christians, who say that they don't believe in absolute truth? Or what good will it do simply to quote the Bible in your evangelistic Bible study when somebody in the group says that the Jesus Seminar has disproved the reliability of the Gospels? If pastors fail to do their homework in these areas, then there will remain a substantial portion of the population—unfortunately, the most intelligent and therefore most influential people in society, such as doctors, educators, journalists, lawyers, business executives, and so forth—who will remain untouched by their ministry.

As I travel, I've also had the experience of meeting other people who've told me of how they've been saved from apparent apostasy through reading an apologetic book or seeing a video of a debate. In their case apologetics has been the means by which God has brought about their perseverance in the faith. Now, of course, apologetics cannot guarantee perseverance, but it can help and in some cases may, in the providence of God, even be necessary. For example, after a lecture at Princeton University on arguments for the existence of God, I was approached by a young man who wanted to talk with me. Obviously trying to hold back the tears, he told me that a couple of years earlier he had been struggling with doubts and was on the brink of abandoning his faith. Someone then gave him a video of one of my debates. He said, "It saved me from losing my faith. I cannot thank you enough."

I said, "It was the Lord who saved you from falling."

"Yes," he replied, "but he used you. I can't thank you too much." I told him how thrilled I was for him and asked him about his future plans. "I'm graduating this year," he told me, "and I plan to go to seminary. I'm going into the pastorate." Praise God for the victory in this young man's life!

But Christian apologetics does much more than safeguard against lapses. The positive, upbuilding effects of apologetic training are even more evident. American churches are filled with Christians who are idling in intellectual neutral. As Christians, their minds are going to waste. One result of this is an immature, superficial faith. People who simply ride the roller coaster of emotional experience are cheating

3. Critical notice of Ian G. Barbour, *Religion in an Age of Science*, reviewed by John K. La Shell, *Journal of the Evangelical Theological Society* 36 (1993): 261.

themselves out of a deeper and richer Christian faith by neglecting the intellectual side of that faith. They know little of the riches of deep understanding of Christian truth, of the confidence inspired by the discovery that one's faith is logical and fits the facts of experience, and of the stability brought to one's life by the conviction that one's faith is objectively true. One of the most gratifying results of the annual apologetics conferences held by the Evangelical Philosophical Society in local churches during the course of our annual conventions is to see the light come on in the minds of many laymen when they discover for the first time in their lives that there are good reasons to believe that Christianity is true and that there is a part of the body of Christ that they never knew existed that wrestles regularly with the intellectual content of the Christian faith.[4]

I also see the positive effects of apologetics when I debate on university campuses. Typically I'll be invited onto a campus to debate some professor who has a reputation of being especially abusive to Christian students in his classes. We'll have a public debate on, say, the existence of God, or Christianity versus humanism, or some such topic. Again and again I find that while most of these men are pretty good at beating up intellectually on an eighteen-year-old in one of their classes, they can't even hold their own when it comes to going toe-to-toe with one of their peers. John Stackhouse once remarked to me that these debates are really a Westernized version of what missiologists call a "power encounter." I think that's a perceptive analysis. Christian students come away from these encounters with a renewed confidence in their faith, their heads held high, proud to be Christians, and bolder in speaking out for Christ on their campus.

Many Christians do not share their faith with unbelievers simply out of fear. They're afraid that the non-Christian will ask them a question or raise an objection that they can't answer. And so they choose to remain silent and thus hide their light under a bushel, in disobedience to Christ's command. Apologetics training is a tremendous boost to evangelism, for nothing inspires confidence and boldness more than knowing that one has good reasons for what one believes and good answers to the typical questions and objections that the unbeliever may raise. Sound training in apologetics is one of the keys to fearless evangelism. In this and many other ways apologetics helps to build up the body of Christ by strengthening individual believers.

3) *Evangelizing unbelievers*. Few people would disagree with me that apologetics strengthens the faith of Christian believers. But many will say that apologetics is not very useful in evangelism. As noted earlier, they claim that nobody comes to Christ through arguments. (I don't know how many times I've heard this said.)

Now this dismissive attitude toward apologetics' role in evangelism is certainly not the biblical view. As one reads the Acts of the Apostles, it's evident that it was the apostles' standard procedure to argue for the truth of the Christian worldview, both with Jews and pagans (e.g., Acts 17:2–3, 17; 19:8; 28:23–24). In dealing with

---

4. For more information on these extraordinary lay conferences, go to www.epsociety.org.

Jewish audiences, the apostles appealed to fulfilled prophecy, Jesus' miracles, and especially Jesus' resurrection as evidence that he was the Messiah (Acts 2:22–32). When they confronted Gentile audiences who did not accept Jewish Scripture, the apostles appealed to God's handiwork in nature as evidence of the existence of the Creator (Acts 14:17). Then appeal was made to the eyewitness testimony to the resurrection of Jesus to show specifically that God had revealed himself in Jesus Christ (Acts 17:30–31; 1 Cor. 15:3–8).

Frankly, I can't help but suspect that those who regard apologetics as futile in evangelism just don't do enough evangelism. I suspect that they've tried using apologetic arguments on occasion and found that the unbeliever remained unconvinced. They then draw a general conclusion that apologetics is ineffective in evangelism.

Now to a certain extent such persons are just victims of false expectations. When you reflect that only a minority of people who hear the gospel will accept it and that only a minority of those who accept it do so for intellectual reasons, we shouldn't be surprised that the number of people with whom apologetics is effective is relatively small. By the very nature of the case, we should expect that most unbelievers will remain unconvinced by our apologetic arguments, just as most remain unmoved by the preaching of the cross.

Well, then, why bother with that minority of a minority with whom apologetics is effective? First, because every person is precious to God, a person for whom Christ died. Like a missionary called to reach some obscure people group, the Christian apologist is burdened to reach that minority of persons who will respond to rational argument and evidence.

But, second—and here the case differs significantly from the case of the obscure people group—this people group, though relatively small in numbers, is huge in influence. One of these persons, for example, was C. S. Lewis. Think of the impact that one man's conversion continues to have! I find that the people who resonate most with my apologetic work tend to be engineers, people in medicine, and lawyers. Such persons are among the most influential in shaping our culture today. So reaching this minority of persons will yield a great harvest for the kingdom of God.

In any case, the general conclusion that apologetics is ineffective in evangelism is hasty. Lee Strobel recently remarked to me that he has lost count of the number of people who have come to Christ through his books *The Case for Christ* and *The Case for Faith*. Speakers such as Josh McDowell and Ravi Zacharias have brought thousands to Christ through apologetically-oriented evangelism. Nor, if I may speak personally, has it been my experience that apologetics is ineffective in evangelism. We continually are thrilled to see people committing their lives to Christ through apologetically-oriented presentations of the gospel. After a talk on arguments for the existence of God or evidence for the resurrection of Jesus or a defense of Christian particularism, I'll sometimes conclude with a prayer of commitment to give one's life to Christ, and the comment cards indicate that students have registered such a commitment. I've even seen students come to Christ just through hearing a defense of the *kalām* cosmological argument!

It's been thrilling, too, to meet people who have come to Christ through reading something I've written. For example, when I was speaking in Moscow a few years ago I met a man from Minsk in Byelorussia. He told me that shortly after the fall of communism he had heard someone reading in Russian my book *The Existence of God and the Beginning of the Universe* over the radio in Minsk. By the end of the broadcast he had become convinced that God exists and yielded his life to Christ. He told me that today he is serving the Lord as an elder in a Baptist church in Minsk. Praise God! Recently, at Texas A&M University, I met a woman attending one of my talks. She told me with tears that for twenty-seven years she had been far away from God and was feeling hopeless and meaningless. Browsing in a Border's bookstore she ran across my book *Will the Real Jesus Please Stand Up?* which contains my debate with John Dominic Crossan, co-chairman of the radical Jesus Seminar, and bought a copy. She said that as she read it, it was as though the light just came on, and she gave her life to Christ. When I asked her what she does, she told me that she is a psychologist who works in a Texas prison for women. Just think of the Christian influence she can have in so desperate an environment!

Stories like these could be multiplied. So those who say that apologetics is not effective with unbelievers must be speaking out of their limited experience. When apologetics is persuasively presented and sensitively combined with a gospel presentation and a personal testimony, the Spirit of God condescends to use it in bringing certain people to himself.

So Christian apologetics is a vital part of the theological curriculum. Our focus in this book will be on the theoretical issues rather than on practical "how-tos." At the same time, I recognize that there remains the question of how to apply the theoretical material learned in this course. I've always thought that this problem was best left to each individual to work out according to the type of ministry to which he feels called. After all, I'm interested not only in training pastors but also systematic theologians, philosophers of religion, and church historians. But it has become clear to me that some people simply don't know how to translate theory into practice. Therefore, I've included a subsection on practical application after each major section of the course. I *know* the theoretical material is practical because I employ it often in evangelism and discipleship and see God use it.

Two Types of Apologetics

The field of apologetics may be broadly divided into two sorts: offensive (or positive) apologetics and defensive (or negative) apologetics. Offensive apologetics seeks to present a positive case for Christian truth claims. Defensive apologetics seeks to nullify objections to those claims. Offensive apologetics tends to subdivide into two categories: natural theology and Christian evidences. The burden of natural theology is to provide arguments and evidence in support of theism independent of authoritative, divine revelation. The ontological, cosmological, teleological, and moral arguments for the existence of God are classical examples of the arguments of natural theology. The goal of Christian evidences is to show why a specifically Christian theism is true. Typical Christian evidences include fulfilled prophecy, the radical personal claims of Christ, the historical reliability of the Gospels, and so forth. A similar subdivision exists within defensive apologetics. In the division corresponding to natural theology, defensive apologetics will address objections to theism. The alleged incoherence of the concept of God and the problem of evil would be the paramount issues here. Corresponding to Christian evidences will be a defense against objections to biblical theism. The objections posed by modern biblical criticism and by contemporary science to the biblical record dominate this field.

In actual practice, these two basic approaches—offensive and defensive—can blend together. For example, one way to offer a defense against the problem of evil would be to offer a positive moral argument for the existence of God precisely on the basis of moral evil in the world. Or again, in offering a positive case for the resurrection of Jesus, one may have to answer objections raised by biblical criticism to the historical credibility of the resurrection narratives. Nonetheless, the overall thrust of these two approaches remains quite distinct: the goal of offensive apologetics is to show that there is some good reason to think that Christianity is true, while the goal of defensive apologetics is to show that no good reason has been given to think that Christianity is false.

It is evident from a glance at the contents page that this book constitutes a course in offensive, rather than defensive, apologetics. Although I hope someday to write a book offering a course in defensive apologetics, I think that a first course in this discipline ought to be positive in nature. There are two related reasons undergirding this conviction. First, a purely negative apologetic only tells you what you ought *not* to believe, not what you should believe. Even if one could succeed in refuting all known objections to Christianity, one would still be left without any reason to think that it is true. In the pluralistic age in which we live, the need for a positive apologetic is especially urgent. Second, by having in hand a positive justification of the Christian faith, one automatically overwhelms all competing worldviews lacking an equally strong case. Thus, if you have a sound and persuasive case for Christianity, you don't have to become an expert in comparative religions and Christian cults so as to offer a refutation of every one of these counter-Christian views. If your positive apologetic is better than theirs, then you have done your job in showing Christianity to be true. Even if you're confronted with an objection which you can't answer, you can still commend your faith as more plausible than its competitors if the arguments and evidence in support of Christian truth claims are stronger than those supporting the unanswered objection. For these reasons, I have sought in this book to lay out a positive case for the Christian faith which, I hope, will be helpful to you in confirming and commending your faith.

For many readers much of this course material will be new and difficult. Nevertheless, *all* of it is important, and if you apply yourself diligently to mastering and interacting personally and critically with this material, you will, I am sure, find it as exciting as it is important.

Part 1

De Fide

1

How Do I Know Christianity Is True?

Before we attempt to build a case for Christianity, we must come to grips with some very fundamental questions about the nature and relationship of faith and reason. Exactly how do we know Christianity to be true? Is it simply by a leap of faith or on the authority of the Word of God, both unrelated to reason? Does religious experience assure us of the truth of the Christian faith, so that no further justification is needed? Or is an evidential foundation for faith necessary, without which faith would be unjustified and irrational? We can better answer these questions if we briefly survey some of the most important representative thinkers of the past.

Historical Background

Medieval

In our historical survey, let's look first at Augustine (354–430) and Thomas Aquinas (1224–1274). Their approaches were determinative for the Middle Ages.

AUGUSTINE

Augustine's attitude toward faith and reason is very difficult to interpret, especially because his views apparently evolved over the years. Sometimes we get the impression that he was a strict authoritarian; that is to say, he held that the ground for faith was sheer, unquestionable, divine authority. This authority might be expressed in either the Scriptures or in the church. Thus, Augustine confessed, "I should not believe the Gospel except as moved by the authority of the Catholic Church."[1] The authority of Scripture he held in even higher esteem than that of the church. Because the Scriptures are inspired by God, they are completely free from error and are therefore to be believed absolutely.[2] Such a view of authority would seem to imply that reason has no role to play in the justification of belief, and sometimes Augustine gives that impression. He asserts that one must first believe before he can know.[3] He was fond of quoting Isaiah 7:9 in the Septuagint version: "Unless you believe you shall not understand." The fundamental principle of the Augustinian tradition throughout the Middle Ages was *fides quaerens intellectum*: faith seeking understanding.

But certain statements of Augustine's make it clear that he was not an unqualified authoritarian. He maintained that authority and reason cooperate in bringing a person to faith. Authority demands belief and prepares man for reason, and reason in turn leads to understanding and knowledge. But at the same time, reason is not entirely absent from authority, for one has to consider whom to believe, and the highest authority belongs to clearly known truth; that is to say, the truth, when it is clearly known, has the highest claim to authority because it demands our assent. According to Augustine, it is our duty to consider what men or what books we ought to believe in order to worship God rightly. Gerhard Strauss, in his book on Augustine's doctrine of Scripture, explains that although for Augustine Scripture is absolutely authoritative and inerrant in itself, it does not carry credibility in itself—that is, people will not automatically accept its authority upon hearing it. Therefore, there must be certain signs (*indicia*) of credibility that make its authority evident. On the basis of these signs, we can believe that the Scripture is the authoritative Word of God and submit to its authority. The principal signs adduced by Augustine on behalf of the authority of Scripture are miracle and prophecy. Though many religions boast of revelations showing the way of salvation, only the Scriptures have the support of miracle and prophecy, which prove it to be the true authority.

Thus, Augustine's authoritarianism would seem to be drastically qualified. Perhaps Augustine's apparent inconsistency is best explained by the medieval understanding of authority. In the early church, authority (*auctoritas*) included not just theological truths but the whole tradition of past knowledge. The relationship between authority and reason was not the same as that between faith and reason. Rather it was the relationship between all past knowledge and present-day understanding. Knowledge of the past was simply accepted on the basis of authority. This seems to have been Augustine's attitude. He distinguishes between what is

---

1. Augustine, *Against the Epistle of Manichaeus Called Fundamental* 5.6.
2. Augustine, *Letters* 82.3; idem *City of God* 21.6.1.
3. Augustine, *On Free Will* 2.1.6.

seen to be true and what is *believed* to be true. We *see* that something is true by either physical perception or rational demonstration. We *believe* that something is true on the basis of the testimony of others. Hence, with regard to miracle and prophecy, Augustine says that the trustworthiness of reports of either past or future events must be believed, not known by the intelligence. Elsewhere he declares that one should believe in God because belief in him is taught in the books of men who have left their testimony in writing that they lived with the Son of God and saw things that could not have happened if there were no God. Then he concludes that one must believe before he can know. Since for Augustine the historical evidence for miracle and prophecy lay in the past, it was in the realm of authority, not reason. Today, on the other hand, we would say that such a procedure would be an attempt to provide a rational foundation for authority via historical apologetics.

Now the obvious question at this point is, Why accept the authority of the writers of the past, whether they be the classical writers or the authors of Scripture? Clearly, if Augustine is to avoid circular reasoning, he cannot say that we should accept the authority of the evangelists because of the authority of Scripture, for it is the evangelists' testimony to miracle and prophecy that is supposed to make evident the authority of Scripture. So Augustine must either come up with some reason to accept the evangelists' testimony as reliable or abandon this historically oriented approach. Since he lacked the historical method, the first alternative was not open to him. Therefore, he chose the second. He frankly admits that the books containing the story of Christ belong to an ancient history that anyone may refuse to believe. Therefore, he turns to the present miracle of the church as the basis for accepting the authority of Scripture. He saw the very existence of the mighty and universal church as an overwhelming sign that the Scriptures are true and divine.

Now notice that Augustine is not basing the authority of Scripture on the authority of the church, for he held the Scripture's authority to exceed even that of the church. Rather, his appeal is still to the sign of miracle, not indeed the Gospel miracles, which are irretrievably removed in the past, but the present and evident miracle of the church. In *The City of God* he states that even if the unbeliever rejects all biblical miracles, he is still left with one stupendous miracle, which is all one needs, namely, the fact of the whole world believing in Christianity without the benefit of the Gospel miracles.[4] It's interesting that, by appealing to a present miracle as the sign of the authority of Scripture, Augustine seems to have implicitly denied authoritarianism, since this sign was not in the past, in the realm of authority where it could only be believed, but in the present, where it could be seen and known. Be that as it may, Augustine's emphases on biblical authority and signs of credibility were to set the tone for subsequent medieval theology.

4. Augustine, *City of God* 22.5.

THOMAS AQUINAS

Aquinas's *Summa contra gentiles*, written to combat Greco-Arabic philosophy, is the greatest apologetic work of the Middle Ages and so merits our attention. Thomas develops a framework for the relationship of faith and reason that includes the Augustinian signs of credibility. He begins by making a distinction within truths about God. On the one hand, there are truths that completely surpass the capability of human reason, for example, the doctrine of the Trinity. On the other hand, many truths lie within the grasp of human reason, such as the existence of God. In the first three volumes of the *Summa contra gentiles*, Thomas attempts to prove these truths of reason, including the existence and nature of God, the orders of creation, the nature and end of man, and so forth. But when he comes to the fourth volume, in which he handles subjects like the Trinity, the incarnation, the sacraments, and the last things, he suddenly changes his method of approach. He states that these things are to be proved by the authority of Holy Scripture, not by natural reason. Because these doctrines surpass reason, they are properly objects of faith.

Now at first blush this seems to suggest that for Aquinas these truths of faith are mysteries, somehow "above logic." But here we must be very careful. For as I read Aquinas, that's not how he defines his terms. Rather he seems to mean that truths of faith surpass reason in the sense that they are neither empirically evident nor demonstrable with absolute certainty. He makes no suggestion that truths of faith transcend Aristotelian logic. Rather there are just no empirical facts which make these truths evident or from which these truths may be inferred. For example, although the existence of God can be proved from his effects, there are no empirical facts from which the Trinity may be inferred. Or again, the eschatological resurrection of the dead cannot be proved, because there is no empirical evidence for this future event. Elsewhere Thomas makes it clear that truths of faith cannot be demonstrated by reason alone, either. He maintains that we Christians must use only arguments that prove their conclusions with absolute certainty; for if we use mere probability arguments, the insufficiency of those arguments will only serve to confirm the non-Christian in his unbelief.[5]

Thus, the distinction Thomas makes between truths of reason and truths of faith is rather like Augustine's distinction between seeing and believing. Truths of reason may be "seen"—that is, either proved with rational certainty or accepted as empirically evident—whereas truths of faith must be believed, since they are neither empirically evident nor rationally provable. This does not mean that truths of faith are incomprehensible or "above logic."

Now because truths of faith can only be believed, does this imply that Thomas is in the end a fideist or an authoritarian? The answer seems clearly no. For like Augustine he proceeds to argue that God provides the signs of miracle and prophecy, which serve to confirm the truths of faith, though not demonstrating them directly. Because of these signs, Aquinas held that a man can see the truths of faith:

---

5. Thomas Aquinas, *Summa theologiae* 1a.32.1; cf. idem, *Summa contra gentiles* 1.9.

"Then they are indeed seen by the one who believes; he would not believe unless he saw that they are worthy of belief on the basis of evident signs or something of this sort."[6] Thomas calls these signs "confirmations," "arguments," and "proofs" for the truths of faith.[7] This seems to make it clear that Aquinas believed there are good grounds for accepting the truths of faith as a whole. The proofs of miracle and prophecy are compelling, although they are indirect. Thus, for example, the doctrine of the Trinity is a truth of faith because it cannot be directly proved by any argument; nevertheless, it is indirectly proved insofar as the truths of faith taken together as a whole are shown to be credible by the divine signs.

Thomas's procedure, then, may be summarized in three steps: (1) Fulfilled prophecies and miracles make it credible that the Scriptures taken together as a whole are a revelation from God. (2) As a revelation from God, Scripture is absolutely authoritative. (3) Therefore, those doctrines taught by Scripture that are neither demonstrably provable nor empirically evident may be accepted by faith on the authority of Scripture. Thus, Aquinas can say that an opponent may be convinced of the truths of faith on the basis of the authority of Scripture as confirmed by God with miracles.[8]

Again the question arises: How do we know that the purported miracles or fulfilled prophecies ever took place? The medieval thinkers, lacking the historical method, could not answer this question. They developed a philosophical framework in which the signs of credibility confirmed the truths of faith, but they had no way of proving the signs themselves. About the only argument was Augustine's indirect proof from the miracle of the church. Thus, Thomas declares,

> Now such a wondrous conversion of the world to the Christian faith is a most indubitable proof that such signs did take place. . . . For it would be the most wondrous sign of all if without any wondrous signs the world were persuaded by simple and lowly men to believe things so arduous, to accomplish things so difficult, and to hope for things so sublime.[9]

A final word might be added. With Aquinas we see the reduction of faith to an epistemological category; that is to say, faith was no longer trust or commitment of the heart, but became a way of knowing, complementary to reason. Faith was essentially intellectual assent to doctrines not provable by reason—hence, Aquinas's view that a doctrine cannot be both known and believed: if you know it (by reason), then you cannot believe it (by faith). Thus, Aquinas diminished the view of faith as trust or commitment. This same intellectualist understanding of faith characterized the documents of the Council of Trent and of Vatican I but was adjusted in the documents of Vatican II.

6. Thomas Aquinas, *Summa theologiae* 2a2ae.1.4 *ad* 2.
7. Thomas Aquinas, *Summa contra gentiles* 3.154; 1.6.
8. Ibid., 1.9.
9. Ibid.

The Enlightenment

The fact that the Enlightenment is also known as the Age of Reason gives us a good clue as to how thinkers of that period regarded the relationship between faith and reason. Nevertheless, there was not complete agreement on this issue, and the two figures we shall survey represent two fundamentally opposed viewpoints.

JOHN LOCKE

The thought of John Locke (1632–1704) was determinative for the eighteenth century. His *Essay Concerning Human Understanding* (1689) laid down the epistemological principles that were to shape religious thought during that age. Though he rejected the philosophical rationalism of Descartes, Locke was nevertheless an ardent theological rationalist. That is to say, he maintained that religious belief must have an evidential foundation and that where such a foundation is absent, religious belief is unwarranted. Locke himself attempted to provide such an evidential foundation.

Locke argued for the existence of God by means of a cosmological argument—indeed, he maintained that the existence of God is "the most obvious truth that reason discovers," having an evidence "equal to mathematical certainty."[10] When one moves beyond such matters of demonstrable reason into matters of faith, Locke insisted that revealed truths cannot contradict reason. God can reveal to us both truths attainable by reason (though reason gives greater certainty of these than does revelation) as well as truths unattainable by reason. The revealed truths unattainable by reason cannot contradict reason, because we shall always be more certain of the truth of reason than we shall be of a purported revelation that contradicts reason. Therefore, no proposition contrary to reason can be accepted as divine revelation. Thus, although we know that a revelation from God must be true, it still lies within the scope of reason to determine if a supposed revelation really is from God and to determine its meaning.[11]

More than that, revelation must not only be in harmony with reason but must itself be guaranteed by appropriate rational proofs that it is indeed divine. Otherwise, one degenerates into irresponsible enthusiasm:

> Revelation is natural reason enlarged by a new set of discoveries communicated by God immediately, which reason vouches the truth of by the testimony and proofs it gives that they come from God. So that he that takes away reason to make way for revelation, puts out the light of both; and does much the same as if he would persuade a man to put out his eyes, the better to receive the remote light of an invisible star by a telescope.[12]

10. John Locke, *An Essay Concerning Human Understanding*, 4.10.1.
11. Ibid., 4.18.5.
12. Ibid., 4.19.4.

Religious enthusiasm was the form of religious expression most scorned by the intellectualist believers of the Age of Reason, and Locke would have nothing to do with it. Only if reason makes plausible that a purported revelation is genuine can that revelation be believed.

Hence, in his subsequent works *The Reasonableness of Christianity* (1695) and *Discourse on Miracles* (1690), Locke argued that fulfilled prophecy and palpable miracles furnish proof of Christ's divine mission. He set forth three criteria for discerning a genuine revelation. First, it must not be dishonoring to God or inconsistent with natural religion and the natural moral law. Second, it must not inform man of things indifferent, insignificant, or easily discovered by natural ability. Third, it must be confirmed by supernatural signs. For Locke, the chief of these signs was miracle. On the basis of Jesus' miracles, we are justified in regarding him as the Messiah and his revelation from God as true.

As the fountainhead for both Deist works and orthodox apologetics, Locke's outlook shaped the religious thought of the eighteenth century. Be they Deist or orthodox, most thinkers of the century after Locke agreed that reason was to be given priority even in matters of faith, that revelation could not contradict reason, and that reason provided the essential foundation to religious belief.

HENRY DODWELL

That is not to say that dissenting voices could not be heard. Henry Dodwell (1700–1784) in his *Christianity Not Founded on Argument* (1742) attacked the prevailing theological rationalism as antithetical to true Christianity. Dodwell was so out of step with his times that he has even been suspected of being an unbeliever who appealed to an arational, subjective basis for religious faith as a subterfuge for undermining the rationality of Christianity. It seems to me, however, that Dodwell is to be taken straightforwardly as a spokesman for the anti-rationalistic religious tradition, which was not altogether absent even during the Enlightenment.

Dodwell argues that matters of religious faith lie outside the determination of reason. God could not possibly have intended that reason should be the faculty to lead us to faith, for faith cannot hang indefinitely in suspense while reason cautiously weighs and reweighs arguments. The Scriptures teach, on the contrary, that the way to God is by means of the heart, not by means of the intellect. Faith is simply a gift of the Holy Spirit. What then is the basis of faith? Dodwell answers, authority—not indeed the arbitrary authority of the church but rather the inner light of a constant and particular revelation imparted separately and supernaturally to every individual. Dodwell's appeal is thus to the inner, faith-producing work of the Holy Spirit in each individual's heart. His subjectively based apologetic appears to have generated no following among the scholars of his day, but later a similar emphasis on the witness of the Spirit by the Wesleys and Whitefield was to be an earmark of the great revivals that opened fresh springs for the dry souls of the English laity.

Contemporary

During the twentieth century, theological discussion of the relationship between faith and reason has replayed many of these same themes.

KARL BARTH AND RUDOLF BULTMANN

Both the dialectical theology championed by Karl Barth (1886–1968) and the existential theology propounded by Rudolf Bultmann (1884–1976) were characterized by a religious epistemology of authoritarianism.

According to Barth, there can be no approach to God whatsoever via human reason. Apart from God's revelation in Christ, human reason comprehends absolutely nothing about God. The fundamental reason for this agnosticism concerning human knowledge of God seems to be Barth's firm commitment to the thesis that God is "wholly other" and therefore transcends all categories of human thought and logic. This belief led Barth to deny the Roman Catholic doctrine of an analogy of being between God and man. According to that doctrine, creation as the product of its Creator shares in an analogous way certain properties possessed most perfectly by God such as being, goodness, truth, and so forth. According to Barth, God is so transcendent that no analogy exists between him and the creature. Hence, it follows that there can be no natural knowledge of God at all. But God has revealed himself to man in Jesus Christ; indeed, Christ is the revelation or Word of God. In him alone there is found an analogy of faith that affords some knowledge of God. But even this knowledge seems to be experiential rather than cognitive: it is a personal encounter with the Word of God, who confronts us now and again through different forms, such as the Bible or preaching. Even in his self-disclosure God remains hidden: "He meets us as the One who is hidden, the One about whom we must admit that we do not know what we are saying when we try to say who He is."[13] God remains incomprehensible and the propositions we assert about him are true in an incomprehensible way.

This might lead one to think that for Barth fideism is the only route by which someone might come to the knowledge of God. This does not, however, seem to be precisely correct. For Barth emphasizes that the personal encounter with the Word of God results entirely from the sovereign, divine initiative. Lost in sin, man cannot even begin to *move* in the direction of faith, so that even a leap of faith is impossible for him. No, it must be God who breaks into man's indolent sinfulness to confront him with the Word of God. As Barth writes, "Knowledge of God is a knowledge completely effected and determined from the side of its object, from the side of God."[14] Or again, "*the fact that* he did come to this decision, *that* he really believed, and that he actually had freedom to enter this new life of obedience and hope—all this was not the work of *his* spirit, but the work

---

13. Karl Barth, *The Knowledge of God and the Science of God according to the Teaching of the Reformation*, trans. J. L. M. Haire and I. Henderson (New York: Scribner's, 1939), 27.
14. Karl Barth, *Dogmatics in Outline*, trans. G. J. Thomson (New York: Philosophical Library, 1947), 24.

of the *Holy* Spirit."[15] Barth believed that the Reformation doctrine of justification by grace through faith is incompatible with any human initiative—even fideism. If knowing God depends wholly on God's grace, then even the act of faith would be a sinful work were it not wholly wrought by God. If it be asked how one knows that it is indeed the Word of God that confronts him and not a delusion, Barth would simply respond that such a question is meaningless. When the Word of God confronts a man, he is not free to analyze, weigh, and consider as a disinterested judge or observer—he can only obey. The authority of the Word of God is the foundation for religious belief.

Like Barth, Bultmann also rejects any human apprehension of the Word of God (which he seems to identify primarily with the call to authentic existence embodied in the gospel) apart from faith. Bultmann construes faith in epistemological categories, opposing it to knowledge based on proof. In the existentialist tradition, he considers it essential to faith that it involves risk and uncertainty. Therefore, rational evidence is not only irrelevant, but actually contrary to faith. Faith, in order to be faith, must exist in an evidential vacuum. For this reason Bultmann denies any significance for the Christian message to the historical Jesus, apart from his bare existence. Bultmann recognizes that Paul in 1 Corinthians 15 does "think that he can guarantee the resurrection of Christ as an objective fact by listing the witnesses who had seen him risen."[16] But he characterizes such historical argumentation as "fatal" because it tries to produce proof for the Christian proclamation.[17] Should an attempt at proof succeed, this would mean the destruction of faith. Only a decision to believe wholly apart from evidence will bring one into contact with the existential significance of the gospel. Bultmann emphasizes that this does not mean that such a step is made arbitrarily or lightheartedly. No, the existential issues of life and death weigh so heavily that this decision to believe is the most important and awesome step a person can take. But it must be taken in the absence of any rational criteria for choice.

This might lead one to think that Bultmann is a pure fideist; but again this does not seem quite correct. For he insists that the very authority of the Word of God strips away all demands for criteria: "As though God had to justify himself to man! As though every demand for justification (including the one concealed in the demand for criteria) did not have to be dropped as soon as the face of God appears!"[18] As Wolfhart Pannenberg explains, the "basic presupposition underlying German Protestant theology as expressed by Barth or Bultmann is that the basis

15. Barth, *Knowledge*, 109.

16. Rudolf Bultmann, *Theologie des Neuen Testaments*, 7th ed., ed. O. Merk (Tübingen: J.C.B. Mohr, 1961), 295.

17. Rudolf Bultmann, "Reply to the Theses of J. Schniewind," in *Kerygma and Myth*, ed. H.-W. Bartsch, trans. R. H. Fuller (London: SPCK, 1953), 1:112.

18. Rudolf Bultmann, "The Case for Demythologizing: A Reply," in *Kerygma and Myth*, ed. H.-W. Bartsch, trans. R. H. Fuller (London: SPCK, 1953), 2:191.

of theology is the self-authenticating Word of God which demands obedience."[19] Thus, it would seem that in both dialectical and existential theology the final appeal is authoritarian.

WOLFHART PANNENBERG

Pannenberg's rigorously evidential approach to theological questions was widely acclaimed as ushering in a new phase in European Protestant theology. In 1961 a circle of young theologians for whom Pannenberg served as the principal spokesman asserted in their manifesto *Offenbarung als Geschichte* [*Revelation as History*] that revelation ought to be understood exclusively in terms of God's acts in history, not as some self-authenticating Word.

Because this "Word," which was understood as God's self-disclosure in a divine-human encounter, needs no external authentication, theology, according to Pannenberg, has depreciated the relevance of history to faith and walled itself off against secular knowledge. On the one hand, Bultmann's existentialist theology neglected objective historical facticity in favor of finding the conditions for authentic human existence in the apostolic proclamation, to which historical facts are thought to be strictly irrelevant. On the other hand, Barth's understanding of peculiarly Christian events as belonging, not to the course of ordinary, investigable history, but rather to redemptive history, which is closed to historical research, equally devalues real history. Both schools share a common motive in their depreciation of the importance of history for faith, namely, the desire to secure for faith an impregnable stronghold against the assaults of modern historical-critical studies. Dialectical theology fled into the harbor of supra-history, supposedly safe from the historical-critical floodtide, while existential theology withdrew from the course of objective history to the subjective experience of human authenticity. Theology's attempt at self-isolationism backfired, however, because the secular sciences turned upon it to criticize and contradict it. "For much too long a time faith has been misunderstood to be subjectivity's fortress into which Christianity could retreat from the attacks of scientific knowledge. Such a retreat into pious subjectivity can only lead to destroying any consciousness of the truth of the Christian faith."[20]

Therefore, if Christianity is to make any meaningful claim to truth, it must, according to Pannenberg, submit to the same procedures of testing and verification that are employed in the secular sciences. This method of verification will be indirect, for example, by means of historical research. A theological interpretation of history will be tested positively by "its ability to take into account all known historical details," and negatively by "the proof that without its specific assertions the acces-

---

19. Wolfhart Pannenberg, ed. *Revelation as History*, trans. D. Granskou (London: Macmillan, 1968), 9.

20. Wolfhart Pannenberg, "The Revelation of God in Jesus of Nazareth," in *New Frontiers in Theology*, vol. 3: *Theology as History*, ed. J. M. Robinson and J. B. Cobb Jr. (New York: Harper & Row, 1967), 131.

sible information would not be at all or would be only incompletely explicable."[21] Since the Christian faith is based on a real past event, and since there is no way to know the past other than by historical-critical research, it follows that the object of Christian faith cannot remain untouched by the results of such research. On the one hand, a kerygmatic Christ utterly unrelated to the real, historical Jesus would be "pure myth"; and on the other hand, a Christ known only through dialectical encounter would be impossible to distinguish from "self-delusion."[22] Therefore, the unavoidable conclusion is that the burden of proving that God has revealed himself in Jesus of Nazareth must fall upon the historian.

Pannenberg acknowledges that if the historical foundation for faith were removed, then Christianity should be abandoned. He is, however, confident that given the historical facts that we now have, this eventuality will not occur. Pannenberg realizes that the results of historical investigation always retain a degree of uncertainty, but nevertheless, through this "precarious and provisional" way a knowledge of the truth of Christianity is possible. Without this factual foundation logically prior to faith, faith would be reduced to gullibility, credulity, or superstition. Only this evidential approach, in contrast to the subjectivism of modern theology, can establish Christianity's truth claim. The historical facts at the foundation of Christianity are reliable, and therefore we can base our faith, our lives, and our future on them.

ALVIN PLANTINGA

Appealing to what he (erroneously, I think) calls the Reformed objection to natural theology, Alvin Plantinga has launched a sustained attack on theological rationalism. Plantinga maintains that belief in God and in the central doctrines of Christianity is both rational and warranted wholly apart from any evidential foundations for belief.

This brings him into conflict with what he calls the evidentialist objection to theistic belief. According to the evidentialist, one is rationally justified in believing a proposition to be true only if that proposition is either foundational to knowledge or is established by evidence that is ultimately based on such a foundation. According to this viewpoint, since the proposition "God exists" is not foundational, it would be irrational to believe this proposition apart from rational evidence for its truth.

But, Plantinga asks, why can't the proposition "God exists" be itself part of the foundation, so that no rational evidence is necessary? The evidentialist replies that only propositions that are properly basic can be part of the foundation of knowledge. What, then, are the criteria that determine whether or not a proposition is properly basic? Typically, the evidentialist asserts that only propositions that are

---

21. Wolfhart Pannenberg, "Redemptive Event and History," in *Basic Questions in Theology*, trans. G. Kehm (Philadelphia: Fortress, 1970), 1:78.

22. Wolfhart Pannenberg, *Jesus—God and Man*, trans. L. L. Wilkins and D. A. Priebe (London: SCM, 1968), 27–28.

self-evident or incorrigible are properly basic. For example, the proposition "The sum of the squares of the two sides of a right triangle is equal to the square of the hypotenuse" is self-evidently true. Similarly, the proposition "I feel pain" is incorrigibly true, since even if I am only imagining my injury, it is still true that I *feel* pain. Since the proposition "God exists" is neither self-evident nor incorrigible, it is not properly basic and therefore requires evidence if it is to be believed. To believe this proposition without evidence is therefore irrational.

Plantinga does not deny that self-evident and incorrigible propositions are properly basic, but he does ask how we know that these are the *only* properly basic propositions or beliefs. If they are, then we are all irrational, since we commonly accept numerous beliefs that are not based on evidence and that are neither self-evident nor incorrigible. For example, take the belief that the world was not created five minutes ago with built-in memory traces, food in our stomachs from the breakfasts we never really ate, and other appearances of age. Surely it is rational to believe that the world has existed longer than five minutes, even though there is no evidence for this. The evidentialist's criteria for proper basicality must be flawed. In fact, what about the status of those criteria? Is the proposition "Only propositions that are self-evident or incorrigible are properly basic" *itself* properly basic? Apparently not, for it is certainly not self-evident or incorrigible. Therefore, if we are to believe this proposition, we must have evidence that it is true. But there is no such evidence. The proposition appears to be just an arbitrary definition—and not a very plausible one at that! Hence, the evidentialist cannot exclude the possibility that belief in God is a properly basic belief.

And in fact, Plantinga maintains, following John Calvin, belief in God is properly basic. Man has an innate, natural capacity to apprehend God's existence even as he has a natural capacity to accept truths of perception (like "I see a tree"). Given the appropriate circumstances—such as moments of guilt, gratitude, or a sense of God's handiwork in nature—man naturally apprehends God's existence. In the same way that certain perceptual beliefs, like "I see a tree," are properly basic given the appropriate circumstances, so belief in God is properly basic in appropriate circumstances. Neither the tree's existence nor God's existence is *inferred* from one's experience of the circumstances. But being in the appropriate circumstances is what renders one's belief *properly* basic; the belief would be irrational were it to be held under inappropriate circumstances. Thus, the basic belief that God exists is not arbitrary, since it is properly held only by a person placed in appropriate circumstances. Similarly, taking belief in God as properly basic does not commit one to the relativistic view that virtually any belief can be properly basic for a normal adult. In the absence of appropriate circumstances, various beliefs taken as basic by certain persons will be arbitrarily and irrationally held. Even in the absence of an adequate criterion of proper basicality to replace the flawed evidentialist criterion, the fact is that we can know that some beliefs are just not *properly* basic. Thus, the Christian who takes belief in God as properly basic can legitimately reject the proper basicality of other beliefs. Plantinga thus insists that his epistemology is not fideistic; the deliverances of reason include not only inferred propositions, but also properly basic propositions. God has so constructed us that we naturally form the belief in his existence under appropriate circumstances, just as we do the belief in perceptual objects, the reality of the past, and so forth. Hence, belief in God is among the deliverances of reason, not faith.

Plantinga emphasizes that the proper basicality of the belief that God exists does not imply its indubitability. This belief is defeasible; that is to say, it can be defeated by other incompatible beliefs which come to be accepted by the theist. In such a case, the individual in question must give up some of his beliefs if he is to remain rational, and perhaps it will be his belief in God that is jettisoned. Thus, for example, a Christian who encounters the problem of evil is faced with a potential defeater of his belief in God. If he is to remain rational in his Christian belief, he must have an answer for the defeater. This is where Christian apologetics comes in; it can help to formulate answers to potential defeaters, such as the Free Will Defense in response to the problem of evil. But Plantinga also argues that in some cases, the original belief itself may so exceed its alleged defeater in rational warrant that it becomes an intrinsic defeater of its ostensible defeater. He gives the example of someone accused of a crime and against whom all the evidence stands, even though that person knows he is innocent. In such a case, that person is not rationally obligated to abandon belief in his own innocence and to accept instead the evidence that he is guilty. The belief that he did not commit the crime intrinsically defeats the defeaters brought against it by the evidence. Plantinga makes the theological application by suggesting that belief in God may similarly intrinsically defeat all the defeaters that might be brought against it. Plantinga suggests that the mechanisms which could produce so powerful a warrant for belief in God are the implanted, natural sense of the divine (Calvin's *sensus divinitatis*), strengthened and accentuated by the testimony of the Holy Spirit.[23]

Plantinga argues that belief in God is not merely *rational* for the person who takes it as properly basic, but that this belief is so warranted that such a person can be said to *know* that God exists. A belief that is merely rational could in fact be false. When we say that a belief is rational, we mean that the person holding it is within his epistemological rights in so doing or that he exhibits no defect in his noetic structure in so believing. But in order that some belief constitutes knowledge, it must be true and in some sense justified or warranted for the person holding it.

The notion of warrant, that quality which differentiates knowledge from merely true belief, is philosophically controversial, and it is to the analysis of this notion that Plantinga then turns. He first exposits and then criticizes all major theories of warrant which are offered by epistemologists today, such as deontologism, reli-

---

23. See his extended discussion in Alvin Plantinga, *Warranted Christian Belief* (New York: Oxford University Press, 2000).

ablism, coherentism, and so forth. Fundamentally, Plantinga's method of exposing the inadequacy of such theories is to construct thought experiments or scenarios in which all the conditions for warrant stipulated by a theory are met and yet in which it is obvious that the person in question does not have knowledge of the proposition which he believes because his cognitive faculties are malfunctioning in forming the belief. This common failing suggests that rational warrant inherently involves the notion of the proper functioning of one's cognitive faculties. But this raises the troublesome question, what does it mean for one's cognitive faculties to be "functioning properly"? Here Plantinga drops a bomb into mainstream epistemology by proposing a peculiarly theistic account of rational warrant and proper functioning, namely, that one's cognitive faculties are functioning properly only if they are functioning as God designed them to.

Although he adds various subtle philosophical qualifications, the basic idea of Plantinga's account is that a belief is warranted for a person just in the case his cognitive faculties are, in forming that belief, functioning in an appropriate environment as God designed them to. The more firmly such a person holds the belief in question, the more warrant it has for him, and if he believes it firmly enough, it has sufficient warrant to constitute knowledge. With respect to the belief that God exists, Plantinga holds that God has so constituted us that we naturally form this belief under certain circumstances; since the belief is thus formed by properly functioning cognitive faculties in an appropriate environment, it is warranted for us, and, insofar as our faculties are not disrupted by the noetic effects of sin, we shall believe this proposition deeply and firmly, so that we can be said, in virtue of the great warrant accruing to this belief for us, to know that God exists.

But what about specifically Christian beliefs? How can one be justified and warranted in holding to Christian theism? In order to answer this question, Plantinga extends his account to include not just the *sensus divinitatis* but also the inner witness or instigation of the Holy Spirit.

The extended account postulates that our fall into sin has had disastrous cognitive and affective consequences. The *sensus divinitatis* has been damaged and deformed, its deliverances muted. Moreover, our affections have been skewed, so that we resist what deliverances of the *sensus divinitatis* remain, being self-centered rather than God-centered. God in his grace needed to find a way to inform us of the plan of salvation which he has made available, and he has chosen to do so by the trifold means of the Scriptures, which lay out the great truths of the gospel, the work of the Holy Spirit, who repairs the cognitive and affective damage of sin so that we can believe the great truths of the gospel, and, finally, faith, which is the principal work of the Holy Spirit produced in believers' hearts. In Plantinga's view the internal instigation of the Holy Spirit is the close analogue of a cognitive faculty in that it, too, is a belief-forming "mechanism." As such the beliefs formed by this process meet the conditions for warrant. Therefore, one can be said to know the great truths of the gospel through the instigation of the Holy Spirit.

Because we know the great truths of the gospel through the Holy Spirit's work, we have no need of evidence for them. Rather they are properly basic for us, both with respect to justification and warrant. Plantinga therefore affirms that "according to the model, the central truths of the Gospel are self-authenticating"; that is to say, "They do not get their evidence or warrant by way of being believed on the evidential basis of other propositions."[24]

Assessment

"How do I know that Christianity is true?" Probably every Christian has asked himself that question. "I believe that God exists, I believe that Jesus rose from the dead, and I've experienced his life-changing power in my life, but how do I *know* it's really true?" The problem becomes especially acute when we're faced with someone who either does not believe in God or Jesus or who adheres to some other world religion. They may demand of us how we know that Christianity is true and to prove it to them. What are we supposed to say? How *do* I know that Christianity is true?

In answering this question, I have found it helpful to distinguish between *knowing* Christianity to be true and *showing* Christianity to be true.

Knowing Christianity to Be True

Here I want to examine two points: first, the role of the Holy Spirit, and second, the role of argument and evidence.

ROLE OF THE HOLY SPIRIT

I think that Dodwell and Plantinga are correct that, fundamentally, the way we know Christianity to be true is by the self-authenticating witness of God's Holy Spirit. Now what do I mean by that? I mean that the experience of the Holy Spirit is veridical and unmistakable (though not necessarily irresistible or indubitable) for him who has it; that such a person does not need supplementary arguments or evidence in order to know and to know with confidence that he is in fact experiencing the Spirit of God; that such experience does not function in this case as a premise in any argument from religious experience to God, but rather is the immediate experiencing of God himself; that in certain contexts the experience of the Holy Spirit will imply the apprehension of certain truths of the Christian religion, such as "God exists," "I am condemned by God," "I am reconciled to God," "Christ lives in me," and so forth; that such an experience provides one not only with a subjective assurance of Christianity's truth, but with objective knowledge of that truth; and that arguments and evidence incompatible with that truth are overwhelmed by the experience of the Holy Spirit for him who attends fully to it.

24. Ibid., 261–62.

It seems to me that the New Testament teaches such a view with respect to both the believer and the unbeliever alike. Now at first blush it might seem self-defeating or perhaps circular for me to appeal to scriptural proof texts concerning the witness of the Spirit, as if to say that we believe in the Spirit's witness because the Scripture says there is such a witness. But insofar as ours is an "in-house" discussion among Christians, it is entirely appropriate to lay out what Scripture teaches on religious epistemology. In interacting with a non-Christian, by contrast, one would simply say that we Christians do in fact experience the inner testimony of God's Spirit.

The Believer

First, let's look at the role of the Holy Spirit in the life of the believer. When a person becomes a Christian, he automatically becomes an adopted son of God and is indwelt with the Holy Spirit: "for in Christ Jesus you are all sons of God, through faith. . . . And because you are sons, God has sent the Spirit of his Son into our hearts, crying, 'Abba! Father!'" (Gal. 3:26; 4:6 esv). Paul emphasizes the point in Romans 8. Here he explains that it is the witness of the Holy Spirit with our spirit that allows us to know that we are God's children: "For you did not receive the spirit of slavery to fall back into fear, but you have received the spirit of sonship. When we cry, 'Abba! Father!' it is the Spirit himself bearing witness with our spirit that we are children of God" (Rom. 8:15–16 rsv). Paul uses the term *plerophoria* (complete confidence, full assurance) to indicate that the believer has knowledge of the truth as a result of the Spirit's work (Col. 2:2; 1 Thess. 1:5; cf. Rom. 4:21; 14:5; Col. 4:12). Sometimes this is called "assurance of salvation" by Christians today; and assurance of salvation entails certain truths of Christianity, such as "God forgives my sin," "Christ has reconciled me to God," and so on, so that in having assurance of salvation one has assurance of these truths.

The apostle John also makes quite clear that it is the Holy Spirit within us who gives believers conviction of the truth of Christianity. "But you have been anointed by the Holy One, and you all know . . . the anointing which you received from him abides in you, and you have no need that any one should teach you; as his anointing teaches you about everything, and is true, and is no lie, just as it has taught you, abide in him" (1 John 2:20, 27 rsv). Here John explains that it is the Holy Spirit who teaches the believer the truth of divine things. John is clearly echoing the teaching of Jesus himself, when he says, "But the Counselor, the Holy Spirit, whom the Father will send in my name, he will teach you all things, and bring to your remembrance all that I have said to you" (John 14:26 rsv). Now the truth that the Holy Spirit teaches us is not, I'm convinced, the subtleties of Christian doctrine. There are too many Spirit-filled Christians who differ doctrinally for that to be the case. What John is talking about is the inner assurance the Holy Spirit gives of the basic truths of the Christian faith, what Plantinga calls the great truths of the gospel. This assurance does not come from human arguments but directly from the Holy Spirit himself.

Now someone might point to 1 John 4:1–3 (ESV) as evidence that the testimony of the Holy Spirit is not self-authenticating, but needs to be tested:

> Beloved, do not believe every spirit, but test the spirits to see whether they are of God; for many false prophets have gone out into the world. By this you know the Spirit of God: every spirit which confesses that Jesus Christ has come in the flesh is of God, and every spirit which does not confess Jesus is not of God. This is the spirit of antichrist.

But such an understanding would be a misinterpretation of the passage. John is not talking about testing the witness of the Spirit in our own hearts; rather he's talking about testing people who come to you claiming to be speaking by the Holy Spirit. He referred to the same people earlier: "Children, it is the last hour; and as you have heard that antichrist is coming, so now many antichrists have come; therefore we know that it is the last hour. They went out from us, but they were not of us" (1 John 2:18–19 ESV). John never encourages the believer to doubt the witness of the Spirit in his own heart; rather he says that if someone else comes claiming to speak by the Holy Spirit, then, since the situation is external to oneself and involves additional truth claims not immediately apprehended, we must test that person in order to determine if his claim is true. But in our own lives, the inner witness of God's Spirit is sufficient to assure us of the truths to which he testifies.

John also underlines other teachings of Jesus on the work of the Holy Spirit. For example, according to Jesus it is the indwelling Holy Spirit that gives the believer certainty of knowing that Jesus lives in him and that he is in Jesus, in the sense of being united with him:

> And I will pray the Father, and he will give you another Counselor, to be with you for ever, even the Spirit of truth, whom the world cannot receive, because it neither sees him nor knows him; you know him, for he dwells with you, and will be in you. . . . In that day you will know that I am in my Father, and you in me, and I in you. (John 14:16–17, 20 RSV)

John teaches the same thing: "And by this we know that he abides in us, by the Spirit which he has given us. . . . By this we know that we abide in him and he in us, because he has given us of his own Spirit" (1 John 3:24; 4:13 RSV). John uses his characteristic phrase "by this we know" to emphasize that as Christians we have a confident knowledge that our faith is true, that we really do abide in God, and God really does live in us. In fact John goes so far as to contrast the confidence which the Spirit's testimony brings to that brought by human evidence:

> This is he who came by water and blood, Jesus Christ, not with the water only but with the water and the blood. And the Spirit is the witness, because the Spirit is the truth. There are three witnesses, the Spirit, the water, and the blood; and these three agree. If we receive the testimony of men, the testimony of God is greater; for

this is the testimony of God that he has borne witness to his Son. He who believes in the Son of God has the testimony in himself. He who does not believe God has made him a liar, because he has not believed in the testimony that God has borne to his Son. (1 John 5:6–10 RSV)

The "water" here probably refers to Jesus' baptism, and the "blood" to his crucifixion, those being the two events which marked the beginning and end of his earthly ministry. "The testimony of men" is therefore nothing less than the apostolic testimony to the events of Jesus' life and ministry. Though John had laid such great weight on precisely that apostolic testimony in his Gospel (John 20:31; 21:24), here he declares that even though we quite rightly receive this testimony, still the inner testimony of the Holy Spirit is even greater! As Christians we have the testimony of God living within us, the Holy Spirit who bears witness with our spirit that we are children of God.

Thus, although arguments and evidence may be used to support the believer's faith, they are never properly the basis of that faith. For the believer, God is not the conclusion of a syllogism; he is the living God of Abraham, Isaac, and Jacob dwelling within us. How then does the believer know that Christianity is true? He knows because of the self-authenticating witness of God's Spirit who lives within him.

The Unbeliever

But what about the role of the Holy Spirit in the life of an unbeliever? Since the Holy Spirit does not indwell him, does this mean that he must rely only upon arguments and evidence to convince him that Christianity is true? No, not at all. According to the Scripture, God has a different ministry of the Holy Spirit especially geared to the needs of the unbeliever. Jesus describes this ministry in John 16:7–11 (RSV):

It is to your advantage that I go away, for if I do not go away, the Counselor will not come to you; but if I go, I will send him to you. And when he comes, he will convince the world concerning sin and righteousness and judgment: concerning sin, because they do not believe in me; concerning righteousness, because I go to the Father, and you will see me no more; concerning judgment, because the ruler of this world is judged.

Here the Holy Spirit's ministry is threefold: he convicts the unbeliever of his own sin, of God's righteousness, and of his condemnation before God. The unbeliever so convicted can therefore be said to know such truths as "God exists," "I am guilty before God," and so forth.

This is the way it has to be. For if it weren't for the work of the Holy Spirit, no one would *ever* become a Christian. According to Paul, natural man left to himself does not even seek God: "None is righteous, no, not one; no one understands, no one seeks for God" (Rom 3:10–11 ESV). Unregenerate man cannot understand spiritual things: "The unspiritual man does not receive the gifts of the Spirit of God, for they are folly to him, and he is not able to understand them because they are spiritually discerned" (1 Cor. 2:14 RSV). And he is hostile to God: "For the mind that is set on the flesh is hostile to God; for it does not submit to God's law; indeed, it cannot" (Rom. 8:7 ESV). As Jesus said, men love darkness rather than light. Left to himself, natural man would never come to God.

The fact that we do find people who are seeking God and are ready to believe in Christ is evidence that the Holy Spirit has already been at work, convicting them and drawing them to him. As Jesus said, "No one can come to me unless the Father who sent me draws him" (John 6:44 ESV).

Therefore, when a person refuses to come to Christ, it is never just because of lack of evidence or because of intellectual difficulties: at root, he refuses to come because he willingly ignores and rejects the drawing of God's Spirit on his heart. No one in the final analysis really fails to become a Christian because of lack of arguments; he fails to become a Christian because he loves darkness rather than light and wants nothing to do with God. But anyone who responds to the drawing of God's Spirit with an open mind and an open heart can know with assurance that Christianity is true, because God's Spirit will convict him that it is. Jesus said, "My teaching is not mine, but his who sent me; if any man's will is to do his will, he shall know whether the teaching is from God or whether I am speaking on my own authority" (John 7:16–17 RSV). Jesus affirms that if anyone is truly seeking God, then he will know that Jesus' teaching is truly from God.

So then for the unbeliever as well as for the believer, it is the testimony of God's Spirit that ultimately assures him of the truth of Christianity. The unbeliever who is truly seeking God will be convinced of the truth of the Christian message.

Therefore, we find that for believer and unbeliever alike it is the self-authenticating work of the Holy Spirit that supplies knowledge of Christianity's truth. Thus, I would agree that belief in the God of the Bible is a properly basic belief and emphasize that it is the ministry of the Holy Spirit that supplies the circumstances for its proper basicality. And because this belief is formed in response to the self-disclosure of God himself, who needs no external authentication, it is not merely rational for us, but constitutes knowledge. We can know Christianity's truth.

ROLE OF ARGUMENT AND EVIDENCE

But what about the second point: the role of argument and evidence in knowing Christianity to be true? I've already said that it is the self-authenticating witness of the Holy Spirit that gives us the fundamental knowledge of Christianity's truth. Therefore, the only role left for argument and evidence to play is a subsidiary role. I think Martin Luther correctly distinguished between what he called the magisterial and ministerial uses of reason. The *magisterial use* of reason occurs when reason stands over and above the gospel like a magistrate and judges it on the basis of argument and evidence. The *ministerial use* of reason occurs when reason submits to and serves the gospel. In light of the

Spirit's witness, only the ministerial use of reason is legitimate. Philosophy is rightly the handmaid of theology. Reason is a tool to help us better understand and defend our faith; as Anselm put it, ours is a faith that seeks understanding. A person who knows that Christianity is true on the basis of the witness of the Spirit may also have a sound apologetic which reinforces or confirms for him the Spirit's witness, but it does not serve as the basis of his belief. If the arguments of natural theology and Christian evidences are successful, then Christian belief is warranted by such arguments and evidences for the person who grasps them, even if that person would still be warranted in their absence. Such a person is doubly warranted in his Christian belief, in the sense that he enjoys two sources of warrant.

One can envision great benefits of having such a dual warrant of one's Christian beliefs. Having sound arguments for the existence of a Creator and Designer of the universe or evidence for the historical credibility of the New Testament records of the life of Jesus in addition to the inner witness of the Spirit could increase one's confidence in the veracity of Christian truth claims. On Plantinga's epistemological model, at least, one would then have greater warrant for believing such claims. Greater warrant could in turn lead an unbeliever to come to faith more readily or inspire a believer to share his faith more boldly. Moreover, the availability of independent warrant for Christian truth claims apart from the Spirit's witness could help predispose an unbeliever to respond to the drawing of the Holy Spirit when he hears the gospel and could provide the believer with support in times of spiritual dryness or doubt when the Spirit's witness seems eclipsed. One could doubtless think of many other ways in which the possession of such dual warrant for Christian beliefs would be beneficial. Should a conflict arise between the witness of the Holy Spirit to the fundamental truth of the Christian faith and beliefs based on argument and evidence, then it is the former which must take precedence over the latter, not vice versa.

A Danger

There is a danger in all this so far. Some persons might say that we should never seek to defend the faith. Just preach the gospel and let the Holy Spirit work! But this attitude is unbalanced and unscriptural, as we'll see in a moment. For now, let's just note in passing that as long as reason is a minister of the Christian faith, Christians should employ it.

An Objection

Some people disagree with what I've said about the role of argument and evidence. They would say that reason can be used in a magisterial role, at least by the unbeliever. They ask how else we could determine which is true, the Bible, the Qur'an, or the Book of Mormon, unless we use argument and evidence to judge them. The Muslim or the Mormon also claims to have a witness of God's Spirit or a "burning in the bosom" which authenticates to him the truth of his scriptures. Christian claims to a subjective experience seem to be on a par with similar non-Christian claims.

But how is the fact that other persons claim to experience a self-authenticating witness of God's Spirit relevant to *my* knowing the truth of Christianity via the Spirit's witness? The existence of an authentic and unique witness of the Spirit does not exclude the existence of false claims to such a witness. How, then, does the existence of false claims of the Spirit's witness to the truth of a non-Christian religion do anything logically to undermine the fact that the Christian believer does possess the genuine witness of the Spirit? Why should I be robbed of my joy and assurance of salvation simply because someone else falsely pretends, sincerely or insincerely, to the Spirit's witness? If a Mormon or Muslim falsely claims to experience the witness of God's Spirit in his heart, that does nothing to undermine the veridicality of my experience.

But someone may insist, "But how do you know that your experience isn't also spurious?" That question has already been answered: the experience of the Spirit's witness is self-authenticating for him who really has it. The Spirit-filled Christian can know immediately that his claim to the Spirit's witness is true despite the false claims made by persons adhering to other religions.

Perhaps the most plausible spin to put on this objection is to say that false claims to a witness of the Holy Spirit ought to undermine my confidence in the reliability of the cognitive faculties which form religious beliefs, since those faculties apparently so often mislead people. The fact that so many people apparently sincerely, yet falsely, believe that God's Spirit is testifying to them of the truth of their religious beliefs ought therefore to make us very leery concerning our own experience of God.

There are at least two things wrong with this construal of the objection. First, the Christian needn't say that non-Christian religious experience is simply spurious. It may well be the case that adherents of other religions do enjoy a veridical experience of God as the Ground of Being on whom we creatures are dependent or as the Moral Absolute from whom values derive or even as the loving Father of mankind. So we're not at all committed to claiming that the cognitive faculties responsible for people's religious beliefs are fundamentally unreliable. Second, the objection unjustifiably assumes that the witness of the Holy Spirit is the product of human cognitive faculties or is indistinguishable from their outputs. In fact, non-Christian religious experience, such as Buddhist or Hindu religious experience, is typically very different from Christian experience. Why should I think that when a Mormon claims to experience a "burning in the bosom" he is having an experience qualitatively indistinguishable from the witness of the Holy Spirit that I enjoy? I see no reason to think that non-veridical religious experiences are indistinguishable from the witness of the Holy Spirit. One way to get some empirical evidence for this would be simply to ask ex-Mormons and Muslims who have become Christians if their experience of God in Christianity is identical to what they had before their conversion.

Someone might say, "But can't neuroscientists artificially induce in the brain religious experiences which are non-veridical and yet seem to be like the witness of the Holy Spirit?" In fact, this is not true. The sort of religious experiences which have been artificially induced by brain stimulus have been more akin to pantheistic religious experiences, a sense of oneness with the All, rather than Christian experience of God's personal presence and love. But more importantly, the fact that a non-veridical experience can be induced which is qualitatively identical to a veridical experience does absolutely nothing to undermine the fact that there are veridical experiences and that we are rational in taking our experiences to be veridical. Otherwise, one would have to say that because neuroscientists can artificially cause us to see and hear things that aren't really there, our senses of sight and hearing are unreliable or untrustworthy! Just because a neurologist could stimulate my brain to make me think that I'm having an experience of God is no proof at all that on some occasion when he is not stimulating my brain that I do not have a genuine experience of God. So the objection to a self-authenticating witness of the Spirit on the basis of false claims to such an experience does not undermine my rationally trusting in the deliverances of the Holy Spirit's witness.

Moreover, let me suggest two theological reasons why I think those Christians who support the magisterial role of reason are mistaken. First, such a role would consign most Christians to irrationality. The vast majority of the human race have neither the time, training, nor resources to develop a full-blown Christian apologetic as the basis of their faith. Even the proponents of the magisterial use of reason at one time in the course of their education presumably lacked such an apologetic. According to the magisterial role of reason, these persons should not have believed in Christ until they finished their apologetic. Otherwise, they would be believing for insufficient reasons. I once asked a fellow seminary student, "How do you know Christianity is true?" He replied, "I really don't know." Does that mean he should give up Christianity until he finds rational arguments to ground his faith? Of course not! He knew Christianity is true because he knew Jesus, regardless of rational arguments. The fact is that we can know the truth whether we have rational arguments or not.

Second, if the magisterial role of reason were legitimate, then a person who had been given poor arguments for Christianity would have a just excuse before God for not believing in him. Suppose someone had been told to believe in God on the basis of an invalid argument. Could he stand before God on the judgment day and say, "God, those Christians only gave me a lousy argument for believing in you. That's why I didn't believe"? Of course not! The Bible says all men are without excuse. Even those who are given no good reason to believe and many persuasive reasons to disbelieve have no excuse, because the ultimate reason they do not believe is that they have deliberately rejected God's Holy Spirit.

Therefore, the role of rational argumentation in knowing Christianity to be true is the role of a servant. A person knows Christianity is true because the Holy Spirit tells him it is true, and while argument and evidence can be used to support this conclusion, they cannot legitimately overrule it.

Showing Christianity to Be True

Such are the roles of the Holy Spirit and of argument in *knowing* Christianity to be true. But what about their roles in *showing* Christianity to be true? Here things are somewhat reversed.

ROLE OF REASON

Let's look first at the role of argument and evidence in showing that Christianity is true. Here we're concerned about how to prove to another person that our faith is true. Even if I myself know personally on the basis of the Spirit's witness that Christianity is true, how can I demonstrate to somebody else that what I believe is true?

Consider again the case of the Christian confronted with an adherent of some other world religion who also claims to have a self-authenticating experience of God. William Alston points out that this situation taken in isolation results in an epistemic standoff.[25] For neither person knows how to convince the other that he alone has a veridical, rather than delusory, experience. This standoff does not undermine the rationality of the Christian's belief, for even if his process of forming his belief is as reliable as can be, there's no way he can give a noncircular proof of this fact. Thus his inability to provide such a proof does not nullify the rationality of his belief. But although he is rational in retaining his Christian belief, the Christian in such circumstances is at a complete loss as to how to show his non-Christian friend that he is correct and that his friend is wrong in his respective beliefs.

How is one to break this deadlock? Alston answers that the Christian should do whatever he can to search for common ground on which to adjudicate the crucial differences between their competing views, seeking to show in a noncircular way which of them is correct. If, by proceeding on the basis of considerations that are common to both parties, such as sense perception, rational self-evidence, and common modes of reasoning, the Christian can show that his own beliefs are true and those of his non-Christian friend false, then he will have succeeded in showing that the Christian is in the better epistemic position for discerning the truth about these matters. Once apologetics is allowed to enter the picture, the objective difference between their epistemic situations becomes crucial, for since the non-Christian only *thinks* he has a self-authenticating experience of God, when in fact he does not, the power of the evidence and argument may, by God's

25. William Alston, "Religious Diversity and Perceptual Knowledge of God," *Faith and Philosophy* 5, no. 4 (1988): 442–43.

grace, crack his false assurance of the truth of his faith and persuade him to place his faith in Christ.

The task of showing that Christianity is true involves the presentation of sound and persuasive arguments for Christian truth claims. Accordingly, we need to ask ourselves how it is that one proves something to be true. A statement or proposition is true if and only if it corresponds to reality—that is to say, reality is just as the statement says that it is. Thus, the statement "The Cubs won the 1993 World Series" is true if and only if the Cubs won the 1993 World Series. In order to prove a proposition to be true, we present arguments and evidence which have that proposition as the conclusion. Such reasoning can be either deductive or inductive.

Deductive Arguments

In a sound deductive argument, the conclusion follows inevitably from the premises. The two prerequisites of a sound deductive argument are that the premises be true and the logic be valid. If the premises are true but the logic is fallacious, then the argument is invalid. An example of an invalid argument would be:

1) If God exists, objective moral values exist.
2) Objective moral values exist.
3) Therefore, God exists.

Although both the premises are true, the conclusion does not follow logically from them, because the argument commits the fallacy known as "affirming the consequent." On the other hand, an argument can be logically valid but still unsound, because it has false premises. An example of such an unsound argument would be:

1) If Jesus were not Lord, he would be a liar or a lunatic.
2) Jesus was neither a liar nor a lunatic.
3) Therefore, Jesus is Lord.

This is a valid argument, inferring the negation of the first premise's antecedent based on the negation of its consequent. But the argument is still unsound, because the first premise is false: there are other, better alternatives, for example, that Jesus as described in the Gospels is a legend. Hence, in presenting a deductive argument for some Christian truth claim we need to be careful to construct arguments which are logically valid and have true premises.

Inductive Arguments

An inductive argument is an argument of which the premises may be true and the logical inferences valid but the conclusion still be false. In such reasoning the evidence and rules of inference are said to "underdetermine" the conclusion; that is to say, they render the conclusion plausible or likely, but do not guarantee its truth. For example, a sound inductive argument would be:

1) Groups A, B, and C were composed of similar persons suffering from the same disease.
2) Group A was administered a certain new drug, group B was administered a placebo, and group C was not given any treatment.
3) The rate of death from the disease was subsequently lower in group A by 75 percent in comparison with both groups B and C.
4) Therefore, the new drug is effective in reducing the death rate from said disease.

The conclusion is quite likely true based on the evidence and rules of inductive reasoning, but it is not inevitably true; maybe the people in group A were just lucky or some unknown variable caused their improvement.

Although inductive reasoning is part and parcel of everyday life, the description of such reasoning is a matter of controversy among philosophers. One way of understanding inductive reasoning is by means of the probability calculus. Probability theorists have formulated various rules for accurately calculating the probability of particular statements or events given the truth or occurrence of certain other statements or events. Such probabilities are called conditional probabilities and are symbolized Pr (A | B). This is to be read as the probability of A on B, or A given B, where A and B stand for particular statements or events. Probabilities range between 0 and 1, with 1 representing the highest and 0 the lowest probability. Thus, a value >.5 indicates some positive probability of a statement or event and <.5 some improbability, while .5 would indicate a precise balance between the two.

Many of the typical cases of inductive reasoning involve inferences from sample cases to generalizations—for example, the probability of Jones's contracting lung cancer given that he is a smoker—and so have greater relevance to scientific than to philosophical concerns. Still a philosophical or theological position can constitute a hypothesis, and that hypothesis can be argued to be more probable than not, or more probable than a particular competing hypothesis, given various other facts taken as one's evidence. In such cases, the apologist may have recourse to Bayes' Theorem, which lays down formulas for calculating the probability of a hypothesis (H) on given evidence (E).

One form of Bayes' Theorem is the following:

$$\Pr(H|E) = \frac{\Pr(H) \times \Pr(E|H)}{\Pr(H) \times \Pr(E|H) + \Pr(\neg H) \times \Pr(E|\neg H)}$$

In order to compute the probability of (H | E), we plug in numerical values for the various probabilities in the numerator and denominator. In philosophical, as opposed to scientific, discussions this is usually impossible to do with precision, so we must be content with vague approximations like "highly improbable," which is represented as << .5 or "highly probable," which is represented as >> .5, or roughly equal, which is represented as ≈ .5. Such vague approximations may still prove useful in arguing for one's hypothesis.

In the numerator we multiply the intrinsic probability of (H) by (H)'s explanatory power (E | H). The intrinsic probability of (H) does not mean the probability of (H) taken in utter isolation, but merely in isolation from the specific evidence E. The intrinsic probability of (H) is the conditional probability of (H) relative to our general background knowledge (B), or Pr (H | B). Similarly, (B) is implicit in (H)'s explanatory power (E | H&B). The formula takes (B) tacitly as assumed. The Pr (E | H) registers our rational expectation of E given that H is the case. If E would be surprising on H, then Pr (E | H) < .5, whereas if we are not surprised to find E, given H, than Pr (E | H) is > .5.

In the denominator of the formula, we take the product of (H)'s intrinsic probability and explanatory power and add to it the product of the intrinsic probability and explanatory power of the denial of (H). Notice that the lower this latter product is, the better it is for one's hypothesis. For in the limit case that Pr (¬H) × Pr (E | ¬H) is zero, then the numerator and denominator have the same number, so that the ratio is equal to 1, which means that one's hypothesis is certain given the evidence. So one will want to argue that while one's hypothesis has great intrinsic probability and explanatory power, the denial of the hypothesis has low intrinsic probability and explanatory power.

The drawback of appeals to Bayes' Theorem in understanding inductive reasoning is that the probabilities involved in the calculus can seem inscrutable, and thus the conditional probability of one's hypothesis incalculable. Nonetheless, Bayesian approaches to arguments for God's existence and to the problem of miracles, as well as the so-called problem of evil, have been fashionable among apologists in recent years.

A different approach to inductive reasoning which is apt to be more useful in apologetics is provided by inference to the best explanation. In inference to the best explanation, we are confronted with certain data to be explained. We then assemble a pool of live options consisting of various explanations for the data in question. From the pool of live options we then select that explanation which, if true, best explains the data. Just what criteria go toward making an explanation the best is disputed; but among the commonly acknowledged criteria will be properties such as explanatory scope, explanatory power, ad hoc–ness, and so on. The best explanation is taken to be the true explanation of the data. One problem with this approach to inductive reasoning is that there is no guarantee that the best explanation is true. It may just be the best of a bad lot, and the true explanation remains unknown to us, outside the pool of live options we have assembled.

Good Arguments

The Christian apologist may employ both deductive and inductive arguments in defense of Christian theism. In order for the arguments to be good ones, the premises need to have a particular epistemic status for us. But what sort of status is that? Certainty is an unrealistic and unattainable ideal. Were we to require that we have certainty of the truth of an argument's premises, the result for us would be skepticism. What we're looking for is a comparative criterion: the premises in a good argument will have greater plausibility than their respective denials.

Plausibility is to a great extent a person-dependent notion. Some people may find a premise plausible while others do not. Accordingly, some people will agree that a particular argument is a good one, while others will say that it is a bad argument. Given our diverse backgrounds and biases, we should expect such disagreements. Obviously, the most persuasive arguments will be those which are based on premises which enjoy the support of widely accepted evidence or seem intuitively to be true. But in cases of disagreement we simply have to dig deeper and ask what reasons we each have for thinking a premise to be true or false. When we do so, we may discover that it is we who have made the mistake. After all, one can present bad arguments for a true conclusion! But we might find instead that our partner in conversation has no good reason for rejecting our premise or that his rejection is based on misinformation, or ignorance of the evidence, or a fallacious objection. In such a case we may persuade him by giving him better information or evidence or by gently correcting his error. Or we may find that the reason he denies our premise is that he doesn't like the conclusion it's leading to, and so to avoid that conclusion he denies a premise which he really ought to find quite plausible. Ironically, it is thus possible, as Plantinga has observed, to move someone from knowledge to ignorance by presenting him with a valid argument based on premises he knows to be true for a conclusion he doesn't want to accept! No better illustration of this can be given than the natural man's refusing to believe in God or Christ at the expense of adopting some outlandish hypothesis which he ought to know is false (for example, that the universe came into being uncaused out of nothing or that Jesus was an alien from outer space).

Some Christian believers might be troubled by the notion that one's apologetic case for Christianity yields only probability rather than certainty. But the fact that Christianity can only be shown to be probably true need not be troubling when two things are kept in mind: (1) that we attain no more than probability with respect to almost everything we infer (for example, that smoking contributes to lung cancer or that it is safe to cross the street) without detriment to the depth of our conviction, and that even our non-inferred, basic beliefs may not be held with any sort of absolute certainty (for example, my memory belief that I had waffles for breakfast on Monday); and (2) that even if we can only *show* Christianity to be probably true, nevertheless we can on the basis of the Spirit's witness *know* Christianity to be true with a deep assurance that far outstrips what the evidence in our particular situation might support (think analogously of the person convinced of his own innocence even though all the evidence stands against him). To demand logically demonstrative proofs as a precondition for making a religious commitment is therefore just being unreasonable.

Since we cannot hope to persuade everybody, our aim should be to make our cumulative apologetic case as persuasive as possible. This can best be done by appealing to facts which are widely accepted or to intuitions that are commonly shared (common sense). When we appeal to expert testimony, our authorities should not be partisan but neutral or even anti-Christian. And of course, the persuasiveness of an argument as it is presented on any particular occasion may depend on a host of arational considerations, such as courteousness, openness, genuine concern for the listener, and so forth.

ROLE OF THE HOLY SPIRIT

Now we come to the second point: the role of the Holy Spirit in showing Christianity to be true. The role of the Holy Spirit is to use our arguments to convince the unbeliever of the truth of Christianity. When one presents reasons for his faith, one is not working apart from or against the Holy Spirit. To return to a point mentioned earlier: it is unbalanced and unscriptural to simply preach the gospel *if* the unbeliever has questions or objections.

First, it's unbalanced because it assumes that the Holy Spirit works only through preaching. But he can work through rational argumentation, too. We should appeal to the head as well as to the heart. If an unbeliever objects that the Bible is unreliable because it is a translation of a translation of a translation, the answer is not to tell him to get right with God. The answer is to explain that we have excellent manuscripts of the Bible in the original Greek and Hebrew languages—and *then* tell him to get right with God!

But second, it's unscriptural to refuse to reason with an unbeliever. Look at Paul. It was Paul's standard procedure to present reasons for the truth of the gospel and so defend the faith:

> And Paul went in, as was his custom, and for three weeks he argued with them from the scriptures, explaining and proving that it was necessary for the Christ to suffer and to rise from the dead. . . . So he argued in the synagogue with the Jews and the devout persons, and in the market place every day with those who chanced to be there. . . . And he entered the synagogue and for three months spoke boldly, arguing and pleading about the kingdom of God. . . . And he expounded the matter to them from morning till evening, testifying to the kingdom of God and trying to convince them about Jesus both from the law of Moses and from the prophets. And some were convinced by what he said, while others disbelieved. (Acts 17:2–3, 17; 19:8; 28:23–4 RSV)

Indeed, Scripture actually *commands* us to be prepared to give such a defense to an unbeliever: "Always being ready to make a defense to every one who asks you to give an account for the hope that is in you" (1 Pet. 3:15b AT). So, as Christians, we are to have an apologetic case ready to show that Christianity is true. To ignore the unbeliever's questions or objections is therefore both unbalanced and unscriptural. Of course, it is true that we can never argue anyone into the kingdom of God. Conversion is exclusively the role of the Holy Spirit. But the Holy Spirit may use our arguments to draw people to himself.

A Danger

Now there is also a danger in all this. There is the danger that in evangelism we may focus our attention on the argument instead of on the unbeliever. In doing evangelism we must never let apologetics distract us from our primary aim of communicating the gospel. Indeed, I'd say that with most people there's no need to use apologetics at all. Only use rational argumentation after sharing the gospel and when the unbeliever still has questions. If you tell him, "God loves you and has a wonderful plan for your life," and he says he doesn't believe in God, don't get bogged down at that point in trying to prove the existence of God to him. Tell him, "Well, at this point I'm not trying to convince you that what the Bible says is *true*; I'm just trying to share with you what the Bible *says*. After I've done that, then perhaps we can come back to whether there are good reasons to believe that what it says is true." Remember our primary aim in evangelism is to present Christ.

An Objection

Some would disagree with what I've said about the role of the Holy Spirit in showing Christianity to be true. They would contend that the believer and the unbeliever have no common ground on which to argue; therefore it is futile to try to convince an unbeliever that Christianity is true. I think I've already indicated what our common ground with unbelievers is: the laws of logic and the facts of experience. Starting from these, we build our case for Christianity.

But in addition, I think that the example of Jesus and the apostles confirms the validity of such an approach. Jesus appealed to miracles and to fulfilled prophecy to prove that his claims were true (Luke 24:25–27; John 14:11). What about the apostles? In dealing with Jews, they appealed to fulfilled prophecy, Jesus' miracles, and especially Jesus' resurrection. A model apologetic for Jews is Peter's sermon on the day of Pentecost in Acts 2. In verse 22 he appeals to Jesus' miracles. In verses 25–31 he appeals to fulfilled prophecy. In verse 32 he appeals to Christ's resurrection. By means of these arguments the apostles sought to show Jews that Christianity is true.

In dealing with non-Jews, the apostles sought to show the existence of God through his handiwork in nature (Acts 14:17). In Romans 1, Paul says that from nature alone all men can know that God exists (Rom. 1:20). According to Michael Green in his book *Evangelism in the Early Church*, the standard procedure of the apostles in dealing with Gentiles was to point to nature to show God's existence.

Paul also appealed to eyewitness testimony of the resurrection of Jesus to show further that Christianity is true (1 Cor. 15:3–8). So it is quite apparent, I think, that both Jesus and the apostles were not afraid to argue for the truth of what they proclaimed. This doesn't imply that they didn't trust the Holy Spirit to bring people to God. Rather they trusted the Holy Spirit to use their arguments to bring people to God.

Therefore, in showing Christianity to be true, it is the role of argument and evidence to show that the central tenets of the Christian worldview are true. And it is the role of the Holy Spirit to use these arguments, as we lovingly present them, to bring people to Christ.

Conclusion

In summary, we've seen that in answering the question "How do I know Christianity is true?" we must make a distinction between *knowing* that it is true and *showing* that it is true. We *know* Christianity is true primarily by the self-authenticating witness of God's Spirit. We *show* Christianity is true by presenting good arguments for its central tenets.

What, then, should be our approach in using apologetics with an unbeliever? It should be something like this:

> My friend, I know Christianity is true because God's Spirit lives in me and assures me that it is true. And you can know it is true, too, because God is knocking at the door of your heart, telling you the same thing. If you're sincerely seeking God, then God will give you assurance that the gospel is true. Now to try to show you it's true, I'll share with you some arguments and evidence that I really find convincing. But should my arguments seem weak and unconvincing to you, that's my fault, not God's. It only shows that I'm a poor apologist, not that the gospel is untrue. Whatever you think of my arguments, God still loves you and holds you accountable. I'll do my best to present good arguments to you. But ultimately you have to deal, not with arguments, but with God himself.

Practical Application

The foregoing discussion has profound practical application both in our Christian walk and in our evangelism. With regard to our Christian walk, it helps us to have a proper assurance of the truth of our faith. A student once remarked to me after class, "I find this view so liberating!" He had struggled for some time to sort out the relation between faith and reason, but without success. Christians often fall into the extremes of fideism or theological rationalism. But the view just expounded enables us to hold to a rational faith which is supported by argument and evidence without our making that argument and evidence the foundation of our faith. It is tremendously liberating to be able to show an unbeliever that our faith is true without being dependent upon the vagaries of argument and evidence for the assurance that our faith is true; at the same time we know confidently and without embarrassment that our faith is true, as can the unbeliever as well, without our falling into relativistic subjectivism.

This view also underlines the vital importance of cultivating the ministry of the Holy Spirit in our lives. For though all Christians are indwelt by the Spirit, not all are filled with the Spirit. The New Testament teaches that we can grieve the Holy Spirit of God by sin (Eph. 4:30) and quench the Spirit by repressing his working in our lives (1 Thess. 5:19). The Christian who is not filled with the Spirit may often be wracked with doubts concerning his faith. I can testify personally that my intellectual doubts seem most poignant when I am in a carnal condition. But when a Christian is walking in the Spirit, then, although his intellectual questions may remain, he can *live* with those questions, without their robbing his faith of its vitality. As the source of the assurance that our faith is true, the Holy Spirit's ministry in our lives needs to be cultivated by spiritual activities that help us to walk close to God, such as Bible study, prayer, devotional reading, inspirational music, evangelism, and Spirit-filled worship.

In evangelism, too, this view enables us to give the unbeliever rational arguments and evidence for the truth of the gospel, instead of challenging him to "just have faith." I have met many non-Christians who came from conservative Christian backgrounds and who were turned off to the gospel by having their honest questions squelched and being told to just believe. By contrast, I recently received the following note from a Canadian student with whom I had chatted after one of my lectures:

> I wish to thank you for speaking with me and for putting time into your busy life in order to converse with a second-year university student. I also wish to thank you for never once bringing the word *faith* into the conversation. I've always felt that as soon as that word is brought up as an argument, the conversation can no longer continue, as it is an inarguable point. You were able to intelligently debate using logical points without resorting to the use of the informal logical fallacies. In return, I truly hope I was able to provide the same sort of intelligent debate.

At the same time, however, this view reminds us that unbelief is at root a spiritual, not an intellectual, problem. Sometimes an unbeliever will throw up an intellectual smoke screen so that he can avoid personal, existential involvement with the gospel. In such a case, further argumentation may be futile and counterproductive, and we need to be sensitive to moments when apologetics is and is not appropriate. If we sense the unbeliever's arguments and questions are not sincere, we may do better to simply break off the discussion and ask him, "If I answered that objection, would you then really be ready to become a Christian?" Tell him lovingly and forthrightly that you think he's throwing up an intellectual smoke screen to keep from confronting the real issue: his sin before God. Apologetics is thus most appropriate and effective when the unbeliever is spiritually open and sincerely seeking to know the truth.

That leads to a final point. Many times a person will say, "That argument wasn't effective because the unbeliever I shared it with wasn't convinced." Here we have to be very careful. In the first place, don't expect an unbeliever to just roll over and play dead the minute he hears your apologetic argument. Of course, he's going to disagree! Think of what's at stake for him! You need to be prepared to listen carefully to his objections and questions, to engage him in dialogue, and to continue the conversation as long as is profitable. Effectiveness in using apologetics in evangelism requires study, practice, and revision in light of experience, not just pat answers. Second, remember that being "convincing" is person-relative. Some people will simply refuse to be convinced. Hence, an argument cannot be said to be ineffective because some people remain unconvinced by it. When one reflects on the fact that "the gate is narrow, and the way is hard that leads to life, and those who find it are few" (Matt. 7:14 rsv), it should not surprise us if most people find our apologetic unconvincing. But that does not mean that our apologetic is ineffective; it may only mean that many people are closed-minded.

What we need to develop is an apologetic that is both cogent and persuasive to as many people as possible. But we mustn't be discouraged and think that our apologetic is ineffective if many or even most people find our arguments unconvincing. Success in evangelism is simply communicating Christ in the power of the Holy Spirit and leaving the results to God. Similarly, effectiveness in apologetics is presenting cogent and persuasive arguments for the gospel in the power of the Holy Spirit and leaving the results to God.

Literature Cited or Recommended

Historical Background

Augustine. *Against the Epistle of Manichaeus Called Fundamental.* Translated by Richard Stothert. In *The Nicene and Post-Nicene Fathers.* Vol. 4. *The Writings Against the Manichaeans and Against the Donatists*, edited by Philip Schaff. Reprint, 125–50. Grand Rapids, Mich.: Eerdmans, 1956.

———. *City of God.* 3 vols. Translated by D. B. Zema, et al. Introduction by Etienne Gilson. Fathers of the Church. New York: Fathers of the Church, 1950–54. See particularly 21.6.1; 22.5.

———. *Confessions.* Translated by V. J. Bourke. Fathers of the Church. New York: Fathers of the Church, 1953.

———. *Letters.* Vol. 1. Translated by Sister Wilfrid Parsons. Fathers of the Church. Washington: Catholic University of America, 1951–56. See particularly letters 22, 28, 82, 147.

———. *On True Religion.* Translated by J. H. Burleigh. Introduction by Louis O. Mink. Chicago: H. Regnery, 1959. See particularly §24–25.

———. *The Teacher; The Free Choice of the Will; Grace and Free Will.* Translated by R. P. Russell. Fathers of the Church. Washington, D.C.: Catholic University of America, 1968.

Barth, Karl. *Dogmatics in Outline*. Translated by G. J. Thomson. New York: Philosophical Library, 1947.

————. *The Knowledge of God and the Service of God according to the Teaching of the Reformation*. Translated by J. L. M. Haire and I. Henderson. New York: Scribner's, 1939.

Bultmann, Rudolf. "The Case for Demythologizing: A Reply." In *Kerygma and Myth*, edited by H.-W. Bartsch. Translated by R. H. Fuller, 2:181–94. London: SPCK, 1953.

————. "Reply to the Theses of J. Schniewind." In *Kerygma and Myth*, edited by H. W. Bartsch. Translated by R. H. Fuller, 2:102–33. London: SPCK, 1953.

————. *Theologie des Neuen Testaments*. 7th ed. Edited by O. Merk. Tübingen: J. C. B. Mohr, 1961.

Cragg, Gerald R. *Reason and Authority in the Eighteenth Century*. Cambridge: Cambridge University Press, 1964.

Dodwell, Henry. *Christianity Not Founded on Argument*. 3rd. ed. London: M. Cooper, 1743.

Gilson, Etienne. *Reason and Revelation in the Middle Ages*. New York: Scribner's, 1938.

Locke, John. *An Essay Concerning Human Understanding*. Edited with an introduction by P. H. Nidditch. Oxford: Clarendon, 1975.

————. *The Works of John Locke*. 11th ed. Vol. 7: *The Reasonableness of Christianity*. London: W. Oldridge & Son, 1812.

————. *The Works of John Locke*. 11th ed. Vol. 9: *A Discourse on Miracles*. London: W. Oldridge & Son, 1812.

Pannenberg, Wolfhart. *Jesus—God and Man*. Translated by L. L. Wilkins and D. A. Priebe. London: SCM, 1968.

————. "Redemptive Event and History." In *Basic Questions in Theology*, translated by G. Kehm, 1:15–80. Philadelphia: Fortress, 1970.

————. "Response to the Discussion." In *New Frontiers in Theology*. Vol. 3 of *Theology as History*. Edited by J. M. Robinson and J. B. Cobb Jr. New York: Harper & Row, 1967.

————. ed. *Revelation as History*. Translated by D. Granskou. London: Macmillan, 1968.

————. "The Revelation of God in Jesus of Nazareth." In *New Frontiers in Theology*. Vol. 3 of *Theology as History*. Edited by J. M. Robinson and J. B. Cobb Jr., 101–33. New York: Harper & Row, 1967.

Plantinga, Alvin. "The Foundations of Theism: a Reply." *Faith and Philosophy* 3 (1986): 298–313.

————. "Is Belief in God Rational?" In *Rationality and Religious Belief*, edited by C. F. Delaney, 7–27. Notre Dame, Ind.: University of Notre Dame Press, 1979.

————. "Reason and Belief in God." In *Faith and Rationality*, edited by Alvin Plantinga and Nicholas Wolterstorff, 16–93. Notre Dame, Ind.: University of Notre Dame Press, 1983.

————. "Self-Profile." In *Alvin Plantinga*, edited by James E. Tomberlin and Peter Van Inwagen, 55–64 Dordrecht, Holland: D. Reidel, 1985.

————. "The Twin Pillars of Christian Scholarship." Grand Rapids, Mich.: Calvin College and Seminary, 1990.

————. *Warrant: The Current Debate*. New York: Oxford University Press, 1993.

————. *Warrant and Proper Function*. New York: Oxford University Press, 1993.

————. *Warranted Christian Belief*. New York: Oxford University Press, 2000.

Stephen, Leslie. *History of English Thought in the Eighteenth Century*. 3rd ed. 2 vols. New York: Harcourt, Brace, & World; Harbinger, 1962.

Strauss, Gerhard. *Schriftgebrauch, Schriftauslegung, und Schriftbeweis bei Augustin*. Beiträge zur Geschichte der biblischen Hermeneutik 1. Tübingen: J. C. B. Mohr, 1959.

Thomas Aquinas. *On the Truth of the Catholic Faith [Summa contra gentiles]*. 4 vols. Translated with notes by A. C. Pegis et al. Notre Dame, Ind.: University of Notre Dame Press, 1975. See particularly 1.3, 5, 6, 9; 3.99–103, 154.

————. *Summa theologiae*. 60 vols. London: Eyre & Spottiswoode for Blackfriars, 1964. See particularly la.32.1; 1a.105.8; 2a2ael.4; 3a43.1–4; 3a55.6.

Assessment

Alston, William P. *Perceiving God: the Epistemology of Religious Experience*. Ithaca, N.Y.: Cornell University Press, 1991.

————. "Religious Diversity and Perceptual Knowledge of God." *Faith and Philosophy 5*, no. 4 (1988): 433–48.

Caputo, John D. *Radical Hermeneutics*. Bloomington, Ind.: Indiana University Press, 1979.

Evans, C. Stephen and Merold Westphal, eds. *Christian Perspectives on Religious Knowledge*. Grand Rapids, Mich.: Eerdmans, 1993.

Geivett, R. Douglas and Brendan Sweetman, eds. *Contemporary Perspectives on Religious Epistemology*. New York: Oxford University Press, 1992.

Green, Michael. *Evangelism in the Early Church*. Grand Rapids, Mich.: Eerdmans, 1970.

Hackett, Stuart. *Oriental Philosophy*. Madison, Wis.: University of Wisconsin Press, 1979.

————. *The Resurrection of Theism*. 2nd ed. Grand Rapids, Mich.: Baker, 1982.

Hick, John. *Faith and Knowledge*. Ithaca, N.Y.: Cornell University Press, 1957.

Kvanvig, Jonathan L., ed. *Warrant in Contemporary Epistemology*. Lanham, Md.: Rowman & Littlefield, 1996.

Marsh, James L., John D. Caputo, and Merold Westphal. *Modernity and Its Discontents*. New York: Fordham University Press, 1992.

Mavrodes, George. *Belief in God*. New York: Random House, 1970.

Part 2

De Homine

2

The Absurdity of Life
without God

One of the apologetic questions that contemporary Christian theology must treat in its doctrine of man is what has been called "the human predicament," that is to say, the significance of human life in a post-theistic universe. Logically, this question ought, it seems to me, to be raised prior to and as a prelude to the question of God's existence.

Historical Background

The apologetic for Christianity based on the human predicament is an extremely recent phenomenon, associated primarily with Francis Schaeffer. Often it is referred to as "cultural apologetics" because of its analysis of post-Christian culture. This approach constitutes an entirely different sort of apologetics than the traditional models, since it is not concerned with epistemological issues of justification and warrant. Indeed, in a sense it does not even attempt to show in any positive sense that Christianity is true; it simply explores the disastrous consequences for human existence, society, and culture if Christianity should be false. In this respect, this approach is somewhat akin to existentialism: the precursors of this approach were also precursors of existentialism, and much of its analysis of the human predicament is drawn from the insights of twentieth-century atheistic existentialism.

Blaise Pascal

One of the earliest examples of a Christian apology appealing to the human predicament is the *Pensées* of the French mathematician and physicist Blaise Pascal (1623–1662). Having come to a personal faith in Christ in 1654, Pascal had planned to write a defense of the Christian faith entitled *L'Apologie de la religion chrétienne*, but he died of a debilitating disease at the age of only thirty-nine years, leaving behind hundreds of notes for the work, which were then published posthumously as the *Pensées*.[1]

Pascal's approach is thoroughly Christocentric. The Christian religion, he claims, teaches two truths: that there is a God whom men are capable of knowing, and that there is an element of corruption in men that renders them unworthy of God. Knowledge of God without knowledge of man's wretchedness begets pride, and knowledge of man's wretchedness without knowledge of God begets despair, but knowledge of Jesus Christ furnishes man knowledge of both simultaneously. Pascal invites us to look at the world from the Christian point of view and see if these truths are not confirmed. His *Apology* was evidently to comprise two divisions: in the first part he would display the misery of man without God (that man's nature is corrupt) and in the second part the happiness of man with God (that there is a Redeemer).[2] With regard to the latter, Pascal appeals to the evidences of miracle and especially fulfilled prophecy. In confirming the truth of man's wretchedness Pascal seeks to unfold the human predicament.

For Pascal the human condition is an enigma. For man is at the same time miserable and yet great. On the one hand, his misery is due principally to his uncertainty and insignificance. Writing in the tradition of the French skeptic Montaigne, Pascal repeatedly emphasizes the uncertainty of conclusions reached via reason and the senses. Apart from intuitive first principles, nothing seems capable of being known with certainty. In particular, reason and nature do not seem to furnish decisive evidence as to whether God exists or not. As man looks around him, all he sees is darkness and obscurity. Moreover, insofar as his scientific knowledge is correct, man learns that he is an infinitesimal speck lost in the immensity of time and space. His brief life is bounded on either side by eternity, his place in the universe is lost in the immeasurable infinity of space, and he finds himself suspended, as it were, between the infinite microcosm within and the infinite macrocosm without. Uncertain and untethered, man flounders in his efforts to lead a meaningful and happy life. His condition is characterized by inconstancy, boredom, and anxiety. His relations with his fellow men are warped by self-love; society is founded on mutual deceit. Man's justice is fickle and relative, and no fixed standard of value may be found.

---

1. The definitive ordering and numbering of these notes is that of Louis Lafuma, and the *Pensées* are cited in reference to the number of each fragment.

2. Blaise Pascal, *Pensées* 29.

Despite their predicament, however, most people, incredibly, refuse to seek an answer or even to think about their dilemma. Instead, they lose themselves in escapisms. Listen to Pascal's description of the reasoning of such a person:

> I know not who sent me into the world, nor what the world is, nor what I myself am. I am terribly ignorant of everything. I know not what my body is, nor my senses, nor my soul and that part of me which thinks what I say, which reflects upon itself as well as upon all external things, and has no more knowledge of itself than of them.
>
> I see the terrifying immensity of the universe which surrounds me, and find myself limited to one corner of this vast expanse, without knowing why I am set down here rather than elsewhere, nor why the brief period appointed for my life is assigned to me at this moment rather than another in all the eternity that has gone before and will come after me. On all sides I behold nothing but infinity, in which I am a mere atom, a mere passing shadow that returns no more. All I know is that I must soon die, but what I understand least of all is this very death which I cannot escape.
>
> As I know not whence I come, so I know not whither I go. I only know that on leaving this world I fall for ever into nothingness or into the hands of a wrathful God, without knowing to which of these two states I shall be everlastingly consigned. Such is my condition, full of weakness and uncertainty. From all this I conclude that I ought to spend every day of my life without seeking to know my fate. I might perhaps be able to find a solution to my doubts; but I cannot be bothered to do so, I will not take one step towards its discovery.[3]

Pascal can only regard such indifference as insane. Man's condition ought to impel him to seek to discover whether there is a God and a solution to his predicament. But people occupy their time and their thoughts with trivialities and distractions, so as to avoid the despair, boredom, and anxiety that would inevitably result if those diversions were removed.

Such is the misery of man. But mention must also be made of the greatness of man. For although man is miserable, he is at least capable of *knowing* that he is miserable. The greatness of man consists in thought. Man is a mere reed, yes, but he is a *thinking* reed. The universe might crush him like a gnat; but even so, man is nobler than the universe because he *knows* that it crushes him, and the universe has no such knowledge. Man's whole dignity consists, therefore, in thought. "By space the universe encompasses and swallows me up like a mere speck; by thought I comprehend the universe." Man's greatness, then, lies not in his having the solution to his predicament, but in the fact that he alone in all the universe is aware of his wretched condition.

> What a chimaera then is man, what a novelty, what a monster, what chaos, what a subject of contradiction, what a prodigy! Judge of all things, yet an imbecile earth-

3. Ibid., 11.

worm; depositary of truth, yet a sewer of uncertainty and error; pride and refuse of the universe. Who shall resolve this tangle?[4]

Pascal hopes that by explaining man's greatness as well as his misery, he might shake people out of their lethargy to think about their condition and to seek a solution.

Pascal's analysis of the human predicament leads up to his famous Wager argument, by means of which he hopes to tip the scales in favor of theism.[5] The founder of probability theory, Pascal argues that when the odds that God exists are even, then the prudent man will gamble that God exists. This is a wager that all men must make—the game is in progress and a bet must be laid. There is no opting out: you have already joined the game. Which then will you choose—that God exists or that he does not? Pascal argues that since the odds are even, reason is not violated in making either choice; so reason cannot determine which bet to make. Therefore, the choice should be made pragmatically in terms of maximizing one's happiness. If one wagers that God exists and he does, one has gained eternal life and infinite happiness. If he does not exist, one has lost nothing. On the other hand, if one wagers that God does not exist and he does, then one has suffered infinite loss. If he does not in fact exist, then one has gained nothing. Hence, the only prudent choice is to believe that God exists.

Now Pascal does believe that there is a way of getting a look behind the scenes, to speak, to determine rationally how one should bet, namely, the proofs of Scripture of miracle and prophecy, which he discusses in the second half of his work. But for now, he wants to emphasize that even in the absence of such evidence, one still ought to believe in God. For given the human predicament of being cast into existence and facing either eternal annihilation or eternal wrath, the only reasonable course of action is to believe in God: "for if you win, you win all; if you lose, you lose nothing."[6]

Fyodor Dostoyevsky

Another apologetic based on the human predicament may be found in the magnificent novels of the great nineteenth-century Russian writer Fyodor Dostoyevsky (1821–1881). (May I add that I think the obsession of contemporary evangelicals with the writings of authors like C. S. Lewis to the neglect of writers like Dostoyevsky is a great shame? Dostoyevsky is a far, far grander writer.) The problem that tortured Dostoyevsky was the problem of evil: how can a good and loving God exist when the world is filled with so much suffering and evil? Dostoyevsky presented this problem in his works so persuasively, so poignantly, that certain passages of his, notably "The Grand Inquisitor" section from his *Brothers Karamazov*,

4. Ibid., 217, 246.
5. Ibid., 343.
6. Ibid.

are often reprinted in anthologies as classic statements of the problem of evil. As a result, some people are under the impression that Dostoyevsky was himself an atheist and that the viewpoint of the Grand Inquisitor is his own.

Actually, he sought to carry through a two-pronged defense of theism in the face of the problem of evil. Positively, he argued that innocent suffering may perfect character and bring one into a closer relation with God. Negatively, he tried to show that if the existence of God is denied, then one is landed in complete moral relativism, so that no act, regardless how dreadful or heinous, can be condemned by the atheist. To live consistently with such a view of life is unthinkable and impossible. Hence, atheism is destructive of life and ends logically in suicide.

Dostoyevsky's magnificent novels *Crime and Punishment* and *The Brothers Karamazov* powerfully illustrate these themes. In the former a young atheist, convinced of moral relativism, brutally murders an old woman. Though he knows that on his presuppositions he should not feel guilty, nevertheless he is consumed with guilt until he confesses his crime and gives his life to God. The latter novel is the story of four brothers, one of whom murders their father because his atheist brother Ivan had told him that moral absolutes do not exist. Unable to live with the consequences of his own philosophical system, Ivan suffers a mental collapse. The remaining two brothers, one of whom is unjustly accused of the parricide and the other a young Russian orthodox monk, find in what they suffer the perfection of their character and a nearness to God.

Dostoyevsky recognizes that his response to atheism constitutes no positive proof of Christianity. Indeed, he rejects that there could be such. Men demand of Christ that he furnish them "bread and circuses," but he refuses to do so. The decision to follow Christ must be made in loneliness and anxiety. Each person must face for himself the anguish of a world without God and in the solitude of his own heart give himself to God in faith.

Søren Kierkegaard

The Danish existentialist of the late nineteenth century, Søren Kierkegaard (1813–1855), also presents a sort of negative apologetic for the Christian faith. He thinks of life as being lived on three different planes or stages: the aesthetic stage, the ethical stage, and the religious stage. Man in the aesthetic stage lives life only on the sensual level, a life that is self- and pleasure-centered. This need not be a gross hedonism. Man on this level could be very cultivated and even circumspect; but nevertheless his life revolves around himself and those material things—whether sex, art, music, or whatever—that bring him pleasure. The paradox of life on this level is that it leads ultimately to unhappiness. The self-centered, aesthetic man finds no ultimate meaning in life and no true satisfaction. Thus, the aesthetic life leads finally to boredom, a sort of sickness with life.

But this is not the end, for only at this point is a person ready to live on the second plane of existence, the ethical plane. The transition to the ethical stage of

life is a sort of leap motivated by dissatisfaction to a higher level, where one affirms transpersonal moral values and guides life by those objective standards. No
longer is life lived only for self and for pleasure; rather one is constrained to seek
the ethical good and to change one's conduct to bring it into conformity with
that good. Thus, man in the ethical stage is the moral man. But life on this level,
too, ends in unhappiness. For the more one tries sincerely to bring one's life into
conformity with the objective standards of the good, the more painfully aware
one is that one cannot do it. Thus, the ethical life, when earnestly pursued, leads
ultimately to guilt and despair.

But there is one more stage along life's way: the religious stage. Here one finds
forgiveness of sins and a personal relationship with God. Only here, in intimate
communion with one's Creator, does man find authentic existence and true fulfillment. Again, Kierkegaard represents the transition to this stage from the ethical
as a leap. The decision to believe is a criterionless choice, a leap of faith into the
dark. Although man can be given no rational grounds to leap, unless he does so,
he will remain in despair and inauthentic existence.

Francis Schaeffer

As I remarked earlier, Francis Schaeffer (1912–1984) is the thinker most responsible
for crafting a Christian apologetic based on the so-called modern predicament.
According to Schaeffer, there can be traced in recent Western culture a "line of
despair," which penetrates philosophy, literature, and the arts in succession. He
believes the root of the problem lies in Hegelian philosophy, specifically in its denial
of absolute truths. Hegel developed the famous triad of thesis-antithesis-synthesis,
in which contradictions are seen not as absolute opposites, but as partial truths,
which are synthesized in the whole. Ultimately all is One, which is absolute and
non-contradictory. In Schaeffer's view, Hegel's system undermined the notion of
particular absolute truths (such as "That act is morally wrong" or "This painting is
aesthetically ugly") by synthesizing them into the whole. This denial of absolutes has
gradually made its way through Western culture. In each case, it results in despair,
because without absolutes man's endeavors degenerate into absurdity. Schaeffer
believes that the Theater of the Absurd, abstract modern art, and modern music
such as compositions by John Cage are all indications of what happens below the
line of despair. Only by reaffirming belief in the absolute God of Christianity can
man and his culture avoid inevitable degeneracy, meaninglessness, and despair.

Schaeffer's efforts against abortion may be seen as a logical extension of this
apologetic. Once God is denied, human life becomes worthless, and we see the
fruit of such a philosophy in the abortion and infanticide now taking place in
Western society. Schaeffer warns that unless Western man returns to the Christian
world and life view, nothing will stop the trend from degenerating into population control and human breeding. Only a theistic worldview can save the human
race from itself.

Assessment

The Loss of God and Immortality

Man, writes Loren Eiseley, is the Cosmic Orphan. He is the only creature in the universe who asks, "Why?" Other animals have instincts to guide them, but man has learned to ask questions.

"Who am I?" he asks. "Why am I here? Where am I going?" Since the Enlightenment, when modern man threw off the shackles of religion, he has tried to answer these questions without reference to God. But the answers that have come back were not exhilarating, but dark and terrible. "You are the accidental by-product of nature, a result of matter plus time plus chance. There is no reason for your existence. All you face is death."

Modern man thought that when he had gotten rid of God, he had freed himself from all that repressed and stifled him. Instead, he discovered that in killing God, he had only succeeded in orphaning himself.

For if there is no God, then man's life becomes absurd.

If God does not exist, then both man and the universe are inevitably doomed to death. Man, like all biological organisms, must die. With no hope of immortality, man's life leads only to the grave. His life is but a spark in the infinite blackness, a spark that appears, flickers, and dies forever. Compared to the infinite stretch of time, the span of man's life is but an infinitesimal moment; and yet this is all the life he will ever know. Therefore, everyone must come face to face with what theologian Paul Tillich has called "the threat of non-being." For though I know now that I exist, that I am alive, I also know that someday I will no longer exist, that I will no longer be, that I will die. This thought is staggering and threatening: to think that the person I call "myself" will cease to exist, that I will be no more!

I remember vividly the first time my father told me that someday I would die. Somehow, as a child, the thought had just never occurred to me. When he told me, I was filled with fear and unbearable sadness. And though he tried repeatedly to reassure me that this was a long way off, that did not seem to matter. Whether sooner or later, the undeniable fact was that I would die and be no more, and the thought overwhelmed me. Eventually, like all of us, I grew to simply accept the fact. We all learn to live with the inevitable. But the child's insight remains true. As the French existentialist Jean-Paul Sartre observed, several hours or several years make no difference once you have lost eternity.

Whether it comes sooner or later, the prospect of death and the threat of non-being is a terrible horror. I met a student once who did not feel this threat. He said he had been raised on the farm and was used to seeing the animals being born and dying. Death was for him simply natural—a part of life, so to speak. I was puzzled by how different our two perspectives on death were and found it difficult to understand why he did not feel the threat of non-being. Years later, I think I found my answer in reading Sartre. Sartre observed that death is not threatening so long as we view it as the death of the other, from a third-person standpoint, so to speak. It is only when we internalize it and look at it from the first-person perspective—"my death: I am going to die"—that the threat of non-being becomes real. As Sartre points out, many people never assume this first-person perspective in the midst of life; one can even look at one's own death from the third-person standpoint, as if it were the death of another or even of an animal, as did my friend. But the true existential significance of my death can only be appreciated from the first-person perspective, as I realize that I am going to die and forever cease to exist.

And the universe, too, faces a death of its own. Scientists tell us that the universe is expanding, and the galaxies are growing farther and farther apart. As it does so, it grows colder and colder, and its energy is used up. Eventually all the stars will burn out, and all matter will collapse into dead stars and black holes. There will be no light at all; there will be no heat; there will be no life; only the corpses of dead stars and galaxies, ever expanding into the endless darkness and the cold recesses of space—a universe in ruins. This is not science fiction. The entire universe marches irreversibly toward its grave. So not only is the life of each individual person doomed; the entire human race is doomed. The universe is plunging toward inevitable extinction—death is written throughout its structure. There is no escape. There is no hope.

The Absurdity of Life without God and Immortality

If there is no God, then man and the universe are doomed. Like prisoners condemned to death, we await our unavoidable execution. There is no God, and there is no immortality. And what is the consequence of this? It means that life itself is absurd. It means that the life we have is without ultimate significance, value, or purpose. Let's look at each of these.

NO ULTIMATE MEANING WITHOUT GOD AND IMMORTALITY

If each individual person passes out of existence when he dies, then what ultimate meaning can be given to his life? Does it really matter whether he ever existed at all? It might be said that his life was important because it influenced others or affected the course of history. But this shows only a relative significance to his life, not an ultimate significance. His life may be important relative to certain other events, but what is the ultimate significance of any of those events? If all the events are meaningless, then what can be the ultimate significance of influencing any of them? Ultimately it makes no difference.

Look at it from another perspective: Scientists say that the universe originated in an explosion called the "Big Bang" about thirteen billion years ago. Suppose the Big Bang had never occurred. Suppose the universe had never existed. What ultimate difference would it make? The universe is doomed to die anyway. In the end it makes no difference whether the universe ever existed or not. Therefore, it is without ultimate significance.

The same is true of the human race. Mankind is a doomed race in a dying universe. Because the human race will eventually cease to exist, it makes no ultimate difference whether it ever did exist. Mankind is thus no more significant than a swarm of mosquitoes or a barnyard of pigs, for their end is all the same. The same blind cosmic process that coughed them up in the first place will eventually swallow them all again.

And the same is true of each individual person. The contributions of the scientist to the advance of human knowledge, the researches of the doctor to alleviate pain and suffering, the efforts of the diplomat to secure peace in the world, the sacrifices of good people everywhere to better the lot of the human race—all these come to nothing. In the end they don't make one bit of difference, not one bit. Each person's life is therefore without ultimate significance. And because our lives are ultimately meaningless, the activities we fill our lives with are also meaningless. The long hours spent in study at the university, our jobs, our interests, our friendships—all these are, in the final analysis, utterly meaningless.

In his poem "The End of the World" Archibald MacLeish portrays life as an idiotic circus, until one day the show is over:

> Quite unexpectedly, as Vasserot
> The armless ambidextrian was lighting
> A match between his great and second toe,
> And Ralph the lion was engaged in biting
> The neck of Madame Sossman while the drum
> Pointed, and Teeny was about to cough
> In waltz-time swinging Jocko by the thumb
> Quite unexpectedly the top blew off:
>
> And there, there overhead, there, there hung over
> Those thousands of white faces, those dazed eyes,
> There in the starless dark, the poise, the hover,
> There with vast wings across the cancelled skies,
> There in the sudden blackness the black pall
> Of nothing, nothing, nothing—nothing at all.[7]

This is the horror of modern man: because he ends in nothing, he is nothing.

But it's important to see that it is not just immortality that man needs if life is to be meaningful. Mere duration of existence does not make that existence meaningful. If man and the universe could exist forever, but if there were no God, their existence would still have no ultimate significance. I once read a science-fiction story in which an astronaut was marooned on a barren chunk of rock lost in outer

7. In *Major American Poets*, ed. Oscar Williams and Edwin Long (New York: New American Library, 1962), 436.

space. He had with him two vials: one containing poison and the other a potion that would make him live forever. Realizing his predicament, he gulped down the poison. But then to his horror, he discovered he had swallowed the wrong vial—he had drunk the potion for immortality. And that meant that he was cursed to exist forever—a meaningless, unending life. Now if God does not exist, our lives are just like that. They could go on and on and still be utterly without meaning. We could still ask of life, "So what?" So it's not just immortality man needs if life is to be ultimately significant; he needs God and immortality. And if God does not exist, then he has neither.

Twentieth-century man came to understand this. Read *Waiting for Godot* by Samuel Beckett. During this entire play two men carry on trivial conversation while waiting for a third man to arrive, who never does. Our lives are like that, Beckett is saying; we just kill time waiting—for what, we don't know. In a tragic portrayal of man, Beckett wrote another play in which the curtain opens revealing a stage littered with junk. For thirty long seconds, the audience sits and stares in silence at that junk. Then the curtain closes. That's all.

French existentialists Jean-Paul Sartre and Albert Camus understood this, too. Sartre portrayed life in his play *No Exit* as hell—the final line of the play are the words of resignation, "Well, let's get on with it." Hence, Sartre writes elsewhere of the "nausea" of existence. Man, he says, is adrift in a boat without a rudder on an endless sea. Camus, too, saw life as absurd. At the end of his brief novel *The Stranger*, Camus's hero discovers in a flash of insight that the universe has no meaning and there is no God to give it one. The French biochemist Jacques Monod seemed to echo those sentiments when he wrote in his work *Chance and Necessity*, "Man finally knows he is alone in the indifferent immensity of the universe."

Thus, if there is no God, then life itself becomes meaningless. Man and the universe are without ultimate significance.

No Ultimate Value without God and Immortality

If life ends at the grave, then it makes no difference whether one has lived as a Stalin or as a saint. Since one's destiny is ultimately unrelated to one's behavior, you may as well just live as you please. As Dostoyevsky put it: "If there is no immortality, then all things are permitted." On this basis, a writer like Ayn Rand is absolutely correct to praise the virtues of selfishness. Live totally for self; no one holds you accountable! Indeed, it would be foolish to do anything else, for life is too short to jeopardize it by acting out of anything but pure self-interest. Sacrifice for another person would be stupid. Kai Nielsen, an atheist philosopher who attempts to defend the viability of ethics without God, in the end admits,

> We have not been able to show that reason requires the moral point of view, or that all really rational persons, unhoodwinked by myth or ideology, need not be individual egoists or classical amoralists. Reason doesn't decide here. The picture I have painted

for you is not a pleasant one. Reflection on it depresses me. . . . Pure practical reason, even with a good knowledge of the facts, will not take you to morality.[8]

But the problem becomes even worse. For, regardless of immortality, if there is no God, then any basis for objective standards of right and wrong seems to have evaporated. All we are confronted with is, in Jean-Paul Sartre's words, the bare, valueless fact of existence. Moral values are either just expressions of personal taste or the by-products of socio-biological evolution and conditioning. In the words of one humanist philosopher, "The moral principles that govern our behavior are rooted in habit and custom, feeling and fashion."[9] In a world without God, who is to say which actions are right and which are wrong? Who is to judge that the values of Adolf Hitler are inferior to those of a saint? The concept of morality loses all meaning in a universe without God. As one contemporary atheistic ethicist points out, "To say that something is wrong because . . . it is forbidden by God, is perfectly understandable to anyone who believes in a law-giving God. But to say that something is wrong . . . even though no God exists to forbid it, is *not* understandable. . . ." "The concept of moral obligation [is] unintelligible apart from the idea of God. The words remain but their meaning is gone."[10] In a world without a divine lawgiver, there can be no objective right and wrong, only our culturally and personally relative, subjective judgments. This means that it is impossible to condemn war, oppression, or crime as evil. Nor can one praise brotherhood, equality, and love as good. For in a universe without God, good and evil do not exist—there is only the bare valueless fact of existence, and there is no one to say that you are right and I am wrong.

NO ULTIMATE PURPOSE WITHOUT GOD AND IMMORTALITY

If death stands with open arms at the end of life's trail, then what is the goal of life? To what end has life been lived? Is it all for nothing? Is there no reason for life? And what of the universe? Is it utterly pointless? If its destiny is a cold grave in the recesses of outer space, the answer must be yes—it is pointless. There is no goal, no purpose, for the universe. The litter of a dead universe will just go on expanding and expanding—forever.

And what of man? Is there no purpose at all for the human race? Or will it simply peter out someday, lost in the oblivion of an indifferent universe? The English writer H. G. Wells foresaw such a prospect. In his novel *The Time Machine* Wells's time traveler journeys far into the future to discover the destiny of man. All he finds is a dead earth, save for a few lichens and moss, orbiting a gigantic red sun. The only sounds are the rush of the wind and the gentle ripple of the sea. "Beyond these lifeless sounds," writes Wells, "the world was silent. Silent? It would be hard to convey the stillness of it. All the sounds of man, the bleating of

8. Kai Nielsen, "Why Should I Be Moral?" *American Philosophical Quarterly* 21 (1984): 90.
9. Paul Kurtz, *Forbidden Fruit* (Buffalo, N.Y.: Prometheus, 1988), 73.
10. Richard Taylor, *Ethics, Faith, and Reason* (Englewood Cliffs, N.J.: Prentice Hall, 1985), 90, 84.

sheep, the cries of birds, the hum of insects, the stir that makes the background of our lives—all that was over."[11] And so Wells's time traveler returned. But to what?—to merely an earlier point on the purposeless rush toward oblivion. When as a non-Christian I first read Wells's book, I thought, "No, no! It can't end that way!" But if there is no God, it will end that way, like it or not. This is reality in a universe without God: there is no hope; there is no purpose. It reminds me of T. S. Eliot's haunting lines:

> This is the way the world ends
> This is the way the world ends
> This is the way the world ends
> Not with a bang but a whimper.[12]

What is true of mankind as a whole is true of each of us individually: we are here to no purpose. If there is no God, then our life is not fundamentally different from that of a dog. I know that's harsh, but it's true. As the ancient writer of Ecclesiastes put it: "The fate of the sons of men and the fate of beasts is the same. As one dies so dies the other; indeed, they all have the same breath and there is no advantage for man over beast, for all is vanity. All go to the same place. All come from the dust and all return to the dust" (Eccles. 3:19–20 AT). In this book, which reads more like a piece of modern existentialist literature than a book of the Bible, the writer shows the futility of pleasure, wealth, education, political fame, and honor in a life doomed to end in death. His verdict? "Vanity of vanities! All is vanity" (1:2 ESV). If life ends at the grave, then we have no ultimate purpose for living.

But more than that: even if it did not end in death, without God life would still be without purpose. For man and the universe would then be simple accidents of chance, thrust into existence for no reason. Without God the universe is the result of a cosmic accident, a chance explosion. There is no reason for which it exists. As for man, he is a freak of nature—a blind product of matter plus time plus chance. Man is just a lump of slime that evolved rationality. There is no more purpose in life for the human race than for a species of insect; for both are the result of the blind interaction of chance and necessity. As one philosopher has put it: "Human life is mounted upon a subhuman pedestal and must shift for itself alone in the heart of a silent and mindless universe."[13]

What is true of the universe and of the human race is also true of us as individuals. Insofar as we are individual human beings, we are the result of certain combinations of heredity and environment. We are victims of a kind of genetic and environmental roulette. Biologists like Richard Dawkins regard man as an electro-chemical machine controlled by its mindless genes. If God does not exist,

11. H. G. Wells, *The Time Machine* (New York: Berkeley, 1957), chap. 11.
12. T. S. Eliot, "The Hollow Men," in *Collected Poems 1909–1962* (New York: Harcourt, Brace, Jovanovich, 1934). Reprinted by permission of the publisher.
13. W. E. Hocking, *Types of Philosophy* (New York: Scribner's, 1959), 27.

then you are just a miscarriage of nature, thrust into a purposeless universe to live a purposeless life.

So if God does not exist, that means that man and the universe exist to no purpose—since the end of everything is death—and that they came to be for no purpose, since they are only blind products of chance. In short, life is utterly without reason.

Do you understand the gravity of the alternatives before us? For if God exists, then there is hope for man. But if God does not exist, then all we are left with is despair. Do you understand why the question of God's existence is so vital to man? As Francis Schaeffer aptly put it, "If God is dead, then man is dead, too."

Unfortunately, the mass of mankind do not realize this fact. They continue on as though nothing has changed. I'm reminded of Nietzsche's story of the madman who in the early morning hours burst into the marketplace, lantern in hand, crying, "I seek God! I seek God!" Since many of those standing about did not believe in God, he provoked much laughter. "Did God get lost?" they taunted him. "Or is he hiding? Or maybe he has gone on a voyage or emigrated!" Thus they yelled and laughed. Then, writes Nietzsche, the madman turned in their midst and pierced them with his eyes.

> "Whither is God?" he cried, "I shall tell you. *We have killed him*—you and I. All of us are his murderers. But how have we done this? How were we able to drink up the sea? Who gave us the sponge to wipe away the entire horizon? What did we do when we unchained this earth from its sun? Whither is it moving now? Away from all suns? Are we not plunging continually? Backward, sideward, forward, in all directions? Is there any up or down left? Are we not straying as through an infinite nothing? Do we not feel the breath of empty space? Has it not become colder? Is not night and more night coming on all the while? Must not lanterns be lit in the morning? Do we not hear anything yet of the noise of the gravediggers who are burying God? . . . God is dead. . . . And we have killed him. How shall we, the murderers of all murderers, comfort ourselves?"[14]

The crowd stared at the madman in silence and astonishment. At last he dashed his lantern to the ground. "I have come too early," he said. "This tremendous event is still on its way—it has not yet reached the ears of man." People did not yet truly comprehend the consequences of what they had done in killing God. But Nietzsche predicted that someday people would realize the implications of their atheism; and this realization would usher in an age of nihilism—the destruction of all meaning and value in life. The end of Christianity, wrote Nietzsche, means the advent of nihilism. This most gruesome of guests is standing already at the door. "Our whole European culture is moving for some time now," wrote Nietzsche, "with a tortured tension that is growing from decade to decade, as toward a

---

14. Friedrich Nietzsche, "The Gay Science," in *The Portable Nietzsche*, ed. and trans. W. Kaufmann (New York: Viking, 1954), 95.

catastrophe: restlessly, violently, headlong, like a river that wants to reach the end, that no longer reflects, that is afraid to reflect."[15]

Most people still do not reflect on the consequences of atheism and so, like the crowd in the marketplace, go unknowingly on their way. But when we realize, as did Nietzsche, what atheism implies, then his question presses hard upon us: how *shall* we, the murderers of all murderers, comfort ourselves?

The Practical Impossibility of Atheism

About the only solution the atheist can offer is that we face the absurdity of life and live bravely. Bertrand Russell, for example, wrote that we must build our lives upon "the firm foundation of unyielding despair."[16] Only by recognizing that the world really is a terrible place can we successfully come to terms with life. Camus said that we should honestly recognize life's absurdity and then live in love for one another.

The fundamental problem with this solution, however, is that it is impossible to live consistently and happily within such a worldview. If one lives consistently, he will not be happy; if one lives happily, it is only because he is not consistent. Francis Schaeffer has explained this point well. Modern man, says Schaeffer, resides in a two-story universe. In the lower story is the finite world without God; here life is absurd, as we have seen. In the upper story are meaning, value, and purpose. Now modern man lives in the lower story because he believes there is no God. But he cannot live happily in such an absurd world; therefore, he continually makes leaps of faith into the upper story to affirm meaning, value, and purpose, even though he has no right to, since he does not believe in God. Modern man is totally inconsistent when he makes this leap, because these values cannot exist without God, and man in his lower story does not have God.

Let's look again, then, at each of the three areas in which we saw that life is absurd without God, in order to show how modern man cannot live consistently and happily with his atheism.

MEANING OF LIFE

First, the area of meaning. We saw that without God, life has no meaning. Yet philosophers continue to live as though life does have meaning. For example, Sartre argued that one may create meaning for his life by freely choosing to follow a certain course of action. Sartre himself chose Marxism.

Now this is utterly inconsistent. It is inconsistent to say that life is objectively absurd and then to say that one may create meaning for his life. If life is really absurd, then man is trapped in the lower story. To try to create meaning in life

---

15. Friedrich Nietzsche, "The Will to Power," trans. W. Kaufmann, in *Existentialism from Dostoyevsky to Sartre* , 2nd ed., ed. with an introduction by W. Kaufmann (New York: New American Library, Meridian, 1975), 130–31.

16. Bertrand Russell, "A Free Man's Worship," in *Why I Am Not a Christian*, ed. P. Edwards (New York: Simon & Schuster, 1957), 107.

represents a leap to the upper story. But Sartre has no basis for this leap. Without God, there can be no objective meaning in life. Sartre's program is actually an exercise in self-delusion. For the universe does not really acquire meaning just because *I* happen to give it one. This is easy to see: for suppose I give the universe one meaning, and you give it another. Who is right? The answer, of course, is neither one. For the universe without God remains objectively meaningless, no matter how *we* regard it. Sartre is really saying, "Let's *pretend* the universe has meaning." And this is just fooling ourselves.

The point is this: if God does not exist, then life is objectively meaningless; but man cannot live consistently and happily knowing that life is meaningless; so in order to be happy he pretends that life has meaning. But this is, of course, entirely inconsistent—for without God, man and the universe are without any real significance.

VALUE OF LIFE

Turn now to the problem of value. Here is where the most blatant inconsistencies occur. First of all, atheistic humanists are totally inconsistent in affirming the traditional values of love and brotherhood. Camus has been rightly criticized for inconsistently holding both to the absurdity of life and to the ethics of human love and brotherhood. The two are logically incompatible. Bertrand Russell, too, was inconsistent. For though he was an atheist, he was an outspoken social critic, denouncing war and restrictions on sexual freedom. Russell admitted that he could not live as though ethical values were simply a matter of personal taste, and that he therefore found his own views "incredible." "I do not know the solution," he confessed.[17] The point is that if there is no God, then objective right and wrong cannot exist. As Dostoyevsky said, "All things are permitted."

But Dostoyevsky also showed in his novels that man cannot live this way. He cannot live as though it is perfectly all right for soldiers to slaughter innocent children. He cannot live as though it is all right for dictatorial regimes to follow a systematic program of physical torture of political prisoners. He cannot live as though it is all right for dictators like Pol Pot or Saddam Hussein to exterminate millions of their own countrymen. Everything in him cries out to say these acts are wrong—really wrong. But if there is no God, he cannot. So he makes a leap of faith and affirms values anyway. And when he does so, he reveals the inadequacy of a world without God.

The horror of a world devoid of value was brought home to me with new intensity several years ago as I viewed a BBC television documentary called "The Gathering." It concerned the reunion of survivors of the Holocaust in Jerusalem, where they rediscovered lost friendships and shared their experiences. Now I had heard stories of the Holocaust before and had even visited Dachau and Buchenwald, and I thought I was beyond shocking by further tales of horror. But I found

17. Bertrand Russell, Letter to the *Observer*, October 6, 1957.

that I was not. Perhaps I had been made more sensitive by the recent birth of our beautiful baby girl, so that I applied the situations to her as they were related on the television. In any case, one woman prisoner, a nurse, told of how she was made the gynecologist at Auschwitz. She observed that pregnant women were grouped together by the soldiers under the direction of Dr. Mengele and housed in the same barracks. Some time passed, and she noted that she no longer saw any of these women. She made inquiries. "Where are the pregnant women who were housed in that barracks?" "Haven't you heard?" came the reply. "*Dr. Mengele used them for vivisection.*"

Another woman told of how Mengele had bound up her breasts so that she could not suckle her infant. The doctor wanted to learn how long an infant could survive without nourishment. Desperately this poor woman tried to keep her baby alive by giving it pieces of bread soaked in coffee, but to no avail. Each day the baby lost weight, a fact that was eagerly monitored by Dr. Mengele. A nurse then came secretly to this woman and told her, "I have arranged a way for you to get out of here, but you cannot take your baby with you. I have brought a morphine injection that you can give to your child to end its life." When the woman protested, the nurse was insistent: "Look, your baby is going to die anyway. At least save yourself." And so this mother felt compelled *to take the life of her own baby*. Dr. Mengele was furious when he learned of it because he had lost his experimental specimen, and he searched among the dead to find the baby's discarded corpse so that he could have one last weighing.

My heart was torn by these stories. One rabbi who survived the camp summed it up well when he said that at Auschwitz it was as though there existed a world in which all the Ten Commandments were reversed: "Thou shalt kill, thou shalt lie, thou shalt steal . . ." Mankind had never seen such a hell.

And yet, if God does not exist, then in a sense, our world *is* Auschwitz: there is no right and wrong; *all things* are permitted. But no atheist, no agnostic, can live consistently with such a view of life. Nietzsche himself, who proclaimed the necessity of living "beyond good and evil," broke with his mentor Richard Wagner precisely over the issue of the composer's anti-Semitism and strident German nationalism. Similarly Sartre, writing in the aftermath of the Second World War, condemned anti-Semitism, declaring that a doctrine that leads to extermination is not merely an opinion or matter of personal taste, of equal value with its opposite.[18] In his important essay "Existentialism Is a Humanism," Sartre struggles vainly to elude the contradiction between his denial of divinely pre-established values and his urgent desire to affirm the value of human persons. Like Russell, he could not live with the implications of his own denial of ethical absolutes.

Neither can Richard Dawkins. For although he solemnly pronounces, "There is at bottom no design, no purpose, no evil, no good, nothing but pointless indif-

---

18. Jean-Paul Sartre, "Portrait of the Antisemite," trans. M. Guiggenheim, in *Existentialism*, 330.

ference. . . . We are machines for propagating DNA,"[19] he is a patent moralist. He declares himself mortified that Enron executive Jeff Skilling regards Dawkins's *The Selfish Gene* as his favorite book because of its perceived Social Darwinism.[20] He characterizes "Darwinian mistakes" like pity for someone unable to pay us back or sexual attraction to an infertile member of the opposite sex as "blessed, precious mistakes" and calls compassion and generosity "noble emotions."[21] He denounces the doctrine of original sin as "morally obnoxious."[22] He vigorously condemns such actions as the harassment and abuse of homosexuals, religious indoctrination of children, the Incan practice of human sacrifice, and prizing cultural diversity in the case of the Amish over the interests of their children.[23] He even goes so far as to offer his own amended Ten Commandments for guiding moral behavior, all the while marvelously oblivious to the contradiction with his ethical subjectivism.[24]

A second problem for the atheist is that if God does not exist and there is no immortality, then all the evil acts of men go unpunished and all the sacrifices of good men go unrewarded. But who can live with such a view? Richard Wurmbrand, who has been tortured for his faith in communist prisons, says,

> The cruelty of atheism is hard to believe when man has no faith in the reward of good or the punishment of evil. There is no reason to be human. There is no restraint from the depths of evil which is in man. The communist torturers often said, "There is no God, no Hereafter, no punishment for evil. We can do what we wish." I have heard one torturer even say, "I thank God, in whom I don't believe, that I have lived to this hour when I can express all the evil in my heart." He expressed it in unbelievable brutality and torture inflicted on prisoners.[25]

The English theologian Cardinal Newman once said that if he believed that all the evils and injustices of life throughout history were not to be made right by God in the afterlife, "Why I think I should go mad." Rightly so.

And the same applies to acts of self-sacrifice. A number of years ago, a terrible mid-winter air disaster occurred when a plane leaving the Washington, D.C., airport smashed into a bridge spanning the Potomac River, plunging its passengers into the icy waters. As the rescue helicopters came, attention was focused on one man who again and again pushed the dangling rope ladder to other passengers rather

19. Richard Dawkins, *Unweaving the Rainbow* (London: Allen Lane, 1998), cited in Lewis Wolpert, *Six Impossible Things before Breakfast* (London: Faber and Faber, 2006), 215. Unfortunately, Wolpert's reference is mistaken. The quotation seems to be a pastiche from Richard Dawkins, *River Out of Eden: A Darwinian View of Life* (New York: Basic, 1996), 133, and Richard Dawkins, "The Ultraviolet Garden," Lecture 4 of 7 Royal Institution Christmas Lectures (1992), http://physicshead.blogspot.com/2007/01/ richard-dawkins-lecture-4-ultraviolet.html. Thanks to my assistant Joe Gorra for tracking down this reference.
20. Richard Dawkins, *The God Delusion* (New York: Houghton-Mifflin, 2006), 215.
21. Ibid., 221.
22. Ibid., 251.
23. Ibid., 23, 313–17, 326, 328, 330.
24. Ibid., 264.
25. Richard Wurmbrand, *Tortured for Christ* (London: Hodder & Stoughton, 1967), 34.

than be pulled to safety himself. Six times he passed the ladder by. When they came again, he was gone. He had freely given his life that others might live. The whole nation turned its eyes to this man in respect and admiration for the selfless and good act he had performed. And yet, if the atheist is right, that man was not noble—he did the stupidest thing possible. He should have gone for the ladder first, pushed others away if necessary in order to survive. But to die for others he did not even know, to give up all the brief existence he would ever have—what for? For the atheist there can be no reason. And yet the atheist, like the rest of us, instinctively reacts with praise for this man's selfless action. Indeed, one will probably never find an atheist who lives consistently with his system. For a universe without moral accountability and devoid of value is unimaginably terrible.

Purpose of Life

Finally, let's look at the problem of purpose in life. Unable to live in an impersonal universe in which everything is the product of blind chance, atheists sometimes begin to ascribe personality and motives to the physical processes themselves. It is a bizarre way of speaking and represents a leap from the lower to the upper story. For example, the brilliant Russian physicists Zeldovich and Novikov, in contemplating the properties of the universe, ask, why did "Nature" choose to create this sort of universe instead of another? "Nature" has obviously become a sort of God-substitute, filling the role and function of God. Francis Crick halfway through his book *The Origin of the Genetic Code* begins to spell nature with a capital *N* and elsewhere speaks of natural selection as being "clever" and as "thinking" of what it will do. Sir Fred Hoyle, the English astronomer, attributes to the universe itself the qualities of God. For Carl Sagan the "Cosmos," which he always spelled with a capital letter, obviously fills the role of a God-substitute. Though these men profess not to believe in God, they smuggle in a God-substitute through the back door because they cannot bear to live in a universe in which everything is the chance result of impersonal forces.

Moreover, the only way that most people who deny purpose in life live happily is either by making up some purpose—which amounts to self-delusion as we saw with Sartre—or by not carrying their view to its logical conclusions. Take the problem of death, for example. According to Ernst Bloch, the only way modern man lives in the face of death is by subconsciously borrowing the belief in immortality that his forefathers held to, even though he himself has no basis for this belief, since he does not believe in God. Bloch states that the belief that life ends in nothing is hardly, in his words, "sufficient to keep the head high and to work as if there were no end." By borrowing the remnants of a belief in immortality, writes Bloch, "modern man does not feel the chasm that unceasingly surrounds him and that will certainly engulf him at last. Through these remnants, he saves his sense of self-identity. Through them the impression arises that man is not perishing, but only that one day the world has the whim no longer to appear to him." Bloch concludes, "This quite shallow courage feasts on a borrowed credit card. It lives from earlier hopes and the support that they once had provided."[26] Modern man no longer has any right to that support, since he rejects God. But in order to live purposefully, he makes a leap of faith to affirm a reason for living.

Finding ourselves cast into a mindless universe with no apparent purpose or hope of deliverance from thermodynamic extinction, the temptation to invest one's own petty plans and projects with objective significance and thereby to find some purpose to one's life is almost irresistible. Thus, the outspoken atheist and Nobel Prize–winning physicist Steven Weinberg at the close of his much acclaimed popularization of contemporary cosmology *The First Three Minutes*, writes:

> However all these problems may be solved, and whichever cosmological model proves correct, there is not much comfort in any of this. It is almost irresistible for humans to believe that we have some special relation to the universe, that human life is not just a more-or-less farcical outcome of a chain of accidents reaching back to the first three minutes, but that somehow we were built in from the beginning. . . . It is very hard to realize that this is all just a tiny part of an overwhelmingly hostile universe. It is even harder to realize that this present universe has evolved from an unspeakably unfamiliar early condition, and faces a future extinction of endless cold or intolerable heat. The more the universe seems comprehensible, the more it also seems pointless.
>
> But if there is no solace in the fruits of our research, there is at least some consolation in the research itself. Men and women are not content to comfort themselves with tales of gods and giants, or to confine their thoughts to the daily affairs of life; they also build telescopes and satellites and accelerators and sit at their desks for endless hours working out the meaning of the data they gather. The effort to understand the universe is one of the very few things that lifts human life a little above the level of farce, and gives it some of the grace of tragedy.[27]

There is something strange about Weinberg's moving description of the human predicament: *tragedy* is an evaluative term. Weinberg sees the pursuit of scientific research as raising human life above the level of farce to the level of tragedy. But on naturalism, what is the basis for such an evaluative differentiation? Weinberg evidently sees a life devoted to scientific pursuits as truly meaningful, and therefore it's too bad that so noble a pursuit should be extinguished. But why on naturalism should the pursuit of science be any different from slouching about doing nothing? Since there is no objective purpose to human life, none of our pursuits has any objective significance, however important and dear they may seem to us subjectively.

Daniel Dennett recently betrayed a similar inconsistency. Speaking at a conference in New Orleans, Dennett opened his talk by showing a short film that encapsulated what he wanted to convey. It showed a group of young African men

26. Ernst Bloch, *Das Prinzip Hoffnung*, 2nd ed., 2 vols. (Frankfurt am Main: Suhrkamp Verlag, 1959), 2:360–1.

27. Steven Weinberg, *The First Three Minutes* (London: Andre Deutsch, 1977), 154–55.

playing with a soccer ball, kicking it into the air and adroitly catching it on their feet in quite amazing ways, while never letting the ball touch the ground. Meanwhile a silent narration played across the screen, describing the unfathomable vastness of the cosmos in space and time and contrasting the tininess and brevity of human existence. We are here for a mere twinkling of the eye and then gone forever. The punch line of the film finally came: "We'd better not blow it." That was the end. "What a strange film!" I thought to myself. What does it mean on an atheistic view to "blow it"? If there is no objective purpose for the human race, then how can one miss that purpose? Like *tragedy*, "blowing it" is an evaluative notion which finds no foothold in an atheistic universe. The boys' skill and evident joy in playing football is no more meaningful a pursuit on atheism than some other kid's staying home and drinking himself into a stupor. But even atheists recognize that some of life's pursuits are more objectively meaningful and worthwhile than others.

While participating in a conference on Intelligent Design two years ago, I had the opportunity to have dinner with the agnostic philosopher of science Michael Ruse one evening at an Atlanta steakhouse. During the course of the meal, Michael asked me, "Bill, are you satisfied with where you are in your career as a philosopher?" I was rather surprised by the question and said, "Well, yes, basically, I guess I am—how about you?" He then related to me that when he was just starting out as a philosopher of science, he was faced with the choice of vigorously pursuing his career or just taking it rather easy. He said that he then thought of the anguished words of the character played by Marlin Brando at the close of the film *On the Waterfront*: "I coulda been a contender!" Michael told me that he decided he didn't want to reach the end of his life and look back in regret and say, "I coulda been a contender!" I was struck by those words. As a Christian I am commanded by the Lord "to contend for the faith that was once for all delivered to the saints" (Jude 3 ESV). But what point is there for an atheist or agnostic to be a "contender"—a contender for what? Since there is no objective purpose in life, the only answer can be, to contend for one's own made-up purposes—hence, the irresistible tendency to treat career advancement and fame as though they really were objectively important ends, when in fact they are nothing.

The Human Predicament

The dilemma of modern man is thus truly terrible. The atheistic worldview is insufficient to maintain a happy and consistent life. Man cannot live consistently and happily as though life were ultimately without meaning, value, or purpose. If we try to live consistently within the framework of the atheistic worldview, we shall find ourselves profoundly unhappy. If instead we manage to live happily, it is only by giving the lie to our worldview.

Confronted with this dilemma, modern man flounders pathetically for some means of escape. In a remarkable address to the American Academy for the Advancement of Science in 1991, Dr. L. D. Rue, confronted with the predicament of modern man, boldly advocated that we deceive ourselves by means of some "Noble Lie" into thinking that we and the universe still have value.[28] Claiming that "the lesson of the past two centuries is that intellectual and moral relativism is profoundly the case," Dr. Rue muses that the consequence of such a realization is that one's quest for personal wholeness (or self-fulfillment) and the quest for social coherence become independent from one another. This is because on the view of relativism the search for self-fulfillment becomes radically privatized: each person chooses his own set of values and meaning. "There is no final, objective reading on the world or the self. There is no universal vocabulary for integrating cosmology and morality." If we are to avoid "the madhouse option," where self-fulfillment is pursued regardless of social coherence, and "the totalitarian option," where social coherence is imposed at the expense of personal wholeness, then we have no choice but to embrace some Noble Lie that will inspire us to live beyond selfish interests and so achieve social coherence. A Noble Lie "is one that deceives us, tricks us, compels us beyond self-interest, beyond ego, beyond family, nation, [and] race." It is a lie, because it tells us that the universe is infused with value (which is a great fiction), because it makes a claim to universal truth (when there is none), and because it tells me not to live for self-interest (which is evidently false). "But without such lies, we cannot live."

This is the dreadful verdict pronounced over modern man. In order to survive, he must live in self-deception. But even the Noble Lie option is in the end un-workable. For if what I have said thus far is correct, belief in a Noble Lie would not only be necessary to achieve social coherence and personal wholeness for the masses, but it would also be necessary to achieve one's *own* personal wholeness. For one cannot live happily and consistently on an atheistic worldview. In order to be happy, one must believe in objective meaning, value, and purpose. But how can one believe in those Noble Lies while at the same time believing in atheism and relativism? The more convinced you are of the necessity of a Noble Lie, the less you are able to believe in it. Like a placebo, a Noble Lie works only on those who believe it is the truth. Once we have seen through the fiction, then the Lie has lost its power over us. Thus, ironically, the Noble Lie cannot solve the human predicament for anyone who has come to see that predicament.

The Noble Lie option therefore leads at best to a society in which an elitist group of *illuminati* deceive the masses for their own good by perpetuating the Noble Lie. But then why should those of us who are enlightened follow the masses in their deception? Why should we sacrifice self-interest for a fiction? If the great lesson of the past two centuries is moral and intellectual relativism, then why (if we could) pretend that we do not know this truth and live a lie instead? If one answers, "for the sake of social coherence," one may legitimately ask why I should sacrifice my self-interest for the sake of social coherence. The only answer the relativist can give

28. Loyal D. Rue, "The Saving Grace of Noble Lies," address to the American Academy for the Advancement of Science, February 1991.

is that social coherence is in my self-interest—but the problem with this answer is that self-interest and the interest of the herd do not always coincide. Besides, if (out of self-interest) I do care about social coherence, the totalitarian option is always open to me: forget the Noble Lie and maintain social coherence (as well as my self-fulfillment) at the expense of the personal wholeness of the masses. Generations of Soviet leaders who extolled proletarian virtues while they rode in limousines and dined on caviar in their country *dachas* found this alternative quite workable. Rue would undoubtedly regard such an option as repugnant. But therein lies the rub. Rue's dilemma is that he obviously values deeply both social coherence and personal wholeness for their own sakes; in other words, they are objective values, which according to his philosophy do not exist. He has already leapt to the upper story. The Noble Lie option thus affirms what it denies and so refutes itself.

The Success of Biblical Christianity

But if atheism fails in this regard, what about biblical Christianity? According to the Christian worldview, God does exist, and man's life does not end at the grave. In the resurrection body man may enjoy eternal life and fellowship with God. Biblical Christianity therefore provides the two conditions necessary for a meaningful, valuable, and purposeful life for man: God and immortality. Because of this, we can live consistently and happily. Thus, biblical Christianity succeeds precisely where atheism breaks down.

Now I want to make it clear that I have not yet shown biblical Christianity to be true. But what I have done is clearly spell out the alternatives. If God does not exist, then life is futile. If the God of the Bible does exist, then life is meaningful. Only the second of these two alternatives enables us to live happily and consistently. Therefore, it seems to me that even if the evidence for these two options were absolutely equal, a rational person ought to choose biblical Christianity. It seems to me positively irrational to prefer death, futility, and destruction to life, meaningfulness, and happiness. As Pascal said, we have nothing to lose and infinity to gain.

Practical Application

The foregoing discussion makes clear the role I conceive cultural apologetics to play: it is not one's whole apologetic but rather an introduction to positive argumentation. It serves to lay out in a dramatic way the alternatives facing the unbeliever in order to create a felt need in him. When he realizes the predicament he is in, he will see why the gospel is so important to him; and many a non-Christian will be impelled by these considerations alone to give his life to Christ.

In sharing this material with an unbeliever, we need to push him to the logical conclusions of his position. If I am right, no atheist or agnostic really lives consistently with his worldview. In some way he affirms meaning, value, or purpose without an adequate basis. It is our job to discover those areas and lovingly show him where those beliefs are groundless. We need not attack his values themselves—for they are probably largely correct—but we may agree with him concerning them, and then point out only that he lacks any foundation for those values, whereas the Christian has a foundation. Thus, we need not make him defensive by a frontal attack on his personal values; rather we offer him a foundation for the values he already possesses.

I have found the appeal to moral values to be an especially powerful apologetic to university students. Although students may give lip service to relativism, my experience is that 95 percent can be very quickly convinced that objective moral values do exist after all. All you have to do is produce a few illustrations and let them decide for themselves. Ask what they think of the Hindu practice of *suttee* (burning widows alive on the funeral pyres of their husbands) or the ancient Chinese custom of crippling women for life by tightly binding their feet from childhood to resemble lotus-blossoms. Point out that without God to provide a transcultural basis for moral values, we're left with socio-cultural relativism, so that such practices are morally unobjectionable—which scarcely anyone can sincerely accept.

Of course, sometimes you find hard-liners, but usually their position is seen to be so extreme that others are repulsed by it. For example, at a meeting of the Society of Biblical Literature a few years ago, I attended a panel discussion on "Biblical Authority and Homosexuality," in which all the panelists endorsed the legitimacy of homosexual activity. One panelist dismissed scriptural prohibitions of such activity on the grounds that they reflect the cultural milieu in which they were written. Since this is the case for all of Scripture's commands (it wasn't written in a vacuum), he concluded that "there are no timeless, normative, moral truths in Scripture." In discussion from the floor, I pointed out that such a view leads to socio-cultural relativism, which makes it impossible to criticize *any* society's moral values, including those of a society which persecutes homosexuals. He responded with a fog of theological double-talk and claimed that there's no place outside Scripture where we can find timeless moral values either. "But that just *is* what we mean by moral relativism," I said. "In fact, on your view there's no content to the notion of the goodness of God. He might as well be dead. And Nietzsche recognized that the death of God leads to nihilism." At this point another panelist came in with that knock-down refutation: "Well, if you're going to get pejorative, we might as well not discuss it."

I sat down, but the point wasn't lost on the audience. The next man who stood up said, "Wait a minute. I'm rather confused. I'm a pastor and people are always coming to me, asking if something they have done is wrong and if they need forgiveness. For example, isn't it always wrong to abuse a child?" I couldn't believe the panelist's response. She replied: "What counts as abuse differs from society to society, so we can't really use the word 'abuse' without tying it to a historical context." "Call it whatever you like," the pastor insisted, "but child abuse is damaging to children. Isn't it wrong to damage children?" And still she wouldn't admit it! This sort of hardness of heart ultimately backfires on the moral relativist and exposes in the minds of most people the bankruptcy of such a worldview.

In sharing this material with an unbeliever, it's important also to ask ourselves exactly what part of our case his objections are meant to refute. Thus, if he says that values are merely social conventions pragmatically adopted to ensure mutual survival, what does this purport to refute? Not that life without God really is without value, for this the objection admits. Therefore, it would be a mistake to react by arguing that values are not social conventions but are grounded in God. Rather the objection is really aimed at the claim that one cannot live as though values do not exist; it holds that one may live by social conventions alone.

Seen in this light, however, the objection is entirely implausible, for we have argued precisely that man cannot live as though morality were merely a matter of social convention. We believe certain acts to be genuinely wrong or right. Therefore, one ought to respond to the unbeliever on this score by saying, "You're exactly right: if God does not exist, then values are merely social conventions. But the point I'm trying to make is that it's impossible to live consistently and happily with such a worldview." Push him on the Holocaust or some issue of popular concern like ethnic cleansing, apartheid, or child abuse. Bring it home to him personally, and if he's honest and you are not threatening, I think he will admit that he does hold to some absolutes. Thus, it's very important to analyze exactly what the unbeliever's objection actually attacks before we answer.

I believe that this mode of apologetics can be very effective in helping to bring people to Christ because it does not concern neutral matters but cuts to the heart of the unbeliever's own existential situation. I remember once, when I was delivering a series of talks at the University of Birmingham in England, that the audience the first night was very hostile and aggressive. The second night I spoke on the absurdity of life without God. This time the largely same audience was utterly subdued: the lions had turned to lambs, and now their questions were no longer attacking but sincere and searching. The remarkable transformation was due to the fact that the message had penetrated their intellectual facade and struck at the core of their existence. I would encourage you to employ this material in evangelistic dorm meetings and fraternity/sorority meetings, where you can compel people to really *think* about the desperate human predicament in which we all find ourselves.

Literature Cited or Recommended

Historical Background

Dostoyevsky, Fyodor. *The Brothers Karamazov*. Translated by C. Garnett. Foreword by M. Komroff. New York: New American Library, Signet Classics, 1957.

————. *Crime and Punishment*. Translated by C. Garnett. Introduction by E. Simmons. New York: Modern Library, 1950.

Kierkegaard, Søren. *Either/Or*. Translated by D. F. Swenson and L. M. Swenson. Princeton: Princeton University, 1944. Volume 1 describes the first stage of life and Volume 2 the second.

————. *Fear and Trembling*. Edited and translated with an introduction and notes by H. V. Hong and E. N. Hong. Princeton: Princeton University Press, 1983. This handles the religious stage.

Morris, Thomas V. *Making Sense of It All: Pascal and the Meaning of Life*. Grand Rapids, Mich.: Eerdmans, 1992.

Pascal, Blaise. *Pensées*. Edited by Louis Lafuma. Translated by John Warrington. Everyman's Library. London: Dent, 1960.

Schaeffer, Francis. *Escape from Reason*. Downers Grove, Ill.: InterVarsity, 1968.

————. *The God Who Is There*. Downer's Grove, Ill.: InterVarsity, 1968.

————. *How Should We Then Live?* Wheaton, Ill.: Crossway Books, 1976.

Assessment

Beckett, Samuel. *Waiting for Godot*. New York: Grove, 1956.

Bloch, Ernst. *Das Prinzip Hoffnung*. 2nd ed. 2 vols. Frankfurt am Main: Suhrkamp Verlag, 1959.

Camus, Albert. *The Myth of Sisyphus and Other Essays*. Translated by J. O'Brien. New York: Vintage, 1959.

————. *The Stranger*. Translated by S. Gilbert. New York: Vintage, 1958.

Crick, Francis. "Why I Study Biology." *Washington University Magazine*. Spring 1971, 20–24.

Dawkins, Richard, *The God Delusion*. New York: Houghton-Mifflin, 2006.

————. *River out of Eden: A Darwinian View of Life*. New York: Basic Books, 1996.

————. "The Ultraviolet Garden," Lecture 4 of 7 Royal Institution Christmas Lectures (1992), http://physicshead.blogspot.com/2007/01/richard-dawkins-lecture-4-ultra-violet.html.

————. *Unweaving the Rainbow*. London: Allen Lane, 1998.

Eliot, T. S. "The Hollow Men." In *The Complete Poems and Plays*. New York: Harcourt, Brace, 1934.

Encyclopaedia Britannica, 15th ed. *Propaedia*, s.v. "The Cosmic Orphan," by Loren Eiseley.

Hocking, W. E. *Types of Philosophy*. New York: Scribner's, 1959.

Hoyle, Fred. *From Stonehenge to Modern Cosmology*. San Francisco: W. H. Freeman, 1972.

Kaufmann, Walter, ed. "Existentialism from Dostoyevsky to Sartre." In *Existentialism from Dostoyevsky to Sartre*. 2nd ed., edited by W. Kaufmann, 11–51. New York: New American Library, Meridian, 1975.

Kurtz, Paul. *Forbidden Fruit*. Buffalo, N.Y.: Prometheus, 1988.

Monod, Jacques. *Chance and Necessity*. Translated by A. Wainhouse. New York: Alfred A. Knopf, 1971.

Moreland, J. P. *Scaling the Secular City*, chap. 4. Grand Rapids, Mich.: Baker, 1987.

Moreland, J. P. and Kai Nielsen. *Does God Exist?* Nashville: Thomas Nelson, 1990. Repr. ed.: Prometheus Books, 1993. Part 2 is an excellent debate over ethics without God.

Nielsen, Kai. "Why Should I Be Moral? Revisited." *American Philosophical Quarterly* 21 (1984): 81–91.

Nietzsche, Friedrich. "The Gay Science." In *The Portable Nietzsche*, edited and translated by W. Kaufmann, 93–102. New York: Viking, 1954.

———. "The Will to Power." Translated by Walter Kaufmann. In *Existentialism from Dostoyevsky to Sartre*. 2nd ed., edited with an introduction by W. Kaufmann, 130–32. New York: New American Library, Meridian, 1975.

Novikov, I. D., and Ya B. Zeldovich. "Physical Processes Near Cosmological Singularities." *Annual Review of Astronomy and Astrophysics* 11 (1973): 387–410.

Rue, Loyal D. "The Saving Grace of Noble Lies." Unpublished address to the American Academy for the Advancement of Science, February 1991.

Russell, Bertrand. "A Free Man's Worship." In *Why I Am Not a Christian*, edited by P. Edwards, 104–16. New York: Simon & Schuster, 1957.

———. Letter to the *Observer*, 6 October 1957.

Sagan, Carl. *Cosmos*. New York: Random House, 1980.

Sartre, Jean-Paul. *Being and Nothingness*. Translated with an introduction by H. E. Barnes. New York: Washington Square, 1966.

———. "Existentialism Is a Humanism." Translated by P. Mairet. In *Existentialism from Dostoyevsky to Sartre*. 2nd ed., edited with an introduction by W. Kaufmann, 345–69. New York: New American Library, Meridian, 1975.

———. *Nausea*. Translated by L. Alexander. London: H. Hamilton, 1962.

———. *No Exit*. Translated by S. Gilbert. New York: Alfred A. Knopf, 1963.

———. "Portrait of the Antisemite." Translated by M. Guggenheim. In *Existentialism from Dostoyevsky to Sartre*. 2nd ed., edited with an introduction by W. Kaufmann, 329–45. New York: New American Library, Meridian, 1975.

———. "The Wall." Translated by L. Alexander. In *Existentialism from Dostoyevsky to Sartre*. 2nd ed., edited with an introduction by W. Kaufmann, 281–99. New York: New American Library, Meridian, 1975.

Taylor, Richard. *Ethics, Faith, and Reason*. Englewood Cliffs, N.J.: Prentice-Hall, 1985. An excellent illustration of the desperate lengths to which an ethicist is driven once a divine moral law giver is denied.

Wells, H. G. *The Time Machine*. New York: Berkeley, 1957.

Wolpert, Lewis. *Six Impossible Things before Breakfast*. London: Faber and Faber, 2006.

Wurmbrand, Richard. *Tortured for Christ*. London: Hodder & Stoughton, 1967.

Part 3

De Deo

3

The Existence of God (1)

We've seen that only if God exists can there be hope for a solution to the human predicament. Therefore, the question of the existence of God is vital for us today. Most people would probably agree that this question does have great existential significance but at the same time deny that it is a question to which rational argumentation is relevant. The conventional wisdom is that it's impossible to "prove" the existence of God and that, therefore, if we are going to believe in God, we must "take it by faith" that God exists.

But the last half century has witnessed a remarkable resurgence of interest in natural theology, that branch of theology that seeks to provide warrant for belief in God's existence apart from the resources of authoritative, propositional revelation. Today, in contrast to just a generation ago, natural theology is a vibrant field of study.

On April 8, 1966, *Time* magazine carried a dramatic cover with just three words emblazoned in red upon the black background. The words read: "Is God Dead?" The article described the movement then current among American theologians to proclaim the death of God. But at the same time that theologians were writing God's obituary, a new generation of philosophers was rediscovering his vitality. Just a few years after its death-of-God issue, *Time* ran a similar red-on-black cover story, only this time the question read, "Is God Coming Back to Life?" That's how it must have seemed to those theological morticians of the 1960s! During the 1970s interest in philosophy of religion continued to grow, and in 1980 *Time* found itself

93

running another major story entitled "Modernizing the Case for God," in which it described the movement among contemporary philosophers to refurbish the traditional arguments for God's existence. *Time* marveled:

> In a quiet revolution in thought and argument that hardly anybody could have foreseen only two decades ago, God is making a comeback. Most intriguingly, this is happening not among theologians or ordinary believers, but in the crisp intellectual circles of academic philosophers, where the consensus had long banished the Almighty from fruitful discourse.[1]

According to the article, the late Roderick Chisholm believes that the reason that atheism was so influential a generation ago is that the brightest philosophers were atheists; but today, he says, many of the brightest philosophers are theists and are using a tough-minded intellectualism in defense of that belief that was formerly lacking on their side of the debate.

The face of Anglo-American philosophy has been transformed as result. In the fall of 2001 the secularist journal *Philo* carried an article by a leading atheist philosopher lamenting what he called "the desecularization of academia that evolved in philosophy departments since the late 1960s." He writes:

> Naturalists passively watched as realist versions of theism, most influenced by Plantinga's writings, began to sweep through the philosophical community, until today perhaps one-quarter or one-third of philosophy professors are theists, with most being orthodox Christians. . . . Theists in other fields tend to compartmentalize their theistic beliefs from their scholarly work; they rarely assume and never argue for theism in their scholarly work. If they did, they would be committing academic suicide or, more exactly, their articles would quickly be rejected. . . . But in philosophy, it became, almost overnight, "academically respectable" to argue for theism, making philosophy a favored field of entry for the most intelligent and talented theists entering academia today.[2]

He concludes, "God is not 'dead' in academia; he returned to life in the late 1960s and is now alive and well in his last academic stronghold, philosophy departments."

This is the testimony of a prominent atheist philosopher to the change that has taken place before his eyes in Anglo-American philosophy. I think he's probably exaggerating when he estimates that one-quarter to one-third of American philosophers are theists; but what his estimates do reveal is the *perceived impact* of Christian philosophers upon this field. Today all of the various traditional arguments for God's existence find prominent, intelligent proponents, who defend these arguments in books published by the finest academic presses, in articles in

1. "Modernizing the Case for God," *Time*, April 7, 1980, 65–66.
2. Quentin Smith, "The Metaphilosophy of Naturalism," *Philo* 4, no. 2 (2001): 3–4.

professional journals of philosophy, and in papers presented at meetings of professional philosophical societies.

Now atheists are hitting back. In the aftermath of the 9/11 terrorist attacks by Muslim jihadists, secularists have become remarkably aggressive both in the United States and Europe, denouncing religious belief in general with an almost evangelical fervor. Lumping evangelical Christians in with Islamic terrorists, popular writers like Richard Dawkins, Daniel Dennett, and Sam Harris have championed atheism in their best-selling books and warned of the dire effects of religious belief upon society. Behind these popular writings stand more substantive critiques of theistic arguments like J. Howard Sobel's *Logic and Theism* and Michael Martin's *Companion to Atheism*. We are witnesses to a mighty struggle for the mind and soul of America in our day, and Christians cannot be indifferent to it.

Historical Background
Ever since Plato, philosophers and theologians have tried to provide a rational basis for belief in God. In this section, we shall briefly survey some of the traditional theistic arguments as developed by various thinkers.

Ontological Argument
The ontological argument attempts to prove from the very concept of God that God exists: if God is conceivable, then he must actually exist. This argument was formulated by Anselm and defended by Scotus, Descartes, Spinoza, Leibniz, and, in modern times, Norman Malcolm, Charles Hartshorne, and Alvin Plantinga, among others. We shall examine the Anselmian argument.

Anselm (1033–1109) wanted to find a single argument that would prove not only that God exists, but also that he has all the superlative attributes Christian doctrine ascribes to him. Having almost given up the project, Anselm landed upon the following reasoning:[3] God is the greatest conceivable being. This is true by definition, for if we could conceive of something greater than God, then *that* would be God. So nothing greater than God can be conceived. It is greater to exist in reality than merely in the mind. Anselm gives the example of a painting. Which is greater: the artist's idea of the painting or the painting itself as it really exists? Obviously the latter; for the painting itself exists not only in the artist's mind, but in reality as well. Similarly, if God existed only in the mind, then something greater than him could be conceived, namely, his existing not only in the mind, but in reality as well. But God is the greatest conceivable being. Hence, he must exist not merely in the mind, but in reality as well. Therefore, God exists.

Another way of putting this, says Anselm, is the following: a being whose non-existence is inconceivable is greater than a being whose non-existence is conceivable. But God is the greatest conceivable being. Therefore, God's non-

---

3. Anselm, *Proslogion* 2–3.

existence must be inconceivable. There is no contradiction involved in this notion. Therefore, God must exist.

This deceptively simple argument is still hotly debated today.

Cosmological Argument

In contrast to the ontological argument, the cosmological argument assumes that something exists and argues from the existence of that thing to the existence of a First Cause or a Sufficient Reason of the cosmos. This argument has its roots in Plato and Aristotle and was developed by medieval Islamic, Jewish, and Christian thinkers. It has been defended by such great minds as Plato, Aristotle, ibn Sīna, al-Ghāzalī, ibn Rushd, Maimonides, Anselm, Aquinas, Scotus, Descartes, Spinoza, Berkeley, Locke, and Leibniz. The cosmological argument is really a family of different arguments, which can be conveniently grouped under three main types.

AL-GHĀZALĪ

The *kalām* cosmological argument originated in the attempts of Christian thinkers to rebut Aristotle's doctrine of the eternity of the universe and was developed by medieval Islamic theologians into an argument for the existence of God.[4] Let's look at the formulation of this argument by al-Ghāzalī (1058–1111). He reasons, "Every being which begins has a cause for its beginning; now the world is a being which begins; therefore, it possesses a cause for its beginning."[5] In support of the first premise, that every being that begins has a cause for its beginning, Ghāzalī reasons: anything that begins to exist does so at a certain moment of time. But since, prior to the thing's existence, all moments are alike, there must be some cause that determines that the thing comes to exist at that moment rather than earlier or later. Thus, anything that comes to exist must have a cause.

The second premise is that the world, or the universe, began to exist. In support of this premise Ghāzalī argues that it is impossible that there should be an infinite regress of events in time, that is to say, that the series of past events should be beginningless. He gives several reasons for this conclusion. For one thing, the series of past events comes to an end in the present—but the infinite cannot come to an end. It might be pointed out that even though the series of events has one end in the present, it can still be infinite in the other direction because it has no beginning. But Ghāzalī's point may be that if the regress of past events were infinite, then it would be impossible for the present moment to arrive. For it is impossible to cross the infinite to get to today. So today could never arrive, which is absurd, for here we are!

Second, if the number of past events were infinite, that would lead to infinites of different sizes. For suppose Jupiter completes an orbit once every twelve years

---

4. "*Kalām*" is the Arabic word for speech and came to denote a statement of theological doctrine and ultimately the whole movement of medieval Islamic theology.

5. Al-Ghāzalī, *Kitab al-Iqtisad fi'l-I'tiqad*, cited in S. de Beaurecueil, "Gazzali et S. Thomas d'Aquin: Essai sur la preuve de l'existence de Dieu proposée dans l'Iqtisad et sa comparaison avec les 'voies' Thomiste," *Bulletin de l'Institut Francais d'Archaeologie Orientale* 46 (1947): 203.

and Saturn once every thirty years and the sphere of the stars once every thirty-six thousand years. If the universe is eternal and these planets have been orbiting from eternity, then each of these bodies has completed an infinite number of orbits, and yet one will have completed twice as many or thousands of times as many orbits as another, which is absurd.

Finally, if we take the orbits completed by just one of these planets, we may ask, is the number of orbits it has completed odd or even? It would have to be one or the other, and yet it is absurd to say the infinite is odd or even. For these reasons, the universe must have had a beginning. It therefore follows that there must be a cause of its beginning, which Ghāzalī identifies with God, the Eternal.

THOMAS AQUINAS

The Thomist cosmological argument is based on the impossibility of an infinite regress of simultaneously operating causes. It seeks a Cause that is First, not in the temporal sense, but in the sense of rank or source. Although Thomas Aquinas (1225–1274) did not originate this line of reasoning, he is famous for his clear summary of it in his Five Ways of proving that God exists.[6] We'll look at his first three ways, which are different versions of the argument for a First Cause.

The First Way is his proof for an Unmoved Mover based on motion. We see in the world that things are in motion. But anything that is in motion is being moved by something else. For a thing that has the potential to move cannot actualize its own potential; some other thing must cause it to move. But this other thing is also being moved by something else, and that is also being moved by something else, and so on. Now this series of things being moved by other things cannot go on to infinity. For in such a series, the intermediate causes have no power of their own but are mere instruments of a first cause.

It is important to keep in mind that Aquinas is thinking here of causes that all act simultaneously like the gears of a machine, not successively like falling dominoes. So if you take away the first cause, all you have left are the powerless instrumental causes. It does not matter if you have an infinity of such causes; they still could not cause anything. For example, a watch could not run without a spring even if it had an infinite number of gears; a train could not move without an engine even if it had an infinite number of box cars. Aquinas concludes that there must be a first cause of motion in every causal series. For all self-moving things—including humans, animals, and plants—this would be the individual soul, which is an unmoved mover. But souls themselves come to be and pass away and thus cannot account for the eternal motion of the heavenly spheres. In order to account for this cosmic motion, we must postulate an absolutely Unmoved Mover, the First Cause of all motion, and this is God.

The Second Way attempts to prove the existence of a First Cause of existence based on causation in the world. We observe that causes are ordered in series. Now nothing

---

6. Thomas Aquinas, *Summa theologiae* 1 a.2, 3 cf. idem *Summa contra gentiles* 1.13.

can be self-caused, because then it would have to bestow existence on itself, which is impossible. Everything that is caused is therefore caused by something else. Aquinas thinks here of the same sort of simultaneous causal series as he did in the First Way, except that here the causes are causes of existence, not motion. The existence of any object depends on a whole array of contemporary causes, of which each in turn depends on other causes, and so forth. But such a causal series cannot go on to infinity for the same reason explained above. Therefore, there must be a First Cause of the existence of everything else, which is simply uncaused; and this everyone calls "God."

The Third Way is the proof for an Absolutely Necessary Being based on the existence of contingent beings. We see in the world beings whose existence is not necessary but only possible. That is to say, these beings do not have to exist, for we see them come to be and pass away. If they were necessary, they would always exist. But all beings cannot be contingent beings, for if everything were merely contingent, then at some point in time everything would cease to exist. Aquinas here presupposes the past eternity of the world and appears to reason that in infinite time all possibilities would be realized. Hence, if every being, including matter itself, were only a contingent being, then it is possible that nothing would exist. Thus, given infinite past time, this possibility would be realized and nothing would exist. But then nothing would now exist, since out of nothing, nothing comes. Since this is obviously absurd, not all beings must be contingent beings. Some being or beings must be necessary. In fact, Aquinas believed that there were many necessary beings: the heavenly bodies, angels, even matter itself.

Now he continues, where do these necessary beings get their necessity—from themselves or from another? Thomas here distinguishes between a thing's essence and existence. A thing's essence is its nature, that set of properties which it must possess in order to be what it is. For example, the essence of man is "rational animality." If anything lacked either of these properties, it would not be a man. A thing's existence, on the other hand, is its being. Now if a being is not necessary in itself, this means that its essence is distinct from its existence. It does not belong to its nature to exist. For example, I could think of the nature of an angel without ever knowing whether or not an angel actually exists. Its essence is distinct from its existence. Hence, if such a being is to exist, something else must conjoin to its essence an act of existence. Then it would exist. But there cannot be an infinite regress of necessary beings that get their existence from another. (The reasoning is the same as that in the First Way against an infinite regress.) So there must be a First Being, which is absolutely necessary in itself. In this Being, essence and existence are not distinct; in some mysterious way its nature is existence. Hence, according to Aquinas, God is Being itself subsisting (*ipsum esse subsistens*). God is pure Being and is the source of being to everything else, whose essences do not involve their existing.

G. W. F. LEIBNIZ

The Leibnizian cosmological argument was developed by the German mathematician and philosopher G. W. F. Leibniz (1646–1716) and is often confused with the

Thomist cosmological argument. But Leibniz does not argue for the existence of an Uncaused Cause, but for the existence of a Sufficient Reason for the universe.[7] The difference will become clear as we proceed.

"The first question which should rightly be asked," wrote Leibniz, "will be, *Why is there something rather than nothing?*" That is, why does anything at all exist? There must be an answer to this question, because "*nothing happens without a sufficient reason.*"[8] Leibniz's famous Principle of Sufficient Reason holds that there must be a reason or rational explanation for the existence of one state of affairs rather than another. Why does the universe exist? The reason cannot be found in any single thing in the universe, for each is contingent itself and does not have to exist. Nor is the reason to be found in the whole aggregate of such things, for the world is just the collection of these contingent beings and is therefore itself contingent. Nor can the reason be found in the prior causes of things, for these are just past states of the universe and do not explain why there are any such states, any universe, at all. Leibniz asks us to imagine that a series of geometry books has been copied from eternity; such an infinite regress would still not explain why such books exist at all. But the same is true with regard to past states of the world: even should these be infinite; we have yet to discover a sufficient reason for the existence of an eternal universe. Therefore, the reason for the universe's existence must be found outside the universe, in a being whose sufficient reason is self-contained; it is its own sufficient reason for existing and is the reason the universe exists as well. This Sufficient Reason of all things is God, whose own existence is to be explained only by reference to himself. That is to say, God is a metaphysically necessary being.

This proof is clearly different from the Thomist argument: there is no reference to the distinction between essence and existence or to the argument against an infinite causal regress. Indeed, Leibniz is not seeking a cause at all, but an explanation for the world. Thomas concludes to an Uncaused Cause, but Leibniz to a Self-Explanatory Being. Many philosophers have confused these and come up with the notion of God as a Self-Caused Being, which neither Aquinas nor Leibniz defended.

Thus, there is a variety of cosmological arguments, which need to be kept distinct, for objections to one version may prove inapplicable to another.

Teleological Argument

Perhaps the oldest and most popular of all the arguments for the existence of God is the teleological argument. It is the famous argument from design, and it infers an intelligent designer of the universe, just as we infer an intelligent designer for

---

7. G. W. F. von Leibniz, "On the Ultimate Origin of Things," in *Leibniz Selections*, ed. P. Wiener (New York: Scribner's, 1951), 527–28; idem, "Monadology," in *Selections*, 540; idem, *Theodicy*, trans. E. M. Huggard (London: Routledge & Kegan Paul, 1951), 127.

8. Leibniz, "Nature and Grace," in *Selections*, 527.

any product in which we discern evidence of purposeful adaptation of means to some end (*telos*).

PLATO AND ARISTOTLE

The ancient Greek philosophers were impressed with the order that pervades the cosmos, and many of them ascribed that order to the work of an intelligent mind who fashioned the universe. The heavens in constant revolution across the sky were especially awesome to the ancients. Plato's Academy lavished extensive time and thought on the study of astronomy because, Plato believed, it was the science that would awaken man to his divine destiny. According to Plato, there are two things that "lead men to believe in the gods": the argument based on the soul, and the argument "from the order of the motion of the stars, and of all things under the dominion of the mind which ordered the universe."[9] What a lovely statement of the divine design evident throughout the universe! Plato employed both of these arguments to refute atheism and concluded that there must be a "best soul" who is the "maker and father of all," the "King," who ordered the primordial chaos into the rational cosmos we observe today.[10]

An even more magnificent statement of divine teleology is to be found in a fragment from a lost work of Aristotle entitled *On Philosophy*. Aristotle, too, was struck with wonder by the majestic sweep of the glittering host across the night sky of ancient Greece. Philosophy, he said, begins with this sense of wonder about the world:

> For it is owing to their wonder that men both now begin and at first began to philosophize; they wondered originally at the obvious difficulties, then advanced little by little and stated difficulties about greater matters, e.g. about the phenomena of the moon and those of the sun, and about the stars and about the genesis of the universe.[11]

Anyone who has personally studied the heavens must lend a sympathetic ear to these men of antiquity who gazed up into the night sky, as yet undimmed by pollution and the glare of city lights, and watched the slow but irresistible turn of the cosmos, replete with its planets, stars, and familiar constellations, across their view and wondered, what is the cause of all this? Aristotle concluded that the cause was divine intelligence. He imagined the impact that the sight of the world would have on a race of men who had lived underground and never beheld the sky:

> When thus they would suddenly gain sight of the earth, seas, and the sky; when they should come to know the grandeur of the clouds and the might of the winds;

9. Plato, *Laws* 12.966e.
10. Plato, *Laws* 10.893b-899c; idem *Timaeus*.
11. Aristotle, *Metaphysica* 1.982610–15.

when they should behold the sun and should learn its grandeur and beauty as well as its power to cause the day by shedding light over the sky; and again, when the night had darkened the lands and they should behold the whole of the sky spangled and adorned with stars; and when they should see the changing lights of the moon as it waxes and wanes, and the risings and settings of all these celestial bodies, their courses fixed and changeless throughout all eternity—when they should behold all these things, most certainly they would have judged both that there exist gods and that all these marvelous works are the handiwork of the gods.[12]

In his *Metaphysics* Aristotle proceeded to argue that there must be a First Unmoved Mover, which is God, a living, intelligent, incorporeal, eternal, and most good being who is the source of order in the cosmos. Hence, from earliest times men, wholly removed from biblical revelation, have concluded on the basis of design in the universe that a divine mind must exist.

THOMAS AQUINAS

We've already seen that Thomas Aquinas in his first three Ways argued for the existence of God via the cosmological argument. His Fifth Way, however, represents the teleological argument. He notes that we observe in nature that all things operate toward some end, even when those things lack consciousness. For their operation hardly ever varies and practically always turns out well, which shows that they really do tend toward a goal and do not hit upon it merely by accident. Thomas is here expressing the conviction of Aristotelian physics that everything has not only a productive cause but also a final cause or goal toward which it is drawn. To use an example of our own, poppy seeds always grow into poppies and acorns into oaks. Now nothing, Aquinas reasons, that lacks consciousness tends toward a goal unless it is under the direction of someone with consciousness and intelligence. For example, the arrow does not tend toward the bull's eye unless it is aimed by the archer. Therefore, everything in nature must be directed toward its goal by someone with intelligence, and this we call "God."

WILLIAM PALEY

Undoubtedly, the high point in the development of the teleological argument prior to our time came with William Paley's brilliant formulation in his *Natural Theology* of 1804. Paley combed the sciences of his day for evidences of design in nature and produced a staggering catalogue of such evidences, based, for example, on the order evident in bones, muscles, blood vessels, comparative anatomy, and particular organs throughout the animal and plant kingdoms. So conclusive was Paley's evidence that Leslie Stephen in his *History of English Thought in the Eighteenth Century* wryly remarked that "if there were no hidden flaw in the reasoning, it would be impossible to understand, not only how any should resist, but

12. Aristotle, *On Philosophy*.

how anyone should ever have overlooked the demonstration."[13] Although most philosophers—who have undoubtedly never read Paley—believe that his sort of argument was dealt a crushing and fatal blow by David Hume's critique of the teleological argument, Paley's argument, which was written nearly thirty years after the publication of Hume's critique, is in fact not vulnerable to most of Hume's objections, as Frederick Ferré has pointed out.[14] Paley opens with a statement of the famous "watch-maker argument":

> In crossing a heath, suppose I pitched my foot against a stone, and were asked how the stone came to be there; I might possibly answer, that, for anything I knew to the contrary it had lain there forever: nor would it perhaps be very easy to show the absurdity of this answer. But suppose I had found a *watch* upon the ground, and it should be inquired how the watch happened to be in that place; I should hardly think of the answer which I had before given, that, for anything I knew, the watch might have always been there. Yet why should not this answer serve for the watch as well as for the stone? Why is it not as admissible in the second case, as in the first? For this reason, and for no other, viz. that, when we come to inspect the watch, we perceive (what we could not discover in the stone) that its several parts are framed and put together for a purpose, e.g. that they are so formed and adjusted as to produce motion, and that motion so regulated as to point out the hour of the day; that if the different parts had been differently shaped from what they are, of a different size from what they are, or placed after any other manner, or in any other order, than that in which they are placed, either no motion at all would have been carried on in the machine, or none which would have answered the use that is now served by it. To reckon up a few of the plainest of these parts, and of their offices, all tending to one result: We see a cylindrical box containing a coiled elastic spring, which, by its endeavor to relax itself, turns round the box. We next observe a flexible chain (artificially wrought for the sake of flexure) communicating the action of the spring from the box to the fusee. We then find a series of wheels, the teeth of which catch in, and apply to each other, conducting the motion from the fusee to the balance, and from the balance to the pointer; and at the same time, by the size and shape of those wheels, so regulating that motion, as to terminate in causing an index, by an equable and measured progression, to pass over a given space in a given time. We take notice that the wheels are made of brass in order to keep them from rust; the springs of steel, no other metal being so elastic; that over the face of the watch there is placed a glass, a material employed in no other part of the work; but in the room of which, if there had been any other than a transparent substance, the hour could not be seen without opening the case. This mechanism being observed (it requires indeed an examination of the instrument, and perhaps some previous knowledge of the subject, to perceive and understand it; but being once, as we have said, observed and understood), the inference, we think, is inevitable; that the watch must have

---

13. Leslie Stephen, *History of English Thought in the Eighteenth Century*, 2 vols., 2nd ed. (London: Smith, Elder, 1881), 1:408.

14. Frederick Ferré, Introduction to *Natural Theology: Selections*, by William Paley (Indianapolis: Bobbs-Merrill, 1963), xi–xxxii.

had a maker; that there must have existed, at some time, and at some place or other, an artificer or artificers, who formed it for the purpose which we find it actually to answer; who comprehended its construction, and designed its use.[15]

This conclusion, Paley continues, would not be weakened if I had never actually seen a watch being made nor knew how to make one. For we recognize the remains of ancient art as the products of intelligent design without having ever seen such things made, and we know the products of modern manufacture are the result of intelligence even though we may have no inkling how they are produced. Nor would our conclusion be invalidated if the watch sometimes went wrong. The purpose of the mechanism would be evident even if the machine did not function perfectly. Nor would the argument become uncertain if we were to discover some parts in the mechanism that did not seem to have any purpose, for this would not negate the purposeful design in the other parts. Nor would anyone in his right mind think that the existence of the watch was accounted for by the consideration that it was one out of many possible configurations of matter and that some possible configuration had to exist in the place where the watch was found. Nor would it help to say that there exists in things a principle of order, which yielded the watch. For one never knows a watch to be so formed, and the notion of such a principle of order that is not intelligent seems to have little meaning. Nor is it enough to say the watch was produced from another watch before it and that one from yet a prior watch, and so forth to infinity. For the design is still unaccounted for. Each machine in the infinite series evidences the same design, and it is irrelevant whether one has ten, a thousand, or an infinite number of such machines—a designer is still needed.

Now the point of the analogy of the watch is this: just as we infer a watchmaker as the designer of the watch, so ought we to infer an intelligent designer of the universe:

> For every indication of contrivance, every manifestation of design, which existed in the watch, exists in the works of nature, of being greater and more, and that in a degree which exceeds all computation. I mean, that the contrivances of nature surpass the contrivances of art, in the complexity, subtilty, and curiosity of the mechanism; and still more, if possible, do they go beyond them in number and variety: yet, in a multitude of cases, are not less evidently contrivances, not less evidently accommodated to their end, or suited to their office, than are the most perfect products of human ingenuity.[16]

Here Paley begins his cataloging of the contrivances of nature bespeaking divine design. He concludes that an intelligent designer of the universe exists, and he closes with a discussion of some of the attributes of this cosmic architect.

15. Paley, *Natural Theology*, 3–4.
16. Ibid., 13.

Moral Argument

The moral argument for the existence of God implies the existence of a Being that is the embodiment of the ultimate Good, which is the source of the objective moral values we experience in the world. The reasoning at the heart of the moral argument goes all the way back to Plato, who argued that things have goodness insofar as they stand in some relation to the Good, which subsists in itself. With the advent of Christian theism, the Good became identified with God himself.

THOMAS AQUINAS

Aquinas's Fourth Way is a type of moral argument. He observes that we find in the world a gradation of values: some things are more good, more true, more noble, and so forth, than other things. Such comparative terms describe the varying degrees to which things approach a superlative standard: the most good, most true, and so forth. There must therefore exist something that is the best and truest and noblest thing of all. Aquinas believed that whatever possesses a property more fully than anything else is the cause of that property in other things. Hence, there is some being that is the cause of the existence, goodness, and any other perfection of finite beings, and this being we call "God."

WILLIAM SORLEY

Perhaps the most sophisticated development of the moral argument prior to our day is that of William Sorley (1855–1935), professor of moral philosophy at Cambridge University until 1933, in his Gifford Lectures, *Moral Values and the Idea of God* (1918). Sorley believed that ethics provides the key to metaphysics, and he argues that God as the ground of the natural and moral orders best provides for a rational, unified view of reality. He begins by arguing that reality is characterized by an objective moral order, which is as real and independent of our recognition of it as the natural order of things is. He admits that in a sense one cannot prove that objective values exist, but insists that in this same sense one cannot prove that the external world exists either! Thus, the moral order and the natural order are on equal footing. On the same ground that we assume the reality of the world of objects, we assume the reality of the moral order of objective value. Now obviously Sorley does not mean we perceive value with our five senses in the way we do physical objects. We discern value in some non-empirical way, and just as we are rational to assume that some objective natural order lies behind our sense perceptions, so we are rational to assume that some objective moral order lies behind our perceptions of value. Our perceptions of both value and physical objects are simply givens of experience.

Our perception of a realm of objective value does not mean for Sorley that everyone has an innate and accurate knowledge of specific moral values. In his *The Ethics of Naturalism* (1885) he had refuted the historical, evolutionary approach to ethics, and now he turns to refute psychological, sociological explanations of value. The fundamental error of all these approaches is that they confuse the subjective origin of our moral judgments and the objective value to which the judgments refer. Just because the origin of our moral judgments can be historically or sociologically explained does not mean there are no objective, corresponding values in reality. In fact, Sorley argues that our moral judgments are not infallible and that we do not know the content of the moral ideal that we ever seek to approach.

Where, then, does objective moral value reside? Sorley answers: in persons. The only beings that are bearers of intrinsic moral value are persons; non-personal things have merely instrumental value in relation to persons. Only persons have intrinsic value, because meaningful moral behavior requires purpose and will.

The foregoing analysis of moral value provides the ground for Sorley's moral argument for God. We have seen that the natural order and the moral order are both part of reality. Therefore, the question is: what worldview can combine these two orders into the most coherent explanatory form? According to Sorley, there are three competing worldviews: theism, pluralism, and monism.

Turning first to theism, Sorley believes that the most serious objection to this worldview is the problem of evil. Basically, the problem here is that the natural order and the moral order seem to be working at cross-purposes with each other: the natural order often fails to realize the good that ought to be realized. Sorley, however, thinks this objection is answerable. The objection, he says, tends to confuse moral purpose with personal happiness; because personal happiness is often not realized, it is assumed that moral purpose has been frustrated. But Sorley points out that the realization of moral purpose cannot be equated with the realization of personal happiness. In other words, just because we are not happy about some situation does not imply that the situation ought not to be. In general, Sorley argues that suffering and evil are possible in a theistic worldview if finite minds are gradually recognizing moral ends that they are free to accept or reject.

Indeed, Sorley argues that the theistic account of the natural and moral orders is the superior worldview. For we have seen that moral values or ideals are an objective part of reality and that they reside in persons. The problem is that no finite person has ever fully realized all moral value. The moral ideal is nowhere fully actualized in the finite world, though it is presently valid, that is, binding and obligatory for the finite world. But how can something be objective and valid if it does not exist? Physical laws, by contrast, are fully realized in the world. So no further explanation of their validity is required. Therefore, if the moral ideal is to be valid for reality, it must be fully realized in an existent that is both personal and eternal, that is, God.

Sorley then proceeds to refute the other two alternatives, pluralism and monism. Against pluralism, which holds that the moral ideal resides in a plurality of finite beings, Sorley argues that the moral values are eternally valid and so cannot reside in temporally finite persons. Against monism, which holds that the universe is constituted by a single non-personal reality of which minds are mere modes, Sorley maintains that it leaves no room for purposeful endeavor or real freedom, because "is" and "ought to be" are identical and everything simply is as it is.

Hence, concludes Sorley, this reasoning, although not a rigid demonstration, shows that theism offers the most reasonable and unified explanation of reality. The moral order is the order of an infinite, eternal Mind who is the architect of nature and whose moral purpose man and the universe are slowly fulfilling.

Assessment

As a result of years of study and reflection, I have come to share Leibniz's conviction that "nearly all the means which have been employed to prove the existence of God are good and might be of service, if we perfect them."[17] My experience of debating these arguments orally and in print with atheist and agnostic philosophers has only served to confirm this conviction in my mind.[18] Whole books have been written on each of these arguments, and the reader wishing to go deeper is referred to the bibliography for those resources. In our limited space I shall formulate each argument, sketch a defense of its premises, and consider the most important objections brought against it.

Leibnizian Cosmological Argument

A simple statement of a Leibnizian cosmological argument might run as follows:[19]

1) Anything that exists has an explanation of its existence, either in the necessity of its own nature or in an external cause.
2) If the universe has an explanation of its existence, that explanation is God.
3) The universe exists.
4) Therefore, the universe has an explanation of its existence. (from 1, 3)
5) Therefore, the explanation of the existence of the universe is God. (from 2, 4)

Is this a good argument? The conclusion follows validly from the premises, so the only question is whether the three premises are more plausibly true than their denials.

17. Gottfried Wilhelm Leibniz, *New Essays on the Understanding*, trans. Alfred G. Langley (New York: Macmillan, 1896), 505.

18. See my debates with Antony Flew, *Does God Exist?* ed. Stan Wallace, with responses by K. Yandell, P. Moser, D. Geivett, M. Martin, D. Yandell, W. Rowe, K. Parsons, and William Wainwright (Aldershot: Ashgate, 2003); with Walter Sinnott-Armstrong, *God? A Debate between a Christian and an Atheist* (New York: Oxford University Press, 2003); and with Paul Kurtz, *God and Ethics: A Contemporary Debate*, ed. Nathan King and Robert Garcia, with responses by L. Antony, W. Sinnott-Armstrong, J. Hare, D. Hubin, S. Layman, M. Murphy, and R. Swinburne (Lanham, Md.: Rowman & Littlefield, 2008), as well as the debates listed at www.reasonablefaith.org.

19. I'm indebted to Stephen T. Davis, "The Cosmological Argument and the Epistemic Status of Belief in God," *Philosophia Christi* 1 (1999): 5–15, for the inspiration for this formulation of the argument.

The Principle of Sufficient Reason

Premise (1) is a modest version of the Principle of Sufficient Reason. It circumvents the typical objections to strong versions of that principle.[20] For (1) merely requires any existing *thing* to have an explanation of its existence. This premise is compatible with there being brute *facts* about the world.[21] What it precludes is that there could exist things which just exist inexplicably. According to (1) there are two kinds of being: necessary beings, which exist of their own nature and so have no external cause of their existence, and contingent beings, whose existence is accounted for by causal factors outside themselves. Numbers, sets, and other mathematical objects would be prime candidates for the first sort of thing, while familiar physical objects like people and planets and stars would be examples of the second kind of thing.

The principle enunciated in (1) seems quite plausible, at least more so than its denial. Richard Taylor gives the illustration of finding a translucent ball on the forest floor while walking in the woods.[22] One would find the claim quite bizarre that the ball simply exists inexplicably; and just increasing the size of the ball, even until it becomes co-extensive with the cosmos, would do nothing to eliminate the need for an explanation of its existence.

Crispin Wright and Bob Hale agree that explicability is the default position and that exceptions to the principle therefore require justification. Nonetheless they maintain that an exception is justified in the case of the universe. Why? Because the explanation of any physical state of affairs S must be found in a causally prior state of affairs in which S does not exist.[23]   For example, the explanation why a certain horse exists is that two other horses were bred with the result that they caused the new horse to be conceived and come into existence. So any explanation of why the universe exists must be found in a causally prior state of affairs in which the universe does not exist. But, Wright and Hale object, since a physically empty world couldn't cause anything, the demand for an explanation of the universe becomes absurd. So the principle enunciated in (1) doesn't apply in the case of the universe.

This objection, however, plainly begs the question in favor of atheism. For unless one assumes in advance that the universe is all there is, there's just no reason to

20. For such objections, see Jordan Howard Sobel, *Logic and Theism: Arguments For and Against Beliefs in God* (Cambridge: Cambridge University Press, 2004), 200–228. But even the strong version is not without its defenders; see Alexander R. Pruss, *The Principle of Sufficient Reason: A Reassessment* (Cambridge: Cambridge University Press, 2006).

21. What about the existence of the fact itself? A fact may be taken to be a true proposition. As abstract objects independent of sentences, propositions exist necessarily, if they exist at all. What is contingent about them is their truth value (whether they are true or false). So the proposition exists by a necessity of its own nature, while its truth value may or may not have an explanation.

22. Richard Taylor, *Metaphysics*, 4th ed., Foundations of Philosophy (Englewood Cliffs, N. J.: Prentice-Hall, 1991), 100–101.

23. Crispin Wright and Bob Hale, "Nominalism and the Contingency of Abstract Objects," *Journal of Philosophy* 89 (1992): 128.

think that the state of affairs causally prior to the existence of the universe which explains why the universe exists has to be a *physical* state of affairs. The explanation of why the physical universe exists could be some causally prior, non-physical state of affairs. If one assumes that that's impossible, then one is just begging the question in favor of atheism. The theist will regard Wright and Hale's maxim about the nature of explanation as not at all restrictive, since the explanation of why the physical universe exists can and should be provided in terms of a causally prior non-physical state of affairs involving God's existence and will.

The Explanation of the Universe

Premise (2) might seem at first blush to be a very bold assertion on the part of the theist. But, in fact, (2) is logically equivalent to the typical atheist response to Leibniz that on the atheistic worldview the universe simply exists as a brute contingent thing. Atheists typically assert that, since there is no God, it is false that everything has an explanation of its existence, for the universe, in this case, just exists inexplicably. So in affirming that

A. If atheism is true, then the universe has no explanation of its existence,

atheists are also affirming the logically equivalent claim that

A'. If the universe has an explanation of its existence, then atheism is not true,

that is to say, that God exists. Hence, most atheists are implicitly committed to (2).

Moreover, (2) seems quite plausible in its own right, for the universe, by definition, includes all of physical reality. So the cause of the universe must (at least causally prior to the universe's existence) transcend space and time and therefore cannot be physical or material. But there are only two kinds of things that could fall under such a description: either an abstract object (like a number) or else a mind (a soul, a self). But abstract objects don't stand in causal relations. This is part of what it means to be abstract. The number 7, for example, doesn't cause anything. So if the universe has an explanation of its existence, that explanation must be a transcendent, unembodied Mind which created the universe—which is what most people have traditionally meant by the word "God."

Finally, premise (3) states the obvious, that there is a universe. Since the universe exists, it follows that God exists.

The Contingency of the Universe

One way for the atheist or agnostic to try to escape the force of this argument is to say that while the universe has an explanation of its existence, as premise (1) requires, that explanation lies not in an external ground but in the necessity of its own nature. The universe exists necessarily. This is, however, an extremely bold suggestion which atheists have not been eager to embrace. We have, one can safely say, a strong sense of the universe's contingency. A possible world in which no concrete objects exist certainly seems conceivable. We generally trust our modal intuitions on other familiar matters (for example, our sense that the planet earth exists contingently, not necessarily, even though we have no experience of its non-existence). If we are to do otherwise with respect to the universe's contingency, then the non-theist needs to provide some reason for his skepticism other than his desire to avoid theism.

Still, it would be desirable to have some stronger argument for the universe's contingency than our modal intuitions alone. Could the Thomist cosmological argument help us here? The difficulty with appeal to the Thomist argument is that it is very difficult to show that things are, in fact, contingent in the special sense required by the argument. Certainly things are naturally contingent in that their continued existence is dependent upon a myriad of factors including particle masses and fundamental forces, temperature, pressure, entropy level, and so forth, but this natural contingency does not suffice to establish things' metaphysical contingency in the sense that being must be continually added to their essences lest they be spontaneously annihilated.

Nevertheless, I think we do have good grounds for thinking that the universe does not exist by a necessity of its own nature. It's easy to conceive of the non-existence of any and all of the objects we observe in the world; indeed, prior to a certain point in the past, when the universe was very dense and very hot, none of them did exist. What about the fundamental particles or the building blocks of matter, like quarks? Well, it's easy to conceive of a world in which all of the fundamental particles composing some macroscopic object were replaced by other quarks. A universe consisting of a totally different collection of quarks, say, seems quite possible. But if that's the case, then the universe does not exist by a necessity of its own nature. For a universe composed of a wholly different collection of quarks is not the same universe as ours. To illustrate, ask yourself whether the shoes you're wearing could have been made of steel? Certainly we can imagine that you could have had a pair of steel shoes in the same shape as the shoes you're wearing; but that's not the question. The question is whether the very shoes you're wearing could have been made of steel. I think the answer is obviously not. They would be a different pair of shoes, not the same pair of shoes you have on. The same is true of the universe. If it were composed of a different collection of quarks, then it would be a different universe, not the same universe. Since quarks are the fundamental building blocks of material objects, one cannot say, as we might say of macroscopic objects, that while they are contingent, the stuff of which they are made is necessary, for there is no further stuff beyond quarks. No atheist will, I think, dare to suggest that some quarks, though looking just like ordinary quarks, have the special occult property of being necessary, so that any universe that exists would have to include them. It's all or nothing here. But no one thinks that every quark exists by a necessity of its own nature. It follows that the universe does not exist by a necessity of its own nature either.

The Principle of Sufficient Reason Once More

There's one last way that the atheist might try to escape the argument. He might say that while there are no beings that exist necessarily, nevertheless it is necessary that something or other exist. Bede Rundle agrees with the theist that it is impossible that nothing exist.[24] But he thinks that the proper conclusion to be drawn from this fact is not that a necessary being exists, but that, necessarily, some contingent being or other exists. (This is akin to saying that while, necessarily, every object has a shape, nonetheless there is no particular shape which everything necessarily has. In the same way, it's necessary that something or other exists but there isn't anything that exists necessarily.) In short, premise (1) is, on Rundle's view, false after all. The universe exists contingently and inexplicably. Some universe must exist, but there is no explanation why this universe exists.

Alexander Pruss has pointed out that Rundle's view has an extremely implausible consequence.[25] It's plausible that no conjunction of claims about the non-existence of various things entails, say, that a unicorn exists. After all, how could the fact that certain things do *not* exist entail that some other contingent thing does exist? But on Rundle's view the conjunction "There are no mountains, there are no people, there are no planets, there are no rocks, . . . [including everything that is not a unicorn]" entails that there is a unicorn! For if it is necessary that contingent beings exist, and none of the other contingent beings listed exist, then the only thing left is a unicorn. Hence, a conjunction about the non-existence of certain things entails that a unicorn exists, which seems absurd.

Moreover, on Rundle's view there is nothing which would account for *why* there exist contingent beings in every possible world.[26] Since there is no metaphysically necessary being, there is nothing that could cause contingent beings to exist in every possible world and no explanation why every world includes contingent beings. There is no strict logical inconsistency in the concept of a world devoid of contingent beings. What accounts for the fact that in every possible world contingent beings exist? Given the infinity of broadly logically possible worlds, the odds that in all of them contingent beings just happen inexplicably to exist is infinitesimal. Hence, the probability of Rundle's hypothesis is effectively zero.

---

24. Bede Rundle, *Why Is There Something Rather Than Nothing?* (Oxford: Oxford University Press, 2004).

25. Alexander Pruss, critical notice of Bede Rundle, *Why Is There Something Rather Than Nothing? Philosophia Christi* 7 (2005): 210.

26. For those unfamiliar with talk of possible worlds, see the explanation provided in the next chapter in our discussion of the ontological argument.

Conclusion

Thus, the premises of this Leibnizian argument all seem to me to be more plausible than their negations. It therefore follows logically that the explanation for why the universe exists is to be found in God. It seems to me, therefore, that this is a good argument for God's existence.

Moreover, the Leibnizian argument is reinforced by the support which the *kalām* cosmological argument adds to premises (1) and (2). An essential property of a being that exists by a necessity of its own nature is that it be eternal, that is to say, without beginning or end. If the universe is not eternal, then it could fail to exist and so does not exist by a necessity of its own nature. But it is precisely the aim of the *kalām* cosmological argument to show that the universe is not eternal but had a beginning. It would follow that the universe must therefore be contingent in its existence. Not only so; the *kalām* argument shows the universe to be contingent in a very special way: it came into existence out of nothing. The atheist who would answer Leibniz by holding that the existence of the universe is a brute fact, an exception to the Principle of Sufficient Reason, is thus thrust into the very awkward position of maintaining, not merely that the universe exists eternally without explanation, but rather that for no reason at all it magically popped into being out of nothing, a position which might make theism look like a welcome alternative. Thus, the *kalām* argument not only constitutes an independent argument for a transcendent Creator but also serves as a valuable supplement to the Leibnizian argument.

Kalām Cosmological Argument

The *kalām* cosmological argument may be formulated as follows:

1) Whatever begins to exist has a cause.
2) The universe began to exist.
3) Therefore, the universe has a cause.

Conceptual analysis of what it means to be a cause of the universe then aims to establish some of the theologically significant properties of this being.

Whatever Begins to Exist Has a Cause

Premise (1) seems obviously true—at the least, more so than its negation. First and foremost, it's rooted in the metaphysical intuition that something cannot come into being from nothing. To suggest that things could just pop into being uncaused out of nothing is to quit doing serious metaphysics and to resort to magic. Second, if things really could come into being uncaused out of nothing, then it becomes inexplicable why just anything and everything do not come into existence uncaused from nothing. Finally, the first premise is constantly confirmed in our experience. Atheists who are scientific naturalists thus have the strongest of motivations to accept it.

When I first wrote *The* Kalām *Cosmological Argument*, I figured that few atheists would deny the first premise and assert that the universe sprang into existence uncaused out of nothing, since I believed they would thereby expose themselves as persons interested only in an academic refutation of the argument and not in really discovering the truth about the universe. To my surprise, however, many atheists have taken this route. For example, Quentin Smith, commenting that philosophers are too often adversely affected by Heidegger's dread of "the nothing," concludes that "the most reasonable belief is that we came from nothing, by nothing, and for nothing"[27]—a nice ending to a sort of Gettysburg address of atheism, perhaps.

Similarly, the late J. L. Mackie, in refuting the *kalām* cosmological argument, turns his main guns on this first step: "There is *a priori* no good reason why a sheer origination of things, not determined by anything, should be unacceptable, whereas the existence of a god [*sic*] with the power to create something out of nothing is acceptable."[28] Indeed, he believes *creatio ex nihilo* raises problems: (i) If God began to exist at a point in time, then this is as great a puzzle as the beginning of the universe. (ii) Or if God existed for infinite time, then the same arguments would apply to his existence as would apply to the infinite duration of the universe. (iii) If it be said that God is timeless, then this, says Mackie, is a complete mystery.

Now notice that Mackie never *refutes* the principle that whatever begins to exist has a cause. Rather, he simply demands what good reason there is *a priori* to accept it. He writes, "As Hume pointed out, we can certainly conceive an uncaused beginning-to-be of an object; if what we can thus conceive is nevertheless in some way impossible, this still requires to be shown."[29] But, as many philosophers have pointed out, Hume's argument in no way makes it plausible to think that something could really come into being without a cause. Just because I can imagine an object, say a horse, coming into existence from nothing, that in no way proves that a horse really could come into existence that way. The defender of the *kalām* argument is claiming that it is *really* impossible for something to come uncaused

27. *Theism, Atheism, and Big Bang Cosmology* (Oxford: Clarendon, 1993), 135. Smith's most recent criticism of the *kalām* cosmological argument is also a denial of the first premise, despite Smith's avowal that he now accepts the conclusion that the universe has a cause for its existence. Quentin Smith, "Kalām Cosmological Arguments for Atheism," in *The Cambridge Companion to Atheism*, ed. Michael Martin, Cambridge Companions to Philosophy (Cambridge: Cambridge University Press, 2007), 182–98. Smith's current position is that the initial singular point of the universe is not real and that therefore the sequence of instantaneous states of the universe is a beginningless series converging toward zero as a limit. Each state is caused by its predecessor and there is no first state. Any non-zero interval or state, such as the first second of the universe's existence, "is not caused by any or all of its instantaneous states and is not caused by any external cause" (ibid., 189). Smith takes "the beginning of the universe" to refer to the Planck era, that state which lasts until 10^{-43} second after the singularity. As a state of non-zero duration, the beginning of the universe therefore has no cause of any sort. The universe therefore comes into being uncaused out of nothing.

28. J. L. Mackie, *The Miracle of Theism* (Oxford: Clarendon, 1982), 94.

29. Ibid., 89.

from nothing. Does Mackie sincerely believe that things can pop into existence uncaused, out of nothing? Does anyone in his right mind really believe that, say, a raging tiger could suddenly come into existence uncaused, out of nothing, in this room right now? The same applies to the universe: if prior to the existence of the universe, there was absolutely nothing—no God, no space, no time—how could the universe possibly have come to exist?[30]

In fact, Mackie's appeal to Hume at this point is counterproductive. For Hume himself clearly believed in the causal principle. In 1754 he wrote to John Stewart, "But allow me to tell you that I never asserted so absurd a Proposition as *that anything might arise without a cause*: I only maintain'd, that our Certainty of the Falsehood of that Proposition proceeded neither from Intuition nor Demonstration, but from another source."[31] Even Mackie confesses, "Still this [causal] principle has some plausibility, in that it is constantly confirmed in our experience (and also used, reasonably, in interpreting our experience)."[32] So why not accept the truth of the causal principle as plausible and reasonable—at the very least more so than its denial?

Because, Mackie thinks, in this particular case the theism implied by affirming the principle is even more unintelligible than the denial of the principle. It makes more sense to believe that the universe came into being uncaused out of nothing than to believe that God created the universe out of nothing.

But is this really the case? Consider the three problems Mackie raises with *creatio ex nihilo*. Certainly, the proponent of the *kalām* argument would not hold (i) that God began to exist or (ii) that God has existed for an infinite number of, say, hours, or any other unit of time. But what is wrong with (iii), that God is, without creation, timeless? I would argue that God exists timelessly without creation and in time subsequent to creation.[33] This may be "mysterious" in the sense of "wonderful" or "awe-inspiring," but it is not, so far as I can see, unintelligible; and Mackie gives us no reason to think that it is. Moreover, there is also an alternative which Mackie failed to consider: (iv) prior to creation God existed in an undifferentiated time in which hours, seconds, days, and so forth simply do not exist. Because this time is undifferentiated, it is not incompatible with the *kalām* argument that an infinite regress of events cannot exist. It seems to me, therefore, that Mackie is entirely unjustified in rejecting the first step of the argument as not being intuitively obvious, plausible, and reasonable.

Other critics have said that premise (1) is true only for things *in* the universe, but it is not true *of* the universe itself. But why think that the universe is an excep-

---

30. Elsewhere Mackie reveals his true sentiments: "I myself find it hard to accept the notion of self-creation *from nothing*, even *given* unrestricted chance. And how *can* this be given, if there really is nothing?" (J. L. Mackie, *Times Literary Supplement*, 5 February 1982, 126).

31. David Hume, *The Letters of David Hume*, 2 vols., ed. J. Y. T. Greig (Oxford: Clarendon, 1932), 1:187.

32. Mackie, *Theism*, 89.

33. See my *Time and Eternity* (Wheaton, Ill.: Crossway, 2001).

tion to the rule? As Arthur Schopenhauer once remarked, the causal principle is not something you can dismiss like a cab once you've arrived at your desired destination. Moreover, the objection misconstrues the nature of the causal principle. Premise (1) does not state a merely physical law like the law of gravity or the laws of thermodynamics, which are valid for things within the universe. Premise (1) is not a physical principle. Rather it is a metaphysical principle: being cannot come from non-being; something cannot come into existence uncaused from nothing. The principle therefore applies to all of reality, and it is thus metaphysically absurd that the universe should pop into being uncaused out of nothing.

Daniel Dennett, misstating the first premise as "Everything that exists must have a cause," accordingly asks, "What caused God?"[34] This retort merely caricatures the argument. In fact, apart from certain Enlightenment rationalists, who by "cause" meant merely "sufficient reason," no orthodox theist of any prominence has ever asserted that everything has a cause or that God is self-caused, a notion rightly rejected by Aquinas as metaphysically impossible. Things that *begin to exist* must have causes. In fact, Dennett himself recognizes that a being "outside of time . . . is nothing with an *initiation* or *origin* in need of explanation. What does need its origin explained is the concrete Universe itself."[35] Dennett rightly sees that a being which exists eternally, since it never comes into being, has no need of a cause, as do things which have an origin. So Dennett actually affirms the first premise, which will lead him, as we'll see, to the remarkable position that the universe must have caused itself to come into being.

Sometimes it is said that quantum physics furnishes an exception to premise (1), since on the sub-atomic level events are said to be uncaused. In the same way, certain theories of cosmic origins are interpreted as showing that the whole universe could have sprung into being out of the sub-atomic vacuum or even out of nothingness. Thus the universe is said to be the proverbial "free lunch."

This objection, however, is based on misunderstandings. In the first place, not all scientists agree that sub-atomic events are uncaused. A great many physicists today are quite dissatisfied with this view (the so-called Copenhagen Interpretation) of quantum physics and are exploring deterministic theories like that of David Bohm. Thus, quantum physics is not a proven exception to premise (1).[36] Second, even on the traditional, indeterministic interpretation, particles do not come into being out of nothing. They arise as spontaneous fluctuations of the energy contained in the sub-atomic vacuum, which constitutes an indeterministic

34. Daniel Dennett, *Breaking the Spell: Religion as a Natural Phenomenon* (NewYork: Viking, 2006), 242.

35. Ibid., 244.

36. There are at least ten different interpretations of quantum mechanics, many of which are fully deterministic, and no one knows which, if any of these, is correct. Even so determined a naturalist as the physicist Victor Stenger admits, "Other viable interpretations of quantum mechanics remain with no consensus on which, if any, is the correct one"; hence, we have to remain "open to the possibility that causes may someday be found for such phenomena." Victor Stenger, *Has Silence Found God?* (Amherst, N.Y.: Prometheus, 2003), 188–89, 173.

cause of their origination. Third, the same point can be made about theories of the origin of the universe out of a primordial vacuum. Popular magazine articles touting such theories as getting "something from nothing" simply do not understand that the vacuum is not nothing but is a sea of fluctuating energy endowed with a rich structure and subject to physical laws. Such models do not therefore involve a true origination *ex nihilo*.[37]

Neither do theories such as Alexander Vilenkin's quantum creation model. Vilenkin invites us to envision a small, closed, spherical universe filled with a so-called false vacuum and containing some ordinary matter. If the radius of such a universe is small, classical physics predicts that it will collapse to a point; but quantum physics permits it to "tunnel" into a state of inflationary expansion. If we allow the radius to shrink all the way to zero, there still remains some positive probability of the universe's tunneling to inflation. Now Vilenkin equates the initial state of the universe explanatorily prior to tunneling with nothingness. But this equivalence is patently mistaken. As Vilenkin's own diagram in his recent book illustrates,[38] the quantum tunneling is at every point a function from something to something (Fig. 3.1).

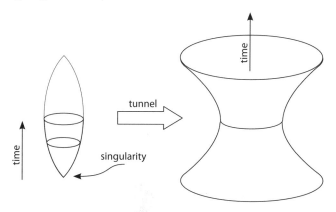

Fig. 3.1: Vilenkin's model of quantum creation. Note that the tunneling is at every point from something to something; the origin of the initial point remains unexplained.

37. As Kanitscheider explains, "The violent microstructure of the vacuum has been used in attempts to explain the origin of the universe as a long-lived vacuum fluctuation. But some authors have connected with this legitimate speculations [*sic*] far-reaching metaphysical claims, or at most they couched their mathematics in a highly misleading language, when they maintained 'the creation of the universe out of nothing.'... From the philosophical point of view it is essential to note that the foregoing is far from being a spontaneous generation of everything from naught, but the origin of that embryonic bubble is really a causal process leading from a primordial substratum with a rich physical structure to a materialized substratum of the vacuum. Admittedly this process is not deterministic, it includes that weak kind of causal dependence peculiar to every quantum mechanical process." Bernulf Kanitscheider, "Does Physical Cosmology Transcend the Limits of Naturalistic Reasoning?" in *Studies on Mario Bunge's "Treatise,"* ed. Weingartner and G. J. W. Doen (Amsterdam: Rodopi, 1990), 346–74.

38. Alex Vilenkin, *Many Worlds in One: The Search for Other Universes* (New York: Hill and Wang, 2006), 180.

For quantum tunneling to be truly from nothing, the function would have to have only one term, the posterior term. Another way of seeing the point is to reflect on the fact that to have no radius (as is the case with nothingness) is not to have a radius, whose measure is zero. Thus, there is no basis for the claim that quantum physics proves that things can begin to exist without a cause, much less that the universe could have sprung into being uncaused from literally nothing.

That Vilenkin has not truly grasped how radical is being's coming from non-being is evident from his incredulity at the claim of the Hartle-Hawking model that an infinite universe should similarly arise from nothing. He exclaims, "The most probable thing to pop out of nothing is then an infinite, empty, flat space. I find this very hard to believe!"[39] Vilenkin finds it easier to believe that an itsy-bitsy universe should pop into being out of nothing. He thereby evinces a lack of understanding of the metaphysical chasm that separates being from non-being. If something can come from nothing, then the size and shape of the object is just irrelevant.

THE UNIVERSE BEGAN TO EXIST

If we agree that whatever begins to exist has a cause, what evidence is there to support the crucial second step in the argument, that the universe began to exist? We'll examine both deductive, philosophical arguments and inductive, scientific arguments in support of (2).

Philosophical Arguments:
1) The Impossibility of an Actually Infinite Number of Things
This argument can also be formulated in three steps:

1) An actually infinite number of things cannot exist.
2) A beginningless series of events in time entails an actually infinite number of things.
3) Therefore, a beginningless series of events in time cannot exist.

Let's examine each premise in turn.

(1) *An actually infinite number of things cannot exist.* In order to understand this first premise, we need to understand what an actual infinite is. There is a difference between a potential infinite and an actual infinite. An actual infinite is a collection of definite and discrete members whose number is greater than any natural number $0, 1, 2, 3 \ldots$ This sort of infinity is used in set theory to designate sets that have an infinite number of members, such as $\{0, 1, 2, 3 \ldots\}$. The symbol for this kind of infinity is the Hebrew letter aleph: $\aleph$. The number of members in the set of natural numbers is $\aleph_0$. By contrast, a potential infinite is a collection that is increasing toward infinity as a limit but never gets there. The symbol for this kind of infinity is the lemniscate: ∞. Such a collection is really indefinite, not infinite.

---

39. Ibid., 191.

For example, any finite distance can be subdivided into potentially infinitely many parts. You can just keep on dividing parts in half forever, but you will never arrive at an actual "infinitieth" division or come up with an actually infinite number of parts. Now premise (1) asserts, not that a potentially infinite number of things cannot exist, but that an actually infinite number of things cannot exist.

It is frequently alleged that this sort of argument has been cut off at the knees by the work of the nineteenth-century mathematician Georg Cantor on the actual infinite and by subsequent developments in set theory, which have legitimized the notion of the actual infinite. But this allegation is far too hasty. It not only begs the question against denials of the mathematical legitimacy of the actual infinite on the part of certain mathematicians (so-called Intuitionists), but, more seriously, it begs the question against anti-realist views of mathematical objects. These are distinct questions, run together by such recent critics of the argument as Howard Sobel and Graham Oppy.[40] Most anti-realists would not go to the Intuitionistic extreme of denying mathematical legitimacy to the actual infinite—hence, the defiant declaration of the great German mathematician David Hilbert: "No one shall be able to drive us from the paradise that Cantor has created for us."[41] They would simply insist that acceptance of the mathematical legitimacy of certain notions does not imply a commitment to the metaphysical reality of various objects. In Hilbert's view, "The infinite is nowhere to be found in reality. It neither exists in nature nor provides a legitimate basis for rational thought. . . . The role that remains for the infinite to play is solely that of an idea."[42] Cantor's system and set theory may be taken to be simply a universe of discourse, a mathematical system based on certain adopted axioms and conventions. On anti-realist views of mathematical objects such as Balaguer's Fictionalism or Yablo's Figuralism or Chihara's Constructibilism, mathematical discourse is not in any way abridged, but there are, notwithstanding, no mathematical objects, let alone an infinite number of them.[43] One may consistently hold that while the actual infinite is a fruitful and consistent concept within the postulated universe of discourse, it cannot be transposed into the real world, for this would involve counter-intuitive absurdities.

40. Sobel, *Logic and Theism*, 181–89, 198–99; Graham Oppy, *Philosophical Perspectives on Infinity* (Cambridge: Cambridge University Press, 2006), 291–93.

41. David Hilbert, "On the Infinite," in *Philosophy of Mathematics*, ed. with an introduction by Paul Benacerraf and Hillary Putnam (Englewood Cliffs, N.J.: Prentice-Hall, 1964), 141.

42. Ibid., 151.

43. Mark Balaguer, *Platonism and Anti-Platonism in Mathematics* (New York: Oxford University Press, 1998), part 2; idem, "A Theory of Mathematical Correctness and Mathematical Truth," *Pacific Philosophical Quarterly* 82 (2001): 87–114; *Stanford Encyclopedia of Philosophy*, s.v. "Platonism in Metaphysics," by Mark Balaguer (Summer 2004), ed. Edward N. Zalta, http://plato.stanford.edu/archives/ sum2004/entries/platonism/; Stephen Yablo, "A Paradox of Existence," in *Empty Names, Fiction, and the Puzzles of Non-Existence*, ed. Anthony Everett and Thomas Hofweber (Stanford: Center for Study of Language and Information, 2000), 275–312; idem, "Go Figure: A Path through Fictionalism," in *Figurative Language*, ed. Peter A. French and Howard K. Wettstein, Midwest Studies in Philosophy 25 (Oxford: Blackwell, 2001), 72–102; Charles S. Chihara, *Constructibility and Mathematical Existence* (Oxford: Clarendon, 1990); idem, *A Structural Account of Mathematics* (Oxford: Clarendon, 2004).

Ludwig Wittgenstein enunciated perhaps the best strategy for showing the metaphysical impossibility of the actual infinite when he quipped, "I wouldn't dream of trying to drive anyone from this paradise. I would do something quite different: I would try to show you that it is not a paradise—so that you'll leave of your own accord. I would say, 'You're welcome to this; just look about you.'"[44] If an actually infinite number of things could exist, this would spawn all sorts of absurdities. We can construct thought experiments illustrating what it would be like if an actually infinite number of things were to exist, in order to evoke a sense of how absurd such a world would be. Let me share one of my favorites, Hilbert's Hotel, the brainchild of David Hilbert.[45]

As a warm-up, let's first imagine a hotel with a finite number of rooms. Suppose, furthermore, that all the rooms are occupied. When a new guest arrives asking for a room, the proprietor apologizes, "Sorry, all the rooms are full," and that's the end of the story. But now let us imagine a hotel with an infinite number of rooms and suppose once more that *all the rooms are occupied*. There is not a single vacant room throughout the entire infinite hotel. Now suppose a new guest shows up, asking for a room. "But of course!" says the proprietor, and he immediately shifts the person in room #1 into room #2, the person in room #2 into room #3, the person in room #3 into room #4, and so on, out to infinity. As a result of these room changes, room #1 now becomes vacant and the new guest gratefully checks in. But remember, before he arrived, all the rooms were already occupied!

But the situation becomes even stranger. For suppose an infinity of new guests shows up at the desk, each asking for a room. "Of course, of course!" says the proprietor, and he proceeds to shift the person in room #1 into room #2, the person in room #2 into room #4, the person in room #3 into room #6, and so on out to infinity, always putting each former occupant into the room with a number twice his own. Because any natural number multiplied by two always equals an even number, all the guests wind up in even-numbered rooms. As a result, all the odd-numbered rooms become vacant, and the infinity of new guests is easily accommodated. And yet, before they came, all the rooms were already occupied! In fact, the proprietor could repeat this process *infinitely many times* and so always accommodate new guests, despite the fact that the hotel is completely full! As one student remarked to me, if Hilbert's Hotel could exist, it would have to have a sign posted outside: No Vacancy—Guests Welcome.

But Hilbert's Hotel is even stranger than the great German mathematician made it out to be. Just ask yourself the question: what happens if some of the guests start to check out? Suppose the guests in rooms #1, #3, #5 . . . check out. In this case an infinite number of people has left the hotel, and half the rooms are now empty.

44. Ludwig Wittgenstein, *Lectures on the Foundations of Mathematics*, ed. Cora Diamond (Sussex, England: Harvester, 1976), 103.

45. The story of Hilbert's Hotel is related in George Gamow, *One, Two, Three, Infinity* (London: Macmillan, 1946), 17.

Now suppose the proprietor doesn't like having a half-empty hotel (it looks bad for business). No matter! By shifting occupants as before, but in reverse order, he transforms his half-vacant hotel into one that is jammed to the gills! You might think that by such maneuvers the proprietor could always keep this strange hotel fully occupied. But you would be wrong. For suppose that the persons in rooms #4, #5, #6 . . . checked out. At a single stroke the hotel would be virtually emptied, the guest register reduced to but three names, and the infinite converted to finitude. And yet it would remain true that the *same number* of guests checked out this time as when the guests in rooms #1, #3, #5 . . . checked out! In both cases we subtracted the *identical number* of guests from the *identical number* of guests and yet did not arrive at an identical result. In fact one can subtract equal quantities from equal quantities and get any quantity between zero and infinity as the remainder. Can anyone believe that such a hotel could exist in reality?

Hilbert's Hotel is absurd. Since nothing hangs on the illustration's involving a hotel, the argument, if successful, would show in general that it is impossible for an actually infinite number of things to exist. Students sometimes react to such illustrations as Hilbert's Hotel by saying that we don't understand the nature of infinity and, hence, these absurdities result. But this attitude is simply mistaken. Infinite set theory is a highly developed and well-understood branch of mathematics, and these absurdities can be seen to result precisely because we *do* understand the notion of a collection with an actually infinite number of members. Hilbert's illustration merely serves to bring out in a practical and vivid way what the mathematics necessarily implies; for if an actually infinite number of things were possible, then such a hotel must be possible. Hence, it logically follows that if such a hotel is impossible, then so is the real existence of an actual infinite.[46]

What can the argument's critic say at this point? Mackie, Sobel, and Oppy try, in Oppy's words, to "outsmart" the proponent of the argument by embracing the conclusion of his *reductio ad absurdum* argument: Hilbert's Hotel is possible after all.[47] The problem with this strategy is that it could be used to legitimize any conclusion, no matter how absurd, so long as one has the chutzpah to embrace it. What we want is some sort of reason to think that such a hotel is really possible. Here Oppy has no more to say than "these allegedly absurd situations are just what one ought to expect if there were . . . physical infinities." This response only reiterates, in effect, that if an actual infinite were to exist, then the relevant situations would result, which is not in dispute. The situations would, after all, not be effective illustrations if they would not result! Rather the question is whether these situations really are absurd. It is indisputable that if an actually infinite number of things

46. Students frequently ask if God, therefore, cannot be infinite. The question is based on a misunderstanding. When we speak of the infinity of God, we are not using the word in a mathematical sense to refer to an aggregate of an infinite number of finite parts. God's infinity is, if you will, qualitative, not quantitative. It means that God is metaphysically necessary, morally perfect, omnipotent, omniscient, eternal, etc.

47. Graham Oppy, *Philosophical Perspectives on Infinity*, 48; cf. Mackie, *Theism*, 93; Sobel, *Logic and Theism*, 186–87.

were to exist, then we should find ourselves landed in an Alice-in-Wonderland world populated with oddities like Hilbert's Hotel. Merely reiterating that "If there were physical infinities, these situations are just what we ought to expect" does nothing to allay one's suspicions that such a world is metaphysically absurd. Moreover, Oppy says nothing about what would happen in cases of inverse operations like subtraction with infinite quantities, as when an infinite number of guests check out of the hotel. In trans-finite arithmetic, inverse operations of subtraction and division are prohibited because they lead to contradictions; but in reality, one cannot stop people from checking out of the hotel if they so desire!

Again, it's worth reiterating that nothing in the argument need be construed as an attempt to undermine the theoretical system bequeathed by Cantor to modern mathematics. Indeed, some of the most eager enthusiasts of the system of transfinite mathematics are only too ready to agree that these theories have no relation to the real world. The case against the real existence of the actual infinite says nothing about the use of the idea of the infinite in conceptual mathematical systems.

2) *A beginningless series of events in time entails an actually infinite number of things.* This second premise is pretty obvious. If the universe never began to exist, then prior to the present event there have existed an actually infinite number of previous events. Thus, a beginningless series of events in time entails an actually infinite number of things, namely, events.

3) *Therefore, a beginningless series of events in time cannot exist.* If the above two premises are true, then the conclusion follows logically. The series of past events must be finite and have a beginning. Since the universe is not distinct from the series of events, the universe therefore began to exist.

Philosophical Arguments:
(2) The Impossibility of Forming an Actually Infinite Collection of Things by Adding One Member after Another

It's important to note that this second argument is distinct from the foregoing argument, for it does not deny that an actually infinite number of things can exist. It denies that a collection containing an actually infinite number of things can be *formed* by adding one member after another. So even if the first philosophical argument were deemed to be unsound, the critic of the *kalām* cosmological argument must still contend with this independent argument for the second premise. This argument, too, can be formulated in three steps:

1) The series of events in time is a collection formed by adding one member after another.

2) A collection formed by adding one member after another cannot be actually infinite.

3) Therefore, the series of events in time cannot be actually infinite.

Let's take a look at each premise.

1) *The series of events in time is a collection formed by adding one member after another.* This may seem rather obvious. The past did not spring into being whole and entire but was formed sequentially, one event occurring after another. Notice, too, that the direction of this formation is "forward," in the sense that the collection grows with time. Although we sometimes speak of an "infinite regress" of events, in reality an infinite past would be an "infinite progress" of events with no beginning and its end in the present.

As obvious as this first premise may seem at first blush, it is, in fact, a matter of great controversy. It presupposes a certain view of time which is variously called the tensed or dynamic or, following the convenient nomenclature of J. M. E. McTaggart, who first distinguished these views of time, the A-Theory of time. According to the A-Theory, things/events in time are not all equally real: the future does not yet exist and the past no longer exists; only things which are present are real. Temporal becoming is an objective feature of reality: things come into being and go out of being. By contrast, on what McTaggart called the B-Theory of time or the tenseless or static theory of time all events in time are equally real, and temporal becoming is an illusion of human consciousness. *Pastness, presentness,* and *futurity* are at most relative notions: for example, relative to the persons living in the year 2050 the people and events of 2000 are past, but relative to the persons living in 1950 the people and events of 2000 are future. Things and events in time are objectively ordered by the relations *earlier than, simultaneous with,* and *later than,* which are tenseless relations that are unchanging and hold regardless of whether the related events are past, present, or future relative to some observer. B-Theorists typically unify time with space into a four-dimensional, geometrical entity called spacetime, all of whose points are equally real and none of which is objectively present. On a B-Theory of time, premise (1) is false, for the past, like the future, exists tenselessly and there is no question of the series of events' being formed sequentially.

The question, then, is which of these two competing theories of time is true? Unfortunately, an adjudication of this issue here would take us too far afield. Everyone agrees that the commonsense view is that the difference between past, present, and future is real and objective, and as a result of over a decade of intensive research on this question my studied opinion is that there is no reason to abandon the commonsense view of this matter.[48] Therefore, I am convinced that the A-Theory of time is correct and, accordingly, that premise (1) is true. Given that the vast majority of people share this conviction, I think that an argument based upon this premise will provoke little objection on this score.

2) *A collection formed by adding one member after another cannot be actually infinite.* This is the crucial step. It's important to realize that this impossibility has nothing to do with the amount of time available: no matter how much time one

---

48. See my *Time and Eternity* for a consideration of the arguments for and against these theories of time and my defense of the A-Theory.

has available, an actual infinite cannot be formed. This may seem obvious in the case of someone's trying to count to infinity: no matter how many numbers he counts, he can always add one more before arriving at infinity. Now someone might say that while an infinite collection cannot be formed by beginning at a point and adding members, nevertheless, an infinite collection could be formed by never beginning but ending at a point, that is to say, ending at a point after having added one member after another from eternity. But this method seems even more unbelievable than the first method. If one cannot count to infinity, how can one count down from infinity?

Sometimes this problem is described as the impossibility of traversing the infinite. In order for us to have "arrived" at today, temporal existence has, so to speak, traversed an infinite number of prior events. Richard Gale protests, "This argument depends on an anthropomorphic sense of 'going through' a set. The universe does not go through a set of events in the sense of planning which to go through first, in order to get through the second, and so on."[49] Of course not; but on an A-Theory of time the universe does endure through successive intervals of time. It arrives at its present event-state only by enduring through a series of prior event-states. So before the present event could occur, the event immediately prior to it would have to occur; and before that event could occur, the event immediately prior to it would have to occur; and so on *ad infinitum*. So one gets driven back and back into the infinite past, making it impossible for any event to occur. Thus, if the series of past events were beginningless, the present event could not have occurred, which is absurd.

Sometimes critics indict this argument as a slight-of-hand trick like Zeno's paradoxes of motion. Zeno argued that before Achilles could cross the stadium, he would have to cross halfway; but before he could cross halfway, he would have to cross a quarter of the way; but before he could cross a quarter of the way, he would have to cross an eighth of the way, and so on to infinity. It is evident that Achilles could not arrive at any point! Therefore, Zeno concluded, motion is impossible. Now even though Zeno's argument is very difficult to refute, nobody really believes that motion is impossible. Even if Achilles must pass through an infinite number of halfway points in order to cross the stadium, somehow he manages to do so. The argument against the impossibility of traversing an infinite past, some critics allege, must commit the same fallacy as Zeno's paradox.

But such an objection fails to reckon with two crucial disanalogies of an infinite past to Zeno's paradoxes: whereas in Zeno's thought experiments the intervals traversed are *potential* and *unequal*, in the case of an infinite past the intervals are *actual* and *equal*. The claim that Achilles must pass through an infinite number

---

49. Richard Gale, "The Failure of Classic Theistic Arguments," in *The Cambridge Companion to Atheism*, ed. Michael Martin, Cambridge Companions to Philosophy (Cambridge: Cambridge University Press, 2007), 92–93. Gale's framing the argument in terms of a "set of events" is maladroit, since we are not talking about a set but about a series of events which elapse one after another. Cf. Russell's statement cited below (n. 52).

of halfway points in order to cross the stadium is question-begging, for it already assumes that the whole interval is a composition of an infinite number of points, whereas Zeno's opponents, like Aristotle, take the line as a whole to be conceptually prior to any divisions which we might make in it. Moreover, Zeno's intervals, being unequal, sum to a merely finite distance, whereas the intervals in an infinite past sum to an infinite distance. Thus, his thought experiments are crucially disanalogous to the task of traversing an infinite number of equal, actual intervals to arrive at our present location.

Mackie and Sobel object that this sort of argument illicitly presupposes an infinitely distant starting point in the past and then pronounces it impossible to travel from that point to today. But if the past is infinite, they say, then there would be no starting point whatever, not even an infinitely distant one. Nevertheless, from any given point in the past, there is only a finite distance to the present, which is easily "traversed."[50] But in fact no proponent of the *kalām* argument of whom I am aware has assumed that there was an infinitely distant starting point in the past. The fact that there is *no beginning* at all, not even an infinitely distant one, seems only to make the problem worse, not better. To say that the infinite past could have been formed by successive addition is like saying that someone has just succeeded in writing down all the negative numbers, ending at 0. And, we may ask, how is the claim that from any given moment in the past there is only a finite distance to the present even relevant to the issue? The defender of the *kalām* argument could agree to this happily. For the issue is how the *whole* series can be formed, not a finite portion of it. Do Mackie and Sobel think that because every *finite* segment of the series can be formed by successive addition the whole *infinite* series can be so formed? That is as logically fallacious as saying because every part of an elephant is light in weight, the whole elephant is light in weight. The claim is therefore irrelevant.

We can heighten the absurdity of the sequential formation of an actual infinite by imagining, with al-Ghāzalī, two beginningless series of coordinated events. He envisions our solar system's existing from eternity past, the orbital periods of the planets being so coordinated that for every one orbit which Saturn completes Jupiter completes 2.5 times as many. If they have been orbiting from eternity, which planet has completed the most orbits? The correct mathematical answer is that they have completed precisely the same number of orbits. But this seems absurd, for the longer they revolve the greater becomes the disparity between them, so that they progressively approach a limit at which Saturn has fallen infinitely far behind Jupiter. Yet, being now actually infinite, their respective completed orbits are somehow magically identical. Indeed, they will have "attained" infinity from eternity past: the number of completed orbits is always the same. Moreover, Ghāzalī asks, will the number of completed orbits be even or odd? Either answer seems absurd. We might be tempted to deny that the number of completed or-

---

50. Mackie, *Theism*, 93; Sobel, *Logic and Theism*, 182.

bits is either even or odd. But post-Cantorian transfinite arithmetic gives a quite different answer: the number of orbits completed is both even and odd![51] For a cardinal number n is even if there is a unique cardinal number m such that $n = 2m$, and n is odd if there is a unique cardinal number m such that $n = 2m + 1$. In the envisioned scenario the number of completed orbits is (in both cases!) $\aleph_0$, and $\aleph_0 = 2\aleph_0 = 2\aleph_0 + 1$. So Jupiter and Saturn have each completed both an even and an odd number of orbits, and that number has remained equal and unchanged from all eternity, despite their ongoing revolutions and the growing disparity between them over any finite interval of time. This strikes me as absurd.

It gets even worse. Suppose we meet a man who claims to have been counting down from infinity and who is now finishing: ..., -3, -2, -1, 0. We could ask, why didn't he finish counting yesterday or the day before or the year before? By then an infinite time had already elapsed, so that he should already have finished. Thus, at no point in the infinite past could we ever find the man finishing his countdown, for by that point he should already be done! In fact, no matter how far back into the past we go, we can never find the man counting at all, for at any point we reach he will already have finished. But if at no point in the past do we find him counting, this contradicts the hypothesis that he has been counting from eternity. This shows again that the formation of an actual infinite by never beginning but reaching an end is as impossible as beginning at a point and trying to reach infinity.

Hence, set theory has been purged of all temporal concepts; as Russell says, "Classes which are infinite are given all at once by the defining properties of their members, so that there is no question of 'completion' or of 'successive synthesis.'"[52] The only way an actual infinite could come to exist in the real world would be by being created all at once, simply in an instant. It would be a hopeless undertaking to try to form it by adding one member after another.

3) *Therefore, the series of events in time cannot be actually infinite.* Given the truth of the premises, the conclusion logically follows. If the universe did not begin to exist a finite time ago, then the present moment would never arrive. But obviously it has arrived. Therefore, we know that the universe is finite in the past and began to exist.

We thus have two separate philosophical arguments to prove that the universe began to exist, one based on the impossibility of an actually infinite number of things and one on the impossibility of forming an actually infinite collection by successive addition. If one wishes to deny the beginning of the universe, he must refute, not one, but both of these arguments.

51. See Wacław Sierpiński, *Cardinal and Ordinal Numbers*, Polska Akademia Nauk Monografie Matematyczne 34 (Warsaw: Państwowe Wydawnictwo Naukowe, 1958), 146.
52. Bertrand Russell, *Our Knowledge of the External World*, 2nd ed. (New York: W. W. Norton, 1929), 170.

Scientific Arguments:
(3) The Expansion of the Universe

Now some people find philosophical arguments dubious or difficult to follow; they prefer empirical evidence. So I now turn to an examination of two remarkable scientific confirmations of the conclusion already reached by philosophical argument alone. Before I do so, however, I want to note in passing that the sort of philosophical problems with the infinity of the past which we have discussed are now being recognized in scientific papers by leading cosmologists and philosophers of science.[53] For example, Ellis, Kirchner, and Stoeger ask, "Can there be an infinite set of really existing universes? We suggest that, on the basis of well-known *philosophical* arguments, the answer is No."[54] Similarly, noting that an actual infinite is not constructible and therefore not actualizable, they assert, "This is precisely why a realised past infinity in time is not considered possible from this standpoint—since it involves an infinite set of completed events or moments."[55] These misgivings represent endorsements of both of the *kalām* arguments which I defended above. Ellis and his colleagues conclude, "The arguments against an infinite past time are strong—it's simply not constructible in terms of events or instants of time, besides being conceptually indefinite."[56]

The physical evidence for the expansion of the universe comes from what is undoubtedly one of the most exciting and rapidly developing fields of science today: astronomy and astrophysics. Prior to the 1920s, scientists had always assumed that the universe was stationary and eternal. Tremors of the impending earthquake that would topple this traditional cosmology were first felt in 1917, when Albert Einstein made a cosmological application of his newly discovered gravitational theory, the General Theory of Relativity (GR). To his chagrin, Einstein found that GR would not permit an eternal, static model of the universe unless he fudged the equations in order to offset the gravitational effect of matter. As a result Einstein's universe was balanced on a razor's edge, and the least perturbation—even the transport of matter from one part of the universe to another—would cause the universe either to implode or to expand. By taking this feature of Einstein's model seriously, the Russian mathematician Alexander Friedman and the Belgian astronomer Georges Lemaître were able to formulate independently in the 1920s solutions to his equations which predicted an expanding universe.

The monumental significance of the Friedman-Lemaître model lay in its historization of the universe. As one commentator has remarked, up to this time the idea of the expansion of the universe "was absolutely beyond comprehension. Throughout

53. Besides the paper by Ellis et al. cited below, see also Rüdiger Vaas, "Time before Time: Classifications of Universes in contemporary cosmology, and how to avoid the antinomy of the beginning and eternity of the world," http://arXiv.org/abs/physics/0408111 (2004).

54. G. F. R. Ellis, U. Kirchner, and W. R. Stoeger, "Multiverses and Physical Cosmology," http://arXiv: astro-ph/0305292 v3 (28 August 2003), 14 (my emphasis).

55. Ibid.

56. Ibid.

all of human history the universe was regarded as fixed and immutable and the idea that it might actually be changing was inconceivable."[57] But if the Friedman-Lemaître model were correct, the universe could no longer be adequately treated as a static entity existing, in effect, timelessly. Rather the universe has a history, and time will not be matter of indifference for our investigation of the cosmos.

In 1929 the American astronomer Edwin Hubble showed that the light from distant galaxies is systematically shifted toward the red end of the spectrum. This red-shift was taken to be a Doppler effect indicating that the light sources were receding in the line of sight. Incredibly, what Hubble had discovered was the expansion of the universe predicted by Friedman and Lemaître on the basis of Einstein's GR. It was a veritable turning point in the history of science. "Of all the great predictions that science has ever made over the centuries," exclaims John Wheeler, "was there ever one greater than this, to predict, and predict correctly, and predict against all expectation a phenomenon so fantastic as the expansion of the universe?"[58]

The Standard Model

According to the Friedman-Lemaître model, as time proceeds, the distances separating the galaxies become greater. It's important to appreciate that as a GR-based theory, the model does not describe the expansion of the material content of the universe into a preexisting, empty space, but rather the expansion of space itself. The galaxies are conceived to be at rest with respect to space but to recede progressively from one another as space itself expands or stretches, just as buttons glued to the surface of a balloon will recede from one another as the balloon inflates. As the universe expands, it becomes less and less dense. This has the astonishing implication that as one reverses the expansion and extrapolates back in time, the universe becomes progressively denser until one arrives at a state of infinite density at some point in the finite past. This state represents a singularity at which spacetime curvature, along with temperature, pressure, and density, becomes infinite. It therefore constitutes an edge or boundary to spacetime itself. P. C. W. Davies comments,

> If we extrapolate this prediction to its extreme, we reach a point when all distances in the universe have shrunk to zero. An initial cosmological singularity therefore forms a past temporal extremity to the universe. We cannot continue physical reasoning, or even the concept of spacetime, through such an extremity. For this reason most cosmologists think of the initial singularity as the beginning of the universe. On this view the big bang represents the creation event; the creation not only of all the matter and energy in the universe, but also of spacetime itself.[59]

57. Gregory L. Naber, *Spacetime and Singularities: an Introduction* (Cambridge: Cambridge University Press, 1988), 126–27.

58. John A. Wheeler, "Beyond the Hole," in *Some Strangeness in the Proportion*, ed. Harry Woolf (Reading, Mass.: Addison-Wesley, 1980), 354.

59. P. C. W. Davies, "Spacetime Singularities in Cosmology," in *The Study of Time III*, ed. J. T. Fraser (Berlin: Springer Verlag, 1978), 78–79.

The term "Big Bang," originally a derisive expression coined by Fred Hoyle to characterize the beginning of the universe predicted by the Friedman-Lemaître model, is thus potentially misleading, since the expansion cannot be visualized from the outside (there being no "outside," just as there is no "before" with respect to the Big Bang).[60]

The standard Big Bang model, as the Friedman-Lemaître model came to be called, thus describes a universe which is not eternal in the past, but which came into being a finite time ago. Moreover—and this deserves underscoring—the origin it posits is an absolute origin out of nothing. For not only all matter and energy, but space and time themselves come into being at the initial cosmological singularity. As physicists John Barrow and Frank Tipler emphasize, "At this singularity, space and time came into existence; literally nothing existed before the singularity, so, if the Universe originated at such a singularity, we would truly have a creation *ex nihilo*."[61] Thus, we may graphically represent spacetime as a cone (Fig. 3.2).

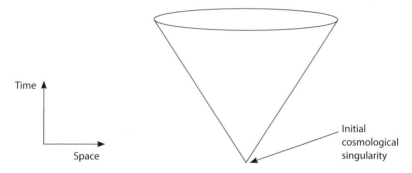

Fig. 3.2: Conical representation of Standard Model spacetime. Space and time begin at the initial cosmological singularity, before which literally nothing exists.

60. As Gott, Gunn, Schramm, and Tinsley write: "The universe began from a state of infinite density about one Hubble time ago. Space and time were created in that event and so was all the matter in the universe. It is not meaningful to ask what happened before the big bang; it is somewhat like asking what is north of the North Pole. Similarly, it is not sensible to ask where the big bang took place. The point-universe was not an object isolated in space; it was the entire universe, and so the only answer can be that the big bang happened everywhere." J. Richard Gott III, James E. Gunn, David N. Schramm, and Beatrice M. Tinsley, "Will the Universe Expand Forever?" *Scientific American*, March 1976, 65.

The Hubble time is the time since the singularity if the rate of expansion has been constant. The singularity is a point only in the sense that the distance between any two points in the singularity is zero. Anyone who thinks that there must be a place in the universe where the Big Bang occurred still has not grasped that it is space itself which is expanding; it is the two-dimensional *surface* of an inflating balloon which is analogous to three-dimensional space. The spherical surface has no center and so no location where the expansion begins. The analogy of the North Pole with the beginning of time should not be pressed, since the North Pole is not an edge to the surface of the globe; the beginning of time is more like the apex of a cone. But the idea is that just as one cannot go further north than the North Pole, so one cannot go earlier than the initial singularity.

61. John Barrow and Frank Tipler, *The Anthropic Cosmological Principle* (Oxford: Clarendon, 1986), 442.

On such a model the universe originates *ex nihilo* in the sense that at the initial singularity it is true that *there is no earlier spacetime point* or it is false that *something existed prior to the singularity.*

Now such a conclusion is profoundly disturbing for anyone who ponders it. For the question cannot be suppressed: *why did the universe come into being?* Sir Arthur Eddington, contemplating the beginning of the universe, opined that the expansion of the universe was so preposterous and incredible that "I feel almost an indignation that anyone should believe in it—except myself."[62] He finally felt forced to conclude, "The beginning seems to present insuperable difficulties unless we agree to look on it as frankly supernatural."[63] The problem of the origin of the universe, in the words of one astrophysical team, thus "involves a certain metaphysical aspect which may be either appealing or revolting."[64]

The Steady State Model

Revolted by the stark metaphysical alternatives presented by an absolute beginning of the universe, certain theorists have been understandably eager to subvert the Standard Model and restore an eternal universe. The first such attempt came in 1948 with the first competitor to the Standard Model, namely, the Steady State Model of the universe. According to this theory, the universe is in a state of cosmic expansion, but as the galaxies recede, new matter is drawn into being *ex nihilo* in the voids created by the galactic recession (Fig. 3.3).

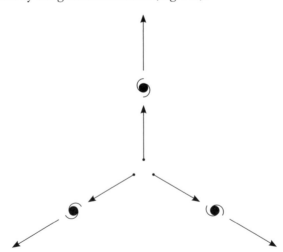

Fig. 3.3: Steady State Model. As the galaxies mutually recede, new matter comes into existence to replace them. The universe thus constantly renews itself and so never began to exist.

62. Arthur Eddington, *The Expanding Universe* (New York: Macmillan, 1933), 124.
63. Ibid., 178.
64. Hubert Reeves, Jean Audouze, William A. Fowler, and David N. Schramm, "On the Origin of Light Elements," *Astrophysical Journal* 179 (1973): 912.

If one extrapolates the expansion of the universe back in time, the density of the universe never increases because the matter and energy simply vanish as the galaxies mutually approach!

The Steady State theory never secured a single piece of experimental verification; its appeal was purely metaphysical. Instead, observational astronomy made it increasingly evident that the universe had an evolutionary history. But the decisive refutation of the Steady State Model came with two discoveries which constituted, in addition to the galactic red-shift, the most significant evidence for the Big Bang theory: the primordial nucleosynthesis of the light elements and the microwave background radiation. Although the heavy elements were synthesized in the stars, stellar nucleosynthesis could not manufacture the abundant light elements such as helium and deuterium. These could only have been created in the extreme conditions present in the first moment of the Big Bang. In 1965 a serendipitous discovery revealed the existence of a cosmic background radiation predicted in the 1940s by George Gamow on the basis of the Standard Model. This radiation, now shifted into the microwave region of the spectrum, consists of photons emitted during a very hot and dense phase of the universe. In the minds of most cosmologists, the cosmic background radiation decisively discredited the Steady State Model.

Oscillating Models

The Standard Model was based on the assumption that the universe is largely the same in every direction. In the 1960s and 1970s some cosmologists suggested that by denying that assumption, one might be able to craft an Oscillating Model of the universe and thus avert the absolute beginning predicted by the Standard Model. If the internal gravitational pull of the mass of the universe were able to overcome the force of its expansion, then the expansion could be reversed into a cosmic contraction, a Big Crunch. If the matter of the universe were not evenly distributed, then the collapsing universe might not coalesce at a point, but quantities of matter might pass by one another, so that the universe would appear to bounce back from the contraction into a new expansion phase. If this process could be repeated indefinitely, then an absolute beginning of the universe might be avoided (Fig. 3.4).

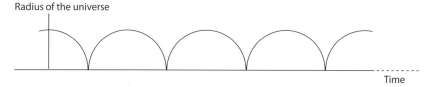

Radius of the universe

Time

Fig. 3.4: Oscillating Model. Each expansion phase is preceded and succeeded by a contraction phase, so that the universe in concertina-like fashion exists beginninglessly and endlessly.

Such a theory is extraordinarily speculative, but again there were metaphysical motivations for adopting this model. The prospects of the Oscillating Model were severely dimmed in 1970, however, by Roger Penrose and Stephen Hawking's formulation of the Singularity Theorems which bear their names. The theorems disclosed that under very generalized conditions an initial cosmological singularity is inevitable, even for inhomogeneous universes. Reflecting on the impact of this discovery, Hawking notes that the Hawking-Penrose Singularity Theorems "led to the abandonment of attempts (mainly by the Russians) to argue that there was a previous contracting phase and a non-singular bounce into expansion. Instead almost everyone now believes that the universe, and time itself, had a beginning at the big bang."[65]

Despite the fact that no spacetime trajectory can be extended through a singularity, the Oscillating Model exhibited a stubborn persistence. Two further strikes were lodged against it. First, there are no known physics which would cause a collapsing universe to bounce back to a new expansion. If, in defiance of the Hawking-Penrose Singularity Theorems, the universe rebounds, this is predicated upon a physics which is as yet unknown. Second, attempts by observational astronomers to discover the mass density sufficient to generate the gravitational attraction required to halt and reverse the expansion continually came up short. In January of 1998 astronomical teams from Princeton, Yale, the Lawrence Berkeley National Laboratory, and the Harvard-Smithsonian Astrophysics Institute reported at the American Astronomical Society meeting that their various tests all showed that "the universe will expand forever."[66] A spokesman for the Harvard-Smithsonian team stated that they were now at least 95 percent certain that "the density of matter is insufficient to halt the expansion of the universe."[67]

At the same time, observations of the red-shifts of supernovae yielded unexpected results that have thrown the discussion of the universe's fate into a wholly new arena and served to render questions of its density irrelevant. The red-shift data gathered from the distant supernovae indicate that, far from decelerating, the cosmic expansion is actually accelerating! There is some sort of mysterious "dark energy" in the form of either a variable energy field (called "quintessence") or, more probably, a positive cosmological constant or vacuum energy which at a certain point in the evolution of the cosmos kicks the expansion into a higher gear, causing the expansion to proceed more rapidly. Consequently, even high density universes may expand forever; a potentially infinite future is no longer the privileged prerogative of low density universes. Highly accurate recent measurements of the cosmic microwave background radiation by the Wilkinson Microwave Anisotropy Probe (WMAP) indicate, "For the theory that fits our data, the Universe will expand forever."[68]

65. Stephen Hawking and Roger Penrose, *The Nature of Space and Time*, The Isaac Newton Institute Series of Lectures (Princeton, N. J.: Princeton University Press, 1996), 20.

66. Associated Press News Release, January 9, 1998.

67. Ibid.

68. See http://map.gsfc.nasa.gov/m_mm/mr_limits.html.

Vacuum Fluctuation Models

Physicists realized that a physical description of the universe prior to the Planck time (10^{-43} second after the Big Bang singularity) would require the introduction of quantum physics in addition to GR. On the sub-atomic level so-called virtual particles are thought to arise due to fluctuations in the energy locked up in the vacuum, particles which the Heisenberg Indeterminacy Principle allows to exist for a fleeting moment before dissolving back into the vacuum. In 1973 Edward Tryon speculated whether the universe might not be a long-lived virtual particle, whose total energy is zero, born out of the primordial vacuum. This seemingly bizarre speculation gave rise to a new generation of cosmogonic theories which we may call Vacuum Fluctuation Models. These models were closely related to an adjustment to the Standard Model known as Inflation. In an attempt to explain the astonishing large-scale smoothness of the universe, certain theorists proposed that between 10^{-35} and 10^{-33} second after the Big Bang singularity, the universe underwent a phase of super-rapid, or inflationary, expansion which served to push the inhomogeneities out beyond our event horizon. Prior to the inflationary era the universe was merely empty space, or a vacuum, and the material universe was born when the vacuum energy was converted into matter via a quantum mechanical phase transition. In most inflationary models, as one extrapolates backward in time, beyond the Planck time, the universe continues to shrink down to the initial singularity. But in Vacuum Fluctuation Models, it was hypothesized that prior to inflation the Universe-as-a-whole was not expanding. This Universe-as-a-whole is a primordial vacuum which exists eternally in a steady state. Throughout this vacuum sub-atomic energy fluctuations constantly occur, by means of which matter is created and mini-universes are born (Fig. 3.5).

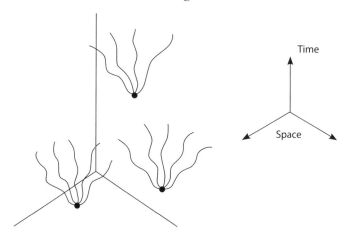

Fig. 3.5: Vacuum Fluctuation Models. Within the vacuum of the wider Universe, fluctuations occur which grow into mini-universes. Ours is but one of these, and its relative beginning does not imply a beginning for the Universe-as-a-whole.

Our expanding universe is but one of an indefinite number of mini-universes conceived within the womb of the greater Universe-as-a-whole. Thus, the beginning of our universe does not represent an absolute beginning, but merely a change in the eternal, uncaused Universe-as-a-whole.

Vacuum Fluctuation Models did not outlive the decade of the 1980s. Not only were there theoretical problems with the production mechanisms of matter, but these models faced a deep internal incoherence. According to such models, it is impossible to specify precisely when and where a fluctuation will occur in the primordial vacuum which will then grow into a universe. Within any finite interval of time there is a positive probability of such a fluctuation's occurring at any point in space. Thus, given infinite past time, universes will eventually be spawned at *every* point in the primordial vacuum, and, as they expand, they will begin to collide and coalesce with one another. Thus, given infinite past time, we should by now be observing an infinitely old universe, not a relatively young one. One theorist tried to avoid this problem by stipulating that fluctuations in the primordial vacuum only occur infinitely far apart, so that each mini-universe has infinite room in which to expand.[69] Not only is such a scenario unacceptably ad hoc, but it doesn't even solve the problem. For given infinite past time, each of the infinite regions of the vacuum will have spawned an open universe which by now will have entirely filled that region, with the result that all of the individual mini-universes would have coalesced.

About the only way to avert the problem would be to postulate an expansion of the primordial vacuum itself; but then we're right back to the absolute origin implied by the Standard Model. According to quantum cosmologist Christopher Isham these models were therefore jettisoned long ago and "nothing much" has been done with them since.[70]

Chaotic Inflationary Model

Inflation also forms the context for the next alternative: the Chaotic Inflationary Model. Inflationary theory, though criticized by some as unduly "metaphysical," has been widely accepted among cosmologists. One of the most fertile of the inflation theorists has been the Russian cosmologist Andrei Linde, who has championed his Chaotic Inflationary Model.[71] In Linde's model inflation *never* ends: each inflating domain of the universe when it reaches a certain volume gives rise via inflation to another domain, and so on, *ad infinitum* (Fig. 3.6).

69. J. R. Gott III, "Creation of Open Universes from de Sitter Space," *Nature* 295 (1982): 304–7. One might also try to avoid the difficulty of coalescing universes by holding that the mini-universes break off from the mother universe to become separate worlds. But see pp. 145–46.

70. Christopher Isham, "Quantum Cosmology and the Origin of the Universe," lecture presented at the conference "Cosmos and Creation," Cambridge University, July 14, 1994.

71. See, e.g., A. D. Linde, "The Inflationary Universe," *Reports on Progress in Physics* 47 (1984): 925–86; idem, "Chaotic Inflation," *Physics Letters* 1298 (1983): 177–81. For a critical review of inflationary scenarios, including Linde's, see John Earman and Jesus Mosterin, "A Critical Look at Inflationary Cosmology," *Philosophy of Science* 66 (1999): 1–49.

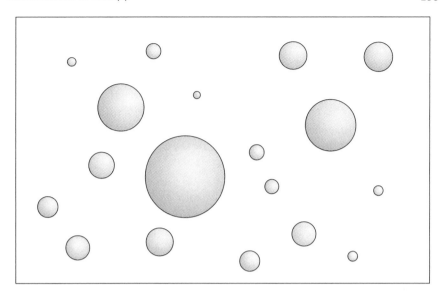

Fig. 3.6: Chaotic Inflationary Model. The wider universe produces via inflation separate domains which continue to recede from one another as the wider space expands.

Linde's model thus has an infinite future. But Linde is troubled at the prospect of an absolute beginning. He writes, "The most difficult aspect of this problem is not the existence of the singularity itself, but the question of what was *before* the singularity. . . . This problem lies somewhere at the boundary between physics and metaphysics."[72] Linde therefore proposed that chaotic inflation is not only endless, but beginningless. Every domain in the universe is the product of inflation in another domain, so that the singularity is averted and with it as well the question of what came before (or, more accurately, what caused it). Our observable universe turns out to be but one bubble in a wider, eternal multiverse of worlds.

In 1994, however, Arvind Borde and Alexander Vilenkin showed that any space-time eternally inflating toward the future cannot be "geodesically complete" in the past, that is to say, there must have existed at some point in the indefinite past an initial singularity. Hence, the multiverse scenario cannot be past eternal. They write:

> A model in which the inflationary phase has no end . . . naturally leads to this question: Can this model also be extended to the infinite past, avoiding in this way the problem of the initial singularity? . . . This is in fact not possible in future-eternal inflationary spacetimes as long as they obey some reasonable physical conditions: such models must necessarily possess initial singularities. . . . The fact that inflationary spacetimes are past incomplete forces one to address the question of what, if anything, came before.[73]

72. Linde, "Inflationary Universe," 976.
73. A. Borde and A. Vilenkin, "Eternal Inflation and the Initial Singularity," *Physical Review Letters* 72 (1994): 3305, 3307.

In response, Linde concurred with the conclusion of Borde and Vilenkin: there must have been a Big Bang singularity at some point in the past.[74]

In 2003 Borde and Vilenkin in cooperation with Alan Guth were able to strengthen their conclusion by crafting a new theorem independent of the assumption of the so-called "weak energy condition," which partisans of past-eternal inflation might have denied in an effort to save their theory.[75] The new theorem, in Vilenkin's words, "appears to close that door completely."[76] Inflationary models, like their predecessors, thus failed to avert the beginning predicted by the Standard Model.

Quantum Gravity Models

At the close of their analysis of Linde's Chaotic Inflationary Model, Borde and Vilenkin say with respect to Linde's metaphysical question, "The most promising way to deal with this problem is probably to treat the Universe quantum mechanically and describe it by a wave function rather than by a classical spacetime."[77] For "it follows from the theorem that the inflating region has a boundary in the past, and some new physics (other than inflation) is necessary to determine the conditions of that boundary. Quantum cosmology is the prime candidate for this role."[78] They thereby bring us to the next class of models which we shall consider, namely, Quantum Gravity Models.

Vilenkin and, more famously, James Hartle and Stephen Hawking have proposed models of the universe which Vilenkin candidly calls exercises in "metaphysical cosmology."[79] Both the Hartle-Hawking and the Vilenkin models eliminate the initial singularity by transforming the conical geometry of classical spacetime into a smooth, curved geometry having no edge (Fig. 3.7). This is accomplished by the introduction of imaginary numbers for the time variable in Einstein's gravitational equations, which effectively eliminates the singularity.

By positing a finite (imaginary) time on a closed surface prior to the Planck time rather than an infinite time on an open surface, such models actually seem to support, rather than undercut, the fact that time and the universe had a beginning. Such theories, if successful, would enable us to model the beginning of the universe without an initial singularity involving infinite density, temperature,

74. Andrei Linde, Dmitri Linde, and Arthur Mezhlumian, "From the Big Bang Theory to the Theory of a Stationary Universe," *Physical Review D* 49 (1994): 1783–1826. Linde has since tried to suggest a way to escape the conclusion of a beginning ("Inflation and String Cosmology," http://arXiv:hep-th/0503195v1 (March 24, 2005), 13. But he does not succeed in extending past spacetime paths to infinity, which is a necessary condition of the universe's having no beginning.

75. Arvind Borde, Alan Guth, and Alexander Vilenkin, "Inflation Is Not Past-Eternal," http://arXiv: gr-qc/0110012v1 (Oct. 1, 2001): 4. The article was updated in January 2003.

76. Alexander Vilenkin, "Quantum Cosmology and Eternal Inflation," http://arXiv:gr-qc/0204061v1 (April 18, 2002): 10.

77. Borde and Vilenkin, "Eternal Inflation," 3307.

78. Vilenkin, "Quantum Cosmology and Eternal Inflation," 11.

79. A. Vilenkin, "Birth of Inflationary Universes," *Physical Review D* 27 (1983): 2854. See J. Hartle and S. Hawking, "Wave Function of the Universe," *Physical Review D* 28 (1983): 2960–75; A. Vilenkin, "Creation of the Universe from Nothing," *Physical Letters* 117B (1982): 25–8.

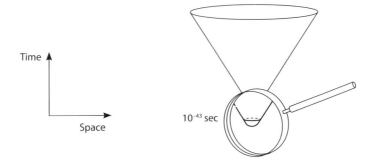

Fig. 3.7: Quantum Gravity Model. In the Hartle-Hawking version, spacetime is "rounded off" prior to the Planck time, so that although the past is finite, there is no edge or beginning point.

pressure, and so on. As Barrow points out, "This type of quantum universe has not always existed; it comes into being just as the classical cosmologies could, but it does not start at a Big Bang where physical quantities are infinite."[80] Barrow points out that such models are "often described as giving a picture of 'creation out of nothing,'" the only caveat being that in this case "there is no definite . . . point of creation."[81] Having a beginning does not entail having a beginning point. Even in the Standard Model, theorists sometimes "cut out" the initial singular point without thinking that therefore spacetime no longer begins to exist and the problem of the origin of the universe is thereby resolved. Time begins to exist just in case for any finite temporal interval, there are only a finite number of equal temporal intervals earlier than it. That condition is fulfilled for Quantum Gravity Models as well as for the Standard Model. According to Vilenkin, "The picture presented by quantum cosmology is that the universe starts as a small, closed 3-geometry and immediately enters the regime of eternal inflation, with new thermalized regions being constantly formed. In this picture, the universe has a beginning but no end."[82] Thus, Quantum Gravity models, like the Standard Model, imply the beginning of the universe.

Perhaps it will be said that such an interpretation of Quantum Gravity models fails to take seriously the notion of "imaginary time." Introducing imaginary numbers for the time variable in Einstein's equation has the peculiar effect of making the time dimension indistinguishable from space. But in that case, the imaginary time regime prior to the Planck time is not a spacetime at all, but a Euclidean four-dimensional space. Construed realistically, such a four-space would be evacuated of all temporal becoming and would simply exist timelessly. Hawking describes it as "completely self-contained and not affected by anything outside itself. It would be neither created nor destroyed. It would just BE."[83]

80. John D. Barrow, *Theories of Everything* (Oxford: Clarendon, 1991), 68.
81. Ibid., 67–68.
82. Alexander Vilenkin, "Quantum Cosmology and Eternal Inflation," 11.
83. Stephen Hawking, *A Brief History of Time* (New York: Bantam, 1988), 136.

The question which arises for this construal of the model is whether such an imaginary time regime should be interpreted realistically or instrumentally. On this score, there can be little doubt that the use of imaginary quantities for time is a mere mathematical device without ontological significance. For, first, there is no intelligible physical interpretation of imaginary time on offer. What, for example, would it mean to speak of the lapse of an imaginary second or of a physical object's enduring through two imaginary minutes? Second, time is metaphysically distinct from space, its moments being ordered by an *earlier than* relation which does not similarly order points in space. But this essential difference is obscured by imaginary time. Thus, "imaginary time" is most plausibly construed as a mathematical contrivance. Barrow observes,

> physicists have often carried out this "change time into space" procedure as a useful trick for doing certain problems in ordinary quantum mechanics, although they did not imagine that time was *really* like space. At the end of the calculation, they just swop back into the usual interpretation of there being one dimension of time and three . . . dimensions of . . . space. [84]

Hawking simply declines to reconvert to real numbers. If we do, then the singularity reappears. Hawking admits, "Only if we could picture the universe in terms of imaginary time would there be no singularities. . . . When one goes back to the real time in which we live, however, there will still appear to be singularities."[85] Hawking's model is thus a way of redescribing a universe with a singular beginning point in such a way that that singularity is transformed away; but such a redescription is not realist in character.

Vilenkin recognizes the use of imaginary time as a mere "computational convenience" without ontological significance.[86] Remarkably, so does Hawking in other contexts.[87] This precludes their models' being construed realistically as accounts of the origin of the spacetime universe in a timelessly existing four-space. Rather their theories are ways of modeling the real beginning of the universe *ex nihilo* in such a way as to not involve a singularity. What brought the universe into being remains unexplained on such accounts.

String Scenarios
We come finally to the extreme edge of cosmological speculation: string cosmology. These scenarios are based on an alternative to the standard quark model of

84. Barrow, *Theories of Everything*, 66–67.
85. Hawking, *Brief History of Time*, 138–39.
86. Vilenkin, *Many Worlds in One*, 182.
87. The clearest example of Hawking's instrumentalism is his description in *The Nature of Space and Time* of particle pair creation in terms of an electron's quantum tunneling in Euclidean space (with time being imaginary) and an electron/positron pair's accelerating away from each other in Minkowski spacetime. This description is directly analogous to the Hartle-Hawking cosmological model; and yet no one would construe particle pair creation as literally the result of an electron's transitioning out of a timelessly existing four-space into our classical spacetime.

elementary particle physics. So-called string theory (or M-theory) conceives of the fundamental building blocks of matter to be, not particles like quarks, but tiny, vibrating, one-dimensional strings of energy. String theory is so complicated and embryonic in its development that all its equations have not yet even been stated, much less solved. But that has not deterred some cosmologists from trying to envision cosmological scenarios based on concepts of string theory to try to avert the beginning predicted by customary Big Bang cosmology.

Two sorts of scenarios have been proposed. The first of these is the Pre-Big Bang Scenario championed by the Italian physicists Gabriele Veneziano and Maurizio Gasperini.[88] They conceive of the Big Bang as the transitional event between a contraction phase chronologically prior to the Big Bang and the observed expansion phase after it. Such a rebound is postulated on the basis of limits which the size and symmetries of strings set to the increase in quantities like spacetime curvature, density, temperature, and so forth. Prior to the Big Bang a black hole formed in the eternally preexisting, static vacuum space and collapsed to the maximum allowed values of such quantities before rebounding in the current expansion observed today (Fig. 3.8).

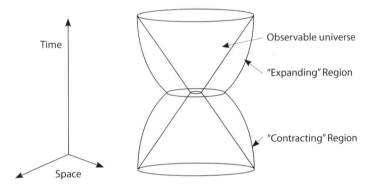

Fig. 3.8: Pre-Big Bang Scenario. Our observable universe results from the rebound of the collapse of a black hole in a wider preexisting vacuum space.

The scenario differs from the old oscillating models in that the prior contraction is conceived to take place within a wider, static space and to proceed from infinity. If the expansion will go on forever, then the contraction has gone on forever. The further one regresses into the infinite past, the less dense the universe becomes, as one approaches a limit in the infinite past of a nearly empty universe consisting of an ultra-thin gas of radiation and matter. As one moves forward in time, the material contents of various regions of space begin to collapse into black holes. But rather than collapsing to singularities, these black holes reach a maximum of

88. Gabriele Veneziano, "A Simple/Short Introduction to Pre-Big Bang Physics/Cosmology," http://arXiv:hep-th/9802057v2 (March 2, 1998); M. Gasperini, "Looking Back in Time beyond the Big Bang," *Modern Physics Letters A* 14/16 (1999): 1059–66; M. Gasperini, "Inflation and Initial Conditions in the Pre-Big Bang Scenario," *Physics Review D* 61 (2000): 87301–305; M. Gasperini and G. Veneziano, "The Pre-Big Bang Scenario in String Cosmology," http://arXiv:hep-th/0207130v1 (July 12, 2002).

spacetime curvature, density, and so on, before rebounding into expansion phases. Our universe is just one of these collapsing and rebounding regions within the wider universe. Thus, an absolute beginning of the universe is averted.

Although the Pre-Big Bang Scenario is based on a non-existent theory and is dogged with problems concerning how to join the pre- and post-Big Bang phases together, these purely physical problems pale in comparison to the deep conceptual difficulties attending such a scenario. Like the old Vacuum Fluctuation Models, the Pre-Big Bang Scenario postulates an eternal, static space in which our observable universe originates via a Big Bang event a finite time ago. But since there is a positive probability of a black hole's forming in any patch of pre-existing space, such an event, given infinite past time, would have happened infinitely long ago, which is inconsistent with the finite age of our observable universe. Moreover, all the pre-Big Bang black holes should in infinite time have coalesced into one massive black hole coextensive with the universe, so that the post-Big Bang universe ought to be observed as infinitely old. Similarly, such a static wider universe, if it is a closed system, should, given infinite past time, have already arrived at a state of thermodynamic equilibrium, in contradiction to the observed disequilibrium (more on this in the sequel). In their efforts to explain the origin of the observable universe from a pre-Big Bang condition, Gasperini and Veneziano have been singularly inattentive to the problematic issues arising from their supposition of a wider, eternally pre-existing space. What they have done, in effect, is to treat the past as a potentially infinite process approaching an infinitely distant limit, rather than as an actually infinite sequence of events having no beginning but an end in the present.

The more celebrated of the string scenarios has been the so-called Ekpyrotic Scenario championed by Paul Steinhardt.[89] In the most recent revision, the Cyclic Ekpyrotic Scenario, we are asked to envision two three-dimensional membranes (or "branes" for short) existing in a five-dimensional spacetime (Fig. 3.9). One of these branes is our universe. These two branes are said to be in an eternal cycle in which they approach each other, collide, and retreat again from each other. It is the collision of the other brane with ours that causes the expansion of our universe. With each collision, the expansion is renewed. Ripples in the branes are said to account for the large-scale structure of our three-dimensional universe. Thus, even though our universe is expanding, it never had a beginning.

Again, wholly apart from its speculative nature, the Ekpyrotic Scenario has been plagued with problems.[90] But let that pass. Perhaps all these problems can somehow be solved. The more important point is that it turns out that, like the Chaotic Inflationary Model, the Cyclic Ekpyrotic Scenario cannot be eternal in the past. With the formulation of their stronger theorem Borde, Guth, and

---

89. See http://feynman.princeton.edu/~steinh/.

90. For typical criticisms see especially Gary Felder, Andret Frolov, Lev Kaufman, and Andrei Linde, "Cosmology with Negative Potentials," http://arXiv:hep-th/0202017v2 (February 16, 2002) and the therein cited literature, particularly the studies by David Lyth.

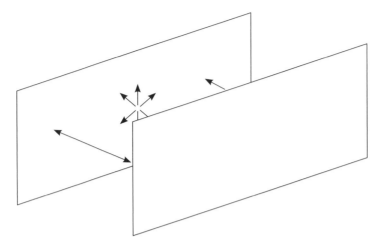

Fig. 3.9: Cyclic Ekpyrotic Scenario. Two three-dimensional membranes in an eternal cycle of approach, collision, and retreat. With each collision the expansion of our universe is re-invigorated.

Vilenkin were able to generalize their earlier results on inflationary models in such a way to extend their conclusion to other models. Indeed, the new theorem implies that any universe which has on average been globally expanding at a positive rate is geodesically incomplete in the past and therefore has a past boundary. Specifically, they note, "Our argument can be straightforwardly extended to cosmology in higher dimensions," specifically brane-cosmology like Steinhardt's.[91] According to Vilenkin, "It follows from our theorem that the cyclic universe is past-incomplete,"[92] that is to say, the need for an initial singularity has not been eliminated. Therefore, such a universe cannot be past-eternal. Steinhardt has himself come to recognize this implication of the theorem for Ekpyrotic Scenarios and so now acknowledges that on his scenario the universe has a past boundary at some point in the metrically finite past.[93]

Summary

The history of twentieth-century cosmogony has, in one sense, been a series of failed attempts to craft acceptable non-standard models of the expanding universe in such a way as to avert the absolute beginning predicted by the Standard Model. This parade of failures can be confusing to the layman, leading him mistakenly to

91. Borde, Guth, and Vilenkin, "Inflation Is Not Past-Eternal," 4. See also Alexander Vilenkin, "Quantum Cosmology and Eternal Inflation," 11.

92. Alexander Vilenkin, personal communication.

93. See www.phy.princeton.edu/~steinh/ under "Answers to Frequently Asked Questions: Has the cyclic model been cycling forever?" Steinhardt seeks to mollify the impact of the Borde-Guth-Vilenkin theorem by maintaining that clocks run progressively faster as one approaches the past boundary, so that elapsed time becomes what he calls "semi-infinite." This trick does nothing to abrogate the finitude of the past or the beginning of the universe.

infer that the field of cosmology is in constant flux, as new theories of the universe's origin continually come and go, with no assured results. In fact, the Standard Model's prediction of an absolute beginning has persisted through a century of astonishing progress in theoretical and observational cosmology and survived an onslaught of alternative theories. With each successive failure of alternative cosmogonic theories to avoid the absolute beginning of the universe predicted by the Standard Model, that prediction has been corroborated. It can be confidently said that no cosmogonic model has been as repeatedly verified in its predictions and as corroborated by attempts at its falsification, or as concordant with empirical discoveries and as philosophically coherent, as the Standard Big Bang Model.

A watershed of sorts appears to have been reached in 2003 with Borde, Guth, and Vilenkin's formulation of their theorem establishing that any universe which has on average over its past history been in a state of cosmic expansion cannot be eternal in the past but must have a spacetime boundary. Theorists intent on avoiding the absolute beginning of the universe could previously always take refuge in the period prior to the Planck time, an era so poorly understood that one commentator has compared it with the regions on the maps of ancient cartographers marked "Here there be dragons!"—it can be filled with all sorts of chimeras. But the Borde-Guth-Vilenkin theorem does not depend upon any particular physical description of the universe prior to the Planck time, being based instead on deceptively simple physical reasoning which will hold regardless of our uncertainty concerning that era. It single-handedly sweeps away the most important attempts to avoid the absolute beginning of the universe, especially the darling of current cosmologists, the eternal inflationary multiverse. Vilenkin pulls no punches: "It is said that an argument is what convinces reasonable men and a proof is what it takes to convince even an unreasonable man. With the proof now in place, cosmologists can no longer hide behind the possibility of a past-eternal universe. There is no escape, they have to face the problem of a cosmic beginning."[94]

Of course, in view of the metaphysical issues raised by the prospect of a beginning of the universe, we may be confident that the quest to avert the absolute beginning predicted by the Standard Model will continue unabated. Such efforts are to be encouraged, and we have no reason to think that such attempts at falsification of the prediction of the Standard Model will result in anything other than further corroboration of its prediction of a beginning. While scientific evidence is always provisional, there can be little doubt in this case where the evidence points.

Scientific Arguments:
(4) The Thermodynamic Properties of the Universe
As if this were not enough, there is a second scientific confirmation for the beginning of the universe, the evidence from thermodynamics. According to the second law of thermodynamics, processes taking place in a closed system always tend

94. Vilenkin, *Many Worlds in One*, 176.

toward a state of equilibrium. In other words, unless energy is constantly being fed into a system, the processes in the system will tend to run down and quit. For example, if I had a bottle that was a sealed vacuum inside, and I introduced into it some molecules of gas, the gas would spread itself out evenly inside the bottle. It is virtually impossible for the molecules to retreat, for example, into one corner of the bottle. This is why when you walk into a room, the air in the room never separates suddenly into oxygen at one end and nitrogen at the other. It's also why when you step into your bath you may be confident that it will be an even temperature instead of frozen solid at one end and boiling at the other. It's clear that life would not be possible in a world in which the second law of thermodynamics did not hold.

Cosmological Implications of the Second Law

Now our interest in the law is what happens when it is applied to the universe as a whole. For the universe is, on the atheistic view, a gigantic closed system, since it is everything there is and there is nothing outside it. Already in the nineteenth century, scientists realized that the application of the second law to the universe as a whole implied a grim eschatological conclusion: given sufficient time, the universe will eventually come to a state of equilibrium and suffer "heat death." Once the universe reaches this state, no further change is possible. The universe is dead.

But this apparently firm projection raised an even deeper question: if, given sufficient time, the universe will suffer heat death, then why, if it has existed forever, is it not now in a state of heat death? If in a finite amount of time the universe will inevitably come to equilibrium, from which no significant further change is physically possible, then it should already be at equilibrium by now, if it has existed for infinite time. Like a ticking clock, it should by now have run down. Since it has not yet run down, this implies, in the words of Richard Schlegel, that "in some way the universe must have been *wound up*."[95]

The nineteenth-century German physicist Ludwig Boltzmann offered a daring hypothesis in order to explain why we do not find the universe in a state of heat death or thermodynamic equilibrium.[96] Boltzmann hypothesized that the universe as a whole *does*, in fact, exist in an equilibrium state, but that over time fluctuations in the energy level occur here and there throughout the universe, so that by chance alone there will be isolated regions where disequilibrium exists. Boltzmann referred to these isolated regions as "worlds." We should not be surprised to see our world in a highly improbable disequilibrium state, he maintained, since in the ensemble of all worlds there must exist by chance certain worlds in disequilibrium, and ours just happens to be one of these.

---

95. Richard Schlegel, "Time and Thermodynamics," in *The Voices of Time*, ed. J. T. Fraser (London: Penguin, 1968), 511.

96. Ludwig Boltzmann, *Lectures on Gas Theory*, trans. Stephen G. Brush (Berkeley: University of California Press, 1964), §90, pp. 446–48.

The problem with Boltzmann's hypothesis was that if our world were merely a fluctuation in a sea of diffuse energy, then it is overwhelmingly more probable that we should be observing a much tinier region of disequilibrium than we do. In order for us to exist, a smaller fluctuation would have sufficed and is much more probable than one so large as the observable universe. Moreover, even a colossal fluctuation that produced our world instantaneously by an enormous accident is inestimably more probable than a progressive decline in entropy over billions of years to fashion the world we see. In fact, Boltzmann's hypothesis, if adopted, would force us to regard the past as illusory, everything having the mere appearance of age, and the stars and planets as illusory, mere "pictures" as it were, since that sort of world is vastly more probable given a state of overall equilibrium than a world with genuine, temporally and spatially distant events. Therefore, Boltzmann's hypothesis has been universally rejected by the scientific community, and the present disequilibrium is usually taken to be just a result of the initial low entropy condition mysteriously obtaining at the beginning of the universe.

Eschatological Scenarios

The advent of relativity theory and its application to cosmology altered the shape of the eschatological scenario predicted on the basis of the second law of thermo-dynamics but did not materially affect the fundamental question. Assuming that there is no positive cosmological constant fueling the expansion of the universe, that expansion will decelerate over time. Two radically different eschatological scenarios then present themselves. If the density of the universe exceeds a certain critical value, then the internal pull of the universe's own gravity will eventually overcome the force of the expansion and the universe will collapse in upon itself in a fiery Big Crunch. Beatrice Tinsley described such a scenario:

> If the average density of matter in the universe is great enough, the mutual gravi-tational attraction between bodies will eventually slow the expansion to a halt. The universe will then contract and collapse into a hot fireball. There is no known physical mechanism that could reverse a catastrophic big crunch. Apparently, if the universe becomes dense enough, it is in for a hot death.[97]

If the universe is fated to re-contraction, then as it contracts the stars gain energy, causing them to burn more rapidly so that they finally explode or evaporate. As everything in the universe grows closer together, the black holes begin to gobble up everything around them and eventually begin themselves to coalesce. In time, "all the black holes finally coalesce into one large black hole that is coextensive with the universe," from which the universe will never reemerge.[98] There is no known physics that would permit the universe to bounce back to a new expansion prior to a final singularity or to pass through the singularity into a subsequent state.

97. Beatrice Tinsley, "From Big Bang to Eternity?" *Natural History Magazine* (October 1975), 103.
98. Duane Dicus, et al., "The Future of the Universe," *Scientific American*, March 1983, 99.

On the other hand, if the density of the universe is equal to or less than the critical value, then gravity will not overcome the force of the expansion and the universe will expand forever at a progressively slower rate. Tinsley described the fate of this universe:

> If the universe has a low density, its death will be cold. It will expand forever at a slower and slower rate. Galaxies will turn all of their gas into stars, and the stars will burn out. Our own sun will become a cold, dead remnant, floating among the corpses of other stars in an increasingly isolated Milky Way.[99]

At 10^{30} years the universe will consist of 90 percent dead stars, 9 percent supermassive black holes formed by the collapse of galaxies, and 1 percent atomic matter, mainly hydrogen. Elementary particle physics suggests that thereafter protons will decay into electrons and positrons, so that space will be filled with a rarefied gas so thin that the distance between an electron and a positron will be about the size of the present galaxy. At 10^{100} years, the commencement of the so-called Dark Era, some scientists believe that the black holes themselves will dissipate by a strange effect predicted by quantum mechanics. The mass and energy associated with a black hole so warp space that they are said to create a "tunnel" or "worm-hole" through which the mass and energy are ejected in another region of space. As the mass of a black hole decreases, its energy loss accelerates, so that it is eventually dissipated into radiation and elementary particles. Eventually all black holes will completely evaporate and all the matter in the ever-expanding universe will be reduced to a thin gas of elementary particles and radiation. Because the volume of space constantly increases, the universe will never actually arrive at equilibrium, since there is always more room for entropy production. Nonetheless, the universe will become increasingly cold, dark, dilute, and dead.

Very recent discoveries provide strong evidence that there is effectively a positive cosmological constant which causes the cosmic expansion to accelerate rather than decelerate. Paradoxically, since the volume of space increases exponentially, allowing greater room for further entropy production, the universe actually grows farther and farther from an equilibrium state as time proceeds. But the acceleration only hastens the cosmos's disintegration into increasingly isolated material patches no longer causally connected with similarly marooned remnants of the expanding universe. Each of these patches faces, in turn, thermodynamic extinction. Therefore, the grim future predicted on the basis of the second law remains fundamentally unaltered.

Thus, the same pointed question raised by classical physics persists: why, if the universe has existed forever, is it not now in a cold, dark, dilute, and lifeless state? In contrast to their nineteenth-century forbears, contemporary physicists have come to question the implicit assumption that the universe is past eternal. Davies reports,

99. Tinsley, "Big Bang," 105.

Today, few cosmologists doubt that the universe, at least as we know it, did have an origin at a finite moment in the past. The alternative—that the universe has always existed in one form or another—runs into a rather basic paradox. The sun and stars cannot keep burning forever: sooner or later they will run out of fuel and die.

The same is true of all irreversible physical processes; the stock of energy available in the universe to drive them is finite, and cannot last for eternity. This is an example of the so-called second law of thermodynamics, which, applied to the entire cosmos, predicts that it is stuck on a one-way slide of degeneration and decay towards a final state of maximum entropy, or disorder. As this final state has not yet been reached, it follows that the universe cannot have existed for an infinite time.[100]

Davies concludes, "The universe can't have existed forever. We know there must have been an absolute beginning a finite time ago."[101]

Oscillating Models

During the 1960s and 1970s some scientists tried to escape this conclusion by arguing that the universe oscillates in and out from eternity, and so never reaches a final state of equilibrium (Fig. 3.4). But wholly apart from the difficulties mentioned earlier, the fact is that the thermodynamic properties of oscillating models imply the very beginning of the universe that their proponents sought to avoid. For entropy is conserved from cycle to cycle in such models, which has the effect of generating larger and longer oscillations with each successive cycle (Fig. 3.10).

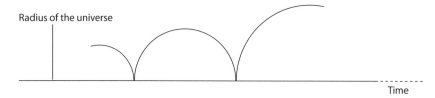

Fig. 3.10: Oscillating Model with entropy increase. Due to the conservation of entropy each successive oscillation has a larger radius and longer expansion time.

Therefore, if one traced the expansions back in time they would get smaller and smaller and smaller. One scientific team explains, "The effect of entropy production will be to enlarge the cosmic scale, from cycle to cycle. . . . Thus, looking back in time, each cycle generated less entropy, had a smaller cycle time, and had a smaller cycle expansion factor then [*sic*] the cycle that followed it."[102] Therefore, in the words of another scientific team, "the multicycle model has an infinite future, but

100. Paul Davies, "The Big Bang—and Before," The Thomas Aquinas College Lecture Series, Thomas Aquinas College, Santa Paula, Calif., March 2002.

101. Paul Davies, "The Big Questions: In the Beginning," ABC Science Online, interview with Phillip Adams, http://aca.mq.edu.au/pdavieshtml.

102. Dicus, "Cosmological Future," 1, 8.

only a finite past."[103] Indeed, astronomer Joseph Silk estimates on the basis of the current level of entropy in the universe that it could not have gone through more than 100 previous oscillations.[104]

Even if this difficulty were avoided, a universe oscillating from eternity past would require an infinitely precise tuning of initial conditions in order to persist through an infinite number of successive bounces. A universe rebounding from a single, infinitely long contraction is, if entropy increases during the contracting phase, incompatible with the initial low entropy condition of our expanding phase. Postulating an entropy decrease during the contracting phase in order to escape this problem would violate the second law. In either case such a universe involves a radical fine-tuning of a very special sort, since the initial conditions have to be set at $-\infty$ in the past.[105]

Baby Universes

Is there some other plausible way of holding onto the eternality of the past in the face of the universe's disequilibrium state? Speculations have been floated in eschatological discussions about our universe's begetting future "baby universes." It has been conjectured that black holes may be portals of wormholes through which bubbles of false vacuum energy can tunnel to spawn new expanding baby universes, whose umbilical cords to our universe may eventually snap as the wormholes close up, leaving the baby universe an independently existing spacetime (Fig. 3.11). Perhaps we might imagine that our observable universe is just one of the newly birthed offspring of an infinitely old, preexisting universe.

The conjecture of our universe's spawning future offspring by such a mechanism was the subject of a bet between Stephen Hawking and James Preskill, which Hawking in 2004 finally admitted, in an event much publicized in the press, that he had lost.[106] The conjecture would require that information locked up in a black hole could be utterly lost forever by escaping to another universe. One of the last holdouts, Hawking finally came to agree that quantum theory requires that information is preserved in black hole formation and evaporation. The implica-

103. I.D. Novikov and Ya. B. Zeldovich, "Physical Processes Near Cosmological Singularities," *Annual Review of Astronomy and Astrophysics* 11 (1973): 401–2.

104. Joseph Silk, *The Big Bang*, 2nd ed. (San Francisco: W. H. Freeman, 1989), 311–12.

105. Cosmologist George Ellis remarks: "The problems are related: first, initial conditions have to be set in an extremely special way at the start of the collapse phase in order that it is a Robertson-Walker universe collapsing; and these conditions have to be set in an acausal way (in the infinite past). It is possible, but a great deal of inexplicable fine tuning is taking place: how does the matter in widely separated causally disconnected places at the start of the universe know how to correlate its motions (and densities) so that they will come together correctly in a spatially homogeneous way in the future? Secondly, if one gets that right, the collapse phase is unstable, with perturbations increasing rapidly, so only a very fine-tuned collapse phase remains close to Robertson-Walker even if it started off so, and will be able to turn around as a whole (in general many black holes will form locally and collapse to a singularity). G. F. R. Ellis to James Sinclair, January 25, 2006.

Ellis then pointedly asks, "Who focused the collapse so well that it turns around nicely?"

106. For a firsthand account see James Preskill's website www.theory.caltech.edu/~preskill/jp-24jul04.html.

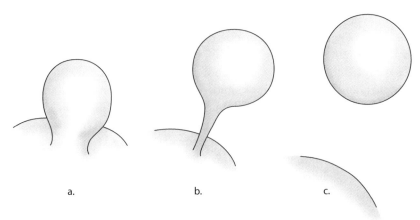

a.   b.   c.

Fig. 3.11. Birth of a baby universe. A baby universe spawned from its mother universe eventually becomes a disconnected and causally isolated spacetime.

tions? "There is no baby universe branching off, as I once thought. The information remains firmly in our universe. I'm sorry to disappoint science fiction fans, but if information is preserved, there is no possibility of using black holes to travel to other universes."[107] Even if Hawking had won the bet, could such an eschatological scenario be in any case successfully extrapolated into the past, such that our universe is one of the baby universes spawned by the mother universe or by an infinite series of ancestors? It seems not, for while such baby universes appear as black holes to observers in the mother universe, an observer in the baby universe itself will see the Big Bang as a white hole spewing out energy. But this is in sharp contrast to our observation of the Big Bang as a low-entropy event with a highly constrained geometrical structure.

Inflationary Multiverse

Inflationary theory has been exploited by some theorists in an attempt to revive Boltzmann's explanation of why we find ourselves in a universe thermodynamically capable of sustaining observers. The question here, in the words of Dyson, Kleban, and Susskind, is "whether the universe can be a naturally occurring fluctuation, or must it be due to an external agent which starts the system out in a specific low entropy state?"[108] According to generic inflationary theory, our universe exists in a

107. S. W. Hawking, "Information Loss in Black Holes," http://arXiv:hep-th/0507171v2 (15 September 2005): 4.

108. Lin Dyson, Matthew Kleban, and Leonard Susskind, "Disturbing Implications of a Cosmological Constant," http://arXiv.org/abs/hep-th/0208013v3 (November 14, 2002), 4. Their point of departure is Henri Poincaré's argument that in a closed box of randomly moving particles every configuration of particles, no matter how improbable, will eventually recur, given enough time; given infinite time, every configuration will recur infinitely many times. Eschewing a global perspective in favor of a restriction to our causally connected patch of the universe, they argue for the inevitability of cosmological Poincaré recurrences, allowing the process of cosmogony to begin anew. N.B. that even if bubble universes decay before the Poincaré recurrences could happen, there is still enough time for the invasion of Boltzmann brains, discussed below.

true vacuum state with an energy density that is nearly zero; but earlier it existed in a false vacuum state with a very high energy density. If we hypothesize that the conditions determining the energy density and evolution of the false vacuum state were just right, then the false vacuum will expand so rapidly that, as it decays into bubbles of true vacuum, the "bubble universes" formed in this sea of false vacuum, though themselves expanding at enormous rates, will not be able to keep up with the expansion of the false vacuum and so will find themselves increasingly separated with time (Fig. 3.12).

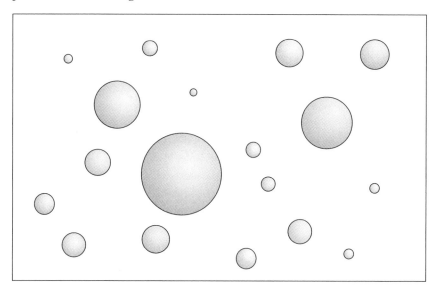

Fig. 3.12. Bubbles of true vacuum in a sea of false vacuum. As the inflating false vacuum decays, bubbles of true vacuum form in the false vacuum, each constituting an expanding universe. Though rapidly expanding, the bubbles will not coalesce because the false vacuum continues to expand at an even more rapid rate.

Moreover, each bubble is subdivided into domains bounded by event horizons, each domain constituting an observable universe. Observers internal to such a universe will observe it to be open and infinite, even though externally the bubble universe is finite and geometrically closed. Despite the fact that the multiverse is itself finite and geometrically closed, the false vacuum will, according to the theory, go on expanding forever. New bubbles of true vacuum will continue to form in the gaps between the bubble universes and become themselves isolated worlds.

The proposed solution to the problem, then, is essentially the same as Boltzmann's. Among the infinity of worlds generated by inflation there will be some worlds that are in a state of thermodynamic disequilibrium, and only such worlds can support observers. It is therefore not surprising that we find the world in a state of disequilibrium, since that is the only kind of world that we could observe.

But then the proposed solution is plagued by the same failing as Boltzmann's hypothesis. In a multiverse of eternally inflating vacua most of the volume will be occupied by high entropy, disordered states incapable of supporting observers. There are two ways in which observable states can exist: first, by being part of a relatively young, low entropy world, or, second, by being a thermal fluctuation in a high entropy world. Even though young universes are constantly nucleating out of the false vacuum, their volumes will be small in comparison with the older bubbles. Disordered states will therefore be on average strongly predominant. That implies that observers are much more likely to be the result of thermal fluctuations than the result of young, low entropy conditions.

But then the objection once again arises that it is incomprehensibly more probable that a much smaller region of disequilibrium should arise via a fluctuation than a region as large as our observable universe. Roger Penrose calculates that the odds of our universe's initial low entropy condition's coming into existence are on the order of one part in $10^{10(123)}$.[109] He comments, "I cannot even recall seeing anything else in physics whose accuracy is known to approach, even remotely, a figure like one part in $10^{10\,(123)}$."[110] By contrast, the odds of our solar system's being formed instantly by random collisions of particles is about $1{:}10^{10(60)}$, a vast number, but inconceivably smaller than $10^{10(123)}$. (Penrose calls it "utter chicken feed" by comparison.[111]) Thus, in the multiverse of worlds, observable states involving such an initial low entropy condition will be an incomprehensibly tiny fraction of all the observable states there are. If we are just one random member of an ensemble of worlds, we should therefore be observing a smaller world.

Adopting the multiverse hypothesis to explain our ordered observations would thus result once more in a strange sort of illusionism. It would be overwhelmingly more probable that there really isn't a vast, orderly universe out there, despite our observations; it's all an illusion. Indeed, the most probable state which is adequate to support our ordered observations is an even smaller "universe" consisting of a single brain which appears out of the disorder via a thermal fluctuation. In all probability, then, you alone exist, and everything you observe around you, even your physical body, is illusory! Some cosmologists have, in melodramatic language reminiscent of grade-B horror movies of the 1950s, dubbed this problem "the invasion of the Boltzmann brains."[112] Boltzmann brains are much more plenteous in the ensemble of universes than ordinary observers, and, therefore, each of us ought to think that he is himself a Boltzmann brain if he believes that the universe is but

109. Roger Penrose, "Time-Asymmetry and Quantum Gravity," in *Quantum Gravity 2*, ed. C. J. Isham, R. Penrose, and D. W. Sciama (Oxford: Clarendon, 1981), 249; cf. Hawking and Penrose, *Nature of Space and Time*, 34–5.

110. Penrose, "Time-Asymmetry," 249.

111. Roger Penrose, *The Road to Reality* (New York: Alfred A. Knopf, 2005), 762–65.

112. For literature see Don N. Page, "Return of the Boltzmann Brains," (November 15, 2006), http://arXiv:hep-th/0611158. See especially Andrei Linde, "Sinks in the Landscape, Boltzmann Brains, and the Cosmological Constant Problem," http://arXiv:hep-th/0611043 and the articles by Dyson, et al., by Bousso and Freivogel, and by Banks cited below.

one member of an ensemble of worlds. Since that seems crazy, that fact strongly disconfirms the hypothesis that there is a multiverse old enough and big enough to have evolved sufficient volume to account for our low entropy condition's appearing by chance.

One might try to avoid the problem by holding that no bubble universe eternally inflates, so that what one theorist calls "respectable, ordinary observers like us" dominate on average. But as Bousso and Freivogel protest, "Such a conclusion would be shocking and is at odds with our current, admittedly crude, understanding of the string landscape."[113] They therefore advise that we avoid the problem by shunning the "global point of view" in favor of a purely local picture of our "causal diamond," that is, the spacetime patch which an observer can causally influence and be influenced by. "In the local picture, the causal diamond is all there is. No-one can go and probe the exponentially large regions allegedly created by the cosmological expansion, so we do not consider them to be part of reality."[114] Taken as serious metaphysics, one can only regard this proposal as an outrageous example of Verificationism at work. Our inability to probe areas outside our causal diamond gives absolutely no warrant for thinking that these regions are unreal and therefore cosmically irrelevant.[115] Moreover, regarding the wider universe as literally unreal would be to give up the multiverse hypothesis, so that we are right back where we started in trying to explain our observed disequilibrium!

By contrast, if we postulate the finitude of past time and space, such problems are avoided.[116] The reason for the observed disequilibrium state is that spacetime

113. R. Bousso and B. Freivogel, "A paradox in the global description of the multiverse," http://arXiv: hep-th/0610132, 6.

114. Ibid., 7.

115. Even on the local point of view we still face the problem of the Poincaré recurrences (n. 108). Dyson, Kleban, and Susskind recognize that the fatal weakness of the hypothesis that our observable universe is the result of such a chance recurrence is that there are "far more probable ways of creating livable ('anthropically acceptable') environments" than those that begin in a low entropy condition. Susskind thinks that the recurrence problems can be avoided because the bubble universes decay into terminal states in which life can never again arise before the recurrences have time to take place. But Banks points out that the problem of the Boltzmann Brains remains unresolved: "The real prediction is that the dominant form of intelligent life in the DKS universe is a form created spontaneously with knowledge of a spurious history, which lives just long enough to realize that its memories are faulty. . . . The DKS model . . . appears to founder on the bizarre phenomenon of Boltzmann's brain" (T. Banks, "Entropy and Initial Conditions in Cosmology," http://arXiv-hep-th/0701146 v1 [January 1, 2007], 16, 31).

116. Dyson, Kleban, and Susskind respond to such a suggestion as follows: "Another possibility is that an unknown agent intervened in the evolution and for reasons of its own restarted the universe in the state of low entropy characterizing inflation. However, even this does not rid the theory of the pesky recurrences. Only the first occurrence would evolve in a way that would be consistent with usual expectations" (Dyson, Kleban, and Susskind, "Disturbing Implications of a Cosmological Constant," 20–21). But so saying, they have misconstrued the hypothesis. The hypothesis was not of an external agent which "restarted" the universe but of "an external agent which *starts the system out* in a specific low entropy state" (ibid., 4). On such a hypothesis "some unknown agent initially started the inflation high up on its potential, and the rest is history" (Ibid., 2). On this hypothesis the recurrence problems do even not arise. By contrast, Dyson, Kleban, and Susskind are finally driven to suggest that "perhaps the only reasonable conclusion is that we

had an absolute beginning in a low entropy condition a finite time ago and is on its way toward states of increasing disorder.

In any case it is now widely acknowledged that a future-eternal inflationary universe, which constitutes the *sine qua non* for the multiverse proposal, cannot be past-eternal. Linde, you'll recall, once proposed that a model of the universe which is eternally inflating toward the future might also be extended infinitely into the past, but the Borde-Guth-Vilenkin Theorem closed the door on that possibility. The attempt to revive the Boltzmann hypothesis thus relies upon a mechanism which itself requires the finitude of the past and so a beginning of time and space.

Summary

Thermodynamics implies that the universe had a beginning. In a certain respect, the evidence of thermodynamics is even more impressive than the evidence afforded by the expansion of the universe. For while an accurate physical description of the universe prior to the Planck time remains and perhaps always will remain unknown, thereby affording room for speculations aimed at averting the origin of time and space implied by the expanding cosmos, no such uncertainty attends the laws of thermodynamics and their application. Indeed, thermodynamics is so well established that this field is virtually a closed science.[117] Even though we may not like it, concludes Davies, we must say on the basis of the thermodynamic properties of the universe that the universe's energy was somehow simply "put in" at the creation as an initial condition.[118] Prior to the creation, says Davies, the universe simply did not exist.[119]

THE UNIVERSE HAS A CAUSE

On the basis of the four arguments for the finitude of the past, we have good grounds for affirming the second premise of the *kalām* cosmological argument, that *the universe began to exist*. From the first premise—that *whatever begins to exist has a cause*—and the second premise, it follows logically that *the universe has a cause*. This conclusion ought to stagger us, to fill us with awe, for it means that the universe was brought into existence by *something* which is greater than and beyond it.

---

do not live in a world with a true cosmological constant" (ibid., 21), a desperate hypothesis which flies in the face of the evidence and fails in any case to address the global problem.

117. One recalls Eddington's remark: "The second law of thermodynamics holds, I think, the supreme position among the laws of Nature. If someone points out to you that your pet theory of the universe is in disagreement with Maxwell's equations—then so much the worse for Maxwell's equations. If it is found to be contradicted by observation, well, these experimentalists do bungle things sometimes. But if your theory is found to be against the second law of thermodynamics I can give you no hope; there is nothing for it but collapse in deepest humiliation." Arthur S. Eddington, *The Nature of the Physical World* (New York: Macmillan), 74.

118. P. C. W. Davies, *The Physics of Time Asymmetry* (London: Surrey University Press, 1974), 104.

119. My thanks to James Sinclair for his comments on the section concerning scientific arguments for the universe's beginning.

Or does it? Dennett, as we have seen, agrees that the universe must have a cause of its beginning. But, he claims, the cause of the universe is itself; the universe brought itself into being! Dennett writes:

> What does need its origin explained is the concrete Universe itself, and as Hume . . . long ago asked: Why not stop at the material world? It . . . does perform a version of the ultimate bootstrapping trick; it creates itself *ex nihilo*. Or at any rate out of something that is well-nigh indistinguishable from nothing at all.[120]

Here Dennett spoils his radical idea by waffling at the end: maybe the universe did not create itself out of nothing but at least out of something well-nigh indistinguishable from nothing. This caveat evinces a lack of appreciation of the metaphysical chasm between being and nothingness. There is no third thing between being and non-being; if anything at all exists, however ethereal, it is something and therefore not nothing. So what could this mysterious something be? Dennett does not tell us. In fact, he seems somewhat impatient with the question. He complains:

> This leads in various arcane directions, into the strange precincts of string theory and probability fluctuations and the like, at one extreme, and into ingenious nitpicking about the meaning of "cause" at the other. Unless you have a taste for mathematics and theoretical physics on the one hand, or the niceties of scholastic logic on the other, you are not apt to find any of this compelling, or even fathomable.[121]

How strange that Dennett, who fancies himself, unlike Christian dullards, to be among the "brights," should indict an argument because it appeals only to the inquisitive and the intelligent! In any case, the appeal of the argument is irrelevant; if even Dennett's complaint were correct, it constitutes at best a piece of friendly, atheistic advice to believers about the limited utility of the *kalām* cosmological argument in evangelism. We can thank Professor Dennett for his advice, while still demanding an account of the origin of the universe.

The best sense I can make of Dennett's suggestion is to construe it as an endorsement of a model of quantum creation such as is offered by his Tufts University colleague Alexander Vilenkin. It will be recalled that Vilenkin equates the initial state of the universe explanatorily prior to quantum tunneling with nothingness. Unfortunately, we saw that this equivalence is clearly mistaken (perhaps Dennett's waffling betrays an understanding of this fact). Thus, on Vilenkin's model we are still left wondering what caused the initial state of the universe to come into being.

Dennett's answer is: the universe, in the ultimate boot-strapping trick, created itself! Dennett's bold hypothesis would at least help to resolve the objection that if something can come into being out of nothing, then it becomes inexplicable why anything and everything does not come into being out of nothing. On Dennett's

---

120. Dennett, *Breaking the Spell*, 244.
121. Ibid., 242.

view the coming of the universe into being is causally constrained: it creates itself. Of course, that still leaves us wondering why other things, say, bicycles and hot dogs and wombats, do not have the same capacity; but never mind. As Aquinas argued, self-creation is metaphysically absurd, since in order to cause itself to come into being, the universe would have to already exist. One is thus caught in a vicious circle. Aquinas made the point with respect to an eternally existing universe, but his argument is even more forceful with respect to a universe with a beginning. For in the latter case the universe must be not only explanatorily prior to itself but even, it seems, chronologically prior to itself, which is incoherent. Thus, Dennett's imaginative suggestion is wholly untenable.

The Nature of the First Cause

It therefore follows that the universe has an external cause. Conceptual analysis enables us to recover a number of striking properties which must be possessed by such an ultra-mundane being. For as the cause of space and time, this entity must transcend space and time and therefore exist atemporally and non-spatially (at least without the universe).[122] This transcendent cause must therefore be changeless and immaterial, since timelessness entails changelessness, and changelessness implies immateriality. Such a cause must be beginningless and uncaused, at least in the sense of lacking any antecedent causal conditions, since there cannot be an infinite regress of causes. Ockham's Razor (the principle which states that we should not multiply causes beyond necessity) will shave away further causes. This entity must be unimaginably powerful, since it created the universe without any material cause.

Finally, and most remarkably, such a transcendent cause is plausibly to be taken to be personal. Three reasons can be given for this conclusion. First, as Richard Swinburne points out, there are two types of causal explanation: scientific explanations in terms of laws and initial conditions and personal explanations in terms of agents and their volitions.[123] For example, if I come into the kitchen and find the kettle boiling, and I ask Jan, "Why is the kettle boiling?" she might answer, "The heat of the flame is being conducted via the copper bottom of the kettle to the water, increasing the kinetic energy of the water molecules, such that they vibrate so violently that they break the surface tension of the water and are thrown off in the form of steam." Or she might say, "I put it on to make a cup of tea. Would you like some?" The first provides a scientific explanation, the second a personal explanation. Each is a perfectly legitimate form of explanation; indeed, in certain contexts it would be wholly inappropriate to give one rather than the other. Now a first state of the universe *cannot* have a scientific explanation, since there is noth-

---

122. Or, alternatively, the cause exists changelessly in an undifferentiated time in which temporal intervals cannot be distinguished. On this view God existed literally before creation but there was no moment, say, one hour or one million years before creation. For discussion of this alternative see my *Time and Eternity*, chap. 6.

123. Richard Swinburne, *The Existence of God*, rev. ed. (Oxford: Clarendon, 1991), 32–48.

ing before it, and therefore it cannot be accounted for in terms of laws operating on initial conditions. It can only be accounted for in terms of an agent and his volitions, a personal explanation.

Second, the personhood of the cause of the universe is implied by its time-lessness and immateriality. The only entities we know of which can possess such properties are either minds or abstract objects, like numbers. But abstract objects do not stand in causal relations. Indeed, their acausal nature is definitive for abstract objects; that is why we call them abstract.[124] Numbers, for example, cannot cause anything. Therefore, the transcendent cause of the origin of the universe must be of the order of mind.

Third, this same conclusion is also implied by the fact that we have in this case the origin of a temporal effect from a timeless cause. We've concluded that the beginning of the universe was the effect of a first cause. By the nature of the case, that cause cannot have any beginning of its existence or any prior cause. Nor can there have been any changes in this cause, either in its nature or operations, prior to the beginning of the universe. It just exists changelessly without beginning, and a finite time ago it brought the universe into existence. Now this is exceedingly odd. The cause is in some sense eternal and yet the effect which it produced is not eternal but began to exist a finite time ago. How can this be? If the necessary and sufficient conditions for the production of the effect are eternal, then why isn't the effect eternal? How can all the causal conditions sufficient for the production of the effect be changelessly existent and yet the effect not also be existent along with the cause? How can the cause exist without the effect?

One might say that the cause came to exist or changed in some way just prior to the first event. But then the cause's beginning or changing would be the first event, and we must ask all over again for its cause. And this cannot go on forever, for we know that a beginningless series of events cannot exist. There must be an absolutely first event, before which there was no change, no previous event. We know that this first event must have been caused. The question is: How can a first event come to exist if the cause of that event exists changelessly and eternally? Why isn't the effect co-eternal with its cause?

To illustrate: Let's say the cause of water's freezing is subzero temperatures. If the temperature were eternally below zero degrees Centigrade, then any water around would be eternally frozen. If the cause exists eternally, the effect must also exist eternally. But this seems to imply that if the cause of the universe existed eternally, the universe would also have existed eternally. And this we know to be false.

One way to see the difficulty is by reflecting on the different types of causal rela-tions. In event/event causation, one event causes another. For example, the brick's striking the window pane causes the pane to shatter. This kind of causal relation clearly involves a beginning of the effect in time, since it is a relation between events which

---

124. See discussion in Paul Copan and William Lane Craig, *Creation out of Nothing: A Biblical, Philo-sophical, and Scientific Exploration* (Grand Rapids, Mich.: Baker, 2004), 168–70.

occur at specific times. In state/state causation one state of affairs causes another state of affairs to exist. For example, some wood's floating on water is caused by the displaced water's having a certain weight. In this sort of causal relation, the effect need not have a beginning: the wood could theoretically be floating eternally on the water. If the wood begins to float on the water, then this will be a case of event/event causation: the wood's beginning to float is the result of its being thrown into the water. Now the difficulty that arises in the case of the cause of the beginning of the universe is that we seem to have a peculiar case of state/event causation: the cause is a timeless state but the effect is an event that occurred at a specific moment in the finite past. Such state/event causation doesn't seem to make sense, since a state sufficient for the existence of its effect should have a state as its effect.

There seems to be only one way out of this dilemma, and that is to say that the cause of the universe's beginning is a personal agent who freely chooses to create a universe in time. Philosophers call this type of causation "agent causation," and because the agent is free, he can initiate new effects by freely bringing about conditions which were not previously present. For example, a man sitting changelessly from eternity could freely will to stand up; thus, a temporal effect arises from an eternally existing agent. Similarly, a finite time ago a Creator endowed with free will could have freely brought the world into being at that moment. In this way, the Creator could exist changelessly and eternally but choose to create the world in time. By "choose" one need not mean that the Creator changes his mind about the decision to create, but that he freely and eternally intends to create a world with a beginning. By exercising his causal power, he therefore brings it about that a world with a beginning comes to exist.[125] So the cause is eternal, but the effect is not. In this way, then, it is possible for the temporal universe to have come to exist from an eternal cause: through the free will of a personal Creator.

On the basis of a conceptual analysis of the conclusion implied by the *kalām* cosmological argument, we may therefore infer that a personal Creator of the universe exists, who is uncaused, beginningless, changeless, immaterial, timeless, spaceless, and unimaginably powerful. This, as Thomas Aquinas was wont to remark, is what everybody means by "God."

Objections

Now certain thinkers have objected to the intelligibility of this conclusion. For example, Adolf Grünbaum, a prominent philosopher of space and time and a vociferous critic of theism, has marshaled a whole troop of objections against inferring God as the Creator of the universe.[126] As these are very typical, a brief review of his objections should be quite helpful.

---

125. Such an exercise of causal power plausibly brings God into time, if he was not temporal already. For more on God's relationship to time, see my response to Grünbaum's final objection below.

126. Adolf Grünbaum, "The Pseudo-Problem of Creation in Physical Cosmology," in *Physical Cosmology and Philosophy*, ed. John Leslie, Philosophical Topics (New York: Macmillan, 1990), 92–112.

Grünbaum's objections fall into three groups. Group I seeks to cast doubt upon the concept of "cause" in the argument: (1) When we say that everything has a cause, we use the word "cause" to mean something that transforms previously existing materials from one state to another. But when we infer that the universe has a cause, we must mean by "cause" something that creates its effect out of nothing. Since these two meanings of "cause" are not the same, the argument is guilty of equivocation and is thus invalid. (2) It does not follow from the necessity of there being a cause that the cause of the universe is a conscious agent. (3) It is logically fallacious to infer that there is a *single* conscious agent who created the universe.

But these objections do not seem to present any insuperable difficulties: (1) The univocal concept of "cause" employed throughout the argument is the concept of something which brings about or produces its effects. Whether this production involves transformation of already existing materials or creation out of nothing is an incidental question. Thus, the charge of equivocation is groundless. (2) The personhood of the cause does not follow from the two premises of the cosmological argument proper, but rather from a conceptual analysis of the notion of a first cause of the beginning of the universe, as we have seen. (3) The inference to a single cause of the origin of the universe seems justified in light of the principle, commonly accepted in science, that one should not multiply causes beyond necessity. One is justified in inferring only causes such as are necessary to explain the effect in question; positing any more would be gratuitous. Since the universe is a single effect originating in the Big Bang event, we have no grounds for inferring a plurality of causes.

The objections of Group II relate the notion of causality to the temporal series of events: (1) Causality is logically compatible with an infinite, beginningless series of events. (2) If everything has a cause of its existence, then the cause of the universe must also have a cause of its existence.

Both of these objections, however, seem to be based on misunderstandings. (1) It is not the concept of causality which is incompatible with an infinite series of past events. Rather the incompatibility, as we have seen, is between the notion of an actually infinite number of things and the series of past events. The fact that causality has nothing to do with it may be seen by reflecting on the fact that the philosophical arguments for the beginning of the universe would work even if the events were all spontaneous, causally unconnected events. (2) The argument does not presuppose that everything has a cause. Rather the operative causal principle is that *whatever begins to exist has a cause*. Something that exists eternally and, hence, without a beginning would not need to have a cause. This is not special pleading for God, since the atheist has always maintained the same thing about the universe: it is beginningless and uncaused. The difference between these two hypotheses is that the atheistic view has now been shown to be untenable.

Group III objections are aimed at the alleged claim that creation from nothing surpasses all understanding: (1) If creation out of nothing is incomprehensible, then it is irrational to believe in such a doctrine. (2) An incomprehensible doctrine cannot explain anything.

But with regard to (1), creation from nothing is not incomprehensible in Grünbaum's sense. By "incomprehensible" Grünbaum appears to mean "unintelligible" or "meaningless." But the statement that a finite time ago a transcendent cause brought the universe into being out of nothing is clearly a meaningful statement, not mere gibberish, as is evident from the very fact that we are debating it. We may not understand *how* the cause brought the universe into being out of nothing; but then it is even more incomprehensible, in this sense, how the universe could have popped into being out of nothing without *any* cause, material or productive. One cannot avert the necessity of a cause by positing an absurdity. (2) The doctrine, being an intelligible statement, obviously does constitute a purported explanation of the origin of the universe. It may be a metaphysical rather than a scientific explanation, but it is no less an explanation for that.

Grünbaum has one final objection against inferring a cause of the origin of the universe: the cause of the Big Bang can be neither *after* the Big Bang (since backward causation is impossible) nor *before* the Big Bang (since time begins at or after the Big Bang). Therefore, the universe's beginning to exist cannot have a cause.[127] But this argument pretty clearly confronts us with a false dilemma. For why couldn't God's creating the universe be *simultaneous* (or coincident) with the Big Bang? On the view I've defended at length elsewhere, God may be conceived to exist timelessly (or in an undifferentiated time) without the universe and in time from the moment of creation. Perhaps an analogy from physical cosmology will be illuminating. The initial Big Bang singularity is not considered to be part of physical time, but to constitute a boundary to time. Nevertheless, it is causally connected to the universe. In an analogous way, we could say that God's timeless eternity is, as it were, a boundary of time which is causally, but not temporally, prior to the origin of the universe. It seems to me, therefore, that it is not only coherent but also plausible in light of the *kalām* cosmological argument that God, insofar as he exists changelessly alone without creation, is timeless and that he enters time at the moment of creation in virtue of his causal relation to the temporal universe. Given that time began to exist, the most plausible view of God's relationship to time is that he is timeless without creation and temporal subsequent to creation.

None of Grünbaum's objections, therefore, seems to undermine the credibility of the *kalām* cosmological argument for God as the Personal Creator of the universe.

We thus have so far two good arguments for the existence of God: the Leibnizian cosmological argument and the *kalām* cosmological argument. But there's more to come!

---

127. Adolf Grünbaum, "Pseudo-Creation of the Big Bang," *Nature* 344 (1990): 821–22.

4

The Existence of God (2)

Teleological Argument

The teleological argument for God's existence has come roaring back into prominence in recent years. The explanatory adequacy of the neo-Darwinian mechanisms of random mutation and natural selection with respect to observed biological complexity has been sharply challenged, as advances in microbiology have served to disclose the breathtaking complexity of the micro-machinery of a single cell, not to speak of higher level organisms. The field of origin of life studies is in turmoil, as all the old scenarios of the chemical origin of life in the primordial soup have collapsed, and no new, better theory is on the horizon. And the scientific community has been stunned by its discovery of how complex and sensitive a nexus of initial conditions must be given in order for the universe even to permit the origin and evolution of intelligent life.

Undoubtedly, it is this last discovery which has most served to reopen the books on the teleological argument. Due to sociological factors surrounding the neo-Darwinian theory of biological evolution, captured most poignantly in the public image of the Scopes trial, biologists have been for the most part extremely loath so much as even to contemplate a design hypothesis, lest they let a creationist foot in the door; but cosmologists, largely untainted by this controversy, have been much more open to entertain seriously the alternative of design. The discovery of cosmic fine-tuning for intelligent life has led many scientists to conclude that such a delicate balance of physical constants and quantities as is requisite for life cannot be dismissed as mere coincidence but cries out for some sort of explanation.

Cosmic Fine-Tuning

What is meant by "fine-tuning"? The physical laws of nature, when given mathematical expression, contain various constants (such as the gravitational constant) whose values are not determined by the laws themselves; a universe governed by such laws might be characterized by any of a wide range of values for these constants. Take, for example, a simple law like Newton's law of gravity $F = Gm_1m_2/r^2$. According to this law, the gravitational force F between two objects depends not just on their respective masses m_1 and m_2 and the distance between them r, but also on a certain quantity G which is constant regardless of the masses and distance. The law doesn't determine what value G actually has. In addition to these constants, moreover, there are certain arbitrary physical quantities, such as the entropy level, which are simply put into the universe as boundary conditions on which the laws of nature operate. They are therefore also independent of the laws. By "fine-tuning" one means that small deviations from the actual values of the constants and quantities in question would render the universe life-prohibiting or, alternatively, that the range of life-permitting values is exquisitely narrow in comparison with the range of assumable values.

We can cite various examples of cosmic fine-tuning.[1] The world is conditioned principally by the values of the fundamental constants α (the fine structure constant, or electromagnetic interaction), α_G (gravitation), α_w (the weak force), α_s (the strong force), and m_n/m_e (the ratio between the mass of a proton and the mass of an electron). When one assigns different values to these constants or forces, one discovers that the proportion of observable universes, that is to say, universes capable of supporting intelligent life, is shockingly small. Just a slight variation in some of these values would render life impossible. For example, according to the physicist P. C. W. Davies, changes in either α_G or α_w of only one part in 10^{100} would have prevented a life-permitting universe. In investigating the initial conditions of the Big Bang, one also confronts two arbitrary parameters governing the expansion of the universe: Ω_0, related to the density of the universe, and H_0, related to the speed of the expansion. Observations indicate that at 10^{-43} second after the Big Bang the universe was expanding at a fantastically special rate of speed with a total density close to the critical value on the borderline between recollapse and everlasting expansion. Stephen Hawking estimates that a decrease in the expansion rate of even one part in a hundred thousand million million one second after the Big Bang would have resulted in the universe's recollapse long ago; a similar increase would have precluded the galaxies' condensing out of the expanding matter. At the Planck time, 10^{-43} second after the Big Bang, the density of the universe must have apparently been within about one part in 10^{60} of the critical density at which space

---

1. For discussion of examples of fine-tuning, see John D. Barrow and Frank J. Tipler, *The Anthropic Cosmological Principle* (Oxford: Clarendon, 1986); John Leslie, "The Prerequisites of Life in Our Universe," in *Newton and the New Direction in Science*, ed. G. V. Coyne, M. Heller, J. Zycinski (Vatican: Citta del Vaticano, 1988); Martin Rees, *Just Six Numbers* (New York: Basic, 2000); Robin Collins, *The Well-Tempered Universe* (forthcoming).

is flat. Most theorists today think that this so-called flatness problem has been adequately explained by an early inflationary era in the history of the universe. As we have seen, according to inflationary theory, the energy density of the primordial false vacuum state overwhelmed even the intense gravitational attraction generated by the extremely high matter density of the early universe, causing a super-rapid, or inflationary, expansion, during which the universe grew from atomic proportions to a size larger than the observable universe in a fraction of a microsecond. Because the universe has inflated to such enormous dimensions, space appears to be flat, just as the surface of the Earth appears flat to its tiny surface dwellers. But inflation only serves to raise a new problem: the fine-tuning of the cosmological constant Λ which drives inflation and is responsible for the recently discovered acceleration of the universe's expansion. The cosmological constant is inexplicably fine-tuned to around one part in 10^{120}. Classical cosmology serves to highlight another parameter, S, the entropy per baryon in the universe. The structure of the Big Bang must have been severely constrained in order that thermodynamics as we know it should have arisen. As we have seen, Oxford physicist Roger Penrose calculates that the odds of the special low entropy condition having arisen sheerly by chance in the absence any constraining principles is at least as small as about one part in $10^{10^{(123)}}$ in order for our universe to exist.

Laymen might think that if the constants and quantities had assumed different values, then other forms of life might well have evolved. But this is not the case. By "life" scientists mean that property of organisms to take in food, extract energy from it, grow, adapt to their environment, and reproduce. The point is that in order for the universe to permit life so defined, whatever form organisms might take, the constants and quantities have to be incomprehensibly fine-tuned. In the absence of fine-tuning, not even atomic matter or chemistry would exist, not to speak of planets where life might evolve!

Sometimes people will object that in universes governed by *different* laws of nature, such disastrous consequences might not result from varying the values of the constants and quantities. We needn't deny that possibility. Maybe in a universe governed by different equations, the gravitational constant G could have a greatly different value and yet life still exist. But such universes are irrelevant to the argument. All we need to show is that among possible universes governed by the *same* equations (but having different values of the constants and quantities) as the actual universe, life-permitting universes are extraordinarily improbable. John Leslie gives the following illustration: imagine a solitary fly resting on a large, blank area of the wall. A single shot is fired, and the bullet strikes the fly. Now, even if the rest of the wall outside the blank area is covered with flies, such that a randomly fired bullet would probably hit one, nevertheless it remains highly improbable that a single, randomly fired bullet would strike the solitary fly within the large, blank area. In the same way, we need only concern ourselves with universes governed by the same equations in order to determine the probability of the existence of a life-permitting universe. Thus, although sloppy formulations of the fine-tuning argument are sometimes framed in terms of nature's laws' being fine-tuned, thereby leading to speculations of what universes governed by different laws of nature would be like, the correct formulation concerns universes governed by the same laws of nature as ours, but with different values of the constants and quantities. Because the equations remain the same, we can predict what the world would be like, if, say, the gravitational constant were doubled.

Explaining the Fine-Tuning

In a sense more easy to discern than to articulate this fine-tuning of the universe seems to manifest the presence of a designing intelligence. The inference to design is best thought of, not as an instance of reasoning by analogy (as it is often portrayed), but as a case of inference to the best explanation.[2] Leslie speaks of the need for what he calls a "tidy explanation." A tidy explanation is one that not only explains a certain situation but also reveals in doing so that there is something to be explained. Leslie provides a whole retinue of charming illustrations of tidy explanations at work. Suppose, for example, that Bob is given a new car for his birthday. There are millions of license plate numbers, and it is therefore highly unlikely that Bob would get, say, CHT 4271. Yet that plate on his birthday car would occasion no special interest. But suppose Bob, who was born on August 8, 1949, finds BOB 8849 on the license plate of his birthday car. He would be obtuse if he shrugged this off with the comment, "Well, it had to have *some* license plate number, and any number is equally improbable . . ." But what makes this case different than the other?

An answer has recently been offered by William Dembski in his *The Design Inference*.[3] He furnishes a ten-step Generic Chance Elimination Argument, which delineates the common pattern of reasoning that he believes underlies chance-elimination arguments. Dembski's analysis can be used to formalize what Leslie grasped in an intuitive way. What makes an explanation a tidy one is not simply the fact that the *explanandum* (the thing to be explained) is some improbable event, but the fact that the event also conforms to some independently given pattern, resulting in what Dembski calls "specified complexity." It is this specified complexity (high improbability + an independent pattern) that tips us off to the need for an explanation in terms of more than mere chance.

Regardless of whether one adopts Dembski's analysis of design inferences or some alternative approach,[4] the key to detecting design is to eliminate the two

---

2. See Peter Lipton, *Inference to the Best Explanation* (London: Routledge, 1991).

3. William A. Dembski, *The Design Inference: Eliminating Chance through Small Probabilities,* Cambridge Studies in Probability, Induction, and Decision Theory (Cambridge: Cambridge University Press, 1998).

4. An alternative approach is offered by Robin Collins. He employs Bayes' Theorem to argue that the cosmic fine-tuning is much more probable on the hypothesis of theism than on the hypothesis of a single, atheistic universe and that therefore the evidence of fine-tuning strongly confirms theism over its rival hypothesis.

competing alternatives of physical necessity and chance. Accordingly, a teleological argument appealing to cosmic fine-tuning might be formulated as follows:

1) The fine-tuning of the universe is due to either physical necessity, chance, or design.
2) It is not due to physical necessity or chance.
3) Therefore, it is due to design.

Three Alternative Accounts of Fine-Tuning

Premise (1), properly understood, should not be controversial. Recall that by "fine-tuning" cosmologists do not mean "designed" or "deliberately adjusted to high specification" or some such intentional expression; that would make the argument question-begging. Rather "fine-tuning" is a neutral expression that has to do with the constants and quantities' being just right for the existence of intelligent life. There is little doubt that the universe is fine-tuned in this neutral sense. Even if some of the evidence of fine-tuning should prove to be mistaken, the multiplicity of lines of evidence for the fine-tuning of certain constants and quantities as well as the number and variety of the constants and quantities that exhibit fine-tuning give ample grounds for thinking that fine-tuning is here to stay and cannot be just written off as a colossal blunder on the part of the scientific community.[5]

Moreover, premise (1) seems to exhaust the alternatives. If someone can think of another alternative, then he is free to suggest it. In the absence of a specific suggestion, however, we are justified in thinking that (1) includes all the alternatives, since necessity and chance seem to exhaust the alternatives to design.

The soundness of the argument will therefore depend on the plausibility of premise (2).

Physical Necessity

Can the cosmic fine-tuning be plausibly attributed to physical necessity? According to this alternative, the constants and quantities must have the values they do, and there was really no chance or little chance of the universe's not being life-permitting. Now, on the face of it, this alternative seems extraordinarily implausible. It requires us to believe that a life-prohibiting universe is virtually physically impossible. But surely it does seem possible. If the primordial matter and anti-matter had been differently proportioned, if the universe had expanded just a little more slowly, if the entropy of the universe were marginally greater, any of these adjustments and

---

5. Ernan McMullin concludes, "It seems safe to say that later theory, no matter how different it may be, will turn up approximately the same . . . numbers. And the numerous constraints that have to be imposed on these numbers . . . seem both too specific and too numerous to evaporate entirely. . . . A dozen or more constraints have been pointed out. . . . Might they all be replaced? . . . It surely seems a very long shot." Ernan McMullin, "Anthropic Explanation in Cosmology," paper delivered at the conference "God and Physical Cosmology," University of Notre Dame, January 30–February 1, 2003.

more would have prevented a life-permitting universe, yet all seem perfectly possible physically. The person who maintains that the universe must be life-permitting is taking a radical line which requires strong proof. But there is none; this alternative is simply put forward as a bare possibility.

Sometimes physicists do speak of a yet to be discovered Theory of Everything (T.O.E.), but such nomenclature is, like so many of the colorful names given to scientific theories, quite misleading. A T.O.E. actually has the limited goal of providing a unified theory of the four fundamental forces of nature, to reduce gravity, electromagnetism, the strong force, and the weak force to one fundamental force carried by one fundamental particle. Such a theory will, we hope, explain why these four forces take the values they do, but it will not even attempt to explain literally everything.

For example, in the most promising candidate for a T.O.E. to date, super-string theory or M-Theory, the physical universe must be 11-dimensional, but why the universe should possess just that number of dimensions is not addressed by the theory. Moreover, M-Theory fails to predict uniquely our universe. Stephen Hawking recently addressed this question at a cosmology conference at the University of California, Davis. Notice the alternative answers which he identifies to the question he poses:

> Does string theory, or M theory, predict the distinctive features of our universe, like a spatially flat four dimensional expanding universe with small fluctuations, and the standard model of particle physics? Most physicists would rather believe string theory uniquely predicts the universe, than the alternatives. These are that the initial state of the universe, is prescribed by an outside agency, code named God. Or that there are many universes, and our universe is picked out by the anthropic principle.[6]

These represent precisely the three alternatives laid out in premise (1). Hawking argues that the first alternative, physical necessity, is a vain hope: "M theory cannot predict the parameters of the standard model. Obviously, the values of the parameters we measure must be compatible with the development of life. . . . But within the anthropically allowed range, the parameters can have any values. So much for string theory predicting the fine structure constant." He wrapped up by saying,

> Even when we understand the ultimate theory, it won't tell us much about how the universe began. It cannot predict the dimensions of spacetime, the gauge group, or other parameters of the low energy effective theory. . . . It won't determine how this energy is divided between conventional matter, and a cosmological constant, or quintessence. . . . So to come back to the question. . . . Does string theory predict

---

6. S. W. Hawking, "Cosmology from the Top Down," paper presented at the Davis Cosmic Inflation Meeting, U. C. Davis, May 29, 2003.

the state of the universe? The answer is that it does not. It allows a vast landscape of possible universes, in which we occupy an anthropically permitted location.

In fact, this idea of a "cosmic landscape" predicted by string theory has become something of a phenom in its own right.[7] It turns out that string theory allows around 10^{500} different possible universes governed by the present laws of nature, so that the theory does not at all render the observed values of the constants and quantities physically necessary. Moreover, even though there may be a huge number of possible universes lying within the life-permitting region of the cosmic landscape, nevertheless that life-permitting region will be unfathomably tiny compared to the entire landscape, so that the existence of a life-permitting universe is fantastically improbable.[8] Indeed, given the multiplicity of constants that require fine-tuning, it is far from clear that 10^{500} possible universes is enough to guarantee that even one life-permitting world will appear by chance in the landscape![9]

All this has been said with respect to the constants alone; there is still nothing to explain the arbitrary quantities put in as boundary conditions. Davies comments,

> Even if the laws of physics were unique, it doesn't follow that the physical universe itself is unique. . . . the laws of physics must be augmented by cosmic initial conditions. . . . There is nothing in present ideas about "laws of initial conditions" remotely to suggest that their consistency with the laws of physics would imply uniqueness. Far from it. . . . It seems, then, that the physical universe does not have to be the way it is: it could have been otherwise.[10]

7. See Leonard Susskind, *The Cosmic Landscape: String Theory and the Illusion of Intelligent Design* (New York: Little, Brown, & Co., 2006). Susskind apparently believes that the discovery of the cosmic landscape undercuts the argument for design, when in fact precisely the opposite is true. Susskind doesn't seem to appreciate that the 10^{500} worlds in the cosmic landscape are not real but merely possible universes consistent with M-Theory. To find purchase for the anthropic principle mentioned by Hawking as the third alternative, one needs a plurality of real universes, which string theory alone does not provide.

8. If only one universe out of 10^{120} has the life-permitting value of the cosmological constant, then, given 10^{500} possible universes, the number of universes with the life-permitting value will be only $10^{500} \div 10^{120} = 10^{380}$. To the novice this may sound as if most of the worlds are then life-permitting, when in fact 10^{380} is an inconceivably small fraction of 10^{500}, so that almost all of the possible universes will be life-prohibiting. To see the point, imagine that we have a million possible universes and the odds of a life-permitting universe are one out of a hundred. So the total number of life-permitting universes will be 1,000,000 $\div$ 100 = 10,000. So the total number of life-permitting universes is $10^6 \div 10^2 = 10^4$. One sees that 10^4 is a tiny fraction of 10^6, for only 10,000 out of the one million worlds are life-permitting, while a whopping 990,000 are life-prohibiting.

9. For example, since the values of at least some of the constants are independent, we must multiply the individual probabilities of the constants to find the probability of two constants' both being finely tuned together. So if the odds of the cosmological constant's having the value it does is 1 out of 10^{120} and the odds of the gravitational constant's having the value it does is 1 out of 10^{100}, then their joint probability will be one chance out of $10^{120+100} = 10^{220}$. If we keep adding constants until we get a life-permitting universe, before too long we'll have run out of possible universes and so will have exhausted all the probabilistic resources!

10. Paul Davies, *The Mind of God* (New York: Simon & Schuster, 1992), 169. I take Davies to mean by the laws of physics the laws with the actual values of the constants. Otherwise he is confusing there being different values of the constants with there being different laws.

The extraordinarily low entropy condition of the early universe would be a good example of an arbitrary quantity which seems to have just been put in at the creation as an initial condition. There is no reason to think that showing every constant and quantity to be physically necessary is anything more than a pipedream.

Chance

Considerations of Probability

What, then, of the alternative of chance? One may seek to eliminate this hypothesis either by appealing to the specified complexity of cosmic fine-tuning or by arguing that the fine-tuning is significantly more probable on design (theism) than on the chance hypothesis (atheism). It is sometimes objected that it is meaningless to speak of the probability of our finely tuned universe's existing because there is, after all, only one universe. But the following illustration from John Barrow clarifies the sense in which a life-permitting universe is improbable. Take a sheet of paper and place upon it a red dot. That dot represents our universe. Now alter slightly one or more of the finely tuned constants and physical quantities which have been the focus of our attention. As a result we have a description of another universe, which we may represent as a new dot in the proximity of the first. If that new set of constants and quantities describes a life-permitting universe, make it a red dot; if it describes a universe which is life-prohibiting, make it a blue dot. Now repeat the procedure arbitrarily many times until the sheet is filled with dots. What one winds up with is a sea of blue with only a few pin-points of red. That is the sense in which it is overwhelmingly improbable that the universe should be life-permitting. There are simply a vastly greater proportion of more life-prohibiting universes in our local area of possible universes than there are life-permitting universes.

It might be objected that we do not know if all these possible universes are equally probable. This amounts, in effect, to the claim that the actual range of possible values for a certain constant or quantity may be very narrow. But even if that were the case, when one has many variables requiring fine-tuning, the probability of a life-permitting universe's existing is still very small. Moreover, in the absence of any physical reason to think that the values are constrained, we are justified in assuming a principle of indifference to the effect that the probability of our universe's existing will be the same as the probability of any other universe which is represented on our sheet.

Barrow's illustration also helps to avoid a possible misunderstanding. Some people say that the existence of any universe is equally improbable and yet some universe must exist. The fine-tuning of the universe is said to be like a lottery in which any individual's winning is fantastically and equally improbable but which some individual has to win. Just as the winner of such a lottery should not conclude that the lottery must be rigged just because he won, so we should not conclude that there is a cosmic designer just because our universe exists. The fallacy in this reasoning is that we are not trying to explain the existence of our universe; rather it is the existence of a life-permitting universe that demands explanation. We're not asking why our dot exists but why a red dot exists. Thus, the proper lottery analogy to the fine-tuning of the universe is a lottery in which a single white ball is mixed into a billion billion billion black balls, and a ball is then selected randomly from the collection. True, any ball that rolls down the chute will be fantastically and equally improbable; nevertheless, it is overwhelmingly more probable that whichever ball rolls down the chute, it will be black rather than white. Similarly, the existence of any particular universe is equally improbable; but it is incomprehensibly more probable that whichever universe exists will be life-prohibiting rather than life-permitting. It is the enormous, specified improbability of a life-permitting universe that presents the hurdle for the chance hypothesis.

The Anthropic Principle

Some theorists have tried to support the chance hypothesis by appeal to the so-called Anthropic Principle. As formulated by Barrow and Tipler, the Anthropic Principle states that any observed properties of the universe which may at first appear astonishingly improbable can only be seen in their true perspective after we have accounted for the fact that certain properties could not be observed by us, since we can only observe properties which are compatible with our own existence. The implication is that we ought not to be surprised at observing the universe to be as it is and therefore no explanation of its fine-tuning need be sought.

The argument is, however, based on confusion. Barrow and Tipler have confused the true claim

A. If observers who have evolved within a universe observe its constants and quantities, it is highly probable that they will observe them to be fine-tuned for their existence.

with the false claim

A′. It is highly probable that a universe exist which is finely tuned for the evolution of observers within it.

An observer who has evolved within the universe should regard it as highly probable that he will find the constants and quantities of the universe fine-tuned for his existence; but he should not infer that it is therefore highly probable that such a fine-tuned universe exist. Leslie gives the illustration of your being dragged before a firing squad of one hundred trained marksmen to be executed. The command is given: "Ready! Aim! Fire!" You hear the deafening roar of the guns. And then you observe that you're still alive, that all the one hundred trained marksmen missed! Now what do you conclude? "I really shouldn't be surprised at the improbability of their all missing because if they hadn't all missed, then I wouldn't be here to be surprised about it. Since I am here, there's nothing to be explained!" Of course not! While it's correct that you shouldn't be surprised that you don't observe that you are dead (since if you were dead, you could not observe the fact), nevertheless, it doesn't follow that you shouldn't be surprised that you do observe that you are alive. In view of the enormous improbability of the marksmen's all missing, you ought to be very surprised that you observe that you are alive and so suspect that more than chance alone is involved, even though you're not surprised that you don't observe that you are dead.

The Many Worlds Hypothesis

Theorists now recognize that the Anthropic Principle can legitimately be employed only when it is conjoined to a Many Worlds Hypothesis, according to which a World Ensemble of concrete universes exists, actualizing a wide range of possibilities. The Many Worlds Hypothesis is essentially an effort on the part of partisans of the chance hypothesis to multiply their probabilistic resources in order to reduce the improbability of the occurrence of fine-tuning. The very fact that otherwise sober scientists must resort to such a remarkable hypothesis is a sort of backhanded compliment to the design hypothesis. It shows that the fine-tuning does cry out for explanation. But is the Many Worlds Hypothesis as plausible as the design hypothesis?

If the Many Worlds Hypothesis is to commend itself as a plausible hypothesis, then some plausible mechanism for generating the many worlds needs to be to be explained. The best shot at providing a plausible mechanism comes from inflationary cosmology, which is often employed to defend the view that our universe is but one domain (or "pocket universe") within a vastly larger universe, or multiverse. Vilenkin is one who vigorously champions the idea that we live in a multiverse. At the heart of Vilenkin's view is the theory of future-eternal, or everlasting, inflation. In order to ensure that inflation will go on forever, Vilenkin hypothesizes that the primordial scalar fields determining the energy density and evolution of the false vacuum are characterized by a certain slope which issues in a false vacuum expanding so rapidly that, as it decays into pockets of true vacuum, the "island universes" thereby generated in this sea of false vacuum, though themselves expanding at enormous rates, cannot keep up with the expansion of the false vacuum and so find themselves increasingly separated with time. Moreover, each island is subdivided into subdomains which Vilenkin calls O-regions, each constituting an observable universe bounded by an event horizon. Despite the fact that the multiverse is finite and geometrically closed, the false vacuum will, according to the theory, go on expanding forever. New pockets of true vacuum will continue to form in the gaps between the island universes and become themselves isolated worlds.

Now at this point Vilenkin executes a nifty piece of legerdemain. As the island universes expand, their central regions eventually grow dark and barren, while stars are forming at their ever-expanding perimeters. We should think of the decay of false vacuum to true vacuum going on at the islands' expanding boundaries as multiple Big Bangs. From the global perspective of the inflating multiverse, these Big Bangs occur successively, as the island boundaries grow with time (Fig. 4.1).

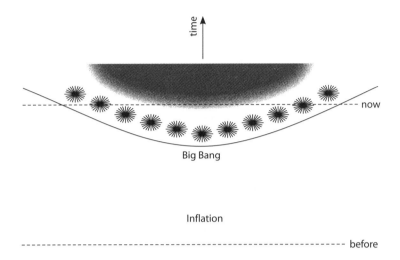

Fig. 4.1: A global perspective on an island universe. As the island expands with time, its central region grows dark and cold in accordance with the second law of thermodynamics, while at its perimeter new star-producing regions are constantly being formed. These regions are causally unconnected and so constitute different O-regions, or observable universes, within the island universe, each traceable back to a Big Bang event.

In the global time of the multiverse, each island is at any time finite in size though constantly growing. Now comes the sleight of hand. When we consider the internal, cosmic time of each island universe, each observer will trace it back to an initial Big Bang event. We can then string together these various Big Bang events as occurring simultaneously (Fig. 4.2). Big Bangs which will occur in the global future are, from the internal point of view, to be regarded as present. As a result, the infinite, temporal series of successive Big Bangs is converted into an infinite, spatial array of simultaneous Big Bangs. Hence, from the internal point of view each island universe is infinite in extent. As Vilenkin puts it, "The infinity of time in one view is thus transformed into the infinity of space in the other."[11]

Vilenkin's deft transformation seems to presuppose a static or B-Theory of time[12] or, as it is sometimes called, four-dimensionalism or spacetime realism. For if temporal becoming is an objective feature of reality, then the global fu-

11. Alex Vilenkin, *Many Worlds in One: The Search for Other Universes* (New York: Hill and Wang, 2006), 99.

12. Recall our distinguishing two views of time on 123.

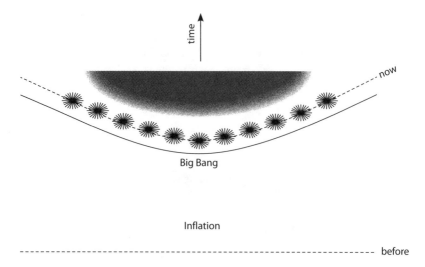

Fig. 4.2: An internal perspective on an island universe. The Big Bangs in which the various O-regions originate will be regarded as occurring simultaneously. Thus, the infinity of time on the global perspective is converted into an infinity of space on the internal perspective. Though finite in size from a global perspective, each island will be regarded as infinite in size by its inhabitants.

ture is potentially infinite only, and future O-regions do not in any sense exist. If there is a global tide of becoming, then there is no actually infinite collection of O-regions after all. Internal observers, unaware of the global perspective, are simply mistaken in their taking the successive Big Bang events to be occurring simultaneously. Once again, we see how issues in the philosophy of time impinge crucially on scientific debates.[13]

But if an infinite ensemble of simultaneous universes does not actually exist, Vilenkin's attempt to explain away the fine-tuning of the universe for intelligent life collapses. For if, in fact, an infinite array of universes does not yet exist, if most of them lie in the potentially infinite future and are therefore unreal, then there actually exist only as many observable universes as can have formed since any island's origin in the finite past. Moreover, since the Borde-Guth-Vilenkin theorem requires that the multiverse itself cannot be extended into the infinite past, there can be only as many island universes now in existence as have formed in the false vacuum since the multiverse's inception at its boundary in the finite past. Given the incomprehensible improbability of the constants' all falling randomly into the life-permitting range, it may well be highly improbable that a life-permitting island universe should have decayed this soon out of the false vacuum. In that case the sting of fine-tuning has not been removed.

13. In my *Time and Eternity*, I defend the privileged nature of the global perspective. There I was considering the universe alone, so that the preferred time is cosmic time. But if a multiverse exists, then the global time will not be the cosmic time of any island universe but the proper time of the multiverse as a whole.

Vilenkin's whole multiverse scenario depends in any case on the hypothesis of future-eternal inflation, which in turn, it will be recalled, is based upon the existence of certain primordial scalar fields which govern inflation. Although Vilenkin observes that "inflation is eternal in practically all models suggested so far,"[14] he also admits, "Another important question is whether or not such scalar fields really exist in nature. Unfortunately, we don't know. There is no direct evidence for their existence."[15] This lack of evidence ought to temper the confidence with which the Many Worlds Hypothesis is put forward.

Wholly apart from its speculative nature, however, the Many Worlds Hypothesis faces a potentially lethal problem. Simply stated, if our universe is but one member of an infinite World Ensemble of randomly varying universes, then it is overwhelmingly more probable that we should be observing a much different universe than that which we in fact observe. Recall our discussion of Ludwig Boltzmann's Many Worlds Hypothesis for why we do not find the universe in a state of "heat death" or thermodynamic equilibrium.[16] The problem with Boltzmann's daring Many Worlds Hypothesis was that if our world were merely a fluctuation in a sea of diffuse energy, then it is overwhelmingly more probable that we should be observing a much tinier region of disequilibrium than we do.

Now a precisely parallel problem attends the Many Worlds Hypothesis as an explanation of fine-tuning. As we have seen, Roger Penrose calculates that the odds of our universe's low entropy condition obtaining by chance alone are on the order of $1:10^{10^{(123)}}$, an inconceivable number. If our universe were but one member of a collection of randomly ordered worlds, then it is vastly more probable that we should be observing a much smaller universe.[17] Adopting the Many Worlds Hypothesis to explain away fine-tuning would thus result in a bizarre illusionism: it is far more probable that all our astronomical, geological, and biological estimates of age are wrong and that the appearance of our large and old universe is a massive illusion (recall the dreaded Boltzmann brains). Or again, if our universe is but one member of a World Ensemble, then we ought to be observing highly extraordinary events, like horses popping into and out of existence by random collisions, or perpetual motion machines, since these are vastly more probable than all of nature's constants and quantities falling by chance into the virtually infinitesimal life-permitting range. Observable universes like those are much more plenteous in the ensemble of universes than worlds like ours and, therefore, ought to be observed by us if the universe were but one member of an ensemble

14. Vilenkin, *Many Worlds in One*, 214.
15. Ibid., 61.
16. See 146–50.
17. Roger Penrose, *The Road to Reality* (New York: Alfred A. Knopf, 2005), 762–65. The odds of our solar system's being formed instantly by random collisions of particles is, according to Penrose, about $1:10^{10^{(60)}}$, a vast number, but inconceivably smaller than $10^{10^{(123)}}$. Penrose concludes that anthropic explanations are so "impotent" that it is actually "misconceived" to appeal to them to explain the special features of the universe.

of worlds. Since we do not have such observations, that fact strongly disconfirms the multiverse hypothesis. On atheism, at least, it is therefore highly probable that there is no World Ensemble.

For these reasons the Many Worlds Hypothesis is severely disabled as a candidate for the best explanation of the observed cosmic fine-tuning. Since the alternative of chance stands or falls with the Many Worlds Hypothesis, that explanation is seen to be very implausible.

It therefore seems that the fine-tuning of the universe is plausibly due neither to physical necessity nor to chance. It follows that the fine-tuning is therefore due to design, unless the design hypothesis can be shown to be even more implausible than its competitors.

The Design Hypothesis

The implication of the design hypothesis is that there exists a Cosmic Designer who fine-tuned the initial conditions of the universe for intelligent life. Such a hypothesis supplies a personal explanation of the fine-tuning of the universe. Is this explanation implausible? Detractors of design sometimes object that on this hypothesis the Cosmic Designer himself remains unexplained. This objection is what Richard Dawkins calls "the central argument of my book" *The God Delusion*.[18] He summarizes his argument as follows:

1) One of the greatest challenges to the human intellect has been to explain how the complex, improbable appearance of design in the universe arises.
2) The natural temptation is to attribute the appearance of design to actual design itself.
3) The temptation is a false one because the designer hypothesis immediately raises the larger problem of who designed the designer.
4) The most ingenious and powerful explanation is Darwinian evolution by natural selection.
5) We don't have an equivalent explanation for physics.
6) We should not give up the hope of a better explanation arising in physics, something as powerful as Darwinism is for biology.

Therefore, God almost certainly does not exist.

This argument is jarring because the atheistic conclusion "Therefore, God almost certainly does not exist" doesn't follow from the six previous statements even if we concede that each of them is true and justified. At most, all that follows is that we should not infer God's existence on the basis of the appearance of design in the universe. But that conclusion is quite compatible with God's existence and

18. Richard Dawkins, *The God Delusion* (New York: Houghton Mifflin, 2006), 157–58.

even with our justifiably believing in God's existence. Maybe we should believe in God on the basis of the cosmological argument or the ontological argument or the moral argument. Maybe our belief in God isn't based on arguments at all but is grounded in religious experience or in divine revelation. The point is that rejecting design arguments for God's existence does nothing to prove that God does not exist or even that belief in God is unjustified.

In any case, several of the steps of Dawkins' argument are plausibly false. Step (5) alludes to the cosmic fine-tuning which has been the focus of our discussion. Dawkins has nothing by way of explanation for it, and therefore the hope expressed in step (6) represents nothing more than the faith of a naturalist. Moreover, consider step (3). Dawkins' claim here is that one is not justified in inferring design as the best explanation of the complex order of the universe because then a new problem arises: who designed the Designer?

This rejoinder is flawed on at least two counts. First, in order to recognize an explanation as the best, one needn't have an explanation of the explanation. This is an elementary point concerning inference to the best explanation as understood in the philosophy of science. If archaeologists digging in the earth were to discover things looking like arrowheads and hatchet heads and pottery shards, they would be justified in inferring that these artifacts are not the chance result of sedimentation and metamorphosis, but products of some unknown group of people, even though they had no explanation of who these people were or where they came from. Similarly, if astronauts were to come upon a pile of machinery on the back side of the moon, they would be justified in inferring that it was the product of intelligent agents, even if they had no idea whatsoever who these agents were or how they got there. In order to recognize an explanation as the best, one needn't be able to explain the explanation. In fact, so requiring would lead to an infinite regress of explanations, so that nothing could ever be explained and science would be destroyed! So in the case at hand, in order to recognize that intelligent design is the best explanation of the appearance of design in the universe, one needn't be able to explain the Designer.

Second, Dawkins thinks that in the case of a divine Designer of the universe, the Designer is just as complex as the thing to be explained, so that no explanatory advance is made. This objection raises all sorts of questions about the role played by simplicity in assessing competing explanations; for example, how simplicity is to be weighed in comparison with other criteria like explanatory power, explanatory scope, and so forth. But leave those questions aside. Dawkins's fundamental mistake lies in his assumption that a divine Designer is an entity comparable in complexity to the universe. As an unembodied mind, God is a remarkably simple entity. As a non-physical entity, a mind is not composed of parts, and its salient properties, like self-consciousness, rationality, and volition, are essential to it. In contrast to the contingent and variegated universe with all its inexplicable constants and quantities, a divine mind is startlingly simple. Certainly such a mind may have complex ideas—it may be thinking, for example, of the infinitesimal calculus—but the mind itself is a remarkably simple entity. Dawkins has evidently confused a mind's ideas, which may, indeed, be complex, with a mind itself, which is an incredibly simple entity. Therefore, postulating a divine mind behind the universe most definitely does represent an advance in simplicity, for whatever that is worth.

It seems to me therefore that of the three proffered alternatives—physical necessity, chance, or design—the most plausible of the three is the hypothesis of design. Thus, the teleological argument based on the fine-tuning of the universe fares well as a sound and persuasive argument for a Designer of the cosmos.

Moral Argument

Like the cosmological argument, the moral argument is a family of diverse arguments for the existence of God, but in this case springing from moral considerations. The version I find most convincing is the argument for God on the basis of the objectivity of moral values and duties. A very simple and straightforward formulation of this argument is as follows:

1) If God does not exist, objective moral values and duties do not exist.
2) Objective moral values and duties do exist.
3) Therefore, God exists.

Although the argument as such does not reach the conclusion that God is the basis of objective moral values and duties, such a claim tends to be implicit in premise (1) and emerges in the defense of that premise against objections.

God and Objective Morals

Every one of us guides his life, however inconsistently, by a certain set of values. But are the values we hold dear and guide our lives by mere social conventions akin to driving on the left- versus right-hand side of the road or mere expressions of personal preference akin to having a taste for certain foods rather than others? Or are they valid independently of our apprehension of them, and if so, what is their foundation? Are there things which I ought not to do and other things which I ought to do? Or is this sense of obligation a mere illusion due to sociological and psychological conditioning? Many philosophers have argued that if God does not exist, then morality is ultimately subjective and non-binding. We might act in precisely the same ways that we do in fact act, but in the absence of God such actions would no longer count as good or evil, right or wrong, since in the absence of God, objective moral values and duties do not exist.

In order to unpack this point, it will be helpful to distinguish between moral values and moral duties. When we speak of moral values, we're talking about whether something is good or bad; when we talk about moral duties we are concerned with whether something is right or wrong. Although we are apt to equate what is right with what is good and what is wrong with what is bad, a little reflection reveals this to be mistaken. Right and wrong have to do with moral obligation, what I ought or ought not to do. But obviously, I am not morally obligated to do something just because it would be good for me to do it. For example, it's a good thing to become a chemist, but that doesn't imply that it is therefore my duty to become a chemist. For it is also good to become a firefighter or a diplomat or a doctor, and I can't become all of them. Moreover, there are occasionally circumstances in which I am, tragically, confronted with nothing but bad choices (think of *Sophie's Choice*), but it is not therefore wrong of me to choose one, since I must choose. So there is a conceptual difference between something's being good (or bad) and something's being right (or wrong). The former has to do with something's worth, while the latter concerns something's obligatoriness. In premise (1) we're concerned with the question whether without God there would be an objective distinction between good and evil and between right and wrong.

Let me say something as well to clarify the distinction between something's being objective and something's being subjective. To say that something is objective is to say that it is independent of what people think or perceive. By contrast, to say that something is subjective is just to say that it is not objective; that is to say, it is dependent on what human persons think or perceive. So, for example, the distinction between being on Mars and not being on Mars is an objective distinction; a particular rock's being on Mars is in no way dependent upon our beliefs. By contrast, the distinction between "here" and "there" is not objective: whether a particular event at a certain spatial location occurs here or occurs there depends upon a person's point of view.

To say that there are objective moral values is to say that something is good or evil independently of whether any human being believes it to be so. Similarly to say that we have objective moral duties is to say that certain actions are right or wrong for us independently of whether any human being believes them to be so. For example, to say that the Holocaust was objectively wrong is to say that it was wrong even though the Nazis who carried it out thought that it was right, and it would still have been wrong even if the Nazis had won World War II and succeeded in exterminating or brainwashing everybody who disagreed with them so that it was universally believed that the Holocaust was right. The claim of premise (1) is that if there is no God, then moral values and duties are not objective in this sense.

Consider, then, moral values. If theism is false, why think that human beings have objective moral value? After all, on the naturalistic view, there's nothing special about human beings. They're just accidental byproducts of nature which have evolved relatively recently on an infinitesimal speck of dust called the planet Earth, lost somewhere in a hostile and mindless universe, and which are doomed to perish individually and collectively in a relatively short time. Richard Dawkins' assessment of human worth may be depressing, but why, on atheism, is he mistaken when he says, "There is at bottom no design, no purpose, no evil, no good, nothing but pointless indifference. . . . We are machines for propagating DNA. . . . It is every living object's sole reason for being"?[19]

Atheist philosophers who are humanists do not seem to have faced squarely the consequences of their naturalism. For example, humanist philosopher Paul Kurtz insists that human flourishing is "the be-all and end-all" of human life,[20] while affirming like Dawkins that "the discoveries of Copernicus and Darwin . . . have [undermined] the belief that we are fundamentally different from all other species."[21] He muses that "many [people] still refuse to accept the full implications of these discoveries."[22] They "still seek to find a special place for the human species in the scheme of things."[23] Kurtz is doubtlessly thinking of theists. Ironically, however, it is precisely humanists themselves who seek to find a special place for the human species in the scheme of things, who refuse to accept the full implications of reducing human beings to just another animal species. For humanists continue to treat human beings as *morally* special in contrast to other species.

What justification is there for this differential treatment? On a naturalistic view moral values are just by-products of socio-biological evolution. Just as a troupe of baboons exhibit co-operative behavior and even altruistic, sacrificial behavior because evolution has determined it to be advantageous in the struggle for survival, so their primate cousins *homo sapiens* exhibit similar behavior for the same reason. As philosopher of science Michael Ruse explains,

> The position of the modern evolutionist . . . is that humans have an awareness of morality . . . because such an awareness is of biological worth. Morality is a biological adaptation no less than are hands and feet and teeth. . . . Considered as a rationally justifiable set of claims about an objective something, ethics is illusory. I appreciate that when somebody says "Love thy neighbor as thyself," they think they are referring above and beyond themselves. . . . Nevertheless, . . . such reference is truly without foundation. Morality is just an aid to survival and reproduction, . . . and any deeper meaning is illusory.[24]

As a result of socio-biological pressures, there has evolved among *homo sapiens* a sort of "herd morality" which functions well in the perpetuation of our species in the struggle for survival. But on the atheistic view there doesn't seem to be anything about *homo sapiens* that makes this morality objectively true. If the film of evolutionary history were rewound and shot anew, very different creatures with a very different set of values might well have evolved. By what right do we regard

---

19. Cited in Lewis Wolpert, *Six Impossible Things before Breakfast* (London: Faber and Faber, 2006), 215. But see n.19 of chap. 2 above.

20. Paul Kurtz, *The Courage to Become* (Westport, Conn.: Praeger, 1997), 125.

21. Ibid., 5–6.

22. Ibid., 6.

23. Ibid., 53.

24. Michael Ruse, "Evolutionary Theory and Christian Ethics," in *The Darwinian Paradigm* (London: Routledge, 1989), 262, 268–89.

our morality as objective rather than theirs? To think that human beings are special is to be guilty of specie-ism, an unjustified bias toward one's own species.

Thus, if there is no God, then any basis for regarding the herd morality evolved by *homo sapiens* as objectively true seems to have been removed. So, if theism is false, it is hard to see what basis remains for the affirmation of objective moral values and in particular of the special value of human beings.

Second, if theism is false, then what is the basis for objective moral duties? Crudely put, on the atheistic view human beings are just animals, and animals have no moral obligations to one another. The ethicist Richard Taylor powerfully illustrates the point. He invites us to imagine human beings living in a state of nature without any customs or laws. Suppose one of them kills another one and takes his goods. Taylor reflects:

> Such actions, though injurious to their victims, are no more unjust or immoral than they would be if done by one animal to another. A hawk that seizes a fish from the sea *kills* it, but does not *murder* it; and another hawk that seizes the fish from the talons of the first *takes* it, but does not *steal* it—for none of these things is forbidden. And exactly the same considerations apply to the people we are imagining.[25]

Why think that if God does not exist, we would have any moral obligations to do anything? Who or what imposes these moral duties upon us? As Taylor says, "the concept of moral obligation [is] unintelligible apart from the idea of God. The words remain, but their meaning is gone."[26]

Thus, if atheism is true, it becomes impossible to condemn war, oppression, or crime as evil. Nor can one praise brotherhood, equality, or love as good. It doesn't matter *what* you do—for there is no right and wrong; all things are permitted. To be sure, some actions—say rape or incest—may not be biologically or sociologically advantageous, and so, in the course of human development, have become taboo. But that does absolutely nothing to show that rape or incest is really *wrong*. On the atheistic view, there's nothing really wrong about raping someone. Such behavior goes on all the time in the animal kingdom. If, as Kurtz states, "the moral principles that govern our behavior are rooted in habit and custom, feeling and fashion,"[27] then the rapist who chooses to flout the herd morality is doing nothing more serious than acting unfashionably. So if theism is false, it's very hard to understand what basis remains for objective moral duties.

Now it's important that we remain clear in understanding the issue before us. The question is *not*: Must we believe in God in order to live moral lives? There's no reason to think that atheists and theists alike may not live what we normally characterize as good and decent lives. Similarly, the question is *not*: Can we formulate a system of ethics without reference to God? If the non-theist grants that human

25. Richard Taylor, *Ethics, Faith, and Reason* (Englewood Cliffs, N.J.: Prentice-Hall, 1985), 14.
26. Ibid., 83–84.
27. Paul Kurtz, *Forbidden Fruit* (Buffalo, N.Y.: Prometheus, 1988), 73.

beings do have objective value, then there's no reason to think that he cannot work out a system of ethics with which the theist would also largely agree. Or again, the question is *not*: Can we recognize the existence of objective moral values without reference to God? The theist will typically maintain that a person need not believe in God in order to recognize, say, that we should love our children.

All of the above misunderstandings of the argument are based on confusing God's existence with *belief* in God's existence. The argument is not that *belief* in God's existence is necessary for the objective reality of moral values and duties, but that God is necessary for the objective reality of moral values and duties. Nor is the argument that God is necessary for our knowledge of moral values and duties. I have been astonished at the confusion of moral ontology with moral epistemology on the part of prominent moral philosophers responding to premise (1).[28] Moral ontology deals with the *reality* of moral values and properties; moral epistemology deals with our *knowledge* of moral truths. As far as moral epistemology is concerned, I can appeal to all the same mechanisms, such as moral intuition and reflection, by means of which humanist thinkers are confident that they accurately discern the good and the right. In fact, the Bible actually teaches that God's moral law is "written on the hearts" of all men, so that even those who do not know God's law "do naturally the things of the law" as "their conscience bears witness to them" (Rom. 2:14–15 AT). If that is the case, a theist's moral epistemology need not differ broadly from the humanist's own moral epistemology. Epistemological objections are thus red herrings which need not detain us. I'm contending that theism is necessary that there might be moral goods and duties, not that we might discern the moral goods and duties that there are. As Kurtz puts it, "The central question about moral and ethical principles concerns their ontological foundation. If they are neither derived from God nor anchored in some transcendent ground, are they purely ephemeral?"[29]

So what response can naturalistic thinkers make to premise (1)? Some philosophers, equally averse to anchoring moral values in some non-theistic transcendent ground as in God, try to maintain the existence of objective moral principles or moral properties in the context of a naturalistic worldview. But the advocates of such theories are typically at a loss to justify their starting point. If there is no God, then it's hard to see any reason for thinking that the herd morality evolved by *homo sapiens* is objectively true or that the property of moral goodness supervenes on certain natural states of such creatures.

28. See the response by Walter Sinnott-Armstrong in our *God? A Debate between a Christian and an Atheist* (New York: Oxford University Press, 2003), and by Sinnott-Armstrong and Louise Antony in Paul Kurtz and my *God and Ethics: A Contemporary Debate*, ed. Nathan King and Robert Garcia (Lanham, Md.: Rowman & Littlefield, 2008). Ironically, the distinction between moral ontology and moral epistemology is drawn with wonderful clarity by Sinnott-Armstrong himself in his "Moral Skepticism and Justification," in *Moral Knowledge?* ed. Walter Sinnott-Armstrong and Mark Timmons (New York: Oxford University Press, 1996), 4–8.

29. Kurtz, *Forbidden Fruit*, 65.

It seems that the atheistic humanist must simply insist, with the Dartmouth ethicist Walter Sinnott-Armstrong, that whatever contributes to human flourishing is morally good and whatever detracts from human flourishing is bad and take that as his explanatory stopping point.[30] But the problem is that such an explanatory stopping point seems premature because of its arbitrariness and implausibility. Why, given atheism, think that inflicting harm on other people would have any moral dimension at all? Why would it be wrong to hurt another member of our species? Sinnott-Armstrong answers, "It simply is. Objectively. Don't you agree?"[31] Of course, I agree that it *is* wrong, since I am a theist. But I can't see any reason to think that it *would be* wrong if atheism were true. Sinnott-Armstrong thinks that rape is wrong, even though the physical activity that counts as rape among human beings goes on all the time in the animal kingdom—just as acts that count as murder and theft when done by one human to another occur constantly between members of other animal species—without any moral significance whatsoever. This is surely strange and cries out for explanation. As Michael Ruse has argued, we can well conceive of extra-terrestrial rational beings for whom rape would not be immoral.[32] Were they to visit Earth, why should they respect the values that have evolved among *homo sapiens*? Had our own evolutionary history gone differently, creatures with a different set of moral values might have existed here. All this underlines the arbitrariness of Sinnott-Armstrong's explanatory ultimate.

The naturalist might try to meet this objection by holding that moral properties supervene necessarily on certain natural states. But then the question as to the plausibility of this explanatory ultimate arises. The claim that moral properties necessarily supervene on certain physical states of affairs at best gives us reason to think that if moral properties do supervene on certain natural states, then they do so necessarily. But that gives us no reason at all to think that, given a naturalistic worldview, there are any moral properties or that they do supervene on natural states. Why think that on an atheistic view of the world the curious, non-physical property of moral goodness would supervene on a human female's nursing her infant? Why, given naturalism, would the strange, non-physical property of moral badness supervene on a man's leaving a shop carrying certain items for which he has not left the currency demanded by the shop owner? I see no reason to think that a full specification of all the natural properties of a situation would determine or fix any moral properties of that situation. If our approach to meta-ethical theory is to be serious metaphysics rather than just a "shopping list" approach, whereby one simply helps oneself to the supervenient moral properties or principles needed to do the job, then some sort of explanation is required for why moral properties supervene on certain natural states or why such principles are

---

30. Walter Sinnott-Armstrong, "Why Traditional Theism Cannot Provide an Adequate Foundation for Morality," in *God and Ethics*.

31. Walter Sinnott-Armstrong, "There Is No Good Reason to Believe in God," in *God? A Debate*, 34.

32. Michael Ruse, "Is Rape Wrong on Andromeda?"

true. It is insufficient for the naturalist to point out that we do, in fact, apprehend the goodness or obligatoriness of some feature of human existence, for that only goes to establish the objectivity of moral values and duties, which just is premise (2) of the moral argument!

Some philosophers think that moral truths, being necessarily true, cannot have an explanation of their truth. I think we can agree that many moral principles are necessarily true. But that doesn't prove that they cannot have an explanation. The crucial presupposition of these philosophers—that necessary truths cannot stand in relations of explanatory priority to one another—is far from evident and, indeed, seems plainly false. For example, the classical theist will say that the statement "A plurality of persons exists" is necessarily true because "God exists" is necessarily true and God is essentially a Trinity. To give a non-theological example, many mathematicians would say that "2+3=5" is necessarily true because the Peano axioms for standard arithmetic are necessarily true. Or again, many metaphysicians would hold that the statement "No event precedes itself" is necessarily true because "Temporal becoming is an essential and objective feature of time" is necessarily true. It would be utterly implausible to suggest that the relation of explanatory priority holding between the relevant statements could go either way.

Given the arbitrariness and implausibility of non-explanatory assertions of the objectivity of human values and duties, we need to ask whether moral values and duties can be plausibly anchored in some transcendent, non-theistic ground. Let's call this view Atheistic Moral Platonism. Atheistic Moral Platonists affirm that objective moral values do exist but are not grounded in God. Indeed, moral values have no further foundation. They just exist.

It is difficult, however, even to comprehend this view. What does it mean to say, for example, that the moral value *Justice* just exists? It's hard to know what to make of this. It is clear what is meant when it is said that a person is just; but it is bewildering when it is said that in the absence of any people, *Justice* itself exists. Moral values seem to exist as properties of persons, not as mere abstractions—or at any rate it's hard to know what it is for a moral value to exist as a mere abstraction.[33] Curiously, since the abstract object *Justice* is not itself just, it would seem to follow that in the absence of any people justice does not exist—which seems to contradict the hypothesis. Atheistic Moral Platonists seem to lack any adequate foundation in reality for moral values but just leave them floating in an unintelligible way.

Second, the nature of moral duty or obligation seems incompatible with Atheistic Moral Platonism. Let's suppose for the sake of argument that moral values do exist

33. Moreover, we might wonder how we could ever come to have any knowledge of this abstract realm. Realists about mathematical objects have faced this same conundrum. The suggestion by realist mathematician Kurt Gödel that we have some mysterious intuitive access to the realm of mathematical objects has been ridiculed by naturalistic philosophers of mathematics. Similarly, it is no clearer how I could know the content of the moral realm than how I could know what is going on in some remote village in Nepal with which I have no contact.

independently of God. Suppose that values like *Mercy, Justice, Love, Forbearance,* and the like just exist. How does that result in any moral obligations for me? Why would I have a moral duty, say, to be merciful? Who or what lays such an obligation on me? On this view moral vices such as *Greed, Hatred,* and *Selfishness* also presumably exist as abstract objects. Why am I obligated to align my life with one set of these abstractly existing objects rather than any other? Theism, by contrast, provides a plausible basis for moral duty, as we shall see.

Thirdly, it is fantastically improbable that just that sort of creature would emerge from the blind evolutionary process that corresponds to the abstractly existing realm of moral values. This seems to be an utterly incredible coincidence when one thinks about it. It is almost as though the moral realm *knew* that we were coming. As William Sorley saw, it is far more plausible to regard both the natural realm and the moral realm as under the hegemony of a divine Creator and Lawgiver than to think that these two entirely independent orders of reality just happened to mesh.

In short, on an atheistic, naturalistic worldview, there just seems to be no basis for affirming the existence of objective moral values and duties. Certainly we have a sense of morality, but on naturalism that sense is an illusion wrought by socio-biological conditioning.

Objectivity of Moral Values and Duties

Premise (2) of the moral argument asserts that, in fact, objective moral values and duties do exist. The way in which moral theorists test competing ethical theories is by assessing how well they cohere with our moral experience. I take it that in moral experience we do apprehend a realm of objective moral values and duties, just as in sensory experience we apprehend a realm of objectively existing physical objects. Just as it is impossible for us to get outside our sensory input to test its veridicality, so there is no way to test independently the veridicality of our moral perceptions. As Sorley emphasized, there is no more reason to deny the objective reality of moral values than the objective reality of the physical world. In the absence of some defeater, we rationally trust our perceptions, whether sensory or moral.

But what about the claim that moral values and duties are illusions fostered in us by socio-biological evolution? Doesn't that constitute a defeater for premise (2)? Here we must distinguish carefully the two ways in which the claim that our moral beliefs are byproducts of socio-biological evolution might constitute a defeater of (2).[34] On the one hand, such a claim might be taken as a defeater of the *truth* of (2). That is to say, the claim might be that since our moral beliefs have been instilled in us through socio-biological pressures, those beliefs are false and

---

34. See Plantinga's understanding of what he calls the Freud and Marx objection to theistic belief. Early on, Plantinga had dismissed Freud and Marx's objections to religious belief as instances of the genetic fallacy ("The Foundations of Theism: A Reply," *Faith and Philosophy* 3 [1986]: 308), but he later came to see them as attacks upon the warrant for theistic belief (*Warranted Christian Belief* [Oxford: Oxford University Press, 2000], 136–42, 151–52).

so objective moral values and duties do not exist. So construed, the objection is a textbook example of the genetic fallacy, which is the attempt to falsify a belief by explaining how that belief originated. Such reasoning is fallacious, since a belief could be true regardless of how it came to be held. In particular, if God exists, then objective moral values and duties exist regardless of how conditioned we may be by the evolutionary process. So the objection at best proves only that our subjective perception of moral values and duties has evolved. But if moral values are gradually discovered, not invented, then our gradual and fallible apprehension of the moral realm no more undermines the objective reality of that realm than our gradual, fallible apprehension of the physical world undermines the objectivity of that realm.

But there's a second, more powerful way in which the socio-biological claim might be construed: not as a defeater of the truth of (2) but of the *warrant* for (2). That is to say, given that our moral beliefs have been determined by socio-biological pressures, we have no warrant for believing (2) to be true. Because our moral beliefs have been selected by evolution, not for their truth, but for their survival value, we can have no confidence in the deliverances of our moral experience. So even if (2) were true, we would still have no warrant for believing it to be true. The problem with this construal of the objection is that it turns out to be question-begging and even self-defeating. First, it's question-begging because it presupposes that naturalism is true.[35] If there is no God, then our moral experience is, plausibly, illusory. I said as much in my defense of premise (1). But why think that naturalism is true? To undermine the warrant which our moral experience gives to our moral beliefs, much more must be done than hold out the possibility that naturalism may be true. For if theism is true, then our moral experience, even if conditioned by biology and society, is probably not wholly illusory but is reliable to some degree. In the absence of a proof of naturalism, the warrant which our moral experience lends to (2) remains undefeated. Second, the objection is self-defeating because, on naturalism, *all* our beliefs, not just our moral beliefs, have been selected for survival value, not truth, and are therefore unwarranted.[36] In particular, the belief in naturalism and the socio-biological account of moral belief is unwarranted. So the objection undermines its own warrant and is therefore incapable of being rationally affirmed. But then it cannot defeat the warrant for premise (2).

Most of us think that in moral experience we do apprehend objective values and obligations. Ruse himself confesses in another context, "The man who says that it is morally acceptable to rape little children is just as mistaken as the man who says, 2+2=5."[37] Speaking several years ago on a Canadian university campus, I noticed a poster put up by the Sexual Assault & Information Center. It read: "Sexual

35. See Plantinga's response to the Freud and Marx objection to theistic belief in *Warranted Christian Belief*, 194–98.

36. This is Plantinga's celebrated evolutionary argument against naturalism *Warrant and Proper Function* (Oxford: Oxford University Press, 1993), 216–37; *Warranted Christian Belief*, 227–40.

37. Michael Ruse, *Darwinism Defended* (London: Addison-Wesley, 1982), 275.

Assault: No One Has the Right to Abuse a Child, Woman, or Man." Most of us recognize that sexual abuse of another person is wrong. Actions like rape, torture, child abuse, and brutality aren't just socially unacceptable behavior—they're moral abominations. By the same token, love, generosity, equality, and self-sacrifice are really good. People who fail to see this are just morally handicapped, and there is no reason to allow their impaired vision to call into question what we see clearly.

Ethicist David Brink thinks that the objectivity of moral values is thus the default position. "There might be no objective moral standards. . . . But this would be a revisionary conclusion, to be accepted only as the result of extended and compelling argument that the commitments of ethical objectivity are unsustainable."[38] Indeed, I think that we are and should be more confident of the truth of premise (2) than we are of the premises in any argument for moral nihilism. In light of the warrant conferred on (2) by our moral experience, arguments for moral nihilism will always include some premise which is less warranted than (2) and which is therefore to be denied.

The Euthyphro Dilemma

From the two premises it follows logically that God exists. Notice that in defending the two premises, we have not committed ourselves to any particular account of the relationship between God and moral values or duties. Nevertheless, the most popular objection raised against the moral argument is essentially a challenge to basing moral values and duties in God. The objection, first recorded in Plato's dialogue *Euthyphro*, goes as follows: either something is good because God wills it or else God wills something because it is good. If it is good just because God wills it, then what is good becomes arbitrary. God could have willed that hatred and jealousy be good, and then we should have been obligated to hate and envy one another. But that seems implausible; at least some moral goods seem to be necessary. But if we say instead that God wills something because it is good, then whether something is good or bad is independent of God. In that case, it seems that moral value exists independently of God, which undermines premise (1) of our moral argument. If God were not to exist, then objective moral values and duties would exist anyway.

The Euthyphro Dilemma can thus be construed as an argument for Atheistic Moral Platonism. Now we've already seen that such a theory has major deficits. This suggests that the dilemma allegedly forcing us to such a position is a false one and that we may escape the horns of the dilemma by finding a third alternative. I think that an appropriately formulated divine command theory of ethics, such as has been articulated by Robert Adams, Philip Quinn, William Alston, and others,[39] supplies such an alternative: our moral duties are constituted by the

---

38. David O. Brink, "The Autonomy of Ethics," in *The Cambridge Companion to Atheism*, ed. Michael Martin, Cambridge Companions to Philosophy (Cambridge: Cambridge University Press, 2007), 149.

39. Philip L. Quinn, *Divine Commands and Moral Requirements* (Oxford: Clarendon, 1978); Janine Marie Idziak, *Divine Command Morality: Historical and Contemporary Readings* (Lewiston, N.Y.: Edwin Mellen Press, 1980); Robert Merrihew Adams, *Finite and Infinite Goods* (Oxford: Oxford University Press, 2000);

commands of an essentially just and loving God. For any action *A* and moral agent *S*, we can explicate the notions of moral requirement, prohibition, and permission of *A* for *S* as follows:

> *A* is *required* of *S* if and only if a just and loving God commands *S* to do *A*.
>
> *A* is *forbidden* to *S* if and only if a just and loving God commands *S* not to do *A*.
>
> *A* is *permitted* for *S* if and only if a just and loving God does not command *S* not to do *A*.

Since our moral duties are grounded in the divine commands, they are not independent of God.

Neither are God's commands arbitrary, for they are the necessary expressions of his just and loving nature. God is essentially compassionate, fair, kind, impartial, and so forth, and his commandments are reflections of his own character. God's character is definitive of moral goodness; it serves as the paradigm of moral goodness. Thus, the morally good/bad is determined by reference to God's nature; the morally right/wrong is determined by reference to his will. The divine will or commands come into play as a source of moral obligation, not moral value. As necessary expressions of his nature, God's commands are not arbitrary, and so we need not trouble ourselves about counterfactuals with impossible antecedents like "If God were to command child abuse . . ." On the customary understanding, counterfactuals with impossible antecedents have no non-vacuous truth value. Even if we reject the customary semantics and allow that some counterfactuals with impossible antecedents may be non-vacuously true or false, how are we to assess the truth value of a statement with an antecedent like this? It is like wondering whether, if there were a round square, its area would equal the square of one of its sides. And what would it matter how one answered, since what is imagined is logically incoherent? I don't see that the divine command theorist is committed to the non-vacuous truth of the counterfactual in question or that anything of significance hangs on his thinking it to be non-vacuously true or false.

If the non-theist should demand, "Why pick God's nature as definitive of the Good?" the answer is that God, by definition, is the greatest conceivable being, and a being which is the paradigm of goodness is greater than one which merely exemplifies goodness. Unless we are nihilists, we have to recognize some ultimate standard of value, and God is the least arbitrary stopping point.

William Alston, "What Euthyphro Should Have Said," in *Philosophy of Religion: A Reader and Guide*, ed. William L. Craig (Edinburgh: Edinburgh University Press, 2001; New Brunswick, N.J.: Rutgers University Press, 2001), 283–98. It is striking that Brink, "The Autonomy of Ethics," 152–54, takes no cognizance of these authors, nor of the alternative they offer; the only theistic account he knows is voluntarism, which is not defended by any philosopher in my acquaintance.

The moral argument thus brings us to a personal, necessarily existent being who is the locus and source of moral goodness. It thereby complements in an important way the conclusions of the cosmological and teleological arguments.

ONTOLOGICAL ARGUMENT

Some readers may be surprised to find here a defense of the ontological argument. Many thinkers would agree with Arthur Schopenhauer's dismissal of the argument as "a charming joke."[40] But a number of recent, prominent philosophers such as Norman Malcolm, Charles Hartshorne, and Alvin Plantinga not only take the argument seriously but consider it to be sound. Since the formulation and defense of the argument provided by Plantinga are the most sophisticated in the long history of the ontological argument, profiting from the missteps and oversights of his predecessors, Plantinga's version of the argument has the best chance of being cogent and will therefore serve as the springboard for our discussion.

In his version of the argument, Plantinga appropriates the insight of Gottfried Wilhelm Leibniz that the ontological argument assumes that the concept of God is possible. That is to say, the argument assumes that the concept "God" or "greatest conceivable being" is a coherent concept or, employing the semantics of possible worlds, that there is a possible world in which God exists.

Possible Worlds

For those who are unfamiliar with the semantics of possible worlds, let me explain that by "a possible world" one does not mean a planet or even a universe, but rather a maximal description of reality, or a way reality might be. Perhaps the best way to think of a possible world is as a huge conjunction $p \ \& \ q \ \& \ r \ \& \ s \ldots$, whose individual conjuncts are the propositions $p, q, r, s, \ldots$ A possible world is a conjunction which comprises every proposition or its contradictory, so that it yields a maximal description of reality—nothing is left out of such a description. By negating different conjuncts in a maximal description we arrive at different possible worlds:

$$W_1: p \ \& \ q \ \& \ r \ \& \ s \ldots$$
$$W_2: p \ \& \ \neg q \ \& \ r \ \& \ \neg s \ldots$$
$$W_3: \neg p \ \& \ \neg q \ \& \ r \ \& \ s \ldots$$
$$W_4: p \ \& \ q \ \& \ \neg r \ \& \ s \ldots$$

$\ldots$

$\ldots$

$\ldots$

Only one of these descriptions will be composed of conjuncts all of which are true and so will be the way reality actually is, that is to say, the actual world.

---

40. I note that in his fifteen pages devoted to the ontological argument in *The God Delusion*, Richard Dawkins only ridicules but does not refute the argument (Dawkins, *The God Delusion*, 80–95).

Since we're talking about possible worlds, the various conjuncts which a possible world comprises must be capable of being true both individually and together. For example, the proposition *The Prime Minister is a prime number* is not even possibly true, for numbers are abstract objects which could not conceivably be identical with a concrete object like the Prime Minister. Therefore, no possible world will have that proposition as one of its conjuncts; rather its negation will be a conjunct of every possible world. Such a proposition is necessarily false, that is to say, it is false in every possible world. By contrast, the proposition *George McGovern is the president of the United States* is false in the actual world but could be true and so is a conjunct of some possible worlds. To say that George McGovern is the president of the United States in some possible world is to say that there is a maximal description of reality having the relevant proposition as one of its conjuncts. Similarly, to say that God exists in some possible world is to say that the proposition *God exists* is true in some maximal description of reality.

Leibniz's insight into the ontological argument was that the argument assumes that the proposition *God exists* (or *A greatest conceivable being exists* or *A perfect being exists*) is possibly true, that is to say, God exists in some possible world. For if the concept of God is incoherent or impossible, then the word "God" cannot possibly refer to anything, any more than the words "square circle" could refer to something. The expression "greatest conceivable being" would in that case just be an incoherent combination of words.

Plantinga's Ontological Argument

Now in his version of the argument, Plantinga conceives of God as a being which is "maximally excellent" in every possible world. Plantinga takes maximal excellence to entail such excellent-making properties as omniscience, omnipotence, and moral perfection. A being which has maximal excellence in every possible world would have what Plantinga calls "maximal greatness." Now the property of maximal greatness, Plantinga avers, is possibly exemplified, that is to say, there is a possible world in which a maximally great being exists. But then this being must exist in a maximally excellent way in every possible world, including the actual world. Therefore, God exists.

We can formulate Plantinga's version of the ontological argument as follows:

1) It is possible that a maximally great being exists.
2) If it is possible that a maximally great being exists, then a maximally great being exists in some possible world.
3) If a maximally great being exists in some possible world, then it exists in every possible world.
4) If a maximally great being exists in every possible world, then it exists in the actual world.

5) If a maximally great being exists in the actual world, then a maximally great being exists.

6) Therefore, a maximally great being exists.

It might surprise you to learn that premises (2)–(5) of this argument are relatively uncontroversial. Most philosophers would agree that if God's existence is even possible, then he must exist. The principal issue to be settled with respect to Plantinga's ontological argument is what warrant exists for thinking the key premise "It is possible that a maximally great being exists" to be true.

In dealing with this issue, it's crucial that we distinguish clearly between metaphysical and merely epistemic possibility. The first concerns what is really possible; the second concerns what is consistent with what we know. One is tempted to say, "It's possible that God exists, and it's possible that he doesn't exist!" But this assertion is true only with respect to epistemic possibility: for all we know, God may exist or he may not exist. On the other hand, if God is conceived as a maximally great being, then his existence is either necessary or impossible, regardless of our epistemic uncertainty. To illustrate: some extraordinarily difficult mathematical equation may be beyond our ability to grasp, and so we say that it's possible that the equation is true and it's possible that it is false. But we thereby merely confess our epistemic uncertainty concerning the equation's truth value. As a piece of mathematics, the equation itself is either necessarily true or necessarily false. In the same way, the epistemic entertainability of premise (1) (or its denial) does not guarantee its metaphysical possibility.

Intuitive Warrant for Premise (1)

That being said, however, it remains the case that the concept of a maximally great being is intuitively a coherent notion and, hence, it might be argued, possibly instantiated. In order for the ontological argument to fail, the concept of a maximally great being must be incoherent, like the concept of a married bachelor. The concept of a married bachelor is not a strictly self-contradictory concept (as is the concept of a married unmarried man), and yet it is obvious, once one understands the meaning of the words "married" and "bachelor," that nothing corresponding to that concept can exist. By contrast, the concept of a maximally great being does not seem even remotely incoherent. This provides some *prima facie* warrant for thinking that it is possible that a maximally great being exists.

But won't this appeal to intuition lead to metaphysical excess? One of the most important strategies employed by detractors of the ontological argument has been to construct parodies of the argument which are designed to defeat the *prima facie* warrant which premise (1) is said to enjoy. By showing that analogous ideas like the idea of "a most perfect island" or the idea of "a necessarily existent lion" also seem *prima facie* to be coherent concepts, critics have tried to show that one is forced by the logic of the ontological argument to postulate the existence of all sorts of ridiculous beings.

But we may plausibly reply that the idea of God differs crucially from the parodies traditionally put forward by the argument's detractors. For one thing, the properties that go to make up maximal excellence as Plantinga defines it have intrinsic maximum values, whereas the excellent-making properties of things like islands do not. For example, omniscience is the property of knowing only and all truths. It's impossible to know any more truths than that. By contrast, in the case of islands, there could always be more palm trees or native dancing girls! Thus, there cannot be a most perfect or greatest conceivable island. Moreover, it is far from clear that there even are objective excellent-making properties of things like islands, for the excellence of islands seems to be relative to one's interests—does one prefer a desert island or an island boasting the finest resort hotels?

The idea of something like a necessarily existent lion also seems incoherent. For as a necessary being, such a beast would have to exist in every possible world we can conceive. But any animal which could exist in a possible world in which the universe is composed wholly of a singularity of infinite spacetime curvature, density, and temperature just is not a lion. By contrast, a maximally excellent being, if it is immaterial, could transcend such physical limitations and so be conceived as necessarily existent.

Perhaps the greatest challenge to the appeal to intuition as warrant for premise (1) is that it seems intuitively coherent in the same way to conceive of what we might call a quasi-maximally great being, for example, one which is in every other respect maximally excellent except that it does not know truths about future contingent events. Why is the key premise of the ontological argument more plausibly true than a parallel premise "It is possible that a quasi-maximally great being exists"? If we are warranted in thinking that a maximally great being exists, aren't we equally warranted in thinking that a quasi-maximally great being exists?

Maybe not; for maximal greatness is logically incompatible with quasi-maximal greatness. Since a maximally great being is by definition omnipotent, no concrete object can exist independently of its creative power. As an omnipotent being, a maximally great being must have the power to freely refrain from creating anything at all, so that there must be possible worlds in which nothing other than the maximally great being exists. But that entails that if maximal greatness is possibly exemplified, then quasi-maximal greatness is not. A quasi-excellent being (that is, a being which has lots of excellent properties but which does not exist in every possible world) may exist in many worlds (worlds in which the maximally great being has chosen to create it), but such a being would lack necessary existence and thus not be quasi-maximally great. Hence, if maximal greatness is possibly exemplified, quasi-maximal greatness is impossible. Thus, our intuition that a maximally great being is possible is not undermined by the claim that a quasi-maximally great being is also intuitively possible, for we see that the latter intuition depends on the assumption that a maximally great being cannot possibly exist, which begs the question.

Still, skeptics about our ability to discern what is possible/impossible will insist that we have no way of knowing *a priori* whether maximal greatness or quasi-maximal greatness is possibly exemplified. It cannot be both, but we have no idea if either is possible. Our intuitions about modal notions like possibility are unreliable guides.

We might plausibly reply to this objection that the intuition that a maximally great being possibly exists has priority over any intuition that a quasi-maximally great being possibly exists. The latter intuition seems to depend on the former, and yet upon reflection we come to lose the latter intuition through the realization that if a maximally great being is possible then a quasi-maximally great being is not. Thus, our *prima facie* warrant for premise (1) remains.

A Posteriori Warrant for Premise (1)

Still, we might wonder whether, in the face of such skepticism, anything more can be offered in defense of premise (1) than our modal intuitions alone. Plantinga provides a clue when he says that if we "carefully ponder" premise (1) and the alleged objections to it, if we "consider its connections with other propositions we accept or reject" and we still find it compelling, then we are within our rational rights in accepting it.[41] Such a procedure is a far cry from the sort of *a priori* speculations decried by the modal skeptic. Even if we cannot determine *a priori* whether maximal greatness is possibly exemplified, we may come to believe on the basis of *a posteriori* considerations that it is possible that a maximally great being exist.

For example, other theistic arguments like Leibniz's cosmological argument, the moral argument, and conceptualist arguments for God as a ground of abstract objects or necessary truths may lead us to think that it is plausible that a maximally great being exists. We've already looked at the Leibnizian cosmological argument and the moral argument. A conceptualist argument for God's existence might be formulated as follows:

1) Abstract objects, such as numbers and propositions, are either independently existing realities or else concepts in some mind.
2) Abstract objects are not independently existing realities.
3) If abstract objects are concepts in some mind, then an omniscient, metaphysically necessary being exists.
4) Therefore, an omniscient, metaphysically necessary being exists.

41. Plantinga, *The Nature of Necessity*, 221.

A defense of premise (1) would involve a refutation of nominalism, the view that abstract objects do not exist at all. Premise (2) rejects Platonism with respect to abstract objects, most plausibly on the grounds of their causal isolation and hence irrelevance to what exists or transpires in the world. Premise (3) excludes the grounding of abstract objects in some human mind, for there are too many such objects to be grounded in anything less than an infinite intelligence and, since many of these objects exist necessarily, they cannot in any case be grounded in the mind of a merely contingent being. Thus, one is brought to the existence of an omniscient, necessary mind as the foundation of the existence of abstract objects. I remain uncertain of this argument, chiefly due to reservations about its first premise, which would require us to reject various nominalistic alternatives to conceptualism such as fictionalism, constructibilism, figuralism, and so forth. Still, prominent philosophers such as Plantinga have endorsed it.

Thus, the cosmological argument leads to a metaphysically necessary being which is the ground of existence for any concrete reality, the moral argument to a locus of moral value which must be as metaphysically necessary as the moral values it grounds, and the conceptualist argument to an omniscient, metaphysically necessary intelligence as the foundation of abstract objects.

Considerations of simplicity might also come into play here. For example, it is simpler to posit one metaphysically necessary, infinite, omniscient, morally perfect being than to think that three separate necessary beings exist exemplifying these respective excellent-making properties. Similarly, with respect to quasi-maximally great beings, Swinburne's contention seems plausible that it is simpler (or perhaps less ad hoc) to posit either zero or infinity as the measure of a degreed property than to posit some inexplicably finite measure. Thus, it would be more plausible to think that maximal greatness is possibly instantiated than quasi-maximal greatness. On the basis of considerations like these, we might well consider ourselves to be warranted in believing that it is possible that a maximally great being exists.

The question which arises at this point is whether the ontological argument has not then become question-begging. An argument is question-begging if one's only reason for accepting a premise in the argument is that one already accepts the conclusion, so that one in effect reasons in a circle. In the present case it might seem that the reason one thinks that it is possible that a maximally great being exists is that one has good reasons to think that a maximally great being does exist.

But this misgiving may arise as a result of thinking of the project of natural theology in too linear a fashion. The theistic arguments need not be taken to be like links in a chain, in which one link follows another so that the chain is only as strong as its weakest link. Rather they are like links in a coat of chain mail, in which all the links reinforce one another so that the strength of the whole exceeds that of any single link. The ontological argument might play its part in a cumulative case for theism, in which a multitude of factors simultaneously conspire to lead one to the global conclusion that God exists. In that sense Anselm was wrong in thinking that he had discovered a single argument which, standing independently of all the rest, served to demonstrate God's existence in all his greatness. Nevertheless, his argument does encapsulate the thrust of all the arguments together to show that God, the Supreme Being, exists.

Practical Application

One of the things that most incenses contemporary non-theists is that Christians believe in God without having any evidence of God's existence. The material in the last two chapters will enable you to shatter that stereotype. Even though I argued in chapter 1 that we can know that God exists wholly apart from evidence, nevertheless the evidence for God's existence which we have surveyed makes it more probable than not that God exists. If you will master the material in these chapters, you will completely disarm the unbeliever of his chief complaint and excuse for his unbelief.

What is the force of these arguments? We needn't claim that we can prove to the unbeliever that God exists. In the minds of most people the word *prove* or *proof* connotes a mathematical demonstration. There's just no reason to set the bar so unrealistically high. It's a better strategy to set the bar low and then really exceed all expectations. So we should simply claim that "There are good arguments for the existence of God" or "In light of the evidence it's more probable than not that God exists" or even more modestly, "The arguments make it rational to believe that God exists." If the unbeliever asks us if we're saying that atheism or agnosticism is irrational, we should say, "I'm not interested in making personal judgments about whether non-theists are rational or not in what they believe. I'm just saying that there are good arguments for God's existence." Worldviews, as such, are neither rational nor irrational; rather people are either rational or not in holding to the worldviews they do. A person can be rational in believing something that is false, if he thinks that he has good arguments for that view. Thus, the same worldview may be rational for some people to hold and irrational for others. So whether atheism is rational for some people or not is really quite beside the point. The issue is rather whether atheism is true. What we aspire to show is that atheism is false, not that it is irrational for anybody to hold. We do that by presenting good arguments for theism. Remember: persons are rational; arguments are sound. We're interested in whether there are sound arguments for God's existence based on premises which are more plausible than their denials. We don't need to make a personal judgment on the rationality or irrationality of non-theists. Such an approach has the advantage of not offending the person we're trying to convince. We're simply saying to him, "Here are some arguments for God's existence that I think are really good. What do you think of them?"

I'd encourage you to memorize the premises of each of the arguments we've discussed. Most of the formulations are very brief so that this is easily done. So doing has a couple of advantages. First, it enables you always to have at your fingertips an answer to anyone who asks you for the reason for your hope (1 Pet. 3:15). As a result you will find tremendous confidence and boldness in talking about your faith with non-believers. Most unbelievers are ignorant of natural theology and have never confronted a Christian who is ready to offer carefully formulated arguments for his belief in God. Having logically valid, clearly formulated arguments is going to make you look smart and increase your credibility in their eyes, which will only make your witness more effective. Second, a huge advantage of laying out the premises of each argument is that it enables you to stay on track and not be misled by red herrings which the unbeliever will drag across your path. Always ask yourself when confronted with an objection, "Exactly which premise of the argument does the objection challenge?" Many times you'll find that the objection doesn't really challenge any premise and so is irrelevant to the argument! For example, I can almost guarantee that if you present the moral argument, the response will be either "How dare you say that nonbelievers can't live good moral lives!" or else "You don't have to believe in God in order to know right from wrong!" These objections are aimed at straw men and so are irrelevant to the argument. By writing out the premises on a piece of paper for your non-believing friend, you can help him to see what is and is not relevant and to have something to take with him from the conversation.

I also find it helpful to be able to lay out a cumulative case comprising several arguments for God's existence. It's funny, but it's been my experience that just being able to name several arguments for God's existence (even without giving the premises!) astonishes many people and lends weight to theism's credibility. The arguments themselves show how the God hypothesis makes sense of a broad range of the facts of human experience and therefore how very powerful a hypothesis it is. As I mentioned earlier, we should think of the arguments like a coat of chain mail in which the links reinforce one another. Many unbelievers have been taught to raise stock objections, like "That argument only proves a Designer of the universe, not a Creator" or "That argument only proves that there is a Creator of the universe, not that he is good." One can freely admit that the cosmological argument doesn't prove the goodness of the Creator; that attribute is shown instead by the moral argument; and the cosmological argument proves that there is a personal Creator of the universe, even if the teleological argument does not. Having a variety of arguments not only reinforces common conclusions but also rounds out the nature of the being whose existence they prove.

Of course, it goes without saying that we should present these arguments with gentleness and respect. We mustn't be quarrelsome with a non-believer, or we'll only succeed in alienating him. Having solid arguments will actually help you to remain calm in the face of angry attacks because you will realize how misled many people are and will respond to them with compassion. When you have good reasons for what you believe and know the answers to objections to your arguments, then there's just no reason to get hot under the collar. Instead you'll find it a pleasure to discuss these important and interesting questions with people who do not yet believe.

Some of you may be wondering, "But how could I possibly share all this material in an evangelistic contact?" Here we must simply exercise a little common sense and be sensitive to where the other person is in his thinking. Of course, you don't lay all this stuff about actual and potential infinity, the expanding universe, fine-tuning, Boltzmann Brains, supervenient moral properties, and the possibility of maximal greatness on the poor non-Christian at once! You need to understand how deep his thinking and background concerning these subjects are in order to know just what to relate to him. You start simple and go deep as he has further questions. I know this material is effective, because I've seen God use it when it's communicated with sensitivity.

For example, my wife, Jan, was once talking to a gal in the student union who said that she did not believe in God. Jan replied, "Well, what do you think of the argument for a first cause?" "What's that?" she said. Jan explained, "Everything we see has a cause, and those causes have causes, and so on. But this can't go back forever. There had to be a beginning and a first cause which started the whole thing. This is God." Now that was obviously a very simple statement of the *kalām* cosmological argument. The young woman responded, "I guess God exists after all." She wasn't ready to place her faith in Christ at that point, but at least she had moved one step closer, away from her atheism.

When one talks with a person who has a deeper understanding of these issues, then of course one must go deeper. For example, many years ago when we were studying in Germany on a research fellowship, we met a Polish physicist who was there on a similar fellowship. As we chatted, she mentioned that physics had destroyed her belief in God and that life had become meaningless to her. "When I look out at the universe all I see is blackness," she explained, "and when I look within myself all I see is blackness." (What a poignant statement of the modern predicament!)

Well, at that point Jan volunteered, "Oh, you should read Bill's doctoral dissertation. He uses physics to prove God exists." So we loaned her my dissertation to read on the cosmological argument. Over the ensuing days, she became progressively more excited. When she got to the section on astronomy and astrophysics, she was positively elated. "I *know* these scientists that you are quoting!" she exclaimed in amazement. By the time she reached the end, her faith had been restored. "Thank you for helping me to believe that God exists," she said.

We answered, "Would you like to know him in a personal way?" Then we made an appointment to meet her that evening at a restaurant. Meanwhile we prepared from memory our own hand-printed Four Spiritual Laws.

After supper we opened the booklet and began, "Just as there are physical laws that govern the physical universe, so there are spiritual laws that govern your relationship to God . . ."

"Why, physical laws! Spiritual laws!" she exclaimed. "This is just for me!" When we got to the circles at the end representing two lives and asked her which circle represented her life, she put her hand over the circles and said, "Oh, this is so personal. I cannot answer now." So we encouraged her to take the booklet home and to give her life to Christ.

When we saw her the next day, her face was radiant with joy. She told us of how she had gone home and in the privacy of her room prayed to receive Christ. She then flushed all the wine and tranquilizers on which she had been relying down the toilet. She was a truly transformed individual. We gave her a *Good News for Modern Man* and explained the importance of maintaining a devotional life with God. Our paths then parted for several months. But when we saw her again she was still enthusiastic in her faith, and her most precious possessions were her Good News Bible and her hand-made Four Spiritual Laws. So it was a great victory for God. It was one of the most vivid illustrations I've seen of how the Holy Spirit can use arguments and evidence to draw someone to a saving knowledge of God.

Let me add few words about each of the arguments in particular. The Leibnizian cosmological argument has a tremendous philosophical pedigree, historically speaking. It is based upon a very deep-seated metaphysical puzzle, namely, why does anything at all exist? This question has bothered philosophers for literally millennia. In sharing the argument, we should try to evoke a sense of the mystery of existence in unbelievers. Nevertheless, I must confess that I've not had much occasion to use the Leibnizian cosmological argument in evangelism. My suspicion is that it's too abstract to be comprehensible to most people. But for philosophically-minded people the argument may be appealing. The key to the argument will be the first premise. Unbelievers recognize no other exception to this principle apart from the universe itself; but why should the universe be an exception? We saw that attempts to justify an exemption for the universe turned out to be question-begging. Use an illustration like Richard Taylor's story of the ball in the woods, which we keep increasing in size until it becomes co-extensive with the universe, to motivate acceptance of the principle. I personally like this argument very much.

As for the *kalām* cosmological argument, I have found it very useful in evangelism. Just recently Jan and I were on a trip to China with the Society of Christian Philosophers, where we had the chance to participate in conference at Fudan University in Shanghai. There I heard a presentation from a Chinese graduate student in philosophy that floored me: it was a defense of *kalām* arguments for the finitude of the past! I said to Jan, "I wonder if he's hit upon these arguments independently." After his presentation, I gave him a booklet in Chinese of my article on the existence of God and the beginning of the universe. The next day when we saw him, he could hardly contain his excitement. "I had no idea that someone else has had similar thoughts about this," he said. "When I read your booklet, I was so thrilled—in fact, I cried!" We gave him further materials on the existence of God and the resurrection of Christ, which he gratefully received. A bridge had been built through the *kalām* cosmological argument.

The *kalām* argument is also a natural bridge to sharing with Muslims, having, as it does, so rich a heritage in medieval Islamic thought. I'm not sure how I feel about this, but I've been told by Muslim apologists how much they've appreciated my work because they use my arguments all the time in debates with atheists! That made me realize all the more how important it is that Christians be trained to share these arguments, lest they be co-opted by Muslims. At any rate the *kalām* argument gives us a point in common with Muslims from which we may go on to share the gospel.

Probably the most common response that you'll get to the *kalām* cosmological argument is the retort, "What caused God?" This is usually put with an air of triumph, as though it were a profound and unanswerable question, a stake in the heart of theism. I am just amazed to hear this childish question even on the lips of intelligent professors. In fact, the question is easy to answer. Recently speaking at Oxford University, I was put this question, so I patiently explained that the first premise of the argument is not that "Everything has a cause" but that "Everything that *begins to exist* has a cause," and since God didn't begin to exist, he doesn't require a cause. Indeed, an eternal being *cannot* have an antecedent cause. So God is simply uncaused. Afterwards, Richard Cunningham, the Inter-Varsity Director for the United Kingdom, took me aside and said, "Bill, your answer was fine, but you need to help people see just how dumb the question is by poking a little fun at it." So when I was in Cambridge the next week and was asked the same question, I said, "You know, that's really a meaningless question. It's like wracking your brain wondering, 'What is the cause of the First Uncaused Cause?'" That got a laugh out of the audience and did seem a more effective way of communicating the point. Asking for God's cause is sort of like asking for a bachelor's wife.

I also find that most people don't understand the Big Bang theory. They seem to think that there was a super-dense pellet of material existing in empty space from time immemorial which then blew up. You need to help them see that this is a complete misunderstanding of the model. Explain to them that according to the theory all matter and energy, even physical space and time themselves, came into being at the Big Bang: there was literally nothing before it (that is to say, there wasn't anything before it). So the cause of the universe has to be a transcendent being. Don't let them try to wriggle out by saying that we don't understand the physics of the very early universe, for the Borde-Guth-Vilenkin theorem we discussed does not depend upon having a physical theory of this era.

As for the teleological argument, the great advantage of the fine-tuning version is that it enables you to do an end run around the emotionally loaded question of biological evolution and to show that in order for evolution to take place anywhere in the universe the initial cosmic conditions had to be incomprehensibly fine-tuned. This version of the argument enjoys the strategic advantage that instead of bucking a widely accepted scientific theory, it is wholly in line with accepted scientific thinking. Therefore, belief in evolution is a non-issue; we're not asking the unbeliever to abandon his belief in biological evolution.

With respect to the moral argument, notice that the argument is formulated in terms of objective morals rather than moral absolutes. The term *absolute* is misleading and can raise unnecessary obstacles in the unbeliever's mind. An action can be objectively wrong without its being absolutely wrong. Killing another person may be wrong in some circumstances and right in others (as when a policeman shoots a terrorist); but in each set of circumstances there will be objectively right and wrong things to do, right to kill in some circumstances and wrong in others. What we're interested in is objectivity, not absoluteness.

In my experience, the moral argument is the most effective argument for the existence of God. I say this grudgingly because my favorite is the cosmological argument. But cosmological and teleological arguments don't really hit people where they live and so can be dismissed as curiosities. But the moral argument cannot be so brushed aside. Every day that you get up you answer the question of whether there are objective moral values and duties by how you live. It's unavoidable.

Moreover, this argument has tremendous force because students have been indoctrinated to believe both premises. They've just never put them together to see the inevitable implication. On the one hand, they've been taught to believe that moral relativism is true, that moral values and duties are culturally and even personally relative and that you have no right to judge another. They've been told the evolutionary story and believe that morality is the byproduct of nature and nurture. On the other hand, they're steeped in political correctness and the values it entails. For example, the sentiment expressed above that no one has the right to judge another is not meant to be a denial of moral obligation but rather the affirmation of the obligation to be tolerant and open-minded. The conviction is that it is wrong to judge another. Although students give lip service to relativism, they don't really believe it nor do they live that way. Just ask them, "So, do you really think that it would be all right if the government rounded up all homosexuals and threw them into concentration camps the way the Nazis did? You don't really have a problem with racial discrimination, I suppose? You think there's nothing really bad about wife beating or child abuse?" You can make the point especially effectively by using moral atrocities perpetrated in the name of religion. "You think it's okay for Catholic priests to sexually abuse little boys and that the Church did nothing wrong in trying to cover it up? I guess you don't have any problem with the Crusades or the Inquisition. On your view, there's nothing really wrong about imposing your beliefs on another person, right?" If you're dealing with someone who is an honest inquirer I can guarantee that 95 percent of the time that person will agree that there are objective moral values and duties.

Now this puts the unbeliever in a real dilemma. Realize that you don't need to *prove* the premises of the argument to be true. The premises in a sound argument just need to be true. So long as the non-believer believes the premises to be true, then he's logically committed to believing the conclusion as well. If he's to avoid the argument's conclusion, he must deny one of the premises. But which one? He believes them both. This quandary can lead to some really strange conversations. I remember one case in which the nonbeliever I was talking with would jump back and forth between the premises. When we talked about the first premise, he'd agree with it and deny the second. But when we talked about the second, he'd agree with it and deny the first. And so back and forth we went, with him unable to make up his mind! This may seem funny, but in fact it's pathetic to see someone floundering in this way in a vain attempt to avoid God.

Very frequently, non-theists in the free thought crowd respond to the moral argument by attacking the morality taught in the Bible or pointing to seeming moral atrocities commanded by God in the Bible like the slaughter of the Canaanites. "The God of the Hebrew Bible is a moral monster!" they'll declare. This attempt to turn the tables is a red herring, and you shouldn't be fooled by it. Just ask yourself: which premise of the moral argument does it refute? Certainly not the second! Indeed, in order to denounce God's actions recorded in the Bible as immoral, one must presuppose that objective moral values exist. So the objection actually presupposes belief in the second premise. So what about the first premise, that if God does not exist, objective moral values and duties do not exist? Is that premise in any way defeated by the objection? Well, no; stories of atrocities in the Bible do nothing to undermine the naturalistic account of morality. Can you imagine trying to refute Michael Ruse by pointing to stories in the Bible?

So what does the objection prove? At the very most, it would prove that certain biblical writers got it wrong in attributing these commands to God. That conclusion wouldn't even faze a theist who is outside the Judaeo-Christian tradition. And even in the case of Jews and Christians, what adjustments to their theology would such a conclusion necessitate? Certainly, it wouldn't require them to give up the existence of God or his moral perfection. Rather, they would be forced at most to give up biblical inerrancy. So doing would require them to adjust their doctrine of biblical inspiration so as not to imply inerrancy. That would doubtless be a major adjustment, but it would be wholly irrelevant to divine command moral theory. What we come to see, then, is that this attack upon the portrayal of God in the Hebrew Bible is not really an attack upon divine command moral theory or God's moral perfection but is rather an attack upon biblical inerrancy and so should be treated as such.[42] It does nothing to defeat the moral argument for God's existence. So if you keep your head and don't get distracted by irrelevancies, I think you'll find the moral argument for God to be very defensible and extremely persuasive.

Which brings us finally to the ontological argument. It's been said that probably no one in the history of mankind has come to believe in God on the basis of

42. For responses to such objections see Paul Copan, *That's Just Your Interpretation* (Grand Rapids, Mich.: Baker, 2001); idem, *How Do You Know You're Not Wrong?* (Grand Rapids, Mich.: Baker, 2005).

the ontological argument. That's not really true—one of my fellow grad students who was writing his dissertation on the ontological argument told me that his adviser had come to believe that the argument was sound—but still the point is undeniable that it hasn't played much of a role in evangelism. After a long period of skepticism about the argument, I came to believe that the argument is not merely sound but a good one. I've not used it in evangelism simply because it's so difficult for people to understand and because there are other, more compelling arguments. I did finally use it as part of a cumulative case in a talk at a Veritas Forum at Ohio University this past year, but all the questions from the audience concerned the other arguments. I'd like to use it more often. Remember: you don't need to prove a premise to someone in order for the argument to be a good one for him. So long as he believes the premises to be true, he is rationally obliged to accept the conclusion. So we may simply present the argument to the unbeliever as a conditional: if God's existence is even possible, then God exists. That alone is a mind-boggling revelation! We could grant, if we wish, that we can't prove in a non-question-begging way that God's existence is possible, but still rightly insist that if the unbeliever agrees that God's existence is possible, then he's logically committed to the conclusion that God exists. That should give him something to think about!

So I encourage you to master these arguments and learn to communicate them with sensitivity. One of my apologetics teachers once advised, "Know your subject profoundly and share it simply." If you can't answer an unbeliever's objection on some point, admit it and refer him to literature on the subject that can satisfy his question. In an age of increasing atheism and agnosticism, we cannot afford to forgo an apologetic for this most basic of all Christian beliefs: the existence of God.

Literature Cited or Recommended

Historical Background

Al-Ghāzalī. "The Jerusalem Tract." Translated and edited by A. L. Tibawi. *The Islamic Quarterly* 9 (1965): 95–122.

———. *Kitab al-Iqtisad fi'l-I'tiqad.* Cited in Beaurecueil, S. de. "Gazzali et S. Thomas d'Aqin: Essai sur la preuve de l'existence de Dieu proposée dans l'Iqtisad et sa comparaison avec les 'voies' Thomistes." *Bulletin de l'Institut Francais d'Archaeologie Orientale* 46 (1947): 199–238.

———. *Tahafut al-Falasifah* [*Incoherence of the Philosophers*]. Translated by Sabih Ahmad Kamali. Lahore, Pakistan: Pakistan Philosophical Congress, 1958.

Anselm. *Proslogion.* In *Anselm of Canterbury,* 4 vols., edited and translated by Jaspar Hopkins and Herbert Richardson. London: SCM, 1974. See particularly 2, 3.

Aristotle. *The Works of Aristotle.* 12 vols. Edited by W. D. Ross. Oxford: Clarendon, 1908–1952.

Chroust, Anton-Hermann. "A Cosmological (Teleological) Proof for the Existence of God in Aristotle's *On Philosophy*." In *Aristotle: New Light on His Lost Works*. London: Routledge & Kegan Paul, 1972. 2:159–74.

Craig, William Lane. *The Cosmological Argument from Plato to Leibniz*. New York: Barnes & Noble, 1980.

Hume, David. *Dialogues Concerning Natural Religion*. Edited with an introduction by Norman Kemp Smith. New York: Bobbs-Merrill, 1947.

Leibniz, G. W. F. von. "Monadology." In *Leibniz Selections*, edited by P. Wiener, 533–52. New York: Scribner's, 1951.

———. "On the Ultimate Origin of Things." In *Leibniz Selections*, edited by P. Wiener, 345–55. New York: Scribner's, 1951.

———. "The Principles of Nature and of Grace, Based on Reason." In *Leibniz Selections*, edited by P. Wiener, 522–33. New York: Scribner's, 1951.

———. *Theodicy: Essays on the Goodness of God, the Freedom of Man, and the Origin of Evil*. Translated by E. M. Huggard. London: Routledge & Kegan Paul, 1951.

"Modernizing the Case for God," *Time*, April 7, 1980, 65–66.

Paley, William. *Natural Theology: Selections*. Edited with an introduction by F. Ferré. Indianapolis: Bobbs-Merrill, 1963.

Plantinga, Alvin, ed. *The Ontological Argument*. Garden City, N.Y.: Doubleday, 1965.

Plato. *The Dialogues of Plato*. 4 vols. 4th ed., rev. Translated with introductions and analyses by B. Jowett. Oxford: Clarendon, 1953.

Smith, Quentin, "The Metaphilosophy of Naturalism" *Philo* 4/2(2001); http://www.philoonline.org/library/smith_4_2.htm.

Sorley, William R. *Moral Values and the Idea of God*. New York: Macmillan, 1930.

Stephen, Leslie. *History of English Thought in the Eighteenth Century*. 2 vols. 2nd ed. London: Smith, Elder, 1881.

Tennant, F. R. *Philosophical Theology*. 2 vols. Cambridge: Cambridge University Press, 1930. His teleological argument is in volume 2.

Thomas Aquinas. *On the Truth of the Catholic Faith*. Edited and translated by Anton C. Pegis, et al. Notre Dame, Ind.: University of Notre Dame Press, 1975. See particularly 1.13.

———. *Summa theologiae*. 60 vols. London: Eyre & Spottiswoode for Blackfriars, 1964. See particularly 1a.2, 3.

Assessment

Adams, Robert Merrihew. *Finite and Infinite Goods*. Oxford: Oxford University Press, 2000.

———. "Flavors, Colors, and God." In *The Virtue of Faith*. New York: Oxford University Press, 1987.

Alston, William. "What Euthyphro Should Have Said." In *Philosophy of Religion: a Reader and Guide*, edited by William L. Craig, 283–98. Edinburgh: Edinburgh University Press, 2001; New Brunswick, N. J.: Rutgers University Press, 2001.

Balaguer, Mark, *Platonism and Anti-Platonism in Mathematics*. New York: Oxford University Press, 1998.

————. *Stanford Encyclopedia of Philosophy*, s.v. "Platonism in Metaphysics," by Mark Balaguer (Summer 2004). Edited by Edward N. Zalta, http://plato.stanford.edu/archives/sum2004/ entries/platonism/

————. "A Theory of Mathematical Correctness and Mathematical Truth," *Pacific Philosophical Quarterly* 82 (2001): 87–114.

Barrow, John D. *Theories of Everything*. Oxford: Clarendon Press, 1991.

Barrow, John D. and Frank J. Tipler. *The Anthropic Cosmological Principle*. Oxford: Clarendon, 1986. A compendious update of Paley's catalogue.

Boa, Kenneth and Robert M. Bowman. *20 Compelling Evidences That God Exists*. Tulsa, Okla.: RiverOak, 2002.

Boltzmann, Ludwig, *Lectures on Gas Theory*. Translated by Stephen G. Brush. Berkeley: University of California Press, 1964.

Borde, A. and A. Vilenkin, "Eternal Inflation and the Initial Singularity." *Physical Review Letters* 72 (1994): 3305–8.

Borde, A., Alan Guth, and Alexander Vilenkin, "Inflation Is Not Past-Eternal." http://arXiv: gr-qc/0110012v1 (October 1, 2001).

Bousso, R. and B. Freivogel, "A paradox in the global description of the multiverse." http:// arXiv:hep-th/0610132.

Brink, David O. "The Autonomy of Ethics." In *The Cambridge Companion to Atheism*, edited by Michael Martin, 149–65. Cambridge Companions to Philosophy. Cambridge: Cambridge University Press, 2007.

Burrill, Donald R. *The Cosmological Arguments*. Garden City, N.Y.: Doubleday, 1967.

Chihara, Charles S., *Constructibility and Mathematical Existence*. Oxford: Clarendon, 1990.

————. *A Structural Account of Mathematics*. Oxford: Clarendon Press, 2004.

Collins, Robin. "A Scientific Argument for the Existence of God: The Fine-Tuning Design Argument." In *Reason for the Hope Within*, edited by Michael J. Murray, 47–75. Grand Rapids, Mich.: Eerdmans, 1999.

————. *The Well-Tempered Universe: God, Fine-Tuning, and the Laws of Nature*. 2 vols. (forthcoming).

Copan, Paul. *How Do You Know You're Not Wrong?* Grand Rapids, Mich.: Baker, 2005.

————. *That's Just Your Interpretation*. Grand Rapids, Mich.: Baker, 2001.

Copan, Paul and William Lane Craig. *Creation out of Nothing: A Biblical, Philosophical, and Scientific Exploration*. Grand Rapids, Mich.: Baker, 2004.

Copan, Paul and Paul Moser, eds. *The Rationality of Theism*. London: Routledge, 2003.

Craig, William Lane. *The Kalām Cosmological Argument*. New York: Barnes & Noble, 1979.

————. ed. *Philosophy of Religion: A Reader and Guide*. New Brunswick, N. J.: Rutgers University Press, 2001.

————. *Time and Eternity*. Wheaton, Ill.: Crossway Books, 2001.

Craig, William Lane and Antony Flew. *Does God Exist?* Edited by Stan Wallace. With responses by K. Yandell, P. Moser, D. Geivett, M. Martin, D. Yandell, W. Rowe, K. Parsons, and Wm. Wainwright. Aldershot, England: Ashgate, 2003.

Craig, William Lane and Paul Kurtz. *God and Ethics: A Contemporary Debate*. Edited by Nathan King and Robert Garcia, with responses by L. Antony, W. Sinnott-Armstrong, J. Hare, D. Hubin, S. Layman, M. Murphy, and R. Swinburne. Lanham, Md.: Rowman & Littlefield, 2007.

Craig, William Lane and J. P. Moreland, eds. *Companion to Natural Theology*. Oxford: Blackwell, forthcoming. An outstanding collection of lengthy articles treating the principal thesitic arguments by Robin Collins, William Lane Craig, Stewart Goetz, Kai Man Kwan, Mark Linville, Lydia and Timothy McGrew, Robert Maydole, J. P. Moreland, Alexander Pruss, Victor Reppert, and Charles Taliaferro.

Craig, William Lane and Walter Sinnott-Armstrong. *God? A Debate between a Christian and an Atheist*. New York: Oxford University Press, 2003.

Craig, William Lane and Quentin Smith. *Theism, Atheism, and Big Bang Cosmology*. Oxford: Clarendon Press, 1993.

Davies, P. C. W. "The Big Bang—and Before." The Thomas Aquinas College Lecture Series. Thomas Aquinas College. Santa Paula, Calif., March 2002.

———. "The Big Questions: In the Beginning." ABC Science Online, interview with Phillip Adams, http://aca.mq.edu.au/pdavieshtml.

———. *The Mind of God*. New York: Simon & Schuster, 1992.

———. *The Physics of Time Asymmetry*. London: Surrey University Press, 1974.

———. "Spacetime Singularities in Cosmology." In *The Study of Time III*, edited by J. T. Fraser, N. Lawrence, D. Park, 74–91. Berlin: Springer, 1978.

Davis, Stephen T. "The Cosmological Argument and the Epistemic Status of Belief in God." *Philosophia Christi* 1 (1999): 5–15.

———. *God, Reason, and Theistic Proofs*. Grand Rapids, Mich.: Eerdmans, 1997.

Dawkins, Richard. *The God Delusion*. New York: Houghton Mifflin, 2006.

Dembski, William A. *The Design Inference: Eliminating Chance through Small Probabilities*. Cambridge Studies in Probability, Induction, and Decision Theory. Cambridge: Cambridge University Press, 1998.

Dennett, Daniel, *Breaking the Spell: Religion as a Natural Phenomenon*. New York: Viking, 2006.

Dicus, Duane, et al. "Effects of Proton Decay on the Cosmological Future." *Astrophysical Journal* 252 (1982): 1–9.

———. et al. "The Future of the Universe." *Scientific American*, March 1983, 90–101.

Denton, Michael. *Evolution: A Theory in Crisis*. Bethesda, Md.: Adler & Adler, 1986.

———. *Nature's Destiny: How the Laws of Biology Reveal Purpose in the Universe*. New York: Free Press, 1998.

———. et al. "Disturbing Implications of a Cosmological Constant." http://arXiv.org/abs/hep-th/0208013v3 (November 14, 2002).

Earman, John and Jesus Mosterin, "A Critical Look at Inflationary Cosmology." *Philosophy of Science* 66 (1999): 1–49.

Eddington, Arthur. *The Expanding Universe*. New York: Macmillan, 1933.

———. *Space, Time, and Gravitation*. 1920; repr. ed. Cambridge: Cambridge University Press, 1987.

Ellis, G. F. R., U. Kirchner, and W. R. Stoeger. "Multiverses and Physical Cosmology." http://arXiv:astro-ph/0305292 v3 (August 28, 2003).

Felder, Gary, Andret Frolov, Lev Kaufman, and Andrei Linde. "Cosmology with Negative Potentials." http://arXiv:hep-th/0202017v2 (February 16, 2002).

Gale, Richard M. "The Failure of Classic Theistic Arguments." In *The Cambridge Companion to Atheism*, edited by Michael Martin, 86–101. Cambridge Companions to Philosophy. Cambridge: Cambridge University Press, 2007.

———. *On the Existence and Nature of God*. New York: Cambridge University Press, 1991.

Gamow, George. *One, Two, Three, . . . Infinity*. London: Macmillan, 1946.

Ganssle, Gregory E. "Necessary Moral Truths and the Need for Explanation." *Philosophia Christi* 2 (2000): 105–12.

Gasperini, M. "Inflation and Initial Conditions in the Pre-Big Bang Scenario." *Physics Review D* 61 (2000): 87301–305.

———. "Looking Back in Time beyond the Big Bang." *Modern Physics Letters A* 14/16 (1999): 1059–66.

Gasperini, M. and G. Veneziano. "The Pre-Big Bang Scenario in String Cosmology." http://arXiv:hep-th/0207130v1 (July 12, 2002).

Gott III, J. R., "Creation of Open Universes from de Sitter Space." *Nature* 295 (1982): 304–7.

Gott, J. Richard, et al. "Will the Universe Expand Forever?" *Scientific American*, March 1976, 62–79.

Grünbaum, Adolf. "Pseudo-Creation of the Big Bang." *Nature* 344 (1990): 821–22.

———. "The Pseudo-Problem of Creation in Physical Cosmology." In *Physical Cosmology and Philosophy*, edited by John Leslie. Philosophical Topics, 92–112. New York: Macmillan, 1990.

Hackett, Stuart. *The Resurrection of Theism*. 2nd ed. Grand Rapids, Mich.: Baker, 1982.

Haldane, J. J. and J. J. C. Smart. *Atheism and Theism*. Great Debates in Philosophy. London: Blackwell, 1996.

Hartle, J. and S. Hawking. "Wave Function of the Universe." *Physical Review D* 28 (1983): 2960–75.

Hawking, Stephen. *A Brief History of Time*. New York: Bantam, 1988.

———. "Information Loss in Black Holes." http://arXiv:hep-th/0507171v2 (September 15, 2005).

Hawking, Stephen and Roger Penrose. *The Nature of Space and Time*. The Isaac Newton Institute Series of Lectures. Princeton, N. J.: Princeton University Press, 1996.

Hick, John. *Arguments for the Existence of God*. London: Macmillan, 1971.

Hilbert, David, "On the Infinite." In *Philosophy of Mathematics*, edited with an introduction by Paul Benacerraf and Hillary Putnam, 183–201. Englewood Cliffs, N.J.: Prentice-Hall, 1964.

Hume, David. *The Letters of David Hume.* 2 vols. Edited by J. Y. T. Greig. Oxford: Clarendon, 1932.

Idziak, Janine Marie. *Divine Command Morality: Historical and Contemporary Readings.* Lewiston, N.Y.: Edwin Mellen Press, 1980.

Isham, C. J. "Creation of the Universe as a Quantum Process." In *Physics, Philosophy, and Theology*, edited by R. J. Russell, W. R. Stoeger, and G. V. Coyne. Vatican City State: Vatican Observatory, 1988.

————. "Quantum Theories of the Creation of the Universe." Unpublished paper, a preliminary version of which appears in *Interpreting the Universe as Creation.* Edited by V. Brummer. The Netherlands: Pharos, 1991.

————. "Space, Time, and Quantum Cosmology." Paper presented at the conference "God, Time, and Modern Physics." Science and Religion Forum, March 1990.

Jastrow, Robert. *God and the Astronomers.* New York: W. W. Norton, 1978.

Kanitscheider, Bernulf. "Does Physical Cosmology Transcend the Limits of Naturalistic Reasoning?" In *Studies on Mario Bunge's "Treatise,"* edited by P. Weingartner and G. J. W. Doen, 346–74. Amsterdam: Rodopi, 1990.

Kurtz, Paul. *The Courage to Become.* Westport, Conn.: Praeger, 1997.

————. *Forbidden Fruit.* Buffalo, N.Y.: Prometheus, 1988.

Leslie, John. "The Prerequisites of Life in Our Universe." In *Newton and the New Direction in Science*, edited by G. V. Coyne, M. Heller, and J. Zycinski, 97–119. Vatican: Citta del Vaticano, 1988.

————. *Universes.* London: Routledge, 1989.

Linde, A. D. "Chaotic Inflation." *Physics Letters* 1298 (1983): 177–81.

————. "The Inflationary Universe." *Reports on Progress in Physics* 47 (1984): 925–86.

————. "Sinks in the Landscape, Boltzmann Brains, and the Cosmological Constant Problem." http://arXiv:hep-th/0611043.

Linde, A. D. and Arthur Mezhlumian. "From the Big Bang Theory to the Theory of a Stationary Universe." *Physical Review D* 49 (1994): 1783–1826.

Lipton, Peter. *Inference to the Best Explanation.* London: Routledge, 1991.

Mackie, J. L. Critical notice of *The Creation*, by Peter Atkins. *Times Literary Supplement* 5 (February 1982), 126.

————. *The Miracle of Theism.* Oxford: Clarendon, 1982.

Martin, Michael, ed. *The Cambridge Companion to Atheism.* Cambridge Companions to Philosophy. Cambridge: Cambridge University Press, 2007.

Maydole, Robert. "The Modal Perfection Argument for the Existence of God." *Philo* 6 (2003): 299–313.

McMullin, Ernan. "Anthropic Explanation in Cosmology." Paper delivered at the conference "God and Physical Cosmology," University of Notre Dame, January 30–February 1, 2003.

Naber, Gregory L. *Spacetime and Singularities: an Introduction*. Cambridge: Cambridge University Press, 1988.

Novikov, I. D., and Ya. B. Zeldovich. "Physical Processes Near Cosmological Singularities." *Annual Review of Astronomy and Astrophysics* 11 (1973): 387–410.

Nowacki, Mark R. *The Kalām Cosmological Argument for God*. Studies in Analytic Philosophy. Buffalo, N.Y.: Prometheus Books, 2007.

Oderberg, David S. "Traversal of the Infinite, the 'Big Bang,' and the Kalām Cosmological Argument." *Philosophia Christi* 4 (2002): 303–34.

Oppy, Graham. *Arguing about Gods*. Cambridge: Cambridge University Press, 2006.

———. *Ontological Arguments and Belief in God*. Cambridge: Cambridge University Press, 1995.

———. *Philosophical Perspectives on Infinity*. Cambridge: Cambridge University Press, 2006.

Page, Don N. "Return of the Boltzmann Brains." http://arXiv:hep-th/0611158 (November 15, 2006).

Penrose, Roger. *The Road to Reality*. New York: Alfred A. Knopf, 2005.

———. "Time-Asymmetry and Quantum Gravity." In *Quantum Gravity 2*, edited by C. J. Isham, R. Penrose, and D. W. Sciama, 245–72. Oxford: Clarendon, 1981.

Plantinga, Alvin. *The Nature of Necessity*. Oxford: Clarendon, 1974. See particularly the section on the ontological argument.

———. "Two Dozen (or So) Theistic Arguments." Paper presented at the 33rd Annual Philosophy Conference, Wheaton College, October 23–25, 1986. Reprinted as an appendix to Deane-Peter Baker, ed. *Alvin Plantinga*, 203–27. Cambridge: Cambridge University Press.

Pruss, Alexander R. Critical notice of *Why Is There Something Rather Than Nothing?* by Bede Rundle. *Philosophia Christi* 7 (2005): 209–13.

———. *The Principle of Sufficient Reason: A Reassessment*. Cambridge: Cambridge University Press, 2006.

Quinn, Philip L. *Divine Commands and Moral Requirements*. Oxford: Clarendon Press, 1978.

Rees, Martin. *Just Six Numbers*. New York: Basic Books, 2000.

Reeves, Hubert, Jean Audouze, William A. Fowler, and David N. Schramm. "On the Origin of Light Elements." *Astrophysical Journal* 179 (1973): 909–30.

Rundle, Bede. *Why Is There Something Rather Than Nothing?* Oxford: Oxford University Press, 2004.

Ruse, Michael. *Darwinism Defended*. London: Addison-Wesley, 1982.

———. "Evolutionary Theory and Christian Ethics." In *The Darwinian Paradigm*, 262–69. London: Routledge, 1989.

Russell, Bertrand. *Our Knowledge of the External World*. 2nd ed. New York: W. W. Norton, 1929.

Schlegel, Richard, "Time and Thermodynamics." In *The Voices of Time*, edited by J. T. Fraser. London: Penguin, 1968.

Sierpiński, Wacław. *Cardinal and Ordinal Numbers*. Polska Akademia Nauk Monografie Matematyczne 34. Warsaw: Państwowe Wydawnictwo Naukowe, 1958.

Silk, Joseph. *The Big Bang*. 2nd ed. San Francisco: W. H. Freeman, 1989.

Sinnott-Armstrong, Walter. "Moral Skepticism and Justification." In *Moral Knowledge*, edited by Walter Sinnott-Armstrong and Mark Timmons, 3–48. New York: Oxford University Press, 1996.

———. "Why Traditional Theism Cannot Provide an Adequate Foundation for Morality." In *God and Ethics: A Contemporary Debate*, edited by Nathan King and Robert Garcia. Lanham, Md.: Rowman & Littlefield, 2008.

Smith, Quentin. "Kalām Cosmological Arguments for Atheism." In *The Cambridge Companion to Atheism*, edited by Michael Martin, 182–98. Cambridge Companions to Philosophy. Cambridge: Cambridge University Press, 2007.

———. "The Metaphilosophy of Naturalism." *Philo* 4 (2001): 195–215. Also available online http://www.qsmithwmu.com/metaphilosophy_of_naturalism.htm.

Sobel, Jordan Howard. *Logic and Theism: Arguments For and Against Beliefs in God*. Cambridge: Cambridge University Press, 2004.

Susskind, Leonard. *The Cosmic Landscape: String Theory and the Illusion of Intelligent Design*. New York: Little, Brown, 2006.

Swinburne, Richard. *The Existence of God*. Rev. ed. Oxford: Clarendon, 1991.

Taylor, Richard. *Ethics, Faith, and Reason*. Englewood Cliffs, N.J.: Prentice-Hall, 1985.

———. *Metaphysics*. 4th ed. Foundations of Philosophy. Englewood Cliffs, N.J.: Prentice-Hall, 1991.

Tinsley, Beatrice. "From Big Bang to Eternity?" *Natural History Magazine*, October 1975, 102–5.

Vaas, Rüdiger. "Time before Time: Classifications of Universes in contemporary cosmology, and how to avoid the antinomy of the beginning and eternity of the world." http://arXiv.org/abs/physics/0408111 (2004).

Veneziano, Gabriele. "A Simple/Short Introduction to Pre-Big Bang Physics/Cosmology." http://arXiv:hep-th/9802057v2 (March 2, 1998).

Vilenkin, Alex. "Birth of Inflationary Universes." *Physical Review D* 27 (1983): 2848–55.

———. "Creation of the Universe from Nothing." *Physical Letters* 117B (1982): 25–8.

———. *Many Worlds in One: The Search for Other Universes*. New York: Hill and Wang, 2006.

———. "Quantum Cosmology and Eternal Inflation." http://arXiv:gr-qc/0204061v1 (April 18, 2002).

Wainwright, William J. *Religion and Morality*. Ashgate Philosophy of Religion Series. Aldershot, England: Ashgate, 2005.

Wheeler, John A. "Beyond the Hole." In *Some Strangeness in the Proportion*, edited by Harry Woolf, 341–75. Reading, Mass.: Addison-Wesley, 1980.

Wittgenstein, Ludwig. *Lectures on the Foundations of Mathematics*. Edited by Cora Diamond. Sussex, England: Harvester, 1976.

Wolpert, Lewis. *Six Impossible Things before Breakfast*. London: Faber and Faber, 2006.

Wright, Crispen and Bob Hale. "Nominalism and the Contingency of Abstract Objects." *Journal of Philosophy* 89 (1992): 111–35.

Yablo, Stephen. "Go Figure: A Path through Fictionalism." In *Figurative Language*, edited by Peter A. French and Howard K. Wettstein. Midwest Studies in Philosophy 25, 72–102. Oxford: Blackwell, 2001.

———. "A Paradox of Existence." In *Empty Names, Fiction, and the Puzzles of Non-Existence*, edited by Anthony Everett and Thomas Hofweber, 275–312. Stanford: Center for Study of Language and Information, 2000.

Part 4

De Creatione

5

The Problem of Historical
Knowledge

"The uniqueness and the scandal of the Christian religion," writes George Ladd, "rest in the mediation of revelation through historical events." Christianity is not a code for living or a philosophy of religion; rather it is rooted in real events of history. To some this is scandalous, because it means that the truth of Christianity is bound up with the truth of certain historical facts, such that if those facts should be disproved, so would Christianity. But at the same time, this makes Christianity unique because, unlike most other world religions, we now have a means of verifying its truth by historical evidence.

This, however, brings us face-to-face with the problem of historical knowledge; that is to say, how is it possible to learn anything about the human past with any degree of assurance? On the popular level, this expresses itself in the attitude that history is uncertain and irrelevant to us today. It has been said that history is a series of lies that everyone has decided to agree on. On the scholarly level, the problem finds expression in the outlook of historical relativism, which denies the objectivity of historical facts. This outlook has profound implications for Christian theology in the areas of apologetics, hermeneutics, and the doctrine of revelation, to name a few. It would make it impossible to demonstrate historically the accuracy of the biblical narratives, since the past cannot be objectively established. One would be free to impose whatever meaning one chose upon the narratives, since facts have no meaning. And one could leave aside the doctrine of the inerrancy of Scripture, since it would be meaningless to speak of "errors" if historical relativism were true. Therefore, it is imperative that the Christian scholar handle certain critical issues in the philosophy of history as a prelude to an examination of the biblical documents themselves.

Historical Background

Though people have written histories from earliest times, historiography as a science is a product of the modern age.

Medieval Period

To understand the development of this science and its impact upon apologetics, let's turn back to the Middle Ages.

MEDIEVAL DEARTH OF HISTORIOGRAPHY

After the Patristic age, the West, in contrast to the Byzantine lands, lapsed into a period of intellectual and cultural decline that lasted from the fifth to the eleventh centuries. Only in ecclesiastical circles were literacy and learning retained, for the masses were to a great extent illiterate. Most of the medieval histories of this time consisted of chronicles that simply listed events and their dates. Around A.D. 900 historiography almost completely disappeared. For the medieval historians, the biblical writers and the Church Fathers on the one hand, together with the classical writers and poets on the other, were considered "authors" or authorities, whose testimony was not questioned. Their successors counted as mere "writers" or "compilers," who adduced the testimony of authorities. Thus, verbatim reiteration became a virtue, and a writer describing the history of the recent past, for which no authorities could be adduced, often felt obliged to apologize to his readers for writing in his own words.

The character of medieval historical writing as reiteration of authorities was largely determined by Isidore, Bishop of Seville (d. 636), who argued in his *Etymologies* that since history, as contrasted to both fable and myth, narrates what truly took place, it must be an eyewitness account. Therefore, the narration of past events is simply a matter of compilation of the testimonies of authorities, who were taken to be eyewitnesses. Writing history consisted of copying one's sources. This historiographical method has been called the "scissors and paste" method by modern historians such as R. G. Collingwood, who emphasize the historian's liberty to criticize his sources.

Although the eleventh and twelfth centuries experienced a revival of culture and learning, this had little effect on historiography. With important exceptions, history continued in the main to be a recapitulation of authorities; and by the thirteenth century history as a literary form had collapsed back into chronicle. It is instructive to note that when in 1286 the administration of the University of

Paris drew up a booklist of all the texts necessary for basic reading at the university, only three out of 140 were historical in nature. It was not until the fifteenth century that modern historiography was born, and not until even later that history became a widely read literary genre.

IMPACT ON APOLOGETICS

Given this circumstance, it would be unrealistic to expect a historical apologetic for the Christian faith from medieval thinkers. What then could be done to commend rationally the Christian faith to unbelievers? Some thinkers, epitomized by Anselm, sought to prove the deity and incarnation of Christ (and hence the truth of the biblical books authorized by him) by *a priori* reasoning alone. At the conclusion of *Cur Deus Homo* Anselm's dialogue partner confesses:

> All things you have said seem to me reasonable and incontrovertible. And by the solution of the single question proposed, do I see the truth of all that is contained in the Old and New Testament. For, in proving that God became man by necessity, leaving out what was taken from the Bible . . . you convince both Jews and Pagans by the mere force of reason. And the God-man himself originates the New Testament and approves the Old. And, as we must acknowledge him to be true, so no one can dissent from anything contained in these books.[1]

Anselm's deductive approach circumvented the need for any historical investigation of the facts, since everything was proved by deductive reasoning from intuitively obvious premises.

On the other hand, we find very early on, and then with increasing sophistication in the thirteenth century, the development of a philosophical framework well suited for historical argumentation, even if it was itself devoid of such argumentation. According to this approach, one supported the authority of Scripture by the empirical signs of credibility, mainly miracle and prophecy. Those were the chief signs employed by Augustine to justify belief in the authority of Scripture. Although early scholasticism tended to follow Anselm's *a priori* approach, during the thirteenth century this approach became less convincing, and increasing weight was given instead to the external signs.

According to Thomas Aquinas, the truths of faith, while unprovable directly, can nevertheless be confirmed or proved indirectly by means of miracle and prophecy. For Aquinas, miracle is the most important sign of credibility. It confirms the truths of faith in two ways: it confirms the truth of what the miracle worker teaches, and it makes known God's presence in the miracle worker. Hence, he says with regard to Christ's miracles: "Christ wrought miracles in order to confirm his teaching, and in order to demonstrate the divine power that was his."[2] I shall argue in the next chapter that this approach to the interpretation of miracle is

---

1. Anselm, *Cur Deus homo* 2.22.
2. Thomas Aquinas, *Summa theologiae* 3a.43.3.

essentially correct. For Aquinas, therefore, the crucial problem is *historical*: how do I know that the miracles in question ever occurred? Here there is danger of reasoning in a circle: miracles confirm that the Scripture is from God; therefore, what it teaches is authoritatively true; therefore, the miracles recorded in Scripture really occurred. Now Aquinas himself never so reasons—he just leaves the historical question unanswered. But the philosophical framework he constructs is well suited to historical argumentation for the events in question, thus filling the gap and avoiding circularity.

Because the medievals lacked the historical method, they could not argue in any substantial way for the historicity of the events recorded in the Gospels. About the only proof they offered for the historicity of the miracles and fulfilled prophecies was the origin and growth of the Christian church. But with the rise of historical consciousness, that deficit could be remedied and the medieval framework could be filled out with historical evidences.

Modern Period

Modern apologetics has been to a great extent historical apologetics. Let's examine briefly how this came to pass.

RISE OF HISTORICAL CONSCIOUSNESS

It is probably no coincidence that the rise of historical apologetics parallels the rise of modern historiography. The modern science of historical study was born in the Italian Renaissance. The first stirrings of the Renaissance spirit in Italy found expression in the search for ancient manuscripts. The humanists cultivated the use of classical Latin and Greek and found their greatest delight in the discovery of documents of antiquity in those languages. They developed the skills of historical criticism; on the basis of internal criteria alone Lorenzo Valla was able to expose the famous Donation of Constantine, on the basis of which the Catholic Church claimed secular authority over Italy, as a forgery. Despite this embarrassment, for nearly a century the papacy supported the humanist writers, and learning and the arts flourished in Rome. In search of ancient manuscripts, Italian humanists visited the monasteries of Northern Europe, and the new learning spread, eventually making its way into the university chairs of Germany and into cultivated circles elsewhere. France, after its invasion of Italy in 1494, thoroughly imbibed the spirit of the Italian Renaissance. Before the end of the fifteenth century, Oxford University was already offering courses in classical Greek and Latin, and Cambridge University soon followed suit.

The embodiment of the ideal Renaissance humanist was Erasmus, who occupied much of his life translating classical works into Latin and editing the Greek New Testament. Lorenzo Valla sought to restore the original Greek text of the New Testament through the use of ancient manuscripts. Erasmus published Valla's corrections as annotations on the New Testament in 1505, and they provided the model for Erasmus's edition of the Greek New Testament in 1516.

The Protestant Reformation spurred the development of the science of history by turning attention to the Patristic age in order to accentuate the Roman Catholic Church's departures from the faith of the Fathers. In their effort to demonstrate that Catholic doctrines and institutions were not of divine origin, but were human accretions not present in the early church, the Reformers stimulated historical research. And, of course, the Catholic Counter-reformers had a tremendous stake in the study of history, because for the Catholic Church a defense of a historical tradition was a defense of the Catholic faith.

By the end of the seventeenth century, the most successful practitioners of the science of history were Catholics of the scholarly orders. Historical writing also became popular literature. Every class in European society took interest in the new historical scholarship and sought to use it to support its own point of view. During the sixteenth and seventeenth centuries, historical writing became one of the most popular literary forms, avidly sought by a growing reading public. It has been estimated that between 1460 and 1700 more than 2.5 million copies of seventeen of the most prominent ancient historians were published in Europe. During the eighteenth century this interest intensified. According to J. Westfall Thompson, "No other age had such a voracious interest in historical literature as the eighteenth century. Everyone read and talked history."[3]

Impact on Apologetics

Without the rise of modern historical consciousness the development of historical apologetics would have been impossible. Protestant apologists were especially effective during the seventeenth and eighteenth centuries in their use of historical arguments for the faith. The course of this development is quite interesting. Although Hugo Grotius may rightly be called the father of modern apologetics, he had important precursors in Juan Luis Vives and Philippe de Mornay.

Vives was a Spanish humanist educated in Paris. He lived very much in the mainstream of European life and traveled so frequently to England and throughout the Continent that Erasmus called him an amphibious animal! After his fifth stay in England, he left for the Netherlands, never to return to Spain. From 1538–1540 he worked on his apology *De veritate fidei christianae*. He died in 1540, and the book was published in 1543. In Vives we find a blend of medieval theology with humanist methodology. That is to say, Vives was a Thomist who accepted the framework of the signs of credibility, but as a humanist he began to provide historical reasons for the credibility of Scripture.

His work tries to deal critically with the question of why Christ is mentioned primarily in Christian sources. He speaks of the true history of Christ and provides a list of historical facts about Jesus. He provides both internal and external evidence for the authenticity of the Gospels. His arguments are primitive and

3. J. Westfall Thompson and Bernard J. Holm, *A History of Historical Writing*, 2 vols. (New York: Macmillan, 1942), 2:94.

amount to little more than assertion, but they are the first glimmerings of a historical approach to the credibility of Scripture. Vives is significant because in him we see the links between modern historical apologetics and the Renaissance rise of historical consciousness on the one hand, and the medieval framework of the signs of credibility on the other.

Mornay, one of the most important Reformed leaders of the late sixteenth century, was a veteran of the Huguenot persecution in France and founder of the Protestant Académie de Saumur. In 1581, writing in French instead of Latin, Mornay penned his treatise *De la vérité de la religion chrestienne*. Although never quoting Vives, Mornay nonetheless appears to have been influenced by him, judging by parallel structure and passages between their works.

Mornay makes explicit his appeal to history: he claims that one can prove the divinity of Christ by means of philosophy and history. He says, "The philosopher thinks only of nature; the historian only of his documents. And from the two we have concluded the deity of Christ and the truth of our Scriptures."[4] Hence, his case is based on what he calls arguments and testimonies. The historical material is brought to bear in the final chapter, demonstrating that "the Gospel truly contains the history and doctrine of Jesus, Son of God."[5] Here he argues for the reliability of the Gospel accounts on the basis of the disciples' unwavering witness even unto death. He appeals to the great number of witnesses, to the changed lives of the disciples, and to the conversion of Paul as evidence for the historicity of the resurrection. Again, his arguments are not sophisticated by modern standards; but they represent an important advance over his predecessors in the development of historical apologetics.

A renowned expert in international law and himself a historical writer, Hugo Grotius was the first to provide a developed historical argument for Christianity in his *De veritate religionis christianae* (1627). He openly expressed his appreciation of the works of his predecessors, Vives and Mornay. *De veritate* is divided into six books: book one defends a cosmological argument and demonstrates God's revelation in Israel's history; book two contains historical proofs for Jesus' miracles and resurrection; book three treats the authority of Scripture; book four demonstrates Christianity's superiority to paganism; book five contains the proof from prophecy to show Christianity's superiority to Judaism; and book six refutes the Islamic religion.

Grotius clearly understood the importance of the science of history for the truth of the Christian faith. He discriminates between the methods employed in mathematics, physics, ethics, and history. In historical proofs we must rely on testimony free from all suspicion of falsity—otherwise the whole structure and use of history collapses. He notes that many historical narrations are commonly

---

4. Philippe de Mornay, *De la vérité de la religion chrestienne* (Anvers: Imprimerie de Christofle Plantin, 1581), Preface.
5. Ibid., 835.

accepted as true on no other ground than authority; but the history of Christ is attested by strong proofs that declare it to be true.

Grotius begins by pointing out that it is certain that Jesus of Nazareth was an actual historical person living in Judea under the reign of Tiberius. This fact is acknowledged in historical writings from Christians, Jews, and pagans alike. Further, he was put to death and thereafter worshiped by men. The reason for this worship was that he had performed various miracles during his life. Many of the early Christians such as Polycarp, Irenaeus, Athenagoras, Origen, Tertullian, Clement of Alexandria, and so forth were raised in other religions, yet came to worship this man Jesus as God, because they had made a diligent inquiry and discovered that he had wrought many miraculous deeds. Moreover, none of their opponents—neither Celsus nor Julian nor the Rabbinic doctors—could deny that Jesus had done these miracles. It is not possible to explain away Jesus' miracles as either wrought by nature or by the devil. With regard to the first of these possibilities, it is not naturally possible that terrible diseases and infirmities should be cured by the sound of a man's voice or his mere touch. As to the second, Christ's teaching was diametrically opposed to Satan, so that his miracles could hardly be attributed to demonic power.

Grotius then argues that Christ's resurrection can also be proved by credible reasons. He points out that the apostles claimed to be eyewitnesses of the risen Christ. They even appealed to the testimony of five hundred brethren who had seen Jesus after his resurrection. Now it would have been impossible for so many to conspire together to perpetrate such a hoax. And what was there to gain by lying? They could expect neither honor, nor wealth, nor worldly profit, nor fame, nor even the successful propagation of their doctrine. If they lied, says Grotius, it had to be for the defense of their religion. But in this case, they either sincerely believed that this religion was true or they did not. If not, then they would never have chosen it for their own and rejected the safer, more customary religions. But if they believed it to be true, then the resurrection of Jesus cannot be avoided. For had he not risen, contrary to his prediction, that would have destroyed the very foundation of any faith the disciples had. Moreover, their own religion prohibited lying and any bearing of false witness. And besides this, no one, and especially so many, would be willing to die for a lie that they themselves had made up, a lie that would bring them absolutely no worldly good. And it is clear from their writings that the apostles were not madmen. Finally, the conversion of the apostle Paul bore witness to the reality of the resurrection.

Grotius concludes by handling two theoretical problems. First, to those who object that the resurrection is impossible, Grotius simply replies that it involves no logical contradiction to say that a dead man has been restored to life. Second, the significance of the resurrection Grotius finds in its confirming the new doctrine taught by Jesus, especially in light of Jesus' prediction that he would rise from the dead.

In his argument for Jesus' resurrection, Grotius presents his opponents with a dilemma. Given the authenticity of the Gospels and 1 Corinthians, the apostolic testimony to the event of the resurrection can only be denied if the apostles were either lying or sincerely mistaken. But neither of these are reasonable. Therefore, the resurrection must be a historical event. We find here in rudimentary form the dilemma that would be sharpened and pressed by subsequent generations of Christian apologists against their Deist opponents.

The period between Blaise Pascal (d. 1662) and Pierre Bayle's skeptical *Diction-naire historique et critique* (1695) has been called the golden age of classical French apologetics. This period included thinkers such as Malebranche, Huet, Bossuet, and Abbadie. The tone for this era—and indeed for that of the next century—was set by Pascal's disciple Filleau de la Chaise in his *Discours sur les preuves des livres de Moyse* (1672). He was important because he inaugurated as a self-conscious methodology in apologetics the method of proof *par les faits* (by the facts).

Filleau held that the proper method of persuading people of the truth of the Christian religion does not consist in trying to make its theological mysteries comprehensible or reasonable, but in showing that the mysteries are entailed in the truth of certain indisputable historical facts. He states:

> If men know anything with assurance, it is the facts; and of everything that falls within their knowledge, there is nothing in which it would be more difficult to deceive them and over which there would be less occasion for dispute. And thus, when one will have made them see that the Christian religion is inseparably attached to facts whose truth cannot be sincerely contested, they must submit to all that it teaches or else renounce sincerity and reason.[6]

This method of proving Christianity by the facts was in French apologetics a logical extension of the function of the signs of credibility in attesting the truths of faith coupled with the historical method. Because truths of faith are above reason, they cannot be directly proved but can nevertheless be indirectly confirmed by miracle and prophecy. Similarly, Filleau contended that we may prove the mysteries of the faith, not directly, but indirectly by the historical facts that entail their truth.

Thus, French apologists began to make a bifurcation between the *contenant* and the *contenu* of the faith. Roughly rendered, the distinction contrasted the "container" of the faith to the "content" of the faith. Though the content of the Christian religion, that is, the body of theological doctrines, may be above reason, nonetheless the container of this religion, that is, the historical events of the gospel story, is demonstrable by the facts; hence, the *contenu* is indirectly proved by historical verification of the *contenant*. Under the influence of this conception, there

---

6. Filleau de la Chaise, "Discours sur les livres de Moise," in *Discours sur les "Pensées" de M. Pascal*, ed. with an introduction by V. Gitaud (Paris: Editions Bossard, 1922), 104–5.

was during the seventeenth and eighteenth centuries a marked swing in French apologetics toward historical apologies.

In eighteenth-century England there was a similar turn toward empirical, historical proofs of Christianity. Although John Locke set the pattern for English thought in this century by his defense of the reasonableness of Christianity on the basis of Jesus' miracles in his *The Reasonableness of Christianity* (1695), it was Charles Leslie who enunciated clearly the method of proving Christianity by the facts in his *Short and Easie Method with the Deists* (1697).

The short and easy method recommended by Leslie is the historical proof of the matters of fact on which Christianity is founded. He argues that when one examines the biblical narratives as one would any matter of fact, one will find them to be historically reliable. Hence, he maintains that one must either reject all the historical works of classical antiquity or else admit the Gospel accounts along with them. Following in Locke's footsteps, Leslie helped to set the tone for the hundreds of historical apologies published in England during the next century.

There was a subtle, yet decisive, difference between French and English historical apologetics. Both agreed that revelation may be discerned by what the medievals called the signs of credibility (miracle and prophecy), but they differed in the following way. By making a distinction between the *contenant* and the *contenu*, the French thinkers underscored the bifurcation between truths of reason and truths of faith, the latter being in themselves rationally incomprehensible and only indirectly verifiable; the English apologists tended to dissolve the distinction between truths of reason and truths of faith, the upper story collapsing down into the lower, so that all truths became in a sense truths of reason, demonstrable by philosophy, science, history, and so forth. When English writers spoke of truths above reason, they did not generally mean mysterious or incomprehensible truths, as did their French counterparts; rather they meant simply truths that we lack the necessary facts to prove. But in both cases, it was the methodology of history that they counted on to carry the weight of the case for the truth of the Christian faith.

Nineteenth and Twentieth Centuries
During the nineteenth and twentieth centuries the parallel development of historiography and historical apologetics was disrupted.

HISTORICISM, RELATIVISM, AND POSTMODERNISM
The nineteenth century saw the greatest advances in the science of history that had theretofore occurred. The climax of this development came in the school of historicism, shaped by the prodigious influence of the German historian Leopold von Ranke. Von Ranke, through his doctoral students and in turn through their students, was responsible for shaping a whole generation of great historians. The earmark of nineteenth-century historicism was objectivity. The task of the historian was to uncover the objective facts, and let those facts speak for themselves. The subjective element—the historian's own personality, biases, outlook, milieu, and so

forth—did not enter the historical equation. Von Ranke's goal in doing history, to use his famous phrase, was to describe the past "*wie es eigentlich gewesen ist*" (as it actually was). He apparently saw no reason, given the enormous industry that he brought to his research and that he instilled in his students, why this goal could not be achieved.

During the twentieth century there came a sharp reaction to von Ranke's naïve objectivism. The school of historical relativism emphasized the inextricable subjective element in the writing of history. In the United States, relativism was associated particularly with the historians Charles Beard and Carl Becker. Against von Ranke, they denied that historical facts are "out there," waiting to be discovered. Facts do not bear their own meaning piggy-back; it is the historian who must ascribe meaning to the facts. And the historian, who is himself a product of his time and place in history, cannot assume the point of a neutral observer in writing history. The personal element is always in the equation. Von Ranke's goal of describing the past as it really was is illusory; rather, the historian must himself reconstruct the past on the basis of the present. Ironically, the viewpoint of historical relativism is often referred to today as historicism, so that this term now means exactly the opposite of what it meant in the nineteenth century.

During the 1970s the postmodernist critique of objective canons of rationality and truth revitalized the old debate between historical objectivists and relativists. Rooted in Continental philosophy and hermeneutics and in the anti-realism of Wittgenstein, there has emerged a powerful postmodernist current of relativism which flows through virtually every academic field, including history. Calling the conflict between objectivism and relativism the "central cultural opposition of our time," Richard Bernstein remarks, "Relativism, a stream in the philosophy of the past two hundred years that began as a trickle, has swelled in recent times into a roaring torrent."[7] As a result, he observes, "There is an uneasiness that has spread throughout intellectual and cultural life. It affects almost every discipline and every aspect of culture."[8] In 1986, writing in the journal *History and Theory*, F. R. Ankersmit called for the abandonment of what he termed the old "epistemological," or objectivist, philosophy of history.[9] The objectivist approach aimed at specifying the conditions under which we are justified in believing the historian's statements about the past to be true, whereas the narrative approach is concerned only with the interpretation of texts and makes no distinction between the historian's language and what that language is about. The narrative approach tends to ignore the intent of the original author and evaluates texts only on aesthetic or non-cognitive grounds, while the objectivist hermeneutical

7. Richard J. Bernstein, *Beyond Objectivism and Relativism* (Oxford: Basil Blackwell, 1983), 7, 13.
8. Ibid., 1.
9. F. R. Ankersmit, "The Dilemma of Contemporary Anglo-Saxon Philosophy of History," in "Knowing and Telling History: The Anglo-Saxon Debate," *History and Theory* Beiheft 25 (1986): 1–27. Cf. F. R. Ankersmit, *History and Tropology: The Rise and Fall of Metaphor* (Berkeley: University of California Press, 1994; idem, in K. Jenkins, *The Postmodern History Reader* (New York: Routledge, 1997).

approach seeks to discern the author's intent and so to penetrate more deeply into the past. Narrative non-realists are thus unconcerned with historical truth of narratives or with what actually happened. Hayden White, for example, believes that because historical events must be embedded by the historian in narratives involving a plot structure which is his own construction, historical writing is not different from fictional writing and should be assessed only by means of literary and aesthetic criteria.[10]

Indeed, it is not clear whether there really is such a thing as the past on a thoroughgoing postmodernist view, since the multiplicity of historical reconstructions and texts seems to lead to multiple pasts, none of which is privileged. Moreover, radical postmodernists like Keith Jenkins deny that there is any extra-linguistic reality corresponding to the historian's statements, since there are no facts independent of a description that constitutes a fact. Thus, Jenkins asserts that the idea that facts/reality can exist independently of the historian "is an implausible idea."[11] All we are left with is inter-textuality, the interplay of texts, not extra-linguistic facts. A more moderate non-realist like Leon Goldstein affirms the existence of the unique, actual past, but denies that it concerns him as a historian. As Goldstein puts it, "the standpoint of God does not enter into the work of historians attempting to constitute the human past."[12] Goldstein remains objectivist in affirming that ultimately there is one interpretation of the past which best accords with the evidence, but he is non-realist or constructionist in that it is a matter of indifference to him whether the historian's construction corresponds to reality as it actually was in the past. Contemporary historical relativism thus comprises two challenges to any claim to know the past as it actually happened: (1) non-realism, or constructionism, the view that all we know are historical reconstructions of the past, rather than the past itself, and (2) non-objectivism, or subjectivism, the view that no historical reconstruction can legitimately claim to be superior to alternative reconstructions.

IMPACT ON APOLOGETICS

One might expect that during the nineteenth century the historical apologetic for Christianity would flower. Seeing instead that it withered away, we might suspect that the historical method had simply gotten too big for its theological britches and had exposed the Gospels as historically unreliable documents. That would, however, be misleading. The chief obstacle to a historical case for the Gospels, as

10. Hayden White, "The Burden of History," in *Tropics of Discourse: Essays in Cultural Criticism* (Baltimore: Johns Hopkins University Press, 1978), 27–50. "Tropics" or "tropology" derives from the Latin *tropus*, meaning "metaphor" or "figure of speech"; postmodernists take historical writing to be inherently metaphorical and non-literal.

11. Keith Jenkins, "Introduction: On Being Open about Our Closures," in *The Postmodern History Reader* (London: Routledge, 1997), 17.

12. Leon J. Goldstein, "*History and the Primacy of Knowing*," in "The Constitution of the Historical Past," History and Theory Beiheft 16 (1977): 29–52. See also his *Historical Knowing* (Austin, Tex.: University of Texas Press, 1976).

we shall see, was the nineteenth century's conviction that miracles had no place in a historical narrative. Because this presupposition was accepted into biblical criticism, the historical method assumed great importance there, whereas it did not take hold in apologetics. The nineteenth century's enthusiasm for the historical may be seen in the old quest for the historical Jesus. One after another life of Jesus appeared during this century, each trying to rediscover the non-miraculous Jesus behind the supernatural figure of the Gospels. Indeed, in that movement one may see the greatest weakness of von Ranke's method exemplified: apparently unaware of the personal element they all brought to their research, each writer reconstructed a historical Jesus after his own image. There was Strauss's Hegelian Jesus, Renan's sentimental Jesus, Bauer's non-existent Jesus, Ritschl's liberal Jesus, and so forth. To paraphrase George Tyrell, each one looked down the long well of history and saw his own face reflected at the bottom.[13] The movement finally ground to a halt in skepticism, since no non-miraculous Jesus could be uncovered in the Gospel traditions. Rather than accept the supernatural Jesus as historical, however, biblical critics ascribed that belief to the theology of the early church, which they said had so overlaid the traditions about the historical Jesus that he was no longer recoverable.

During the twentieth century, the historical method—usually called the historical-critical method—continued to play the decisive role in biblical exegesis. But both dialectical and existential theology severed the theological truth of the Gospel from the facts concerning the historical Jesus. Hence, any historical apologetic was conceived to be worse than useless, since it focused on the historical Jesus instead of the Christ of faith—a distinction introduced by the German theologian Martin Kähler at the close of the nineteenth century and subsequently taken up into dialectical and existential theology. It is only since the second half of this century that a new quest of the historical Jesus has begun, this time more cautious and chastened; and once more historical apologetics is beginning to reassert itself. Not even the challenge posed by postmodernist relativism has been able to slow its advance.

Assessment

If a historical apologetic for the Christian faith is to be successful, the objections of historical relativism need to be overcome. This does not mean a return to naive von Rankian historicism. Of course, the subjective element cannot be eliminated. But the question is whether this subjective element need be so predominant that the study of history is vitiated. In order to answer this question, let us examine more closely the objections of historical relativism.

13. George Tyrrell, *Christianity at the Cross-Roads* (London: Longman, Green, 1910), 44.

Objections to the Objectivity of History

The case against the objectivity of history may be summarized under two main points: first, we cannot know anything about the past as it actually happened because we cannot directly observe the past; and second, we cannot reconstruct the past objectively because we are not neutral observers, but rather products of our time, place, culture, circumstances, and so forth. Postmodern relativists will put a linguistic spin on these points: because of our lack of direct access to the past we cannot get outside our linguistic milieu, and the historian's descriptions or representations of the past will be determined by the concepts and language which he brings with him to the task. Let me explain each of these objections in turn.

THE PROBLEM OF LACK OF DIRECT ACCESS

The things and events of the past no longer exist or are happening today, except in the peculiar sense that events of the recent past may be continuing in the present (a war, say, or a session of Congress) and some things existing in the past may have endured to the present (for example, the pyramids). But for the most part, events of the past have ceased, and things of the past no longer exist. Having slipped through our grasp, they are no longer available for direct inspection. At best all we have of the past are the remains and memories of the past, which are in the present. All we seem to know, then, is what exists in the present. How, then, can one avoid skepticism about the past? As historian Patrick Gardiner asks,

> In what sense can I be said to know an event which is in principle unobservable, having vanished behind the mysterious frontier which divides the present from the past? And how can we be sure that anything really happened in the past at all, that the whole story is not an elaborate fabrication, as untrustworthy as a dream or a work of fiction?[14]

Even if one admits the reality of the past, of what relevance is it to the historian? Goldstein points out that historical realism doesn't add anything factually to the historian's store of information; he is still wholly dependent on the present evidence for his reconstructions and inferences about the past.[15] Since past events and things are forever gone, the historian has no way to check if his reconstructions correspond to reality, that is to say, are true. Historical realism and historical truth are otiose for the historian and should therefore be ignored.

Old-line relativists often emphasized the contrast between history and science on this score. The scientist has the objects of his research right in front of him and is free to experiment repeatedly upon them in order to test his hypotheses. By contrast, the historian's objects of research no longer exist and so are not subject to either observation or experiment. Historical knowledge thus fails to measure up to the standards of objectivity set by scientific knowledge.

14. Patrick Gardiner, *The Nature of Historical Explanation* (London: Oxford, 1961), 35.
15. Goldstein, "History and Primacy of Knowing," 30–31.

More recently, however, postmodern relativism has invaded science as well, threatening to undermine the objectivity of the scientific enterprise. Old-line historical relativists prized the objectivity of science because it served them well as a foil for exposing what they considered to be the comparative non-objectivity of historical constructions. But during the 1960s proponents of so-called *Weltanschauung* analyses of scientific theories, such as Thomas Kuhn and Paul Feyerabend, radically challenged the old, positivistic view of science. According to these thinkers, scientific work takes place within the context of an all-embracing worldview (*Weltanschauung*) or paradigm, which is so intimately linked with a given scientific theory that for scientists working within that paradigm, their observations are not neutral, but theory-laden; the very meanings of terms used by them are determined by the theory, so that scientists working within a different paradigm aren't even talking about the same things; and what counts as a fact is determined by a scientist's *Weltanschauung*, so that there are no neutral facts available for assessing the adequacy of two rival theories. On this analysis, scientific change from one theory to another becomes fundamentally arational and is to be explained sociologically. On *Weltanschauung* analyses, scientists find themselves in the same boat with historical relativists, for scientific theories are constructions which are not based on objective facts and cannot claim to describe the world as it actually is. Ironically, then, the old-line relativist complaint that the scientist (unlike the historian) has direct access to the objects of his study has been undercut by postmodernist relativists who challenge the positivist idea that scientists neutrally observe the uninterpreted world around them. The scientist's understanding of the present is just as much a theoretical construction as is the historian's understanding of the past, a construction which cannot be checked for its correspondence with the objective facts, since one's *Weltanschauung* determines what the facts are. The implication is that science and history alike are anti-realist and non-objective.

Now, according to historical relativists, our lack of direct access to the past has two important implications. First, it affects how one views historical facts. According to one famous relativist, Carl Becker, it means that historical facts are only in the mind. The event itself is gone, so all we have are the historian's statements about the event. It is those statements that are historical facts. If one were to reply that the event itself is a historical fact because it had an enduring impact on the course of history, Becker would say it had an impact only because people had "long memories." If everyone forgot the event, it would no longer be a historical fact. Thus, historical events really only exist in your mind, not in the past. The claim of postmodernist philosophers of history like F. R. Ankersmit and Hayden White that historical narratives do not refer to reality at all and therefore constitute their own linguistic universe is the linguistic variant of classical relativism's denial of mind-independent facts.[16] Two further sub-implications follow.

16. See Chris Lorenz, "Historical Knowledge and Historical Reality: A Plea for 'Internal Realism,'" *History and Theory* 33 (1994): 311 for this connection.

The first sub-implication is that facts have no meaning and that the historian must put his own meaning onto the facts. Because the event itself is gone and the facts are only in the historian's mind, this means, in Becker's words, that "even if you could present all the facts, the miserable things wouldn't say anything, would say nothing at all." Therefore, the historian must put his own meaning on the facts. As Becker says, "the event itself, the facts, do not say anything, do not impose any meaning. It is the historian who speaks, who imposes a meaning."[17]

The second sub-implication is that history is largely a result of the historian's own biases, personality, interest, and so forth. Because the historian determines the meaning of the facts himself, the history he writes will be just a reflection of himself. Hayden White gives the following example: "no historical event is *intrinsically tragic*. . . . For in history what is tragic from one perspective is comic from another. . . . The important point is that most historical sequences can be emplotted in a number of different ways, so as to provide different interpretations of those events and to endow them with different meanings."[18] In this way the past is really the product of the present.

There is a second important implication of the historian's not having direct access to the past. There seems to be no way to test the truth of historical facts. A scientist has the method of experimentation to test his hypotheses. But the historian cannot do that, because the events are gone. The scientist at least has the advantage of predictability and repeatability which the historian lacks. So how can the historian test his hypotheses? As Gardiner says,

> We cannot reproduce what we believe to have been the conditions that determined the collapse of the Roman Empire and then watch for the consequences, in the fashion in which we can combine certain chemicals and then see whether the result agrees or disagrees with a prediction of the result of such a combination.[19]

So because the historian cannot directly observe the facts, there is the unsolved problem of how to test for truth in history. This problem has led postmodernist historian Keith Jenkins to proclaim the "end of history."[20] That is to say, a realist understanding of history as an accurate description of the past is no longer tenable. "In fact history now appears to be just one more foundationless, positioned expression in a world of foundationless, positioned expressions."[21]

Thus, the problem of the lack of direct access to the past raises two challenges to those who want to learn something from history: first, what is the nature of historical facts, and second, how can one test the truth of historical facts?

17. Carl Becker, "What Are Historical Facts?" in *The Philosophy of History in Our Time*, ed. H. Meyerhoff (Garden City, N.Y.: Doubleday, 1959), 130–31.
18. White, "Burden of History," 84–85.
19. Gardiner, *Historical Explanation*, 35.
20. Jenkins, "Introduction," 8.
21. Ibid., 6.

THE PROBLEM OF LACK OF NEUTRALITY

The second objection of historical relativists to knowledge of the past as it actually happened is that we cannot reconstruct the past objectively because we are not neutral observers, but are the products of our time, place, culture, language, and so forth. The historian cannot "stand back" and describe what has happened from a neutral perspective because the historian, too, is caught up in the historical flow of events. Henri Pirenne makes the point:

> Historical syntheses depend to a very large degree not only upon the personality of their authors, but upon all the social, religious, or national environments which surround them. It follows, therefore, that each historian will establish between the facts relationships determined by the convictions, the movements, and the prejudices that have molded his own point of view.[22]

Because of this, each new generation must rewrite history in its own way. The history written today will be judged inferior and obsolete by the historians of the next generation. But their work will also be shaped by their culture and so forth. Thus, in the words of philosopher Karl Popper, "There can be no history of the past as it actually did happen; there can only be historical interpretations; and none of them final; and every generation has a right to frame its own."[23] Therefore, history can never be objectively written. The historian always looks at the past through the colored glasses of the present, as determined by his society and environment.

Critique of Historical Relativism

These two basic objections, then, need to be answered before we examine the historical foundations of Christianity: first, the problem of the lack of direct access to the past, which issues in anti-realism; and second, the problem of the lack of neutrality, which issues in subjectivism.

THE PROBLEM OF LACK OF DIRECT ACCESS

The things and events of the past are obviously for the most part gone; the question is whether our lack of direct access to them forces us to become historical constructionists or narrative non-realists. Here it will be helpful to distinguish between constructionism as a methodology and constructionism as a metaphysic.[24] Postmodern relativism at its most radical takes constructionism metaphysically as an ontological thesis about how reality is constituted. Ontological constructionism holds that the historian actually constitutes the past events themselves via his representations; that there really is not nor ever was a past-in-itself, but only a past-for-me, relative to each person. As such, this view implies a fantastic subjec-

---

22. Henri Pirenne, "What Are Historians Trying to Do?" in *Philosophy of History*, 97.

23. Karl Popper, "Has History Any Meaning?" in *Philosophy of History*, 303.

24. P. H. Nowell-Smith, "The Constructionist Theory of History," in "The Constitution of the Historical Past," *History and Theory* Beiheft 16 (1977): 1–2.

tive idealism which flies in the face of our common sense beliefs that things and events of the past really existed independently of oneself before one arrived on the scene, that we share together a common past issuing in a shared present, that after we die the world will go on without us. Indeed, insofar as postmodernist constructionists claim that language constitutes reality and that there is therefore no extralinguistic reality, their position is self-refuting, since those claims, if true, would be descriptive of the way reality is! Given the radical nature of ontological constructionism, Nowell-Smith is surely right when he states that the burden of proof lies on the person who claims that what the historian constructs is not an *account* of past events, but rather the past events themselves. But as we shall see below when we discuss the nature of historical facts, the postmodernist's arguments for ontological constructionism are weak, to say the least.

Moreover, ontological constructionism has some bizarre implications, as Plantinga points out in his biting satire of postmodernist Richard Rorty's claim that "truth is what my peers will let me get away with saying":

> Although this view is very much *au courant* and with-it in the contemporary intellectual world, it has consequences that are peculiar, not to say preposterous. For example, most of us think that the Chinese authorities did something monstrous in murdering those hundreds of young people in Tiananmen Square, and then compounded their wickedness by denying that they had done it. On Rorty's view, however, this is an uncharitable misunderstanding. What the authorities were really doing, in denying that they had murdered those students, was something wholly praiseworthy: they were trying to bring it about that the alleged massacre never happened. For they were trying to see to it that their peers would let them get away with saying that the massacre never happened; that is, they were trying to make it *true* that it never happened; and who can fault them for that? The same goes for those contemporary neo-Nazis who claim that there was no holocaust; from a Rortian view, they are only trying to see to it that such a terrible thing never happened; and what could be more commendable than that? This way of thinking has real possibilities for dealing with poverty and disease: if only we let each other get away with saying that there isn't any poverty and disease—no cancer or AIDS, let's say—then it would be true that there isn't any; and if it were true that there isn't any, then of course there wouldn't *be* any.[25]

The serious point in this justifiably deserved satire is that ontological constructionism is not only obviously ridiculous, but even sinister, in that it lends itself to wicked and self-justifying distortions of history.[26]

25. Alvin Plantinga, *The Twin Pillars of Christian Scholarship* (Grand Rapids, Mich.: Calvin College and Seminary, 1990), 21–22.

26. On this see Gertrude Himmelfarb, "Telling It as You Like It: Postmodernist History and the Flight from Fact," in *Postmodern History Reader*, 164. Zagorin blasts Jenkins's postmodernist historiography on these grounds: "A historiography of the kind Jenkins hopes to see . . . would probably forsake its critical senses and respect for evidence, be thoroughly serviceable to a repressive political orthodoxy, and breed lies and myths without restraint." Perez Zagorin, "Rejoinder to a Postmodernist," *History and Theory* 39

A constructionist might insist that one's construction of the past must be constrained by present evidence. Not only would this not solve the moral problem exposed by Plantinga (one can imagine, for example, someone's destroying present evidence so as to bring about a different past), but a moment's reflection exposes the untenability of such a view. For it is clearly impossible to act only on present evidence, since this would necessitate abandonment of all memory beliefs, including everything we have learned in our research. The very notion of "present evidence" is past-infected, for it has been assembled, digested, catalogued, remembered, and so on. The only present evidence we have is our immediate sensory awareness, which cannot restrain ontological constructionism. Lionel Rubinoff is therefore amply warranted in his observation that postmodern relativism "risks succumbing to all the pitfalls and skeptical implications of the epistemological anarchism that follow from unqualified, radical relativism or subjectivism."[27]

But suppose the philosophical constructionist adopts a more moderate line such as Goldstein's, who holds, it will be remembered, that the past is real independent of our reconstructions, but that we cannot or do not come to know that past. The untenability of even this moderate philosophical constructionism may be seen by reflecting on a case in which every putatively factual statement in a historian's reconstruction of the past happens to be true, where by "true" we understand minimally that a statement "*S*" is true if and only if *S*. So "Snow is white" if and only if snow is white. In such a case the past would have been just as the historian's statements say that it was. Now if the evidence justifies belief in that historian's statements, as Goldstein admits it may, then how could we be said to have knowledge only of the historian's reconstruction and not of the past itself? Perhaps Goldstein would say that in such a case we do not know that the reconstruction corresponds with the past and so we do not have true knowledge of the past, but only a sort of unwitting true belief. But consider the case of a detective who on the basis of the evidence independently offers a reconstruction of a crime which an eyewitness knows to be correct. Wouldn't the detective be said to know what really happened, since he believes exactly what the eyewitness believes and does so on the basis of the evidence? In general, the claim that in order to know something we must be able to know that we know it, that is, to justify our justification, is an epistemological principle which should be rejected.[28] Like the detective, the historian who holds to a correct picture of the past and does so on the basis of justifying evidence by definition knows the past.

Admittedly, Goldstein is right that historical realism doesn't contribute *factually* to the historian's work in the sense of adding one more event to our knowledge

(2000): 208. Fortunately, Jenkins's notion of historiography is "a fantasy rather than something to be taken seriously" (ibid.).

27. Lionel Rubinoff, "Introduction," in *Objectivity, Method and Point of View* (Leiden: E. J. Brill), 3. Cf. J. Appleby, L. Hunt, and M. Jacob, *Telling the Truth about History* (New York: W. W. Norton, 1994), 7.

28. See discussion in Frederick Suppe, "Afterword," in *The Structure of Scientific Theories*, 2nd ed. (Urbana, Ill.: University of Illinois Press, 1977), 717–27.

of the past which we otherwise would have missed. But realism is a philosophical thesis which lends to science and history a significance they would otherwise lack, for on the realist view such enterprises really do tell us something about the world we live in, as opposed to historical or science fiction. Indeed, on Goldstein's view it is hard to see a qualitative difference between the writing of history and the writing of historical novels, since the latter cohere with all known evidence, too. He might insist that history is limited to what the evidence *requires* us to believe; but then what is the rationale for such a limitation if not the fact that history aims at truth about the real past whereas historical novels do not? Moreover, as W. H. Dray points out, historical realism serves a quasi-methodological function in that a real past cannot have incompatible properties, and realism thus serves as a restraint on the anti-realist tendency toward acceptance of multiple, incompatible reconstructions of the past.[29]

But if historical constructionism fails as a metaphysic, what about constructionism as a methodology? As a historiographical methodology, constructionism may be interpreted as the thesis that the historical past should be regarded as what the evidence indicates that it was. The historian reasons, "The evidence is such and such; it would not be such and such unless my hypothesis were true; therefore, my hypothesis is true." So understood there is no incompatibility between historical realism and methodological constructionism. On the contrary, it is precisely the historian's goal, using all his critical skills, to determine what happened in the past by reconstructing it on the basis of the evidence. Of course, in many cases, various proffered reconstructions will be underdetermined by the evidence, so that one does not know which one, if any, is correct; but that in no way implies that there is no objective past or that in other cases where the evidence is clear we cannot know with confidence what really happened. Nowell-Smith points out,

> Some results of historical thinking are so well established that it would be madness to doubt them; others have only the status of being a more probable explanation of the evidence than any rival hypothesis. This is a point on which it is worth while to dwell. Why is it still reasonable to doubt whether there ever was such a person as King Arthur but utterly unreasonable to question the existence of George Washington? The reason is not far to seek. If we took *seriously* the hypothesis that there never was any such person as George Washington, we should be faced with the problem of accounting for the existence of such a vast body of evidence—not testimony, but *evidence*, documents of whose existence and nature we are now aware—that it would soon become obvious that the task is impossible. To put it mildly, the hypothesis that there was no such person is in a very weak position vis-a-vis the hypothesis that there was; and that is all that the standard of proof in history requires.[30]

29. W. H. Dray, "Comment," in *Objectivity, Method and Point of View*, 183.
30. Nowell-Smith, "Constructionist Theory of History," 4.

We shall have more to say below about how the historian weighs the evidence for his hypotheses; but for now the point seems clear that while constructionism fails as a metaphysical thesis, it is a vital part of historical methodology aimed at recovering the real past.

Turning then to the traditional relativist claim that the historian finds himself in a disadvantaged position compared to the scientist due to the greater inaccessibility of the objects of historical study, let me say two things. First, it is naïve to think that the scientist always has direct access to his objects of study. Not only is the scientist largely dependent on the reports of others' research (which, interestingly, constitute for him historical documents) for his own work, but furthermore, the objects of the scientist's research are often only indirectly accessible, especially in the highly theoretical fields like physics. Such theoretical entities as black holes, quarks, and neutrinos are postulated as the best explanations for the observable data, but they themselves cannot be directly observed. It might be thought that this point actually serves to reinforce the relativist's objection, since it is precisely in the case of such theoretical entities that a non-realist interpretation of scientific theories is most plausible. The plausibility of non-realism in the case of high-level theoretical entities, such as those postulated in particle physics, need not be disputed; but what this retort fails to appreciate is that scientific theories also populate the world with very low-level theoretical entities whose real existence is far more difficult to deny, entities such as dinosaurs, Ice Age glaciers, and even galaxies! The relativist will have to swallow hard before denying that such things are real simply because they are not susceptible to direct observation.

Secondly, while the historian does not have direct access to the past, the residue of the past, things that have really existed, is directly accessible to him. The modern historian is not simply dependent on the reports of earlier historians. For example, archaeological data furnish direct access to the objects of the historian's investigation. The renowned English historian R. G. Collingwood states,

> scissors and paste [is] not the only foundation of historical method. Archaeology has provided a wonderfully sensitive method for answering questions to which not only do literary sources give no direct answer but which cannot be answered even by the most ingenious interpretation of them.[31]

Thus, the historian, like the scientist, often has direct access to things he is investigating. Now I'm not confusing the evidence with the events themselves, which are admittedly past; but I am saying, in Van der Dussen's words, that "from the epistemological point of view evidence has the peculiar feature of being itself directly observable and accessible for inspection, while the knowledge it may lead to is not."[32] And archaeology is only one of the means to secure such evidence.

---

31. R. G. Collingwood, *An Autobiography* (London: Oxford University Press, 1939), 135.

32. W. J. Van der Dussen, "The Historian and His Evidence," in *Objectivity, Method and Point of View*, 157; cf. Gardiner, *Historical Explanation*, 39.

As Old Testament scholar R. K. Harrison explains, modern historians are not so heavily dependent on subjective literary sources as before, because the sciences of linguistics, sociology, anthropology, numismatics, and archaeology have become so developed.[33]

In fact, we can at this point draw a very instructive analogy: what history is to the humanities, geology is to the sciences. The major difference between history and geology is the human factor, not the accessibility of the data. Whereas the subject matter of the geologist is the earth's history, the subject matter of the historian is human history. Basically their task is the same. As Collingwood states, "The historian's real work is the reconstruction in thought of a particular historical event; the geologist's, the reconstruction in thought of a particular geological epoch at a particular place."[34]

If this is the case, then the relativists' argument based on the inaccessibility of the past loses all its punch. For the subject matter of the geologist is every bit as indirect as that of the historian, and yet geology is part of science, which has traditionally been the model of objectivity to the relativist. Since lack of direct access cannot preclude geological knowledge, neither can it preclude historical knowledge.

But what, then, of the postmodern relativist's claim that science, as well as history, is non-realist and subjective? It does not appear to be widely appreciated outside the field of philosophy of science—especially by postmodernist theologians who continue to invoke the authority of Thomas Kuhn and to talk freely of paradigms, as though this notion were accepted or even well-defined—that after an initial stir *Weltanschauung* analyses had already been widely discredited by philosophers of science by the late 1970s.[35] Contemporary philosophy of science is post-positivist, post-Kuhnian, and generally realist.

Consider the anti-realist claim that all observation is theory-laden. Taken in the radical sense that our theory actually determines the way the world is, this thesis leads at once to the same subjective idealism implied by ontological constructionism, which is, as Scheffler says, the *reductio ad absurdum* of such a thesis.[36] What about a more moderate claim, that our *Weltanschauung* determines how we observe the independently existing world? Here one need not dispute that observation is theory-laden in the sense that it involves "seeing that something is the case" or "seeing something as a certain kind of thing," which is relative to the observer's background knowledge. For example, if a scientist and a layman enter a laboratory together, the scientist may see an interferometer on the table, while the layman sees only a piece of machinery. Or again, a baseball fan may leap to his feet at seeing a home run at the ballpark, while someone ignorant of the game

---

33. R. K. Harrison, *Introduction to the Old Testament* (Grand Rapids, Mich.: Eerdmans, 1969), 292.

34. R. G. Collingwood, "Croce's Philosophy of History," in *Essays in the Philosophy of History*, ed. W. Debbins (Austin, Tex.: University of Texas Press, 1965), 19.

35. See Suppe, "Afterword," 633–49.

36. Israel Scheffler, *Science and Subjectivity*, 2nd ed. (Indianapolis: Hackett, 1982), 19.

sees only a ball going over the fence. This sort of theory-ladenness characterizes historical observation and writing as well: when a historian describes the history of primitive man in terms of "magic" and "mythology," for example, this is only possible because he is writing from the standpoint of a scientific culture for which the distinction between science and magic is meaningful.[37]

Now I think that it is obvious that this sort of theory-ladenness does nothing to undermine the objectivity of science or history or to support anti-realism. As the great historian of philosophy Frederick Copleston argues, to say that I experience something as *x* is not to imply that it is not in fact *x*. "Why should it?" he asks. "I am aware of an object lying on my table. I see it as a pencil. It by no means follows that the object is not a pencil." Similarly, "It is reasonable to claim that the people who were present at the beheading of King Charles I saw the course of events as the beheading of the king. It by no means follows that this was a purely subjective interpretation or reading of the events."[38] Nor does the failure of someone else to see something as I see it do anything to suggest that either of us fails to see correctly. If an aboriginal fails to see the slender, yellow object on the table as a pencil, that in no way proves that it is not a pencil, as I see it to be. Now, of course, I may be mistaken in seeing *x* as a pencil. But I can discover my mistakes. I can pick up *x* and try to write with it and find that what I thought was a pencil isn't one after all. Here we return to the notion of evidence. "Sometimes," observes Copleston, "the available evidence is such as to eliminate any reasonable doubt about the validity of an interpretation."[39] (Recall the case of George Washington; similarly no scientist could today justifiably hold to a pre-Copernican cosmology or a pre-Harveyian theory of blood circulation.)

Now, to be sure, the evidence itself is also seen as such and such. But for people with shared background knowledge, certain observed facts can simply be taken as data. For example, the layman and the scientist both see the interferometer as machinery, so that that fact is for them a datum; but for a very primitive person, say a troglodyte, that fact would not be a datum. What counts as data or interpretation is thus relative, but in order for much of the evidence available to us to count as data the level of shared background beliefs is not very high at all. Even a caveman could not justifiably see the interferometer as, say, his mate or a saber-toothed tiger. Thus, when the historian or scientist assesses the evidence for a theory, he needn't try to justify all over again every datum which he uses. Some data are reasonably taken as given. As Copleston says, "it is foolish to demand uninterpreted experiential data before we are prepared to admit that historiography is not a purely subjective construction."[40]

37. Lionel Rubinoff, "Historicity and Objectivity," in *Objectivity, Method and Point of View*, 137.

38. Frederick Copleston, "Problems of Objectivity," in *On the History of Philosophy* (London: Search Press, 1979), 54.

39. Ibid., 55.

40. Ibid., 53–54.

The evidence which the historian uses will include texts, as well as artifacts, and here, too, his reconstruction will be limited by the data. Copleston states:

> The historian is not free to interpret the texts as he likes. Some statements may be ambiguous; but there are others, the meaning of which is clearly determined independently of the historian's will. For example, he is not at liberty to deny the fact that Marx asserted the priority of matter to spirit or mind. As far as the historian is concerned, the texts constitute something given, something which limits his reconstruction.[41]

Texts have limits to the meanings which can be seen in them. No one employs postmodern hermeneutics in reading the instructions on a medicine bottle. The fact that texts taken as evidence have limits is of particular importance to our project, since most of the evidence which we shall assess involves the texts of the New Testament.

The above leads to one final point about theory-ladenness. As Suppe explains, it is false that there is a different *Weltanschauung* uniquely correlated with each scientific theory.[42] If the notion of a *Weltanschauung* is defined too broadly, then it just becomes equivalent to one's total-background, experience, beliefs, training, and so forth, in which case the striking fact is that scientists possessing widely different *Weltanschauungen* do employ the same theories and come to agreement on the testing, articulation, and use of such theories. On the other hand, if one tries to narrow the definition of a *Weltanschauung*, then the fact is that scientists involved in research programs on different theories do not necessarily have different *Weltanschauungen*, but clearly understand the competing theory, the observations and evidence that support it, and regularly communicate with one another about such matters. It would be bizarre, for example, to say that all proponents of the standard Big Bang theory have a unique and different *Weltanschauung* than cosmologists who advocated the old Steady State theory, rather than to say that they just disagreed on which theory offered the best explanation of the evidence. Thus, theory-ladenness of observation, insofar as this is a plausible notion, undermines neither science nor history.

The second major thesis of *Weltanschauung* analyses, that the meanings of terms in theories are theory-dependent, has proved even more indefensible.[43] It implies that two different theories could not agree or disagree with each other, in which case it makes no sense to speak of them as alternatives between which a choice is to be made; instead, every theory becomes true by definition and the testing of theories circular (since anything purportedly contradictory to the theory will have a different meaning). This is just a gross distortion of what science is. If one

41. Ibid., 57.

42. Frederick Suppe, "The Search for Philosophic Understanding of Scientific Theories," in *Structure of Scientific Theories*, 218–20.

43. See ibid., 199–208.

adopts a more moderate thesis to the effect that in our formulations of theories the meanings of some of the terms are partially determined by some of the principles of the theory, then one gives up the characteristic claim of *Weltanschauung* analyses that theories are incommensurable and cannot be adjudicated from outside the paradigm. In any case, it is not clear how the incommensurability thesis for scientific theories would apply to the terms of historians' reconstructions of the past, since the latter do not employ theoretical terms and principles, but are formulated in ordinary language.

Finally, the third major claim of *Weltanschauung* analyses, that what counts as a fact is determined by the *Weltanschauung*, is patient of a radical or a moderate interpretation.[44] Radically construed as the thesis that facts about the world are literally determined by our *Weltanschauung*, it leads once again to a sort of solipsism. A more moderate claim, that what one can entertain as a fact is determined by one's *Weltanschauung*, can only be defended when due consideration is given to the criticisms of the first two theses above. There exists a body of evidence which can serve to adjudicate rival theories. While a theory will shape some of the criteria for its assessment, such as which questions the theory should address or what is the appropriate methodology for testing its assertions, still the requirement that an adequate theory be empirically true guarantees that subjective factors will not nullify the objectivity of science. Similarly, in history, while different reconstructions of the past may be prompted by different questions on the part of the historian and no single methodology exists for testing historical reconstructions, still any acceptable reconstruction must make its peace with the empirical evidence.

The appeal of postmodern relativists to *Weltanschauung* analyses of science in order to undermine objectivism in history thus proves vain. According to Suppe, *Weltanschauung* analyses "are not widely viewed as serious contenders for a viable philosophy of science. Contemporary philosophy of science, although strongly influenced by these *Weltanschauungen* views, has gone beyond them and is heading in new directions. The *Weltanschauungen* views, in a word, today are passé, although . . . they continue to be much discussed in the philosophical literature."[45] The turn to realism by contemporary philosophy of science is an encouraging development which can only reinforce historical objectivism.

The Nature of Historical Facts

Now it will be remembered that there were two supposed implications of our lack of direct access to the past. First, there's the problem of the nature of historical facts. Becker says that facts exist only in the mind. He says that the facts are merely the historian's statements about events. But this is clearly untenable. For Becker also says the facts have no meaning. Now surely he doesn't want to say that the historian's statements have no meaning! His position is thus self-refuting. Rather a

---

44. See discussion in ibid., 208–17.
45. Suppe, "Afterword," 633–34.

historical fact is either the historical event itself or a piece of accurate information about that event. Thus, a historian makes statements about the facts.

Seen in this light, Becker's statement that facts exist only in the mind is somewhat silly. His belief forces him to the bizarre conclusion that Lincoln's assassination made a difference in history only because people have long memories, but that if everyone had forgotten Lincoln's death within forty-eight hours, then it would have made no difference at all and would have ceased to be a historical fact! It's difficult to take such an idea seriously. For clearly, Lincoln's death would have made an immense impact on United States history whether *anyone* remembered it or not. It was primarily Lincoln's *absence*, not memories of Lincoln, that made such a difference in United States history. Even if everyone had forgotten that there even was a Lincoln, the absence created by the death of that great man would still have had its devastating results. In other words, the facts exist independently of our minds and still have their impact even long after they are forgotten.

There were two sub-implications arising from the idea that historical facts are just in one's mind. A little reflection will reveal that the first sub-implication, that historical facts have no meaning, is a preposterous notion. For what do we mean by the phrase *facts without meaning*? What in the world is a "meaningless" fact? This is a notion trembling on the brink of self-contradiction. Meaning is inherent in the very concept of *fact*. To describe a fact is to give its meaning. Thus, if I say "It is a fact that Garfield was the twentieth president of the United States," the meaning of the fact, if not obvious enough, is given by simply defining its terms: it is a fact that a man named Garfield was the twentieth man to be the head of the executive branch of the government of the country named the United States. What the fact is *is* its meaning. The notion of a meaningless fact is absurd; there can be no such thing. Insofar as a thing is a fact, it has meaning, because meaning is inherent in the concept of fact. That is the half-truth of the postmodernist's claim that there are no facts independent of a description. The above description of Garfield uses terms that only a person with a political vocabulary could understand. But that in no way implies that the description fails to express a fact about the world. Again, only a scientist will see the object on the table as an interferometer, but that does not imply that there is no interferometer on the table! When postmodernists assert that historians impart meaning to facts, they are often, as White's example of regarding events as either tragic or comic reveals, using the word *meaning* in some evaluative sense such as "significance" or "importance," in which case the varying assessments attributed by people from different perspectives to events in the past do nothing to undermine the objectivity of our knowledge of the course of past events.[46]

46. See the three levels of meaning distinguished by José Carlos Barrera, "Making History, Talking about History," *History and Theory* 40 (2001): 199, the first of which, reference, is independent of narrative and evaluative context. See also Hayden White, *The Content of Form: Narrative Discourse and Historical Representation* (Baltimore: Johns Hopkins University Press, 1987), 10: "It is this need or impulse to rank events with respect to their significance for the culture or group that is writing its own history that makes

The second sub-implication of the relativists' argument that facts are just in the mind is that history is the product of the historian himself. I plan to deal with this argument when I discuss whether the historian can reconstruct the past objectively or whether what he writes is determined by his cultural milieu and so forth. I'll argue that because the facts are not just in his mind but are, as it were, "out there," subjective influences are constrained by the facts themselves.

Testing Historical Hypotheses

The second major implication of the lack of direct access to the data concerns the testability of historical hypotheses. Since the historian cannot perform experiments like a scientist, how can he test his theories? It seems to me that the historian's hypotheses are to be tested like anyone else's: by their logical consistency and their ability to explain the evidence.

The problem arises as to how to apply this test in history. I suggest that the historian applies this test in exactly the same way as the scientist. Whatever model of explanation one adopts in the sciences will do nicely for history as well. One popular model is the hypothetico-deductive model. The scientist invents a hypothesis to provide an explanation of the facts, and then he deduces from the hypothesis specific conditions that would either confirm or disprove his hypothesis. Then he performs certain experiments to see which conditions obtain.

The historian can follow the same procedure. He reconstructs a picture of the past. This is his hypothesis. Then he deduces certain conditions from it that will confirm or disprove his hypothesis. He then checks to see which conditions exist. He does this not by experiments, as the scientist does, but by historical evidence. As Collingwood says, "The historian's picture of the past stands in a peculiar relation to something called evidence. The only way in which the historian can judge of its truth is by considering this relation."[47] Collingwood is saying that the historian's hypothesis must be corroborated by the evidence, for example, archaeological evidence. "By treating coins, pottery, weapons, and other artifacts as evidence," one historian writes, "the historian raises his study to the level of a science. What happened in the past is what the evidence indicates as having happened."[48]

Alternatively, one may employ the more recently developed model of inference to the best explanation. According to this approach, we begin with the evidence

---

a narrative representation of real events possible"; and Robert F. Berkhofer, *Beyond the Great Story: History as Text and Discourse* (Cambridge, Mass.: Belknap Press of Harvard University Press, 1995), 53: "Evidence is not fact until given meaning in accordance with some framework or perspective." Raymond Martin rightly comments on this sense of meaning, "Since there is no limit to the ways in which something can be humanly significant, there is no limit to what events can mean and, hence, no such thing as *the* meaning of events" (Raymond Martin, "Progress in Historical Studies," *History and Theory* 37 [1998]: 33). Still, Martin shows how facts constrain interpretations of them.

47. R. G. Collingwood, *The Idea of History*, ed. T. M. Know (Oxford: Oxford University Press, 1956), 246.

48. William Debbins, "Introduction," in *Essays in the Philosophy of History*, xiv. See also Dray, "Comment," 182.

available to us and then infer what would, if true, provide the best explanation of that evidence. Out of a pool of live options determined by our background beliefs, we select the best of various competing potential explanations to give a causal account of why the evidence is as it is rather than otherwise. The scientist can test his proposed explanation by performing experiments; the historian will test his by seeing how well it elucidates the historical evidence.

The process of determining which historical reconstruction is the best explanation will involve the historian's craft, as various factors will have to be weighed. In his book *Justifying Historical Descriptions*,[49] C. Behan McCullagh lists the factors which historians typically weigh in testing a historical hypothesis:

1) The hypothesis, together with other true statements, must imply further statements describing present, observable data.

2) The hypothesis must have greater *explanatory scope* (that is, imply a greater variety of observable data) than rival hypotheses.

3) The hypothesis must have greater *explanatory power* (that is, make the observable data more probable) than rival hypotheses.

4) The hypothesis must be *more plausible* (that is, be implied by a greater variety of accepted truths, and its negation implied by fewer accepted truths) than rival hypotheses.

5) The hypothesis must be *less ad hoc* (that is, include fewer new suppositions about the past not already implied by existing knowledge) than rival hypotheses.

6) The hypothesis must be *disconfirmed by fewer accepted beliefs* (that is, when conjoined with accepted truths, imply fewer false statements) than rival hypotheses.

7) The hypothesis must so *exceed its rivals* in fulfilling conditions (2)–(6) that there is little chance of a rival hypothesis, after further investigation, exceeding it in meeting these conditions.

Since some reconstructions may fulfill some conditions but be deficient in others, the determination of the best explanation requires skill and may often be difficult. But if the strength and scope of any explanation are very great, so that it explains a large number and variety of facts, many more than any other competing explanation, then, advises McCullagh, it is likely to be true.

In his process of formulating and testing hypotheses the historian is very much like the scientist, especially the geologist or paleontologist, who also lacks direct access to his data and the opportunity of lab experiments on past events. Collingwood gives the conclusion: "The analysis of science in epistemological terms is

---

49. C. Behan McCullagh, *Justifying Historical Descriptions* (Cambridge: Cambridge University Press, 1984), 19.

identical with the analysis of history and the distinction between them as separate kinds of knowledge is an illusion."[50]

One final point needs to be made. The goal of historical knowledge is to obtain probability, not mathematical certainty. An item can be regarded as a piece of historical knowledge when it is related to the evidence in such a way that any reasonable person ought to accept it. This is the situation with all of our inductive knowledge: we accept what has sufficient evidence to render it probable. Similarly, in a court of law, the verdict is awarded to the case that is made most probable by the evidence. Even in a criminal case, in which the burden of proof is highest, the jury is asked to decide if the accused is guilty—not beyond all doubt, which is impossible—but beyond all reasonable doubt. Similarly, in history we should accept the hypothesis that provides the most probable explanation of the evidence.

To summarize, then, we test for truth by assessing historical hypotheses in light of the evidence, and the method of applying this test is the same in history as it is in science. The historian should accept the hypothesis that best explains all the evidence. Thus, the supposed lack of direct access to the data is no stumbling block to testing for truth in history and so gaining an accurate knowledge of the past.

The Problem of Lack of Neutrality

Let's move now to the second major objection to our gaining knowledge from the past: the lack of neutrality. Relativists argue that because we are all shaped by personality and environment, no historian can objectively reconstruct the past. In what I've said already we have begun to expose the fallacies of this objection.

When we judge the truth of a historical work, it is not so important how the knowledge of the past was learned, as *what* the content of that knowledge is. As the historian Maurice Mandelbaum explains, if we say that a historical work is false, we say that it is false because it does not accord with the facts, not because of sociological factors surrounding the historian.[51] As long as historical realism is correct and historical hypotheses must square with the evidence, then the cultural conditioning of the historian is secondary.

Another way of putting this is that it is not so important how the historian comes to arrive at his hypothesis as how his hypothesis is tested. So long as it is tested by the objective facts, it is of secondary importance what factors influenced the historian to come up with his hypothesis in the first place. Thus, Morton White emphasizes that although a number of psychological and social factors may influence the formulation of a hypothesis, the historian still has to submit to objective tests that have nothing to do with personality, milieu, or general worldview.[52] It

50. R. G. Collingwood, "Are History and Science Different Kinds of Knowledge?" in *Essays in the Philosophy of History*, 32.

51. Maurice Mandelbaum, *The Problem of Historical Knowledge* (New York: Harper & Row, 1967), 184.

52. Morton White, "Can History Be Objective?" in *Philosophy of History* (London: Routledge & Kegan Paul), 1957), 199.

is the same situation as in science. This is not to say that there isn't a "logic of discovery" that the scientist (or historian) follows in framing fruitful hypotheses. The point is that so far as the truth of the hypothesis is concerned, it doesn't matter how the historian or scientist comes up with his hypothesis—he could have learned it at his mother's knee, for all that matters. So long as the hypothesis is tested by the facts, there is no danger of sacrificing objectivity.

In reality, relativists recognize that our knowledge of history is not awash in subjectivism. For although they deny historical objectivity, they do not really treat history in so roughshod a manner. This is evident in three ways:

1) *A common core of indisputable historical facts exists.* Thus, one relativist confesses that "there are basic facts which are the same for all historians," facts which it is "the duty" of the historian to present accurately.[53] Even Becker, while saying that facts have no meaning, admits that "some things, some 'facts' can be established and agreed upon"—examples include the date of the Declaration of Independence, Caesar's crossing the Rubicon, the sale of indulgences in 1517, Lincoln's assassination, and so forth.[54] The same goes for postmodernist historians.[55] Not even the most radical theorist is really prepared to abandon history as a hopeless bog of subjectivism. As historian Isaiah Berlin puts it, if someone were to tell us that *Hamlet* was written at the court of Genghis Khan in outer Mongolia, we would not think that he was merely wrong, but that he was out of his mind![56]

But if there is a common, incontrovertible core of historical facts, then the relativist has surrendered his point that the facts do not speak for themselves or that historical objectivity is vitiated. It is a simple truth that, in historian Christopher Blake's words, there "is a very considerable part" of history that is "acceptable to the community of professional historians beyond all question," be they Marxists or liberals, Catholics or Protestants, nineteenth-century Germans or twentieth-century Englishmen.[57] If one were to ask what some of the facts are which make up this backbone of history, I think few historians would disagree with very much of what has been catalogued in a book such as Langer's *Encyclopedia of World History.* Thus, the existence of a common core of historical facts shows that even relativists believe that lack of neutrality does not obviate the objectivity of history.

2) *It is possible to distinguish between history and propaganda.* "All reputable historians," states W. H. Walsh, make a distinction between history and propaganda. The latter may serve some purpose, says Walsh, but, he insists, it is "emphatically

53. E. H. Carr, *What Is History?* (New York: Random House, 1953), 8.

54. Becker, "Historical Facts," 132.

55. Cf. Perez Zagorin, "History, the Referent, and Narrative: Reflections on Postmodernism Now," *History and Theory* 38 (1999): 14; T. L. Haskell, "Objectivity Is Not Neutrality: Rhetoric vs. Practice in Peter Novick's *That Noble Dream,*" *History and Theory* 29 (1990): 155–56.

56. Isaiah Berlin, "The Concept of Scientific History," in *Philosophical Analysis and History*, ed. W. H. Dray (New York: Harper & Row, 1966), 11.

57. Christopher Blake, "Can History Be Objective?" in *Theories of History*, ed. P. Gardiner (Glencoe, Ill.: Free Press, 1959), 331.

not history."[58] A good example of such propaganda was the Soviet practice of rewriting history to serve their political purposes. According to Morton White, when Stalin came to power, he had Russian history rewritten so that it was he and Lenin who led the Bolshevik Revolution instead of Lenin and Trotsky. According to White,

> It has been shown by students of the Russian Revolution that mountains of books, newspapers, pamphlets, decrees, and documents had to be consigned to the "memory hole," mashed to pulp, or brought out in corrected editions in order to substitute for Lenin-Trotsky a new duality-unity, Lenin-Stalin.[59]

White charges that the most dangerous thing about historical relativism is the way it can be used to justify historical distortions. The ultimate result of this totalitarian fiddling with the past is envisioned by George Orwell in *1984*:

> "There is a Party slogan dealing with control of the past," he said. "Repeat it, if you please."
>
> "Who controls the past controls the future; who controls the present controls the past," repeated Winston obediently.
>
> "Who controls the present controls the past," said O'Brien, nodding his head with slow approval. . . .
>
> "I tell you, Winston, that reality is not external. Reality exists in the human mind, and nowhere else. Not in the individual mind, which can make mistakes, and in any case soon perishes; only in the mind of the Party, which is collective and immortal. Whatever the Party holds to be truth *is* truth."[60]

If the facts have no meaning and can be made to say whatever the historian wants, then there is no way to protest this propagandizing of history. On relativist grounds, there is no way to distinguish history from propaganda. But again, not even postmodern relativists can countenance such a notion. Brian Fay reports,

> Postmetaphysical metatheorists as much as any know the difference between propaganda and genuine history; they can recognize the ideological blindness which sanctions revisionist histories bent on denying the existence of the Holocaust, can identify the ways Soviet historiography was contaminated by Stalinist political correctness, can criticize not just the conclusions but the entire practice of racist historiography (such as Nazi Aryan history).[61]

58. W. H. Walsh, *Philosophy of History: An Introduction* (New York: Harper & Row, 1965), 111.

59. Morton White, *Foundations of Historical Knowledge* (New York: Harper & Row, 1965), 268; see also Karl Popper, *The Open Society and Its Enemies*, 5th rev. ed. (London: Routledge & Kegan Paul, 1966).

60. George Orwell, *1984: A Novel* (London: Secker & Warburg, 1949), pt. 3, chap. 2.

61. Brian Fay, "Nothing but History?" *History and Theory* 37 (1998): 84.

Relativists of all stripes want to say that the facts *do* make a difference and that propagandists cannot distort them at will. But the only way to do that is to acknowledge that historical objectivity is in some measure attainable.

3) *It is possible to criticize poor history.* All historians distinguish good history from poor. A good illustration is the reaction to Immanuel Velikovsky's attempt to rewrite ancient history on the basis of worldwide catastrophes caused by extraterrestrial forces in the fifteenth, eighth, and seventh centuries B.C. Velikovsky completely reconstructs ancient history, dismissing entire ancient kingdoms and languages as fictional. In a meticulously documented essay on Velikovsky's theories, archaeologist Edwin Yamauchi incisively criticizes the proposed reconstruction, relentlessly plucking out one support after another by a detailed analysis of ancient documents, archaeology, and philology until the whole structure tumbles down in ruin. His conclusion is succinct: "Velikovsky's reconstruction is a catastrophic history in a double sense. It is a history based on catastrophe, and it is a disastrous catastrophe of history."

Now no relativist could make such a statement. If history is simply the subjective product of the historian's own biases and background, then Velikovsky's views are as good as anybody's. Yet, as Yamauchi observes, the reaction of historians to Velikovsky's proposals was "quite hostile."[62] In saying that such a rewrite is poor history or biased or inaccurate, historians implicitly admit that the facts themselves do say something and are not like a waxen nose that can be pulled and twisted about to suit any historian's whim. So in criticizing poor history the relativist acknowledges the objectivity of history.

Finally, the objection based on lack of neutrality fails to appreciate that the lack of neutrality can be mitigated in a number of ways. Michael Licona lists six factors which can help to mitigate the unavoidable absence of neutrality:[63] (1) proper historical method, including the way in which data are viewed, weighed, and contextualized, correct criteria for testing the adequacy of hypotheses, and fair consideration of competing hypotheses; (2) public acknowledgment of one's horizon and methodology; (3) peer pressure and review by the community of historians; (4) submitting hypotheses to hostile experts, (5) the presence of certain minimal facts which all contemporary historians regard as historical facts and may be taken for granted; (6) a serious effort at detachment from one's biases. Popper says that the best way out of the problem of having unconscious points of view is to state clearly one's view and to recognize that there are also other points of view.[64] Raymond Aron states that "relativism is transcended as soon as the historian ceases to claim a detachment which is impossible, recognizes what

62. Edwin Yamauchi, "Immanuel Velikovsky's Catastrophic History," *Journal of the American Scientific Affiliation* 25 (1973): 138, 134.

63. Michael Licona, "Some Hermeneutical and Historiographical Considerations Pertaining to the Historicity of the Resurrection of Jesus" (Ph.D. thesis, University of Pretoria, forthcoming), chap. 1.

64. Karl Popper, *The Poverty of Historicism* (London: Routledge & Kegan Paul, 1957), 152.

his point of view is, and consequently puts himself in a position to recognize the points of view of others."[65]

Why, then, are histories rewritten each generation? In his classic book *The Problem of Historical Knowledge*, Maurice Mandelbaum provides seven reasons.[66] None of these counts against historical objectivity. Some of the reasons are: new sources and evidence are discovered; recent history always needs to be reworked as we gain perspective on what has happened; new appreciation of a certain form of art, music, literature, and so forth may arise in one generation after another. Far from eliminating knowledge of the past as it actually was, the rewriting of history serves to advance our knowledge of the past as new discoveries are made.

One aspect of the problem of lack of neutrality is of special interest for our inquiry: the presupposition of naturalism or supernaturalism on the part of the historian. Naturalism, in contrast to supernaturalism, holds that every effect in the world is brought about by causes which are themselves also part of the natural order (the spacetime realm of matter and energy). It follows that no naturalist as such can accept the historicity of the miraculous events of the Gospels, such as Jesus' resurrection: he must deny either their miraculous nature or their historicity. The presupposition of naturalism will thus affect the historian's assessment of the evidence of the Gospels. R. T. France has commented:

> At the level of their literary and historical character we have good reasons to treat the Gospels seriously as a source of information on the life and teaching of Jesus, and thus on the historical origins of Christianity. . . . Beyond that point, the decision as to how far a scholar is willing to accept the record they offer is likely to be influenced more by his openness to a "supernaturalist" world-view than by strictly historical considerations.[67]

We have seen, for example, that in inferring to the best explanation, one chooses from a pool of live options a candidate to serve as one's explanation for the evidence. For the naturalist historian confronted with, say, the evidence of the empty tomb and resurrection appearances, the hypothesis that Jesus rose from the dead would most probably not even be a live option.[68] If a supernaturalistic historian were to offer such an explanation of the evidence, his naturalistic colleague would probably find it incredible.

But on what grounds? In a fascinating comment on the criteria for assessing historical hypotheses, McCullagh actually considers the Christian hypothesis of the resurrection of Jesus and observes, "This hypothesis is of greater explanatory scope and power than other hypotheses which try to account for the relevant

---

65. Raymond Aron, "Relativism in History," in *Philosophy of History*, 160.

66. Mandelbaum, *Problem of Historical Knowledge*, 298–304.

67. R.T. France, "The Gospels as Historical Sources for Jesus, the Founder of Christianity," *Truth* 1 (1985): 86.

68. See Peter Lipton, *Inference to the Best Explanation* (London: Routledge, 1991), 122.

evidence, but it is less plausible and more ad hoc than they are. That is why it is difficult to decide on the evidence whether it should be accepted or rejected."[69] The question of whether the resurrection hypothesis is more ad hoc than its rivals can be deferred until our discussion of that event, but for now we may ask why this hypothesis should be considered less plausible than rival hypotheses. Degree of plausibility is defined by McCullagh as the degree to which a hypothesis is implied by accepted knowledge, including both background knowledge and the specific relevant evidence for the hypothesis. Now with respect to the background knowledge alone, the supernaturalist may agree with the naturalist that the resurrection hypothesis has virtually zero plausibility in McCullagh's sense, for nothing in that information alone implies that the resurrection occurred (for the sake of argument, we set aside our experience of the Risen Lord). But by the same token, the hypotheses that the disciples stole the body or that Jesus was taken down from the cross alive, and so forth, also have zero plausibility with respect to the background information alone, for nothing in that information implies that any of these events took place either. That means that the greater plausibility enjoyed by naturalistic hypotheses must derive from the specific evidence itself. But here it is very hard to see how the specific evidence confers greater plausibility on any naturalistic hypothesis than on the resurrection hypothesis; on the contrary, these rival hypotheses, far from being rendered plausible by the evidence, are usually thought to be made implausible by the evidence.

Perhaps McCullagh's claim, then, should have been that the resurrection hypothesis is *more implausible* than rival hypotheses. *Degree of implausibility* is defined as the degree to which our present knowledge implies the falsity of a hypothesis. Now, again dividing present knowledge into background information and specific evidence for the hypothesis, it cannot be that the specific evidence renders the resurrection hypothesis more implausible than its competitors, for that evidence in no way implies the falsity of the resurrection hypothesis. Hence, there must be something in our background knowledge that renders the resurrection hypothesis more implausible than its rivals. I strongly suspect that the reason the naturalist finds the resurrection implausible is because included in our background knowledge of the world is the fact that dead men do not rise, which he takes to be incompatible with Jesus' resurrection. I'll have much more to say about this problem in the next chapter. But in passing we may agree that our background knowledge makes the hypothesis of the natural revivification of Jesus from the dead enormously implausible, in that the causal powers of nature are insufficient to return a corpse to life; but such considerations are simply irrelevant to assessing the implausibility of the hypothesis of the resurrection of Jesus, since according to that hypothesis God raised Jesus from the dead. I should say that the hypothesis that God raised Jesus from the dead has about zero implausibility with respect to our background knowledge—leaving aside any implausibility thought to attend to

---

69. McCullagh, *Justifying Historical Descriptions*, 21.

the hypothesis of God's existence. Only if the naturalist has good reasons to think that God's existence is implausible or his intervention in the world implausible could he justifiably regard the resurrection hypothesis as implausible.

The upshot of this discussion is that the objective facts can lead a historian to abandon his naturalistic stance if a miraculous hypothesis should clearly exceed any naturalistic hypothesis in fulfilling the conditions of a best explanation. Of course, a historian could be so deeply prejudiced in favor of naturalism that he resolutely refuses to accept any miraculous hypothesis. But that is just a fact of psychology, which does not undermine the objectivity of history, any more than does the case of a Marxist historian who shuts his eyes to noneconomic causes of historical development or a Confederate historian who refuses to acknowledge any responsibility of the South in bringing on the Civil War. The point is that naturalism (or supernaturalism) does not inevitably determine how one weighs the evidence. Indeed, one's naturalism might be very lightly held, a sort of unconscious assumption unreflectively embraced as a result of one's upbringing, and quickly abandoned upon the presentation of powerful evidence for a miraculous hypothesis.[70]

All this has been said concerning metaphysical naturalism. But it has been argued, even by Christian thinkers, that there is a sort of methodological naturalism which must be adopted in science and history. According to methodological naturalism, science and, by implication, history just don't deal with supernatural explanations, and so these are left aside. Now in this case the issue does not concern a lack of neutrality; it is merely a question of methodology. For my part, I see no good reason for methodological naturalism in either science or history. But we may simply sidestep the issue, since our purpose is not to show that the historian *qua* historian should accept the miraculous events of the Gospels, any more than our aim was to show that the scientist *qua* scientist should accept the existence of a Creator. A methodological naturalist will simply remain agnostic when speaking professionally about such issues, but acknowledge that as a human being he accepts the supernaturalistic explanations.

Conclusion

Therefore, we can conclude that neither the supposed problem of lack of direct access to the past nor the supposed problem of the lack of neutrality can prevent us from learning something from history. And if Christianity's claims to be a religion rooted in history are true, then history may lead us to a knowledge of God himself.

Practical Application

The content of this chapter has little direct applicability to evangelism. I have never met a non-Christian who overtly objected to the gospel message because of

---

70. See the special issue "Creation/Evolution and Faith," of *Christian Scholar's Review* 21/1 (1991); Alvin Plantinga, "Methodological Naturalism," paper presented at the symposium "Knowing God, Christ, and Nature in the Post-Positivistic Era," University of Notre Dame, April 14–17, 1993.

historical relativism. But in an age self-consciously postmodern, historicism and subjectivism are rampant. As people who believe in an objective revelation mediated through historical events, Christians cannot afford to sacrifice the objectivity of history. Otherwise, the events of the life, death, and resurrection of Jesus cannot be said to be part of the objective past, since the Gospels do not represent objective history. It is critical if we are not to lapse into mere mythology that we defend the objectivity of history and, thus, of the Gospels.

It is therefore heartening to find that the community of professional historians has remained unmoved by the blandishments of postmodern relativists. Nancy Partner observes, "For all the sophistication of the theory-saturated part of the profession, scholars in all the relevant disciplines that contribute to or depend on historical information carry on in all essential ways as though nothing had changed since Ranke, or Gibbon for that matter."[71] One might think that although they go about their task in the same way as before, practicing historians, as a result of the influence of postmodernism, have nonetheless become non-realists about their narratives. But by all accounts such an inference would be mistaken. Practicing historians know better, and even the theorists have largely rejected postmodern approaches to history. Zagorin reports, "In contrast to scholars in the field of literary studies, the American historical profession has been much more resistant to postmodernist doctrines; . . . the latter's influence upon the thinking and practice of historians is not only fading but increasingly destined to fade."[72] Postmodernist doctrines are so obviously self-refuting that it is difficult for most philosophers of history to take them seriously. As Fay complains,

Postmetaphysical theories claim to tell us what is the case about history (and thus invoke the idea of truth); claim that their accounts better fit the evidence than do their rivals' (and thus invoke the idea of objectivity); and claim to reveal something about the ways things are (and thus invoke the idea of reality). Most postmetaphysical metatheories implode because they utilize what they deny is legitimate.[73]

As for practicing historians, Lorenz opines that it's a good thing that they do not take postmodernist views seriously because if they did, "it would be completely incomprehensible why they would actually leave their armchairs to do *research*."[74] Historians know the difference between fiction, which is essentially invented or made up, and history, which requires investigation of a mind-independent reality.

71. Nancy F. Partner, "History in an Age of Reality-Fictions," in *A New Philosophy of History*, ed. Frank Ankersmit and Hans Kellner (Chicago: University of Chicago, 1995), 22.
72. Zagorin, "History, the Referent, and Narrative," 1. He observes that nearly all the well-known philosophers in Great Britain and the United States who have shown greatest interest in philosophy of history have been almost entirely unresponsive or opposed to postmodernist approaches to historiography. Cf. Jenkins' admission, "Most historians . . . have been resistant to that postmodernism which has affected so many of their colleagues in adjacent discourses" (Jenkins, "Introduction," 1).
73. Fay, "Nothing but History?" 84; cf. Zagorin, "History, the Referent, and Narrative."
74. Lorenz, "Historical Knowledge and Historical Reality," 316.

Moreover, when sharing the gospel, one does occasionally encounter non-Christians who seem very skeptical about history. With such persons I think it would be especially effective to share the three ways in which relativists implicitly concede the objectivity of history. If they insist on a complete historical skepticism, then we should explain to them the utter unliveability of such a view. If we are to get along in this world, we need a method of sorting out to the best of our ability what has and has not happened. The results of this procedure will allow for the possibility that the historical foundations of the Christian faith will be as well established as many other purely natural events. Therefore, it would be hypocrisy to admit the one but not the other. Insist on this fundamental dilemma in dealing with the non-believer.

Literature Cited or Recommended

Historical Background

Anselm. *Cur Deus Homo.* In *Basic Writings.* 2nd ed. Translated by S. N. Deane. Introduction by C. Hartshorne. Open Court Library of Philosophy, 171–288. LaSalle, Ill.: Open Court, 1968.

De la Chaise, Filleau. "Discours sur les livres de Moise." In *Discours sur les "Pensées" de M. Pascal,* edited with an introduction by V. Giraud. Collections des chefs-d'oeuvre méconnues. Paris: Editions Bossard, 1922.

Grotius, Hugo. *The Truth of the Christian Religion.* Notes by J. Le Clerc. Translated by J. Clarke. London: 1709.

Kümmel, Werner Georg. *The New Testament: The History of the Investigation of Its Problems.* Translated by S. McL. Gilmour and H. C. Kee. Nashville: Abingdon, 1972.

Ladd, George. "The Knowledge of God: The Saving Acts of God." In *Basic Christian Doctrines,* edited by Carl F. H. Henry, 7–13. New York: Holt, Rinehart, and Winston, 1962.

Leslie, Charles. *A Short and Easie Method with the Deists.* 2nd ed. London: C. Brome, E. Pode, & Geo. Strahan, 1699.

Mornay, Philippe de. *De la vérité de la religion chrestienne.* Anvers: Imprimerie de Christofle Plantin, 1581. Translated as *A Work Concerning the Trueness of the Christian Religion,* by P. Sidney and A. Goldring. London: 1617.

Thomas Aquinas. *Summa theologiae.* 60 vols. London: Eyre & Spottiswoode for Blackfriars, 1964.

Thompson, J. Westfall, and Bernard J. Holm. *A History of Historical Writing.* 2 vols. New York: Macmillan, 1942.

Vives, Juan Luis. *De veritate fidei christianae.* Repr. London: Gregg International, 1964.

Assessment

Ankersmit, F. R. "The Dilemma of Contemporary Anglo-Saxon Philosophy of History." In "Knowing and Telling History: the Anglo-Saxon Debate." *History and Theory* Beiheft 25 (1986): 1–27.

———. *History and Tropology: The Rise and Fall of Metaphor*. Berkeley: University of California Press, 1994.

Appleby, J., L. Hunt, and M. Jacob. *Telling the Truth about History*. New York: W. W. Norton, 1994.

Aron, Raymond. "Relativism in History." In *The Philosophy of History in Our Time*, edited by H. Meyerhoff, 153–62. Garden City, N.Y.: Doubleday, 1959.

Barrera, José Carlos. "Making History, Talking about History." *History and Theory* 40 (2001): 190–205.

Beard, Charles. "That Noble Dream." In *The Varieties of History*, edited by F. Stern, 314–28. Cleveland: World, Meridian, 1956.

Becker, Carl. "What Are Historical Facts?" In *The Philosophy of History in Our Time*, edited by H. Meyerhoff, 120–39. Garden City, N.Y.: Doubleday 1959.

Berkhofer, Robert F. *Beyond the Great Story: History as Text and Discourse*. Cambridge, Mass.: Belknap Press of Harvard University Press, 1995.

Berlin, Isaiah. "The Concept of Scientific History." In *Philosophical Analysis and History*, edited by W. H. Dray. Sources in Contemporary Philosophy. New York: Harper & Row, 1966.

Bernstein, Richard J. *Beyond Objectivism and Relativism: Science, Hermeneutics, and Praxis*. Oxford: Basil Blackwell, 1983.

Blake, Christopher. "Can History Be Objective?" In *Theories of History*, edited by P. Gardiner, 329–43. Glencoe, Ill.: Free Press, 1959.

Carr, E. H. *What Is History?* New York: Random House, Vintage, 1953.

Collingwood, R. G. "Are History and Science Different Kinds of Knowledge?" In *Essays in the Philosophy of History*, edited by W. Debbins, 23–33. Austin, Tex.: University of Texas Press, 1965.

———. *An Autobiography*. London: Oxford, 1939.

———. "Croce's Philosophy of History." In *Essays in the Philosophy of History*, edited by William Debbins, 3–22. Austin, Tex.: University of Texas Press, 1965.

———. *The Idea of History*. Edited by T. M. Know. Oxford: Oxford, Galaxy, 1956.

Copleston, Frederick. "Problems of Objectivity." In *On the History of Philosophy*, 40–65. London: Search Press, 1979.

"Creation/Evolution and Faith." *Christian Scholar's Review* 21/1 (1991).

Debbins, William. "Introduction." In *Essays in the Philosophy of History*, by R. G. Collingwood, edited by W. Debbins. Austin, Tex.: University of Texas Press, 1965.

Donagan, Alan. "Introduction." In *Philosophy of History*, edited by A. Donagan and B. Donagan. Sources in Philosophy, 1–22. New York: Macmillan, 1965.

Dray, W. H. "Comment." In *Objectivity, Method and Point of View: Essays in the Philosophy of History*, 170–90. Philosophy of History and Culture 6. Leiden: E. J. Brill, 1991.

Fay, Brian. "Nothing but History?" *History and Theory* 37 (1998): 83–93.

France, R. T. "The Gospels as Historical Sources for Jesus, the Founder of Christianity." *Truth* 1 (1985): 81–87.

Gardiner, Patrick. *The Nature of Historical Explanation*. London: Oxford, Galaxy, 1961.

Goldstein, Leon J. *Historical Knowing*. Austin, Tex.: University of Texas Press, 1976.

———. "History and the Primacy of Knowing." In "The Constitution of the Historical Past." *History and Theory* Beiheft 16 (1977): 29–52.

Harrison, R. K. *Introduction to the Old Testament*. Grand Rapids, Mich.: Eerdmans, 1969.

Haskell, T. L. "Objectivity Is Not Neutrality: Rhetoric vs. Practice in Peter Novick's *That Noble Dream.*" *History and Theory* 29 (1990): 129–57.

Himmelfarb, Gertrude. "Telling It as You Like It: Postmodernist History and the Flight from Fact." In *Postmodern History Reader*, edited by Keith Jenkins, 158–74. New York: Routledge, 1997.

Jenkins, Keith, ed. *The Postmodern History Reader*. New York: Routledge, 1997.

Licona, Michael. "Some Hermeneutical and Historiographical Considerations Pertaining to the Historicity of the Resurrection of Jesus." Ph.D. thesis, University of Pretoria, forthcoming.

Lipton, Peter. *Inference to the Best Explanation*. London: Routledge, 1991.

Lorenz, Chris. "Can Histories Be True? Narrativism, Positivism, and the 'Metaphorical Turn.'" *History and Theory* 37 (1998): 309–29.

———. "Historical Knowledge and Historical Reality: A Plea for 'Internal Realism.'" *History and Theory* 33 (1994): 297–327.

McCullagh, C. Behan. *Justifying Historical Descriptions*. Cambridge: Cambridge University Press, 1984.

———. "What Do Historians Argue About?" *History and Theory* 43 (2004): 18–38.

Mandelbaum, Maurice. *The Problem of Historical Knowledge*. New York: Harper & Row, Harper Torchbooks, 1967.

Martin, Raymond. "Progress in Historical Studies." *History and Theory* 37 (1998): 14–39.

Novick, P. *That Noble Dream: The "Objectivity Question" and the American Historical Profession*. New York: Cambridge University Press, 1988.

Nowell-Smith, P. H. "The Constructionist Theory of History." In "The Constitution of the Historical Past." *History and Theory* Beiheft 16 (1977): 1–28.

Orwell, George. *1984: A Novel*. London: Secker & Warburg, 1949.

Partner, Nancy F. "Historicity in an Age of Reality-Fictions." In *A New Philosophy of History*, edited by Frank Ankersmit and Hans Kellner, 21–39. Chicago: University of Chicago Press, 1995.

Pirenne, Henri. "What Are Historians Trying to Do?" In *The Philosophy of History in Our Time*, edited by H. Meyerhoff, 87–100. Garden City, N.Y.: Doubleday, 1959.

Plantinga, Alvin. "Methodological Naturalism." Paper presented at the symposium "Knowing God, Christ, and Nature in the Post-Positivistic Era." University of Notre Dame, April 14–17, 1993.

———. *The Twin Pillars of Christian Scholarship*. Grand Rapids, Mich.: Calvin College and Seminary, 1990.

Popper, Karl. "Has History Any Meaning?" In *The Philosophy of History in Our Time*, edited by H. Meyerhoff, 300–312. Garden City, N.Y.: Doubleday, 1959.

———. *The Open Society and Its Enemies*. London: Routledge & Kegan Paul, 1966.

———. *The Poverty of Historicism*. London: Routledge & Kegan Paul, 1957. Repr. New York: Harper & Row, Harper Torchbooks, 1964.

Rubinoff, Lionel. "Historicity and Objectivity." In *Objectivity, Method and Point of View: Essays in the Philosophy of History*. Philosophy of History and Culture 6, 133–53. Leiden: E. J. Brill, 1991.

———. "Introduction: W. H. Dray and the Critique of Historical Thinking." In *Objectivity, Method and Point of View: Essays in the Philosophy of History*. Philosophy of History and Culture 6, 1–11. Leiden: E. J. Brill, 1991.

Scheffler, Israel. *Science and Subjectivity*. 2nd ed. Indianapolis: Hackett, 1982.

Suppe, Frederick, ed. *The Structure of Scientific Theories*. 2nd ed. Urbana, Ill.: University of Illinois Press, 1977. See especially the Introduction and Afterword.

Tyrrell, George. *Christianity at the Cross-Roads*. London: Longman, Green, 1910.

Van der Dussen, W. J. "The Historian and His Evidence." In *Objectivity, Method and Point of View: Essays in the Philosophy of History*, 154–69. Philosophy of History and Culture 6. Leiden: E.J. Brill, 1991.

Walsh, W. H. *Philosophy of History: An Introduction*. New York: Harper & Row, Harper Torchbooks, 1965.

White, Hayden. *The Content of Form: Narrative Discourse and Historical Representation*. Baltimore: Johns Hopkins University Press, 1987.

———. *Tropics of Discourse: Essays in Cultural Criticism*. Baltimore: Johns Hopkins University Press, 1978.

White, Morton. "Can History Be Objective?" In *The Philosophy of History in Our Time*, edited by H. Meyerhoff, 188–202. Garden City, N.Y.: Doubleday, 1959.

———. *Foundations of Historical Knowledge*. New York: Harper & Row, Harper Torchbooks, 1965.

Yamauchi, Edwin. "Immanuel Velikovsky's Catastrophic History." *Journal of the American Scientific Affiliation* 25 (1973): 134–39.

Zagorin, Perez. "History, the Referent, and Narrative: Reflections on Postmodernism Now." *History and Theory* 38 (1999): 1–24.

———. "Rejoinder to a Postmodernist." *History and Theory* 39 (2000): 201–9.

6

The Problem of Miracles

Before we can examine the evidence to see whether the Creator God of the universe has revealed himself in some special way in the world in order to offer us the promise of immortality so necessary for meaningful existence now, we must deal with the problem of whether such divine action is possible in the first place. And if it is, how can it be identified? That is to say, we are confronted with the problem of miracles.

Undoubtedly, one of the major stumbling blocks to becoming a Christian for many people today is that Christianity is a religion of miracles. It asserts that God became incarnate in Jesus of Nazareth, being born of a virgin, that he performed various miracles, exorcised demonic beings, and that, having died by crucifixion, he rose from the dead. But the problem is that these sorts of miraculous events seem to belong to a worldview foreign to modern man—a pre-scientific, superstitious worldview belonging to the ancient and middle ages.

Some theologians have been so embarrassed by this fact that many of them, following Rudolf Bultmann, have sought to demythologize the Bible, thereby removing the stumbling block to modern man. According to Bultmann, no one who uses the radio or electric lights should be expected to believe in the mythological worldview of the Bible in order to become a Christian. He insists that he is not trying to make Christianity more palatable to modern man but is trying merely to remove a false stumbling block so that the true stumbling block—the call to authentic existence symbolized by the cross—might become evident. But in so doing, Bultmann reduces Christianity to little more than the existentialist philosophy of Martin Heidegger. Indeed, some Bultmann disciples like Herbert Braun or Schubert Ogden have pushed Bultmann's views to their logical conclusion and have propounded a Christless and even atheistic Christianity. Such theologies offer man no hope of immortality. If the Christian hope of immortality through eschatological resurrection is to be believed, then contemporary thinkers may well demand of Christians some defense of miracles.

Historical Background

Deist Objections to Miracles

The skepticism of modern man with regard to miracles arose during the Enlightenment, or Age of Reason, which dawned in Europe during the seventeenth century. Thereafter, miracles simply became unbelievable for most of the intelligentsia. The attack upon miracles was led by the Deists. Although Deists accepted the existence of God, his conservation of the world in being, and his general revelation in nature, they strenuously denied that he had revealed himself in any special way in the world. They were therefore very exercised to demonstrate the impossibility of the occurrence of miracles, or at least of the identification of miracles. They were countered by a barrage of Christian apologetic literature defending the possibility and evidential value of miracles. Let's examine now the principal arguments urged by the Deists against miracles and the responses offered by their Christian opponents.

THE NEWTONIAN WORLD-MACHINE

Although the most important philosophical opponents of miracles were Spinoza and Hume, much of the debate was waged against the backdrop of the mechanical worldview of Newtonian physics. In his *Philosophiae naturalis principia mathematica* (1687), Isaac Newton formulated his famous three laws of motion, from which, together with some definitions, he was able to deduce the various theorems and corollaries of his physics. In regarding the world in terms of masses, motions, and forces operating according to these laws, Newton's *Principia* seemed to eliminate the need for God's providence and gave rise to a picture of the universe appropriately characterized as the "Newtonian world-machine."

Newton's model of mechanical explanation was enthusiastically received as the paradigm for explanation in all fields; this attitude reached its height in Pierre Simon de Laplace's belief that a Supreme Intelligence, equipped with Newton's *Principia* and knowing the present position and velocity of every particle in the universe, could deduce the exact state of the universe at any other point in time. When Napoleon remarked to Laplace on the absence of any mention of God in his work, a nonplussed Laplace retorted, "Sire, I have no need of that hypothesis."[1]

---

1. For an account of this famous exchange see Roger Hahn, *Pierre Simon de Laplace 1749–1827: A Determined Scientist* (Cambridge, Mass.: Harvard University Press, 2005), 172.

Such a worldview promoted the Deist conception of God as the creator of the world-machine, who wound it up like a clock and set it running under the laws of matter and motion, never to interfere with it again.

Indeed, this harmoniously functioning world-machine was thought to provide the best evidence that God exists. The eighteenth-century French *philosophe* Diderot exclaimed, "Thanks to the works of these great men, the world is no longer a God; it is a machine with its wheels, its cords, its pulleys, its springs, and its weights."[2] But equally it was thought that such a world system also made it incredible that God should interfere with its operation via miraculous interventions. Diderot's contemporary Voltaire said it was absurd and insulting to God to think that he would interrupt the operations of "this immense machine," since he designed it from the beginning to run according to his divinely decreed, immutable laws.[3] For eighteenth-century Newtonians, such miraculous interventions could only be described as violations of the laws of nature and were therefore impossible.

BENEDICT DE SPINOZA

The philosophical attack upon miracles, however, actually preceded the publication of Newton's *Principia*. In 1670 Benedict de Spinoza in his *Tractatus theologico-politicus* argued against both the possibility and evidential value of miracles. Two of his arguments are of special significance for our discussion.

Miracles Violate the Unchangeable Order of Nature
First, Spinoza argues that nothing happens contrary to the eternal and unchangeable order of nature. He maintains that all that God wills is characterized by eternal necessity and truth. For since there is no difference between God's understanding and his will, it is the same to say that God knows a thing or that God wills a thing. Thus, the same necessity that characterizes God's knowledge characterizes his will. Therefore, the laws of nature flow from the necessity and perfection of the divine nature. If some event contrary to these laws could occur, then the divine will and knowledge would stand in contradiction to nature, which is impossible. To say that God does something contrary to the laws of nature is to say God does something contrary to his own nature. Therefore, miracles are impossible.

Miracles Insufficient to Prove God's Existence
Second, Spinoza believed that a proof of God's existence must be absolutely certain. It is by the unchangeable order of nature that we know that God exists. By admitting miracles, Spinoza warns, we break the laws of nature and thus create doubts about the existence of God, leading us right into the arms of atheism!

Spinoza also develops two sub-points under this objection. First, a miracle could not in any case prove God's existence, since a lesser being such as an angel

2. Denis Diderot, "Philosophical Thoughts," in *Diderot's Philosophical Works*, trans. M. Jourdain (Chicago: Open Court, 1916), 18.
3. *A Philosophical Dictionary* (New York: Harcourt, Brace, & World, 1962), s.v. "Miracles," by Márie François Arouet de Voltaire.

or demon could be the cause of the event. Second, a so-called miracle is simply a work of nature not yet discovered by man. Our knowledge of nature's laws is limited, and just because we cannot explain the cause of a particular event does not imply that it is a miracle having God as its supernatural cause.

DAVID HUME

While Spinoza attacked the possibility of the *occurrence* of a miracle, the eighteenth-century Scottish skeptic David Hume attacked the possibility of the *identification* of a miracle. In his essay "Of Miracles" he presents a two-pronged assault against miracles, which takes the form of an "Even if . . . , but in fact . . ." argument; that is to say, in the first half he argues against miracles while granting certain concessions, and in the second half he argues on the basis of what he thinks is in fact the case. We may differentiate the two halves of his argument by referring to the first as his "in principle" argument and to the second as his "in fact" argument.

"In Principle" Argument

Hume maintains that it is impossible in principle to prove that a miracle has occurred. A wise man, he says, proportions his belief to the evidence. If the evidence makes a conclusion virtually certain, then we may call this a "proof," and a wise man will give wholehearted belief to that conclusion. If the evidence makes a conclusion more likely than not, then we may speak of a "probability," and a wise man will accept the conclusion as true with a degree of confidence proportionate to the probability. Now, Hume argues, even if we concede that the evidence for a particular miracle amounts to a *full proof*, it is still in principle impossible to identify that event as a miracle. Why? Because standing opposed to this proof is an equally full proof, namely the evidence for the unchangeable laws of nature, that the event in question is not a miracle.

Hume seems to imagine a scale in which the evidence is being weighed. On the one side of the scale is the evidence for a particular miracle, which (he concedes for the sake of argument) amounts to a full proof. But on the other side of the scale stands the evidence from all people in all the ages for the regularity of the laws of nature, which also amounts to a full proof. He writes, "A miracle is a violation of the laws of nature, and as a firm and unalterable experience has established these laws, a proof against miracle, from the very nature of the fact, is as entire as any argument from experience can possibly be imagined."[4] Thus, proof stands against proof, and the scales are evenly balanced. Since the evidence does not incline in either direction, the wise man cannot hold to a miracle with any degree of confidence.

Indeed, Hume continues, to prove a miracle has taken place one would have to show that it would be an even *greater* miracle for the testimony in support of the event in question to be false. Thus, with regard to the resurrection, Hume

4. David Hume, *Enquiry Concerning Human Understanding*, 10.1.90.

asks, which would be the greater miracle: that a man should rise from the dead or that the witnesses should either be deceived or try to deceive? He leaves no doubt as to his answer: he asserts that even if all historians agreed that on January 1, 1600, Queen Elizabeth publicly died and was buried and her successor installed, but that a month later she reappeared, resumed the throne, and ruled England for three more years, Hume would not have the least inclination to believe so miraculous an event. He would accept the most extraordinary hypothesis for her pretended death and burial rather than admit such a striking violation of the laws of nature. Thus, even if the evidence for a miracle constituted a full proof, the wise man would not believe in miracles.

"In Fact" Arguments

But in fact, says Hume, the evidence for miracles does not amount to a full proof. Indeed, the evidence is so poor, it does not even amount to a probability. Therefore, the decisive weight falls on the side of the scale containing the full proof for the regularity of nature, a weight so heavy that no evidence for miracle could ever hope to counter-balance it.

Hume gives four reasons why in fact the evidence for miracles is negligible: First, no miracle in history is attested by a sufficient number of educated and honest men, who are of such social standing that they would have a great deal to lose by lying. Second, people crave the miraculous and will believe the most absurd stories, as the abundance of false tales of miracles proves. Third, miracles occur only among barbarous peoples. And fourth, miracles occur in all religions and thereby cancel each other out, since they support contradictory doctrines.

Hume concludes that miracles can never be the foundation for any system of religion. "Our most holy religion is founded on *Faith*, not on reason," pontificates Hume, all the while laughing up his sleeve:

> The Christian Religion not only was at first attended with miracles, but even at this day cannot be believed by any reasonable person without one. Mere reason is insufficient to convince us of its veracity: And whoever is moved by *Faith* to assent to it, is conscious of a continued miracle in his own person, which subverts all the principles of his understanding, and gives him a determination to believe what is most contrary to custom and experience.[5]

In other words, it is a miracle that anyone could be stupid enough to believe in Christianity!

Christian Defense of Miracles

As I indicated earlier, the Christians of the seventeenth and eighteenth centuries were far from lax in responding to the Deists' attacks. Let us look, therefore, at

---

5. Ibid., 10.2.101.

some of their answers to Spinoza and Hume, as well as to the general Newtonian worldview.

Contra Spinoza

First, we shall consider the response to Spinoza's two objections by several of the leading Christian thinkers of that era.

Jean Le Clerc

One of the earliest progenitors of biblical criticism, the French theologian Jean Le Clerc presented in his *Sentimens de quelques théologiens* (1685) an apologetic for Christianity that, he maintained, was invulnerable to Spinoza's attacks. He asserts that the empirical evidence for Jesus' miracles and resurrection is simply more convincing than Spinoza's *a priori* philosophical reasoning. Specifically, against Spinoza's contention that miracles may simply be natural events, Le Clerc rejoins that nobody could sincerely believe Jesus' resurrection and ascension to be natural events comparable to, say, a man's birth. Nor does it suffice to say these events could be caused by unknown natural laws, for why then are not more of these events produced, and how is it that at the very instant Jesus commanded a paralyzed man to walk "the Laws of Nature (unknown to us) were prepared and ready to cause the . . . Paralytic Man to walk"?[6] Both of these considerations serve to show that the miraculous events in the Gospels, which can be established by ordinary historical methods, are indeed of divine origin.

Samuel Clarke

Considerable analysis was brought to the concept of miracle by the English philosopher-theologian Samuel Clarke in his Boyle lectures of 1705. Reflecting Newtonian influence, Clarke asserts that matter has only the power to continue in either motion or rest. Anything that is *done* in the world is done either by God or by created intelligent beings. The so-called natural forces of matter, like gravitation, are properly speaking the effect of God's acting *on* matter at every moment. The upshot of this is that the so-called "course of nature" is a fiction—what we call the course of nature is in reality nothing other than God's producing certain effects in a continual and uniform manner. Thus, a miracle is not contrary to the course of nature, which does not really exist; it is simply an unusual event that God does. Moreover, since God is omnipotent, miraculous events are no more difficult for him than regular events. So the regular order of nature proves the existence and attributes of God, and miracles prove the interposition of God into the regular order in which he acts.

From the miracle itself taken as an isolated event, it is impossible to determine whether it was performed directly by God or by an angel or a demonic spirit. But, according to Clarke, the key to distinguishing between demonic miracles and divine miracles (whether done directly or indirectly by God) is the doctrinal context in

---

6. Jean Le Clerc, *Five Letters Concerning the Inspiration of the Holy Scriptures* (London: [n.p.], 1690), 235–36.

which the miracle occurs. If the miracle is done in support of a doctrine that is contrary to moral law, then we may be sure that it is not a divine miracle. Thus, in order for an event to be a divine miracle, the *doctrinal context* of the event must be at least morally neutral. If two miracles are performed in support of two contrary doctrines, each morally neutral in itself, then the doctrine supported by the greater miracle ought to be accepted as of divine origin. Hence, the correct theological definition of a miracle is: "a work effected in a manner unusual, or different from the common and regular Method of Providence, by the interposition of God himself, or of some intelligent Agent superior to Man, for the proof or Evidence of some particular Doctrine, or in attestation to the Authority of some particular Person." Jesus' miracles thus prove that he was "a Teacher sent from God" who had "a Divine Commission."[7]

Jacob Vernet

The finest apologetic work written in French during the eighteenth century was, in my opinion, Jean Alphonse Turretin and Jacob Vernet's multi-volume *Traité de la vérité de la religion chrétienne* (1730–1788). Turretin, an esteemed professor of Protestant theology at Geneva, wrote the first volume in Latin; Vernet, also a member of the theological faculty at Geneva after 1756, translated Turretin's volume and added nine of his own. The result was a sophisticated and informed response to French Deism based on internal and external Christian evidences.

Vernet defines a miracle as "a striking work which is outside the ordinary course of nature and which is done by God's all-mighty will, such that witnesses thereof regard it as extraordinary and supernatural."[8] Vernet does not, like Clarke, deny that there is a course of nature, but he does insist that the so-called course or order of nature is really composed of incidental states of events, not necessary states. They depend on the will of God, and it is only the constant and uniform procession of events that leads us to think the course of nature is invariable. But God can make exceptions to the general order of things when he deems it important. These miraculous events show that the course of nature "is not the effect of a blind necessity but of a free Cause who interrupts and suspends it when He pleases."[9]

Against the objection that miracles may be the result of an as yet undiscovered law of nature, Vernet replies that when the miracles are diverse and numerous, this possibility is minimized because it is hardly possible that all these unknown, marvelous operations of nature should occur at the same time. One might be able to explain away a single, isolated miracle on this basis, but not a series of miracles of different sorts.

7. Samuel Clarke, *A Discourse Concerning the Unchangeable Obligations of Natural Religion and the Truth and Certainty of the Christian Revelation* (London: W. Batham, 1706), 367–68.
8. Jean Alphonse Turretin, *Traité de la vérité de la religion chrétienne*, 2nd ed., 7 vols., trans. J. Vernet (Geneva: Henri-Albert Gosse, 1745-55), 5:2–3.
9. Ibid., 5:240.

Claude François Houtteville

The French Abbé Claude François Houtteville also argued for the possibility of miracles against Spinoza in his treatise *La religion chrétienne prouvée par les faits* (1740). He defines a miracle as "a striking action superior to all finite power" or more commonly as "a singular event produced outside the chain of natural causes."[10] Given the existence of God, it is at once evident that he can perform miracles, since he not only created the world but preserves it in being and directs all the laws of its operation by his sovereign hand. Against Spinoza's charge that miracles are impossible because natural law is the necessary decree of God's immutable nature, Houtteville responds that natural law is not necessary, but that God is free to establish whatever laws he wills. Moreover, God can change his decrees whenever he wishes. And even if he could not, miracles could be part of God's eternal decree for creation just as much as the natural laws, so that they represent no change in God. Houtteville even suggests that miracles may not be contrary to nature but only to what we know of nature. From God's perspective they could conform to certain laws unknown to us.

Contra Hume

The Christian response to Hume's arguments was as variegated as the response to Spinoza's.

Thomas Sherlock

Thomas Sherlock, the Bishop of London, wrote his immensely popular *Tryal of the Witnesses* (1729) against the Deist Thomas Woolston, but his arguments are relevant to Hume's later critique of miracles. He presents a mock trial in which the apostles are accused of hoaxing the resurrection of Jesus. Woolston's attorney argues that because the resurrection violates the course of nature, no human testimony could possibly establish it, since it has the whole witness of nature against it. Sherlock has a multifaceted reply.

First, on that principle many natural matters of fact would have to be pronounced false. If we admit testimony only when it accords with our prior conceptions, then a man living in a hot climate, for example, would never believe the testimony of others that water could exist in a solid state as ice. Second, the resurrection is simply a matter of sense perception. If we met a man who claimed to have been dead, we would be admittedly suspicious. But of what? Not that he is now alive, for that is evident to our senses, but that he was ever dead. But would we say that it is impossible to prove by human testimony that this man died a year ago? Such evidence is admitted in any court of law. Conversely, if we saw a man executed and later heard he was alive again, we would be suspicious. But of what? Not that he had been dead, but that he was now alive. But again, could we say that it is impossible for human testimony to prove that a man is alive? The point is, we are suspicious

---

10. Claude François Houtteville, *La religion chrétienne prouvée par les faits*, 3 vols. (Paris: Mercier & Boudet, 1740), 1:33.

in these cases not because the facts in question cannot be proved by evidence, but because we tend to believe our own senses rather than reports of others that go contrary to our preconceived opinions of what can and cannot happen. But as a historical fact, the resurrection requires no more ability in the witnesses than to be able to distinguish between a dead man and a living man. Sherlock is willing to grant that in miraculous cases we may require more evidence than usual; but it is absurd to say that such cases admit of no evidence.

Third, and finally, the resurrection contradicts neither right reason nor the laws of nature. Similarly to Houtteville, Sherlock maintains that the so-called course of nature arises from the prejudices and imaginations of men. Our senses tell us what the usual course of things is, but we go beyond our senses when we conclude that it cannot be otherwise. The uniform course of things runs contrary to the resurrection, but that is no proof that it is absolutely impossible. The same Power that created life in the first place can give it to a dead body again—the latter feat is no greater than the former.

Gottfried Less

Less, a German theologian at the University of Göttingen, discusses Hume's objections at length in his *Wahrheit der christlichen Religion* (1758). He defines a miracle as a work beyond the power of all creatures. There are two types of miracles: first degree miracles, which are performed directly by God; and second degree miracles, which are beyond human power but are done by finite spirit beings. Less admits that no more than second degree miracles can be proved, since one cannot be sure when God is acting directly. Miracles are both physically and morally possible: physically because God is the Lord of nature, and morally because miracles constitute part of his plan to confirm divine teaching.

There are two steps in proving that a miracle has occurred. First, one must prove the historicity of the event itself. Second, one must prove that the event is a miracle. Less argues that the testimony of the disciples to Jesus' miracles meets even the stringent conditions laid down by Hume, and that therefore even he should accept the historicity of the Gospel accounts. Although the apostles were unlearned men, all one needs in order to prove that something happened (say, a disease's being cured at a sheer verbal command) is five good senses and common sense. More specifically, Less argues that the miracles of Jesus were witnessed by hundreds of people, friends and enemies alike; that the apostles had the ability to testify accurately to what they saw; that the apostles were of such doubtless honesty and sincerity as to place them above suspicion of fraud; that the apostles, though of low estate, nevertheless had comfort and life itself to lose in proclaiming the gospel; and that the events to which they testified took place in the civilized part of the world under the Roman Empire, in Jerusalem, the capital city of the Jewish nation. Thus, there is no reason to doubt the apostles' testimony concerning the miracles and resurrection of Jesus.

But were these events miracles? Less maintains that they were and turns to a refutation of Hume's arguments. In response to the "in principle" argument, Less argues: first, because nature is the freely willed order of God, a miracle is just as possible as any other event. Therefore, it is just as believable as any other event. Second, testimony to an event cannot be refuted by prior experiences and observations. Otherwise, we should never be justified in believing something outside our present experience; no new discoveries would be possible. Third, there is no contradiction between miracles and experience. Miracles are different events (*contraria*) from experience in general, but not contradictory events (*contradictoria*) to experience in general. For example, the contradiction to the testimony that Jesus raised certain people from the dead and himself so rose three days after his death must necessarily be the exact opposite of this statement, namely, that Jesus never raised anyone from the dead and never himself so rose. This latter statement would have to be proved in order to destroy the evidence for the Gospels. But it would hardly be sufficient to assert that experience in general shows that dead men do not rise, for with this the Christian testimony is in full agreement. Only when the exact opposite is proved to be true could the Christian testimony be said to contradict experience.

As for Hume's "in fact" arguments, these are easily dismissed. First, it has already been shown that the witnesses to the Gospel miracles were abundant and qualified. Second, the fact that people tend to believe miracle stories without proper scrutiny only shows that our scrutiny of such stories ought to be cautious and careful. Third, Jesus' miracles did not occur among a barbarous people, but in Jerusalem. Fourth, Hume's allegation that all religions have their miracles is not in fact true, for no religion other than Christianity claims to be able to prove its teachings through miracles. Less also examines in considerable detail the examples furnished by Hume and finds in each case that the evidence does not approach the evidence for the Gospel miracles.

William Paley

Paley's two-volume *A View of the Evidences of Christianity* (1794) is undoubtedly the finest apologetic work of that era in English, and it exercised such considerable influence that it remained compulsory reading for any applicant to Cambridge University right up until the twentieth century. Primarily a studious investigation of the historical evidence for Christianity from miracles, Paley's treatise constitutes an across-the-board refutation of Hume's arguments. It will be remembered that it was Paley who so masterfully expounded the teleological argument, and he makes clear that in this work he presupposes the existence of God as proved by that argument.

Given the existence of God, miracles are not incredible. For why should it be thought incredible that God should want to reveal himself in the natural world to men, and how could this be done without involving a miraculous element? Further, any antecedent improbability in miracles is not so great that sound historical testimony cannot overcome it. Paley discerns the same fallacy in Hume's argument as did Less. A narrative of a fact can only be said to be contrary to experience if we, being at the time and place in question, observe that the alleged event did not in fact take place.

What Hume really means by "contrary to experience" is simply the lack of similar experience. (To say that a miracle is contrary to universal experience is obviously question-begging, since it assumes in advance that the miracle in question did not occur.) But in this case the improbability that results from our not having similar experiences is equal to the probability that we should have similar experiences. But what probability is there for that? Suppose God wished to inaugurate Christianity with miracles. What is the probability that we should also experience similar events today? Clearly, any such probability is negligible. Conversely, then, any improbability resulting from our lack of such experiences is also negligible. According to Paley, Hume's argument assumes either that the course of nature is invariable or that if it is variable, these variations must be frequent and general. But what grounds are there for either of these assumptions? If the course of nature is the work of an intelligent Being, should we not expect that he would vary the course of nature only infrequently at times of great importance?

As for determining whether a miracle has occurred, Paley considers Hume's account of the matter a fair one: which is more probable in any given case, that the miracle be true or the testimony be false? In answering this question, Paley reminds us, we must not remove the miracle from its theistic and historical context, nor can we ignore how the testimony and evidence arose. According to Paley, the real problem with Hume's skepticism becomes clear when we apply it to a test case: suppose twelve men, whom I know to be honest and reasonable people, were to assert that they saw personally a miraculous event in which it was impossible for them to have been tricked; furthermore, the governor called them before him for an inquiry and sentenced them all to death unless they were to admit the hoax; and they all went to their deaths rather than say they were lying. According to Hume, we should still not believe such men. But such incredulity, says Paley, would not be defended by any skeptic in the world.

Against Hume's "in fact" arguments, Paley maintains that no parallel to the Gospel miracles exists in history. Like Less, he examines Hume's examples in considerable detail and concludes that it is idle to compare such cases with the miracles of the Gospels. Even in cases not easily explained away, there is no evidence that the witnesses have passed their lives in labor and danger and have voluntarily suffered for the truth of what they reported. Thus, the circumstance of the Gospel accounts is unparalleled.

SUMMARY

Christian apologists thus contested Spinoza's and Hume's objections to miracles from a variety of standpoints. It is noteworthy that virtually all the Christian thinkers presupposed the existence of God in their argument. It must be remembered that this was not a case of theism versus atheism, but of Christian theism versus Deism. Moreover, God's existence was not always just assumed: Clarke and Paley formulated sophisticated arguments to justify belief in God. The Christians argued that given the existence of God, miracles are possible because of God's omnipotence (Clarke), because of his conservation of the world in being (Houtteville), and because of his sovereign freedom to act as he wills (Less).

Against the mechanistic Newtonian worldview, they argued variously that the course of nature is really only the regular pattern of the operation of God's will (Clarke), or that it is subject to God's freedom to alter it (Vernet, Houtteville, Less, Paley), or even that it may include within itself the capacity for miraculous events (Sherlock, Houtteville).

Against Spinoza's first objection, the apologists argued that miracles do not contradict God's nature, because the laws of nature do not flow in necessitarian fashion from the being of God, but are freely willed and therefore alterable (Vernet); and miracles as well as the laws could be willed by God from eternity so that their occurrence represents no change in God's decrees (Houtteville). Against his second objection, they maintained that miracles, while not proof of the existence of God, are proof of the *Christian* God. Hence, it is correct to say that the regular order of nature proves God's existence; but it is equally true to say that a miracle proves the action of God in the world (Clarke, Paley).

The Christian thinkers sometimes granted freely that one could not know whether God or a lesser being was at work in the miracle; but here they urged that it was the religious, doctrinal context that allowed one to determine if the miracle was divine (Clarke, Less).

As for Spinoza's charge that a supposed miracle may be caused by an unknown law of nature, Le Clerc responded that it then becomes inexplicable why such events do not recur and why these mysterious laws operated coincidentally at the moment of Jesus' command. Vernet replied that this possibility is negligible when numerous and various miracles occur. And others (Sherlock, Houtteville) granted that such unknown laws might be God's means of acting within the course of nature.

In response to Hume's "in principle" argument they argued: Given God's existence, miracles are as possible as any other event (Less); and the probability that God would reveal himself nullifies any inherent improbability in miracles (Paley). A miracle is a matter of sense perception like any other event, and is therefore capable of being supported by historical testimony (Sherlock). A miracle is not contrary to experience as such, and therefore, the testimony to a miracle cannot be nullified by the testimony to the regular order of other experiences (Less, Paley). The improbability that a miracle should occur in the past is equal to the probability that we should experience such events today, a probability that is slight or non-existent (Paley). Hume's argument, if equably applied, would eliminate not only miracles but many natural matters of fact as well (Sherlock, Less). Hume's argument leads to an indefensible skepticism regarding events amply established by reliable testimony (Paley).

In response to Hume's "in fact" argument, the Christian apologists simply sought to prove that in the case of Jesus' miracles and resurrection, the factual evidence was strong enough to establish the credibility of these events, in contrast to other stories of purported miracles (Less, Paley). In short, miracles are neither impossible nor unidentifiable.

Assessment

We've seen that the problem of miracles occupied a central place in the Deist controversy of the seventeenth and eighteenth centuries. Although the Christians argued vigorously on behalf of miracles, it was undoubtedly the arguments of Spinoza, Hume, and the Deists that posterity gave an eye to, for in the next century D. F. Strauss was able to proceed in his investigation of the life of Jesus on the *a priori* assumption that miracles are impossible. According to Strauss, this is not a presupposition requiring proof; on the contrary, to assume that miracles are possible is a presupposition requiring proof. Strauss asserts that God's interposition in the regular course of nature is "irreconcilable with enlightened ideas of the relation of God to the world."[11] Thus, any supposedly historical account of miraculous events must be dismissed out of hand; "indeed no just notion of the true nature of history is possible, without a perception of the inviolability of the chain of finite causes, and of the impossibility of miracles."[12]

This presupposition governed the remainder of the nineteenth-century Life of Jesus movement. According to Albert Schweitzer, the historian of that movement, by the mid-1860s the question of miracles had lost all importance. He reports, "The exclusion of miracle from our view of history has been universally recognized as a principle of criticism, so that miracle no longer concerns the historian either positively or negatively."[13] This might lead one to think that the Deists had won the debate. But is this in fact the case?

The Newtonian World-Machine

It will be remembered that the backdrop for the Deist controversy was a deterministic view of the universe as a Newtonian world-machine that bound even the hands of God. With the advent of quantum physics, however, a significant element of indeterminacy has been introduced into physics, which a good many thinkers have sought to exploit in defense of miracles or, ironically, as way of explaining divine action in the world without miracles.

---

11. David Friedrich Strauss, *The Life of Jesus Critically Examined*, trans. G. Eliot (London: SCM, 1973), 737.

12. Ibid., 75.

13. Albert Schweitzer, *The Quest of the Historical Jesus*, 3rd ed., trans. W. Montgomery (London: Adam & Charles Black, 1954), 111.

In quantum physics there is an ineradicable element of indeterminacy in the behavior of systems described by quantum physical laws, whether those systems be sub-atomic or macroscopic. For example, in classical physics, if the kinetic energy of an elementary particle is less than its potential energy, then the particle will be unable to surmount a potential barrier which it confronts. But in quantum physics, if the kinetic and potential energies are close, then by means of a phenomenon called "quantum tunneling" the particle can surmount or pass through the barrier. Whether the particle is stopped by or overcomes the barrier cannot be determined on the basis of obtainable information concerning its state prior to its encountering the barrier. It appears to be entirely random whether or not similar particles breach the barrier, and where they end up is a matter of probability. Similarly, an elementary particle fired at a screen cannot be predicted to strike the screen at a specific determined point, as in Newtonian physics. Rather, there is a probability curve describing the various points where it might strike which is highest in a certain area and becomes vanishingly low as one moves away from that area. Theoretically, the particle could end up anywhere. Now since macroscopic objects, like a human body, for example, are composed of sub-atomic particles governed by quantum laws, there is some non-zero probability that each of the particles composing the body should travel to some distant location, and if all the particles did this in concert, the whole body would be "miraculously" transported to another location. Natural laws then become statistical in nature, describing what generally occurs in a number of cases.

This would appear to bring some comfort to the modern defender of miracles, for he may now argue that it is illegitimate to exclude *a priori* a certain event that does not conform to known natural law, since that law cannot be rigidly applied to individual cases. Given quantum indeterminacy, there is at least *some* chance of an event's occurring, regardless of how bizarre it might be.

It seems to me, however, that this appeal to quantum indeterminacy does not settle the problem of miracles. In the first place, not all of nature's laws are affected by quantum indeterminacy. Relativity theory, which, together with quantum theory, underpins the structure of modern physics, enunciates laws which are not statistical or based on indeterminacy. Miracles violating such laws would still be impossible. Secondly, it is not evident that all the Gospel miracles could be explained in conformity to quantum laws. Water might be changed into wine by a spontaneous rearrangement of its sub-atomic constituents, but no such explanation could account for the resurrection of Jesus, which was not simply the resuscitation of a corpse, but the transformation of the body to an immortal and glorified existence.

Thirdly, and most importantly, quantum indeterminacy and the statistical character of certain natural laws show only that one cannot *absolutely* rule out in advance an event not conforming to known laws. Although quantum physics has opened a crack in the door for the defender of miracles, it is not wide enough for him to put his whole case through. As one philosopher of science explains:

> There is no question that most events regarded as significantly "miraculous" in religious contexts would, if they violate Newtonian laws, also be excessively improbable on well-established quantum laws, and therefore would be regarded as violations of these also. Thus, if we consider only the currently accepted theories of physics, the credibility of such miracles is no greater than in Newtonian theory.[14]

It would be crazy, for example, for a person accused of murder, who was known to have been alone in the room with the victim at the time the murder occurred, to offer as his defense the claim that another man quantum tunneled into the room spontaneously, shot the victim dead, and then, before he could be apprehended, spontaneously quantum tunneled back out again. (Come to think of it, maybe such a defendant could get off by being declared not guilty by reason of insanity!) We cannot sidestep the problem of miracles, then, by a disingenuous appeal to quantum indeterminacy or the statistical character of nature's laws. We are still confronted with the question whether violations of nature's laws are possible.

But are miracles in fact "violations of the laws of nature," as Newtonian mechanists claimed? Here it would seem to be of no avail to answer with Clarke that matter has no properties and that the course of nature is simply God's regular action. Not only does modern physics hold that matter does possess certain properties and that certain forces like gravitation and electro-magnetism are real forces operating in the world, but Clarke's view also leads to the strange doctrine of occasionalism, which holds that fire does not really burn wood, for example, but that God causes wood to burn merely upon the occasion of its coming into contact with fire. Nor would it help to answer with Sherlock and Houtteville that nature may contain within itself the power to produce certain effects contrary to its normal operation, for this explanation is unconvincing in cases where the natural laws are sufficiently well known so as to preclude with a high degree of probability the event's taking place. Moreover, this solution threatens to reduce the event in question to a freak of nature, the result of chance, not an act of God.

A better tack, I think, is to ask whether in fact miracles should be characterized as "violations of the laws of nature," as Newtonian mechanists assumed. (It would be well if we could rid ourselves of this characterization, since it is very prejudicial psychologically, smacking of the breaking of a civil law, so that God takes on the appearance of a divine rapist who violates Mother Nature.) An examination of the chief competing schools of thought concerning the notion of a natural law in fact reveals that on each theory the concept of a violation of a natural law is incoherent and that miracles need not be so defined. Broadly speaking, there are

14. Mary Hesse, "Miracles and the Laws of Nature," in *Miracles*, ed. C. F. D. Moule (London: A. R. Mowbray, 1965), 38.

three main views of natural law today: the regularity theory, the nomic necessity theory, and the causal dispositions theory.[15]

According to the regularity theory, the "laws" of nature are not really laws at all, but just descriptions of the way things happen in the world. They describe the regularities which we observe in nature. Now since on such a theory a natural law is just a generalized description of *whatever* occurs in nature, it follows that no event which occurs can violate such a law. Instead, it just becomes part of the description. The law cannot be violated, because it just describes in a certain generalized form everything that does happen in nature.

According to the nomic necessity theory, natural laws are not merely descriptive, but tell us what can and cannot happen in the natural world. They allow us to make certain contrary-to-fact conditional judgments, such as "If the density of the universe were sufficiently high, it would have re-contracted long ago," which a purely descriptivist theory would not permit. Again, however, since natural laws are taken to be universal inductive generalizations, a violation of a natural law is no more possible on this theory than on the regularity theory. So long as natural laws are *universal* generalizations based on experience, they must take account of anything that happens and so would be revised should an event occur which the law did not permit.

Of course, in practice proponents of such theories do not treat natural laws so rigidly. Rather, natural laws are assumed to have implicit in them the assumption "all things being equal." That is to say, the law states what is the case under the assumption that no other natural factors are interfering. When a scientific anomaly occurs, it is usually assumed that some unknown natural factors are interfering, so that the law is neither violated nor revised. But suppose the law fails to describe or predict accurately because some *supernatural* factors are interfering? Clearly the implicit assumption of such laws is that no supernatural factors as well as no natural factors are interfering. Thus, if the law proves inaccurate in a particular case because God is acting, the law is neither violated nor revised. If God brings about some event which a law of nature fails to predict or describe, such an event cannot be characterized as a violation of a law of nature, since the law is valid only under the tacit assumption that no supernatural factors come into play in addition to the natural factors.

On such theories, then, if miracles are to be distinguished from both God's ordinary and special providential acts, then miracles ought to be defined as naturally impossible events, that is to say, events which cannot be produced by the natural causes operative at a certain time and place. Whether an event is a miracle is thus relative to a time and place. Given the natural causes operative at a certain time and place, for example, rain may be naturally inevitable or necessary, but on

---

15. For discussion see Stephen S. Bilinskyj, "God, Nature, and the Concept of Miracle" (Ph.D. dissertation, University of Notre Dame, 1982); Alfred J. Freddoso, "The Necessity of Nature," *Midwest Studies in Philosophy* 11 (1986): 215–42.

another occasion, rain may be naturally impossible. Of course, some events, say, the resurrection, may be absolutely miraculous in that they are at every time and place beyond the productive capacity of natural causes.

According to the causal dispositions theory, things in the world have different natures or essences, which include their causal dispositions to affect other things in certain ways, and natural laws are metaphysically necessary truths about what causal dispositions are possessed by various natural kinds of things. For example, "Salt has a disposition to dissolve in water" would state a natural law. If, due to God's action, some salt failed to dissolve in water, the natural law is not violated, because it is still true that salt has such a disposition. As a result of things' causal dispositions, certain deterministic natural propensities exist in nature, and when such a propensity is not impeded (by God or some other free agent), then we can speak of a natural necessity. On this theory, an event which is naturally necessary must and does actually occur, since the natural propensity will automatically issue in the event if it is not impeded. By the same token, a naturally impossible event cannot and does not actually occur. Hence, a miracle cannot be characterized on this theory as a naturally impossible event. Rather, a miracle is an event which results from causal interference with a natural propensity which is so strong that only a supernatural agent could impede it. The concept of miracle is essentially the same as under the previous two theories, namely, God's acting to cause an event in the sequence of natural events in the absence of any secondary cause of that event, but one just cannot call a miracle "naturally impossible" as those terms are defined in this theory; perhaps we could adopt instead the nomenclature "physically impossible" to characterize miracles.

On none of these theories, then, should miracles be understood as violations of the laws of nature. Rather they are naturally (or physically) impossible events, events which at certain times and places cannot be produced by the relevant natural causes.

Now the question is, what could conceivably transform an event that is naturally impossible into a real historical event? Clearly, the answer is the personal God of theism. For if a transcendent, personal God exists, then he could cause events in the universe that could not be produced by causes within the universe. It is precisely to such a God that the Christian apologists appealed. Given a God who is omnipotent, who conserves the world in being, and who is capable of acting freely, Christian thinkers seem to be entirely justified in maintaining that miracles are possible. Indeed, only if atheism were proved to be true could one rationally deny the epistemic possibility of miracles. For if it is even epistemically possible that a transcendent, personal God exists, then it is equally possible that he has acted in the universe. Therefore, it seems to me that the Christian apologists argued in the main correctly against their Newtonian opponents, and that the natural (or physical) impossibility of miracles in no way precludes their reality.

Spinoza's Objections

As we turn to Spinoza's objections, again it seems to me that the Christian thinkers argued cogently.

OBJECTION BASED ON THE IMMUTABILITY OF NATURE

It would be tempting to dismiss Spinoza's objections simply on the grounds that he was a pantheist, for whom "God" and "Nature" were interchangeable terms. So, of course, a violation of nature's laws would be a violation of God's nature, since they are the same. The question is not whether miracles are possible on a pantheistic worldview, but on a theistic worldview.

But such a refutation would be too easy. The *Tractatus* is a Deistic, not a pantheistic, work, and Spinoza presupposes the traditional understanding of God. In particular, his argument is based on the classic doctrine of divine simplicity, which states that God's knowledge, will, goodness, power, and so forth are all really identical and one with his essence. The question Spinoza raises is, in effect, how can God's knowledge be necessary and his will be contingent, if these are identical? Now contrary to Spinoza, classical theology did not claim that God's knowledge is characterized by necessity. For example, God knows the truth "The universe exists." But God was under no obligation to create the universe. Since creation is a free act, he could have refrained from creating anything at all. If God had not created the world, then he would instead know the truth "No universe exists." Necessarily, then, whatever God knows is true; but it is not necessary that the content of God's knowledge be what it is. Had he created a different world or no world at all, the content of his knowledge would be different. Hence, just as God is free to will differently than he does, so he is able to have different knowledge than he does.

The laws of nature, then, are not known by God necessarily, since, as Vernet said, they depend on God's will. Even if we hold that the laws of nature are necessary truths, God could have willed to create a universe operating according to a different set of laws by creating things having different natures from the things he created. By the same token, the miracles he performs could, as Less and Houtteville pointed out, have been willed by God just as eternally and immutably as the laws. There is just no reason, then, to think that when he causes a naturally impossible event, God's knowledge and will come into conflict.

Spinoza's objection does raise one important point, though. It is very difficult to see how God's knowledge, for example, can be contingent and yet be identical with his essence, which includes necessary existence. How can God be utterly simple if he is in some respects necessary and in others contingent? What this calls into question, however, is not the possibility of miracles, but the doctrine of divine simplicity. This is a doctrine which is fortunately extra-biblical and is rejected as incoherent by the majority of Christian philosophers today.[16]

---

16. For a brief discussion see my and J. P. Moreland's *Philosophical Foundations for a Christian Worldview* (Downer's Grove, Ill.: InterVarsity, 2007), 524–26.

Objection Based on the Insufficiency of Miracles

Spinoza's second objection was that miracles are insufficient to prove God's existence. As it is stated, the objection was simply irrelevant for most of the Christian apologists, for virtually all of them used miracles not as a proof for the existence of God, but as a proof for his action in the world. Hence, Spinoza was really attacking a straw man.

Nevertheless, the supporting reasoning of the objection was relevant to the Christians' position. Spinoza's main point was that a proof for God must be absolutely certain. Since we infer God's existence from the immutable laws of nature, anything that casts doubt on those laws casts doubt on God's existence. Two assumptions seem to underlie Spinoza's reasoning: first, that a proof for God's existence must be demonstratively certain; and second, that God's existence is inferred from natural laws. But Christian apologists denied both of these assumptions. The more empirically minded of them held that a cogent argument for God's existence need not be demonstratively certain. Think, for example, of Paley's teleological argument: while not reaching absolute certainty, it claimed to make it more plausible to believe in God than not. Contemporary philosophers agree that if we were justified in accepting only those conclusions proved with demonstrative certainty, then we should know very, very little indeed. The second assumption fails to take account of the fact that there are other arguments for the existence of God not based on natural laws. For example, Clarke, while sharing Spinoza's concern for demonstrative certainty, nevertheless believed that the ontological and cosmological arguments provided rational grounds for accepting God's existence. So even if natural law were uncertain, that would not for Clarke call into question God's existence.

But is Spinoza's objection in fact true? He seems to think that the admission of a genuine miracle would overthrow the natural law violated by the miracle. Now we have already seen that miracles, properly defined, do not violate natural laws and so do not cast doubt upon their truth. Perhaps Spinoza would insist that were it proven that some event occurred which under current understanding of natural law is thought to be naturally impossible, then rather than admit that a miracle has happened we should instead revise the natural law so as to permit the natural occurrence of such an event. But Clarke and Paley argued more persuasively that a miracle need not overthrow nature's general regularity; a miracle shows at most God's intervention at that particular point. As Richard Swinburne argues, a natural law is not abolished because of one exception; the exception must occur repeatedly whenever the conditions for it are present. If the event will not occur again under identical circumstances, then the law will not be abandoned. A natural law will not be reformulated unless a new version will yield better predictability of future events without being more complicated than the original law. But if the new version does no better in predicting the phenomena and explaining the event in question, then the event will simply remain an unexplained exception to the natural law. Thus,

Spinoza's fear that miracles would destroy the fabric of natural law appears to be unjustified. Rather than leading us into the arms of atheism, exceptions to natural laws could lead us to discern the action of God in the world at that point.

Spinoza's sub-point that miracles could not prove the existence of God, but only of a lesser being, did not strike against most of the Christian apologists because they were not trying to prove the existence of God. Having proved or presupposed God's existence, they used miracles chiefly to show that Christian theism was true.

Nevertheless, Christian apologists were very concerned about how to show in any particular case that a miracle was not demonic but divine. I think that their answer to this problem constitutes one of their most important and enduring contributions to the discussion of miracles. They held that the doctrinal context of the miracle makes it evident if the miracle is truly from God. In this way they drew attention to the religio-historical context in which the miracle occurred as the key to the interpretation of that miracle. This is very significant, for a miracle without a context is inherently ambiguous. This is the problem with Hume's example of the revivification of Queen Elizabeth: the event lacks any religious context and appears as a bald and unexplained anomaly. Hence, one feels a degree of sympathy for Hume's skepticism. But how different it is with the case of Jesus' resurrection! It occurs in the context of and as the climax to Jesus' own unparalleled life and teachings and produced so profound an effect on his followers that they called him Lord and proclaimed salvation for all men in his name. It ought, therefore, to give us serious pause, whereas the resuscitation of Queen Elizabeth would occasion only perplexity. The religio-historical context is crucial to the interpretation of a miraculous event.

Spinoza's concern with lesser spiritual beings like angels and demons would probably not trouble many contemporary minds. Such beings are part of the furniture, so to speak, of a wider theistic worldview, so that no atheist today would seriously concede the Gospel miracles and yet maintain they were performed by angels. It would not seem unwarranted to infer that if such events are genuine miracles, then they were wrought by God.

Spinoza's final sub-point, that a supposed miracle may really be the effect of an unknown law of nature, is not really an objection against the occurrence of miracles, but against the identification of miracles. Granted that miracles are possible, how can we know when one has occurred? This problem has been persuasively formulated in our day by the British philosopher Antony Flew:

> We simply do not have, and could not have, any natural . . . criterion which enables us to say, when faced with something which is found to have actually happened, that here we have an achievement which nature, left to her own unaided devices, could never encompass. The natural scientist, confronted with some occurrence inconsistent with a proposition previously believed to express a law of nature, can

find in this disturbing inconsistency no ground whatever for proclaiming that the particular law of nature has been supernaturally overridden![17]

The response of Sherlock and Houtteville to this objection, that an unknown law of nature is God's means of producing the event, is surely inadequate. For it could just as easily be the case that the event is no act of God at all, just a spontaneous accident of nature without religious significance. Rather I think Le Clerc and Vernet have taken a better tack: when the miracles occur at a momentous time (for example, a man's leprosy vanishing when Jesus spoke the words "Be clean") and do not recur regularly in history, and when the miracles in question are numerous and various, then the chance of their being the result of unknown natural causes is minimal. Since, as we shall see, most critics now acknowledge that Jesus did perform what we may call miracles, this answer to Spinoza and Flew seems to be a cogent defense of the supernatural origin of the Gospel miracles.

Stephen Bilynskyj provides the following criteria for identifying some event E as a miracle:[18]

1) The evidence for the occurrence of E is at least as good as it is for other acceptable but unusual events similarly distant in time and space from the point of the inquiry;
2) An account of the natures and/or powers of the causally relevant natural agents, such that they could account for E, would be clumsy and ad hoc;
3) There is no evidence except the inexplicability of E for one or more natural agents which could produce E;
4) There is some justification for a supernatural explanation of E, independent of the inexplicability of E.

Even if we leave Jesus' miracles aside and focus our attention on his resurrection from the dead, I think that the supernatural nature of that event alone may be successfully defended. We're not asking here whether the facts of the case, such as the empty tomb or resurrection appearances, might be explained in a natural manner. The question is, if Jesus actually did rise from the dead, would we then be justified in inferring a supernatural cause for that event? Here the overwhelming majority of people would say yes. Those who argue against the resurrection try to explain away the facts of the case without allowing that Jesus rose from the dead. I know of no critic who argues that the best explanation of the historical facts is that Jesus rose from the dead, but that his resurrection was no miracle but a perfectly natural occurrence. That would appear to be a somewhat desperate obstinacy.

Two factors undergird this reasoning. First, the resurrection so exceeds what we know of natural causes that it seems most reasonable to attribute it to a su-

17. *Encyclopedia of Philosophy*, s.v. "Miracles," by Antony Flew.
18. Bilynskyj, "God, Nature, and the Concept of Miracle," 222.

pernatural cause. Hume himself asserted that it has never in the history of the
world been heard of that a truly dead man (in Jesus' case for a night, a day, and a
night) has been raised from the dead. Given the length of time that Jesus had been
dead, it would be idle to compare his resurrection with the resuscitation of persons
pronounced clinically dead in hospitals. But more than that: it is very important
to understand that the resurrection was more than the resuscitation of a corpse.
It was not a return to the earthly mortal life; rather it was the transformation of
the body to a new mode of existence, which Paul described as powerful, glorious,
imperishable, and Spirit-directed (1 Cor. 15:42–44). It is inconceivable that such
an event could be the product of natural causes. Moreover, if it were the effect
of purely natural causes, then its singularity in the history of mankind becomes
very difficult to understand—why has it not happened again? In the nearly two
thousand years since that event, no natural causes have been discovered that could
explain it. On the contrary, the advance of science has only served to confirm that
such an event is naturally impossible.

Second, the supernatural explanation is given immediately in the religio-
historical context in which the event occurred. Jesus' resurrection was not merely
an anomalous event, occurring without context; it came as the climax to Jesus' own
life and teachings. As Wolfhart Pannenberg explains,

> The resurrection of Jesus acquires such decisive meaning, not merely because someone
> or anyone has been raised from the dead, but because it is Jesus of Nazareth, whose
> execution was instigated by the Jews because he had blasphemed against God.[19]
>
> Jesus' claim to authority, through which he put himself in God's place, was . . . blas-
> phemous for Jewish ears. Because of this Jesus was then also slandered before the
> Roman Governor as a rebel. If Jesus really has been raised, this claim has been visibly
> and unambiguously confirmed by the God of Israel, who was allegedly blasphemed
> by Jesus.[20]

Thus the religio-historical context furnishes us with the key to the supernatural
character of that event.

One final remark on Spinoza's objection against the identification of a miracle:
his argument, unlike Hume's, does not spring from the nature of historical investigation. Rather, the very eyewitnesses of the event could press Spinoza's objection. But
in this case, the argument leads to an untenable skepticism. There comes a point
when the back of skepticism is broken by the sheer reality of the miracle before
us. I think, for example, of that delightful scene in Dickens's *Christmas Carol* in
which Scrooge is confronted by Marley's ghost, all bound in chains:

19. Wolfhart Pannenberg, "Jesu Geschichte und unsere Geschichte," in *Glaube und Wirklichkeit* (München:
Chr. Kaiser, 1975), 92.

20. Wolfhart Pannenberg, *Jesus—God and Man*, trans. L. L. Wilkins and D. A. Priebe (London: SCM,
1968), 67.

"You don't believe in me," observed the Ghost.

"I don't," said Scrooge.

"What evidence would you have of my reality beyond that of your senses?"

"I don't know," said Scrooge.

"Why do you doubt your senses?"

"Because," said Scrooge, "a little thing affects them. A slight disorder of the stomach makes them cheats. You may be an undigested bit of beef, a blot of mustard, a crumb of cheese, a fragment of underdone potato. There's more gravy than grave about you, whatever you are."

". . . You see this toothpick?" said Scrooge.

"I do," replied the Ghost.

". . . Well!" returned Scrooge, "I have but to swallow this, and be for the rest of my life persecuted by a legion of goblins, all of my own creation. Humbug, I tell you! Humbug!"

At this the spirit raised a frightful cry and shook its chain with such a dismal and appalling noise, that Scrooge held on tight to his chair, to save himself from falling into a swoon. But how much greater was his horror, when the phantom, taking off the bandage round its head . . . its lower jaw dropped down upon its breast!

Scrooge fell upon his knees, and clasped his hands before his face.

"Mercy!" he said. "Dreadful apparition, why do you trouble me?"

"Man of worldly mind!" replied the Ghost, "do you believe in me or not?"

"I do," said Scrooge. "I must."[21]

Such studied skepticism as Scrooge's becomes untenable when confronted with the evident reality of such a striking miracle. Can we imagine, for example, doubting Thomas, when confronted with the risen Jesus, studiously considering whether what he saw palpably before him might not be the effect of an unknown natural cause? Had Jesus himself encountered such skepticism, would he not have attributed it to hardness of heart? In this light, such skepticism need not be demonstratively refuted but is self-condemned. Perhaps Pascal was right in saying that God has given evidence sufficiently clear for those with an open heart, but sufficiently vague so as not to compel those whose hearts are closed.

Hume's Objections

"In Principle" Argument

Hume's "in principle" argument, despite its influence, especially upon biblical scholars, is generally recognized by philosophers today to be, in the words of the

21. Charles Dickens, "A Christmas Carol," in *Christmas Books*, by Charles Dickens (London: Oxford, 1954), 18–19.

philosopher of science John Earman, an "abject failure."[22] Even Hume's admirers try at most to salvage some insightful nugget from his convoluted discussion, typically Hume's maxim that "no testimony . . . is sufficient to establish a miracle, unless this testimony is of such a kind that . . . its falsehood would be more miraculous, than the fact which it endeavours to establish." But, as we shall see, even that maxim requires re-interpretation.

Hume's argument actually falls into two more or less independent claims. On the one hand there is his claim that miracles are by definition utterly improbable; on the other hand there is his claim that no evidence for a purported miracle can serve to overcome its intrinsic improbability. As it turns out, both of these claims are mistaken.

Consider the second claim first, that no amount of evidence can serve to establish a miracle. Stimulated by Hume's argument against miracles, there arose a discussion among probability theorists from Condorcet to John Stuart Mill over how much evidence it takes in order to establish the occurrence of highly improbable events.[23] It was soon realized that if one simply weighed the probability of the event against the reliability of the witness to the event, then we should be led into denying the occurrence of events which, though highly improbable, we reasonably know to have happened. For example, if on the morning news you hear reported that the pick in last night's lottery was 7492871, this is a report of an extraordinarily improbable event, one out of several million, and even if the morning news' accuracy is known to be 99.99 percent, the improbability of the event reported will swamp the probability of the witness's reliability, so that we should never believe such reports. In order to believe the report, Hume would require us to have enough evidence in favor of the morning news's reliability to counter-balance the improbability of the winning pick, which is absurd. Paley was therefore quite correct when he charged that Hume's argument could lead us into situations where we would be forced to deny the testimony of the most reliable witnesses because of general considerations. And that goes not only for miraculous events, but, as Sherlock and Less urged, for non-miraculous events as well, as Hume himself admitted with respect to the man in the tropics confronted with travelers' tales of ice.

Probability theorists saw that what also needs to be considered is the probability that if the reported event has *not* occurred, then the witness's testimony is just as it is. As Mill wrote,

> To know whether a coincidence does or does not require more evidence to render it credible than an ordinary event, we must refer, in every instance, to first principles,

22. John Earman, *Hume's Abject Failure: The Argument against Miracles* (Oxford: Oxford University Press, 2000).

23. See S. L. Zabell, "The Probabilistic Analysis of Testimony," *Journal of Statistical Planning and Inference* 20 (1988): 327–54.

and estimate afresh what is the probability that the given testimony would have been delivered in that instance, supposing the fact which it asserts not to be true.[24]

Thus, to return to our example, the probability that the morning news would announce the pick as 7492871 if some other number had been chosen is incredibly small, given that the newscasters had no preference for the announced number. On the other hand, the announcement is much more probable if 7492871 were the actual number chosen. This comparative likelihood easily counterbalances the high prior improbability of the event reported.

The realization on the part of probability theorists that other factors need to be included in the correct calculation of the probability of some event comes to expression in Bayes' Theorem, which we encountered in chapter 1. Letting M = some miraculous event, E = the specific evidence for that event, and B = our background knowledge apart from the specific evidence, the so-called "odds form" of Bayes' Theorem states:

$$\frac{\Pr(M|E\&B)}{\Pr(\text{not-}M|E\&B)} = \frac{\Pr(M|B)}{\Pr(\text{not-}M|B)} \times \frac{\Pr(E|M\&B)}{\Pr(E|\text{not-}M\&B)}$$

On the left-hand side of the equation $\Pr(M|E\&B)$ represents the probability of the miracle given the total evidence, and $\Pr(\text{not-}M|E\&B)$ represents the probability of the miracle's not occurring given the total evidence. The odds form of Bayes' Theorem gives us the ratio of these two probabilities.[25] If the ratio is 1/1, then M and not-M have the same probability; the odds of M's occurring are, as they say, fifty/fifty, or 50 percent. If we represent this ratio as A/B, what Hume wants to show is that, in principle, A<B—for example, 2/3 or 4/9 or what have you. So given the odds, one could never rationally believe, no matter what the evidence, that a miracle has taken place.

Now whether the miracle is more probable than not will be determined by the ratios on the right hand side of the equation. In the first ratio, the numerator $\Pr(M|B)$ represents the intrinsic probability of the miracle, and the denominator $\Pr(\text{not-}M|B)$ represents the intrinsic probability of the miracle's not occurring. We're asking here which is more probable, M or not-M, relative to our background knowledge alone, abstracting from the specific evidence for M. In the second ratio the numerator $\Pr(E|M\&B)$ represents the explanatory power of the miracle, and the denominator $\Pr(E|\text{not-}M\&B)$ represents the explanatory power

24. J. S. Mill, *A System of Logic*, 2 vols. (London: 1843), bk. 3, chap. 25, §6, cited in Zabell, "Probabilistic Analysis of Testimony," 331.

25. Given this ratio we can also compute the actual probability of M. If we represent the ratio as A/B, then we can compute the probability of M given the total evidence by A/(A+B). So if the ratio is 2/3, then the probability of M given the total evidence is 2/(2+3) = 2/5 = .4, or 40%.

of the miracle's not occurring. We're asking here which best explains the specific evidence we have, M or not-M.

Now notice that even if the ratio of the intrinsic probabilities weighs heavily against M, that improbability can be offset if the ratio representing the explanatory power of M or not-M weighs equally or greater in favor of M. For example, $(1/100) \times (100/1) = 100/100 = 1/1$, or a 50% probability for M.

Unfortunately, Hume never discusses the second ratio representing the explanatory power of the miracle's occurring or not occurring. He focuses almost exclusively on $Pr(M|B)$, the intrinsic probability of a miracle, claiming that it is so inevitably low that no amount of evidence can establish a miracle. But that is plainly wrong, since no matter what non-zero value one assigns to the first ratio, the miracle may be very probable on the total evidence if the second ratio is sufficiently large.[26] So much for Hume's in principle argument!

Hume does say that "no testimony . . . is sufficient to establish a miracle, unless this testimony is of such a kind that . . . its falsehood would be more miraculous, than the fact which it endeavours to establish." This is the closest Hume comes to discerning the remaining factors in the probability calculus. Hume's way of putting his maxim is rhetorically loaded, however, equivocating on the term "miraculous." Since it is not at all miraculous that human testimony be false, any miracle, no matter how small, would seem to be more miraculous than the testimony's being false. Indeed, it would seem almost sacrilegious to suggest, for example, that the disciples' being mistaken would be a greater miracle than Christ's resurrection! But Hume's maxim is not really using "miraculous" in the sense of "naturally impossible." To see this point, suppose, for the sake of argument, that it is more intrinsically probable that Jesus would rise from the dead than that the disciples were either deceivers or deceived. In such a case their testimony may, indeed, be sufficient to establish the fact of Jesus' resurrection, even though Jesus' resurrection is, technically speaking, more miraculous than their testimony's being false. Of course, Hume argues that a miraculous event will always be more improbable than the falsehood of the testimony in support of it. But that only goes to underline the point that the real issue here is the probability of the events, not their miraculousness. The miraculousness of an event is merely the means by which Hume endeavors to show its improbability. It's the improbability of miracle claims that Hume is after. So as Paley correctly discerned and as contemporary thinkers recognize, what

26. A further factor which is neglected by Hume is the remarkable impact of multiple, independent testimony to some event. If two witnesses are each 99% reliable, then the odds of their both independently testifying falsely to some event are only .01 x .01 = .0001, or one out of 10,000; the odds of three such witnesses' being wrong is .01 x .01 x .01 = .000001, or one out of 1,000,000; and the odds of six such witnesses' being mistaken is .01 x .01 x .01 x .01 x .01 x .01 = .000000000001, or one out of 1,000,000,000,000. In fact, the cumulative power of independent witnesses is such that individually they could be *un*reliable more than 50% of the time and yet their testimony combine to make an event of apparently enormous improbability quite probable in light of their testimony. With respect to Jesus' resurrection, it is difficult to know how independent some of the witnesses are—though in the cases of people like Peter, James, and Saul independence is well established.

Hume's maxim, less pejoratively stated, really means is "no testimony is sufficient to establish a miracle, unless this testimony is of such a kind that its falsehood would be more improbable than the fact which it endeavours to establish." Paley accepts Hume's maxim and challenges Hume's argument that it is always more probable that the testimony in support of a miracle is false than that the miracle actually occurred.

There is a slogan beloved in the free thought subculture that "extraordinary events require extraordinary evidence." What we now see is that this seemingly commonsensical slogan is, in fact, false as usually understood. In order to establish the occurrence of a highly improbable event, one need not have lots of evidence. The only plausible sense in which the slogan is true is that in order to establish the occurrence of an event which has a very low intrinsic probability, then the evidence would also have to have a very low intrinsic probability, that is, $Pr(E|B)$ would have to be very low. So, to return to our example of the pick in last night's lottery, it is highly improbable, given our background knowledge of the world, that the morning news would announce just that specific number out of all the numbers that could have been announced. In that Pickwickian sense the evidence for the winning pick is, indeed, extraordinary. But obviously, that isn't the sense that skeptics have in mind when they say that it takes extraordinary evidence to establish the occurrence of an extraordinary event. For that condition is easily met in the Pickwickian sense. The skeptic can't reasonably mean that miraculous events require miraculous evidence, for that would force us to reject any miracle claim, even if wholly natural evidence rendered the miracle more probable than not. What the skeptic seems to be saying by his slogan is that in order to believe rationally in a miraculous event, you must have an enormous amount of evidence. But why think that that is the case? "Because a miracle is so improbable," the skeptic will say. But Bayes' Theorem shows that rationally believing in a highly improbable event doesn't require an enormous amount of evidence. What is crucial is that the evidence be far more probable given that the event did occur than given that it did not. The bottom line is that it doesn't always take a huge amount of evidence to establish a miracle.

J. Howard Sobel takes Hume's maxim to assert that $Pr(M|E\&B) > 1/2$ only if $Pr(M|B) > Pr(\text{not-}M\&E|B)$.[27] Sobel's rendering of "the falsehood of the testimony" as $Pr(\text{not-}M\&E|B)$ is controverted,[28] but his formula does state a necessary condition of $Pr(M|E\&B) > 1/2$. But there is nothing in this formula to show that it is in principle impossible to establish the occurrence of a miracle. One might think that relative to our background knowledge a miracle is always more improbable than the miracle's not occurring and the evidence's being as it is. But that is by

27. Jordan Howard Sobel, *Logic and Theism: Arguments for and against Beliefs in God* (Cambridge: Cambridge University Press, 2004), 316.

28. Earman takes it more plausibly to be $Pr(\text{not-}M|E \& B)$ or $Pr(E|\text{not-}M \& B)$. He concludes, "Hume's Maxim is just the unhelpful tautology that no testimony is sufficient to establish the credibility of a miracle unless it is sufficient to make the occurrence more probable than not" (*Hume's Abject Failure*, 40).

no means the case. Remember that the evidence itself may be extraordinary in the Pickwickian sense of being, like the miracle, highly improbable relative to the background information alone, so that Pr(not-M&E|B) < Pr(M|B). Ironically, the skeptic's own slogan returns to bite him, for the evidence may well be extraordinary, that is, highly improbable relative to our background knowledge, so that Sobel's condition is met.

In order to show that no evidence can in principle establish the historicity of a miracle, Hume needs to show that the intrinsic probability of any miracle claim is so low that it can never be overcome. This takes us back to the first part of Hume's argument, that miracles are by definition utterly improbable. Hume claimed that the uniform experience of mankind supports the laws of nature rather than miracles. Now such an assertion appears at face value to be question-begging. To say that uniform experience is against miracles is implicitly to assume already that all miracle reports are false. Earman interprets Hume to mean, not that uniform experience is against miracles, but that up to the case under investigation, uniform experience has been against miracles; that is to say, as we come to some alleged miracle claim, we do so knowing that all past miracle claims apart from this one have been spurious. Earman interprets Hume to construe Pr(M|B) in terms of *frequency*. Miracles are utterly improbable because they diverge from mankind's uniform experience. But Earman points out that the frequency model of probability simply will not work in this context. For trying to construe the probabilities in Bayes' Theorem as objective frequencies would disqualify many of the theoretical hypotheses of the advanced sciences. For example, scientists are investing long hours and millions of dollars hoping for an observation of an event of proton decay, though such an event has never been observed. On Hume's model of probability such research is a waste of time and money, since the event will have a probability of zero. Earman concludes that in the case of Pr(M|B) the guidance for assigning probability "cannot take the simple minded form" of using the frequency of M-type events in past experience; that frequency may be flatly zero (as in proton decay), but it would be unwise to therefore set Pr(M|B)=0.[29]

How we assess the intrinsic probability of M will depend on how M is characterized. Take the resurrection of Jesus, for example. The hypothesis "Jesus rose from the dead" is ambiguous, comprising two radically different hypotheses. One is that "Jesus rose naturally from the dead"; the other is that "Jesus rose supernaturally from the dead," or that "God raised Jesus from the dead." The former is agreed on all hands to be outrageously improbable. Given what we know of cell necrosis, the hypothesis "Jesus rose naturally from the dead" is fantastically, even unimaginably, improbable. Conspiracy theories, apparent death theories, hallucination theories, twin brother theories—almost any hypothesis, however unlikely, seems more probable than the hypothesis that all the cells in Jesus' corpse spontaneously came back to life again. Accordingly, that improbability will lower greatly the probability that

29. John Earman, "Bayes, Hume, and Miracles," *Faith and Philosophy* 10 (1993): 303.

"Jesus rose from the dead," since that probability will be a function of its two component hypotheses, the one natural and the other supernatural. But the evidence for the laws of nature which renders improbable the hypothesis that Jesus rose naturally from the grave is simply irrelevant to the probability of the hypothesis that God raised Jesus from the dead. Since our interest is in whether Jesus rose supernaturally from the dead, we can assess this hypothesis on its own.

Let us ask, then, what is the intrinsic probability of the hypothesis R= "God raised Jesus from the dead." How we assess $Pr(R|B)$ will depend on whether our background knowledge B includes the facts which support the arguments of natural theology for God's existence, such as the origin of the universe, the fine-tuning of the universe, objective moral values and duties, and so forth. If it does not, the $Pr(R|B)$ will be lower than if it does, for then our evidence E will have to carry the full burden of justifying belief in God's existence as well as Jesus' resurrection. If we let G = God's existence, the Theorem on Total Probability tells us:

$$Pr(R|B) = [Pr(R|G\&B) \times Pr(G|B)] + [Pr(R|\text{not-}G\&B) \times Pr(\text{not-}G|B)]$$

Now $Pr(R|\text{not-}G\&B)$ is 0, since it is impossible for God to raise Jesus if God doesn't exist! So $Pr(R|B)$ reduces to just $Pr(R|G\&B) \times Pr(G|B)$. As we have seen, the classical defenders of miracles did not treat them as arguments for God's existence; rather God's existence was taken to be implied by facts already included in B. So let's include in B all the facts that go to support the premises of the arguments of natural theology. On this basis let's suppose that the probability of God's existence on the background knowledge of the world $Pr(G|B)$ is at least 0.5. The remaining probability to estimate is $Pr(R|G\&B)$, the probability that God would raise Jesus from the dead, given that God exists. We may think of this probability as the degree of expectation that a perfectly rational agent would have that, given G&B, God would raise Jesus of Nazareth from the dead. God has never before intervened to do such a thing, so far as we know, and there are other ways he could vindicate Jesus, should he want to, if he even wants to. So how would a perfectly rational agent assess the risk of betting in this case that, given G&B, God would raise Jesus from the dead? In estimating this probability, we mustn't abstract from the historical context of Jesus' own life, ministry, and teaching, insofar as these can be included in our background knowledge. When we include in B our knowledge of the life of the historical Jesus up to the time of his crucifixion and burial, I don't think we can say that God's raising Jesus is improbable. So just for the sake of illustration let's say that $Pr(R|G\&B) = 0.5$. In that case $Pr(R|B) = 0.5 \times 0.5 = 0.25$, or one out of four. Such an intrinsic improbability is easily outweighed by the other factors in Bayes' Theorem.

Now in fact I think that it is impossible to assign a value to a probability like $Pr(R|G\&B)$ with any sort of confidence, and so $Pr(R|B)$ will remain inscrutable. The difficulty here is that we are dealing with a free agent (the Creator of the universe), and how do we know what he would do with respect to Jesus? But I think we can say that there is no reason to think that Pr(R|G&B) is terribly low, such that Pr(R|B) becomes overwhelmingly improbable. We certainly cannot take Pr(R|G&B) to be terribly low simply because of the infrequency of resurrections, for it may be precisely *because* of the resurrection's uniqueness that it is highly probable that God would choose so spectacular an event as a means of vindicating Jesus.

In any case, I think it is evident that there is no "in principle" argument here against miracles. Rather what will be at stake, as our example of Jesus' resurrection illustrates, is an "in fact" argument that handles a putative miracle claim in its historical context, given the evidence for God's existence. So the Humean skeptic has failed to show that any possible miracle claim has an insuperably low intrinsic probability. Couple this result with our earlier conclusion that even incredibly low intrinsic probabilities can be outweighed by the other factors in Bayes' Theorem, and it is evident why contemporary thinkers have come to see Hume's argument as a failure.[30]

Although the fallaciousness of Hume's reasoning has been recognized by the majority of philosophers writing on the subject today, still a widespread assumption persists that if historical inquiry is to be feasible, then one must adopt a sort of methodological naturalism as a fundamental historiographical principle. According to this outlook, historians must adopt as a methodological principle a sort of "historical naturalism" that excludes the supernatural. Antony Flew, while acknowledging the failure of Hume's argument, has sought to defend the presumption against miracles in historical studies. He writes:

> It is only and precisely by presuming that the laws that hold today held in the past and by employing as canons all our knowledge . . . of what is probable or improbable, possible or impossible, that we can rationally interpret the detritus of the past as evidence and from it construct our account of what actually happened. But in this context, what is impossible is what is physically, as opposed to logically impossible. And "physical possibility" is, and surely has to be, defined in terms of inconsistency with a true law of nature. . . . Our sole ground for characterizing a reported occurrence as miraculous is at the same time a sufficient reason for calling it physically impossible.[31]

This viewpoint is simply a restatement of the nineteenth-century German theologian Ernst Troeltsch's principle of analogy. According to Troeltsch, one of the most basic historiographical principles is that the past does not differ essentially from the present. Though the events of the past are obviously not the same events as those of the present, they must be the same kind of events if historical investigation is to be possible. Troeltsch realized that this principle was incompatible

---

30. I'm indebted to Tim and Lydia McGrew, epistemologists who specialize in confirmation theory, for very interesting and illuminating discussions of Hume's "in principle" argument.

31. *Encyclopedia of Philosophy*, s.v. "Miracles."

with the miraculous events of the Gospels and therefore held that they must be regarded as unhistorical.

In our own day, however, Wolfhart Pannenberg has persuasively argued that Troeltsch's principle of analogy cannot be legitimately employed to banish all non-analogous events from history. According to Pannenberg, analogy, when properly defined, means that in an unclear historical situation we should interpret the facts in terms of known experience. Troeltsch, however, uses analogy to constrict all past events to purely natural events. But, Pannenberg maintains, the fact that an event bursts all analogies to the present cannot be used to dispute its historicity. When, for example, myths, legends, illusions, and the like are dismissed as unhistorical, it is not because they are unusual but because they are analogous to present forms of consciousness to which no historical reality corresponds. When an event is said to have occurred for which no present analogy exists, we cannot automatically dismiss its historicity; to do that we must have an analogy to some known form of consciousness to which no reality corresponds that would suffice to explain the situation.

Pannenberg has thus reformulated Troeltsch's principle of analogy in such a way that it is not the *lack* of an analogy that shows an event to be unhistorical, but the *presence* of a positive analogy to known thought forms that shows a purported miracle to be unhistorical. Hence, he has elsewhere affirmed that if the Easter narratives were shown to be essentially secondary constructions analogous to common comparative religious phenomena, if the Easter appearances were shown to correspond completely to the model of hallucinations, and if the empty tomb tradition were shown to be a late legend, then the resurrection should be evaluated as unhistorical. In this way the lack of an analogy to present experience says nothing for or against the historicity of an event. Pannenberg's use of the principle preserves the analogous structure of the past to the present or to the known, thus making the investigation of history possible without thereby forcing the past into the mold of the present. It would therefore seem that Hume's "in principle" argument fares no better than Spinoza's objections.

"IN FACT" ARGUMENTS

If, then, there is no "in principle" objection to the identification of miracles, what may be said of Hume's "in fact" arguments? All of his points have force, but the fact remains that these general considerations cannot be used to decide the historicity of any particular miracle. They serve to make us cautious in the investigation of any miracle, but the only way the question of historicity can be solved is through such an investigation. Hume's fourth point (that miracles occur in all religions and thereby cancel each other out) does try to preclude an investigation, but it still remains an empirical question whether the evidence for any miracle supporting a counter-Christian claim is as well (or better) attested as the evidence for Jesus' miracles and resurrection. And if the latter should prove to be genuine, then we can forgo the investigation of every single counter-Christian miracle, for most of these pale into insignificance next to the Gospel miracles.

Conclusion

Hence, I think that for the most part the Christian apologists argued correctly against their Deist opponents; and it is sad that the nineteenth century failed to discern this fact. The presupposition against miracles survives in theology only as a hangover from an earlier Deistic age and ought now to be once for all abandoned.

Practical Application

Like the contents of the last chapter, the material shared in this chapter does not, I must confess, admit of much practical application in evangelism. I've never encountered a non-Christian who rejected the gospel because of an overt objection to miracles.

Nevertheless, this section is extremely important because the presupposition of modern biblical criticism has been the impossibility or unidentifiability of miracles, so that an open-minded approach to the Scriptures necessitates a prior defense of the rationality of belief in miracles. For example, the infamous Jesus Seminar, a group of radical New Testament critics committed to reforming the church's view of Jesus, has dismissed most of the New Testament witness to the life of Jesus as unhistorical. In explaining the presuppositions with which its Fellows work, the Jesus Seminar is remarkably candid about its presupposition of the impossibility of miracles. Their Introduction to *The Five Gospels* states:

> The contemporary religious controversy turns on whether the worldview reflected in the Bible can be carried forward into this scientific age and retained as an article of faith. . . . the Christ of creed and dogma . . . can no longer command the assent of those who have seen the heavens through Galileo's telescope.[32]

But why, we might ask, is it impossible in a scientific age to believe in a supernatural Christ? Here things really get interesting. According to the Seminar, the historical Jesus *by definition* must be a non-supernatural figure. At this point they appeal to D. F. Strauss, the nineteenth-century German biblical critic. Strauss's epochal book *The Life of Jesus, Critically Examined* was based squarely in a philosophy of naturalism. According to Strauss, God does not act directly in the world; he acts only indirectly through natural causes. With regard to the resurrection, as we have seen, Strauss states that God's raising Jesus from the dead "is irreconcilable with enlightened ideas of the relation of God to the world."[33] Now look carefully at what the Jesus Seminar says about Strauss:

---

32. R. W. Funk, R. W. Hoover, and the Jesus Seminar, "Introduction" to *The Five Gospels* (New York: Macmillan, 1993), 2.

33. David Friedrich Strauss, *The Life of Jesus, Critically Examined*, trans. George Eliot, ed. with an introduction by Peter C. Hodgson, Lives of Jesus Series (London: SCM, 1973), 736.

Strauss distinguished what he called the "mythical" (defined by him as anything legendary or supernatural) in the Gospels from the historical.... The choice Strauss posed in his assessment of the Gospels was between the supernatural Jesus—the Christ of faith—and the historical Jesus.[34]

Anything that is supernatural is *by definition* not historical. There's no argument given; it's just defined that way. Thus we have a radical divorce between the Christ of faith, or the supernatural Jesus, and the real, historical Jesus. Now the Jesus Seminar gives a ringing endorsement of Strauss's distinction: they say that the distinction between the historical Jesus and the Christ of faith is "the first pillar of scholarly wisdom."[35]

But now the whole quest of the historical Jesus becomes a charade. If we *begin* by presupposing naturalism, then of course what we wind up with is a purely natural Jesus. This reconstructed, naturalistic Jesus is not based on evidence, but on definition. What is amazing is that the Jesus Seminar makes no attempt to defend their naturalism; it is just presupposed.

Gerd Lüdemann, who is the leading German critic of the historicity of Jesus' resurrection, takes it for granted that a historical approach to Jesus of Nazareth must be a naturalistic approach. "Historical criticism," he states, "does not reckon with an intervention of God in history."[36] Thus, the resurrection *cannot* belong to the portrait of the historical Jesus. So what justification does Lüdemann give for this crucial presupposition of the impossibility of miracles? All he offers is a one-sentence allusion to Hume: "Hume ... demonstrated that a miracle is defined in such a way that 'no testimony is sufficient to establish it.'"[37] In my 1997 debate with Lüdemann on the campus of Boston College, when I challenged him on this point, he showed himself impotent to provide any defense of his presupposition apart from his own incredulity.[38]

Similarly, Bart Ehrman, a best-selling New Testament scholar and vociferous ex-Christian, naïvely reiterates the argument of Hume against the identification of miracles, apparently without even knowing its provenance. With respect to Jesus' resurrection, he states, "Because historians can only establish what probably happened, and a miracle of this nature is highly improbable, the historian cannot say it probably occurred."[39] In other words, in calculating the probability of Jesus'

34. Funk, et al., "Introduction," 3.

35. Ibid., 2–3.

36. Gerd Lüdemann, "Die Auferstehung Jesu," in *Fand die Auferstehung wirklich statt?* ed. Alexander Bommarius (Düsseldorf: Parega Verlag, 1995), 16.

37. Gert Lüdemann, *The Resurrection of Jesus*, trans. John Bowden (Minneapolis: Fortress Press, 1994), 12.

38. See William Lane Craig and Gerd Lüdemann, *The Resurrection: Fact or Figment?* ed. Paul Copan with responses by Stephen T. Davis, Michael Goulder, Robert H. Gundry, and Roy Hoover (Downer's Grove, Ill.: InterVarsity, 2000). See especially Davis and Hoover's discussion of this issue, along with my final response.

39. Bart Ehrman, "The Historical Jesus," (The Teaching Company, 2000), pt. 2, p. 50.

resurrection, the only factor Ehrman considers is the intrinsic probability of the resurrection $Pr(R|B)$. He overlooks all of the other factors in the probability calculus. Moreover, he just assumes that the intrinsic probability of Jesus' resurrection is insuperably low, which surely requires some sort of justification. But it gets even worse. For Ehrman offers another version of his objection which is even more obviously fallacious. He asserts, "Since historians can establish only what *probably* happened in the past, they cannot show that miracles happened, since this would involve a contradiction—that the most improbable event is the most probable."[40] In truth, there's no contradiction here at all because we're talking about *two different* probabilities: the probability of the resurrection on our total evidence $Pr(R|E \, \& \, B)$ versus the probability of the resurrection on our background knowledge alone $Pr(R|B)$. It's perfectly possible for the former probability to be high and the latter probability to be low. In any case, there is no contradiction here at all.

When I pointed out these *faux pas* to Ehrman in our 2006 debate on the resurrection at Holy Cross, rather than correct his mistake he pooh-poohed my explanation of the probability calculus as a "mathematical proof for the existence of God."[41] He did not seem to understand that I was not using Bayes' Theorem to prove God's existence or even Jesus' resurrection but rather to explain to him why his own argument based on the improbability of miracles is demonstrably mistaken. It was clear that he understood neither Hume nor Bayes' Theorem. Ironically, Ehrman sought to defend his position by claiming that because the hypothesis "God raised Jesus from the dead" is a statement about God, it "is a theological conclusion . . . not a historical one." Since "historians have no access to God," they "are unable to establish what God does." This claim, whatever it is worth, is logically contradictory with his claim that the resurrection is intrinsically improbable. For if the historian cannot say anything about God, neither can he say that it is improbable that God raised Jesus. The historian would have to say that the probability of Jesus' resurrection is simply inscrutable. Thus, Ehrman's position is literally self-refuting.

Hume had an excuse for his abject failure because the probability calculus hadn't yet been developed in his day. But today New Testament theologians no longer have any excuse for using such fallacious reasoning.

Moreover, I've been surprised to find how often Deistic thinking underlies the flowering dialogue between science and religion on the contemporary scene. For example, in a conference I attended a few years ago at the University of Notre Dame on "Science and Religion in the Post-Positivist Era," Arthur Peacocke claimed that modern cell biology has "radically undermined" the credibility of the virgin birth because it would require God's making a Y-chromosome *de novo* in Mary's ovum—in other words, it would have to be a miracle! Similarly, the stern

40. Bart Ehrman, *The New Testament: A Historical Introduction to the Early Christian Writings*, 3rd ed. (New York: Oxford University Press, 2004), 229.

41. See the transcript at www.reasonablefaith.org/site/PageServer?pagename=debates_main.

remonstrances one often hears from theologians and physicists against inferring a supernatural cause for the origin and order of the universe often conceal a presuppositional bias against miracles, since such acts of God are essentially miracles on a cosmic scale. The presupposition against miracles tends to dominate the science and religion dialogue today, and yet neither the scientists nor the theologians involved whom I have read or talked to about this issue, not being themselves trained in philosophy, are typically able to muster any robust defense of this presupposition.

In addition, I do think that people to whom we talk about Christ do sometimes have covert problems with miracles. They do not formulate their misgivings into an argument; they just find it hard to believe that the miraculous events of the Gospels really occurred. Insofar as we sense this is the case, we need to bring this presupposition out into the open and explain why there are no good grounds for it. Show unbelievers that they have no reasons for rejecting the possibility of miracles and challenge them with the thought that the universe may be a much more wonderful place than they imagine. In my own case, the virgin birth was a stumbling block to my coming to faith—I simply could not believe such a thing. But when I reflected on the fact that God had created the entire universe, it occurred to me that it wouldn't be too difficult for him to create the genetic material necessary for a virgin birth! Once the non-Christian understands who God is, then the problem of miracles should cease to be a problem for him.

Literature Cited or Recommended

Historical Background

Brown, Colin. *Miracles and the Critical Mind*. Grand Rapids, Mich.: Eerdmans, 1984.

Clarke, Samuel. *A Discourse Concerning the Unchangeable Obligations of Natural Religion and the Truth and Certainty of the Christian Revelation*. London: W. Botham, 1706.

Diderot, Denis. "Philosophical Thoughts." In *Diderot's Early Philosophical Works*, translated by M. Jourdain. Open Court Series of Classics of Science and Philosophy 4. Chicago: Open Court, 1916.

Hahn, Roger. *Pierre Simon Laplace 1749–1827: A Determined Scientist*. Cambridge, Mass.: Harvard University Press, 2005.

Houtteville, Claude François. *La religion chrétienne prouvée par les faits*. 3 vols. Paris: Mercier & Boudet, 1740.

Hume, David. *Enquiries Concerning Human Understanding and Concerning the Principles of Morals*. 3rd ed. Edited by P. H. Nidditch. Oxford: Clarendon, 1975. Chapter 10 of the first enquiry constitutes his case against miracles.

Le Clerc, Jean. *Five Letters Concerning the Inspiration of the Holy Scriptures*. London, 1690.

Less, Gottfried. *Wahrheit der christlichen Religion*. 4th ed. Göttingen: Georg Ludewig Förster, 1776.

Paley, William. *A View of the Evidences of Christianity*. 2 vols. 5th ed. London: R. Faulder, 1796; repr. ed.: Westmead, England: Gregg International, 1970.

Sherlock, Thomas. *The Tryal of the Witnesses of the Resurrection of Jesus*. London: J. Roberts, 1729.

Spinoza, Baruch. *Tractatus theologico-politicus*. Trans. Samuel Shirley, with an introduction by Brad S. Gregory. Leiden: E. J. Brill, 1989.

Stephen, Leslie. *History of English Thought in the Eighteenth Century*. 2 vols. 3rd ed. New York: Harcourt, Brace, & World; Harbinger, 1962.

Turretin, J. Alphonse. *Traité de la vérité de la religion chrétienne*. 2nd ed. 7 vols. Translated by J. Vernet. Geneva: Henri-Albert Gosse, 1745–55.

Voltaire, Marie François. *A Philosophical Dictionary*. 2 vols. New York: Harcourt, Brace, & World; Harbinger, 1962. See particularly the article on miracles.

Assessment

Bilinskyj, Stephen S. "God, Nature, and the Concept of Miracle." Ph.D. dissertation. University of Notre Dame Press, 1982.

Craig, William Lane and Gerd Lüdemann. *The Resurrection: Fact or Figment?* Edited by Paul Copan with responses by Stephen T. Davis, Michael Goulder, Robert H. Gundry, and Roy Hoover. Downer's Grove, Ill.: InterVarsity, 2000.

Dickens, Charles. "A Christmas Carol." In *Christmas Books*, by Charles Dickens. Introduced by E. Farejon. London: Oxford University Press, 1954.

Earman, John. "Bayes, Hume, and Miracles." *Faith and Philosophy* 10 (1993): 293–310.

———. *Hume's Abject Failure: The Argument against Miracle*. Oxford: Oxford University Press, 2000. Definitive treatment of Hume's argument.

Ehrman, Bart. "The Historical Jesus." The Teaching Company, 2000.

———. *The New Testament: A Historical Introduction to the Early Christian Writings*. 3rd ed. New York: Oxford University Press, 2004.

Encyclopedia of Philosophy. S.v. "Miracles," by Antony Flew.

Freddoso, Alfred J. "The Necessity of Nature." *Midwest Studies in Philosophy* 11 (1986): 215–42.

Funk, Robert, Roy Hoover, and the Jesus Seminar. "Introduction." In *The Five Gospels*. New York: Macmillan, 1993.

Geivett, R. Douglas and Gary Habermas, eds. *In Defense of Miracles*. Downers Grove, Ill.: InterVarsity, 1997.

Hesse, Mary. "Miracles and the Laws of Nature." In *Miracles*, edited by C. F. D. Moule. London: A. R. Mowbray, 1965.

Lüdemann, Gerd. "Die Auferstehung Jesu." In *Fand die Auferstehung wirklich statt?* Edited by Alexander Bommarius. Düsseldorf: Parega Verlag, 1995.

———. *The Resurrection of Jesus*. Trans. John Bowden. Minneapolis: Fortress Press, 1994.

Mill, J. S. *A System of Logic*. 2 vols. London: 1843.

McGrew, Lydia and Timothy McGrew. "The Argument from Miracles: The Historical Argument for the Resurrection." In *Companion to Natural Theology*, edited by William Lane Craig and J. P. Moreland. London: Blackwell, forthcoming.

Moreland, J. P. and William Lane Craig. *Philosophical Foundations for a Christian Worldview*. Downer's Grove, Ill.: InterVarsity, 2003.

Pannenberg, Wolfhart. "Jesu Geschichte und unsere Geschichte." In *Glaube und Wirklichkeit*. München: Chr. Kaiser, 1975.

————. *Jesus—God and Man*. Translated by L. L. Wilkins and D. A. Priebe. London: SCM, 1968.

Schweitzer, Albert. *The Quest of the Historical Jesus*. 3rd ed. Translated by W. Montgomery. London: Adam & Charles Black, 1954.

Sobel, Jordan Howard. *Logic and Theism: Arguments For and Against Beliefs in God*. Cambridge: Cambridge University Press, 2004.

Strauss, David Friedrich. *The Life of Jesus Critically Examined*. Translated by G. Eliot. Edited with an introduction by P. C. Hodgson. Lives of Jesus Series. London: SCM, 1973.

Swinburne, Richard. *The Concept of Miracle*. New York: Macmillan, 1970.

————. ed. *Miracles*. Philosophical Topics. New York: Macmillan, 1989.

Zabell, S. L. "The Probabilistic Analysis of Testimony." *Journal of Statistical Planning and Inference* 20 (1988): 327–54.

Part 5

De Christo

7

The Self-Understanding of Jesus

The Christian religion stands or falls with the person of Jesus Christ. Judaism could survive without Moses, Buddhism without Buddha, Islam without Mohammed; but Christianity could not survive without Christ. This is because unlike most other world religions, Christianity is belief in a person, a genuine historical individual—but at the same time a special individual, whom the church regards as not only human, but divine. At the center of any Christian apologetic therefore must stand the person of Christ; and very important for the doctrine of Christ's person are the personal claims of the historical Jesus. Did he claim to be divine? Or did he regard himself as a prophet? Or was he the exemplification of some highest human quality such as love or faith? Who did Jesus of Nazareth claim to be?

Historical Background
Before we explore this problem, let's take a brief look at the recent historical background of Jesus research.

Life of Jesus Movement
During the late eighteenth and nineteenth centuries, post-Enlightenment European theology strove to find the historical Jesus behind the figure portrayed in the Gospels. The chief effort of this quest was to write a life of Jesus as it supposedly really was, without the supernatural accretions found in the Gospels. One after

another of these lives of Jesus appeared, each author thinking to have uncovered the real man behind the mask.

Early lives of Jesus tended to portray him as a spiritual man who was forced to make claims about himself that he knew were false in order to get the people to listen to his message. For example, Karl Bahrdt in his *Ausführung des Plans und Zwecks Jesu* (1784–1792) maintained that Jesus belonged to a secret order of Essenes, dedicated to weaning Israel from her worldly messianic expectations in favor of spiritual, religious truths. In order to gain a hearing from the Jews, Jesus claimed to be the Messiah, planning to spiritualize the concept of Messiah by hoaxing his death and resurrection. To bring this about, Jesus provoked his arrest and trial by his triumphal entry into Jerusalem. Other members of the order, who secretly sat on the Sanhedrin, ensured his condemnation. Luke the physician prepared Jesus' body by means of drugs to withstand the rigors of crucifixion for an indefinite time. By crying loudly and slumping his head, Jesus feigned his death on the cross, and a bribe to the centurion guaranteed that his legs would not be broken. Joseph of Arimathea, another member of the order, took Jesus to a cave, where he resuscitated Jesus by his ministrations. On the third day, they pushed aside the stone over the mouth of the cave, and Jesus came forth, frightening away the guards and appearing to Mary and subsequently to his other disciples. Thereafter, he lived in seclusion among the members of the order.

Similar to Bahrdt's theory was Karl Venturini's life of Jesus in his *Natürliche Geschichte des grossen Propheten von Nazareth* (1800–1802). As a member of a secret society, Jesus sought to persuade the Jewish nation to substitute the idea of a spiritual Messiah for their conception of a worldly Messiah. But his attempt backfired: he was arrested, condemned, and crucified. However, he was taken down from the cross and placed in the tomb alive, where he revived. A member of the secret society, dressed in white, frightened away the guards at the tomb, and other members took Jesus from the tomb. During forty days thereafter he appeared to various disciples, always to return to the secret place of the society. Finally, his energy spent, he retired permanently.

Much of the early Life of Jesus movement was spent in trying to provide natural explanations for Jesus' miracles and resurrection. The high water mark of the natural explanation school came in H. E. G. Paulus's *Das Leben Jesu* (1828), in which Paulus devised all sorts of clever explanations to explain away the substance of the Gospel miracles while still accepting the form of the factual accounts.

But with his *Das Leben Jesu, kritisch bearbeitet* (1835), D. F. Strauss sounded the death knell for this school. According to Strauss, the miraculous events in the Gospels never happened; rather they are myths, legends, and editorial additions. Jesus was a purely human teacher who made such an impression on his disciples that after his death they applied to him the myths about the Messiah that had evolved in Judaism. Thus, out of the Jesus of history evolved the Christ of the Gospels—the Messiah, the Lord, the incarnate Son of God. Though such a mythological Jesus never actually existed, nevertheless the myth embodies a profound truth, namely, the Hegelian truth of the unity of the infinite and the finite, of God and man—not, indeed, of God and the individual man Jesus, but of God and mankind as a whole. Strauss was a self-confessed pantheist, and it was this truth that the myth of the God-man embodied.

The reaction in Germany against Strauss was virulent, but the Life of Jesus movement did not return to a supernatural view of Jesus. The question of miracles was dead, and the chief issue that remained was the interpretation of the man behind the myth. With the rise of liberal theology in the second half of the nineteenth century, Jesus became a great moral teacher. The kingdom of God was interpreted by Albrecht Ritschl and Wilhelm Herrmann as an ethical community of love among mankind. Although Jesus employed apocalyptic language, his real meaning, according to Ritschl, was ethical. He lived in complete devotion to his vocation of founding this kingdom and therefore serves as the model of the ethical life for all people. According to Herrmann, Jesus completely identified with the moral ideal of the kingdom of God and is thus God's unique representative among men.

Up until this point all of the researchers shared the optimistic view that a purely human Jesus was discoverable behind the Gospel traditions, that indeed a life of Jesus was possible. By this time New Testament criticism had evolved the two-source hypothesis—that is, that the synoptic problem was to be solved by postulating Matthew and Luke's use of Mark and another source of sayings of Jesus, arbitrarily designated Q. It was believed that in these two most primitive sources the true, historical Jesus was to be found.

This optimism received a crushing blow at the hands of William Wrede in his theory of the "Messianic secret." Wrede was exercised by the question, why does Jesus, according to Mark, always seek to conceal his identity as the Messiah, commanding people to tell no one who he really is? Wrede's ingenious answer was that since Jesus never made such divine claims about himself, Mark had to come up with some reason why people are unaware of Jesus' messianic claims, which the Christian church had written back into the Gospel traditions and had asserted were made by Jesus. To get around this problem Mark invented the "Messianic secret" motif, that is, the notion that Jesus had tried to conceal his identity, and Mark wrote his Gospel from the perspective of this motif. The consequence of Wrede's theory was that it now became clear that even the most primitive sources about Jesus were theologically colored and that therefore a biography of the historical Jesus was impossible.

Albert Schweitzer and the End of the Old Quest

Thus, according to Albert Schweitzer, the historian of this intriguing movement, the old Life of Jesus movement ground to a halt in nearly complete skepticism. The liberal Jesus who went forth proclaiming the ethical kingdom of God and the brotherhood of man never existed but is a projection of modern theology. We do not know who Jesus really was, says Schweitzer; he comes to us as a man unknown. What we do know about him is that he actually believed the end of the world was near and that he died in his fruitless attempt to usher in the eschatological kingdom of God. Schweitzer intimates that Jesus may have been psychologically deranged; hence his eschatological expectation and suicidal course of action. Schweitzer thus not only pronounced the final rites over the liberal Jesus, but he was instrumental in the rediscovery of the eschatological element in Jesus' preaching.

The net result of the old quest of the historical Jesus was the discovery of theology in even the earliest sources of the Gospels. This was taken to imply that a biography of the man Jesus could not be written. The theology of the early church had so colored the documents that it was no longer possible to extract the Jesus of history from the Christ of faith.

Dialectical and Existential Theology

This conviction characterized theology during the first half of the twentieth century. For dialectical and existential theology, the Jesus of history receded into obscurity behind the Christ of faith. Karl Barth took almost no cognizance of New Testament criticism regarding Jesus. It is the Christ proclaimed by the church that encounters us today. The events of the Gospels are *geschichtlich*, but not *historisch*, a distinction that could be rendered as *historic*, but not *historical*. That is to say, those events are of great importance for history and mankind, but they are not accessible to ordinary historical research like other events. Even though the later Barth wanted to place more emphasis on the historicity of the events of the Gospels, he never succeeded in placing them in the ordinary world of space and time. What really mattered to him was not the historical Jesus, but the Christ of faith.

Similarly, Bultmann held that all that could be known about the historical Jesus could be written on a 4 x 6 index card[1] but that this lack of information was inconsequential. Like Strauss, he held the Gospel narratives to be mythologically colored throughout. And he, too, sought by demythologizing to find the central truth expressed in the myth. He turned, not to Hegel, but to Heidegger for the proper interpretation of the Christ-myth in terms of authentic existence in the face of death. It was this Christ-idea that was significant for human existence; as for the historical Jesus, the mere "*dass* seines Gekommenseins"—the *that* of his coming—that is to say, the mere fact of his existence, is enough.

The New Quest of the Historical Jesus

Some of Bultmann's disciples, however, such as Ernst Käsemann, could not agree with their master that the mere fact of Jesus' existence was enough to warrant our acceptance of the meaning of the Christ-idea as constitutive for our lives today. Unless there is some connection between the historical Jesus and the Christ of

1. As Bultmann finely put it, "In my opinion, of the life and personality of Jesus we can now know as good as nothing" (Rudolph Bultmann, *Jesus* [Tübingen: J.C.B. Mohr, 1951], 11).

faith, then the latter reduces to pure myth, and the question remains why this myth should be thought to embody a truth that supplies the key to my existence. Thus, New Testament criticism heralded a "new quest of the historical Jesus," but this time considerably more cautious and modest than the old quest.

Those pursuing the new quest are painfully conscious of the presence of theology in the Gospel narratives and are reluctant to ascribe to the historical Jesus any element that may be found in the theology of the early church. Indeed, James Robinson actually differentiates between the historical Jesus and the Jesus of history. The latter is the Jesus who really lived; the former is the Jesus that can be *proved* as a result of historical research. Robinson says that the new quest concerns only the historical Jesus, not the Jesus of history. Accordingly, Robinson believes that because of the presence of theology in the Gospels, the burden of proof rests on the scholar who would ascribe some fact to the historical Jesus, not on the scholar who would deny that fact. In other words, we ought to presuppose that unless some putative feature of the historical Jesus can be proven to be authentic, we ought to regard it as inauthentic, as a product of Christian theology.

Robinson's distinction between the historical Jesus and the Jesus of history is one that has been made in so many words by a number of prominent Jesus scholars. For example, John Meier, whose voluminous and ongoing study of the life of Jesus, *A Marginal Jew*, has made him perhaps the most eminent Jesus researcher, differentiates between the historical Jesus and the person who actually lived. According to Meier the historical Jesus or the Jesus of history (Meier uses the terms synonymously) "is a modern abstraction and construct. By the Jesus of history I mean the Jesus whom we can 'recover' and examine using the scientific tools of modern historical research."[2] Meier notes that "this definition is not some arbitrary invention of mine; it is the commonly accepted one in present Jesus-of-history research."[3] Meier contrasts the historical Jesus with what he calls "the real Jesus." The opening lines of Meier's first chapter of his first volume cleanly distinguish the two: "The historical Jesus is not the real Jesus. The real Jesus is not the historical Jesus."[4] Now we might think that by "the real Jesus" Meier means the human person who actually lived and wrought. But that would be a mistake. For Meier the real Jesus is also a modern abstraction and construct, but a fuller one. Meier characterizes the real Jesus as "a reasonably complete record of public words and deeds" of Jesus.[5] Later he refers to the real Jesus as "a reasonably complete biographical portrait."[6] So neither the historical Jesus nor even the real Jesus are for Meier the person who actually lived. In addition to these two abstractions, there is a third abstraction lurking in the wings which Meier calls the "total reality" of

2. John P. Meier, *A Marginal Jew*: vol. 1: *The Roots of the Problem and the Person,* Anchor Bible Reference Library (New York: Doubleday, 1991), 25.

3. Ibid., 1:34.

4. Ibid., 1:21.

5. Ibid., 1:22.

6. Ibid., 1:24.

Jesus, which is "everything he ... ever thought, felt, experienced, did, and said."[7] Since even this is not a living, flesh-and-blood person but a description, one cannot help but wonder what has happened to the actual person Jesus of Nazareth.

Robinson's further claim that there exists a differential burden of proof upon Jesus researchers, such that only those who regard some element of the Gospels as authentic are required to provide evidence in support of their assertion, seems to underlie a great deal of New Testament criticism, although it has been sharply criticized.[8] For example, the only way in which the scholars involved in the much publicized Jesus Seminar of the Westar Institute can make the judgment that so much of the Jesus tradition in the Gospels is doubtful or inauthentic would seem to be by presupposing an approach much like Robinson's.[9] Otherwise, the greatest percentage of the tradition would have to be classified under the unexciting but straightforward label "cannot be proven authentic or inauthentic" (a category which the Seminar does not countenance). For almost all of the typical "criteria of authenticity" employed in such studies to detect historical sayings and events in the life of Jesus—such as dissimilarity to Christian teaching, multiple attestation, linguistic Semitisms, traces of Palestinian milieu, retention of embarrassing material, coherence with other authentic material, and so forth[10]—can only be properly used positively, to demonstrate authenticity. In other words, the criteria state sufficient, not necessary, conditions of historicity. Treating the criteria of authenticity as necessary rather than sufficient conditions of historicity would lead to the reconstruction of a historical Jesus who was utterly unaffected by the Jewish milieu in which he was raised and who had no impact whatsoever on the early church which followed him, which is crazy. The criteria are therefore not designed to be employed negatively. Failure to meet the criteria does not imply the inauthenticity of a saying or event—unless, that is, one is tacitly presupposing Robinson's principle that Jesus traditions are to be assumed to be inauthentic unless and until they are proven to be authentic.

More specifically, one of the more celebrated members of the Seminar, John Dominic Crossan, seems to presuppose Robinson's methodology in his much discussed work *The Historical Jesus: The Life of a Mediterranean Jewish Peasant* (1991). After sorting out Jesus traditions into various strata from early to late and determining the number of times a saying of Jesus is attested, Crossan chooses to "bracket the singularities"—that is, to ignore any saying only singly attested, even if it is found in the earliest, first stratum. The reason he gives for this procedure is that the saying could have been created by the source itself. But by the same token it

---

7. Ibid., 1:21.

8. See Morna Hooker, "On Using the Wrong Tool," *Theology* 75 (1972): 570–81.

9. See Robert W. Funk and Roy W. Hoover, eds., *The Five Gospels: What Did Jesus Really Say?* (New York: Macmillan, 1993).

10. For helpful discussions, see Robert H. Stein, "The Criteria for Authenticity," in *Gospel Perspectives I*, ed. R.T. France and David Wenham (Sheffield, England: JSOT Press, 1980), 225–63; Craig A. Evans, "Authenticity Criteria in Life of Jesus Research," *Christian Scholar's Review* 19 (1989): 6–31.

could very well be authentic. Multiple attestation of a saying counts positively in favor of its authenticity, but the want of multiple attestation cannot be taken as a strike against authenticity—*unless* one is assuming that sayings are presumed to be inauthentic until proven authentic. Without this assumption there can be no grounds for thinking that the historical Jesus which Crossan reconstructs on the attenuated basis of multiply attested material alone, while bracketing or ignoring all other traditions about him which are not multiply attested, will not be but a pale shadow or lopsided distortion of the person who actually lived.

Or again, Bart Ehrman, a best-selling New Testament scholar, while explaining factors like multiple attestation and dissimilarity positively as critieria of authenticity, repeatedly inverts them to try to demonstrate inauthenticity. For example, he renders the negative verdict, "Some of the best known traditions of Jesus' birth cannot be accepted as historically reliable when gauged by our criteria,"[11] when at most he should have said that these traditions cannot be positively proven to be historical when gauged by these criteria. In fact, the Virgin Birth and Jesus' being born in Bethlehem are multiply and independently attested, but Ehrman doubts their historicity because they are *not* more widely attested. Similarly, he rejects the historicity of such events as the Virgin Birth, Jesus' claiming to be the Son of Man, his Triumphal Entry into Jerusalem, his passion predictions, and the crowd's calling for Jesus' crucifixion—all of which are multiply and independently attested—on the grounds that they are *not* dissimilar to early Christian beliefs.[12] So to argue is to pervert the criteria; for while multiple attestation and dissimilarity are positive evidence for authenticity, single attestation and similarity to Christian beliefs are not evidence of inauthenticity—unless, once more, one is assuming that the Gospels are inauthentic until they are proven to be authentic on some point.

During the previous generation the assumption enunciated by Robinson that Jesus traditions are to be ascribed to the theological activity of the early church unless they can be positively proven to have originated in Jesus' life and ministry took on the status of a sort of methodological dogma of critical scholarship. But increasingly this dogma has been called into question. Most scholars today would be reluctant to adopt such a methodological approach to the Gospels, even given their theological coloring. Such an approach assumes that history and theology are mutually exclusive categories, such that wherever theology is present in the Gospels, that automatically counts against their historical accuracy. But what justification is there for this assumption? Some feature of the Gospel portrait of Jesus, such as the dividing of his garments at the crucifixion or the piercing of Jesus' side, could be both historical and regarded by the evangelist as pregnant with theological significance. Since one cannot assume *a priori* that history and theology are mutually exclusive, the only way to justify that conclusion with respect to the Gospels

11. Bart Ehrman, "The Historical Jesus," (The Teaching Company, 2000), pt. 1, p. 53. The context makes clear that Ehrman means that these traditions should be regarded as historically unreliable.

12. Ibid., pt. 1, p. 49; pt. 2, pp. 37, 38, 48.

would be to carry out a historical examination of the Gospels. But since such an investigation aims to discover whether the presence of theology in the Gospels precludes their historical credibility, this examination cannot itself be based on the assumption that these categories are mutually exclusive in the Gospels.

Of course, Robinson would contend that such an examination was carried out in the first quest and yielded a negative verdict concerning the compatibility of history and theology in the Gospels. But such an examination was far from conclusive. The Roman historian A. N. Sherwin-White has compared the Gospels quite favorably with Roman history with respect to external confirmation of narrated events.[13] In the book of Acts, he asserts, the historicity of the narrative is indisputable.[14] Yet Acts is just as much propaganda as the Gospels. Moreover, in the Gospels wherever Jesus comes into the Jerusalem orbit, the external confirmation inevitably begins. Therefore, in Sherwin-White's judgment, the historical trustworthiness of the accounts of the Galilean ministry, which is by nature less susceptible to external confirmation, ought to be presumed. Thus, according to Sherwin-White's analysis, not only are the categories of history and theology not mutually exclusive, but the Gospels enjoy such external confirmation that their trustworthiness ought to be presumed even in cases where specific confirmation is lacking. It can be safely concluded that the assumption that the Gospels' status as theological documents militates against their also being historically reliable narratives has not been substantiated and that therefore the methodological principle of "inauthentic until proven authentic" is unfounded. The pursuit of such a methodology threatens to construct a theoretical and historical Jesus which is in fact very unlike the man who actually lived—in which case the whole enterprise becomes rather pointless.

A Third Quest

In recent years some biblical scholars have spoken of a third quest of the historical Jesus, a quest which one observer has aptly characterized as "the Jewish reclamation of Jesus."[15] One has reference to a movement of increasing momentum among Jewish scholars studying the New Testament which assesses Jesus appreciatively and seeks to reincorporate him as far as possible into the fold of Judaism. Spearheaded by the work of men like C. G. Montefiore (*The Synoptic Gospels*, 1909), Israel Abrahams (*Studies in Pharisaism and the Gospels*, 1917, 1929), and Joseph Klausner (*Jesus of Nazareth: His Life, Times, and Teaching*, 1922), the movement has

13. A. N. Sherwin-White, *Roman Society and Roman Law in the New Testament* (Oxford: Clarendon, 1963), 186–89.

14. Sherwin-White's contention has been powerfully driven home by the epochal study by Colin Hemer, *The Book of Acts in the Setting of Hellenistic History*, ed. Conrad H. Gempf, Wissenschaftliche Untersuchungen zum Neuen Testament 49 (Tübingen: J. C. B. Mohr, 1989). Through a painstaking analysis of papyrological, epigraphical, and other evidence Hemer demonstrates convincingly the wealth of historical material contained in the book of Acts and thus, by implication, Luke's care as a historian.

15. Donald A. Hagner, *The Jewish Reclamation of Jesus* (Grand Rapids, Mich.: Zondervan, 1984).

swelled in recent years and includes among contemporary scholars Samuel Sandmel (*We Jews and Jesus*, 1965), Schalom Ben-Chorin (*Bruder Jesus: Der Nazarener in Jüdischer Sicht*, 1967,) David Flusser (*Jesus*, 1969), Pinchas Lapide (*Der Rabbi von Nazareth*, 1974), and, perhaps most significant, the Qumran scholar Geza Vermes (*Jesus the Jew*, 1973; *The Religion of Jesus the Jew*, 1993). A number of non-Jewish scholars have also devoted themselves to demonstrating the rightful interpretation of Jesus in the context of Jewish thought and culture, principally E. P. Sanders (*Jesus and Judaism*, 1985). Confluent with this movement is the Scandinavian school of thought headed by Birger Gerhardsson (*Memory and Manuscript*, 1961), which sees rabbinic models of teaching and transmission of tradition as the key to understanding Jesus' teachings, and its extension by the German New Testament scholar Rainer Riesner (*Jesus als Lehrer*, 1981), who shows that memorization and recitation were commonly employed techniques in the home, synagogue, and elementary school, and finds many typical mnemonic aids in Jesus' teaching, which would facilitate its accurate preservation.

Jewish scholars have for the most part concentrated their attention on the ethical teachings of Jesus, with a view toward emphasizing his continuity, rather than rupture, with Judaism. The New Questers' criteria of authenticity are generally eschewed, the Gospels' record of Jesus' teaching being treated with much more trust, especially in light of its consonance with Jewish ethical teaching. But even the assimilation of this single facet of the historical Jesus, namely, Jesus as ethical teacher, to first-century Judaism has not been without its difficulties for Jewish scholars. Jesus' sense of personal authority to correct the Torah and contradict Jewish tradition goes down hard for faithful Jews. As Ben-Chorin admits, "The sense of the unique, absolute authority that is evident from this way of acting remains deeply problematic for the Jewish view of Jesus."[16] When Jewish scholars do consider the personal claims or self-understanding of Jesus, the majority conclude that Jesus did believe himself to be the Messiah, though, of course, they consider him to have been tragically deluded in this opinion.

Another interesting feature of contemporary scholarship's understanding of Jesus to which the third quest has contributed significantly is what one critic has called "the eclipse of mythology."[17] From Strauss through Bultmann, the category of myth was taken to be key to the Gospel portrait of Jesus, and any historical reconstruction would have to proceed by means of "demythologizing" this portrait. Today, however, scarcely any scholar thinks of myth as an important interpretive category for the Gospels. The Jewish reclamation of Jesus has helped to make unnecessary any understanding of the Gospels' portrait as significantly shaped by mythology. Although contemporary scholars may be no more prepared to believe

16. S. Ben-Chorin, *Jesus in Judenthum* (Wuppetal: R. Brockhaus, 1970), 41, cited in Hagner, *Reclamation*, 105.

17. Craig A. Evans, "Life-of-Jesus Research and the Eclipse of Mythology," *Theological Studies* 54 (1993): 3–36.

in the supernatural character of Jesus' miracles and exorcisms than were scholars of previous generations, they are no longer willing to ascribe such stories to the influence of Hellenistic divine man (*theios anēr*) myths;[18] rather Jesus' miracles and exorcisms are to be interpreted in the context of first-century Jewish beliefs and practices. Vermes, for example, has drawn attention to the ministries of the charismatic miracle workers and/or exorcists Honi the Circle-Drawer (first century B.C.) and Hanina ben Dosa (first century A.D.), and interprets Jesus of Nazareth as a Jewish *hasid* or holy man. In contrast to Schweitzer's assessment of the place of miracle with respect to the old quest, today the consensus of scholarship holds that miracle-working and exorcisms (bracketing the question of their supernatural character) most assuredly do belong to any historically acceptable reconstruction of Jesus' ministry.

Assessment

As we enter the twenty-first century after his death, Jesus of Nazareth, now as always, continues to exert his power of fascination over the minds of men and women. From sensational films and popular-level speculations to scholarly debates in academic societies, journals, and monographs, Jesus is a matter of controversy. Who did this first-century Galilean take himself to be? A political or social revolutionary? A practitioner of magical arts? A sort of social gadfly, the Jewish equivalent of a Greek cynic philosopher? A Jewish rabbi or prophet? The Messiah? The Son of God? Who did Jesus think that he was?

The Historical Jesus

In asking such a question, I take for granted that we want to know what Jesus thought about himself. The primary object of the quest of the historical Jesus is Jesus himself, not some abstraction manufactured by the historian. To regard Meier's abstractions as the object of historical inquiry is at best misleading and implies some bizarre conclusions as well. Neither Meier's "total reality of Jesus," nor "real Jesus," nor "historical Jesus" is a flesh-and-blood human being who actually lived. The entities referred to by Meier are in fact collections of propositions or statements. The total reality of Jesus seems to be the collection of all true propositions about Jesus. The real Jesus seems to be the collection of all true propositions about the public life of Jesus. The historical Jesus seems to be the collection of all propositions about Jesus which can be rendered probable by historical research. What is evident is that these collections of propositions are none of them persons and, as such, are not the object of the historian's study. Rather historians study the persons and events referred to by those propositions. If "Jesus" refers, not to

18. For a critique, see Barry L. Blackburn, "'Miracle Working' in Hellenism (and Hellenistic Judaism)," in *Gospel Perspectives VI*, ed. David Wenham and Craig Blomberg (Sheffield, England: JSOT Press, 1986), 185–218; see also Edwin Yamauchi, "Magic or Miracle? Diseases, Demons, and Exorcisms," in *Gospel Perspectives VI*, 89–183.

the man Jesus, but to the abstraction called "the historical Jesus," then virtually every sentence about Jesus in Meier's massive volumes turns out to be false. For the historical Jesus, contrary to Meier's assertions, was not born in Nazareth, did not speak Greek, and did not die by crucifixion. As a collection of propositions the historical Jesus is not a human being and so was never born, never spoke any language, and could not die. Only a person can do such things, and on Meier's account the historical Jesus is not a person. As such the historical Jesus is not the object of the historian's inquiry. What Meier and the rest of us really want to know is whether the person Jesus of Nazareth was born in Nazareth, spoke Greek, was executed by crucifixion, and so forth.

Meier states that the failure to distinguish between the real Jesus and the historical Jesus has led to "endless confusion" in the quest of the historical Jesus.[19] In fact, it is the distinction as drawn by Meier which is terribly confused. As a good historian Meier is really after the Jesus who actually lived, and to assign Jesus' proper name to collections of propositions can only lead to confusion.[20]

Now, obviously, there is some sort of distinction to be drawn between what Jesus was actually like and what historical inquiry can establish about Jesus; but it is not a distinction between two Jesuses. We try to find out what Jesus was actually like by means of what historical inquiry can establish about Jesus. Because historical inquiry is uncertain, our conclusions will be provisional. But they will be conclusions *about Jesus,* that is, about the actual person who is the referent of our descriptive statements. In both ordinary language and in the history of research, phrases like "the historical Jesus" and "the real Jesus" typically refer to the individual who actually lived, and to use them as names of classes of propositions is misleading. We can draw the needed distinctions in a more philosophically discriminating and less confusing way. By so doing we shall avoid the illusion that in investigating Jesus historically we are not studying the real Jesus who actually lived and wrought.

19. Meier, *A Marginal Jew,* 1:21.

20. For similar confusion see James D. G. Dunn, *Jesus Remembered: Christianity in the Making I* (Grand Rapids, Mich.: Eerdmans, 2003), 126–27, 130–31, 827, 876, 882. Dunn recognizes that although the historical Jesus is always identified as a construction of historical research, in practice the phrase is used to refer to Jesus himself. It seems to me that this slide is inevitable and unremarkable for any historian who is not a narrative non-realist. For his part Dunn distinguishes between Jesus himself and Jesus remembered—as though accurate memories of Jesus would not be memories of Jesus himself! Although Dunn asserts that the only reasonable objective for a quest of the historical Jesus is Jesus remembered, he inconsistently goes on to argue that from the impact Jesus made on the traditions about him, we can, in fact, discern something of the person who made that impact. This leads Dunn to the bizarre conclusion that "the Jesus tradition *is* Jesus remembered. And the Jesus thus remembered *is* Jesus . . ." (p. 335), from which it follows that Jesus himself is a tradition! Once again the person Jesus of Nazareth has disappeared from view. What Dunn should say, and wants to say, I think, is that in the Synoptic tradition we find preserved memories of what Jesus said and did; those memories are largely accurate; we can, therefore, know a good deal about Jesus; and there is no competing portrait of Jesus that is as historically credible as the one delivered to us by the tradition and that can be used to overturn the conclusions drawn on the basis of that tradition.

As we have seen, scholars involved in the quest of the historical Jesus have enunciated a number of so-called criteria for detecting historically authentic features of Jesus. It is absolutely crucial to the study of the historical Jesus that these criteria be correctly stated and applied. As already mentioned, it is somewhat misleading to call these "criteria," for they aim at stating sufficient, not necessary, conditions of historicity. This is easy to see: suppose a saying is multiply attested and dissimilar but not embarrassing. If embarrassment were a necessary condition of authenticity, then the saying would have to be deemed inauthentic, which is wrong-headed, since its multiple attestation and dissimilarity are sufficient for authenticity. Of course, the criteria are defeasible, meaning that they are not infallible guides to authenticity. They might be better called "Indications of Authenticity." Had the expression not already been appropriated, the medieval "Signs of Credibility" would have been the perfect cognomen for the criteria.

In point of fact, what the criteria really amount to are statements about the effect of certain types of evidence upon the probability of various sayings or events. For some saying or event S, evidence of a certain type E, and our background information B, the criteria would state that, all things being equal, $\Pr(S \mid E\&B) > \Pr(S \mid B)$. In other words, all else being equal, the probability of some event or saying is greater given, for example, its multiple attestation than it would have been without it.

What are some of the factors that might serve the role of E in increasing the probability of some saying or event S? The following are some of the most important: (1) *Historical congruence*: S fits in with known historical facts concerning the context in which S is said to have occurred; (2) *Independent, early attestation*: S appears in multiple sources which are near to the time at which S is alleged to have occurred and which depend neither upon each other nor upon a common source; (3) *Embarrassment*: S is awkward or counterproductive for the persons who serve as the source of information for S; (4) *Dissimilarity*: S is unlike antecedent Jewish thought-forms and/or unlike subsequent Christian thought-forms; (5) *Semitisms*: traces in the narrative of Aramaic or Hebraic linguistic forms; (6) *Coherence*: S is consistent with already established facts about Jesus.

Notice that these "criteria" do not presuppose the general reliability of the Gospels. Rather they focus on a particular saying or event and give evidence for thinking that specific element of Jesus' life to be historical, regardless of the general reliability of the document in which the particular saying or event is reported. These same "criteria" are thus applicable to reports of Jesus found in the apocryphal Gospels, or rabbinical writings, or even the Qur'an. Of course, if the Gospels can be shown to be generally reliable documents, so much the better! But the "criteria" do not depend on any such presupposition. They serve to help spot historical kernels even in the midst of historical chaff. Thus we need not concern ourselves with defending the Gospels' general reliability or every claim attributed to Jesus in the Gospels; if even some of his radical personal claims are authentic, that will be enough to give us insight in Jesus' self-understanding.

Denial of Christ's Divine Claims

In 1985 a prominent New Testament scholar named Robert Funk founded a think tank in Southern California which he called the Jesus Seminar. The ostensible purpose of the Seminar was to uncover the historical person Jesus of Nazareth using the best methods of scientific, biblical criticism. In Funk's view the historical Jesus has been overlaid by Christian legend, myth, and metaphysics and thus scarcely resembled the Christ figure presented in the Gospels and worshiped by the church today. The goal of the Seminar is to strip away these layers and to recover the authentic Jesus who really lived and taught.

In so doing, Funk hopes to ignite a revolution which will bring to an end what he regards as an age of ignorance. He blasts the religious establishment for "not allowing the intelligence of high scholarship to pass through pastors and priests to a hungry laity."[21] He sees the Jesus Seminar as a means of disabusing laymen of the mythological figure they have been taught to worship and bringing them face-to-face with the real Jesus of history.

The degree to which the Gospels have allegedly distorted the historical Jesus is evident in the edition of the Gospels published by the Jesus Seminar. Called *The Five Gospels* because it includes the so-called *Gospel of Thomas* along with Matthew, Mark, Luke, and John, their version prints in red only those words of Jesus which the fellows of the Seminar determine to be authentic, actually spoken by Jesus. As it turns out, less than 20 percent of the sayings attributed to Jesus are printed in red.

The real, historical Jesus turns out to have been a sort of itinerant, social critic, the Jewish equivalent of a Greek Cynic philosopher. He never claimed to be the Son of God or to forgive sins or to inaugurate a new covenant between God and man. His crucifixion was an accident of history; his corpse was probably thrown into a shallow dirt grave where it rotted away or was eaten by wild dogs.

These conclusions play havoc with the popular apologetic for Christian faith based on the claims of Christ. According to popular apologetics, Jesus claimed to be God, and his claims were either true or false. If they were false, then either he was intentionally lying or else he was deluded. But neither of these alternatives is plausible. Therefore, his claims cannot be false; he must be who he claimed to be, God incarnate, and we must decide whether we shall give our lives to him or not. Now certainly the majority of scholars today would agree that Jesus was neither a liar nor a lunatic; but that does not mean that they acknowledge him as Lord. Rather, many would say that the Jesus who claimed to be divine is a legend, a theological product of the Christian church. Thus, the dilemma posed by traditional apologetics is undercut, for Jesus himself never claimed to be God.

Defense of Christ's Divine Claims

Obviously, Jesus of Nazareth didn't go about Palestine introducing himself to people as God. The Gospels do not portray him in such a way, nor is it consistent

21. Robert Funk, "The Issue of Jesus," *Forum* 1 (1985): 8.

with the Christian doctrine of the incarnation, which holds that Jesus as a man had an ordinary human consciousness, even if it was supernaturally informed. Rather Jesus' divine self-understanding is evident explicitly in the Christological titles he used by way of self-reference and implicitly by his teaching and behavior.

THE CHRISTOLOGICAL TITLES

Those who deny that Jesus made any personal claims implying divinity face the very severe problem of explaining how it is that the worship of Jesus as Lord and God came about at all in the early church. It does little good to say that the early church wrote its beliefs about Jesus back into the Gospels, for the problem is the very origin of those beliefs themselves. Studies by New Testament scholars such as Larry Hurtado of the University of Edinburgh, Martin Hengel of Tübingen University, C. F. D. Moule of Cambridge, and others have proved that within twenty years of the crucifixion a full-blown Christology proclaiming Jesus as God incarnate existed. How does one explain this worship by monotheistic Jews of one of their countrymen whom they had accompanied during his lifetime, apart from the claims of Jesus himself? The great church historian Jaroslav Pelikan points out that all the early Christians shared the conviction that salvation was the work of a being no less than Lord of heaven and earth and that the redeemer was God himself. He observes that the oldest Christian sermon, the oldest account of a Christian martyr, the oldest pagan report of the church, and the oldest liturgical prayer (1 Cor. 16:22) all refer to Christ as Lord and God. He concludes, "Clearly it was the message of what the church believed and taught that 'God' was an appropriate name for Jesus Christ."[22] But if Jesus never made any such claims, then the belief of the earliest Christians in this regard becomes inexplicable.

In the Gospels there are a number of self-descriptions used by Jesus which provide insight into his self-understanding. Until recently, critical scholars have been quite skeptical of the authenticity of such self-descriptions. In 1977 a group of seven British theologians, headed by John Hick of the University of Birmingham, caused a great stir in the press and among laymen by publishing a book provocatively entitled *The Myth of God Incarnate*. In it they asserted that today the majority of New Testament scholars agree that the historical Jesus of Nazareth never claimed to be the Messiah or the Lord or the Son of God or indeed any of the divine titles that are attributed to Christ in the Gospels. Rather, these titles developed later in the Christian Church and were written back into the traditions handed down about Jesus, so that in the Gospels he appears to claim these titles for himself. Thus, the divine Christ of the Gospels who appears as God incarnate is a myth and ought to be rejected.

---

22. Jaroslav Pelikan, *The Christian Tradition: A History of the Development of Doctrine*, vol. 1: *The Emergence of the Catholic Tradition* (100–600), 173.

Today no such skeptical consensus exists. On the contrary, the balance of scholarly opinion on Jesus' use of Christological titles may have actually tipped in the opposite direction.

Messiah

For example, it is increasingly acknowledged as likely that Jesus of Nazareth did consider himself to be Israel's promised Messiah. Israel's ancient hope for an Anointed One (*mashiach*) of God had revived in the century immediately preceding Jesus' birth. Of the various sorts of messianic figures in Jewish hope, the most important and widespread was the expectation of a mighty king of Davidic descent who would throw off Israel's oppressors and restore the Davidic throne in Jerusalem. Written during the period of Roman occupation of Jerusalem prior to its destruction in A.D. 70, the pseudepigraphical *Psalms of Solomon* breathe out passionately the Jewish yearning for a royal messianic deliverer:

> See, Lord, and raise up for them their king,
>> the son of David, to rule over your servant Israel
>> in the time known to you, O God.
> Undergird him with the strength to destroy the unrighteous rulers,
>> to purge Jerusalem from gentiles
>> who trample her to destruction;
>> in wisdom and in righteousness to drive out
>> the sinners from the inheritance; . . .
>
> He will gather a holy people
>> whom he will lead in righteousness;
> and he will judge the tribes of the people
>> that have been made holy by the Lord their God.
> He will not tolerate unrighteousness (even) to pause among them,
>> and any person who knows wickedness shall not live with them. . . .
>
> He will judge peoples and nations in the wisdom of his righteousness.
> And he will have gentile nations serving under his yoke, . . .
>
> And he will purge Jerusalem
>> (and make it) holy as it was even from the beginning,
> (for) nations to come from the ends of the earth to see his glory,
> . . .
> And he will be a righteous king over them, taught by God.
> There will be no unrighteousness among them in his days,
>> for all shall be holy,
>> and their king shall be the Lord Messiah. (17.21–32)

The psalmist goes on to extol "the beauty of the king of Israel": he will be "compassionate to all the nations," "free from sin," "not weaken(ing) in his days," "powerful in the holy spirit," "faithfully and righteously shepherding the Lord's flock" (18.34–42). More than a warrior king, the royal Messiah would be a spiritual shepherd to Israel.

It is, of course, indisputable that the New Testament church regarded Jesus as the promised Messiah. The title *Christos* (Messiah) became so closely connected with the name "Jesus" that for Paul it is practically a surname: "Jesus Christ" (cf. the less frequent "Christ Jesus"). The very name borne by the followers of Jesus within ten years of his death—Christians—bears witness to the centrality of their belief that Jesus was the Messiah. Mark's Gospel opens with the words "the beginning of the Gospel of Jesus Christ, the Son of God" (1:1), just as John's Gospel closes with the explanation that it was written "that you may believe that Jesus is the Christ, the Son of God" (20:31). The question, then, is whether they arrived at this common conviction on their own, or did it represent Jesus' own self-understanding?

Unless Jesus himself made messianic pretensions, it is difficult to explain the unanimous and widespread conviction that Jesus was the Messiah. Why, in the absence of any messianic claims on Jesus' part, would Jesus' followers come to think of him as Messiah at all, and why was there no non-messianic form of the Jesus movement? Craig Evans reflects, "The force of this point seems lost on many who claim that the recognition of Jesus as Messiah originated only in the post-Easter setting. Had there been no messianic element in Jesus' teaching or activity . . . then it is very hard to understand where post-Easter Messianism came from. The resurrection alone cannot account for this widespread belief, for there is no pre-Christian messianic tradition that viewed resurrection as in some way evidence of a person's messianic identity."[23] With respect to this last point, Martin Hengel emphasizes that the notion "that a righteous man via resurrection from the dead was appointed as Messiah, is absolutely without analogy. Neither resurrection nor translation [into Paradise] have anything to do with Messiahship. Indeed, the suffering righteous man attains a place of honor in Paradise, but there is never any question of messianic majesty and transfer of eschatological functions in this connection."[24] "Had he been crucified for messianic claims, then—and only then—belief in his resurrection would have had to become belief in the resurrection of the crucified Messiah."[25]

---

23. Craig Evans, "Authenticating the Activities of Jesus," in *Authenticating the Activities of Jesus*, ed. Bruce Chilton and Craig Evans, New Testament Tools and Studies 28/2 (Leiden: E. J. Brill, 1999), 25.

24. Martin Hengel, "Jesus, the Messiah of Israel: The Debate about the 'Messianic Mission' of Jesus," in *Authenticating the Activities of Jesus*, 327.

25. Martin Hengel, *The Son of God*, trans. John Bowden (Philadelphia: Fortress, 1976), 63, citing N. A. Dahl, "Der gekreuzigte Messias," in *Der historische Jesus und der kerygmatische Christus*, ed. H. Ristow and K. Matthiae (1960), 161.

The Gospels unambiguously present Jesus as having a Messianic sense of identity. Of the texts in which Jesus displays his conviction that he was indeed the Messiah, the most famous is Peter's confession:

> And Jesus went on with his disciples, to the villages of Caesarea Philippi, and on the way he asked his disciples, "Who do men say that I am?" And they told him, "John the Baptist; and others say Elijah; and others one of the prophets." And he asked them, "But who do you say that I am?" Peter answered him "You are the Christ." And he charged them to tell no one about him. (Mark 8:27–30 RSV)

That people should be interested in the nature of Jesus' pretensions is both natural and to be expected. Luke and John independently attest that John the Baptist had been confronted with a similar question, which forms the backdrop for his prediction of the coming of one "mightier than I . . . the thong of whose sandals I am not worthy to untie" (Luke 3:15–16; John 1:19–27 RSV). The disciples, who had left their families and livelihoods to follow Jesus, would certainly have asked themselves who it was that they were following. Peter's answer receives independent attestation from John 6:69 (ESV), where Peter declares to Jesus, "We have believed, and have come to know, that you are the Holy One of God" (cf. Mark 1:24; Acts 3:14).

The mention of John the Baptist brings to mind the account of John's final message to Jesus found in the Q material shared by Matthew and Luke. From prison John sends disciples to Jesus with the following question: "Are you he who is to come, or shall we look for another?" (Matt. 11:3; Luke 7:19 RSV). The expression "he who is to come" obviously harks back to John's proclamation, independently attested in Mark and John, of "him who comes after me" (Mark 1:7; John 1:27). The credibility of such an embassage by John is supported not only by its presence in such early tradition, but also by the awkwardness of John's apparently wavering faith (criterion of embarrassment). Jesus' answer to John appeals to the signs that would herald the establishment of God's kingdom in Israel: "Go and tell John what you have seen and heard: the blind receive their sight, the lame walk, lepers are cleansed, and the deaf hear, the dead are raised up, the poor have good news preached to them. And blessed is the one who is not offended by me" (Luke 7:22–23 ESV; cf. Matt. 11:4–6). The signs mentioned by Jesus are a blend of prophecies from Isaiah 35:5–6; 26:19; and 61:1. The latter prophecy explicitly mentions being God's anointed one. That Jesus' contemporaries saw these signs as earmarks of the Messiah's coming is evident from a remarkable passage in the Dead Sea scrolls kept by the Essenes at Qumran (4Q521). The passage first predicts the advent of Messiah: "[For the hea]vens and the earth shall listen to his Messiah [and all t]hat is in them shall not turn away from the commandments of the holy ones." It then goes on to describe what the Lord will do at that time: "He will honor the pious upon the th[ro]ne of the eternal kingdom, setting prisoners free, opening the eyes of the blind, raising up those who are bo[wed down.] . . . and the Lord shall do glorious things which have not been done, just as he said. For he will heal the injured, he shall make alive the dead, he shall proclaim good news to the afflicted." Here we have associated with the Messiah just that same pastiche of prophetic signs listed by Jesus in answer to John's question! The criteria of Palestinian milieu and coherence with other authentic material, coupled with the criterion of embarrassment, as well as the story's presence in early tradition reinforce one another in leading to the conclusion that Jesus in fact saw himself as God's Messiah.

Even more convincing than Jesus' sayings in demonstrating his messianic self-understanding are Jesus' deeds. Jesus' Triumphal Entry into Jerusalem at the beginning of the last week of his life is a dramatic, public, provocative assertion of his messianic status. This event is multiply attested by Mark and John (Mark 11:1–11; John 12:12–19). Although their accounts differ in various circumstantial details, they fully agree on the core of the story: that one week before his death Jesus of Nazareth rode into Jerusalem seated on a colt and was hailed by the crowds who had come to Jerusalem to celebrate the annual Passover feast with shouts of "Hosanna! Blessed is he who comes in the name of the Lord!" in anticipation of the coming of the Davidic kingdom.

In every other account of Jesus' movements, he goes by foot. What, then, is he doing when he mounts a donkey's colt and rides down the Mount of Olives into Jerusalem? The answer is that Jesus is deliberately fulfilling the prophecy of Zechariah 9:9–10 (ESV):

> Rejoice greatly, O daughter of Zion!
>> Shout aloud, O daughter of Jerusalem!
> Behold, your king is coming to you;
>> righteous and having salvation is he,
> humble and mounted on a donkey,
>> on a colt, the foal of a donkey.
>
> I will cut off the chariot from Ephraim
>> and the war horse from Jerusalem;
> and the battle bow shall be cut off,
>> and he shall speak peace to the nations;
> his rule shall be from sea to sea,
>> and from the River to the ends of the earth.

Jesus is deliberately and provocatively claiming to be the promised king of Israel who will inaugurate his reign of peace. His action is like a living parable, acted out to disclose his true identity.[26]

---

26. For other examples of acting out Scripture in Judaism see Craig Evans, "Jesus and Zechariah's Messianic Hope," in *Authenticating the Activities of Jesus*, 373–88.

Skeptical critics have challenged the historicity of the narrative because Zechariah 9:9 was not interpreted as a messianic prophecy until later Judaism. But the spirit of Zechariah's prophecy pervades *Psalms of Solomon* 17–18, which also connect the images of a king and a shepherd of the people (cf. Zechariah 11) and speak of his dominion of peace. In any case, this consideration, far from detracting from the historical credibility of the narrative, actually supports it, for it makes improbable the early church's developing such a story based on Zechariah 9:9 (which is not even cited as a proof text by Mark, in contrast to the later accounts in Matt. 21:4–5; John 12:15–16) alone, in the absence of any such event. So by the criterion of dissimilarity, in this instance from antecedent Judaism, we should see the event as belonging to our picture of the historical Jesus. Jesus himself might well have interpreted the passage messianically, especially given its more irenic and humble portrayal of Israel's king. As for the crowd, it was Jesus' own disciples, who already doubtless believed in his Messiahship and who accompanied him to the feast, who initiated the acclamation of Jesus as he rode from Bethphage into Jerusalem.

Skeptical scholars have also questioned the historicity of the incident because so public a demonstration would have provoked Jesus' immediate arrest by the Roman authorities. But this conjectural objection is very weak. According to Mark's account "he entered Jerusalem and went into the temple. And when he had looked around at everything, as it was already late, he went out to Bethany with the twelve" (11:11 ESV). Jesus doesn't cleanse the temple; he doesn't even give a stirring speech. He just looks around—and leaves. His triumphal entry into the city was not something that the Roman authorities were expecting or would have understood, nor would a man on a slow-moving donkey with no show of weapons have appeared to them as a military threat; and Jesus' procession probably just melted into the Passover crowd once it got to Jerusalem. Nonetheless, the Triumphal Entry displays Jesus' royal messianic self-consciousness and reveals who he took himself to be. He identified himself with the Shepherd-King predicted by Zechariah.

The clearest indication of Jesus' messianic self-consciousness emerges by reflecting on his execution. The plaque nailed to his cross recording the charge for which Jesus was crucified is multiply attested as stating that Jesus was executed as "the King of the Jews" (Mark 15:26; John 19:19). This was never a Christian title for Jesus, so by the criterion of dissimilarity as well it probably represents the actual charge against him. Therefore, according to Craig Evans, "the majority of scholars . . . accept the *titulus* and its wording as historical and genuine."[27] Indeed, Dunn says that "his execution on the charge of being a messianic pretender ('king of the Jews') is generally reckoned to be part of the bedrock data in the Gospel tradition."[28]

27. Craig Evans, "Authenticating the Activities of Jesus," 24.
28. James D. G. Dunn, "Can the Third Quest Hope to Succeed?" in *Authenticating the Activities of Jesus*, 34. Cf. Wright's judgment: "There can be no doubt, historically speaking, that Jesus was executed as a messianic pretender" (N. T. Wright, *Christian Origins and the Question of God*, vol. 2: *Jesus and the Victory of God* [Minneapolis: Fortress Press, 1996], 522).

The speculation on the part of certain skeptical scholars that Jesus was arrested simply as a troublemaker or disturber of the peace is therefore wholly implausible. One may profitably compare here Josephus's account of another Jesus arrested during a feast in Jerusalem in A.D. 62:

> Four years before the war, when the city was enjoying profound peace and prosperity, there came to the feast at which it is the custom of all Jews to erect tabernacles to God, one Jesus, son of Ananias, a rude peasant, who, standing in the temple, suddenly began to cry out, "A voice from the east, a voice from the west, a voice from the four winds; a voice against Jerusalem and the sanctuary, a voice against the bridegroom and the bride, a voice against all the people." Day and night he went about all the alleys with this cry on his lips. Some of the leading citizens, incensed at these ill-omened words, arrested the fellow and severely chastised him. But he, without a word on his own behalf or for the private ear of those who smote him, only continued his cries as before. Thereupon, the magistrates, supposing, as was indeed the case, that the man was under some supernatural impulse, brought him before the Roman governor; therefore, although flayed to the bone with scourges, he neither sued for mercy nor shed a tear, but, merely introducing the most mournful of variations into his ejaculation, responded to each stroke with "Woe to Jerusalem!" When Albinus, the governor, asked him who and whence he was and why he uttered these cries, he answered him never a word, but unceasingly reiterated his dirge over the city, until Albinus pronounced him a maniac and let him go.[29]

The parallels between the proceedings against these two Jesuses reinforce the historical credibility of the Gospel accounts. Notice Albinus's principal concerns: who Jesus was, whence he came, and why he was doing such things. Doubtless these would have been Pilate's concerns as well. The difference in the respective outcomes of these inquests is most plausibly explained by the fact that whereas Jesus ben Ananias was deemed a harmless troublemaker, Jesus of Nazareth had made messianic pretensions which had to be treated much more seriously.[30] Had Jesus simply been disrupting the temple or disturbing the peace during Passover season, his case need not have gone any further than did the case of Jesus ben Ananias.

Virtually all critics acknowledge that during the ensuing week Jesus did cause some sort of disruption in the temple, an action multiply attested in all four Gospels, resulting in a temporary cessation in the commercial activities there. The last sentence of Zechariah's prophecy, which prompted Jesus' Triumphal Entry into Jerusalem, is: "There shall no longer be traders in the house of the Lord on

29. Josephus *Jewish Wars* 6.300–309.
30. In Evans's view, in contrast to Jesus ben Ananias, "Jesus [of Nazareth] provided the grounds for a sentence of death from both the Jewish authorities (i.e., capital blasphemy) and the Roman authorities (i.e., treason and sedition).... The messianic dimension of Jesus' activities is unmistakable" (Craig A. Evans, "What Did Jesus Do?" in *Jesus under Fire*, ed. J. P. Moreland and Michael J. Wilkins [Grand Rapids, Mich.: Zondervan, 1995], 111).

that day" (Zech. 14:21 AT).[31] Jesus' assertion of his authority in the temple, the supreme locus of Jewish religious life and authority, fits with his royal messianic self-consciousness. At his trial, according to the Synoptics, a centerpiece of the case brought against Jesus was a saying on his part having to do with the temple's destruction and Jesus' rebuilding it in three days (Mark 14:58), a saying also attested in John 2:19. In Jewish thinking God is the one who built the temple (Ex. 15:17; *Jub.* 1.17; cf. *1 En.* 90.28–29; 11Q Temple 29.8–10) and who threatens the destruction of the temple (Jer. 7:12–13; 26:4–6, 9; cf. *1 En.* 90.28–29). The charges brought against Jesus, that he threatened the destruction of the temple and promised to rebuild it, show that he was being charged with arrogating to himself divine roles.[32] Jesus' refusal to respond to these charges provokes the high priest's direct demand: "Are you the Messiah, the Son of the Blessed?" (Mark 14:61 AT). The connection between the charge and Caiaphas's question may be seen by the messianic reading given to 2 Samuel 7:12–14 by one of the Dead Sea Scrolls. The passage in Samuel concerns David's desire to build for God a temple, and the Lord's reserving that right for David's son Solomon:

> When your days are fulfilled and you lie down with your fathers, I will raise up your offspring after you, who shall come forth from your body, and I will establish his kingdom. He shall build a house for my name, and I will establish the throne of his kingdom forever. I will be his father and he will be my son. (2 Sam. 7:12–14 RSV)

In scroll 4Q174 this passage is quoted and interpreted as a prophecy of the Messiah: "He is the branch of David who will arise with the interpreter of the Law who [ ] in Zi[on in the la]st days according as it is written: 'I will raise up the tent of David that has falle[n]' (Amos 9:11), who will arise to save Israel" (1:10–13). It is the Messiah, the Davidic branch prophesied by Isaiah and Jeremiah (Isa. 11:1; Jer. 33:14–16), who will build the temple and will be God's Son. Caiaphas's question, given such messianic expectations, would have been natural, demanding whether Jesus claimed to be the Messiah, God's Son, who would fulfill this prophecy by destroying the present temple and replacing it with his own. Jesus' pretensions to be the Messiah could in turn be presented to the Roman authorities as treasonous; hence, his execution as "King of the Jews." The conspiracy of so many factors, each enjoying ratification independently by factors such as multiple attestation, Palestinian milieu, dissimilarity, and so forth, makes for an extraordinarily powerful case that Jesus of Nazareth did regard himself as the promised Messiah. Hengel concludes, "If Jesus never possessed a messianic consciousness of divine mission,

---

31. Following the NRSV translation "traders" rather than "Canaanites."

32. Robert H. Gundry, *Mark: A Commentary on His Apology for the Cross* (Grand Rapids, Mich.: Eerdmans, 1993), 900. Gundry argues that the historical authenticity of the charges brought against Jesus is further supported by the lack of harmony between Mark 14:58 and 13:32. The false witnesses had evidently mingle-mangled Jesus' prediction of the temple's destruction with his predictions of his resurrection in Mark 8:31; 9:31; 10:34, a confusion which is not apt to be a later Christian creation.

nor spoke of the coming, or present, 'Son of Man,' nor was executed as a messianic pretender—as is maintained by radical criticism untroubled by historical
arguments—then the emergence of Christology, indeed, the entire early history
of primitive Christianity, is incomprehensible."[33]

This is not to say that Jesus thought of himself as the man to lead a violent
revolt against the Roman authorities and to establish David's throne by force. Such
a move would be wholly inconsistent with the ethical teachings of Jesus. More
than anything else, this rejection of the militaristic aspects of the messianic office
by Jesus provides the key to Wrede's Messianic Secret motif, as Wrede himself
later came to see.[34] To claim openly to be the Messiah, given the popular image
of the Messiah as a military conqueror, would have tended to obscure rather than
elucidate the true nature of God's kingdom and Jesus' mission.

In concluding that Jesus understood himself to be the promised Messiah, we
have not yet arrived at a clearly divine self-understanding. Scholars typically take
Messiah to be a purely human figure and identify a number of Jewish reformers
as would-be Messiahs. For example, during the second Jewish revolt (132–135)
Bar Kokhba may have been regarded by his followers as the Messiah (Jerusalem
Talmud Ta'anit 4.5).[35] Still, the concept of the Messiah is often of an extraordinarily
exalted figure, and the leaders of renewal movements who are typically identified as
messianic pretenders were not, in fact, given and did not claim that title, so far as
we know.[36] Figures like Judas the Galilean and Simon bar Giora may have aspired
to be king over Israel, but that office is obviously not in itself messianic—not every
Jewish king is the Davidic Messiah.[37] In the *Psalms of Solomon* Messiah was to be
not merely a military ruler but much more a spiritual leader of his people:

> There will be no unrighteousness among them in his day
>> for all shall be holy,
>> and their king shall be the Lord Messiah. . . .
> He will strike the earth with the word of his mouth forever;
>> he will bless the Lord's people with wisdom and happiness.
>> And he himself (will be) free from sin, (in order) to rule a great people. . . .

33. Hengel, "Jesus, the Messiah of Israel," 327. Cf. Wright's conclusion: "Messiahship . . . was central to
Jesus' self-understanding" (Wright, *Christian Origins and the Question of God*, 2: 538).

34. See Werner Zager and Hans Rollmann, "Unveröffentlichte Briefe William Wredes zur Problematisierung des messianischen Selbstverständnisses Jesu," *Zeitschrift für neuere Theologiegeschichte* 8 (2001):
274–322.

35. See discussion of the sources in Craig A. Evans, *Jesus and His Contemporaries: Comparative Studies*
(Leiden: Brill, 2001), chap. 4.

36. For a review of messianic claimants around Jesus' time see Evans, *Jesus and His Contemporaries*, chap.
2. A great deal of Evans's case for identifying many Jewish revolutionaries, e.g., Menachem the son of Judas
the Galilean, as messianic figures is, one has to say, based on inference and conjecture.

37. Cf. Josephus's comment: "Now Judea was full of robberies; and as the several companies of the
seditious lighted upon any one to head them, he was created a king immediately" (*Antiquities of the Jews*
17.10.8 [285]).

And he will not weaken in his days, (relying) upon his God,
>for God made him
>powerful in the holy spirit
>and wise in the counsel of understanding,
>with strength and righteousness. . . .
Faithfully and righteously shepherding the Lord's flock,
>he will not let any of them stumble in their pasture. . . .
This is the beauty of the king of Israel
>which God knew,
>to raise him over the house of Israel to discipline it. (17.32–42)

It scarcely needs to be said that the typical revolutionary, reformer, or prophet could hardly aspire to such a status. In rabbinic tradition Bar Kokhba himself, having claimed to be the Messiah, was slain because he could not pass a certain superhuman test which laid down necessary conditions of messianic status.[38] While such a legend or defamation doubtless reflects later disillusionment with the man, still the requirement that Messiah display supernatural powers is striking.

But even more exalted images of the Messiah existed. Isaiah declared,

For to us a child is born,
>to us a son is given;
and the government will be upon his shoulder,
>and his name will be called
"Wonderful Counselor, Mighty God,
>Everlasting Father, Prince of Peace."
Of the increase of his government and of peace
>there will be no end,
upon the throne of David, and over his kingdom,
>to establish it, and to uphold it
with justice and with righteousness
>from this time forth and for evermore. (Isa. 9:6–7 RSV)

Here the Davidic king is called "Mighty God," and his reign is said to endure forever, motifs which are echoed in the *Psalms of Solomon*. Again, in the first-century *Similitudes of Enoch* we are presented with "the Lord of the Spirits and his Messiah," who is also called "that Son of Man." Of him we read,

Even before the creation of the sun and the moon, before the creation of the stars, he was given a name in the presence of the Lord of the Spirits. He will become a

---

38. "Bar Koziba reigned two and a half years, and then said to the Rabbis, 'I am the Messiah.' They answered, 'Of Messiah it is written that he smells and judges: let us see whether he [Bar Koziba] can do so.' When they saw that he was unable to judge by the scent, they slew him" (Babylonian Talmud Sanhedrin 93b).

staff for the righteous ones in order that they may lean on him and not fall. He is the light of the gentiles and he will become the hope of those who are sick in their hearts. All those who dwell upon the earth shall fall and worship before him; they shall glorify, bless, and sing the name of the Lord of the Spirits. For this purpose he became the Chosen One; he was concealed in the presence of (the Lord of the Spirits) prior to the creation of the world, and for eternity. (*1 En.*48.3–6)

Here the Messiah is understood to be a preexistent, God-like figure. Thus, the messianic options available at the time of Jesus included not only prophet, priest, and king, but also a heavenly Messiah.[39]

In Jesus' case the proclamation of John the Baptist, that after him would come one mightier than him who would baptize with the Holy Spirit, is seen as the fulfillment of Malachi 3:1 (RSV): "Behold, I send my messenger to prepare the way for me, and the Lord whom you seek will suddenly come to his temple" and Isaiah 40:3 (ESV): "A voice cries, 'In the wilderness prepare the way of the Lord, make straight in the desert a highway for our God.'" Notice that, according to these prophecies, it is *the Lord himself* who is coming (cf. Isa. 40:5, 9–11). The relevant question to be posed here is not whom John expected,[40] but, as the person coming in self-conscious fulfillment of John's predictions, who Jesus took himself to be. It is intriguing that in the Q saying by Jesus on the person of John the Baptist (Matt. 11:10; Luke 7.27), Jesus himself identifies John as the messenger of Malachi 3:1. In that same discourse Jesus goes on to speak of himself as the Son of Man who has come after John (Matt.11:19; Luke 7:34). Such a divine-human figure would sensibly fulfill the divine and human facets of John's prediction.[41]

We might interpret prophetic descriptions of the Messiah in terms of divinity as religious hyperbole and therefore take Jesus' claim to be the Messiah as startling but not super-human. But then again, if we find in Jesus' other personal claims and activities indications of a divine self-understanding, then his taking himself to be Israel's promised Messiah may also involve an implicit claim to divinity.

The Son of God

We've already seen that at his trial Caiaphas challenged Jesus as to his being the Son of God. This is a status to which Jesus often lays claim in the Gospels. Here we'll examine three texts in which he does so.

First, consider Jesus' parable of the wicked tenants of the vineyard (Mark 12:1–9). In this parable, the owner of the vineyard sends servants to the tenants of the

39. John J. Collins, *The Scepter and the Star: The Messiahs of the Dead Sea Scrolls and Other Ancient Literature*, Anchor Bible Reference Library (New York: Doubleday, 1995), 102–94.

40. As thought by Dunn, *Jesus Remembered*, 369–71.

41. Paul's letters also give early evidence of the Christ's being taken to be God in human form (Phil. 2:5–8). Hengel comments, "The discrepancy between the shameful death of a Jewish state criminal and the confession that depicts this executed man as a pre-existent divine figure who becomes man and humbles himself to a slave's death is . . . without analogy in the ancient world" (Hengel, *Son of God*, p. 1). Hengel goes on to show that this idea is pre-Pauline.

vineyard to collect its fruit. The vineyard symbolizes Israel (cf. Isa. 5:1–7), the owner is God, the tenants are the Jewish religious leaders, and the servants are prophets sent by God. The tenants beat and reject the owner's servants. Finally, the owner decides that he has one left to send: his only beloved son. "They will respect my son," he says. But instead, the tenants kill the son because he is the heir to the vineyard.

Even skeptical scholars like those in the Jesus Seminar recognize the authenticity of this parable, since it is also found in one of their favorite sources, the *Gospel of Thomas* (65), and so is by their reckoning multiply attested.[42] Moreover, as Evans has emphasized, the parable not only reflects the actual experience of absentee landowners in the ancient world but also employs stock images and themes found in rabbinic parables: Israel as a vineyard, God as the owner, unworthy rebellious tenants, the figure of a son, and so on, so that it coheres well with a Jewish milieu.[43] There are, furthermore, aspects of the parable which render unlikely its later origin in the Christian church, for example, the concern over who should possess the vineyard after it is taken from the present tenants and the absence of the resurrection of the slain son. The parable also contains interpretative nuances rooted in the Aramaic targums (paraphrases) of Isaiah 5 which were in use in Jesus' day. Evans concludes, "When understood properly and in full context, everything about the parable of the wicked vineyard tenants—including its context in the New Testament Gospels—argues that it originated with Jesus, not with the early church."[44]

What, then, does this parable tell us about Jesus' self-understanding? It tells us that he thought of himself as God's only Son, distinct from all the prophets, God's final messenger, and even the heir of Israel itself. Notice that one cannot delete the figure of the son from the parable as an inauthentic, later addition, for then the parable lacks any climax and point. Moreover, the uniqueness of the son is not only explicitly stated but inherently implied by the tenants' stratagem of murdering the heir in order to claim possession of the vineyard. So this parable discloses to us that the historical Jesus believed and taught that he was the only Son of God.

Jesus' self-concept as God's Son comes to explicit expression in Matthew 11:27 (RSV cf. Luke 10:22): "All things have been delivered to me by my Father; and no one knows the Son except the Father; and no one knows the Father except the Son and anyone to whom the Son chooses to reveal him." Again there is good reason to regard this as an authentic saying of the historical Jesus. It is a Q saying of Jesus and therefore very early. The saying has been shown to go back to an

---

42. On the derivative character of the Thomas version see Charles L. Quarles, "The Use of the Gospel of Thomas in the Research on Historical Jesus of John Dominic Crossan," *Catholic Biblical Quarterly* 69 (2007): 517–36.

43. Craig A. Evans, *Fabricating Jesus* (Downers Grove, Ill.: InterVarsity, 2006), 132–35.

44. Ibid., 138.

original Aramaic version, which counts in favor of its authenticity.[45] Moreover, it is unlikely that the church invented this saying because it says that the Son is unknowable—"no one knows the Son except the Father"—which would exclude even Jesus' followers from knowing him. But the conviction of the post-Easter church is that we *can* know the Son (see, e.g., Phil. 3:8–11). Notice, too, that according to the saying the content of Jesus' revelation is the Father, whereas Jesus himself was the content of the church's proclamation. The reference to the Son is almost informal, rather than emphasizing a title like "Son of God." So this saying is unlikely to be the product of later church theology.

This saying has been characterized as a bolt out of the Johannine blue. For what does it tell us about Jesus' self-concept? It tells us that he thought of himself as the exclusive Son of God and the only revelation of God the Father to mankind! It is said by those who deny the saying's authenticity that the unrestricted authority and absoluteness and exclusivity of the postulated relation between the Father and the Son is unparalleled in the pre-Easter Synoptic tradition. But that assumes, implausibly, that passages like Mark 1:11, 27; 3:11; Matthew 7:21–23, and so forth, are not part of the pre-Easter tradition, for they certainly do contemplate Jesus as the absolute, authoritative Son of God and revealer of the Father. As Denaux has rightly emphasized, what we have here is a Johannine Christological affirmation in the earliest stratum of the Gospel traditions, an affirmation which forms a bridge to the high Christology of John's Gospel and yet, in light of passages like Mark 4:10–12; 12:1–11; 13:32; and Matthew 16:17–19; 28:18, is also at home in the Synoptic tradition.[46] On the basis of this saying, we may conclude that Jesus thought of himself as God's Son in an absolute and unique sense and as having been invested with the exclusive authority to reveal his Father God to men.

Finally, another interesting indication of Jesus' sense of being God's Son is his saying concerning the date of the consummation: "But of that day or that hour no one knows, not even the angels in heaven, nor the Son, but only the Father" (Mark 13:32 rsv). It seems highly unlikely that this saying could be the manufacture of Christian theology, especially in light of traditions like Matthew 11:27 (cf. John 5:20; 16:15, 30; 21:17c), because it ascribes ignorance to the Son. The criterion of embarrassment requires the authenticity of the reference to the Son's ignorance. Just how embarrassing the saying was is evident in the fact that although Matthew reproduces it (Matt. 24:36), Luke omits it, and most copyists of Matthew's Gospel also chose to drop the verse (though it is preserved in the best manuscripts). That Mark preserves this saying, despite his emphasis on Jesus' predictive power and foreknowledge (Mark 11:2; 13; 14:13–15, 18, 27–28, 30), is testimony to his

45. Joachim Jeremias, *The Prayers of Jesus*, translated by John Burchard (London: SCM, 1967), 45–46.
46. Adelbert Denaux, "The Q-Logion Mt 11, 27/Lk 10, 22 and the Gospel of John," in *John and the Synoptics*, ed. A. Denaux, Bibliotheca Ephemeridum Theologicarum Lovaniensium 101 (Leuven, Belgium: Leuven University Press, 1992).

faithfulness to the tradition. As Markan commentator Vincent Taylor nicely puts it, "Its offence seals its genuineness."[47]

Some critics have suggested that the early church may have inserted the phrase "nor the Son" into the saying, using an honorific title to compensate for the slight dealt to Jesus by this saying. Not only does this suggestion violate the structure of the saying—the *oude . . . oude* forming a pair so as to say "neither the angels nor the Son"—but it is precisely by the addition of such a phrase that the saying becomes offensive. Without the phrase the saying would contrast what is unknown to men and angels but known to the Father (and by implication to Jesus as the one who exclusively reveals the Father). It is futile to suggest that the early church may have substituted the honorific title "the Son" for some other self-designation on Jesus' part, for it would have been easier and more natural just to omit any such self-reference, so that Jesus' knowledge would not even come into the equation.

On the basis of these three sayings of the historical Jesus, we have good evidence that Jesus thought of himself as the unique Son of God. Once again, however, we are not yet arrived at an unequivocal claim to divinity. For although Hellenistic readers of the Gospels would be apt to interpret the expression "Son of God" in terms of the divine status of the claimant, in a Jewish milieu such a status was not the customary sense of the title. Jewish kings were referred to as God's sons (2 Sam. 7:14; 1 Chron. 17:13; 22:10; Pss. 2:6–7; 89:26–27), and in Wisdom literature the righteous man could be characterized as God's child, having God as his father (Wis. 2.13, 16, 18; 5.5; Sir. 4.10; 51.10). Such generic usage is, however, irrelevant to Jesus' claim to divine Sonship, given the uniqueness and exclusivity of his claim. We have seen that Jesus thought of himself as God's Son in a singular sense that set him apart even from the prophets who had gone before. But what was that sense?

The answer may be, once more, that Jesus thought of himself as God's unique Son in the sense that he was the promised Messiah. *Four Ezra* 7.28–29 speaks of Messiah as God's son but nonetheless as mortal: "My son the Messiah shall be revealed . . . and those who remain shall rejoice four hundred years. And after these years my son the Messiah shall die, and all who have human breath." The Dead Sea Scrolls also show that the Messiah was thought to be God's son. 4Q174 interprets the promise to Solomon in 2 Samuel 7:14 that God will be his father to apply to the Messiah, as we have seen. 4Q246 speaks of a false prince who "will be called the Son of God, and they will call him the son of the Most High" (cf. Luke 1:35). 1QSa 2.11–12 anticipates the time "when [God] has begotten the Messiah," which evinces a messianic interpretation of Psalm 2:7, which concerns the Lord's anointed one (Ps. 2.2). This is the psalm alluded to at Jesus' baptism in the words of the heavenly voice, "You are my beloved son" (Mark 1:11; cf. Acts

47. Vincent Taylor, *The Gospel according to St. Mark*, 2nd ed. (London: Macmillan, 1966), 522.

13:33). The uniqueness of Jesus' Sonship could be a function of the uniqueness of the Messiah.

On the other hand, it must be said in all honesty that these texts do not even approach the sort of absoluteness and exclusivity claimed by Jesus of Nazareth in the sayings we have examined. There is nothing in Dead Sea texts to suggest the filial uniqueness of the Messiah. Being the Messiah might set Jesus apart from all the prophets who had come before him and make him the heir of Israel, as claimed in the parable of the vineyard, but being Messiah would not give him exclusive knowledge of the Father and absolute revelatory significance, as claimed in Matthew 11:27. Moreover, the saying in Mark 13:32 not only discloses Jesus' sense of unique sonship but also presents us with an ascending scale of status from men to angels to the Son to the Father. Thus, amazingly, Jesus' sense of being God's Son involved a sense of proximity to the Father which transcended that of any mortal man (such as a king or prophet) or any angelic being.

Such an exalted conception of God's Son is not foreign to first-century Judaism. The New Testament materials themselves bear witness to this fact (Col. 1:13–20; Heb. 1:1–12). In *4 Ezra* 13, Ezra sees a vision of a man arising out of the sea who is identified by God as "my Son" (13.32, 37) and who proceeds to subdue all the nations. Ezra asks,

> "O sovereign Lord, explain this to me: Why did I see the man coming up from the heart of the sea?"
>
> He said to me, "Just as no one can explore or know what is in the depths of the sea, so no one on earth can see my Son or those who are with him, except in the time of his day." (*4 Ezra* 13.51–52; cf. 13.26)

That there are other persons presently with the Son prior to his earthly appearance suggests that the Son is a preexistent, heavenly figure. This becomes quite clear in 14.9 when Ezra is told that his own life is about to end and that he is going to be with God's Son until he is revealed at the end of time: "You shall be taken up from among men, and henceforth you shall live with my Son and those who are like you, until the times are ended." It is intriguing that there is a differentiation made between the pre-existent Son and the righteous, human dead like Ezra who are with him. The Son is clearly set apart as a supernatural figure.

We have here the same ambiguity with "the Son of God" that we encountered in considering the title "Messiah." These titles are multi-valent and therefore inherently ambiguous without a context. In order to understand more clearly the meaning that Jesus invested in such self-descriptions, we shall need to look at the Christological significance of Jesus' teaching and actions. But before we do so, there is one more title, the most significant of all, which demands our attention.

The Son of Man

It is highly likely that Jesus thought of himself as and claimed to be the Son of Man.[48] This was Jesus' favorite self-description and is the title found most frequently in the Gospels (over eighty times). Yet remarkably, this title is found only once outside the Gospels in the rest of the New Testament (Acts 7:56). That shows that the designation of Jesus as "the Son of Man" was not a title that arose in later Christian usage and was then written back into the Jesus traditions. Even in the Gospels, only Jesus uses this title; others may confess him as the Messiah or the Son of God, but never as the Son of Man. On the basis of the criterion of dissimilarity we can say with confidence that Jesus called himself "the Son of Man." Dunn concludes, "When we encounter a thoroughly consistent and distinctive feature—a tradition which depicts Jesus regularly using the phrase 'son of man' and virtually no other use of the phrase—it simply beggars scholarship to deny that this feature stemmed from a remembered speech usage of Jesus himself."[49]

The key question then becomes the theological significance of the phrase. Some critics maintain that in calling himself "Son of Man" Jesus merely meant "a human person," just as the Old Testament prophet Ezekiel referred to himself as "a son of man," or even "I" or "one," as in later rabbinic use of the Aramaic equivalent. But with Jesus there is a crucial difference. For Jesus did not refer to himself as "a son of man," but as "*the* Son of Man." The use of the phrase with the definite article, *ho huios tou anthropou*, is consistent throughout the Gospels, whereas the Hebrew equivalent *ben hadam* occurs only in 1QS 10.20 and the Aramaic *bar enasha* is unknown, in contrast to the frequent instances of the indefinite phrases *ben 'adam* and *bar enash*. It is sometimes said that the existence of certain parallel passages in the Gospels where "the Son of Man" occurs in one passage and the first person pronoun "I" occurs in the other (Matt. 5:11/Luke 6:22; Matt. 10:32–33/Luke 12:8–9; Mark 8:27/Matt. 16:13) shows an awareness in the transmission of the tradition that the two expressions are synonymous and that Jesus used *bar enasha* as a personal indexical term like "I" and "me." But such an inference confuses sense and reference. The tradition does, indeed, support Jesus' use of the expression as a means of self-reference; but it does not follow that because the two expressions are co-referential they have the same meaning. This is an elementary semantic point; the king, for example, may refer to himself as "the King" or as "I," but obviously "the King" does not mean "I." The parallel passages show merely that the tradents of the tradition understood that the person designated in Jesus' sayings by the expression *bar enasha* was Jesus. Thus, the inference that because Jesus used *bar enasha* to refer to himself he did not use the expression as a title is quite erroneous.[50]

48. See Ben Witherington, III, *The Christology of Jesus* (Minneapolis: Fortress Press, 1990), 233–62; see also Gundry, *Mark*, 118–19, 587, and the therein cited literature, as well as Seyoon Kim, *The Son of Man as the Son of God* (Grand Rapids, Mich.: Eerdmans, 1985).

49. Dunn, "Can the Third Quest Hope to Succeed?" 47.

50. Cf. the Beloved Disciple's use of a descriptive title to refer to himself, on the assumption that he is the author of John's Gospel. That obviously does not make "the Beloved Disciple" a personal indexical

Rather by use of the definite article Jesus was directing attention to the divine eschatological figure of Daniel 7:13–14 (ESV). Daniel describes his vision in the following way:

> I saw in the night visions,
>
> and behold, with the clouds of heaven
>   there came one like a son of man,
> and he came to the Ancient of Days
>   and was presented before him.
> And to him was given dominion
>   and glory and kingdom,
> that all peoples, nations, and languages
>   should serve him;
> his dominion is an everlasting dominion,
>   which shall not pass away,
> and his kingdom one
>   that shall not be destroyed.

That Jesus believed in the eschatological appearance of the figure described in Daniel's vision is multiply attested in Markan and Q sayings (Mark 8:38; 13:26–27; Matt. 10:32–33/Luke 12:8–9; Matt. 24:27, 37, 39/Luke 17:24, 26, 30). In Daniel's vision the figure looks like a human being, but he comes on the clouds of heaven, and to him is given a dominion and glory which is God-like. The *Similitudes of Enoch* present a similar vision of the preexistent Son of Man (*1 En.* 48.3–6 cited above; cf. 62.7) who "shall depose the kings from their thrones and kingdoms" (*1 En.* 46.5) and shall sit "upon the throne of his glory" (*1 En.* 69.29). We have also mentioned the Danielic vision of *4 Ezra* 13, in which Ezra sees "something like the figure of a man come up out of the heart of the sea," whom the Most High identifies as "my son" (*4 Ezra* 13.37) and who preexists with the Most High. The point in mentioning these passages is not that people listening to Jesus would have recognized his allusions to such works or ideas—which they evidently did not—but rather that the construal of Daniel's Son of Man as a divine-human figure would be neither anachronistic nor un-Jewish for Jesus. By using the oblique, self-referential expression "the Son of Man," Jesus prevented a prematurely transparent revelation of his super-human and messianic dignity.[51]

Some scholars, recognizing Jesus' belief in an eschatological figure called the Son of Man to whom judgment and dominion would be given, have nonetheless tried to avert a radical claim to divinity on Jesus' part by maintaining that Jesus was talking about and expecting someone else! Such an exegesis is sheer fancy. It

term. That the "Son of Man" can appear in the mouths of others (John 12:34; Acts 7:56) proves that it is not a personal indexical.

51. Gundry, *Mark*, 119.

would require us to say that all of the Son of Man sayings used by Jesus to refer either to himself or to an earthly, suffering figure are inauthentic; if even one such saying is authentic, the proposed exegesis is invalidated. For example, Matthew 8:20 (RSV), "Foxes have holes and birds of the air have nests, but the Son of Man has nowhere to lay his head," is generally taken to be authentic but obviously does not refer to some eschatological, cosmic figure. Moreover, in general, this view cannot make sense of Jesus' claim to ultimate authority. There is something of a scholarly consensus, as we shall see, that Jesus had a sense of unsurpassed authority. He put himself in God's place by his words and actions. But then it makes no sense to suppose that he thought that someone else was coming who would judge the world, someone who would, in fact, judge Jesus himself, if Jesus were merely a human prophet or teacher. Jesus' consciousness of unsurpassed authority is incompatible with the view that he thought someone else was the coming Son of Man.

All three of the titles we have examined thus far come together in a remarkable way at Jesus' trial. Mark records,

> And the high priest stood up in the midst, and asked Jesus, "Have you no answer to make? What is it that these men testify against you?" But he was silent and made no answer. Again the high priest asked him, "Are you the Christ, the Son of the Blessed?" And Jesus said, "I am; and you will see the Son of Man sitting at the right hand of Power and coming with the clouds of heaven." And the high priest tore his mantle and said, "Why do we still need witnesses? You have heard his blasphemy. What is your decision?" And they all condemned him as deserving death. (Mark 14:60–64 RSV)

Here in one fell swoop Jesus affirms that he is the Messiah, the Son of God, and the coming Son of Man. He compounds his crime by adding that he is to be seated at God's right hand, a claim that is truly blasphemous in Jewish ears.[52] The trial scene beautifully illustrates how in Jesus' self-understanding all the diverse claims blend together, thereby taking on connotations that outstrip any single term taken out of context.

So are these words of Jesus, which served as the basis for his condemnation by the Sanhedrin and for his delivery to the Roman authorities on charges of treason, authentic? In his meticulous commentary on Mark's Gospel, Robert Gundry argues that the words of the high priest "Son of the Blessed (One)" are likely authentic because this use of a circumlocution for "God," though common among Jews, was not characteristic of Christians; moreover, it appears only here in the Gospel of Mark, who elsewhere prefers the title "Son of God" (1:1; 3:11; 5:7; 15:39). As for Jesus' reply to the high priest's question, Gundry provides several lines of evidence

---

52. See discussion in Darrell L. Bock, *Blasphemy and Exaltation in Judaism and the Final Examination of Jesus*, Wissenschaftliche Untersuchungen zum Neuen Testament 106 (Tübingen: J. C. B. Mohr, 1998); repr. ed.: *Blasphemy and Exaltation in Judaism: The Charge against Jesus in Mark 14:53–65*, Biblical Studies Library (Grand Rapids, Mich.: Baker, 2000).

in support of its authenticity: (1) the combination of sitting at God's right hand and coming with the clouds of heaven appears nowhere in New Testament material except on Jesus' lips; (2) the Son of Man is nowhere else associated with the notion of sitting at God's right hand; (3) the saying exhibits the same blend of oblique self-reference and personally high claims that characterizes other Son of Man sayings (Mark 2:10, 28; 8:38; 13:26); (4) even though Psalm 110:1 concerning sitting at the right hand of God is alluded to frequently in the New Testament, the substitution of "the Power" for "God," though typical for Jewish reverential usage, occurs nowhere else in the New Testament; and (5) Mark is unlikely to have created a prediction to the Sanhedrin which they did not, in fact, see fulfilled.

In addition, Gundry notes the subtlety of the Markan account of the trial, which would escape a later Christian fabricator. Rules for dealing with capital blasphemy cases in the Mishnah (*Sanhedrin* 7.5) concern cases in which a person is accused of having pronounced on some previous occasion the divine name "Yahweh" so as to dishonor God. During the trial the alleged blasphemy of the accused is not actually repeated, but some substitute for the divine name is used. Only at the trial's close is the courtroom cleared, and in the presence of the judges, the lead witness is instructed, "Say expressly what you heard." He then repeats the blasphemous words uttered by the accused, at which all the judges stand and rend their clothes. In Jesus' trial, the blasphemy occurs unexpectedly on the spot, so that only the high priest is standing and tears his garments. If Jesus actually uttered the divine name by saying, "You will see the Son of Man sitting at the right hand of Yahweh," a report of what transpired in Jesus' trial would not include the pronunciation of the divine name itself but some substitute for it, like "the Power." Gundry concludes, "The collocation of capital blasphemy and clothes-rending in *m. Sanh.* 7.5 as well as in Mark favors . . . that Mark's account of Jesus' trial rests on trustworthy information. . . . For though Christians might have fabricated an account so defamatory of the Sanhedrin, Christians are unlikely to have fabricated—or even have been able to fabricate—an account corresponding so subtly to a later idealization of Sanhedrin jurisprudence in cases of capital blasphemy."[53] How did Jesus dishonor God? Gundry answers, "We may best think that the high priest and the rest of the Sanhedrin judge Jesus to have verbally robbed God of incommensurateness and unity by escalating himself to a superhuman level, by portraying himself as destined to sit at God's right hand and come with the clouds of heaven."[54]

For Jesus, then, titles like "Messiah" and "Son of God," which need carry no connotation of divinity, become infused with such a connotation in his self-understanding and usage, just as they do in *1 Enoch* and *4 Ezra*, by his conviction that he is the Danielic Son of Man who is to be seated at God's right hand.

53. Gundry, *Mark*, 917–18.
54. Ibid., 917.

IMPLICIT CHRISTOLOGY

So the skepticism of earlier generations concerning Jesus' use of Christological titles has greatly receded as the Third Quest of the historical Jesus has gained insight into the religio-cultural milieu of first-century Palestinian Judaism. But we may gain additional insight into Jesus' self-understanding by examining his teaching and behavior. Most scholars believe that in what he said and did Jesus made claims that imply the same thing as the titles. In other words, the titles serve only to express *explicitly* what Jesus in his teaching and behavior had already expressed about himself *implicitly*. Let's therefore review some of the implicit personal claims of Jesus widely accepted in New Testament scholarship, wholly apart from the question of Christological titles.

Jesus' Preaching of the Kingdom

One of the undisputed facts about Jesus of Nazareth is the centrality of the advent of the kingdom of God to his proclamation.[55] Moreover, it is clear that Jesus thought of himself as central to the coming of God's kingdom. The scholarly debate continues over whether God's kingdom was thought by Jesus to be already here or not yet arrived (or, as most scholars think, both in a dynamic tension), but in either case it is Jesus who is the vanguard and representative of that kingdom. As we shall see, Jesus carried out a ministry of miraculous healings and exorcisms as signs to the people of the inbreaking of God's kingdom. The question then arises as to Jesus' role in that kingdom. Was he merely a herald of that kingdom or did he have a more significant role to play? Here we encounter the very interesting Q saying of Jesus concerning his twelve disciples' roles in the coming kingdom: "Truly, I say to you, in the new world . . . you who have followed me will also sit on twelve thrones, judging the twelve tribes of Israel" (Matt. 19:28 ESV; cf. Luke 22:28–30). The saying is likely to be authentic, not only because it seems to envision an earthly kingdom which did not immediately materialize, but also because of the awkwardness of envisioning a throne for Judas Iscariot, who was known to have apostatized. Jesus' calling twelve disciples is thus seen to be no accident: the number twelve is significant as corresponding to the number of tribes of the full nation of Israel. This fact has interesting ramifications for Jesus' view of Israel as a political entity; but our interest lies elsewhere. If the twelve disciples are to sit on thrones judging the twelve tribes of Israel, who will be the king over all of Israel? The clear answer is, Jesus himself. He will certainly not be beneath the disciples or outside of Israel, but he will be over the disciples as the King of Israel. In short, Jesus thought of himself as Israel's royal Messiah. Thus Jesus' messianic self-understanding is implicit in his proclamation of the inbreaking of God's kingdom in his person and ministry, wholly apart from his explicit claims.

55. See extended discussion in Meier, *Marginal Jew*, vol. 2: *Mentor, Message, and Miracles*, Anchor Bible Reference Library (New York: Doubleday, 1994), 237–506.

Jesus' Authority

Jesus' personal sense of acting and speaking with divine authority is evident in a number of ways.

First, his authority comes to expression in the content and style of his teaching. These two aspects of his teaching are especially evident in the Sermon on the Mount. The typical rabbinical style of teaching was to quote extensively from learned teachers, who provided the basis of authority for one's own teaching. But Jesus did exactly the opposite. He began, "You have heard that it was said to the men of old . . ." and quoted the Mosaic Law; then he continued, "But I say to you . . ." and gave his own teaching. Jesus thus equated his own authority with that of the divinely given Torah. It's no wonder that Matthew comments, "When Jesus finished these sayings, the crowds were astonished at his teaching, for he taught them as one who had authority, and not as their scribes" (Matt. 7:28–29 rsv).

But it's not just that Jesus placed his personal authority on a par with that of the divine Law. More than that, he adjusted the Law on his own authority. Although Jewish scholars have attempted valiantly to assimilate Jesus' ethical teachings to the tradition of Judaism, Jesus' opposition of his own personal authority to the divine Torah given through Moses is the rock upon which all such attempts are finally broken. Take, for example, Jesus' teaching on divorce in Matthew 5:31–32 (cf. Mark 10:2–12). Here Jesus explicitly quotes the teaching of the Law (Deut. 24:1–4) and opposes to it, on the basis of his own authority, his teaching on the matter. In the Markan passage, he declares that Moses does not represent the perfect will of God on this matter and presumes to correct the Law on his own authority as to what is really the will of God. But no human being, no prophet or teacher or charismatic, has that kind of authority. "Jesus," observes Witherington, "seems to assume an authority over Torah that no Pharisee or Old Testament prophet assumed—the authority to set it aside."[56]

In his provocative dialogue *A Rabbi Talks with Jesus*, the eminent Jewish scholar Jacob Neusner explains that it is precisely on this basis why he, as a Jew, would not have followed Jesus had he lived in first-century Palestine. Explaining that for a Jew the Torah is God's revelation to Moses, he asserts,

> Jews believe in the Torah of Moses . . . and that belief requires faithful Jews to enter a dissent at the teachings of Jesus, on the grounds that those teachings at important points contradict the Torah. . . . And therefore, because that specific teaching was so broadly out of phase with the Torah and covenant of Sinai, I could not then follow him and do not now either. That is not because I am stubborn or unbelieving. It is because I believe God has given a different Torah from the one that Jesus teaches; and that Torah, the one Moses got at Sinai, stands in judgment of the torah of Jesus, as it dictates true and false for all other torahs that people want to teach in God's name.[57]

56. Witherington, *Christology of Jesus*, 65.
57. Jacob Neusner, *A Rabbi Talks with Jesus* (New York: Doubleday, 1993), xii, 5.

Given the supremely authoritative status of the divinely revealed Torah, Jesus' teaching can only appear presumptuous and even blasphemous. In effect, as Robert Hutchinson put it, "Neusner wants to ask Jesus, 'Who do you think you are—God?'"[58] Neusner himself recognizes that "no one can encounter Matthew's Jesus without concurring that before us in the evangelist's mind is God incarnate."[59] But if Jesus' opposition of his personal teaching to the Torah is an authentic facet of the historical Jesus—as even the skeptical scholars of the Jesus Seminar concede—then it seems that Jesus did arrogate to himself the authority of God. According to Robert Guelich, "one must not shy away from the startling antithesis between *God has said to those of old / But I say to you* since here lies not only the key to the antithesis but to Jesus' ministry."[60]

Second, Jesus' use of *amēn* expresses his authority. The expression frequently attributed to Jesus, "Truly, truly I say to you," is historically unique and is recognized on all hands to have been used by Jesus to preface his teaching. It served to mark off his authoritative word on some subject, usually a statement about the inbreaking kingdom of God or about Jesus' own work. Ben Witherington in his acclaimed study of the Christology of Jesus explains the significance of Jesus' use of the phrase "Amen, I say to you":

> It is insufficient to compare it to "thus says the Lord," although that is the closest parallel. Jesus is not merely speaking for Yahweh, but for himself and on his own authority. . . . This strongly suggests that he considered himself to be a person of authority above and beyond what prophets claimed to be. He could attest to his own truthfulness and speak on his own behalf, and yet his words were to be taken as having the same or greater authority than the divine words of the prophets. Here was someone who thought he possessed not only divine inspiration . . . but also divine authority and the power of direct divine utterance. The use of *amen* followed by "I say unto you" must be given its full weight in light of its context—early Judaism.[61]

That Witherington's analysis is correct is evident from the complaint of the orthodox Jewish writer Ahad ha' Am: "Israel cannot accept with religious enthusiasm, as the Word of God, the utterances of a man who speaks in his own name—not 'thus saith the Lord,' but '*I* say unto you.' This 'I' is in itself sufficient to drive Judaism away from the Gentiles forever."[62]

Third, Jesus' authority is especially evident in his role as an exorcist. Embarrassing as it may be to many modern theologians, it is historically certain that

58. Robert J. Hutchinson, "What the Rabbi Taught Me about Jesus," *Christianity Today*, September 13, 1993, 28.
59. Neusner, *A Rabbi Talks with Jesus*, 14.
60. Robert Guelich, *Sermon on the Mount* (Waco, Tex.: Word, 1982), 185.
61. Witherington, *Christology of Jesus*, 188.
62. Ahad ha' Am, "Judaism and the Gospels," in *Nationalism and the Jewish Ethic*, ed. H. Kohn (New York: Schocken, 1962), 298.

Jesus believed he had the power to cast out demons.[63] This was a sign to people of his divine authority. He declared, "But if it is by the finger of God that I cast out demons, then the kingdom of God has come upon you" (Luke 11:20 ESV). This saying, which is recognized by New Testament scholarship as authentic, is remarkable for two reasons. First, it shows that Jesus claimed divine authority over the spiritual forces of evil. Second, it shows that Jesus believed that in himself the kingdom of God had come. According to Jewish thinking, the kingdom of God would come at the end of history when the Lord would reign over Israel and the nations. But Jesus was saying, "My ability to rule the spiritual forces of darkness shows that in me the kingdom of God is already present among you." As Ben Meyer explains in his study of Jesus' aims, "The exorcisms pointed beyond themselves to the dawning of God's reign! In terms of the history of religions, this gives an entirely distinctive profile to the exorcisms of Jesus. They become . . . *signs of the eschaton.*"[64] Jesus' exorcisms signaled that a new era was dawning and that Satan was being decisively cast out. More than that, however; for the advent of God's kingdom was inseparable from the advent of God himself, as Meyer explains:

> Dalman pointed out that in the targumic literature "the reign of God" appears as a reverential circumlocution for "God" (as ruler). Jeremias rightly finds this phenomenon in Jesus' idiom, as well, so that the words "the reign of God is near!" virtually mean "God is near"—at the door or already here![65]

In claiming that in himself the kingdom of God had already arrived, as visibly demonstrated by his exorcisms, Jesus was, in effect, saying that in himself God had drawn near, thus putting himself in God's place.

Finally, Jesus' sense of divine authority comes clearly to expression in his claim to forgive sins. Several of Jesus' parables, which are acknowledged on all hands to have been uttered by the historical Jesus, show that he assumed the prerogative to forgive sins. In parables like the prodigal son, the lost sheep, and so forth, Jesus describes persons who have wandered away from God and are lost in sin. In Jewish thought such a person was irretrievably lost and therefore given up as dead. But Jesus extended forgiveness to such persons and welcomed them back into the fold. The problem is that no one but God had the authority to make such a proclamation. No mere prophet could presume to speak for God on this matter. As Royce Gruenler puts it, Jesus "is consciously speaking as the voice of God on matters that belong only to God. . . . The evidence clearly leads us to affirm that Jesus implicitly claims to do what only God can do, to forgive sins. . . . The religious

---

63. According to Witherington, that Jesus was an exorcist is "one of the most incontestable facts about his ministry," being attested in nearly all layers of tradition and by allusions in sayings, narratives, and summaries (Witherington, *Christology of Jesus*, 201).

64. Ben F. Meyer, *The Aims of Jesus* (London: SCM, 1979), 155–56.

65. Ibid., 136.

authorities correctly understood his claim to divine authority to forgive sinners, but they interpreted his claims as blasphemous and sought his execution."[66]

What Jesus taught in his parables, he acted out in real life. One of the most radical features of the historical Jesus was his practice of inviting prostitutes, toll collectors, and other outcasts into fellowship with him around the dinner table.[67] This was a living illustration of God's forgiveness of them and his invitation of them into fellowship in the kingdom of God. As John Meier explains, in the eyes of religious Jews

> Jesus' table fellowship with the ritually or morally unclean communicated uncleanness to Jesus himself. Jesus, of course, saw it the other way round: he was communicating salvation to religious outcasts. His meals with sinners ... were celebrations of the lost being found, of God's mercy reaching out and embracing the prodigal son returning home. His banquets with sinful Israelites were a preparation and foretaste of the coming banquet in the kingdom of God.[68]

Critics like Crossan who see Jesus' table fellowship as merely a demonstration of Jesus' egalitarianism have missed its most distinctive feature: the reconciliation of sinners and their integration into the kingdom of God. In table fellowship with the immoral and unclean Jesus is acting in the place of God to welcome them into God's kingdom. It's no wonder that the religious authorities saw this presumptuous activity as blasphemous and sought to have him crucified (cf. the reaction to Jesus' claim in Mark 2:1–12 that as the Son of Man he has authority to forgive sins)!

Thus, most New Testament critics acknowledge that the historical Jesus acted and spoke with a self-consciousness of divine authority and that, furthermore, he saw in his own person the coming of the long-awaited kingdom of God and invited people into its fellowship.

Jesus' Miracles

Jesus believed himself to be not only an exorcist but a miracle worker. Recall his reply to the disciples of John the Baptist, "Go and tell John what you hear and see: the blind receive their sight and the lame walk, lepers are cleansed and the deaf

---

66. Royce Gordon Gruenler, *New Approaches to Jesus and the Gospels* (Grand Rapids, Mich.: Baker, 1982), 46, 59, 49. This claim comes to explicit expression in Mark 2:1–12, whose authenticity is defended by Gundry, *Mark*, 110–22.

67. As Meyer explains, through table fellowship the Jewish ritual distinction of clean and unclean and the Jewish moral distinction of righteous and unrighteous, which shaped and permeated the self-understanding of Judaism, came to concrete expression. With respect to Jesus' ignoring such distinctions, Meyer comments, "Nothing ... could have dramatized the gratuity and the present realization of God's saving act more effectively than this unheard of initiative toward sinners" (Meyer, *Aims*, 161). Jesus' iconoclasm in this regard lends credibility to Mark's comment that Jesus consciously overturned Old Testament food laws (Mark 7:19), which underscores the point above concerning his authority to correct the Torah, as is pointed out by Gundry, *Mark*, 356, 367–71.

68. Meier, *Marginal Jew*, 2:303.

hear, and the dead are raised up, and the poor have good news preached to them"
(Matt. 11:4–5 ᴇsᴠ). Dunn comments: "Whatever the 'facts' were, Jesus evidently
believed that he had cured cases of blindness, lameness, and deafness—indeed there
is no reason to doubt that he believed lepers had been cured under his ministry
and dead restored to life."[69]

Moreover, the miracle stories are so widely represented in all strata of the Gospel
traditions that it would be fatuous to regard them as not rooted in the life of Jesus.
Thus, the consensus of New Testament scholarship agrees that Jesus did perform
"miracles"—however one might want to interpret or explain these. At the end of
his long and detailed study of Jesus' miracles Meier concludes,

> The overall attestation of the figure of Jesus as healer of physical infirmities and ill-
> nesses is thus even stronger than the attestation of his activity as an exorcist. . . . In
> sum, the statement that Jesus acted as and was viewed as an exorcist and healer
> during his public ministry has as much historical corroboration as almost any other
> statement we can make about the Jesus of history.[70]

Therefore, it is clear that Jesus at least thought that he had the power to perform
miracles; and in that the majority of New Testament critics agree.

The miracles of Jesus take on a Christological significance in light of the
fact that they, like his exorcisms, were taken to be signs of the in-breaking of
the kingdom of God.[71] This is the sense of Jesus' allusion to Isaiah 35:5–6; 61:1
above.[72] As such, they functioned fundamentally differently from the wonders
performed by Hellenistic magicians or Jewish holy men. Moreover, Jesus' miracles
differed from those of his compatriots Honi and Hanina in that Jesus never prays
for a miracle to be done; he may first express thanks to the Father, but then he
effects it himself. And he does so in his own name, not God's. Moreover, neither
Honi nor Hanina carried out a prophetic ministry, made messianic claims, or
brought any new teaching in conjunction with their miracles. Thus, Jesus' self-
understanding cannot be reduced simply to that of another charismatic Jewish
holy man.

This is remarkable enough in itself; but there is more. For Jesus' claim to be able
to heal miraculously all diseases and infirmities also contains an implicit claim to
divinity. As Howard Kee, a New Testament scholar from Boston University who
has specialized in the study of the Gospel miracles, explains, for Old Testament
Judaism God is the one who heals all Israel's diseases. In this light, Jesus' claim to
heal miraculously, without use of any medical means, takes on a new significance:

69. James D. G. Dunn, *Jesus and the Spirit* (London: SCM, 1975), 60. On the authenticity of the passage, see Witherington, *Christology of Jesus*, 165.

70. Meier, *Marginal Jew*, 2:969–70.

71. As emphasized by Graham H. Twelftree, *Jesus the Miracle Worker* (Downers Grove, Ill.: InterVarsity,
1999).

72. Witherington points out: "The emphasis here is on the present fulfillment of Old Testament hopes
for the messianic or eschatological age" (Witherington, *Christology of Jesus*, 44; cf. 172).

Jesus in effect takes God's place as the healer of Israel.[73] No doctors or medicine are necessary for him—he heals as God heals. Compare Jesus' claim to have healed lepers with 2 Kings 5:7 (RSV): "When the king of Israel read the letter [from the king of Aram concerning Naaman's leprosy], he rent his clothes and said, 'Am I God, to kill and to make alive, that this man sends word to me to cure a man of his leprosy?'" Jesus assumes the place reserved for God in the Old Testament. So his claim to perform miracles is not only amazing in itself, but actually has a deeper significance in implying Jesus' divinity.

Jesus' Prayer Life

Jesus *always* prayed to God as "Father." The German New Testament scholar Joachim Jeremias demonstrated that such practice is attested in every layer of the Gospel traditions (Mark 14:36; Matt. 11:25–26/Luke 10:21; Matt. 26:42; Luke 23:34, 46; John 12:27–28). Behind the Greek word *pater* for Father lies the Aramaic "*abba*" (Mark 14:36), a familial term. This contrasts with what D. R. Bauer calls "the obsolete and formalized Hebrew term '*abi*,'" typically used in Jewish prayers.[74] Jesus thus thought of himself as God's son in an intimate sense. This same intimate form of address to God appears also in early Christian practice (Rom. 8:15; Gal. 4:6–7), doubtlessly preserved in Greek-speaking churches in imitation of Jesus. Since prayer to God as *abba* was part of Christian practice, the mere use of *abba* cannot be said to indicate a filial relationship to God unique to Jesus. But Jesus' practice is noteworthy in that this expression was original to him and was his consistent and only form of address to God. It is also noteworthy that although Jesus may have taught his disciples to pray to God as *Abba*, he never joined with them in praying "*Our* Father . . ." On the contrary, he always referred to God as "my Father." This distinction leads to an odd circumlocution like John 20:17: "my Father and your Father . . . my God and your God." Jesus' prayer life thus hints that he thought of himself as God's Son in a unique sense that set him apart from the rest of the disciples.

Jesus' Status as Arbiter of People's Eternal Destiny

Jesus held that people's attitudes toward himself would be the determining factor in God's judgment on the judgment day. He proclaimed, "I tell you, every one who acknowledges me before men, the Son of man also will acknowledge before the angels of God; but he who denies me before men will be denied before the angels of God" (Luke 12:8-9 RSV).[75] I have no doubt that in this passage Jesus is referring to himself as the Son of Man, not referring to some third figure besides himself. But be that as it may, the point is that whoever the Son of Man may be, Jesus is claiming that people will be judged before

---

73. Comments made in discussion of Kee's paper at the conference "Christianity Challenges the University," Dallas, Tex., February 1985.

74. *Dictionary of Jesus and the Gospels*, s.v., "Son of God," by D. R. Bauer, p. 772, col. 1.

75. A multiply attested Q-saying, the authenticity of 12:8 is defended by Wolfhart Pannenberg, *Jesus—God and Man*, trans. L. L. Wilkins and D. A. Priebe (London: SCM, 1968), 58–60.

him on the basis of their response to Jesus. Think of it: people's eternal destiny is fixed on their response to Jesus. Make no mistake: if Jesus were not divine, then this claim could only be regarded as the most narrow and objectionable dogmatism. For Jesus is saying that people's salvation depends on their confession to Jesus himself.

A discussion of Jesus' implicit self-concept could go on and on. According to Witherington, any adequate theory of Jesus' self-understanding must be able to explain the following thirteen established features of the historical Jesus:

1) his independent approach to the Law
2) his feeding of the 5,000
3) his interpretation of his miracles
4) his proclamation of the kingdom of God as present and in-breaking in his ministry
5) his choosing of twelve disciples
6) his use of *the Son of Man*
7) his use of *amēn*
8) his use of *abba*
9) his distinguishing himself from his contemporaries, including John the Baptist, the Pharisees, Jewish revolutionaries, and the disciples
10) his belief that one's future standing with God hinged on how one reacted to his ministry
11) his understanding that his death was necessary to rectify matters between God and his people
12) his sense of mission to the whole of Israel, especially to sinners and outcasts, which led to table fellowship with such people
13) his raising messianic expectations in a repeated pattern of controversy with his contemporaries.[76]

Although we have not discussed all these matters, enough has been said, I think, to indicate the radical self-concept of Jesus. Here is a man who thought of himself as the promised Messiah, God's only Son, the Danielic Son of Man to whom all dominion and authority would be given, who claimed to act and speak with divine authority, who held himself to be a worker of miracles, and who believed that people's eternal destiny hinged on whether or not they believed in him. Gruenler sums it up: "It is a striking fact of modern New Testament research that the essential clues for correctly reading the implicit Christological self-understanding of Jesus are abundantly clear." There is, he

76. Witherington, *Christology of Jesus*, 268.

concludes, "absolutely convincing evidence" that Jesus did intend to stand in the very place of God himself.[77]

Horst Georg Pöhlmann in his *Abriss der Dogmatik* reports, "In summary, one could say that today there is virtually a consensus concerning that wherein the historical in Jesus is to be seen. It consists in the fact that Jesus came on the scene with an *unheard of authority*, namely with the authority of God, with the *claim of the authority to stand in God's place and speak to us and bring us to salvation*."[78] This involves, says Pöhlmann, an implicit Christology. He concludes:

> This unheard of claim to authority, as it comes to expression in the antitheses of the Sermon on the Mount, for example, is implicit Christology, since it presupposes a unity of Jesus with God that is deeper than that of all men, namely a unity of essence. This . . . claim to authority is explicable only from the side of his deity. This authority only God himself can claim. With regard to Jesus there are only two possible modes of behavior: either to believe that in him God encounters us or to nail him to the cross as a blasphemer. *Tertium non datur*.[79]

There is no third way.[80]

Conclusion

Explicit use of Christological titles like Messiah, the Son of God, and especially the Son of Man, combined with implicit Christological claims made through his teaching and behavior indicates a radical self-understanding on the part of Jesus of Nazareth. Indeed, so extraordinary was the person who Jesus thought himself to be that Dunn at the end of his study of the self-consciousness of Jesus feels compelled to remark, "One last question cannot be ignored: Was Jesus mad?"[81] Dunn rejects the hypothesis that Jesus was insane because it cannot account for the full portrait of Jesus that we have in the Gospels. The balance and soundness of Jesus' whole life and teachings make it evident that he was no lunatic. But notice that by means of these claims of Jesus, on the basis of sayings shown to be authentic, we are brought round again to the same dilemma posed by the traditional apologetic: if Jesus was not who he claimed to be, then he was either a charlatan or a madman, neither of which is plausible. Therefore, why not accept him as the divine Son of God, just as the earliest Christians did?

77. Gruenler, *New Approaches to Jesus and the Gospels*, 74.
78. Horst Georg Pöhlmann, *Abriss der Dogmatik*, 3rd rev. ed. (Düsseldorf: Patmos Verlag, 1966), 230.
79. Ibid.
80. I'm grateful to Robert Bowman, Charles Quarles, and Craig Evans for their helpful suggestions on this section.
81. Dunn, *Jesus and the Spirit*, 86.

Practical Application

It is intellectually gratifying to see how contemporary New Testament criticism has actually served to support rather than undermine a high view of Christ. The refusal of radical critics to draw the obvious Christological implications of unquestionably authentic sayings of Jesus is due not to lack of historical evidence but to their personal anti-metaphysical and, quite frankly, anti-Chalcedonian prejudices. The evidence thus vindicates the approach of the traditional apologetic.

But here a word of caution would be in order. Often one hears people say, "I don't understand all those philosophical arguments for God's existence and so forth. I prefer historical apologetics." I suspect that those who say this think that historical apologetics is easy and will enable them to avoid the hard thinking involved in the philosophical arguments. But this section ought to teach us clearly that this is not so. It is naïve and outdated simply to trot out the dilemma "Liar, Lunatic, or Lord" and adduce several proof texts where Jesus claims to be the Son of God, the Messiah, and so forth. The publicity generated by the Jesus Seminar and *The DaVinci Code* has rendered that approach forever obsolete. Rather, if an apologetic based on the claims of Christ is to work, we must do the requisite spadework of sorting out those claims of Jesus that can be established as authentic, and then drawing out their implications. This will involve not only mastering Greek but also the methods of modern criticism and the criteria of authenticity. Far from being easy, historical apologetics, if done right, is every bit as difficult as philosophical apologetics. The only reason most people think historical apologetics to be easier is because they do it superficially. But, of course, one can do philosophical apologetics superficially, too! My point is that if we are to do a credible job in our apologetics, we need to do the hard thinking and the hard work required, or at least to rely on those who have.

Now in applying this material in evangelism, I think it is often more effective when used defensively than offensively. That is to say, if the unbeliever says Jesus was just a good man or religious teacher, then confront him with Christ's claims. Used offensively to convince someone that Jesus was divine, this apologetic can be derouted on the popular level. Many people will say Jesus was a man from outer space, and the more you argue with them the more they become entrenched in this position. Of course, such a view is hopelessly kooky, so that, oddly enough, this apologetic is probably more effective on the scholarly level than on the popular.

I think that a more effective approach is to argue that Jesus' claims provide the religio-historical context in which his resurrection becomes significant, as it vindicates those claims. Of course, the non-Christian might still say Jesus was from outer space and came back to life like E. T., in which case the most effective strategy is not to argue with him at all but just to point out that no scholar believes such a thing. If you argue with him, this gives the impression that his view is worth refuting and therefore has some credibility, which it does not. So simply brush it aside, and it is to be hoped that the unbeliever, not wishing to feel intellectually isolated, will not take it too seriously either. Taken in conjunction with evidence for the resurrection—and one might add, with the evidence for Jesus' miracles and with fulfilled prophecy, which I have not discussed—the radical claims of Jesus become a powerful apologetic for the Christian faith.

Literature Cited or Recommended

Historical Background

Bartsch, Hans-Werner, ed. *Kerygma and Myth*. 2 vols. Translated by R. H. Fuller. London: SPCK, 1953.

Ben-Chorin, S. *Jesus in Judenthum*. Wuppetal: R. Brockhaus, 1970.

Bultmann, Rudolph. *Jesus*. Tübingen: J. C. B. Mohr, 1951.

Evans, Craig A. "Authenticity Criteria in Life of Jesus Research," *Christian Scholar's Review* 19 (1989): 6–31.

———. "Life-of-Jesus Research and the Eclipse of Mythology." *Theological Studies* 54 (1993): 3–36.

Funk, Robert W. and Roy W. Hoover, eds. *The Five Gospels: What Did Jesus Really Say?* New York: Macmillan, 1993.

Hagner, Donald A. *The Jewish Reclamation of Jesus*. Grand Rapids, Mich.: Zondervan, 1984.

Hemer, Colin. *The Book of Acts in the Setting of Hellenistic History*. Edited by Conrad H. Gempf, Wissenschaftliche Untersuchungen zum Neuen Testament 49. Tübingen: J. C. B. Mohr, 1989.

Hooker, Morna. "On Using the Wrong Tool." *Theology* 75 (1972): 570–81.

Kissinger, W. S. *The Lives of Jesus: A History and Bibliography*. New York: Garland, 1985.

Marshall, I. Howard. *I Believe in the Historical Jesus*. Grand Rapids, Mich.: Eerdmans, 1977.

Paulus, Heinrich Eberh. Gottlob. *Das Leben Jesu, als Grundlage einer reinen Geschichte des Urchristentums*. 2 vols. Heidelberg: C. F. Winter, 1828.

Robinson, James. *A New Quest of the Historical Jesus*. Studies in Biblical Theology 25. London: SCM, 1959.

Schweitzer, Albert. *The Quest of the Historical Jesus*. 3rd ed. Translated by W. Montgomery. London: Adam & Charles Black, 1954.

Sherwin-White, A. N. *Roman Society and Roman Law in the New Testament*. Oxford: Clarendon, 1963.

Stein, Robert H. "The Criteria for Authenticity." In *Gospel Perspectives I*, edited by R. T. France and David Wenham, 225–53. Sheffield, England: JSOT Press, 1980.

Strauss, David Friedrich. *The Life of Jesus Critically Examined*. Translated by G. Eliot. Edited with an introduction by P. C. Hodgson. Lives of Jesus Series. London: SCM, 1973.

Wrede, William. *The Messianic Secret*. Translated by J. O. G. Greig. Cambridge: James Clarke, 1971.

Assessment

Am, Ahad, ha'-. "Judaism and the Gospels." In *Nationalism and the Jewish Ethic*, edited by H. Kohn. New York: Schocken Books, 1962.

Blackburn, Barry L. "Miracle Working in Hellenism and Hellenistic Judaism." In *Gospel Perspectives VI*, edited by David Wenham and Craig Blomberg, 185–218. Sheffield, England: JSOT Press, 1986.

Bock, Darrell L. *Blasphemy and Exaltation in Judaism and the Final Examination of Jesus.* Wissenschaftliche Untersuchungen zum Neuen Testament 106. Tübingen: J. C. B. Mohr, 1998; repr. ed.: *Blasphemy and Exaltation in Judaism: The Charge against Jesus in Mark 14:53–65.* Biblical Studies Library. Grand Rapids, Mich.: Baker, 2000.

Bultmann, Rudolph. *Jesus and the Word.* New York: Scribner's Sons, 1934.

Collins, John J. *The Scepter and the Star: The Messiahs of the Dead Sea Scrolls and Other Ancient Literature.* Anchor Bible Reference Library. New York: Doubleday, 1995.

Crossan, John Dominic. *The Historical Jesus: The Life of a Mediterranean Jewish Peasant.* Edinburgh: T. & T. Clark, 1991.

Denaux, Adelbert. "The Q-Logion Mt 11,27/Lk 10,22 and the Gospel of John." In *John and the Synoptics*, edited by A. Denaux. Bibliotheca Ephemeridum Theologicarum Lovaniensium 101. Leuven, Belgium: Leuven University Press, 1992.

Dictionary of Jesus and the Gospels. Edited by Joel B. Green, Scot McKnight, and I. Howard Marshall. Downers Grove, Ill.: InterVarsity, 1992. A compendium of scholarship on the historical Jesus which ought to be on every Christian apologist's shelf.

Dictionary of Jesus and the Gospels. S.v. "Son of God," by D. R. Bauer.

Dunn, James D.G. "Can the Third Quest Hope to Succeed?" In *Authenticating the Activities of Jesus*, edited by Bruce Chilton and Craig Evans, 31–48. New Testament Tools and Studies 28/2. Leiden: E. J. Brill, 1999.

———. *Christianity in the Making.* Vol. 1: *Jesus Remembered.* Grand Rapids, Mich.: Eerdmans, 2003.

———. *Jesus and the Spirit.* London: SCM, 1975.

Ellis, E. E. "Dating the New Testament." *New Testament Studies* 26 (1980): 487–502.

Evans, Craig A. "Authenticating the Activities of Jesus." In *Authenticating the Activities of Jesus*, edited by Bruce Chilton and Craig Evans, 3–29. New Testament Tools and Studies 28/2. Leiden: E. J. Brill, 1999.

———. "Authenticity Criteria in Life of Jesus Research." *Christian Scholar's Review* 19 (1989): 6–31.

———. *Fabricating Jesus.* Downers Grove, Ill.: InterVarsity, 2006.

———. *Jesus and His Contemporaries: Comparative Studies.* Leiden: Brill, 2001.

———. "Jesus and Zechariah's Messianic Hope." In *Authenticating the Activities of Jesus*, edited by Bruce Chilton and Craig Evans, 373–88. New Testament Tools and Studies 28/2. Leiden: E. J. Brill, 1999.

———. "Life-of-Jesus Research and the Eclipse of Mythology." *Theological Studies* 54 (1993): 3–36.

———. "What Did Jesus Do?" In *Jesus under Fire*, edited by J. P.Moreland and Michael J. Wilkins, 101–11. Grand Rapids, Mich.: Zondervan, 1995.

Funk, Robert W. "The Issue of Jesus." *Forum* 1 (1985): 7–12.

Funk, Robert W. and Roy W. Hoover, eds. *The Five Gospels: What Did Jesus Really Say?* New York: Macmillan, 1993.

Green, Michael. "Jesus and Historical Skepticism." In *The Truth of God Incarnate*, edited by M. Green, 107–39. Grand Rapids, Mich.: Eerdmans, 1977.

———. "Jesus in the New Testament." In *The Truth of God Incarnate*, edited by M. Green, 17–57. Grand Rapids, Mich.: Eerdmans, 1977.

Gruenler, Royce Gordon. *New Approaches to Jesus and the Gospels*. Grand Rapids, Mich.: Baker, 1982.

Guelich, Robert. *Sermon on the Mount*. Waco, Tex.: Word, 1982.

Gundry, Robert H. *Mark: A Commentary on His Apology for the Cross*. Grand Rapids, Mich.: Eerdmans, 1993.

Hagner, Donald A. *The Jewish Reclamation of Jesus*. Grand Rapids, Mich.: Zondervan, 1984.

Hemer, Colin. *The Book of Acts in the Setting of Hellenistic History*. Edited by Conrad H. Gempf. Wissenschaftliche Untersuchungen zum Neuen Testament 49. Tübingen: J. C. B. Mohr, 1989.

Hengel, Martin. "Jesus, the Messiah of Israel: The Debate about the 'Messianic Mission' of Jesus." In *Authenticating the Activities of Jesus*, edited by Bruce Chilton and Craig Evans, 323–49. New Testament Tools and Studies 28/2. Leiden: E. J. Brill, 1999.

———. *The Son of God: The Origin of Christology and the History of Jewish–Hellenistic Religion*. Translated by John Bowden. Philadelphia: Fortress, 1976.

Hick, John, ed. *The Myth of God Incarnate*. London: SCM, 1977.

Hooker, Morna. "On Using the Wrong Tool." *Theology* 75 (1972): 570–81.

Hurtado, Larry W. *Lord Jesus Christ: Devotion to Jesus in Earliest Christianity*. Grand Rapids, Mich.: Eerdmans, 2003.

Hutchinson, Robert J. "What the Rabbi Taught Me about Jesus." *Christianity Today*, September 13, 1993, 27–29.

Jeremias, Joachim. *The Central Message of the New Testament*. London: SCM, 1965.

———. *The Prayers of Jesus*. Translated by John Burchard. London: SCM, 1967.

Kim, Seyoon. *The Son of Man as the Son of God*. Grand Rapids, Mich.: Eerdmans, 1985.

Marshall, I. Howard. *The Origins of New Testament Christology*. Downers Grove, Ill.: Inter-Varsity, 1976.

Meier, John P. *A Marginal Jew*. 3 vols. Anchor Bible Reference Library. New York: Doubleday, 1991, 1994, 2001.

Meyer, Ben F. *The Aims of Jesus*. London: SCM, 1979.

Moreland, J. P. and Michael J. Wilkins, eds. *Jesus under Fire*. Grand Rapids, Mich.: Zondervan, 1995.

Moule, C. F. D. *The Origins of Christology*. Cambridge: Cambridge University Press, 1977.

Pannenberg, Wolfhart. *Jesus—God and Man.* Translated by L. L. Wilkins and D. A. Priebe. London: SCM, 1968.

Pelikan, Jaroslav. *The Christian Tradition: A History of the Development of Doctrine.* Vol. 1: *The Emergence of the Catholic Tradition (100–600).* Chicago: University of Chicago Press, 1971.

Pöhlmann, Horst Georg. *Abriss der Dogmatik.* 3rd rev. ed. Gütersloh: Gerd Mohn, 1980.

Quarles, Charles L. "The Use of the Gospel of Thomas in the Research on Historical Jesus of John Dominic Crossan." *Catholic Biblical Quarterly* 69 (2007): 517–36.

Riesner, Rainer. *Jesus als Lehrer.* Wissenschaftliche Untersuchungen zum Neuen Testament 2/7. Tübingen: J. C. B. Mohr, 1984.

Sherwin-White, A. N. *Roman Law and Roman Society in the New Testament.* Oxford: Clarendon, 1963.

Stein, Robert H. "The Criteria for Authenticity." In *Gospel Perspectives I*, edited by R. T. France and David Wenham, 225–63. Sheffield, England: JSOT Press, 1980.

Taylor, Vincent. *The Gospel according to St. Mark.* 2nd ed. London: Macmillan, 1966.

Trilling, Wolfgang. *Fragen zur Geschichtlichkeit Jesu.* Düsseldorf: Patmos Verlag, 1966.

Twelftree, Graham H. *Jesus the Miracle Worker.* Downers Grove, Ill.: InterVarsity, 1999.

Witherington III, Ben. *The Christology of Jesus.* Minneapolis: Fortress Press, 1990.

Wright, N. T. *Christian Origins and the Question of God.* 3 vols. Minneapolis: Fortress Press, 1992, 1996, 2003.

Yamauchi, Edwin. "Magic or Miracle? Diseases, Demons, and Exorcisms." In *Gospel Perspectives VI*, edited by David Wenham and Craig Blomberg, 89–183. Sheffield, England: JSOT Press, 1986.

Zager, Werner and Hans Rollmann. "Unveröffentlichte Briefe William Wredes zur Problematisierung des messianischen Selbstverständnisses Jesu." *Zeitschrift für neuere Theologiegeschichte* 8 (2001): 274–322.

8

The Resurrection of Jesus

God and immortality: those were the two conditions we saw to be necessary if man is to have a meaningful existence. I have argued that God exists, and now we have come at length to the second consideration, immortality. Against the dark background of modern man's despair, the Christian proclamation of the resurrection is a bright light of hope. The earliest Christians saw Jesus' resurrection as both the vindication of his personal claims and the harbinger of our own resurrection to eternal life. If Jesus rose from the dead, then his claims are vindicated and our Christian hope is sure; if Jesus did not rise, our faith is futile and we fall back into despair. How credible, then, is the New Testament witness to the resurrection of Jesus?

Historical Background
The historical apologetic for the resurrection played a central role in the case of the Christian apologists during the Deist controversy. A review of their arguments and of the reasons for the decline of this form of apologetics will be useful in preparing the way for a contemporary assessment of the resurrection. Too often Christians today employ an apologetic for the resurrection that was suitable for use against eighteenth-century opponents but is today ineffective in dealing with the objections raised by modern biblical criticism.

The Case for the Resurrection in the Traditional Apologetic

The traditional apologetic may be summarized in three steps.

THE GOSPELS ARE AUTHENTIC

The point of this step in the argument was to defend the apostolic authorship of the Gospels. The reasoning was that if the Gospels were actually written by the disciples, then quite simply they were either true accounts or they were lies. Since the Deists granted the apostolic authorship of the Gospels, they were reduced to defending the implausible position that the Gospels were a tissue of deliberate falsehoods. In order to demonstrate the authenticity of the Gospels, Jacob Vernet (whom we met in chapter 4) appeals to both internal and external evidence.

Internal Evidence

Under internal evidence, Vernet notes that the style of writing in the Gospels is simple and alive, what we would expect from their traditionally accepted authors. Moreover, since Luke was written before Acts, and since Acts was written prior to the death of Paul, Luke must have an early date, which speaks for its authenticity. The Gospels also show an intimate knowledge of Jerusalem prior to its destruction in A.D. 70. Jesus' prophecies of that event must have been written prior to Jerusalem's fall, for otherwise the church would have separated out the apocalyptic element in the prophecies, which makes them appear to concern the end of the world. Since the end of the world did not come about when Jerusalem was destroyed, so-called prophecies of its destruction that were really written after the city was destroyed would not have made that event appear so closely connected with the end of the world. Hence, the Gospels must have been written prior to A.D. 70. Further, the Gospels are full of proper names, dates, cultural details, historical events, and customs and opinions of that time. The stories of Jesus' human weaknesses and of the disciples' faults also bespeak the Gospels' accuracy. Furthermore, it would have been impossible for forgers to put together so consistent a narrative as that which we find in the Gospels. The Gospels do not try to suppress apparent discrepancies, which indicates their originality. There is no attempt at harmonization between the Gospels, such as we might expect from forgers. Finally, the style of each particular gospel is appropriate to what we know of the personalities of the traditional authors.

Gottfried Less adds to Vernet's case the further point that the Gospels do not contain anachronisms; the authors appear to have been first-century Jews who were witnesses of the events. William Paley adds a final consideration: the Hebraic and Syriac idioms that mark the Gospels are appropriate to the traditional authors. He concludes that there is no more reason to doubt that the Gospels come from the traditional authors than there is to doubt that the works of Philo or Josephus are authentic, *except* that the Gospels contain supernatural events.

External Evidence

Turning next to the external evidence for the Gospels' authenticity, Vernet argues that the disciples must have left some writings, engaged as they were in giving lessons to and counseling believers who were geographically distant. And what could these writings be if not the Gospels and Epistles themselves? Similarly, Paley reasons that eventually the apostles would have needed to publish accurate narratives of Jesus' history, so that any spurious attempts would be discredited and the genuine Gospels preserved. Moreover, Vernet continues, there were many eyewitnesses who were still alive when the books were written who could testify whether they came from their purported authors or not. Most importantly, the extra-biblical testimony unanimously attributes the Gospels to their traditional authors.

No finer presentation of this point can be found than Paley's extensive eleven-point argument. First, the Gospels and Acts are cited by a series of authors, beginning with those contemporary with the apostles and continuing in regular and close succession. This is the strongest form of historical testimony, regularly employed to establish authorship of secular works; and when this test is applied to the Gospels, their authenticity is unquestionably established. Paley traces this chain of testimony from the Epistle of Barnabas, the Epistle of Clement, and the Shepherd of Hermas all the way up to Eusebius in A.D. 315. Less presents similar evidence, and concludes that there is better testimony for the authenticity of the New Testament books than for *any* classical work of antiquity.

Second, the Scriptures were quoted as authoritative and as one-of-a-kind. As proof Paley cites Theophilus, the writer against Artemon, Hippolitus, Origen, and many others.

Third, the Scriptures were collected very early into a distinct volume. Ignatius refers to collections known as the Gospel and the Apostles, what we today call the Gospels and the Epistles. According to Eusebius, about sixty years after the appearance of the Gospels Quadratus distributed them to converts during his travels. Irenaeus and Melito refer to the collection of writings we call the New Testament.

Fourth, these writings were given titles of respect. Polycarp, Justin Martyr, Dionysius, Irenaeus, and others refer to them as Scriptures, divine writings, and so forth.

Fifth, these writings were publicly read and expounded. Citations from Justin Martyr, Tertullian, Origen, and Cyprian go to prove the point.

Sixth, copies, commentaries, and harmonies were written on these books. Noteworthy in this connection is Tatian's *Diatessaron*, a harmony of the four Gospels, from about A.D. 170. With the single exception of Clement's commentary on the Revelation of Peter, Paley emphasizes, no commentary was ever written during the first three hundred years after Christ on any book outside the New Testament.

Seventh, the Scriptures were accepted by all heretical groups as well as by orthodox Christians. Examples include the Valentinians, the Carpocratians, and many others.

Eighth, the Gospels, Acts, thirteen letters of Paul, 1 John, and 1 Peter were received without doubt as authentic even by those who doubted the authenticity of other books now in the canon. Caius about A.D. 200 reckoned up about thirteen of Paul's letters but insisted that Hebrews was not written by Paul. About twenty years later Origen cites Hebrews to prove a particular point, but noting that some might dispute the authority of Hebrews, he states that his point may be proved from the undisputed books of Scripture and quotes Matthew and Acts. Though he expresses doubt about some books, Origen reports that the four Gospels alone were received without dispute by the whole church of God under heaven.

Ninth, the early opponents of Christianity regarded the Gospels as containing the accounts upon which the religion was founded. Celsus admitted that the Gospels were written by the disciples. Porphyry attacked Christianity as found in the Gospels. The Emperor Julian followed the same procedure.

Tenth, catalogues of authentic Scriptures were published, which always contained the Gospels and Acts. Paley supports the point with quotations from Origen, Athanasius, Cyril, and others.

Eleventh, the so-called apocryphal books of the New Testament were never so treated. It is a simple fact, asserts Paley, that with a single exception, no apocryphal gospel is ever even quoted by any known author during the first three hundred years after Christ. In fact, there is no evidence that any inauthentic gospel whatever existed in the first century, in which all four Gospels and Acts were written. The apocryphal gospels were never quoted, were not read in Christian assemblies, were not collected into a volume, were not listed in the catalogues, were not noticed by Christianity's adversaries, were not appealed to by heretics, and were not the subject of commentaries or collations, but were nearly universally rejected by Christian writers of succeeding ages.

Therefore, Paley concludes, the external evidence strongly confirms the authenticity of the Gospels. Even if it should be the case that the names of the authors traditionally ascribed to the Gospels are mistaken, it still could not be denied that the Gospels do contain the story that the original apostles proclaimed and for which they labored and suffered.

Taken together, then, the internal and external evidence adduced by the Christian apologists served to establish the first step of their case, that the gospels are authentic.

THE TEXT OF THE GOSPELS IS PURE

The second step often taken by the Christian thinkers was to argue that the text of the Gospels is pure. This step was important to ensure that the Gospels we have today are the same Gospels as originally written.

Vernet, in support of the textual purity of the Gospels, points out that because of the need for instruction and personal devotion, these writings must have been copied many times, which increases the chances of preserving the original text. In fact, no other ancient work is available in so many copies and languages, and yet all these various versions agree in content. The text has also remained unmarred by heretical additions. The abundance of manuscripts over a wide geographical distribution demonstrates that the text has been transmitted with only trifling discrepancies. The differences that do exist are quite minor and are the result of unintentional mistakes. The text of the New Testament is every bit as good as the text of the classical works of antiquity.

To these considerations, Less adds that the quotations of the New Testament books in the early church fathers coincide. Moreover, the Gospels could not have been corrupted without a great outcry on the part of orthodox Christians. Against the idea that there could have been a deliberate falsifying of the text, Abbé Houtteville argues that no one could have corrupted all the manuscripts. Moreover, there is no precise time when the falsification could have occurred, since, as we have seen, the New Testament books are cited by the church fathers in regular and close succession. The text could not have been falsified before all external testimony, since then the apostles were still alive and could repudiate any such tampering with the Gospels. In conclusion, Vernet charges that to repudiate the textual purity of the Gospels would be to reverse all the rules of criticism and to reject all the works of antiquity, since the text of those works is less certain than that of the Gospels.

THE GOSPELS ARE RELIABLE

Having demonstrated that the Gospels are authentic and that the text of the Gospels is pure, the Christian thinkers were now in a position to argue that the Gospels are historically reliable. Their argument basically boiled down to a dilemma: if the Gospel accounts of Jesus' miracles and resurrection are false, then the apostles were either deceivers or deceived. Since both of these alternatives are implausible, it follows that the Gospel accounts must be true.

Apostles Neither Deceivers Nor Deceived

Let's turn first to the arguments presented against the second horn of the dilemma: that the apostles were deceived. This alternative embraces any hypothesis holding that Jesus did not rise from the dead, but that the disciples sincerely believed he had.

Humphrey Ditton in his *Discourse Concerning the Resurrection of Jesus Christ* (1712) argues that the apostles could not have been mistaken about the resurrection. In the first place, the witnesses to the appearances were well qualified. There were a great many witnesses, and they had personal knowledge of the facts over an extended period of forty days. It is unreasonable, therefore, to ascribe their experience to imagination or dreaming. Moreover, the disciples were not religious enthusiasts, as is evident from their cool and balanced behavior even in extreme situations. Thomas Sherlock responds to the charge that the evidence for the resurrection consists of the testimony of silly women by pointing out that they, too, had eyes and ears to report accurately what they experienced; and far from being gullible, they were actually disbelieving. He observes also that the women were never in fact used as witnesses to the resurrection in the apostolic preaching. Finally, he adds, the testimony of the men is none the worse off for having the testimony of the women as well. (This exchange obviously took place before the days of feminist consciousness!)

Paley answers the allegation that the resurrection appearances were the result of "religious enthusiasm" (that is, were hallucinations) by arguing that the theory fails on several counts. First, not just one person but many saw Christ appear. Second, they saw him not individually but together. Third, they saw him appear not just once, but several times. Fourth, they not only saw him, but touched him, conversed with him, and ate with him. Fifth and decisively, the religious enthusiasm hypothesis fails to explain the non-production of the body. It would have been impossible for Jesus' disciples to have believed in their master's resurrection if his corpse still lay in the tomb. But it is equally incredible to suppose that the disciples could have stolen the body and perpetrated a hoax. Furthermore, it would have been impossible for Christianity to come into being in Jerusalem if Jesus' body were still in the grave. The Jewish authorities would certainly have produced it as the shortest and completest answer to the whole affair. But all they could do was claim that the disciples had stolen the body. Thus, the hypothesis of religious enthusiasm, in failing to explain the absence of Jesus' corpse, ultimately collapses back into the hypothesis of conspiracy and deceit, which, Paley remarks, has pretty much been given up in view of the evident sincerity of the apostles, as well as their character and the dangers they underwent in proclaiming the truth of Jesus' resurrection.

With Paley's last remark, we return to the first horn of the dilemma: that the disciples were deceivers. This alternative encompasses any hypothesis holding that the disciples knew that the miracles and resurrection of Jesus did not take place, but that they nevertheless claimed that they did.

One of the most popular arguments against this theory is the obvious sincerity of the disciples as attested by their suffering and death. No more eloquent statement of the argument can be found than Paley's: he seeks to show that the original witnesses of the miraculous events of the Gospels passed their lives in labors, dangers, and sufferings, voluntarily undertaken in attestation to and as a consequence of the accounts which they delivered.

Paley argues first from the general nature of the case. We know that the Christian religion exists. Either it was founded by Jesus and the apostles or by others, the first being silent. The second alternative is quite incredible. If the disciples had not zealously followed up what Jesus had started, Christianity would have died at its birth. If this is so, then a life of missionary sacrifice must have been necessary for those first apostles. Such a life is not without its own enjoyments, but they are only such as spring from sincerity. With a consciousness at bottom of hollowness and falsehood, the fatigue and strain would have become unbearable.

There was probably difficulty and danger involved in the propagation of a new religion. With regard to the Jews, the notion of Jesus' being the Messiah was contrary to Jewish hopes and expectations; Christianity lowered the esteem of Jewish law; and the disciples would have had to reproach the Jewish leaders as guilty of an execution that could only be represented as an unjust and cruel murder. As to the Romans, they could have understood the kingdom of God only in terms of an earthly kingdom—thus, a rival. And concerning the heathen, Christianity admitted no other god or worship. Although the philosophers allowed and even enjoined worship of state deities, Christianity could countenance no such accommodation. Thus, even in the absence of a general program of persecution, there were probably random outbursts of violence against Christians. The heathen religions were old and established and not easily overthrown. Those religions were generally regarded by the common people as equally true, by the philosophers as equally false, and by the magistrates as equally useful. From none of these sides could the Christians expect protection. Finally, the nature of the case requires that these early apostles must have experienced a great change in their lives, now involved as they were in preaching, prayer, religious meetings, and so forth.

What the nature of the case would seem to require is in fact confirmed by history. Writing seventy years after Jesus' death, Tacitus narrates Nero's persecution about thirty years after Christ, how the Christians were clothed in the skins of wild beasts and thrown to dogs, how others were smeared with pitch and used as human torches to illuminate the night while Nero rode about in the dress of a charioteer, viewing the spectacle. The testimonies of Suetonius and Juvenal confirm the fact that within thirty-one years after Jesus' death, Christians were dying for their faith. From the writings of Pliny the Younger, Martial, Epictetus, and Marcus Aurelius, it is clear that believers were voluntarily submitting to torture and death rather than renounce their religion. This suffering is abundantly attested in Christian writings as well. Christ had been killed for what he said; the apostles could expect the same treatment. Jesus' predictions in the Gospels of sufferings for his followers were either real predictions come true or were put into his mouth because persecution had in fact come about. In Acts, the sufferings of Christians are soberly reported without extravagance. The epistles abound with references to persecutions and exhortations to steadfastness. In the early writings of Clement, Hermas, Polycarp, and Ignatius, we find the sufferings of the early believers historically confirmed.

It is equally clear that it was for a *miraculous* story that these Christians were suffering. After all, the only thing that could convince these early Christians that Jesus was the Messiah was that they *thought* there was something supernatural about him. The Gospels are a miraculous story, and we have no other story handed down to us than that contained in the Gospels. Josephus's much disputed testimony can only confirm, not contradict, the Gospel accounts. The letters of Barnabas and Clement refer to Jesus' miracles and resurrection. Polycarp mentions the resurrection of Christ, and Irenaeus relates that he had heard Polycarp tell of Jesus' miracles. Ignatius speaks of the resurrection. Quadratus reports that persons were still living who had been healed by Jesus. Justin Martyr mentions the miracles of Christ. No relic of a non-miraculous story exists. That the original story should be lost and replaced by another goes beyond any known example of corruption of even oral tradition, not to speak of the experience of written transmissions.

These facts show that the story in the Gospels was in substance the same story that Christians had at the beginning. That means, for example, that the resurrection of Jesus was always a part of this story. Were we to stop here, remarks Paley, we have a circumstance unparalleled in history: that in the reign of Tiberius Caesar a certain number of persons set about establishing a new religion, in the propagation of which they voluntarily submitted to great dangers, sufferings, and labors, all for a miraculous story which they proclaimed wherever they went, and that the resurrection of a dead man, whom they had accompanied during his lifetime, was an integral part of this story.

Since it has been already abundantly proved that the accounts of the Gospels do stem from their apostolic authors, Paley concludes, then the story must be true. For the apostles could not be deceivers. He asks:

> Would men in such circumstances pretend to have seen what they never saw; assert facts which they had not knowledge of, go about lying to teach virtue; and, though not only convinced of Christ's being an imposter, but having seen the success of his imposture in his crucifixion, yet persist in carrying on; and so persist, as to bring upon themselves, for nothing, and with full knowledge of the consequence, enmity and hatred, danger and death?[1]

The question is merely rhetorical, for the absurdity of the hypothesis of deceit is all too clear.

A second popular argument against the disciples' being deceivers was that their character precludes their being liars. Humphrey Ditton observes that the apostles were simple, common men, not cunning deceivers. They were men of unquestioned moral integrity and their proclamation of the resurrection was solemn and devout. They had absolutely nothing to gain in worldly terms in preaching this doctrine. Moreover, they had been raised in a religion that was vastly different from the one they preached. Especially foreign to them was the idea of the death and resurrection of the Jewish Messiah. This militates against their concocting this idea. The Jewish laws against deceit and false testimony were very severe, which fact would act as a deterrent to fraud. Finally, they were evidently sincere in what they

---

1. William Paley, *A View of the Evidences of Christianity*, 2 vols., 5th ed. (London: R. Faulder, 1796; repr. ed.: Westmead, England: Gregg, 1970), 1:327–28.

proclaimed. In light of their character so described, asks Ditton bluntly, *why not believe the testimony of these men?*

A third argument pressed by the apologists was that the notion of a conspiracy is ridiculous. Vernet thinks it inconceivable that one of the disciples should suggest to the others that they say Jesus was risen when both he and they knew the precise opposite to be true. How could he possibly rally his bewildered colleagues into so detestable a project? And are we then to believe that these men would stand before judges declaring the truth of this product of their imaginations? Houtteville asserts that a conspiracy to fake the resurrection would have had to have been of such unmanageable proportions that the disciples could never have carried it off. Ditton points out that had there been a conspiracy, it would certainly have been unearthed by the disciples' adversaries, who had both the interest and the power to expose any fraud. Common experience shows that such intrigues are inevitably exposed even in cases where the chances of discovery are much less than in the case of the resurrection.

Yet a fourth argument, urged by Less, was that the Gospels were written in such temporal and geographical proximity to the events they record that it would have been almost impossible to fabricate events. Anyone who cared to could have checked out the accuracy of what they reported. The fact that the disciples were able to proclaim the resurrection in Jerusalem in the face of their enemies a few weeks after the crucifixion shows that what they proclaimed was true, for they could never have proclaimed the resurrection under such circumstances had it not occurred.

Fifth, the theft of the body from the tomb by the disciples would have been impossible. Ditton argues that the story of the guard at the tomb is plausible, since the Jews had the ability and motivation to guard the tomb. But in this case, the disciples could not have stolen the body on account of the armed guard. The allegation that the guards had fallen asleep is ridiculous, because in that case they could not have known that it was the disciples who had taken the corpse. Besides, adds Houtteville, no one could have broken into the tomb without waking the guard.

Sixth, even the enemies of Christianity acknowledged Jesus' resurrection. The Jews did not publicly deny the disciples' charge that the authorities had bribed the guard to keep silent. Had the charge been false, they would have openly denounced it. Thus, the enemies of Christianity themselves bore witness to the resurrection.

Seventh and finally, the dramatic change in the disciples shows that they were absolutely convinced Jesus had risen from the dead. They went from the depths of despair and doubt to a joyful certainty of such height that they preached the resurrection openly and boldly and suffered bravely for it.

Thus, the hypothesis of deceit is just as implausible as the hypothesis that the apostles had been deceived. But since neither of these alternatives is reasonable, the conclusion can only be that they were telling the truth and that Jesus rose from the dead.

The Origin of Christianity Proves the Resurrection

In addition to this fundamental dilemma, the Christian apologists also refurbished the old argument from the origin of the church. Suppose, Vernet suggests, that no resurrection or miracles occurred: how then could a dozen men, poor, coarse, and apprehensive, turn the world upside down? If Jesus did not rise from the dead, declares Ditton, then either we must believe that a small, unlearned band of deceivers overcame the powers of the world and preached an incredible doctrine over the face of the whole earth, which in turn received this fiction as the sacred truth of God; or else, if they were not deceivers, but enthusiasts, we must believe that these extremists, carried along by the impetus of extravagant fancy, managed to spread a falsity that not only common folk, but statesmen and philosophers as well, embraced as the sober truth. Because such a scenario is simply unbelievable, the message of the apostles, which gave birth to Christianity, must be true.

The Decline of Historical Apologetics

Paley's *View of the Evidences* (1794) constituted the high-water mark of the historical apologetic for the resurrection. During the nineteenth century this approach dramatically receded. Indeed, it would be difficult to find a significant and influential thinker defending the Christian faith on the basis of the evidence for the resurrection. It seems to me that there were two factors that served to undermine the traditional apologetic.

THE ADVANCE OF BIBLICAL CRITICISM

The first of those was the advance of biblical criticism. In England the Deist controversy subsided, in France it was cut short by the Revolution, but in Germany it was taken up into a higher plane. There is a direct link between Deism and the advance in biblical criticism that began in Germany in the late eighteenth century.

The flood of Deist thought and literature that poured into eighteenth-century Germany from England and France wrought a crisis in German orthodox theology. That theology had been characterized by an extremely rigid doctrine of biblical inspiration and infallibility and by a devotional pietism. The critique of the Deists undermined the faith of many in the inerrancy of Scripture, but their piety would not allow them to join themselves to the Deist camp and reject Christianity. This group of scholars, generally called Rationalists, therefore sought to resolve the crisis by forging a new way between orthodoxy and Deism; namely, they loosed the religious meaning of a text from the historicity of the events described therein. The historical events were only the form, the husk, in which some spiritual, transhistorical truth was embodied. What was of importance was the substance, the kernel, not the mere external trappings. In this way, the Rationalists could accept the Deist critique of miracles but at the same time retain the spiritual truth expressed in these stories. With regard to the resurrection we have seen that many Rationalists adopted some form of the apparent death theory to explain away the resurrection; but for most it still retained its spiritual significance and truth.

The Rationalists thus sought a middle ground between the Deists and the supernaturalists. The Deists and supernaturalists agreed that if the events of the Gospels did not in fact occur, then Christianity was false. But the Rationalists, while holding with the Deists that the events never occurred, nevertheless held with the supernaturalists that Christianity was true. Let's take a look at two of the principal figures in this radical new direction.

Herrmann Samuel Reimarus, a professor of oriental languages at Hamburg, struggled privately with gnawing doubts about the truth of the biblical revelation. From 1730 to 1768 he wrote them down, and his writing evolved into an enormous 4,000-page critique of the Bible. He was troubled by the many contradictions he found in the Bible and could not accept the stories of the flood, the crossing of the Red Sea, and the resurrection of Jesus. He denied miracles and came to accept a Deistic natural religion. Nevertheless, he never published his opinions but only showed his manuscript to a few close friends and two of his children. After his death, Reimarus's daughter gave the manuscript to Gottfried Lessing, who became librarian in Wolfenbüttel. In 1774 Lessing began to publish excerpts from the manuscript, passing them off as anonymous fragments found in the library's archives. In 1777 he published Reimarus's attack on the historicity of Jesus' resurrection, which set German orthodoxy in an uproar.

According to Reimarus, Jesus claimed to have been only an earthly Messiah, and having tried to establish his reign and failed, he was executed. But the disciples stole Jesus' corpse and spread the story of Jesus' resurrection, touting him as a spiritual Messiah so that they could continue the easy life of preaching that they had enjoyed with Jesus while he was alive. Reimarus realized that to maintain this position he must refute the evidence for the historicity of the resurrection. In his mind, this consisted of the witness of the guard at the tomb, the witness of the apostles, and the fulfillment of Old Testament prophecies. Against the testimony of the guard, Reimarus employed the arguments of the English Deists. He argued that the story is improbable in itself and is full of contradictions. He held it to be an invention of Matthew that the other evangelists rejected. In order to undermine the testimony of the apostles, Reimarus capitalized on the inconsistencies and contradictions in the resurrection narratives. If these were not enough, there is the overriding problem of the privacy of Jesus' appearances. The apostles' testimony is suspect because they are the only ones who supposedly saw Christ. Finally, Reimarus made short shrift of the proof from prophecy. The interpretations of the Old Testament passages in question are so strained as to be unconvincing. Besides, the whole procedure begs the question anyway, since it assumes that Jesus was in fact raised from the dead and the prophecies thus apply to him! In conclusion, Reimarus summarized his case:

(1) the guard story is very doubtful and unconfirmed, and it is very probable the disciples came by night, stole the corpse, and said afterward Jesus had arisen; (2) the

disciples' testimony is both inconsistent and contradictory; and (3) the prophecies appealed to are irrelevant, falsely interpreted, and question-begging.[2]

Thus, Christianity is quite simply a fraud.

Among the many who undertook to refute Reimarus was Johann Salomo Semler, a conservative Rationalist. In his earlier *Abhandlung von freier Untersuchung des Canon* (1771) Semler had broken the ground for the new Rationalist approach to the Scriptures. Semler had been the assistant at the University of Halle to S. J. Baumgarten, who chronicled the course of Deism in his *Nachrichten von einer Hallischen Bibliothek* (1748–1751), reviewing almost every English Deist and apologetic work. Semler actually assisted Baumgarten in the reading and translation of Deist literature, and thus became open to Deist influences.

At the same time, Semler had a background in Pietism and had no desire to undermine Christianity. Therefore, he made a distinction between the timeless, spiritual truths in Scripture and the merely local truths. It was his conviction that only the spiritual truths may properly be called the Word of God. He thus introduced into theology the decisive distinction between the Scriptures and the Word of God. Since only the spiritual truths are the Word of God, it is no longer possible to regard the Scriptures as a whole as divinely inspired. Rather, the Word of God is clothed in fallible, human forms, which have only local importance. These fallible forms represent God's and Jesus' accommodation to human weakness. Included among these accommodations is the miraculous element in Scripture. No Christian can be obligated to believe that such events literally happened, for they are not part of the Word of God. Thus, we are free to examine the historical narratives as we would any other ordinary narrative, since inspiration concerns only the timeless truths they embody. Should the narrative be shown to be unhistorical, that is of little consequence, for that cannot have any effect on the Word of God. The proof that certain events are unhistorical is irrelevant to divine truths.

Given his views of Scripture, it seems somewhat surprising to find Semler writing a refutation of Reimarus in his *Beantwortung der Fragmente eines Ungenannten* (1779). Reimarus's bitter attack seems to have forced him back to the orthodox end of the spectrum. But in the way he defends the resurrection, we can see the beginning of the end for the historical apologetic for the resurrection. He emphatically subordinates the resurrection to the teachings of Jesus and removes from it any apologetic significance. According to Semler, Christianity consists of the spiritual doctrines taught by Christ. Reimarus mistakenly thinks that in refuting the three purported grounds for belief in the resurrection, he has thereby struck down the essential truths of Christianity. But this is far from the case, asserts Semler. In the first place, one may be a Christian without believing in the resurrection of Jesus. In the second place, the true ground for belief in the resurrection is the self-evident

---

2. Hermann Samuel Reimarus, *Fragments*, trans. R. S. Fraser, ed. C. H. Talbert, Lives of Jesus Series (London: SCM, 1971), 104.

truth of Christ's teachings. For Semler, belief in Christ's teaching entails belief in Christ's resurrection: "The resurrection of Jesus hangs together with Jesus' life and goal; whoever has experienced his teachings will also believe that God has raised him from the dead."[3] The proof of the resurrection is not the three points mentioned by Reimarus; the proof is the spiritual teachings of Christ. In specific response to Reimarus's refutation of the three purported grounds, Semler grants all three to Reimarus—but for Semler they are simply irrelevant and present no problem once one has abandoned the doctrine of verbal inspiration.

Thus, Semler undercut the traditional apologetic in various ways: while affirming the truth of the resurrection, he nonetheless admitted that belief in the resurrection was not essential to being a Christian; he provided no historical reason to accept the reliability of the gospel accounts with regard to this event; he denied that the resurrection has any power to confirm Christ's teaching; and he instead subordinated the resurrection to the teachings of Christ, the self-evident Word of God, making the latter the proof of the former.

By loosing the Word of God from the Scriptures and making its truth self-attesting, Semler enabled Rational theology to adhere to the doctrines of Christianity while denying their historical basis. During the time between Semler and Strauss, the natural explanation school predominated. The old conspiracy theory of Reimarus was rejected as an explanation for the resurrection of Jesus, and instead the apparent death theory enjoyed popularity among Rationalists. Even F. D. E. Schleiermacher, known as the father of modern theology, accepted this explanation. But the roof really caved in on the traditional apologetic with the advent of David Friedrich Strauss and his hermeneutic of mythological explanation.

Strauss's *Leben Jesu* (1835) marks a watershed in the history of biblical criticism, to which modern form and redaction criticism may be traced. The year 1835 marks a turning point in the history of the Christian faith.

Strauss's approach to the Gospels, and to the resurrection in particular, may be seen as an attempt to forge a third way between the horns of the dilemma posed by the traditional apologetic, which says that if the miracles and resurrection of Jesus are not historical facts, then the apostles were either deceivers or deceived, neither of which is plausible. Reimarus had chosen to defend the first horn, arguing that the disciples had hoaxed the resurrection. Paulus had chosen to defend the second horn, arguing that the disciples had been mistaken about Jesus' return from the dead. What Strauss saw clearly was that neither of these alternatives was plausible, and so he sought a third alternative in the mythological explanation. According to this view, the miraculous events of the gospels never happened, and the gospel accounts of them are the result of a long process of legend and religious imagination:

---

3. Johann Salomo Semler, *Beantwortung der Fragmente eines Ungennanten insbesondere vom Zweck Jesu and seiner Jünger*, 2nd ed. (Halle: Verlag des Erziehungsinstitut, 1780), 266.

In the view of the church, Jesus was miraculously revived; according to the deistic view of Reimarus, his corpse was stolen by the disciples; in the rationalistic view, he only appeared to be dead and revived; according to our view the imagination of his followers aroused in their deepest spirit, presented their Master revived, for they could not possibly think of him as dead. What for a long time was valid as an external fact, first miraculous, then deceptive, finally simply natural, is hereby reduced completely to the state of mind and made into an inner event.[4]

Strauss thus denied that there was any external fact to be explained. The gospel accounts of the resurrection were unreliable legends colored by myth. Hence, the dilemma of "deceivers or deceived" did not arise. The fact that the resurrection was unhistorical did not rob it of its religious significance (here we see the change wrought by Semler), for a spiritual truth may be revealed within the husk of a delusion.

Strauss believed that the chief problem in applying the mythical interpretation to the New Testament is that the first century was no longer an age of myths. But although it was a time of writing, if there was a long period of oral transmission during which no written record existed, then marvelous elements could begin to creep in and grow into historical myths. Strauss recognized as well that adherence to this theory necessitated denying the contemporary authorship of the Gospels and the influence of eyewitnesses. Hence, Strauss regarded it as "the sole object" of his book to examine the internal evidence in order to test the probability of the authors' being eyewitnesses or competently informed writers.[5]

Strauss gave short shrift to the external testimony to the Gospels: he believed Mark to be compiled from Matthew and Luke and hence not based on Peter's preaching; the Matthew mentioned by Papias is not our Matthew; Acts so contradicts Paul that its author could not be his companion; the earliest reference to John is in A.D. 172, and the Gospel's authenticity was disputed by the Alogoi. Nor could living eyewitnesses prevent the accrual of legend: first, the legends could have originated in areas where Jesus was not well known; second, the apostles could not be everywhere at once to correct or suppress unhistorical stories; and third, eyewitnesses themselves would be tempted to fill up the gaps in their own knowledge with stories. Strauss argued that the Jews lagged behind the Romans and Greeks in their historical consciousness; even Josephus's work is filled with marvelous tales. Myths about the Messiah had already arisen between the exile and Christ's day. All that was wanting was the application of these myths with some modification to Jesus by the Christian community.

With regard to the resurrection accounts, Strauss used arguments similar to Reimarus's to demonstrate their unreliability. For example, if the body was em-

4. David Friedrich Strauss, "Herrmann Samuel Reimarus and His 'Apology,'" in *Fragments*, 280–81.

5. David Friedrich Strauss, *The Life of Jesus Critically Examined*, trans. G. Eliot, ed. with an introduction, P.C. Hodgson, Lives of Jesus Series (London: SCM, 1973), 70.

balmed and wrapped, why do the women return for this purpose? Was the body placed in the tomb because it was Joseph's or because it was near? The story of the guard is improbable, and the inconsistencies in the empty tomb narrative are irreconcilable. As for the appearances, why should Jesus command the disciples to go to Galilee when he was going to appear to them in Jerusalem? And why did he command them to stay in Jerusalem when he was going to Galilee? For such reasons, no credence can be given to the gospel stories of the empty tomb or resurrection appearances.

Despite this, Strauss admitted that Paul's challenge in 1 Corinthians 15 concerning living witnesses to an appearance of Jesus before five hundred brethren makes it certain that people were alive at that time who believed they had seen the risen Christ. How is that to be explained? Certainly not by supernatural intervention, for that is unenlightened. "Hence, the cultivated intellect of the present day has very decidedly stated the following dilemma: either Jesus was not really dead, or he did not really rise again."[6] But that Jesus did not die on the cross is the defunct theory of Rationalism; therefore, Jesus did not rise. The correct explanation of the appearances is to be found in the appearance to Paul. His experience makes clear that the appearances were not external to the mind. What happened is that the disciples, convinced that Jesus was the Messiah, began to search the Scriptures after his death. There they found the dying and glorified Messiah of Isaiah 53. So Jesus must be alive! Soon they would see him, especially the women. Having hallucinated appearances of Christ, they would naturally infer that his grave was empty, and by the time they returned from Galilee to Jerusalem, which was certainly not as soon as Pentecost, there was no closed tomb to refute them. In this way belief in Jesus' resurrection originated, and eventually the legendary gospel accounts arose.

Strauss's work completely altered the tone and course of German theology. Gone forever was the central dilemma of the eighteenth-century apologetic for the resurrection. Now the evangelists were neither deceivers nor deceived, but stood at the end of a long process in which the original events were completely reshaped through mythological and legendary influences. The dissolution of the apologists' dilemma did not itself entail that the supernaturalist view was false. But for Strauss the supernaturalist view was not only disproved by the inconsistencies and contradictions noted by Reimarus, but was *a priori* ruled out of court because of the presupposition of the impossibility of miracles. Any event that stood outside the inviolable chain of finite causes was *by definition* mythological. Therefore, the resurrection could not possibly be a miraculous and historical event.

This is the challenge that Strauss has left to Christian apologetics. The position of Bultmann in the twentieth century with regard to the resurrection is virtually the same as Strauss's. It is no longer effective to argue for the resurrection today simply by refuting theories as to who stole the body or that Jesus did not really

6. Ibid., 736.

die. They are no longer the issue. The issue is whether the gospel narratives are historically credible accounts or unhistorical legends.

THE TIDE OF SUBJECTIVISM

The other reason, it seems to me, for the decline in historical apologetics during the nineteenth century was the tide of subjectivism that swept away an objective approach to matters of religious belief. I do not have space to develop this here, but let me say in passing that during the nineteenth century there came a back-lash to the Age of Reason, and Romanticism swept Europe. This was spurred on in England by the Great Awakening, which emphasized the subjective, personal experience of faith. In France, the very emotive, subjective side of thinkers such as Rousseau emerged as a widespread reaction to the prior age of the *philosophes*, which ended in Revolution and the Reign of Terror. In Germany the effect of the philosophy of Kant and surging German Romanticism combined to color religious faith with a strong subjectivism. The net result of this tide of subjectivism was that apologetics moved from objective evidences for faith to emphasizing the moral grounds for faith or the beauties of faith itself. This subjective turn also enabled one to live with the destruction that was increasingly being wrought on the biblical narrative by the hammers of biblical criticism.

Twentieth-Century Developments

Liberal theology, with its cheery view of human perfectibility and progress, could not survive World War I; but its demise brought no renewed interest in the his-toricity of Jesus' resurrection. For the two most influential schools of theological thought that succeeded it were united in their devaluation of the historical with regard to Jesus. Thus, dialectical theology, exemplified by Karl Barth, championed the *doctrine* of the resurrection, but would have nothing to do with the resurrec-tion as an *event of history*. In his commentary on the book of Romans (1919), the early Barth declared, "The resurrection touches history as a tangent touches a circle—that is, without really touching it." Existential theology, exemplified by Rudolf Bultmann, was even more antithetical to the historicity of Jesus' resurrection. Though Bultmann acknowledged that the earliest disciples believed in the literal resurrection of Jesus and that Paul in 1 Corinthians 15 even attempts to prove the resurrection, he nevertheless pronounces such a procedure "fatal." It reduces Christ's resurrection to a nature miracle akin to the resurrection of a corpse, and modern man cannot be reasonably asked to believe in nature miracles before becoming a Christian. Therefore, the miraculous elements of the gospel must be demythologized to reveal the true Christian message: the call to authentic existence in the face of death, symbolized by the cross. The resurrection is merely a symbolic restatement of the message of the cross and essentially adds nothing to it. To appeal to the resurrection as historical evidence, as did Paul, is doubly wrongheaded, for it is the very nature of existential faith that it is a leap without evidence. Thus, to argue historically for the resurrection is contrary to faith. Clearly then, the antipathy of liberal theology to the historicity of Jesus' resurrection remained unrelieved by either dialectical or existential theology.

But a remarkable change came about during the second half of the twentieth century. The first glimmerings of change began to appear in 1953. In that year, as we have said, Ernst Käsemann, a pupil of Bultmann, argued at a colloquy at the University of Marburg that Bultmann's historical skepticism toward Jesus was unwarranted and counterproductive and suggested reopening the question of where the historical about Jesus was to be found. A new quest of the historical Jesus had begun. Three years later in 1956 the Marburg theologian Hans Grass in his influential *Ostergeschehen und Osterberichte* subjected the resurrection itself to historical inquiry and concluded that the resurrection appearances cannot be dismissed as mere subjective visions on the part of the disciples, but were objective visionary events.

Meanwhile the church historian Hans Freiherr von Campenhausen in an equally epochal essay defended the historical credibility of Jesus' empty tomb. During the ensuing years a stream of works on the historicity of Jesus' resurrection flowed forth from German, French, and English presses. By 1968 the old skepticism was a spent force and began dramatically to recede. So complete has been the turn-about during the second half of the century concerning the resurrection of Jesus that I think that it is no exaggeration to speak of a reversal of scholarship on this issue, such that those who deny the historicity of Jesus' resurrection now seem to be the ones on the defensive. Perhaps one of the most significant theological developments in this connection is the theological system of Wolfhart Pannenberg, who bases his entire Christology on the historical evidence for Jesus' ministry and resurrection. This is a development undreamed of in German theology prior to 1950. Equally startling is the declaration of one of the world's leading Jewish theologians, Pinchas Lapide, that he is convinced on the basis of the evidence that Jesus of Nazareth rose from the dead. Also noteworthy is that fact that Christian philosophers, such as Stephen T. Davis and Richard Swinburne, whose own field has undergone a similar renaissance over the last half century, have begun to engage in the discussion of Jesus' resurrection, a development that can only be salutary due to the sophisticated tools of philosophical analysis that they bring to questions like the problem of miracles, personal identity, probability, and so forth. We have truly entered a new era of resurrection scholarship.

Assessment

Historical Study and Jesus' Resurrection
Despite its pivotal nature for our understanding of Jesus, many historical Jesus scholars would probably still agree with Barth that the resurrection is not a legitimate object of historical research and is therefore strictly off-limits for the historian. Even if it occurred, such an event is not open to historical investigation

and can therefore be affirmed only on non-historical grounds, for example, through religious experience or faith.

Structure of the Argument

Before we look at the reasons some critical scholars have offered for placing the resurrection in historical quarantine, it will be helpful to say something about the structure of a historical argument for Jesus' resurrection. Any historical argument for Jesus' resurrection will have two steps, even if these are not clearly delineated: (1) to establish the facts which will serve as historical evidence and (2) to argue that the hypothesis of Jesus' resurrection is the best or most probable explanation of those facts. Step (1) will involve an investigation of the historicity of events such as the discovery of Jesus' empty tomb; step (2) will assess the comparative merits of rival hypotheses offered as explanations of the facts established in step (1).

Bart Ehrman's Objections

With this two-step procedure in mind, consider the claim of Bart Ehrman that there can be no historical evidence for the resurrection of Jesus.[7] Ehrman takes it for granted that historians have no privileged access to what happens in the supernatural realm; they have access only to what happens in the natural world.[8] Therefore a supernatural act by its very nature lies outside the purview of the historian. The historian *qua* historian cannot tell us whether God is the cause of some event; he can at best tell us that certain people regarded an event as miraculous. So, with respect to the resurrection, "Historians . . . have no difficulty whatsoever speaking about the belief in Jesus' resurrection, since this is a matter of public record. For it is a historical fact that some of Jesus' followers came to believe that he had been raised from the dead soon after his execution."[9] But the truth or falsity of that belief is not within the purview of the historian.

Readers who have followed my argument to this point will recognize Ehrman's objection as a variation on Troeltsch's historiographical ban on miracles, which we encountered in chapter 6. Once we differentiate the two steps in a historical argument for the resurrection, however, then it becomes apparent that Ehrman's objection, even if conceded, strikes at most against step (2) of the argument. The resurrection of Jesus is, indeed, a miraculous explanation of the evidence. But the evidence established in step (1) is not itself miraculous. None of the relevant facts is in any way supernatural or inaccessible to the historian. Take the fact that Jesus' tomb was found empty on the Sunday morning following his crucifixion. There is nothing miraculous about the discovery of an empty grave. To give an analogy, after Abraham Lincoln was assassinated, a plot was hatched by enemies of Lincoln to steal his body as it was being transported by train back to Illinois. The

---

7. See http://www.reasonablefaith.org/site/PageServer?pagename=debates_main.

8. Bart D. Ehrman, *The New Testament*, 3rd ed. (Oxford: Oxford University Press, 2004), 16, 294, 227.

9. Bart D. Ehrman, *Jesus: Apocalyptic Prophet of the New Millennium* (Oxford: Oxford University Press, 1999), 231.

historian will obviously want to know whether this plot was foiled or not. Was Lincoln's body missing from the train? Was it successfully interred in the tomb at Springfield? Or take the postmortem appearances of Jesus. A Civil War historian will want to know if Lincoln's closest associates like Secretary of War Stanton and Vice President Johnson experienced appearances of Lincoln alive after his death. These are questions any historian can investigate. And it's the same with the facts relevant to the resurrection hypothesis. Hence, even if Ehrman were correct that the historian, due to a methodological constraint, cannot infer the resurrection of Jesus, he may still investigate the events which constitute the evidence which the resurrection hypothesis seeks to explain.

Indeed, Ehrman himself, after expressing initial skepticism concerning some of those facts, came to regard them all as historically well founded. With respect to Jesus' burial and empty tomb, he judges that "the earliest accounts we have are unanimous in saying that Jesus was in fact buried by this fellow, Joseph of Arimathea, and so it's relatively reliable that that's what happened. We also have solid traditions to indicate that women found this tomb empty three days later."[10] As for the postmortem appearances, Ehrman agrees with virtually all scholars in holding that "we can say with some confidence that some of his disciples claimed to have seen Jesus alive."[11] And we have already seen that he thinks that the historian can establish that shortly after Jesus' execution some of his followers came to believe that he had been raised from the dead; in fact, Ehrman surmises that had Jesus died and no one believed in his resurrection, no new religion would have emerged following his death.[12] So Ehrman himself has no problem with the historian's carrying out, indeed, carrying out successfully, step (1) of a historical argument for the resurrection of Jesus.

Many defenders of the resurrection will be quite content to let the case rest there, leaving the best explanation of these facts to be settled between an inquirer and God—after all, not everything has to be, or even can be, settled historically! In scholarly books on the resurrection, perhaps 90 percent of the space is typically devoted to step (1) of the argument. Take, for example, N. T . Wright's massive study *The Resurrection of the Son of God*, the most important book on Jesus' resurrection today. Wright's argument may be summarized as follows:[13]

1. Early Christians believed in Jesus' (physical, bodily) resurrection.

10. Bart Ehrman, "From Jesus to Constantine: A History of Early Christianity," Lecture 4: "Oral and Written Traditions about Jesus" (The Teaching Company, 2003).
11. Ehrman, *Jesus*, 200.
12. Ehrman, *New Testament*, 276.
13. See my analysis of Wright's loosely formulated seven-step argument in "Wright vs. Crossan on the Resurrection of Jesus," in *The Resurrection: The Crossan-Wright Dialogue,* ed. Robert B. Stewart (Minneapolis and London: Augsburg Fortress and SPCK, 2006), 139–48.

2. The best explanation of that belief is the hypothesis of the disciples' discovery of Jesus' empty tomb and their experience of post-mortem appearances of Jesus.

2.1. The hypothesis of the disciples' discovery of Jesus' empty tomb and their experience of postmortem appearances of Jesus has the explanatory power to account for that belief.

2.2. Rival hypotheses such as spontaneous generation within a Jewish context, dreams about Jesus, cognitive dissonance or a fresh experience of grace following Jesus' death, etc., lack the explanatory power to account for that belief.

3. The best explanation for the facts of Jesus' empty tomb and postmortem appearances is the hypothesis that Jesus rose from the dead.

Virtually the entirety of Wright's book is devoted to establishing points (1) and (2); when it comes to (3) he simply laterals the ball to Gary Habermas, referring the reader to Habermas's treatments of rival hypotheses.[14] Wright has almost nothing to say in defense of the resurrection hypothesis as an explanation for the empty tomb and postmortem appearances; he is content, having firmly established those facts, to invite the modern secularist to reconsider his naturalistic worldview and see if the resurrection hypothesis doesn't make good sense.[15]

But why must we stop there? Why think that step (2) is off limits to the historian? We saw that Troeltsch's principle of analogy can be stood on its head so as not to constrain the historian to purely naturalistic hypotheses. Moreover, we have given objective criteria for the identification of some event as a miracle. So what is the problem? Ehrman seems to suggest that it is the historian's lack of access to the supernatural realm, which prevents his justifiably inferring that some event has a supernatural cause. But this objection is very weak. In the first place, the historian need not have direct access to the explanatory entities postulated by one's hypothesis. Think of the analogy of contemporary physics. Physicists posit all sort of entities to which they have no direct access: strings, higher dimensional membranes, even parallel universes. They postulate such entities as the best explanation for the evidence to which we do have access. Nor is such a procedure unique to theoretical physics; the historical sciences like paleontology, geology, and cosmology do exactly the same thing. Dinosaurs, like quarks, are theoretical entities to which we have no direct access but which are postulated as the best explanation of the evidence we have. Indeed—and here we come to the second point—the historian doesn't have direct access to any of the objects of his study! This was one of the problems we encountered in dealing with the objectivity of history in chapter 5. The past is gone, and things and events of the past can be inferred only indirectly

---

14. N. T. Wright, *Christian Origins and the Question of God*, vol. 3: *The Resurrection of the Son of God* (Minneapolis: Fortress Press, 2003), 718.
    15. Ibid., 710–16.

on the basis of present evidence. Inaccessibility is thus not an epistemologically differentiating feature of natural as opposed to supernatural entities.

Finally, even if we were to concede that the professional historian must as a member of his guild act under the constraint of methodological naturalism, the question remains why we should so act. Why can't I as a philosopher or just as a human being judge that the best explanation for the facts of the case is a miraculous explanation? Indeed, why can't the historian himself, in his off-hours, so to speak, make a similar judgment? Would it not be a tragedy if we were to fail to come to know the truth about reality simply because of a methodological constraint? Apart from some good reason for thinking that inference to a supernatural explanation is irrational, why should we, when we are not acting as professional historians, pay heed to a mere methodological constraint?

John Meier's Reservations

John Meier's reason for prescinding from a historical investigation of Jesus' resurrection is quite different from Ehrman's. Indeed, Meier's reason is so kooky that it would scarcely deserve discussion here, were it not for the status of its exponent. It is sobering to think that the world's preeminent historical Jesus scholar plans to end his voluminous life of Jesus with the crucifixion and burial, with apparently no concern for what German scholars call "das Geschick Jesu" (Jesus' final fate).[16]

As is evident from his treatment of Jesus' miracles, Meier is quite willing to consider the historicity of purportedly miraculous events themselves, even if prescinding from a judgment as to their miraculous nature. Meier does not rule the miracle stories off-limits, as he does the resurrection narratives, but seeks to render a historical judgment about the occurrence of the events while leaving aside the question as to their being supernaturally caused. So why does Meier refuse to investigate the resurrection or to discuss the resurrection narratives? He says that the resurrection is off-limits due to the restrictive definition of the historical Jesus which he will be using throughout his investigation. Recall that Meier defines the historical Jesus or the Jesus of history (the terms are used synonymously) as "a modern abstraction and construct. By the Jesus of history I mean the Jesus whom we can 'recover' and examine using the scientific tools of modern historical research."[17] We have already seen in chapter 7 the problems with this definition, but let that pass. What is it about this definition that precludes the resurrection narratives from being examined with such tools and our recovering the resurrection of Jesus as a part of the historical Jesus? Meier answers that "in the historical-critical context, the 'real' has been defined—and has to be defined—in terms of what exists in this world of time and space, what can be experienced in principle by any observer,

---

16. John P. Meier, *A Marginal Jew*, vol. 1: *The Roots of the Problem and the Person* (New York: Doubleday, 1991), 13.
17. Ibid., 25.

and what can be reasonably deduced and inferred from such experience."[18] Here Meier appears to state three necessary conditions of something's being real—that is, belonging to a reasonably complete biographical portrait of someone—in the context of historical inquiry. Now the three conditions stated by Meier for something's being historically recoverable seem quite unremarkable. So which of those conditions preclude the resurrection from belonging to the historical Jesus?

Here things really become interesting. To my knowledge, Meier never denies that the third condition could be fulfilled, that is to say, that Jesus' resurrection can be reasonably deduced and inferred from such facts as Jesus' empty tomb, his postmortem appearances, and the origin of the Christian Way. What, then, about the second condition, that an event must be experienceable in principle by any observer? Meier denies that the resurrection "is in principle open to the observation of any and every observer,"[19] but he does not explain himself. I see no reason to think that someone sitting in the tomb holding vigil over the body of Jesus would not have observed his resurrection. And again, even if it were true that the resurrection is not in principle observable by anyone, that is still no reason for ignoring the events which go to make up the evidence established in step (1) of a historical argument for the resurrection like the empty tomb, the origin of the disciples' belief in Jesus' resurrection, and so forth. Rather Meier's real reason for denying that the resurrection can be part of the historical Jesus is that Meier doubts that the first condition can be fulfilled. Citing Gerald O'Collins, Meier asserts that "although the 'resurrection is a real, bodily event involving the person of Jesus of Nazareth,' the resurrection of Jesus 'is not an event *in* space and time and hence should not be called historical,' since 'we should require an historical occurrence to be something significant that is known to have happened in our space-time continuum.'"[20]

Here Meier asserts that Jesus' resurrection was an actual, bodily event but that it did not occur in time and space. Accordingly, it can be said to have actually occurred without being "historical" in Meier's idiosyncratic sense, that is, recoverable by the scientific tools of historical research. Now the claim that Jesus' resurrection can be an actual, bodily event involving the person Jesus of Nazareth without being an occurrence in time and space is certainly strange. Unfortunately, Meier does not explain the paradox. But a consultation of O'Collins's article, which is cited by Meier in both volume one and volume two on this score, as well as elsewhere, sheds light on the conundrum.

The key to understanding O'Collins's claim that the resurrection does not occur *in* space and time is his conception of the resurrection as a kind of transition from this-worldly to other-worldly existence. The resurrection, on his view, is Christ's transitioning out of space and time into a new reality. "Through the resurrection

---

18. Ibid., 197.
19. Ibid., vol. 2: *Mentor, Message, and Miracle* (New York: Doubleday, 1994), 525.
20. Ibid., 1:201.

Christ passes out of the empirical sphere of this world to a new mode of existence in the 'other' world of God."[21] Through the resurrection Christ moves outside the ordinary datable, localizable conditions of our experience to become an other-worldly reality. Whereas those raised from the dead by Jesus during his earthly ministry "resume life under normal bodily conditions" so that "their space-time lives continue," Jesus "does not return to life in our space-time continuum."[22] Christ "on the far side of the resurrection" did not continue to exist under the bodily conditions which we experience and within which the historian operates.[23]

Now as an aside, it should be said that O'Collins' claim that Jesus' resurrection did not involve a return to life in our spacetime continuum presupposes a patent misreading of the Gospel narratives, not to speak of Jewish texts. One of the merits of Wright's exhaustive study of ancient texts concerning resurrection from the dead is his demonstration that the notion of resurrection was not a flight to an other-worldly, non-spatio-temporal realm but inherently involved the restoration of life in the realm of space and time.[24] That life was not, of course, a mere reanimation to mortal existence, but it was bodily, physical, and spatio-temporal. O'Collins has turned Jesus' resurrection into Jesus' assumption into heaven on the pattern of Enoch and Elijah, a quite different category than resurrection of the dead.

But let that pass. Let us grant O'Collins that with the resurrection Jesus of Nazareth's four-dimensional earthly existence came abruptly to an end. Still, we might object, the final three-dimensional configuration of that existence had specific spatio-temporal coordinates. It was at that place and time that the resurrection occurred. Pannenberg makes a similar point, observing that if the empty tomb is historical, then the resurrection did occur in space. "If it really took place," he says wryly, "it took place in Palestine and not for instance in America."[25] One might add, "And it took place in time as well, sometime around A.D. 30 and not, for instance, in 1967."

In his response to Pannenberg, O'Collins' conception of the resurrection as a transition becomes crucial. He responds,

> It seems odd, however, to speak of a transition "out of" space, viz. to a reality not locatable in space, taking place in space, viz. in Palestine. For even if the "initial point" of this transition were located in space, this would not justify us in concluding that the transition "took place" in space. Besides it seems preferable to talk of the tomb containing the body of the historical Jesus not as "the initial point" of the transition, but as being the last place where Jesus in the normal historical sense was locatable.[26]

21. G. G. O'Collins, "Is the Resurrection an 'Historical' Event?" *Heythrop Journal* 8 (1967): 384.
22. Ibid., 385.
23. Ibid.
24. Wright, *Christian Origins*, vol. 3; see 3:625–26 for a particularly powerful statement of the point.
25. Wolfhart Pannenberg, *Theology as History*, 265, n.76, cited by O'Collins, "Resurrection," 386.
26. O'Collins, "Resurrection," 387.

We can set aside immediately the red herring of the tomb's not being the initial point of the transition, for no one has suggested that. Rather the idea is that the four-dimensional entity which in its final stages is Jesus' corpse has its terminus at a certain spatial location which is in the tomb. Why not say that the resurrection occurred there (and then)? The answer, says O'Collins, is that a transition out of space ought not to be said to occur in space.

There's something both right and wrong about this answer. Compare a shopper's exiting a grocery store. Does his exiting the store occur in the store? At any point in the store right up to and including its boundary point, the shopper has not yet exited the store. But once he is outside the store, there is no first point at which he can be said to exit the store, for between any exterior point and the store's boundary there is a dense series of closer points at each of which the shopper had already exited the store. So where does his exiting the store occur?

It's evident that O'Collins has unwittingly entangled himself in the ancient Greek paradoxes of motion.[27] Transitional events like stopping, exiting, and dying occur over non-zero intervals of time, and it is conceptually absurd to specify any single spacetime point as the instant of change. There will be either a last instant of the state of the object before the change, with no first instant of its state after the change, or else a first instant of the state of the object after the change, with no last instant of its state before the change. What there cannot be is any instant at which the change itself can coherently be said to occur.

That the ancient paradoxes of motion are, indeed, the culprit behind O'Collins's argument, and not the nature of the resurrection, is evident from the fact that even if the resurrection were conceived as a transformation wholly within space and time, one could not specify a single spacetime point at which it happened. At any point it would either not yet have happened or have already happened.

Nevertheless, just as it is perfectly acceptable to say that the shopper exited the building, say, through the front door rather than the rear entrance in the sense that that was the last location at which he existed prior to being outside the store, so Jesus' transformation to his glorified state can be similarly located in the sense that one can specify the spacetime point at which his corruptible existence ended prior to his being in a glorified state. Moreover, in ordinary language we content ourselves with approximations rather than spacetime points. Just as the historian can determine where someone exited a building or when someone died, there is no realistic objection based on continuity considerations to the historian's determining where and when Jesus' resurrection occurred.

The final irony of Meier's appeal to O'Collins's argument as justification for ignoring the resurrection narratives is that O'Collins, himself a strong proponent of the historical credibility of Jesus' resurrection, in the very same article goes on to insist, "To argue that the resurrection of Christ is not appropriately described

---

27. See the engaging discussion of these paradoxes by Richard Sorabji, *Time, Creation, and the Continuum* (Ithaca, N.Y.: Cornell University Press, 1983), chap. 26.

as an historical event is not to assert that historical evidence and inquiry are irrelevant."[28] He lists three areas of inquiry: (1) the "proclaiming faith" of the disciples can be investigated by the historian; (2) Christ's appearances at definite times and places to a particular number of persons are historical from the side of those who encountered him; and (3) the empty tomb can be the object of investigation by the historian. These are precisely the three independently established facts which I shall argue are best explained by the resurrection of Jesus, namely, the origin of the Christian Way, Jesus' postmortem appearances, and the discovery of Jesus' empty tomb. Even given O'Collins's conclusion that Jesus' resurrection was not "historical" in his Pickwickian sense, still all the evidence for Jesus' resurrection remains intact to be explored by the scientific tools of historical research.

That leads to a final point. O'Collins's argument that the resurrection of Jesus did not occur *in* space and time is the result of a prolonged historical study of the New Testament evidence of the resurrection of Jesus. But in the absence of any such investigation, how does Meier know whether or not Jesus' resurrection, if it took place, took place in space and time and whether it was observable or not? How can he know *a priori* that Wright is not correct that Jesus' resurrection was a spatio-temporal event which was in principle observable by any fair-minded and interested observer? How does he know that Jesus' resurrection can only be affirmed by faith and not through historical investigation, apart from such an investigation?

I can think of only one answer to that question: theology. It is a theological conviction on Meier's part that Jesus' resurrection is affirmable only by faith. Meier's theological commitment intrudes in a comment like the following on Pannenberg's historical approach to the resurrection: "In my opinion, Pannenberg's overall approach to revelation and faith on the one hand and history and reason on the other creates more difficulties than it solves. At times it comes close to saying that the object of faith can be proven by historical research."[29] What is, of course, ironic about this is that Meier eschews theological commitments in his work as a historian, aspiring to approach questions from a theologically neutral stance. But it seems clear that the reason Meier as a historian won't touch the resurrection is that his prior theological commitments preclude this. We can only hope that he will shed those commitments and bring his considerable talents to bear on the question of the historicity of Jesus' postmortem appearances, his empty tomb, the origin of the disciples' belief in his resurrection, and ultimately, upon the event of Jesus' resurrection itself.

Dale Allison's Doubts
Philosophical problems of a different kind make it difficult for Dale Allison, an eminent New Testament scholar, to accept Jesus' literal resurrection.[30] At the heart

---

28. O'Collins, "Resurrection," 385.
29. Meier, *A Marginal Jew*, 2:529.
30. Dale C. Allison, *Resurrecting Jesus: The Earliest Christian Tradition and Its Interpreters* (New York: T. & T. Clark, 2005), 219–28.

of his doubts about a literal resurrection of the dead is the problem of the identity of the resurrection body with the mortal body in cases in which the mortal body has been completely destroyed. If spatio-temporal continuity is a necessary condition of identity over time, then the discontinuity caused by the dissolution of the mortal body implies that the resurrection body is at best a duplicate of the mortal body but is not identical to it. So it would seem impossible in such a case to hold that that very body will be raised.

It's odd that these concerns should cause Allison to have doubts about the literal resurrection of Jesus, since in Jesus' case the mortal body was not destroyed, so that no spatio-temporal discontinuity existed to preclude identity. It was clearly the body in the tomb that was raised (hence, the empty tomb). Even if, in cases in which the mortal body has been utterly dissolved, God has to create a brand-new look-alike out of nothing, how could this conclusion possibly impact the evidence for Jesus' resurrection?

Allison says that in such a case Jesus' resurrection becomes the exception, an aberration. I think this assertion is highly doubtful. In Jewish belief the primary object of the resurrection was the bones of the deceased (hence, the Jewish practice of preserving the bones in ossuaries for the eschatological resurrection), and skeletal remains are amazingly durable, existing even from prehistoric times. Moreover, the world's population explosion guarantees, barring worldwide catastrophe, that there will always be more recently deceased than long deceased. But leave that aside. These doctrinal issues are just irrelevant to a historical assessment of our sources. Suppose we say that when the eschatological resurrection occurs, God elects to raise the (skeletal) remains of any of the dead whose remains still exist and to create new bodies for those deceased who have no remains. How could this possibly affect one's estimation of the historical evidence for Jesus' resurrection?

I frankly think that Allison's real problem is just the all too common prejudice against physical, corporeal immortality. He says, "I believe, rightly or wrongly, in a future existence free from the constraints of material corporeality as we have hitherto known them."[31] Philosophical problems about identity are then exploited in the attempt to justify this prejudice. But those problems at most show that the resurrection bodies of people whose mortal bodies have been utterly dissolved are duplicates of those bodies rather than the numerically identical bodies. That does nothing to undermine a doctrine of physical, corporeal immortality. Allison's scepticism is therefore just an unjustified bias.

Notice that having a duplicate body does nothing to preclude *personal* identity of the deceased and resurrected individual if one believes, as Allison does, in the reality of a soul distinct from the body. Jewish belief was that when the body died, the soul went to be with God until the eschatological resurrection, at which time the remains of the dead would be raised, the body reconstituted, and the soul reunited with the body. By postulating such an intermediate state between death and

31. Ibid., 225.

resurrection, personal identity was ensured, even in cases in which there were no remains to be raised. Problems with personal identity arise only for the theologian who is a materialist or who denies the intermediate state of the soul after death. Since Allison is a dualist, there should be for him no problem at all concerning the personal identity of those raised by God from the dead.

All this goes to show the irrelevance of doubts about bodily identity in the case of those whose mortal bodies have been destroyed to the question of Jesus's literal resurrection.[32] Therefore, I'll not delve into the knotty question of whether spatio-temporal continuity is, in fact, as Allison assumes, a necessary condition of physical identity over time. I simply note that this is hugely controversial, so that it is far from obvious that God could not create a physical object, destroy it, and then recreate that very same object.[33]

Bayes' Theorem and Inference to the Best Explanation

In building a historical case for the resurrection of Jesus, we are engaged in an inductive argument for a particular historical hypothesis. Although Bayes' Theorem can be useful for calculating the probability of some hypothesis on a given body of evidence and while philosophers such as Richard Swinburne have argued for the resurrection hypothesis by Bayesian means,[34] professional historians do not really avail themselves of Bayes' Theorem in the justification of historical hypotheses. One reason is that the values assigned to some of the probabilities involved are little more than conjectures. In the case of Jesus' resurrection the probability of Jesus' resurrection on the background information $\Pr(R \mid B)$ depends, we have seen, on the probability that God would raise Jesus of Nazareth from the dead $\Pr(R \mid G)$, which is speculative. A Bayesian approach will continue to have heuristic value in helping us to discern the relevance of various considerations involved in

32. To summarize, they are irrelevant for four reasons: (1) what is critical with respect to the resurrection of the dead is not bodily identity, but personal identity, which is guaranteed by the enduring soul; (2) Jewish belief was that the bones of the dead would be raised, so that strict bodily identity is not at issue; (3) in Jesus' case bodily identity is unproblematic; and (4) such doctrinal concerns about eschatological resurrection should make no difference to one's appraisal of historical evidence.

33. See, e.g., Trenton Merricks, "There Are No Criteria of Identity over Time," *Noûs* 33 (1998): 106–24, who argues that there are no informative, necessary, and sufficient conditions of identity over time.

34. Richard Swinburne, *The Resurrection of God Incarnate* (Oxford: Oxford University Press, 2003); see also Timothy and Lydia McGrew's contribution to *Companion to Natural Theology*, ed. William L. Craig and J. P. Moreland (Oxford: Blackwell, forthcoming). Plantinga launched a misconceived attack upon Swinburne's Bayesian approach based upon what he called the problem of dwindling probabilities (Alvin Plantinga, *Warranted Christian Belief* [Oxford: Oxford University Press, 2000], 268–80), which drew responses from both Swinburne ("Natural Theology, Its 'Dwindling Probabilities,' and 'Lack of Rapport,'" *Faith and Philosophy* 21 [2004]: 533-46) and McGrew ("Has Plantinga Refuted the Historical Argument?" *Philosophia Christi* 6 [2004]: 7–26). See further Alvin Plantinga, "Historical Arguments and Historical Probabilities: A Response to Timothy McGrew," *Philosophia Christi* 8 (2006): 7–22; Timothy and Lydia McGrew, "On the Historical Argument: A Rejoinder to Plantinga," *Philosophia Christi* 8 (2006): 23–38. Plantinga concedes that the McGrews' Bayesian approach is not compromised by the problem of dwindling probabilities and is a substantial contribution to our understanding of historical arguments.

arguing a case for Jesus' resurrection, for example, how certain arguments lower $Pr(E \mid not\text{-}R\&B)$, while others raise $Pr(E \mid R\&B)$.

An argument for Jesus' resurrection which conforms to actual historiographical practice will be formulated as an inference to the best explanation.[35] According to this approach, we begin with the evidence available to us and then infer what would, if true, provide the best explanation of that evidence. Out of a pool of live options determined by our background beliefs, we select the best of various competing potential explanations to give a causal account of why the evidence is as it is and not otherwise. The process of determining which historical reconstruction is the best explanation will involve the historian's craft, since various factors will have to be weighed, such as explanatory power, explanatory scope, plausibility, degree of being ad hoc, and so on.[36] Since the competing explanations may meet the various criteria to different degrees, the determination of which is the best explanation may be difficult and require a good deal of skill.

In my estimation the hypothesis "God raised Jesus from the dead" furnishes the best explanation of the historical data relevant to Jesus' final fate. The inductive grounds for the inference of this explanation consist primarily in the evidence of three independently established facts: (1) the tomb of Jesus was found empty by a group of his women followers on the first day of the week following his crucifixion, (2) various individuals and groups thereafter experienced on different occasions and under varying circumstances appearances of Jesus alive, and (3) the first disciples came sincerely to believe in Jesus' resurrection in the absence of sufficient antecedent historical influences from either Judaism or pagan religions. If these three facts can be historically established with a reasonable degree of confidence (and it seems to me that they can) and if alternative naturalistic explanations for these facts can be shown to be implausible (and the consensus of scholarship is that they can), then unless the resurrection hypothesis is shown to be even more implausible than its failed competitors (and my experience in debating the comparative merits of the hypotheses convinces me that it cannot), then the preferred explanation ought to be the one given in the documents themselves: God raised Jesus from the dead. The significance of this event is then to be found in the religio-historical context in which it occurred, namely, as the vindication of Jesus' own unparalleled claim to divine authority. I think that the evidence for the resurrection of Jesus is such that a well-informed investigator ought to agree that it is more likely than not to have occurred.

The Evidence for Jesus' Resurrection
As alluded to above, the case for the historicity of the resurrection of Jesus seems to me to rest upon the evidence for three great, independently established facts:

35. For an account see Peter Lipton, *Inference to the Best Explanation* (London: Routledge, 1981).

36. For discussion see C. Behan McCullagh, *Justifying Historical Descriptions* (Cambridge: Cambridge University Press, 1984), 19.

the empty tomb, the resurrection appearances, and the origin of the Christian faith. If these three facts can be established and no plausible natural explanation can account for them as well as the resurrection hypothesis, then one is justified in inferring Jesus' resurrection as the most plausible explanation of the data. Accordingly, let us examine the evidence for each of these facts.

The Empty Tomb

THE FACT OF JESUS' EMPTY TOMB

Here I'll summarize briefly six lines of evidence supporting the fact that the tomb of Jesus was found empty by a group of his women followers on the first day of the week following his crucifixion.

1) *The historical reliability of the story of Jesus' burial supports the empty tomb.* Now you might ask, how does the fact of Jesus' burial prove that his tomb was found empty? The answer is this: if the story of Jesus' entombment is accurate, then the location of Jesus' tomb was known in Jerusalem to both Jew and Christian alike. But in that case, the tomb must have been empty when the disciples began to preach that Jesus was risen. Why? First, the disciples could not have believed in Jesus' resurrection if his corpse still lay in the tomb. It would have been wholly un-Jewish, not to say foolish, to believe that a man was raised from the dead when his body was still in the grave. One of the greatest merits of N. T. Wright's exhaustive study of pre-Christian and Christian beliefs about resurrection is his demonstration that "resurrection" always meant physical, bodily resurrection. He insists, "Let us be quite clear at this point . . . when the early Christians said 'resurrection' they meant it in the sense it bore both in paganism (which denied it) and in Judaism (. . . which affirmed it). 'Resurrection'. . . meant bodily resurrection; and that is what the early Christians affirmed."[37] The suggestion by some critics that the disciples were so convinced of Jesus' resurrection that they never bothered to visit the gravesite is, frankly, rather silly when you think about it (they *never* went back, if not to verify, even to see where the Lord lay?) and contradicts the evidence that the site of the tomb was preserved in Christian memory.

Second, even if the disciples had preached Jesus' resurrection despite his occupied tomb, scarcely anybody else would have believed them. One of the most remarkable facts about the early Christian belief in Jesus' resurrection was that it flourished in the very city where Jesus had been publicly crucified. So long as the people of Jerusalem thought that Jesus' body was in the tomb, few would have been prepared to believe such nonsense as that Jesus had been raised from the dead. And third, even if they had so believed, the Jewish authorities would have exposed the whole affair simply by pointing to Jesus' tomb or perhaps even exhuming the body as decisive proof that Jesus had not been raised. If even no longer identifiable remains lay in the tomb where Jesus had been buried, the burden of proof

37. Wright, *Christian Origins*, 3:209.

would have lain upon the shoulders of those who said that these were *not* Jesus' remains. But no such dispute over the identification of Jesus' corpse ever seems to have taken place. As we shall see, the dispute between Jewish non-Christians and Christians lay elsewhere. To suggest that the Jewish authorities didn't take this business about Jesus' being risen as anything more than a minor nuisance not worth dealing with is, again, fantastic, and contrary to the evidence that they were deeply concerned about squelching the nascent Christian movement (think of their engaging Saul of Tarsus!). Thus, if the story of Jesus' burial is historical, then it is a very short inference to the historicity of the empty tomb as well. For that reason, critics who deny the historicity of the empty tomb feel constrained to argue against the burial account as well.

Unfortunately for those who deny the empty tomb, Jesus' burial in the tomb is one of the best-established facts about Jesus. Space does not permit me to go into all the details of the evidence for the burial. But let me just mention a couple of points:

First, Jesus' burial is multiply attested in extremely early, independent sources. The account of Jesus' burial in a tomb by Joseph of Arimathea is part of Mark's source material for the passion story. This is a very early source which is probably based on eyewitness testimony and which the commentator Rudolf Pesch dates to within seven years of Jesus' crucifixion.[38] Moreover, Paul in 1 Corinthians 15:3–5 quotes an old Christian tradition that he had received from the earliest disciples. Paul probably received this tradition no later than his visit to Jerusalem in A.D. 36 (Gal. 1:18), if not earlier in Damascus. It thus goes back to within the first five years after Jesus' death. The tradition is a summary of the early Christian preaching and may have been used in Christian instruction. Its form would have made it suitable for memorization. Here is what it says:

> . . . that Christ died for our sins in accordance with the Scriptures,
> and that He was buried,
> and that He was raised on the third day in accordance with the Scriptures,
> and that He appeared to Cephas, then to the Twelve.

Notice that the second line of this tradition refers to Jesus' burial.

But, we might wonder, was the burial mentioned by Paul the same event as the burial by Joseph of Arimathea? The answer to that question is made clear by a comparison of the four-line formula passed on by Paul with the Gospel narratives on the one hand and the sermons in the Acts of the Apostles on the other:

---

38. Rudolph Pesch, *Das Markusevangelium*, 2 vols., Herders theologischer Kommentar zum Neuen Testament (Freiburg: Herder, 1976–77), 2:21, 364–77. Mark Allen Powell, chair of the Historical Jesus section of the Society of Biblical Literature reports, "The dominant view. . . [is] that the passion narratives are early and based on eyewitness testimony" (Mark Allen Powell, critical notice of *The Birth of Christianity*, by John Dominic Crossan, *Journal of the American Academy of Religion* 68 (2000): 171.

1 Corinthians 15:3–5	Acts 13:28–31	Mark 15:37–16:7
Christ died . . .	Though they could charge him with nothing deserving death, yet they asked Pilate to have him killed.	And Jesus uttered a loud cry and breathed his last.
he was buried . . .	they took him down from the tree and laid him in a tomb	And he [Joseph] bought a linen shroud, and taking him down, wrapped him in the linen shroud and laid him in a tomb.
he was raised . . .	But God raised him from the dead . . .	"He has risen, he is not here; see the place where they laid him."
he appeared . . .	. . . and for many days he appeared to those who came up with him from Galilee to Jerusalem, who are now his witnesses to the people.	"But go, tell his disciples and Peter that he is going before you to Galilee; there you will see him."

This remarkable correspondence of independent traditions is convincing proof that the four-line formula (which, as is evident from the grammatically unnecessary repetition of "and that" [*kai hoti*] at the head of each line, lists sequentially four distinct events) is a summary in outline form of the basic events of Jesus' passion and resurrection, including his burial in the tomb. We thus have evidence from two of the earliest, independent sources in the New Testament for the burial of Jesus in the tomb.

But that's not all! For further independent testimony to Jesus' burial by Joseph is also found in the sources behind Matthew and Luke and the Gospel of John, not to mention the extra-biblical *Gospel of Peter*. The differences between Mark's account and those of Matthew and Luke suggest that the latter had sources other than Mark alone. These differences are not plausibly explained as Matthew and Luke's editorial changes of Mark because of their sporadic and uneven nature,[39] the inexplicable omission of events like Pilate's interrogation of the centurion, and the agreements in wording between Mathew and Luke in contrast to Mark.[40] The first two considerations could be equally well explained by rejecting the stratigraphic model of the Gospels in favor of oral performances, in which case it will be the stability of the tradition's core of entombment by Joseph that will commend the historicity of the event. Moreover, the third consideration is not so easily explained, for why would Matthew and Luke independently agree in their performances over

39. E.g., Mark's "tomb which had been hewn out of rock" vs. Matthew's "tomb which he hewed in the rock."

40. E.g., Matt. 27:58 = Luke 23:52: "This man went in to Pilate and asked for the body of Jesus"; also the phrase "wrapped it in linen" is identical in Matthew and Luke.

against Mark? Either way, however, whether through independent sources or a common stable tradition, the historicity of Joseph's burial of Jesus shines through. Moreover, we have another independent source for the burial in John's Gospel, as Paul Barnett explains: "Careful comparison of the texts of Mark and John indicate that neither of these Gospels is dependent on the other. Yet they have a number of incidents in common: for example . . . the burial of Jesus in the tomb of Joseph of Arimathea."[41] Finally we have the early apostolic sermons in the book of Acts, which are probably not wholly Luke's creation but preserve the early preaching of the apostles. These also make mention, as we have seen, of Jesus' interment in a tomb. Thus, we have the remarkable number of at least four and perhaps more independent sources for Jesus' burial, some of which are extraordinarily early.

Second, as a member of the Jewish Sanhedrin that condemned Jesus, Joseph of Arimathea is unlikely to be a Christian invention. Joseph is described as a rich man, a member of the Jewish Sanhedrin. The Sanhedrin was a sort of Jewish high court made up of seventy of the leading men of Judaism, which presided in Jerusalem. There was an understandable hostility in the early church toward the Jewish Sanhedrists. In Christian eyes, they had engineered a judicial murder of Jesus. The sermons in Acts, for example, go so far as to say that the Jewish leaders crucified Jesus (Acts 2:23, 36; 4:10)! Given his status as a Sanhedrist—all of whom, Mark reports, voted to condemn Jesus—Joseph is the last person one would expect to care properly for Jesus. Thus, according to the late New Testament scholar Raymond Brown, Jesus' burial by Joseph is "very probable," since it is "almost inexplicable" why Christians would make up a story about a Jewish Sanhedrist who does what is right by Jesus.[42]

For these and other reasons, most New Testament critics concur that Jesus was buried by Joseph of Arimathea in a tomb. According to the late John A. T. Robinson of Cambridge University, the burial of Jesus in the tomb is "one of the earliest and best-attested facts about Jesus."[43] But if this conclusion is correct, then, as I have explained, it is very difficult to deny the historicity of the empty tomb.

2) The discovery of Jesus' empty tomb is multiply attested in very early, independent sources. The pre-Markan passion source in all probability did not end with Jesus' burial but included the event of the women's discovery of Jesus' empty tomb. For the burial story and empty tomb story are really one story, forming a smooth, continuous narrative. They are linked by grammatical and linguistic ties.[44] Furthermore, it seems unlikely that the early Christians would have circulated a story of Jesus'

---

41. Paul Barnett, *Jesus and the Logic of History,* New Studies in Biblical Theology (Grand Rapids, Mich.: Eerdmans, 1997), 104–5.

42. Raymond E. Brown, *The Death of the Messiah,* 2 vols. (Garden City, N.Y.: Doubleday, 1994), 2:1240–41.

43. John A. T. Robinson, *The Human Face of God* (Philadelphia: Westminster, 1973), 131.

44. E.g., the antecedent of "him" (Jesus) in Mark 16:1 is in the burial account (15:43); the women's discussion of the stone over the door presupposes their prior experience of seeing the stone rolled across the entrance (15:46); their visiting the tomb presupposes their noting its location (15:47); the words of the angel, "see the place where they laid him," refers back to Joseph's laying the body in the tomb (15:46).

passion ending in his burial. The passion story is incomplete without victory at the end. Hence, the pre-Markan source probably included and may have ended with the discovery of the empty tomb.

We have seen that in 1 Corinthians 15:3–5 Paul quotes from an extremely early tradition that refers to Christ's burial and resurrection. Although the empty tomb is not explicitly mentioned, a comparison of the four-line formula with the Gospel narratives on the one hand and the sermons in Acts on the other reveals that the third line is, in fact, a summary of the empty tomb narrative, the "he has been raised" mirroring the "he is risen!"[45] Moreover, two features of the tradition plausibly imply the empty tomb. First, the expression "he was buried," followed by the expression "he was raised" implies the empty tomb. The idea that a man could be buried and then be raised from the dead while his body still remained in the grave is a peculiarly modern notion. For first-century Jews there would have been no question but that the tomb of Jesus would have been empty. As E. E. Ellis remarks, "It is very unlikely that the earliest Palestinian Christians could conceive of any distinction between resurrection and physical, 'grave-emptying' resurrection. To them an *anastasis* (resurrection) without an empty grave would have been about as meaningful as a square circle."[46] Therefore, when the tradition states that Christ was buried and he was raised, it automatically implies that an empty tomb was left behind. Given the early date and provenance of this tradition, the drafters could not have believed such a thing were the tomb not empty.

Second, the expression "on the third day" implies the empty tomb. Very briefly summarized, since no one actually saw Jesus rise from the dead, why did the early disciples proclaim that he had been raised "on the third day"? Why not the seventh day? The most likely answer is that it was on the third day that the women discovered the tomb of Jesus empty; and so naturally, the resurrection itself came to be dated on that day. In this case, the expression "on the third day" is a time indicator pointing to the discovery of the empty tomb.

We have, then, extraordinarily early, independent evidence for the fact of Jesus' empty tomb. The discovery of Jesus' empty tomb cannot be written off as a late legendary development.

But there's more! Once again there are good reasons to discern independent sources for the empty tomb in the other Gospels and Acts. Matthew is clearly working with an independent source, for he includes the story of the guard at the tomb, which is unique to his Gospel. Moreover, there are traces of prior tradition

---

45. It is therefore insufficient to say with Allison that while Paul may have *believed* in the empty tomb on theological grounds, he may not have had actual historical knowledge of it (Allison, *Resurrecting Jesus*, 316). See the other two features of the tradition I mention in the text as well. Curiously, Allison himself recognizes that "1 Cor. 15:3–8 must be be a summary of traditional narratives that were told in fuller forms elsewhere" (ibid., 235; cf. his footnote 133). This is but one example of the many internal inconsistencies that characterize Allison's treatment.

46. E. Earle Ellis, ed., *The Gospel of Luke*, New Century Bible (London: Nelson, 1966), 273.

in the non-Matthean vocabulary in his narrative.[47] And the comment "This story has been spread among Jews till this day" (Matt. 28:15) shows that Matthew is responding to prior tradition. Luke also has an independent source, for he relates the story, not found in Mark, of two disciples' verifying the report of the women that the tomb was vacant. The story can't be regarded as a Lukan creation, since the incident is independently attested in John. And, again, given John's independence of the Synoptic Gospels, we have yet another independent attestation of the empty tomb. Finally, in the apostolic sermons in the book of Acts, we again have indirect references to the empty tomb. For example, Peter draws the sharp contrast, "David . . . both died and was buried and his tomb is with us to this day," but "this Jesus God raised up" (Acts 2:29–32 ESV; cf. 13:36–7).

Historians think that they have hit historical paydirt when they have two independent accounts of the same event. But in the case of the empty tomb we have a surfeit of independent sources, no less than six, some of which are among the earliest materials to be found in the New Testament.[48]

3) *The phrase "the first day of the week" reflects ancient tradition.* According to the Markan account, the empty tomb was discovered by the women "on the first day of the week." We've already seen from the Christian tradition quoted by Paul that the earliest Christians proclaimed the resurrection of Jesus "on the third day." As E. L. Bode explains, if the empty tomb story were a late legend, it would almost certainly have been formulated in terms of the accepted and widespread third-day motif. The fact that Mark uses "on the first day of the week" confirms that his tradition is very old, even antedating the third-day reckoning. This fact is confirmed by the linguistic character of the phrase in question. For although "the first day of the week" is very awkward in the Greek (*te mia ton sabbaton*), employing a cardinal instead of an ordinal number and "Sabbath" for "week," the phrase when translated back into Aramaic is perfectly natural. This suggests that the empty tomb tradition is not a late-developing legend.

47. E.g., several words or expressions which are unique in all the New Testament, such as "on the next day," "the preparation day," "deceiver," "guard (of soldiers)," "to make secure," "to seal." The expression "chief priests and Pharisees" is unusual for Matthew and never appears in Mark or Luke. The expression "on the third day" is also non-Matthean; he always uses "after three days." In general only 35 of Matthew's 136 words in the empty tomb story are found in Mark's 138 words. Similarly, only 16 of Luke's 123 words are found in Mark's account. Moreover, Matthew and Luke have only a dozen words in common, which shows the independence of their traditions.

48. It is ironic, then, that Allison deems Jesus' burial by Joseph of Arimathea to be "well attested" and therefore "highly likely," while complaining that scholarly opinion is divided over how many independent souces we have for the empty tomb (Allison, *Resurrecting Jesus*, 300, 354, 362). There is a clear double standard operative here. Notice that as in the case of Joseph's burial of Jesus, multiple, independent attestation militates against the possibility, taken with grave seriousness by Allison, that the empty tomb narrative is an imaginative Christian fabrication or legend (ibid., 311). Its presence, like that of the burial narrative, in such early, independent sources makes such a possibility very unlikely. Notice, too, that the possibility of Christian fabrication or legend is predicated upon an important condition: "Christians might . . . have been able to reason like this without fear of contradiction if the location of Jesus' burial or disposal were unknown, or if too much time had passed since his death" (ibid., 307)—a condition Allison himself admits is unmet (ibid., 232, 362).

4) *The Markan story is simple and lacks legendary development.* Like the burial account, Mark's account is remarkably straightforward and unembellished by theological or apologetic motifs likely to characterize a later legendary account.[49] The resurrection itself is not witnessed or described, and there is no reflection on Jesus' triumph over sin and death, no use of Christological titles, no quotation of fulfilled prophecy, no description of the Risen Lord. Some critics might stumble at the presence of the angel, but really there is no reason to think that the tradition ever lacked the angel. We may choose to excise him as, say, a purely literary figure which provides the interpretation of the vacant tomb, but then we have a narrative that is all the more stark and unadorned (cf. John 20:1–2). To appreciate how restrained Mark's narrative is, one has only to read the account in the *Gospel of Peter*, which describes Jesus' triumphant egress from the tomb as a gigantic figure whose head reaches above the clouds, supported by giant angels, followed by a talking cross, heralded by a voice from heaven, and all witnessed by a Roman guard, the Jewish leaders, and a multitude of spectators! This is how real legends look: they are colored by theological and apologetical developments. By contrast, the Markan account is stark in its simplicity.

5) *The tomb was probably discovered empty by women.* In order to grasp this point, we need to understand two things about the place of women in Jewish society. First, women were not regarded as credible witnesses. This attitude toward the testimony of women is evident in Josephus's description of the rules supposedly left by Moses for admissible testimony: "Let not the testimony of women be admitted, on account of the levity and boldness of their sex" (*Antiquities of the Jews* IV.8.15.§219). No such regulation is to be found in the Pentateuch but is rather a reflection of the patriarchal society of first-century Judaism.

Second, women occupied a low rung on the Jewish social ladder. Compared to men, women were second-class citizens. Consider these rabbinical texts: "Sooner let the words of the Law be burnt than delivered to women!" (Sotah 19a) and again: "Happy is he whose children are male, but unhappy is he whose children are female!" (Kiddushin 82b). The daily prayer of every Jewish man included the benediction "Blessed are you, Lord our God, ruler of the universe, who has not created me a woman" (Berachos 60b).

Now, given their low social status and inability to serve as legal witnesses, it's quite amazing that it is women who are the discoverers of and principal

---

49. Again, it is ironic that Allison recognizes this feature of the empty tomb narrative; but whereas he considers this factor to be very weighty evidence when it comes to the historicity of Jesus' burial by Joseph of Arimathea, he doesn't give it due weight when it comes to the empty tomb (Allison, *Resurrecting Jesus*, 320–21, 356). Cf. his treatment of the proper names associated with the burial narrative and with the empty tomb narrative (ibid., 327, 355), of the application of the criterion of embarrassment to both narratives (ibid., 327–29, 354–55), and of the public knowledge of the burial and the tomb's location (ibid., 313, 316–20, 362). It's strange that Allison doesn't seem to notice that the same arguments which lead to his unqualified verdict of "highly likely" for the burial by Joseph also support the historicity of the empty tomb, which he deems "with great hesitation" to be "historically likely" (Allison, *Resurrecting Jesus*, 332).

witnesses to the empty tomb. If the empty tomb story were a legend, then it is most likely that the male disciples would have been made to be the first to discover the empty tomb. The fact that women, whose testimony was deemed worthless, were the chief witnesses to the fact of the empty tomb can only be plausibly explained if, like it or not, they actually were the discoverers of the empty tomb. Hence, the Gospels are most likely giving an accurate account of this matter.

Skeptical critics have proposed all sorts of creative explanations for the women's role, some of them quite fantastic, such as Crossan's proposal that the women are vestiges of an earlier *Secret Gospel of Mark* (a hypothesis which has blown up in Crossan's face by the demonstration that the *Secret Gospel of Mark* was a fraud perpetrated by Morton Smith). In general the problem with these hypotheses is that any conceivable role for women to play in the narrative would have been better served by men. Some scholars have said that the men were not available because they had all fled. Such a claim is wholly unconvincing, since it depends upon the implausible hypothesis that the disciples, fleeing from the garden, returned all the way back to Galilee (a supposition rightly dubbed "a fiction of the critics") and fails to appreciate that legends by their very nature are no respecters of fact. As Allison insists, "It is the hallmark of legends to sin against the established facts. Why should Mark . . . be more conscientious? Why not bring Peter and other more important disciples on the stage despite what really happened?"[50] Some critics have said that women are made the discoverers of Jesus' empty tomb as Mark's way of explaining why the fact of Jesus' empty tomb had remained unknown until the writing of his Gospel—the women didn't tell anybody! This hypothesis is too clever by half. In the first place we have seen that the empty tomb story is not a late-developing legend but is extremely early. But secondly, are Mark's readers seriously to believe that for thirty years no one in the Jerusalem church ever bothered to ask the women whom Mark placed at the cross about what happened afterward or that even *after* the resurrection appearances the women continued to stonewall? Mark doubtless intended the women's silence to be taken as temporary, since he foreshadows appearances of Jesus to the disciples in Galilee, where the women are commanded to tell the disciples that they will see Jesus. When Mark says, "They said nothing to anyone" (Mark 16:8), he obviously means "as they fled back to the disciples." This is precisely how his earliest literary interpreters Matthew and Luke understood him, and Mark would doubtless have been quite surprised by the suggestion that he meant that the women never said anything to anyone.[51] The contrived

50. Dale C. Allison Jr., "Explaining the Resurrection: Conflicting Convictions," *Journal for the Study of the Historical Jesus* 3 (2005): 128; cf. Allison, *Resurrecting Jesus*, 329–30.

51. See the fine study by Larry Hurtado, "Mission Accomplished: Apologetics, Witness, and Women in Mark's Passion-Resurrection Narratives," paper delivered at the 2005 meeting of the Society of Biblical Literature, forthcoming as "The Women, the Tomb, and the Climax of Mark" in a Festschrift for Sean Freyne to be published by Brill.

nature of these attempts to explain away the women witnesses only reinforces the historical credibility of this feature of the narrative; indeed, probably no other factor has proved so persuasive to scholars of the empty tomb's historicity as the role of the female witnesses.

6) *The earliest Jewish polemic presupposes the empty tomb.* In Matthew 28:11–15 (RSV) we have the earliest Christian attempt to refute the Jewish polemic against the Christian proclamation of the resurrection:

> While they were going, behold, some of the guard went into the city and told the chief priests all that had taken place. And when they had assembled with the elders and taken counsel, they gave a sum of money to the soldiers and said, "Tell people, 'His disciples came by night and stole him away while we were asleep.' And if this comes to the governor's ears, we will satisfy him and keep you out of trouble." So they took the money and did as they were directed; and this story has been spread among the Jews to this day.

Now our interest is not so much in the evangelist's story of the guard at the tomb as in his incidental remark at the end: "This story had been spread among the Jews to this day." This remark reveals that the author was concerned to refute a widespread Jewish explanation of the resurrection. Now what were unbelieving Jews saying in response to the disciples' proclamation that Jesus was risen? That these men are full of new wine? That Jesus' body still lay in the tomb in the hillside? No. They were saying, "The disciples stole away his body." Think about that. "The disciples stole away his body." The Jewish polemic did not deny the empty tomb but instead entangled itself in a hopeless series of absurdities trying to explain it away. In other words, the Jewish claim that the disciples stole the body presupposes that the body was missing.

Skeptical critics have dismissed Matthew's guard story as an apologetic legend. But even if we regard the guard as a Christian apologetic creation, the fact which cannot be denied is that the story was aimed at a widespread Jewish allegation that the disciples had stolen Jesus' body—which implies the empty tomb. That the story is not a Matthean creation out of whole cloth is evident not only in the many non-Matthean linguistic traits noted above, but also by the tradition history presupposed by the narrative. Behind the story evidently lies a developing pattern of assertion and counter-assertion:

Christian: "The Lord is risen!"
Jew: "No, his disciples stole away his body."
Christian: "The guard at the tomb would have prevented any such theft."
Jew: "No, the guard fell asleep."
Christian: "The chief priests bribed the guard to say this."

This pattern probably goes right back to controversies in Jerusalem following the disciples' proclamation of the resurrection.[52] In response to the Christian proclamation of Jesus' resurrection, the Jewish reaction was simply to assert that the disciples had stolen the body. The idea of a guard could only have been a Christian, not a Jewish, development. At the next stage there is no need for Christians to invent the bribing of the guard; it was sufficient to claim that the tomb was guarded. The bribe arises only in response to the second stage of the polemic, the Jewish allegation that the guard fell asleep. This part of the story could only have been a Jewish development, since it serves no purpose in the Christian polemic. At the final stage, the time of Matthew's writing, the Christian answer that the guards were bribed is given.

Thus, the Jewish polemic itself shows that the tomb was empty. This is historical evidence of the highest quality, since it comes not from the Christians but from the very enemies of the early Christian faith.

Taken together these six lines of evidence constitute a powerful case that Jesus' tomb was indeed found empty on the first day of the week by a group of his women followers. As a historical fact, this seems to be well established. According to D. H. Van Daalen, It is extremely difficult to object to the empty tomb on historical grounds; those who deny it do so on the basis of theological or philosophical assumptions.[53] But those assumptions cannot alter the facts themselves. New Testament scholars seem to be increasingly aware of this. According to Jacob Kremer, a New Testament critic who has specialized in the study of the resurrection: "By far most exegetes hold firmly to the reliability of the biblical statements about the empty tomb."[54] In fact in a bibliographical survey of over 2,200 publications on the resurrection in English, French, and German since 1975, Habermas found

---

52. Allison overlooks this developing pattern in confessing that it escapes him why this passage "bears 'the mark of a fairly protracted controversy'" (Allison, *Resurrecting Jesus*, 312). Contrast Meier's judgment: "The earliest fights about the person of Jesus that raged between ordinary Jews and Christian Jews after Easter centered on the Christian claims that a crucified criminal was the Messiah, that God had raised him from the dead" (Meier, *A Marginal Jew*, 2:150). Given the early date of the pre-Markan passion story, there is no need to quarrel with Allison's surmise that the controversy arose between Mark and Matthew, so long as by "Mark" we mean Mark's tradition.

53. D. H. Van Daalen, *The Real Resurrection* (London: Collins, 1972), 41. Allison is a good case in point. He recognizes that "a decent case" can be made for the empty tomb but thinks that there is "a respectable case against it" (Allison, *Resurrecting Jesus*, 331). This supposedly respectable case consists of only two arguments: first, "the ability of early Christians to create fictions" and, second, "the existence of numerous legends about missing bodies" (ibid., 332). But these two considerations show at the very most the possibility that the empty tomb narrative is a legend. This is a possibility we are aware of based on our general background knowledge *prior* to an examination of the specific evidence. These two considerations do nothing to show that, based on an examination of the specific evidence, the narrative of the empty tomb *is* a fiction or legend. Allison's skepticism is rooted in his initial philosophical doubts, which he candidly expresses, about the literal resurrection of Jesus (ibid., 225; cf. 344). That someone exhibiting such proclivity against the empty tomb, doubtless because of his philosophical reservations about the material continuity of the resurrected body with the mortal body, should nonetheless feel compelled to affirm the historicity of the empty tomb is testimony to the strength of the evidence in its favor.

54. Jacob Kremer, *Die Osterevangelien—Geschichten um Geschichte* (Stuttgart: Katholisches Bibelwerk, 1977), 49–50.

that 75 percent of scholars accepted the historicity of the discovery of Jesus' empty tomb.[55] The evidence is so compelling that even a number of Jewish scholars, such as Pinchas Lapide and Geza Vermes, have declared themselves convinced on the basis of the evidence that Jesus' tomb was found empty.

EXPLAINING THE EMPTY TOMB

Now if this is the case, that leads us to our second main point: explaining the empty tomb. Down through history, those who denied the resurrection of Jesus have been obligated to come up with a convincing alternative explanation. In fact, they have come up with only about four:

Conspiracy Hypothesis

According to this explanation, the disciples stole the body of Jesus and lied about his postmortem appearances, thus faking the resurrection. This was, as we saw, the first counter-explanation for the empty tomb, and it was revived by the Deists during the eighteenth century. Today, however, this explanation has been completely given up by modern scholarship. Let's see how it fares when assessed by McCullagh's criteria for justifying historical hypotheses.

1) *The hypothesis, together with other true statements, must imply further statements describing present, observable data.* Virtually any explanation offered for the resurrection will fulfill this first criterion, since such explanations are offered to account for the New Testament witness to Jesus' resurrection and so will imply that the literary evidence contained in the New Testament will exist as a result of the events described in the proposed hypothesis. On the Conspiracy Hypothesis the Gospel accounts are simply deliberate fabrications.

2) *The hypothesis must have greater explanatory scope than rival hypotheses.* The Conspiracy Hypothesis seems to cover the full scope of the evidence, for it offers explanations of the empty tomb, the postmortem appearances, and the origin of the disciples' (supposed) belief in Jesus' resurrection.

3) *The hypothesis must have greater explanatory power than rival hypotheses.* Here doubts begin to arise about the Conspiracy Hypothesis. Take the empty tomb, for example. If the disciples stole Jesus' corpse, then it would be utterly daft to fabricate a story of women's finding the tomb to be empty. Such a story would not be the sort of tale Jewish men would invent. Moreover, the simplicity of the narrative is not well explained by the Conspiracy Hypothesis—where are the Scripture citations, the evidence of fulfilled prophecy? Why isn't Jesus described as emerging from the tomb, as in later forgeries like the *Gospel of Peter*? Neither is the polemic with non-believing Jews well explained. Why isn't Matthew's guard already there in the pre-Markan tradition? Even in Matthew's story the guard is set too late: the body could have been already stolen before the guard arrived on Saturday morning. For a fail-safe alibi against theft of the body, see once more the

55. Gary Habermas, "Experience of the Risen Jesus: The Foundational Historical Issue in the Early Proclamation of the Resurrection," *Dialog* 45 (2006): 292.

Gospel of Peter, where the guard (explicitly identified as Roman) is set immediately upon interment of the corpse.

As for the appearance narratives, similar problems arise. A fabricator would probably describe the appearances in terms of Old Testament theophanies and descriptions of eschatological resurrection (e.g., Dan. 12:2). But then Jesus should appear to the disciples in dazzling glory. And why not a description of the resurrection itself? Why no appearances to Caiaphas or the villains on the Sanhedrin, as Jesus predicted? They could be then branded as the real liars for denying that Jesus did appear to them.

But the explanatory power of the Conspiracy Hypothesis is undoubtedly weakest when it comes to the origin of the disciples' belief in Jesus' resurrection. For the hypothesis is really a denial of that fact; it seeks to explain the mere semblance of belief on the disciples' part. But as critics since Strauss have universally recognized, one cannot plausibly deny that the earliest disciples at least sincerely believed that Jesus was risen from the dead, a conviction on which they staked their very lives, as Paley so eloquently emphasized. The transformation in the lives of the disciples is not credibly explained by the hypothesis of a conspiracy. This shortcoming alone has been enough in the minds of most scholars to sink the old Conspiracy Hypothesis.

4) *The hypothesis must be more plausible than rival hypotheses.* The real Achilles' heel of the Conspiracy Hypothesis is, however, its implausibility. One might mention here the usual objections to the unbelievable complexity of such a conspiracy or the supposed psychological state of the disciples; but the overriding problem is the anachronism of first-century Jews' intending to hoax Jesus' resurrection. The Conspiracy Hypothesis views the disciples' situation through the rearview mirror of Christian history rather than through the eyes of a first-century Jew. There was no expectation of a Messiah who, instead of establishing David's throne and subduing Israel's enemies, would be shamefully executed by the Gentiles as a criminal. Moreover, the idea of eschatological resurrection was unconnected with the idea of Messiah and even incompatible with it. As Wright nicely puts it, if your favorite Messiah got himself crucified, then you either went home or else you got yourself a new Messiah. But the idea of stealing Jesus' corpse and saying that God had raised him from the dead is hardly one that would have entered the minds of the disciples.

5) *The hypothesis must be less ad hoc than rival hypotheses.* Like all conspiracy theories of history, the Conspiracy Hypothesis is ad hoc in postulating that what all the evidence seems to point to is, in fact, mere appearance only, to be explained away by hypotheses for which there is no evidence. Specifically, it postulates motives and ideas in the thinking of the earliest disciples and actions on their part for which there is not a shred of evidence. It can become even more ad hoc, as hypotheses must be multiplied to deal with objections to the theory, for example,

how to account for the appearance to the 500 brethren or the women's role in the empty tomb and appearance stories.

6) *The hypothesis must be disconfirmed by fewer accepted beliefs than rival hypotheses.* The Conspiracy Hypothesis tends to be disconfirmed by our general knowledge of conspiracies, their instability and tendency to unravel. Moreover, it is disconfirmed by accepted beliefs such as the sincerity of the disciples, the nature of first-century Jewish messianic expectations, and so on.

7) *The hypothesis must significantly exceed its rivals in fulfilling conditions (2)–(6).* This condition is obviously not met, since there are better hypotheses, such as the Hallucination Hypothesis, which do not dismiss the disciples' belief in Jesus' resurrection as fraudulent.

No scholar would defend the Conspiracy Hypothesis today. The only place you read about such things is in the popular, sensationalist press or in former propaganda from behind the Iron Curtain.

Apparent Death Hypothesis
A second theory was the apparent death explanation. Critics around the beginning of the nineteenth century such as Heinrich Paulus or Friedrich Schleiermacher defended the view that Jesus was not completely dead when he was taken down from the cross. He revived in the tomb and escaped to convince his disciples he had risen from the dead. Today this hypothesis has also been almost completely given up. Once again, let's apply McCullagh's criteria for the best explanation:

1) *The hypothesis, together with other true statements, must imply further statements describing present, observable data.* Again this condition is easily met.

2) *The hypothesis must have greater explanatory scope than rival hypotheses.* The Apparent Death Hypothesis also provides explanations for the empty tomb, post-mortem appearances, and origin of the disciples' belief in Jesus' resurrection.

3) *The hypothesis must have greater explanatory power than rival hypotheses.* Here the theory begins to founder. Some versions of the Apparent Death Hypothesis are really variations on the Conspiracy Hypothesis, merely substituting the disciples' hoaxing Jesus' death for their stealing Jesus' body. In such cases, the theory shares all the weaknesses of the Conspiracy Hypothesis. A non-conspiratorial version of the theory is also saddled with insuperable difficulties: how to explain the empty tomb, given Jesus' merely apparent death, since a man sealed inside a tomb could not move the stone so as to escape; how to explain the postmortem appearances, since as Strauss mused, the appearance of a half-dead man desperately in need of medical attention would hardly have elicited in the disciples the conclusion that he was the Risen Lord and conqueror of Death; and how to explain the anachronism of the origin of the disciples' belief in Jesus' resurrection, since seeing him again would lead them to conclude that he had not died, not that he was, contrary to Jewish thought (as well as their own eyes), gloriously risen from the dead.

4) *The hypothesis must be more plausible than rival hypotheses.* Here again the theory fails miserably. Roman executioners could be relied upon to ensure that

their victims were dead. Since the exact moment of death by crucifixion was uncertain, executioners could ensure death by a spear thrust into the victim's side,
such as was dealt to Jesus. Moreover, what the theory suggests is virtually physically impossible. The extent of Jesus' tortures was such that he could never have
survived the crucifixion and entombment. The suggestion that a man so critically
wounded then went on to appear to the disciples on various occasions in Jerusalem
and Galilee is pure fantasy.

5) *The hypothesis must be less ad hoc than rival hypotheses.* The Apparent Death
Hypothesis, especially in its conspiratorial instantiations, can become enormously
ad hoc. We are invited to imagine secret societies, stealthily administered potions,
conspiratorial alliances between Jesus' disciples and members of the Sanhedrin,
and so forth, all with nary a scrap of evidence in support.

6) *The hypothesis must be disconfirmed by fewer accepted beliefs than rival hypotheses.* The Apparent Death Hypothesis is massively disconfirmed by medical facts
concerning what would happen to a person who has been scourged and crucified.
It is also disconfirmed by the unanimous evidence that Jesus did not continue
among his disciples after his death.

7) *The hypothesis must significantly exceed its rivals in fulfilling conditions (2)–(6).*
This theory also is hardly a standout. For that reason it has virtually no defenders
among New Testament historians today.

Wrong Tomb Hypothesis

First proposed by Kirsopp Lake in 1907, this theory holds that the belief in Jesus'
empty tomb was based on a simple mistake. According to Lake, the women lost
their way that Sunday morning and happened upon a caretaker at an unoccupied
tomb in the garden. He said something like, "You're looking for Jesus of Nazareth. He is not here." The women, however, were so unnerved that they fled. After
the disciples had experienced visions of Jesus alive, the women's story developed
into the account of their discovery of Jesus' empty tomb. Unlike the previous two
theories considered, Lake's hypothesis generated virtually no following but was
dead almost upon arrival.

1) *The hypothesis, together with other true statements, must imply further statements
describing present, observable data.* This condition is easily met.

2) *The hypothesis must have greater explanatory scope than rival hypotheses.* Lake's
theory doesn't really explain the resurrection appearances. Some additional
hypothesis will have to be conjoined to the Wrong Tomb Hypothesis in order to
explain Jesus' appearances. In that sense the theory fails to have sufficiently wide
explanatory scope.

3) *The hypothesis must have greater explanatory power than rival hypotheses.* Because the Wrong Tomb Hypothesis says nothing to explain the postmortem appearances, it has no explanatory power in that respect. It also is anachronistic in
its explanation of the origin of the disciples' belief in Jesus' resurrection. Merely
going to the wrong tomb and seeing a man there telling them that Jesus is not

there would hardly lead a first-century Jew to conclude that Jesus was risen from the dead—especially if this were reported by women and could not be verified. In fact, the question of verification reveals that Lake's hypothesis has weak explanatory power even with respect to the empty tomb. For any later check of the tomb would have revealed the women's error. After their initial fright, wouldn't the women have attempted to retrace their steps by the light of day? Certainly the disciples themselves would have wanted to verify the empty tomb. The state of the actual tomb could not have remained a matter of complete indifference to a movement in the same locale based on belief in the resurrection of the dead man interred there. And in any case, since the burial site was known to Jew and Christian alike, the Jewish opponents of the Christians would have been only too happy to point out the women's error.

4) *The hypothesis must be more plausible than rival hypotheses.* The Wrong Tomb Hypothesis is also implausible in light of the evidence we do have, for example, that the site of Jesus' tomb was known to Jew and Christian alike in Jerusalem, that the empty tomb story is extremely early and shows no signs of theological development and reflection, and so on. Insofar as the Hallucination Hypothesis proves to be implausible, Lake's theory will share that, too.

5) *The hypothesis must be less ad hoc than rival hypotheses.* Lake's theory is ad hoc in that it treats the evidence selectively and arbitrarily. For example, Lake regards the women's visit to the tomb with the intention of anointing the body as historical but must discount their noting, precisely because of that intention, where the body was laid (Mark 15:47; 16:1). But why accept the one but not the other? Or again, Lake regards the angel's words ascribed to the caretaker, "You're looking for Jesus of Nazareth. He is not here," as authentic but passes over the words, "He is risen!" But all of the angel's message is the language of Christian proclamation if any of it is. Similarly, there are no grounds for taking Mark's "young man" to be a human rather than angelic figure, the Greek word used here being often used of angels and the man's white robe being typical for the Jewish portrait of angels. Moreover, the women's fear and astonishment is a characteristic Markan motif which presupposes the angelic confrontation, so that one cannot regard the women's reaction as traditional and historical while historically excising the angel as a legendary accretion.

6) *The hypothesis must be disconfirmed by fewer accepted beliefs than rival hypotheses.* The Wrong Tomb Hypothesis will be disconfirmed by the generally accepted beliefs that Joseph of Arimathea buried Jesus and thus could point to his burial location, that the empty tomb tradition belongs to very early rather than late tradition, and so on.

7) *The hypothesis must significantly exceed its rivals in fulfilling conditions (2)–(6).* Obviously, nobody thinks that this is the case.

Displaced Body Hypothesis

In one of the few Jewish attempts to deal with the facts concerning Jesus' resurrec-tion, Joseph Klausner in 1922 proposed that Joseph of Arimathea placed Jesus' body in his tomb temporarily, due to the lateness of the hour and the proximity of his own family tomb. But then he moved the corpse later to the criminals' graveyard. Unaware of the displacement of the body, the disciples erroneously inferred Jesus' resurrection from the dead. Although no scholars defend Klausner's hypothesis today, I have seen attempts by popular authors to revive it. In light of what has already been said of other theories, its shortcomings are evident:

1) *The hypothesis, together with other true statements, must imply further statements describing present, observable data.* No problem here.

2) *The hypothesis must have greater explanatory scope than rival hypotheses.* The Displaced Body Hypothesis has narrow explanatory scope. It tries to explain the empty tomb but says nothing about the postmortem appearances and the origin of the disciples' belief in Jesus' resurrection.

3) *The hypothesis must have greater explanatory power than rival hypotheses.* Klaus-ner's hypothesis has no explanatory power vis-à-vis the appearances and the origin of the Christian faith. As for the empty tomb, it faces the same obstacle as the Wrong Tomb Hypothesis: since Joseph and any servants with him knew what they had done with the corpse, the theory is at a loss to explain why the disciples' error was not corrected—unless, that is, one resorts to ad hoc conjectures such as Joseph and his servants' sudden deaths! It might be said that Jesus' corpse would have no longer been identifiable; but that is to miss the point. The point is that the earliest Jewish/Christian disputes about the resurrection were not over the location of Jesus' grave or the identity of the corpse but over why the tomb was empty. Had Joseph displaced the body, the Jewish/Christian polemic would have taken a quite different course.

4) *The hypothesis must be more plausible than rival hypotheses.* The hypothesis is implausible for a number of reasons. So far as we can rely on Jewish sources, the criminals' graveyard was only 50 to 600 yards from the site of Jesus' crucifixion. Jewish practice, furthermore, was to bury executed criminals on the day of their execution, so that is what Joseph would have wanted to accomplish. Therefore, Joseph could and would have placed the body directly in the criminals' graveyard, thereby obviating any need to move it later or defile his own family tomb. Indeed, Jewish law did not even permit the body to be moved later, except to the family tomb (Semachot 13.7). Joseph had adequate time for a simple burial, which prob-ably included washing the corpse and wrapping it up in a sheet with dry spices.

5) *The hypothesis must be less* ad hoc *than rival hypotheses.* The theory is some-what ad hoc in ascribing to Joseph motives and activities for which we have no evidence at all.

6) *The hypothesis must be disconfirmed by fewer accepted beliefs than rival hypotheses.* The theory suffers disconfirmation from what we know about Jewish burial procedures for criminals mentioned above.

7) *The hypothesis must significantly exceed its rivals in fulfilling conditions (2)–(6).* Again, no historian seems to share this estimation.

As we look at these hypotheses proffered to explain the fact of the empty tomb, it is striking that scarcely any modern historian or biblical critic would hold to these theories. They are almost completely passé. You may say to yourselves at this point, "Well, then, what explanation of the empty tomb do modern critics offer who deny the resurrection?" The fact is that they are self-confessedly without any explanation to offer. There simply is no plausible natural explanation available today to account for how Jesus' tomb became empty. If we deny the resurrection of Jesus, we are left with an inexplicable mystery.

Conclusion

We have seen that multiple lines of historical evidence indicate that Jesus' tomb was found empty on Sunday morning by a group of his women followers. Furthermore, no convincing natural explanation is available to account for this fact. This alone might prompt us to believe that the resurrection of Jesus is the best explanation. But there is even more evidence to come.

The Postmortem Appearances
In 1 Corinthians 15:3–8 (RSV), Paul writes:

> For I delivered to you as of first importance what I also received,
>> that Christ died for our sins in accordance with the scriptures,
> and that he was buried,
> and that he was raised on the third day in accordance with the scriptures,
> and that he appeared to Cephas, then to the Twelve.
>> Then he appeared to more than five hundred brethren at one time, most of whom are still alive, though some have fallen asleep. Then he appeared to James, then to all the apostles. Last of all, as to one untimely born, he appeared also to me.

This is a truly remarkable claim. We have here an indisputably authentic letter of a man personally acquainted with the first disciples, and he reports that they actually saw Jesus alive after his death. More than that, he says that he himself also saw an appearance of Jesus. What are we to make of this claim? Did Jesus really appear to people alive after his death?

To answer this question, let's again consider two major points: first, the fact of the resurrection appearances of Jesus; and second, explaining the resurrection appearances.

THE FACT OF THE POSTMORTEM APPEARANCES

Once again, space will not allow me to examine in detail all the evidence for Jesus' post-mortem appearances. But I'd like to examine three main lines of evidence.

1) *Paul's list of eyewitnesses to Jesus' resurrection appearances guarantees that such appearances occurred.* We saw that in 1 Corinthians 15 Paul gives a list of witnesses to Jesus' resurrection appearances. Let's look briefly at each appearance to see whether it is plausible that such events actually took place.

a) *Appearance to Peter.* We have no story in the Gospels telling of Jesus' appearance to Peter. But the appearance is mentioned here in the old Christian tradition quoted by Paul, which originated in the Jerusalem church, and it is vouched by the apostle Paul himself. As we know from Galatians 1:18, Paul spent about two weeks with Peter in Jerusalem three years after his Damascus Road experience. So Paul would know personally whether Peter claimed to have had such an experience. In addition to this, the appearance to Peter is mentioned in another old Christian tradition found in Luke 24:34 (AT): "The Lord has really risen, and has appeared to Simon!" That Luke is working with a tradition here is evident by the awkward way in which it intrudes into his narrative of the Emmaus disciples. So although we have no detailed story of this appearance, it is quite well founded historically. As a result, even the most skeptical New Testament critics agree that Peter saw an appearance of Jesus alive from the dead.

b) *Appearance to the Twelve.* Undoubtedly, the reference here is to that original group of disciples who had been chosen by Jesus during his ministry—less, of course, Judas, whose absence did not affect the formal title of the group. This is the best-attested resurrection appearance of Jesus. It, too, is included in the very early traditional formula that Paul cites, and Paul himself had contact with members of the Twelve. Moreover, we have independent stories of this appearance in Luke 24:36–42 and John 20:19–20. Undoubtedly, the most notable feature of these appearance stories is the physical demonstrations of Jesus' showing his wounds and eating before the disciples. The purpose of the physical demonstrations is to show two things: first, that Jesus was raised *physically*; and second, that he was the *same Jesus* who had been crucified. Thus, they served to demonstrate both *corporeality* and *continuity* of the resurrection body. There can be little doubt that such an appearance occurred, for it is attested in the old Christian tradition, vouched for by Paul, who had personal contact with the Twelve, and is independently described by both Luke and John.

c) *Appearance to five hundred brethren.* The third appearance comes as somewhat of a shock: "then he appeared to more than five hundred brethren at one time"! This is surprising, since we have no mention whatsoever of this appearance elsewhere in the New Testament. This might make one rather skeptical about this appearance, but Paul himself apparently had personal contact with these people, since he knew that some had died. This is seen in Paul's parenthetical comment, "most of whom remain until now, but some have fallen asleep." Why does Paul add this remark? The great New Testament scholar of Cambridge University, C. H. Dodd, replies, "There can hardly be any purpose in mentioning the fact that the most of the 500 are still alive, unless Paul is saying, in effect, 'The witnesses are there to be questioned.'"[56] Notice: Paul could never have said this if the event had not occurred. He could not have challenged people to ask the witnesses if the event had never taken place and there were no witnesses. But evidently there were witnesses to this event, and Paul knew that some of them had died in the meantime. Therefore, the event must have taken place.

I think that this appearance is not related in the Gospels because it probably took place in Galilee. As one puts together the various appearances in the Gospels, it seems that they occurred first in Jerusalem, then in Galilee, and then in Jerusalem again. The appearance to the five hundred would have to be out of doors, perhaps on a hillside outside a Galilean village. In Galilee thousands had gathered to hear Jesus teach during his ministry. Since the Gospels focus their attention on the appearances in Jerusalem, we do not have any story of this appearance to the five hundred because it probably occurred in Galilee. An intriguing possibility is that this was the appearance predicted by the angel in the pre-Markan passion story and described by Matthew (28:16–17).

d) *Appearance to James.* The next appearance is one of the most amazing of all: he appeared to James, Jesus' younger brother. What makes this amazing is that apparently neither James nor any of Jesus' younger brothers believed in Jesus during his lifetime (Mark 3:21, 31–35; John 7:1–10). They didn't believe he was the Messiah, or a prophet, or even anybody special. By the criterion of embarrassment, this is doubtless a historical facet of Jesus' life and ministry. But after the resurrection, Jesus' brothers show up in the Christian fellowship in the upper room in Jerusalem (Acts 1:14). There is no further mention of them until Acts 12:17. This is the story of Peter's deliverance from prison by the angel. What are Peter's first words? "Report this to *James.*" In Galatians 1:19 Paul tells of his two-week visit to Jerusalem about three years after his Damascus Road experience. He says that besides Peter, he saw none of the other apostles *except James* the Lord's brother. Paul at least implies that James was now being reckoned as an apostle. When Paul visited Jerusalem again fourteen years later, he says there were three "pillars" of the church in Jerusalem: Peter, John, and *James* (Gal. 2:9). Finally, in Acts 21:18 James is the sole head of the Jerusalem church and of the council of elders. We hear no more about James in the New Testament; but from Josephus, the Jewish historian, we learn that James was stoned to death illegally by the Sanhedrin sometime after A.D. 60 for his faith in Christ (Josephus, *Antiquities of the Jews* 20.200). Not only James but also Jesus' other brothers became believers and were active in Christian preaching, as we see from 1 Corinthians 9:5 (RSV): "Do we not

56. C. H. Dodd, "The Appearances of the Risen Christ: A study in the form criticism of the Gospels," in *More New Testament Studies* (Manchester: University of Manchester, 1968), 128.

have the right to be accompanied by a wife, as the other apostles and the brothers of the Lord and Cephas?"

Now, how is this to be explained? On the one hand, it seems certain that Jesus' brothers did not believe in him during his lifetime. On the other hand, it is equally certain that they became ardent Christians, active in the church. Jesus' crucifixion would only confirm in James's mind that his elder brother's Messianic pretensions were delusory, just as he had thought. Many of us have brothers. What would it take to make you believe that your brother is the Lord, so that you would die for this belief, as James did? Can there be any doubt that the reason for this remarkable transformation is to be found in the fact that "then he appeared to James"? Even the skeptical New Testament critic Hans Grass admits that the conversion of James is one of the surest proofs of the resurrection of Jesus Christ.[57]

e) *Appearance to "all the apostles."* This appearance was probably to a limited circle of Christian missionaries somewhat wider than the Twelve. For such a group, see Acts 1:21–22. Once again, the facticity of this appearance is guaranteed by Paul's personal contact with the apostles themselves.

f) *Appearance to Saul of Tarsus.* The final appearance is just as amazing as the appearance to James: "Last of all," says Paul, "he appeared to me also." The story of Jesus' appearance to Saul of Tarsus (or Paul) just outside Damascus is related in Acts 9:1–9 and is later told again twice. That this event actually occurred is established beyond doubt by Paul's references to it in his own letters.

This event changed Saul's whole life. He was a rabbi, a Pharisee, a respected Jewish leader. He hated the Christian heresy and was doing everything in his power to stamp it out. He was even responsible for the execution of Christian believers. Then suddenly he gave up everything. He left his position as a respected Jewish leader and became a Christian missionary: he entered a life of poverty, labor, and suffering. He was whipped, beaten, stoned and left for dead, shipwrecked three times, in constant danger, deprivation, and anxiety. Finally, he made the ultimate sacrifice and was martyred for his faith at Rome. And it was all because on that day outside Damascus, he saw "Jesus our Lord" (1 Cor. 9:1).

The list of witnesses of postmortem appearances of Jesus which Paul transmits thus makes it indisputable that individuals and groups had such experiences.

2) *The Gospel accounts provide multiple, independent attestation of postmortem appearances of Jesus.* The Gospels independently attest to postmortem appearances of Jesus, even to some of the same appearances found in Paul's list. Wolfgang Trilling explains,

> From the list in I Cor. 15 the particular reports of the Gospels are now to be interpreted. Here may be of help what we said about Jesus' miracles. It is impossible to "prove" historically a particular miracle. But the totality of the miracle reports permits

57. Hans Grass, *Ostergeschehen und Osterberichte*, 4th ed. (Göttingen: Vandenhoeck & Ruprecht, 1974), 80.

no reasonable doubt that Jesus in fact performed "miracles." That holds analogously for the appearance reports. It is not possible to secure historically the particular event. But the totality of the appearance reports permits no reasonable doubt that Jesus in fact bore witness to himself in such a way.[58]

Trilling's conclusion is actually too modest: for just as we can justifiably infer the historicity of specific miracles of Jesus, such as his feeding of the 5,000, so can we infer the historicity of some of the specific appearances. The appearance to Peter is independently attested by Paul and Luke (1 Cor. 15:5; Luke 24:34) and is universally acknowledged by critics. The appearance to the Twelve is independently attested by Paul, Luke, and John (1 Cor. 15:5; Luke 24:36–43; John 20:19–20) and is again not in dispute, even if many critics are skeptical of the physical demonstrations that attend this appearance. The appearance to the women disciples is independently attested by Matthew and John (Matt. 28:9–10; John 20:11–17) and enjoys, as well, ratification by the criterion of embarrassment, given the low credibility accorded to the testimony of women. It is generally agreed that the absence of this appearance from the list of appearances in the tradition quoted by Paul is a reflection of the same discomfort in citing female witnesses. Finally, that Jesus appeared to the disciples in Galilee is independently attested by Mark, Matthew, and John (Mark 16:7; Matt. 28:16–17; John 21). Taken sequentially, the appearances follow the pattern of Jerusalem—Galilee—Jerusalem, matching the festival pilgrimages of the disciples as they returned to Galilee following the Passover/Feast of Unleavened Bread and traveled again to Jerusalem two months later for Pentecost.

From this evidence what should we conclude? We can call these appearances hallucinations if we want to, but we cannot deny that they occurred. The late New Testament critic of the University of Chicago, Norman Perrin, states, "The more we study the tradition with regard to the appearances, the firmer the rock begins to appear upon which they are based."[59] Lüdemann is even more emphatic: "It may be taken as historically certain that Peter and the disciples had experiences after Jesus' death in which Jesus appeared to them as the risen Christ."[60] The evidence makes it certain that on separate occasions different individuals and groups had experiences of seeing Jesus alive from the dead. This conclusion is virtually indisputable—and therefore undisputed.

---

58. Wolfgang Trilling, *Fragen zur Geschichtlichkeit Jesu* (Düsseldorf: Patmos Verlag, 1966), 153. With respect to Jesus' miracles, Trilling had written: "We are convinced and hold it for historically certain that Jesus did in fact perform miracles. . . . The miracle reports occupy so much space in the Gospels that it is impossible that they could all have been subsequently invented or transferred to Jesus" (ibid.). The fact that miracle working belongs to the historical Jesus is, as we have seen in chapter 7, no longer disputed.

59. Norman Perrin, *The Resurrection According to Matthew, Mark, and Luke* (Philadelphia: Fortress, 1974), 80.

60. Gerd Lüdemann, *What Really Happened to Jesus?* trans. John Bowden (Louisville, Ky.: Westminster John Knox Press, 1995), 80.

3) *The resurrection appearances were physical, bodily appearances.* So far the evidence I've presented does not depend on the nature of the post-mortem appearances of Jesus. I've left it open whether they were visionary or physical in nature. It remains to be seen whether even visionary experiences of the risen Jesus can be plausibly explained on the basis of psychological models. But if the appearances were physical and bodily in nature, then a purely psychological explanation becomes next to impossible. So it is worth examining what we can know about the nature of these appearances.

a) *Paul implies that the appearances were physical.* He does this in two ways. First, he conceives of the resurrection body as physical. Everyone recognizes that Paul does not teach the immortality of the soul alone but the resurrection of the body. In 1 Corinthians 15:42–44 Paul describes the differences between the present earthly body and the future resurrection body, which will be like Christ's. He draws four essential contrasts between the earthly body and the resurrection body:

The earthly body is:	But the resurrection body is:
mortal	immortal
dishonorable	glorious
weak	powerful
natural	spiritual

Only the last contrast could make us think that Paul did not believe in a physical resurrection body. But what does he mean by the words translated here as "natural/spiritual"? The word translated "natural" (*psychikos*) literally means "soul-ish." Obviously, Paul does not mean that our present body is made out of soul. Rather by this word he means "dominated by or pertaining to human nature." Similarly, when he says the resurrection body will be "spiritual" (*pneumatikos*), he does not mean "made out of spirit." Rather, he means "dominated by or oriented toward the Spirit." It is the same sense of the word "spiritual" as when we say that someone is a spiritual person. In fact, look at the way Paul uses exactly those same words in 1 Corinthians 2:14–15 (AT):

> The natural man (*anthropos psychikos*) does not receive the gifts of the Spirit of God, for they are folly to him, and he is not able to understand them, because they are spiritually discerned. The spiritual man (*anthropos pneumatikos*) judges all things but is himself to be judged by no one.

Natural man does not mean "physical man," but "man oriented toward human nature." And *spiritual man* does not mean "intangible, invisible man" but "man oriented toward the Spirit." The contrast is the same in 1 Corinthians 15. The present, earthly body will be freed from its slavery to sinful human nature and become instead fully empowered and directed by God's Spirit. Thus, Paul's doctrine of the resurrection body implies a physical resurrection.

Second, Paul, and indeed all the New Testament, makes a conceptual (if not linguistic) distinction between an appearance of Jesus and a vision of Jesus. The appearances of Jesus soon ceased, but visions continued in the early church.[61] Now the question is: what is the difference between an appearance and a vision? The answer of the New Testament would seem to be clear: a vision, though caused by God, was purely in the mind, while an appearance took place "out there" in the external world.[62] It is instructive to compare here Stephen's vision of Jesus in Acts 7 with the resurrection appearances of Jesus. Though Stephen saw an identifiable, bodily image, what he saw was a vision of a man, not a man who was physically there, for no one else present experienced anything at all. By contrast the resurrection appearances took place in the world "out there" and could be experienced by anybody present. Paul could rightly regard his experience on the Damascus Road as an appearance, even though it took place after Jesus' ascension, because it involved manifestations in the external world, which Paul's companions also experienced to varying degrees. Thus, the conceptual distinction between a vision and an appearance of Jesus also implies that the resurrection appearances were physical.

b) *The Gospel accounts show the appearances were physical and bodily.* Again, two points deserve to be made. First, every resurrection appearance related in the Gospels is a physical, bodily appearance. The unanimous testimony of the Gospels in this regard is quite impressive. If *none* of the appearances was originally a physical, bodily appearance, then it is very strange that we have a completely unanimous testimony in the Gospels that *all* of them were physical, with no trace of the supposed original, non-physical appearances. Such a thorough-going corruption of oral tradition in so short a time, while eyewitnesses were still about, is most unlikely.

Second, if all the appearances were originally non-physical visions, then one is at a complete loss to explain the rise of the Gospel accounts. For physical, bodily appearances would be foolishness to Gentiles and a stumbling block to Jews, since neither, for different reasons, could countenance physical resurrection from the dead but would be quite happy to accept visionary appearances of the deceased. Some critics have suggested that anti-Docetic motives might have prompted the materialization of the appearances. But this suggestion has little to commend it, since Docetists did not, in fact, affirm purely visionary resurrection appearances. Moreover, the Gospel accounts do not evince the rigor of an anti-Docetic apologetic

61. "One can only wonder in what ways, if any, Luke and Paul imagined the original christophanies to differ from later experiences" (Allison, *Resurrecting Jesus*, 261). The answer to this key question is, I think, fairly clear, as I explain in the text. This answer is important, for no matter how real, how tangible, how opaque, visions of the departed may seem to the bereaved, the departed only *appear* to be external, physical, objects. The bereaved recognize that what they experienced was a vision of the deceased.

62. A hallucination, for example, a mirage, would differ from a vision in that a hallucination is not induced by God but is the result of natural or human causes, whereas a vision is caused by God. But a vision, as opposed to a genuine appearance, is still wholly intra-mental and, hence, private, even if it is veridical.

(more would need to be done than Jesus' merely *showing* his wounds, for example), and the appearance traditions ante-date Docetism in any case.

To be perfectly candid, the only grounds for denying the physical, corporeal nature of the postmortem appearances of Jesus is philosophical, not historical: such appearances would be nature miracles of the most stupendous proportions, and that many critics cannot swallow. But in that case one needs to retrace one's steps to think again about what we had to say concerning evidence for the existence of God and concerning the problem of miracles. Most New Testament critics are untrained in philosophy and are, hence, naïve when it comes to these issues.

Thus, on the basis of these three lines of evidence, we can conclude that the fact of Jesus' postmortem appearances to various individuals and groups under a variety of circumstances is firmly established historically and, moreover, that these appearances were bodily and physical. But how do we explain these appearances? That leads me to my second major point.

EXPLAINING THE RESURRECTION APPEARANCES

If one denies that Jesus actually rose from the dead, then he must try to explain away the resurrection appearances psychologically. Strauss believed that the resurrection appearances were merely hallucinations on the part of the disciples. The most prominent defender of the view today is the German New Testament critic Gerd Lüdemann. How does the hypothesis fare when assessed by McCullagh's criteria?

1) *The hypothesis, together with other true statements, must imply further statements describing present, observable data.* As usual, the theory meets this criterion.

2) *The hypothesis must have greater explanatory scope than rival hypotheses.* The Hallucination Hypothesis has narrow explanatory scope. It says nothing to explain the empty tomb. Therefore, one must either deny the fact of the empty tomb and, hence, burial or else conjoin some independent hypothesis to the Hallucination Hypothesis to account for the empty tomb. Allsion is right to remind us that explanatory scope is not the only or even most important criterion for theory assessment and that historical events typically have complex causes.[63] Still, all things being equal, the simpler hypothesis will be preferred, and, since not all things are equal, we shall also consider the Hallucination Hypothesis' explanatory power, plausibility, and so forth before making our final judgment.

Again, the Hallucination Hypothesis says nothing to explain the origin of the disciples' belief in Jesus' resurrection. Although Allison makes a great deal out of the alleged similarities between the postmortem appearances of Jesus and visions of the recently departed on the part of the bereaved, the overriding lesson of such fascinating stories is that the bereaved do not as a result of such experiences, however real and tangible they may seem, conclude that the deceased has returned physically to life—rather the deceased is seen in the afterlife. As Wright observes,

63. Allison, *Resurrecting Jesus*, 347–48.

for someone in the ancient world, visions of the deceased are not evidence that the person is alive, but evidence that he is dead![64] Moreover, in a Jewish context other, more appropriate interpretations of such experiences than resurrection are close to hand. Dunn demands,

> Why did they conclude that it was Jesus *risen from the dead?*—Why not simply a vision of the dead man?—Why not visions "fleshed out" with the apparatus of apocalyptic expectation, coming on the clouds of glory and the like . . .? Why draw the astonishing conclusion that the *eschatological* resurrection had *already* taken place in the case of a *single individual* separate from and prior to the general resurrection?[65]

As Dunn's last question indicates, the inference "he has been raised from the dead," so natural to our ears, would have been wholly unnatural to a first-century Jew. In Jewish thinking there was already a category perfectly suited to describe Peter's postulated experience: Jesus had been assumed into heaven. Allison himself admits, "If there was no reason to believe that his solid body had returned to life, no one would have thought him, against expectation, resurrected from the dead. Certainly visions of or perceived encounters with a postmortem Jesus would not by themselves, have supplied such reason."[66] Thus, even given hallucinations, belief in Jesus' resurrection remains unexplained.

3) *The hypothesis must have greater explanatory power than rival hypotheses.* The Hallucination Hypothesis arguably has weak explanatory power even when it comes to the appearances. Suppose that Peter was one of those individuals who experiences a vision of a deceased loved one. Would this hypothesis suffice to explain the resurrection appearances? Not really, for the diversity of the appearances bursts the bounds of anything found in the psychological casebooks. Jesus appeared not just one time, but many times; not at just one locale and circumstance but at a variety of places and circumstances; not to just one individual, but to different persons; not just to individuals, but to various groups; not just to believers but to unbelievers and even enemies. Positing a chain reaction among the disciples won't solve the problem because people like James and Paul don't stand in the chain. Those who would explain the resurrection appearances psychologically are compelled to construct a composite picture by cobbling together different unrelated cases of hallucinatory experiences, which only serves to underline the fact that there is nothing like the resurrection appearances in the psychological casebooks.

4) *The hypothesis must be more plausible than rival hypotheses.* Lüdemann attempts to make his Hallucination Hypothesis plausible by a psychoanalysis of Peter and

64. For references to ancient pagan and Jewish texts concerning apparitions of the dead, see Craig Keener, *The Gospel of John: A Commentary* (Peabody, Mass.: Hendrickson, 2003), 2:1169.

65. James W. D. G. Dunn, *Jesus and the Spirit* (London: SCM, 1975), 132.

66. Allison, *Resurrecting Jesus*, 324–25. The remaining question is whether bereavement visons in conjunction with the discovery of the empty tomb would have led to the disciples' belief and proclamation of Jesus' resurrection from the dead, on which see below concerning the origin of the Christian Way.

Paul, according to which both labored under guilt complexes which found release in hallucinations of Jesus. But Lüdemann's psychoanalysis is implausible for three reasons: first, Lüdemann's use of depth psychology is based upon certain theories of Jung and Freud which are highly disputed. Second, there is insufficient data to do a psychoanalysis of Peter and Paul. Psychoanalysis is difficult enough to carry out even with patients on the psychoanalyst's couch, so to speak, but it is next to impossible with historical figures. It is for that reason that the genre of psycho-biography is rejected today. Finally, third, what evidence we do have suggests that Paul did *not* struggle with a guilt complex as Lüdemann supposes. Nearly fifty years ago the Swedish scholar Krister Stendahl pointed out that Western readers have tended to interpret Paul in light of Martin Luther's struggles with guilt and sin. But Paul (or Saul) the Pharisee experienced no such struggle. Stendahl writes:

> Contrast Paul, a very happy and successful Jew, one who can say "As to righteousness under the Law [I was] blameless" (Phil. 3.6). That *is* what he says. He experiences no troubles, no problems, no qualms of conscience. He is a star pupil, the student to get the thousand dollar graduate scholarship in Gamaliel's Seminary. . . . Nowhere in Paul's writings is there any indication . . . that psychologically Paul had some problem of conscience.[67]

In order to justify his portrait of a guiltridden Paul, Lüdemann is forced to inter-pret Romans 7 in terms of Paul's pre-Christian experience. But, as Hans Kessler observes, this interpretation is rejected by "almost all expositors" since the late 1920's.[68] So Lüdemann's psychoanalysis is positively implausible.

A second respect in which the Hallucination Hypothesis is implausible is its construal of the appearances as merely visionary experiences. Lüdemann recognizes that the Hallucination Hypothesis depends on the presupposition that what Paul saw on the Damascus Road was the same as what all the *other* disciples experienced: "Anyone who does not share [this] presupposition will not be able to make any sense" out of what he has to say. But this presupposition is groundless. Many of Paul's opponents denied his true apostleship, so Paul is anxious to include himself along with the other apostles who had seen Christ. John Dominic Crossan explains: "Paul *needs* in I Cor 15 to equate his own experience with that of the preceding apostles. To equate, that is, its *validity* and *legitimacy*, but not necessarily its mode or manner. . . . Paul's own entranced revelation should not be presumed to be the model for all others."[69] Paul is trying to bring his experience up to the objectivity and reality of the disciples' experience, not to dilute their experience to a merely visionary seeing. So with respect both to its psychoanalysis of the witnesses and its

67. Krister Stendahl, "Paul among Jews and Gentiles," in *Paul among Jews and Gentiles* (Philadelphia: Fortesss, 1976), 12–13.

68. Hans Kessler, *Sucht den Lebenden nicht bei den Toten,* new ed. (Würzburg: Echter, 1995), 423.

69. John Dominic Crossan, *Jesus: A Revolutionary Bibliography* (San Francisco: Harper San Francisco, 1994), 169.

reduction of the appearances to visionary experiences, the Hallucination Hypothesis suffers from implausibility.

5) *The hypothesis must be less ad hoc than rival hypotheses.* Lüdemann's version of the Hallucination Hypothesis is ad hoc in a number of ways: it assumes that the disciples fled back to Galilee after Jesus' arrest, that Peter was so obsessed with guilt that he projected a hallucination of Jesus, that the other disciples were also prone to hallucinations, and that Paul had a struggle with the Jewish law and a secret attraction to Christianity.

6) *The hypothesis must be disconfirmed by fewer accepted beliefs than rival hypotheses.* Some of the accepted beliefs of New Testament scholars today which tend to disconfirm the Hallucination Hypothesis, at least as Lüdemann presents it, include the belief that Jesus received an honorable burial by Joseph of Arimathea, that Jesus' tomb was discovered empty by women, that psychoanalysis of historical figures is not feasible, that Paul was basically content with his life under the Jewish law, and that the New Testament makes a distinction between a vision and a resurrection appearance.

7) *The hypothesis must significantly exceed its rivals in fulfilling conditions (2)–(6).* The Hallucination Hypothesis remains a live option today and in that respect has outstripped its naturalistic rivals. But the question is whether it outstrips the Resurrection Hypothesis.

From the preceding we come to the conclusion that it is well established that in multiple and varied circumstances, different individuals and groups saw Jesus physically and bodily alive from the dead. Furthermore, there is no good way to explain this away psychologically. So once again, if we reject the resurrection of Jesus as the only reasonable explanation of the resurrection appearances, we are left with an inexplicable mystery.

The Origin of the Christian Faith

The third fact from which the resurrection of Jesus may be inferred is the very origin of the Christian faith. This fact takes pride of place in Wright's historical argument for Jesus' resurrection. Indeed, Wright's entire book *The Resurrection of the Son of God* is probably best understood as the fullest and most sophisticated development of this third point of the overall case, for he actually argues for the historicity of Jesus' empty tomb and postmortem appearances on the basis of the origin of the disciples' belief in Jesus' resurrection. Such a procedure understates the historical evidence for Jesus' resurrection, since independent evidence can be offered on behalf of the empty tomb and postmortem appearances, as we have seen and as most critics recognize. Still, Wright's procedure serves to draw attention to the power of this third point.

THE FACT OF THE ORIGIN OF THE CHRISTIAN FAITH

Even skeptical New Testament scholars admit that the earliest disciples at least *believed* that Jesus had been raised from the dead. In fact, they pinned nearly everything on it; to take just one example: the belief that Jesus was the Messiah. Jews had no conception of a Messiah who, instead of triumphing over Israel's enemies, would be shamefully executed by them as a criminal.

Messiah was supposed to be a triumphant figure who would command the respect of Jew and Gentile alike and who would establish the throne of David in Jerusalem. A Messiah who failed to deliver and to reign, who was defeated, humiliated, and slain by his enemies, is a contradiction in terms. Nowhere do Jewish texts speak of such a "Messiah." Therefore, as Wright emphasizes, "The crucifixion of Jesus, understood from the point of view of any onlooker, whether sympathetic or not, was bound to have appeared as the complete destruction of any messianic pretensions or possibilities he or his followers might have hinted at."[70] It is difficult to overemphasize what a disaster the crucifixion was for the disciples' faith. Jesus' death on the cross spelled the humiliating end for any hopes they had entertained that he was the Messiah.

But the belief in the resurrection of Jesus reversed the catastrophe of the crucifixion. Because God had raised Jesus from the dead, he was seen to be Messiah after all. Thus, Peter proclaims in Acts 2:32, 36 (RSV): "This Jesus God raised up. . . . Let all the house of Israel therefore know assuredly that God has made Him both Lord and Christ—this Jesus whom you crucified." It was on the basis of belief in his resurrection that the disciples could believe that Jesus was the Messiah.

It is no surprise, therefore, that belief in Jesus' resurrection was universal in the early Christian church. Helmut Koester points out that the traditional formula quoted in 1 Corinthians 15:3–7 in which the "gospel" is defined as the death, burial, resurrection, and appearances of Christ makes it probable that this understanding of the gospel goes right back to the very beginning of the church in Jerusalem. "What Paul preached was never the subject of controversy between Paul's Gentile mission and the church in Jerusalem. Jesus' death and resurrection was the event upon which their common proclamation was based."[71] Some critics have speculated whether there was a community of believers exclusively devoted to the sayings of the Q document who had no belief in Jesus' passion and resurrection. But Meier rejects this conjecture, commenting that the only two Q communities that we really know of were Matthew and Luke's churches, and they both valued the passion tradition. "The idea that some first-generation Christian community proclaimed the sayings of Q without any . . . interest in Jesus' death and resurrection is simply not verified by the data. . . ."[72] Günther Bornkamm sums it up: "The Easter faith of the first disciples . . . was not the peculiar experience of a few enthusiasts or a peculiar theological opinion of a few apostles, who in the course

70. Wright, *Christian Origins*, 3:557–58.

71. Helmut Koester, *Ancient Christian Gospels: Their History and Development* (London: SCM, 1990), 51.

72. John Meier, "Dividing Lines in Jesus Research Today," *Interpretation* 50 (1996), 359.

of time had the luck to prevail. No, they were all one in the belief and the confession to the Risen One."[73]

Some critics have sought to avoid this conclusion by maintaining with Bultmann that the earliest disciples did not distinguish between Jesus' resurrection and his ascension into heaven. The primitive proclamation was of Jesus' exaltation, which later became differentiated into his resurrection and ascension. In effect, then, the primitive Christian belief was not in Jesus' resurrection, so there is nothing to be explained beyond belief in his exaltation. Wright is sharply critical of such a suggestion:

> The idea that there was originally no difference for the earliest Christians between resurrection and exaltation/ascension is a twentieth-century fiction, based on a misreading of Paul. Actually, Bultmann's account is slippery at the crucial point: though he says there was no difference between resurrection and ascension, what he means is that *there was no early belief in "resurrection" at all*, since . . . the word "resurrection" and its cognates was not used to denote a non-bodily extension of life in a heavenly realm, however glorious. Plenty of words existed to denote heavenly exaltation; "resurrection" is never one of them. . . . Bultmann therefore has to postulate—though he has covered up this large move—that at some point halfway through the first century someone who had previously believed that Jesus had simply "gone to heaven when he died" began to use, to denote this belief, language which had never meant that before and continued not to mean it in either paganism, Judaism, or Christianity thereafter, namely, the language of resurrection. . . . What is more, Bultmann has to assume that, though this theory about a risen body was a new thing within the already widely diverse Christian church, it took over almost at once, so that all traces of the original view—that Jesus was not raised from the dead, but simply "went to heaven," albeit in an exalted capacity—have dropped out of historical sight.[74]

Given the date, for example, of the tradition quoted by Paul in 1 Corinthians 15:3–5, Bultmann's hypothesis threatens to collapse into a conspiracy theory akin to those of eighteenth-century Deism, which is the *reductio ad absurdum* of his hypothesis. Resurrection, which the evidence shows to be the primitive belief, entails exaltation and—given that Jesus is no longer present— therefore ascension into heaven; but a reverse evolution, from exaltation to physical resurrection and ascension, does not follow from the concept of exaltation.

Thus, the origin of Christianity hinges on the belief of the earliest disciples that God had raised Jesus from the dead. But the question is: how does one explain the origin of that belief? As R. H. Fuller says, even the most skeptical critic must posit some mysterious X to get the movement going.[75] But what was that X?

73. Günther Bornkamm, *Jesus von Nazareth*, 8th ed. (Stuttgart: Kohlhammer, 1968), 159.
74. Wright, *Christian Origins*, 3:625-6.
75. R. H. Fuller, *The Formation of the Resurrection Narratives* (London: SPCK, 1972), 2.

EXPLAINING THE ORIGIN OF THE CHRISTIAN FAITH

If one denies that the resurrection itself was that X, then one must explain the disciples' belief in Jesus' resurrection as the result of either Christian influences, pagan influences, or Jewish influences. That is to say, one must hold that the disciples came to believe in Jesus' resurrection either because of the influence of early Christianity, the influence of pagan religions, or the influence of Jewish beliefs.

Not from Christian Influences

Now clearly the disciples' belief in Jesus' resurrection cannot be explained as a result of Christian influences, simply because there was no Christianity yet. Since the belief in Jesus' resurrection was itself the foundation for Christianity, it cannot be explained as the later product of Christianity.

Not from Pagan Influences

But neither can belief in Jesus' resurrection be explained as the result of pagan influences on the disciples. Back around the turn of the nineteenth to the twentieth century, in the hey-day of the History of Religions school, scholars in comparative religion collected parallels to Christian beliefs in other religious movements, and some thought to explain those beliefs, including belief in Jesus' resurrection, as the result of the influence of such myths.

The movement soon collapsed, however, principally due to two factors: first, scholars came to realize that the parallels are spurious. The ancient world was a virtual cornucopia of myths of gods and heroes. Comparative studies in religion and literature require sensitivity to their similarities and differences, or distortion and confusion inevitably result. Unfortunately, those who adduced parallels to Jesus' resurrection failed to exercise such sensitivity. Many of the alleged parallels are actually apotheosis stories, the divinization and assumption of the hero into heaven (Hercules, Romulus). Others are disappearance stories, asserting that the hero has vanished into a higher sphere (Apollonius of Tyana, Empedocles). Still others are seasonal symbols for the crop cycle, as the vegetation dies in the dry season and comes back to life in the rainy season (Tammuz, Osiris, Adonis). Some are political expressions of Emperor worship (Julius Caesar, Caesar Augustus). None of these is parallel to the Jewish idea of the resurrection of the dead. David Aune, a specialist in comparative ancient Near Eastern literature, concludes, "No parallel to them [resurrection traditions] is found in Graeco-Roman biography."[76] Indeed, most scholars have come to doubt whether properly speaking there really were any myths of dying and rising gods at all. In the Osiris myth, one of the best known symbolic seasonal myths, Osiris does not really come back to life at all but simply continues to exist in the nether realm of the departed. In a recent review of the evidence, T. N. D. Mettinger reports: "From the 1930s . . . a consensus has developed to the effect that the 'dying and rising gods' died but did not return or

---

76. D. E. Aune, "The Genre of the Gospels," in *Gospel Perspectives II*, ed. R. T. France and David Wenham (Sheffield: JSOT Press, 1981), 48.

rise to live again. . . . Those who still think differently are looked upon as residual members of an almost extinct species."[77] Mettinger himself believes that myths of dying and rising did exist in the cases of Dumuzi, Baal, and Melqart; but he recognizes that such symbols are quite unlike the early Christian belief in Jesus' resurrection:

> The dying and rising gods were closely related to the seasonal cycle. Their death and return were seen as reflected in the changes of plant life. The death and resurrection of Jesus is a one-time event, not repeated, and unrelated to seasonal changes. . . . There is, as far as I am aware, no *prima facie* evidence that the death and resurrection of Jesus is a mythological construct, drawing on the myths and rites of the dying and rising gods of the surrounding world. While studied with profit against the background of Jewish resurrection belief, the faith in the death and resurrection of Jesus retains its unique character in the history of religions. The riddle remains.[78]

Notice Mettinger's comment that the belief in Jesus' resurrection may be profitably studied against the background of *Jewish* resurrection beliefs (not pagan mythology). Here we see one of the major shifts in New Testament studies over the last century, what I earlier flagged as the Jewish reclamation of Jesus. Scholars came to realize that pagan mythology is simply the wrong interpretive context for understanding Jesus of Nazareth. Evans has called this shift the "Eclipse of Mythology" in Life of Jesus research.[79] Jesus and his disciples were first-century Palestinian Jews, and it is against that background that they must be understood. The spuriousness of the alleged parallels is just one indication that pagan mythology is the wrong interpretive context for understanding the disciples' belief in Jesus' resurrection.

Second, there is no causal connection between pagan myths and the origin of the disciples' belief in Jesus' resurrection. Jews were familiar with the seasonal deities (Ezek. 8:14–15) and found them abhorrent. Therefore, as Gerhard Kittel notes, there is no trace of cults of dying and rising gods in first-century Palestine.[80] In any case, surely Grass does not exaggerate when he says that it would be "completely unthinkable" that the original disciples would have sincerely come to believe that Jesus of Nazareth was risen from the dead because they had heard of pagan myths about dying and rising seasonal gods.[81]

---

77. Tryggve N. D. Mettinger, *The Riddle of Resurrection: "Dying and Rising Gods" in the Ancient Near East* (Stockholm, Sweden: Almquist & Wiksell International, 2001), 4, 7.

78. Ibid., 221.

79. Craig Evans, "Life-of-Jesus Research and the Eclipse of Mythology," *Theological Studies* 54 (1993): 18, 34.

80. Gerhard Kittel, "Die Auferstehung Jesu," *Deutsche Theologie* 4 (1937): 133–68. In fact Hengel thinks that the belief in the resurrection of the dead served as retardant to the influence of the pagan mystery religions: "The development of the apocalyptic resurrection-, immortality-, and judgment-doctrine in Jewish Palestine explains why—in contrast to Alexandrian Judaism—the Hellenistic mystery religions . . . could gain virtually no influence there" (Martin Hengel, *"Judentum und Hellenismus,"* Wissenschaftliche Untersuchungen zum Neuen Testament 10 [Tübingen: J. C. B. Mohr, 1969], 368–69).

81. Grass, *Ostergeschehen*, 133.

Not from Jewish Influences

The real question, then, is: would the disciples have come to believe that Jesus had been raised from the dead because of Jewish influences? Again, the answer would seem to be no. To understand this, we need to look at what the Jewish conception of the resurrection was. The belief in the resurrection of the dead is explicitly mentioned three times in the Old Testament: Isaiah 26:19, Ezekiel 37, and Daniel 12:2. During the intertestamental period, the belief in the resurrection of the dead became a widespread hope. In Jesus' day this belief was held to by the party of the Pharisees, although it was denied by the party of the Sadducees. So the belief in resurrection was itself nothing new but rather was a prominent Jewish belief.

But the Jewish conception of the resurrection differed in at least two fundamental respects from the resurrection of Jesus. First, in Jewish thought the resurrection always occurred after the end of the world. Joachim Jeremias explains:

> Ancient Judaism did not know of an anticipated resurrection as an event of history. Nowhere does one find in the literature anything comparable to the resurrection of Jesus. Certainly resurrections of the dead were known, but these always concerned resuscitations, the return to the earthly life. In no place in the late Judaic literature does it concern a resurrection to *doxa* [glory] as an event of history.[82]

For a Jew the resurrection always occurred after the end of history. He had no conception of a resurrection within history. We find this typical Jewish frame of mind in the Gospels themselves, for example, John 11:23–24 (esv). Here Jesus is about to raise Lazarus from the dead. He tells Martha, "Your brother will rise again." What is her response? "Martha said to Him, 'I know that he will rise again in the resurrection on the last day.'" She had no inkling of a resurrection within history; she thought that Jesus was talking about the resurrection at the end of the world. I think that it's for this same reason that the disciples had so much trouble understanding Jesus' predictions of his own resurrection. They thought he was talking about the resurrection at the end of the world. Look at Mark 9:9–11 (esv), for example.

> And as they were coming down the mountain, he charged them to tell no one what they had seen, until the Son of Man had risen from the dead. So they kept the matter to themselves, questioning what this rising from the dead might mean. And they asked him, "Why do the scribes say that first Elijah must come?"

Here Jesus predicts his resurrection, and what do the disciples ask? "Why is it that the scribes say that first Elijah must come?" In first-century Judaism it was believed the prophet Elijah would come again before the great and terrible Day of the Lord, the judgment day when the dead would be raised. The disciples could

---

82. Joachim Jeremias, "Die älteste Schicht der Osteruberlieferung," in *Resurrexit*, ed. Edouard Dhanis (Rome: Editrice Libreria Vaticana, 1974), 194.

not understand the idea of a resurrection occurring within history prior to the end of the world. Hence, Jesus' predictions only confused them. Thus, given the Jewish conception of the resurrection, the disciples after Jesus' crucifixion would not have thought that he had been already raised. They would have only looked forward to the resurrection at the last day and, in keeping with Jewish custom, perhaps preserved his tomb as a shrine where his bones could rest until the resurrection.

Second, in Jewish thought, the resurrection was always the resurrection of all the righteous or all the people. They had no conception of the resurrection of an isolated individual. Ulrich Wilckens reports:

> For nowhere do the Jewish texts speak of the resurrection of an individual which already occurs before the resurrection of the righteous in the end time and is differentiated and separate from it; nowhere does the participation of the righteous in the salvation at the end time depend on their belonging to the Messiah, who was raised in advance as "First of those raised by God" (1 Cor. 15:20).[83]

Wilckens' observation that no connection existed between the individual believer's resurrection and the prior resurrection of the Messiah is an understatement. For there existed no belief in Messiah's prior resurrection at all. That is why we find no instances of claims comparable to those of the disciples for Jesus. Wright has been insistent upon this point. "All the followers of those first century messianic movements were fanatically committed to the cause. . . . But in no case right across the century before Jesus and the century after him do we hear of any Jewish group saying that their executed leader had been raised from the dead, and he really was the Messiah after all."[84] Wright invites us to suppose that the disciples were convinced, on other grounds, that Jesus was the Messiah.

> This would not have led the early disciples to say he had been raised from the dead. A change in the meaning of "Messiah," yes (since nobody in the first century supposed that the Messiah would die at the hands of pagans); but not an assertion of his resurrection. No second-Temple Jewish texts speak of the Messiah being raised from the dead. Nobody would have thought of saying, "I believe that so-and-so really was the Messiah; therefore he must have been raised from the dead."[85]

The disciples had no idea of the resurrection of an isolated individual, especially of the Messiah. Therefore, after Jesus' crucifixion, all they could do was wait with longing for the general resurrection of the dead to see their Master again.

For these two reasons, then, we cannot explain the disciples' belief in Jesus' resurrection as a result of Jewish influences. Or, as Wright puts it, some sufficient explanation must be given for these two peculiar mutations of traditional Jewish

---

83. Ulrich Wilckens, "Auferstehung," *Themen der Theologie* 4 (Stuttgart: Kreuz Verlag, 1970), 131.
84. N. T. Wright, lecture at Asbury College and Seminary, 1999.
85. Wright, *Christian Origins*, 3:25.

belief in the resurrection that occurred within early Christianity. Left to themselves, the disciples would never have come to believe that Jesus' resurrection had already occurred. C. F. D. Moule asks:

> If the coming into existence of the Nazarenes, a phenomenon undeniably attested by the New Testament, rips a great hole in history, a hole the size and shape of the Resurrection, what does the secular historian propose to stop it up with? ... The birth and rapid rise of the Christian Church ... *remain an unsolved enigma for any historian who refuses to take seriously the only explanation offered by the Church itself.*[86]

Translation versus Resurrection

But let's push the argument one notch further. Suppose the disciples were not simply "left to themselves" after the crucifixion. Suppose that somehow Jesus' tomb was found empty and the shock of finding the empty tomb caused the disciples to see hallucinations of Jesus. The question is: would they then have concluded that he had been raised from the dead? True, those suppositions face formidable objections in their own right; but let's be generous and suppose for the sake of argument that this is what happened. Would the disciples have concluded that Jesus had been raised from the dead?

The answer would seem to be, no. Hallucinations, as projections of the mind, can contain nothing new. Therefore, given the current Jewish beliefs about life after death, the disciples, were they to project hallucinations of Jesus, would have seen Jesus in heaven or in Abraham's bosom, where the souls of the righteous dead were believed to abide until the resurrection. And such visions would not have caused belief in Jesus' resurrection.

At the most, it would have only led the disciples to say Jesus had been *translated* or *assumed into heaven*, not *raised from the dead*. In the Old Testament, figures such as Enoch and Elijah were portrayed as not having died but as having been translated directly into heaven. In an extra-canonical Jewish writing called The Testament of Job (40), the story is told of the translation of two children killed in the collapse of a house. The children are killed when the house collapses, but when the rescuers clear away the rubble their bodies are not to be found. Meanwhile, the mother sees a vision of the two children glorified in heaven, where they have been translated by God. It needs to be emphasized that for the Jew a translation is not the same as a resurrection. Translation is the bodily assumption of someone out of this world into heaven. Resurrection is the raising up of a dead man in the spacetime universe. They are distinct categories.

Thus, given Jewish beliefs concerning translation and resurrection, the disciples, having seen heavenly visions of Jesus, would not have preached that Jesus had been raised from the dead. At the very most, the empty tomb and hallucinations of Jesus would have caused them to believe in the translation of Jesus into glory, for

---

86. C. F. D. Moule, *The Phenomenon of the New Testament*, Studies in Biblical Theology 2/1 (London: SCM, 1967), 3, 13.

this was consonant with their Jewish frame of thought. But they would not have come to believe that Jesus had been raised from the dead, for this contradicted Jewish belief in at least two fundamental respects.

The origin of Christianity owes itself to the belief of the earliest disciples that God had raised Jesus from the dead. That belief cannot be plausibly accounted for in terms of either Christian, pagan, or Jewish influences. Even if we grant, for the sake of argument, that the tomb was somehow emptied and the disciples saw hallucinations—suppositions which we have seen to be false anyway—the origin of the belief in Jesus' resurrection still cannot be plausibly explained. Such events would have led the disciples to say only that Jesus had been translated into heaven, not resurrected. The origin of the Christian faith is therefore inexplicable unless Jesus really rose from the dead.

Conclusion

Now we are ready to summarize all three of our discussions. First, we saw that numerous lines of historical evidence prove that the tomb of Jesus was found empty by a group of his women followers. Second, we saw that several lines of historical evidence established that on numerous occasions and in different places Jesus appeared physically and bodily alive from the dead to various witnesses. And finally, we saw that the very origin of the Christian faith depends on belief of the earliest disciples that God had raised Jesus of Nazareth from among the dead.

As one reflects on this evidence, it is striking how successfully the historical facts undergirding the inference to the resurrection of Jesus pass the received tests of authenticity. A glance at our case on behalf of the historicity of Jesus' resurrection reveals that much of the evidence I have marshaled is based on an implicit application of the standard criteria of authenticity. For example, here are examples of standard criteria at work in our historical argument for Jesus' resurrection:

1) *Multiple attestation*. We saw that the burial and empty tomb accounts are multiply attested by a remarkable number of independent and sometimes extremely early sources. The resurrection appearances enjoy multiple attestation from Pauline and Gospel traditions, and the latter themselves multiply attest to Jesus' appearances, in some cases the same ones. And, of course, the fact that the first disciples came to believe in Jesus' resurrection is attested throughout the New Testament.

2) *Dissimilarity*. The third point in our case based on the very origin of the Christian faith is a clear example of the application of this criterion, for the argument consists in showing that the origin of the disciples' belief in Jesus' resurrection cannot be explained as the result of either antecedent Jewish influences, because of its dissimilarity, or as a retrojection of Christian theology.

3) *Embarrassment*. Jesus' burial by Joseph of Arimathea is supported by this criterion, since burial by a Sanhedrist is awkward for the church, whose leaders deserted Jesus. The argument for the discovery of the empty tomb by women is an outstanding illustration of the application of this criterion, for their role in the

story was useless, not to say counterproductive, for the early church and would have been much better served by men.

4) *Context and expectation.* Again, the argument concerning the origin of the Christian way appeals to the absence of any expectation in Judaism of an executed, much less rising, Messiah in order to show that the disciples' belief in Jesus' resurrection cannot plausibly be explained as the outgrowth of Jewish beliefs and expectations.

5) *Semitic traces.* Aramaisms play a part in showing that the tradition quoted by Paul in 1 Corinthians 15:3–5 stems from the early church in Jerusalem. We also saw Semitic traces in the account of the empty tomb preserved in the pre-Markan passion story.

6) *Effect.* According to this criterion, an adequate cause must be posited for some established effect. The conversion of James and Paul, the earliest Jewish polemic concerning the disciples' alleged theft of the body, and the disciples' transformation after the crucifixion all constitute effects which point to the resurrection appearances, the empty tomb, and the disciples' coming to believe that Jesus was risen as their sufficient causes.

7) *Principles of embellishment.* It was on the basis of this criterion that I argued that the Markan account of the empty tomb, in contrast to the apologetically and theologically embellished account in the *Gospel of Peter*, was not a late legend.

8) *Coherence.* The very fact that we have three great, independently established facts pointing to the resurrection of Jesus—namely, the empty tomb, the resurrection appearances, and the origin of the Christian faith—is a powerful argument from coherence for the historicity of the resurrection. Moreover, these facts cohere interestingly with each other; for example, the coherence between Jesus' physical resurrection appearances, Paul's teaching on the nature of the resurrection body, and the empty tomb.

9) *Historical congruence.* Elsewhere I have shown the historical congruence of the burial and empty tomb narratives with what we know of first-century Jewish burial practices.[87]

Thus, the complex of facts which we have examined in support of the historicity of Jesus' resurrection passes the same tests for authenticity that serve to establish the authentic core of Jesus' sayings and deeds and therefore deserves to be accorded no less degree of credibility than those facets of the historical Jesus.

Further, we have seen how poorly the typical explanations of these three facts fare when assessed by standard criteria for the justification of historical hypotheses. They are especially weak when it comes to explanatory scope and power and are often highly implausible. But does the Resurrection Hypothesis do any better at explaining this body of evidence? Is it a better explanation than the implausible naturalistic explanations proffered in the past? In order to answer these questions,

---

87. William Lane Craig, *Assessing the New Testament Evidence for the Historicity of the Resurrection of Jesus*, 3rd ed., Studies in the Bible and Early Christianity 16 (Toronto: Edwin Mellen, 2002).

let's recall McCullagh's seven criteria for the testing of a historical hypothesis and apply them to the hypothesis that "God raised Jesus from the dead."

1) *The hypothesis must imply further statements describing present, observable data.* Dialectical theologians like Barth often spoke of the resurrection as a suprahistorical event; but even though the cause of the resurrection is beyond history, that event nonetheless has a historical margin in the empty tomb and resurrection appearances. As J. A. T. Robinson nicely put it, there was not simply nothing to show for it; rather there was *nothing* to show for it (that is, an empty tomb)![88] Moreover, there is the Christian faith itself to show for it. The present, observable data is chiefly in the form of historical texts which form the basis of the historian's reconstruction of the events of Easter.

2) *The hypothesis must have greater explanatory scope than rival hypotheses.* The resurrection hypothesis, we have seen, exceeds counter-explanations like hallucinations or the Wrong Tomb Hypothesis precisely by explaining all three of the great facts at issue, whereas these rival hypotheses only explain one or two.

3) *The hypothesis must have greater explanatory power than rival hypotheses.* This is perhaps the greatest strength of the resurrection hypothesis. The Conspiracy Hypothesis or the Apparent Death Hypothesis just do not convincingly account for the empty tomb, resurrection appearances, or origin of the Christian faith: on these theories the data (for example, the transformation in the disciples, the historical credibility of the narratives) become very improbable. By contrast, on the hypothesis of the resurrection it seems extremely probable that the observable data with respect to the empty tomb, the appearances, and the disciples' coming to believe in Jesus' resurrection should be just as it is.

4) *The hypothesis must be more plausible than rival hypotheses.* The plausibility of Jesus' resurrection grows exponentially as we consider it in its religio-historical context of Jesus' unparalleled life and radical personal claims and in its philosophical context of the arguments of natural theology. Once one abandons the philosophical prejudice against the miraculous, the hypothesis that God should raise Jesus from the dead is no more implausible than its rivals, nor are they more plausible than the resurrection.

5) *The hypothesis must be less ad hoc than rival hypotheses.* It will be recalled that while McCullagh thought that the Resurrection Hypothesis possesses great explanatory scope and power, he nevertheless felt that it was ad hoc, which he defines in terms of the number of new suppositions made by a hypothesis about the past which are not already implied by existing knowledge. So defined, however, it is difficult to see why the Resurrection Hypothesis is extraordinarily ad hoc. It seems to require only one new supposition: that God exists. Surely its rival hypotheses require many new suppositions. For example, the Conspiracy Hypothesis requires us to suppose that the moral character of the disciples was defective, which is certainly not implied by already existing knowledge; the Apparent Death Hypothesis requires the supposi-

88. John A. T. Robinson, *The Human Face of God* (London: SCM, 1973), 136.

tion that the centurion's lance thrust into Jesus' side was just a superficial poke or is an unhistorical detail in the narrative, which again goes beyond existing knowledge; the Hallucination Hypothesis requires us to suppose some sort of emotional preparation of the disciples which predisposed them to project visions of Jesus alive, which is not implied by our knowledge. Such examples could be multiplied. It should be noted, too, that scientific hypotheses regularly include the supposition of the existence of new entities, such as quarks, strings, gravitons, black holes, and the like, without those theories being characterized as ad hoc. Moreover, for the person who is already a theist, the Resurrection Hypothesis does not even introduce the new supposition of God's existence, since that is already implied by his existing knowledge. For that reason we include the arguments of natural theology in our background knowledge. So the Resurrection Hypothesis cannot be said to be ad hoc simply in virtue of the number of new suppositions it introduces.

If our hypothesis is ad hoc, then, it must be for some other reasons. Philosophers of science have found it notoriously difficult to explain what it is exactly that makes a hypothesis ad hoc. There seems to be an ill-defined air of artificiality or contrivedness about a hypothesis deemed to be ad hoc, which can be sensed, if not explained, by those who are seasoned practitioners of the relevant science. Now I think that the sense of discomfiture which many, *even theists*, feel about appealing to God as part of an explanatory hypothesis for some phenomenon in the world is that so doing has this air of being contrived. It just seems too easy when confronted with some unexplained phenomenon to throw up one's hands and say, "God did it!" The universal disapprobation of the so-called "God of the gaps" and the impulse towards methodological naturalism in science and history spring from the sense of illegitimacy attending such appeals to God. Is the hypothesis that "God raised Jesus from the dead" ad hoc in this sense?

I think not. One of the most important contributions of the traditional defenders of miracles was their drawing attention to the religio-historical context in which a purported miracle occurs. A supernatural explanation of the facts of the empty tomb, the resurrection appearances, and the origin of the Christian faith is not ad hoc because those events took place, as we have seen, in the context of and as the climax to Jesus' own unparalleled life, ministry, and personal claims, with which a supernatural hypothesis readily fits. It is also precisely because of this historical context that the resurrection hypothesis does not seem ad hoc when compared to miraculous explanations of other sorts: for example, that a "psychological miracle" occurred, causing normal men and women to become conspirators and liars who would be willingly martyred for their subterfuge; or that a "biological miracle" occurred, which prevented Jesus' expiring on the cross (despite the spear-thrust through his chest, and so forth) or his dying of exposure in the tomb.[89] It is these

89. See Ehrman's appeal in the Q & A period of our debate to precisely such ad hoc miraculous hypotheses, for example, that the make-believe god Zulu sent Jesus into the twelfth dimension (http://www.reasonablefaith.org/site/PageServer?pagename=debates_main).

miraculous hypotheses which strike us as artificial and contrived, not the resurrection hypothesis, which makes abundantly good sense in the context of Jesus' ministry and radical personal claims. Thus, it seems to me that the Resurrection Hypothesis cannot be characterized as excessively ad hoc.

6) *The hypothesis must be disconfirmed by fewer accepted beliefs than rival hypotheses.* I can't think of any accepted beliefs which disconfirm the Resurrection Hypothesis—unless one thinks of, say, "dead men do not rise" as disconfirmatory. But then we're just back to the problem of miracles again. I've argued that this inductive generalization does nothing to disconfirm the hypothesis that God raised Jesus from the dead. By contrast, rival theories are disconfirmed by accepted beliefs about, for example, the instability of conspiracies, the likelihood of death as a result of crucifixion, the psychological characteristics of hallucinatory experiences, and so forth, as we have seen.

7) *The hypothesis must so exceed its rivals in fulfilling conditions (2)–(6) that there is little chance of a rival hypothesis exceeding it in meeting these conditions.* There is certainly little chance of any of the rival hypotheses suggested to date ever exceeding the Resurrection Hypothesis in fulfilling the above conditions. The stupefaction of contemporary scholarship when confronted with the facts of the empty tomb, the resurrection appearances, and the origin of the Christian faith suggests that no better rival is anywhere on the horizon. Once one gives up the prejudice against miracles, it's hard to deny that the resurrection of Jesus is the best explanation of the facts.

In conclusion, therefore, three great, independently established facts—the empty tomb, the resurrection appearances, and the origin of the Christian faith—all point to the same marvelous conclusion: that God raised Jesus from the dead. Given that miracles are possible, this conclusion cannot be debarred to anyone seeking for the meaning to existence who sees therein the hope of eternal life.

Given the religio-historical context in which this event occurred, the significance of Jesus' resurrection is clear: it is the divine vindication of Jesus' radical personal claims. As Wolfhart Pannenberg explains:

> The resurrection of Jesus acquires such decisive meaning, not merely because someone or anyone has been raised from the dead, but because it is Jesus of Nazareth, whose execution was instigated by the Jews because he had blasphemed against God. If this man was raised from the dead, then that plainly means that the God whom he had supposedly blasphemed has committed himself to him. . . . The resurrection can only be understood as the divine vindication of the man whom the Jews had rejected as a blasphemer.[90]

90. Wolfhart Pannenberg, "Jesu Geschichte und unsere Geschichte," in *Glaube und Wirklichkeit* (München: Chr. Kaiser, 1975), 92–94.

Practical Application

The material I've presented on the resurrection can be nicely summarized into an evangelistic message that can be used effectively on university campuses. It can even be used in personal evangelism, if you can arrange with the person with whom you're sharing to set up a time when you can lay out the evidence. Construct a two-step case such as I've laid out, using the three broad facts as your data to be explained and the criteria for assessing historical hypotheses for inferring the resurrection as the best explanation. Then lay out the case as a whole rather than present and discuss it piecemeal, for the impact of the cumulative case is greater.

For example, I was once discussing the gospel with a student who seemed open but was hesitant. I challenged him to consider the evidence for the resurrection of Jesus, and he told me, "If you can prove that Jesus rose from the dead, I'll become a Christian." So I made an appointment to see him the next week to lay out my case. When I met with him again, I submitted the evidence to him for an uninterrupted twenty minutes and then asked him what he thought. He was virtually speechless. I asked, "Are you now ready to become a Christian?" "Well, I don't know," he said indecisively. So I said that he should think about it some more and that I would come back again the following week to see what he had decided. By the third week, he was ready, and together in his dorm room we prayed to invite Christ into his life. It was one of the most thrilling experiences I have had in seeing God use apologetics to draw someone to himself.

Recently we received a call early Saturday morning. The foreign voice on the line announced, "Hello! This is Muhammad al-Islam calling from Oman!" (I've changed the names to protect his identity.) He explained that he was a former Muslim who had lost his faith in Islam and had become an atheist. But recently he had been reading books on Christian apologetics which he had been ordering through Amazon.com and had become convinced that God exists after all. Now he was reading books on the resurrection of Jesus and was nearly convinced. But he had a few questions which he wanted to ask before making the step to follow Christ. We spent the next hour and a half talking about issues surrounding the resurrection of Jesus, and I sensed that in his heart he really did believe but was just reluctant to take that step self-consciously before he had all his ducks in a row. Before we wrapped up our conversation, he said, "You understand that this is not my real name. In my country, if I were to believe in Christ, I would be killed." I then prayed for him and wished him well. I was on cloud nine after the privilege of a conversation like that! And some people think God doesn't use apologetics in evangelism!

Let me encourage you to work up a talk or a case of your own that you can use in evangelistic meetings or contacts. And then always be prepared to give this defense to anyone who calls you to account for the hope that is in you.

Literature Cited or Recommended

Historical Background

Craig, William Lane. *The Historical Argument for the Resurrection of Jesus during the Deist Controversy.* Texts and Studies in Religion 23. Lewiston, N.Y.: Edwin Mellen, 1985.

Ditton, Humphrey. *A Discourse Concerning the Resurrection of Jesus Christ.* London: J. Darby, 1712.

Fuller, Daniel P. *Easter Faith and History.* London: Tyndale, 1968.

Houtteville, Claude François. *La religion chrétienne prouvée par les faits.* 3 vols. Paris: Mercier & Boudet, 1740.

Less, Gottfried. *Wahrheit der christlichen Religion.* Göttingen: G. L. Förster, 1776.

Paley, William. *A View of the Evidences of Christianity.* 2 vols. 5th ed. London: R. Faulder, 1796. Repr. Westmead, England: Gregg, 1970.

Reimarus, Hermann Samuel. *Fragments.* Translated by R. S. Fraser. Edited by C. H. Talbert. Lives of Jesus Series. London: SCM, 1971.

Semler, Johann Salomo. *Abhandlung von freier Untersuchung des Canon.* Texte zur Kirchen- und Theologiegeschichte 5. Gütersloh: G. Mohn, 1967.

———. *Beantwortung der Fragmente eines Ungennanten insbesondere vom Zweck Jesu und seiner Jünger.* 2nd ed. Halle: Verlag des Erziehungsinstituts, 1780.

Sherlock, Thomas. *The Tryal of the Witnesses of the Resurrection of Jesus.* London: J. Roberts, 1729.

Strauss, David Friedrich. "Hermann Samuel Reimarus and His 'Apology.'" In *Fragments,* by H. S. Reimarus, translated by R. S. Fraser. Edited by C. H. Talbert, 44–57. Lives of Jesus Series. London: SCM, 1971.

———. *The Life of Jesus Critically Examined.* Translated by G. Eliot. Edited with an introduction by P. C. Hodgson. Lives of Jesus Series. London: SCM, 1973.

Tholuck, Friedrich August. "Abriss einer Geschichte der Umwälzung, welche seit 1750 auf dem Gebiete der Theologie in Deutschland statt gefunden." In *Vermischte Schriften grösstentheils Apologetischen Inhalts.* 2 vols. Hamburg: Friedrich Perthes, 1859.

Turretin, J. Alph. *Traité de la vérité de la religion chrétienne.* Translated by J. Vernet. 2nd ed. 7 vols. Geneva: Henri Albert Gosse, 1745–55.

Assessment

Allison, Dale C., Jr. "Explaining the Resurrection: Conflicting Convictions," *Journal for the Study of the Historical Jesus* 3 (2005): 217–33.

———. "Resurrecting Jesus." In *Resurrecting Jesus,* 198–375. New York: T. & T. Clark, 2005. The best presentation of skeptical arguments against inferring Jesus' resurrection.

Alsup, John. *The Post-Resurrection Appearances of the Gospel Tradition.* Stuttgart: Calwer Verlag, 1975. This is the most important work on the post-resurrection appearances.

Aune, D. E. "The Genre of the Gospels." In *Gospel Perspectives II,* edited by R. T. France and David Wenham, 9–60. Sheffield: JSOT Press, 1981.

Barnett, Paul. *Jesus and the Logic of History.* New Studies in Biblical Theology. Grand Rapids, Mich.: Eerdmans, 1997.

Blinzler, Josef. "Die Grablegung Jesu in historischer Sicht." In *Resurrexit*, edited by Edouard Dhanis. Rome: Editrice Libreria Vaticana, 1974. The best piece on the burial.

Bode, Edward Lynn. *The First Easter Morning.* Analecta Biblica 45. Rome: Biblical Institute Press, 1970. The best work on the empty tomb.

Brown, Raymond E. *The Death of the Messiah.* 2 vols. Garden City, N.Y.: Doubleday, 1994. The definitive work on Jesus' passion.

Craig, William Lane. *Assessing the New Testament Evidence for the Historicity of the Resurrection of Jesus*, 3rd ed. Studies in the Bible and Early Christianity 16. Lewiston, N.Y.: Edwin Mellen, 2002.

———. "Wright vs. Crossan on the Resurrection of Jesus." In *The Resurrection: The Crossan-Wright Dialogue*, edited by Robert B. Stewart, 139–48. Minneapolis and London: Augsburg Fortress and SPCK, 2006.

Crossan, John Dominic. *Jesus: A Revolutionary Bibliography.* San Francisco: Harper San Francisco, 1994.

Dodd, C. H. "The Appearances of the Risen Christ: A Study in the Form Criticism of the Gospels." In *More New Testament Studies*, 102–33. Manchester: University of Manchester, 1968.

Dunn, James W. D. G. *Jesus and the Spirit.* London: SCM, 1975.

Ehrman, Bart D. "From Jesus to Constantine: A History of Early Christianity." Lecture 4: "Oral and Written Traditions about Jesus." The Teaching Company, 2003.

———. *Jesus: Apocalyptic Prophet of the New Millennium.* Oxford: Oxford University Press, 1999.

———. *The New Testament.* 3rd ed. Oxford: Oxford University Press, 2004.

Ellis, E. Earle, ed. *The Gospel of Luke.* New Century Bible: London: Nelson, 1966.

Evans, Craig A. "Life-of-Jesus Research and the Eclipse of Mythology." *Theological Studies* 54 (1993): 3–36.

Fuller, R. H. *The Formation of the Resurrection Narratives.* London: SPCK, 1972.

Grass, Hans. *Ostergeschehen und Osterberichte.* 4th ed. Göttingen: Vandenhoeck & Ruprecht, 1974. This influential work remains one of the most important overall treatments of the historicity of the resurrection.

Gundry, Robert. *Sōma in Biblical Theology.* Cambridge: Cambridge University Press, 1976. The best work on the second part of 1 Corinthians 15.

Habermas, Gary. "Experience of the Risen Jesus: The Foundational Historical Issue in the Early Proclamation of the Resurrection." *Dialog* 45 (2006): 288–97.

Hengel, Martin. "*Judentum und Hellenismus.*" Wissenschaftliche Untersuchungen zum Neuen Testament 10. Tübingen: J. C. B. Mohr, 1969.

Hurtado, Larry. "Mission Accomplished: Apologetics, Witness, and Women in Mark's Passion-Resurrection Narratives," paper delivered at the 2005 meeting of the Society of Biblical Literature, forthcoming as "The Women, the Tomb, and the Climax of Mark" in a Festschrift for Sean Freyne to be published by Brill.

Jeremias, Joachim. "Die älteste Schicht der Osterüberlieferung." In *Resurrexit*, edited by Edouard Dhanis. Rome: Editrice Libreria Vaticana, 1974.

Kessler, Hans. *Sucht den Lebenden nicht bei den Toten*, new ed. Würzburg: Echter, 1995.

Kittel, Gerhard. "Die Auferstehung Jesu." *Deutsche Theologie* 4 (1937): 133–68.

Klappert, Berthold. "Einleitung." In *Diskussion um Kreuz und Auferstehung*, edited by B. Klappert, 9–52. Wuppertal: Aussaat Verlag, 1971.

Koester, Helmut. *Ancient Christian Gospels: Their History and Development.* London: SCM, 1990.

Kremer, Jacob. *Die Osterevangelien—Geschichten um Geschichte.* Stuttgart: Katholisches Bibelwerk, 1977.

Lehmann, Karl. *Auferweckt am dritten Tag nach der Schrift.* Quaestiones disputatae 38. Freiburg: Herder, 1968. The most important work on the first part of 1 Corinthians 15.

Lipton, Peter. *Inference to the Best Explanation.* London: Routledge, 1981.

Lüdemann, Gerd. *What Really Happened to Jesus?* Trans. John Bowden. Louisville, Ky.: Westminster John Knox Press, 1995.

McCullagh, C. Behan. *Justifying Historical Descriptions.* Cambridge: Cambridge University Press, 1984.

McGrew, Timothy. "Has Plantinga Refuted the Historical Argument?" *Philosophia Christi* 6 (2004): 7–26.

McGrew, Lydia and Timothy McGrew. "The Argument from Miracles." In *Companion to Natural Theology*, edited by William L. Craig and J. P. Moreland. Oxford: Blackwell, forthcoming.

———. "On the Historical Argument: A Rejoinder to Plantinga." *Philosophia Christi* 8 (2006): 23–38.

Meier, John P. "Dividing Lines in Jesus Research Today." *Interpretation* 50 (1996): 355–72.

———. *A Marginal Jew*, vol. 1: *The Roots of the Problem and the Person.* New York: Doubleday, 1991.

———. *A Marginal Jew*, vol. 2: *Mentor, Message, and Miracle.* New York: Doubleday, 1994.

Mettinger, Tryggve N. D. *The Riddle of Resurrection: "Dying and Rising Gods" in the Ancient Near East.* Stockholm, Sweden: Almquist & Wiksell International, 2001.

Moule, C. F. D. *The Phenomenon of the New Testament.* Studies in Biblical Theology 2/1. London: SCM, 1967.

O'Collins, G. G. "Is the Resurrection an 'Historical' Event?" *Heythrop Journal* 8 (1967): 381–87.

Pannenberg, Wolfhart. *Glaube und Wirklichkeit.* München: Chr. Kaiser, 1975.

Perrin, Norman. *The Resurrection according to Matthew, Mark, and Luke.* Philadelphia: Fortress, 1977.

Pesch, Rudolph. *Das Markusevangelium.* 2 vols. Herders theologischer Kommentar zum Neuen Testament. Freiburg: Herder, 1976–77.

Plantinga, Alvin. "Historical Arguments and Historical Probabilities: A Response to Timothy McGrew." *Philosophia Christi* 8 (2006): 7–22.

———. *Warranted Christian Belief.* Oxford: Oxford University Press, 2000.

Powell, Mark Allen. Critical notice of *The Birth of Christianity*, by John Dominic Crossan, *Journal of the American Academy of Religion* 68 (2000): 169–71.

Robinson, John A. T. *The Human Face of God*. London: SCM, 1973.

Sorabji, Richard. *Time, Creation, and the Continuum*. Ithaca, N.Y.: Cornell University Press, 1983.

Swinburne, Richard. "Natural Theology, Its 'Dwindling Probabilities,' and 'Lack of Rapport.'" *Faith and Philosophy* 21 (2004): 533–46.

———. *The Resurrection of God Incarnate*. Oxford: Oxford University Press, 2003.

Stendahl, Krister. *Paul among Jews and Gentiles*. Philadelphia: Fortesss, 1976.

Trilling, Wolfgang. *Fragen zur Geschichtlichkeit Jesu*. Düsseldorf: Patmos Verlag, 1966.

Van Daalen, D. H. *The Real Resurrection*. London: Collins, 1972.

Von Campenhausen, Hans Freiherr. *Der Ablauf der Osterereignisse und das leere Grab*. 3rd rev. ed. Sitzungsberichte der Heidelberger Akademie der Wissenschaften. Heidelberg: Carl Winter, 1966.

Wilckens, Ulrich. *Auferstehung*. Themen der Theologie 4. Stuttgart: Kreuz Verlag, 1970.

Wright, N. T. *Christian Origins and the Question of God*, vol. 3: *The Resurrection of the Son of God*. Minneapolis: Fortress Press, 2003.

Conclusion

The Ultimate Apologetic

Throughout this book we've examined many arguments in support of the Christian faith. I've argued that we can know that Christianity is true because of the self-authenticating witness of God's Holy Spirit and that we can show it to be true by means of rational argumentation and evidence. We have explored the human predicament without God and immortality and seen how it leads to futility and despair. But we have also examined the evidence for a Christian solution to this predicament: evidence that a personal Creator of the universe exists and that Jesus Christ's offer of eternal life to those who believe in him is genuine, being confirmed by his resurrection from the dead. But now I want to share with you what I believe to be the most effective and practical apologetic for the Christian faith that I know of. This apologetic will help you to win more persons to Christ than all the other arguments in your apologetic arsenal put together.

This ultimate apologetic involves two relationships: your relationship with God and your relationship with others. These two relationships are distinguished by Jesus in his teaching on the duty of man: "And one of them, a lawyer, asked him a question to test him. 'Teacher, which is the great commandment in the Law?' And he said to him, 'You shall love the Lord your God with all your heart and with all your soul and with all your mind. This is the great and first commandment. And a second is like it: You shall love your neighbor as yourself. On these two commandments depend all the Law and the Prophets'" (Matt 22:35–40 ESV). The first commandment governs our relationship to God, the second our relationship with our fellow man. Let's examine each of these relationships in turn.

First, our relationship with God. This is governed by the great commandment:

Hear, O Israel; The LORD our God is one LORD; and you shall love the Lord your God with all your heart, and with all your soul, and with all your might. And these words which I command you this day shall be upon your heart; and you shall teach them diligently to your children, and shall talk of them when you sit in your house, and when you walk by the way, and when you lie down, and when you rise. And you shall bind them as a sign upon your hand, and they shall be as frontlets between your eyes. And you shall write them on the doorposts of your house and on your gates. (Deut. 6:4–9 RSV)

Notice the importance given to this commandment—loving God is to be our preoccupation in life. Sometimes we get the idea that our main duty in life is to serve God, perhaps by being a great apologist, and forget, as J. I. Packer reminds us, that our primary aim ought to be to learn to know God:

We both can and must get our life's priorities straight. From current Christian publications you might think that the most vital issue for any . . . Christian in the world today is . . . social witness, or dialogue with other Christians and other faiths, or refuting this or that "-ism," or developing a Christian philosophy and culture, or what have you. But our line of study makes the present day concentration on these things look like a gigantic conspiracy of misdirection. Of course, it is not that; the issues themselves are real and must be dealt with in their place. But it is tragic that, in paying attention to them, so many in our day seem to have been distracted from what was, is, and always will be the true priority for every human being—that is, learning to know God in Christ.[1]

In our relationship with God we are to give him his legal right—namely, all that we have and are. The Christian is to be as a matter of course totally dedicated to God (Rom. 12:1–2) and filled with the Holy Spirit (Eph. 5:18). For his part God gives to us positionally, as we are in Christ, forgiveness of sins (Eph. 1:7), eternal life (Rom. 6:23), adoption as sons (Gal. 4:5), and the availability of unlimited help and power (Eph. 1:18–19). Think of how much that means! Moreover, he gives to us experientially, as we are Spirit-filled, the fruit of the Spirit: love, joy, peace, patience, kindness, goodness, faithfulness, gentleness, and self-control (Gal. 5:22–23). When this relationship is intact, the product in our lives will be righteousness (Rom. 6:16), and the by-product of righteousness is happiness. Happiness is an elusive thing and will never be found when pursued directly; but it springs into being as one pursues the knowledge of God and as his righteousness is realized in us.

The other relationship is our relationship with our fellow man. This is governed by the second great commandment, as Paul explains: "The commandments, 'You shall not commit adultery, You shall not kill, You shall not steal, You shall not covet,' and any other commandment, are summed up in this sentence, 'You shall love your neighbor as yourself'" (Rom. 13:9 RSV). Why is

---

1. J. I. Packer, *Knowing God* (London: Hodden & Stoughton, 1973), 314.

love the great commandment? Simply because all the other commandments are the outworking of love in practice (Rom. 13:10). When we love others, we simply show that we have understood God's love for us, and it is being worked out in our lives toward others. As John says, "If God so loved us, we also ought to love one another" (1 John 4:11 ESV). What does love involve? To begin with, it means possessing the characteristics of love described in 1 Corinthians 13. Can we say, "I am patient and kind; I am not jealous or boastful, arrogant or rude; I am not selfish or irritable or resentful; I am not happy about wrong, but I rejoice in the right; I bear all things, believe all things, hope all things, endure all things"? Moreover, love will involve having a servant's heart, a willingness to count others better than yourself and to serve and look out for their interests as well as your own (Gal. 5:13b–14; Phil. 2:3). Certainly Jesus himself is our supreme model here: think of how he stooped to wash his disciples' dirty feet!

What will be the result when these two relationships are strong and close? There will be a unity and warmth among Christians. There will be a love that pervades the body of Christ; as Paul describes it, "speaking the truth in love, we are to grow up in every way into him who is the head, into Christ, from whom the whole body, joined and knit together by every joint with which it is supplied, when each part is working properly, makes bodily growth and upbuilds itself in love" (Eph. 4:15–16 RSV). And what will be the result of this unity through love? Jesus himself gives us the answer in his prayer for the church: "That they may all be one, just as you, Father, are in me, and I in you, that they also may be in us, so that the world may believe that you have sent me. . . . I in them and you in me, that they may become perfectly one, so that the world may know that you sent me and loved them even as you loved me" (John 17:21–23 ESV). According to Jesus, our love is a sign to all people that we are his disciples (John 13:35); but even more than that, our love and unity are living proof to the world that God the Father has sent his Son Jesus Christ and that the Father loves people even as he loves Jesus. When people see this—our love for one another and our unity through love—then they will in turn be drawn to Christ and will respond to the gospel's offer of salvation. More often than not, it is who you *are* rather than what you *say* that will bring an unbeliever to Christ.

This, then, is the ultimate apologetic. For the ultimate apologetic is—your life.

Index

Additional Online Resources to Enrich Your Study of *Reasonable Faith*

Reasonable Faith was written to equip believers in the fruitful proclamation of Christian truth claims. Now you may download additional study guides, materials, and learning opportunities at *www.ReasonableFaithTools.com*.

Intentionally constructed to enhance the reader's experience, the site extends the book's topics by offering a wealth of free resources:

- Audio and video lectures and debates by Dr. Craig that compliment the book's main topics
- *Reasonable Faith* book samples
- PowerPoints for class or small group presentations
- Interactive message board to discuss *Reasonable Faith* updates
- Study group questions for each chapter
- Recommended print resources for further study and research
- Syllabi for course study
- Dr. Craig's upcoming speaking schedule
- Materials to help tell others about *Reasonable Faith*
- Even more free resources at www.reasonablefaith.org

www.reasonablefaithtools.com